Looking for a Hero

LOOKING FOR A HERO

Staff Sergeant Joe Ronnie Hooper
and the Vietnam War

Peter Maslowski and Don Winslow

University of Nebraska Press • Lincoln and London

ISBN 0-8032-3244-6

Set in Minion and
Gill Sans by G&S Typsetters, Inc.
Designed by Ray Boeche.

Contents

Looking for a Hero

Prologue

With utter disregard for his own safety . . .

Joe Hooper's Medal of Honor citation,
regarding his conduct during a battle in February 1968

Hero.

After reading Staff Sergeant Joe Ronnie Hooper's Medal of Honor file, you know the man was a hero. Before the war was over, he would be widely acclaimed as the war's most highly decorated soldier, the Audie Murphy of Vietnam.

Joe was a squad leader in a unit officially designated Company D, 2nd Battalion, 501st Infantry Regiment, 101st Airborne Division, but informally known as the "Delta Raiders." The Raiders were an unusual front-line rifle company. Hastily formed during the massive manpower buildup for Vietnam, many of its men were originally trained not as infantrymen but as cooks, clerks, mechanics, cryptographers, military policemen, and in other noncombat specialties. Some of the men, including Joe Hooper, had less-than-stellar disciplinary records. A few even came to the unit directly from the stockade.

Now, in the early afternoon of February 21, 1968, under cloudy, misty skies that made visibility extremely poor, the Raiders were a few miles north of Hue, attacking across a broad rice paddy toward a well-entrenched enemy position dug into a small village.

The village was embedded in a dense tangle of trees, thorny vines, and bamboo, some of the latter shooting forty feet skyward. Advancing through such foliage under normal conditions was difficult, but doing it in combat against strongly held enemy positions verged on the impossible.

According to Joe's detailed Medal of Honor file, as the company moved toward a river running parallel to the enemy's first line of fortified bunkers, the enemy met the Raiders with intense fire from machine guns, rockets, and automatic weapons. The stream was about thirty feet wide and up to five feet deep in some places but easily fordable in others. Beyond the stream was an embankment topped by a woodline that marked the village's outer edge. Enemy bunkers were burrowed into the treeline, virtually invisible, spaced about six feet apart and connected by a slender trench. Other bunker-trench lines ran perpendicular to this woodline, some of them spanning the village's entire depth. Covered with alternating layers of bamboo and dried clay, the camouflaged bunkers provided good overhead cover against air and artillery strikes. The North Vietnamese also fortified many of the houses, converting them into mini-bastions.

Overall the enemy designed its defensive positions to catch an approaching force in crisscrossing and enfilade fires. Well protected, amply supplied, and equipped with modern small arms, the defenders were also in high morale, as their determined resistance was about to demonstrate.

Joe Hooper's extraordinary afternoon began along the stream when he rallied five soldiers from his squad and, braving intense enemy fire, spearheaded the attack by splashing across the river and storming into the woodline bunkers, knocking out five of them and thereby opening a gap in the enemy line.

Six feet tall, with bright red hair, blue eyes, and a lopsided, boyish grin, Hooper did not much look like John Wayne, but this mini-attack showed that he was a John Wayne kind of man.

Hooper's men immediately began paying the normal price for battlefield bravery. An assistant machine gunner, PFC Hopkins, fell badly wounded, unable to move. Undeterred by the lead hurtling around the injured soldier, Hooper immediately went to the man's aid and brought him back to safety. No sooner had he dragged this first casualty out of harm's way than he saw that machine gunner PFC Delaney had also been wounded. Without hesitation Sergeant Hooper again put his own life at risk to aid a wounded man. This time the risk was almost fatal. As he raced through a hailstorm of exploding grenades, Hooper was seriously wounded, yet still reached Delaney and carried him back.

Although ordered to stay in the rear for evacuation because of his own injuries, Hooper refused treatment, applied a makeshift bandage to his wounds, grabbed some extra ammunition, and hastened back to his men where, amid continuing fierce fire, he redistributed the ammo and led his small band of Raiders forward again.

After advancing a short distance Hooper noticed that another squad leader, Staff Sergeant Lonnie Thomas, had crawled forward to survey the situation but was so tightly pinned down that he could not move an inch one way or the other. Because several small houses blocked his view of enemy positions farther to the front, Hooper provided covering fire while a fellow trooper, Al Mount, maneuvered between the two houses to try to determine the enemy's location. Mount took only one step into the open area before he was shot in the leg and rendered immobile.

Hooper now went solo, edging to the left under intense gunfire, getting around the houses, where he spotted a triple bunker complex. Three fully manned bunkers spurting machine gun and rifle fire against one man?

Spraying the first bunker with rifle fire and a grenade, Hooper killed all the defenders, then leaped into it. From this protected position he turned his attention on the middle bunker, only ten meters away, and shot all of its occupants. Leaping out of his sheltered haven, Hooper raced around the second bunker and attacked the third one, killing still more defenders and thus rescuing Al Mount and Sergeant Thomas.

Upon returning to his men Hooper also found a number of additional soldiers huddled against the riverbank. These men were reluctant to move forward, but Hooper's dynamic leadership dispelled their fears and inspired them to join the battle.

Just as they moved over the top of the bank, heading back into the fray, the battalion chaplain, William W. Erbach, joined them. Suddenly three North Vietnamese soldiers burst out of the dense brush and fired at the group, hitting Chaplain Erbach. Everyone froze—except Joe, who instantly blazed away, killing two of the North Vietnamese and sending the third into a rapid retreat. Rescuing his fourth wounded man, the sergeant cradled Erbach in his arms, carried him to the rear, and made certain he received medical aid.

Then he returned to the front despite pleas that he have his own wounds treated.

Reunited with his men, Hooper halted them at a line of houses and moved forward alone, doing a personal reconnaissance. Suddenly three enemy snipers sprinted in front of him. He killed one but the other two reached a house about fifty meters away. Securing a Light Anti-Tank Weapon (LAW), he hit the house dead center, killing the two momentary escapees. Next, noticing enemy fire coming from two more "hooches," he destroyed both of them with additional LAWs. Ordering his men to remain where they were, Hooper crawled to the shattered houses to make sure all the occupants were dead.

They were.

Over to the right the enemy was still firing from a shrine but Hooper knocked it out—by himself using a LAW according to one eyewitness, or with the aid of two other soldiers according to a second eyewitness. In any event, Joe now brought his men forward as they quickly overran a small bunker line.

Or at least so it seemed. Now occurred one of those events that even a dreadfully bad novelist would not have the gall to invent. An enemy officer unexpectedly popped out of the supposedly overrun bunkers. As he aimed his rifle at Hooper at point blank range and squeezed the trigger, the sergeant swung his rifle toward the North Vietnamese officer and squeezed the trigger.

Nothing happened. The enemy's rifle jammed and Hooper's was out of bullets. The North Vietnamese officer ran. Joe chased him, drawing his bayonet as he ran. Catching up to the fleeing officer, Joe plunged the bayonet into him, killing the man.

Meanwhile Hooper's squad had come under intense fire from a building fifty meters to the front. Yelling for covering fire, Joe moved behind the building and bounded through a back entrance. A startled defender fired, the bullets shredding the wall behind Hooper, missing his head by less than an inch. Joe fired a burst, tossed a grenade, quickly pulled the pin on another one and hurled it, and then jumped out just before the concussions killed whoever was still alive inside.

By this time Joe had multiple grenade wounds. Despite the substantial loss of blood and the urging of Platoon Leader Lee Grimsley that he get prompt medical treatment, Joe continued leading his men against enemy fire, which seemed undiminished.

His next target was a line of four bunkers connected by a trench that ran along the left side of the Raiders' axis of advance. Gathering up several hand grenades, Joe moved along the trench, tossing grenades into each bunker as he raced past. Two badly stunned enemy soldiers survived the one-man on-slaught, but they were quickly captured. As Joe made this bunker-busting dash, Raider Dale Urban followed closely behind; each time Hooper tossed a grenade into a bunker Urban poured rifle fire into it after the explosion, making doubly sure the bunker was indeed destroyed.

At the fourth bunker the trench made a 90-degree right turn, leading to three more stoutly defended bunkers. Joe's rifle fire drove away two enemy soldiers hiding behind the first of these dug-in positions. Assuming that this bunker was now empty, he climbed on top of it. About twenty feet away, the other two bunkers were spewing machine-gun fire. Joe silenced the first with his rifle.

Then he suddenly heard whispers in the bunker beneath him. He flipped an incendiary grenade inside, wiping out the bunker and its occupants.

Moments later he took out the third bunker.

These seven bunkers were the enemy's last established defensive positions, but isolated pockets of resistance remained. Thirty meters away from Hooper another Raider, Tex Gray, got hit by enemy rounds that shattered his shoulder, and he fell into one of the enemy's narrow trenches. Squeezed in with only one workable arm, Gray was trapped as gunfire raked the ground around him.

Joe sprinted to the wounded man.

As he leaped into the trench to assist Gray, he laid his rifle—which was now empty—on the ground. Lonnie Thomas, the squad leader Joe saved earlier in the day and who had maneuvered his squad parallel to Joe's ever since, tossed him a .45 caliber pistol. But Joe needed both hands to lift Gray so he set the pistol down, too. As he hoisted the wounded man onto his back, an enemy soldier appeared out of nowhere and raised a rifle into Hooper's face.

He wasn't quick enough. Joe grabbed the pistol and killed him, and then carried Gray to safety.

Then he went back. *Again.*

Joe rejoined his men just beyond the enemy's final trench line, where they were receiving fire from an undetermined source. Hooper and Urban thought they located the enemy position but could not see any enemy soldiers there. Putting their rifles on full automatic and firing low, they sprayed the suspected area with full clips. Crawling forward to investigate, Joe found three North Vietnamese officers, their heads turned to pulp from the rifle fire.

Late in the afternoon, three hours after the battle began, enemy resistance ended.

Returning from the three dead officers, Joe reorganized his men, made sure the wounded received aid, and helped establish a defensive perimeter for the night. Only then did he have his own wounds treated. However, emergency first aid in the field was unequal to Hooper's injuries. Finally realizing how badly he was hurt, when daylight of February 22 dawned Hooper consented to medical evacuation.

During the battle Hooper destroyed a dozen bunkers and assisted in eliminating many more; knocked out four houses occupied by enemy forces; killed at least twenty soldiers with rifle fire, grenades, LAWs, and his bayonet; took two prisoners; rescued four wounded soldiers and Chaplain Erbach; and received multiple wounds himself, at least one of them serious.

Equally important to the physical destruction he inflicted on the North Vietnamese was Joe's inspirational behavior. Acting "with utter disregard for his own safety" throughout the battle, he set such a brave example that other men were ashamed to remain behind.

Thus reads the official story of Joe Hooper's afternoon, derived from eight eyewitness accounts, a post-battle study of the terrain and the enemy defenses, and a detailed set of maps with an accompanying chronology of Joe's actions.

For these actions, Joe Ronnie Hooper received the Medal of Honor.[1]

In the spring of 1971 Joe and a platoon sergeant, a kindred spirit named Steve Hawk, huddled together in the pitch of night on an isolated fire base in northern South Vietnam. Hooper began telling Hawk about February 21, 1968, saying he must have performed all those heroic feats because people told him that he did.

But, personally, he did not remember doing many of them.[2]

One

Everybody saw the war movies.
I mean, that was the big thing.

Rusty Cutlip, Joe's boyhood friend,
on growing up in Moses Lake, Washington

His hero was Audie Murphy.

As a kid, Joe Hooper spent hours at the Skyline Drive-In or the Lake Theater in his hometown of Moses Lake, Washington, watching Murphy dispatch Germans in *To Hell and Back*, or gun down bad guys in the endless horse operas that Murphy starred in.

The two had a lot in common—both came from poor, rural backgrounds, both had alcoholic fathers who would disappear for months at a time, both worked out the shame and embarrassment by fighting the biggest opponents they could find.

Both had movie heroes—just as Joe would sit enthralled by Murphy's cinematic exploits in the sterilized, glamorous Hollywood version of war, Murphy himself had scraped up just enough money to go see Gary Cooper as *Sergeant York*. That was the way, after all, that American boys learned about war, about courage, death, and sacrifice.

So Joe watched Audie Murphy, and when it wasn't Murphy in *To Hell and Back* it was John Wayne in *Sands of Iwo Jima* or *Flying Leathernecks*. And he learned the same lesson that thousands of other boys his age—the generation that would go to Vietnam—learned from these movies: War tested your courage and character. If you passed by fighting bravely you entered the ranks of manhood. If you didn't, you were something less than a real man.

But young men saw another "heroic" image on the screen other than the "all-American men" personified by Murphy and Wayne. They also saw *Rebel without a Cause*. James Dean's screen persona was the polar opposite of Murphy's and Wayne's: an alienated loner who was sensitive, almost feminine in his affect. His courage was more emotional than physical. Dean's heroism was rooted not in the unity of men tested together in battle, but in his nonconformity, in being an outcast. When he did fight, it was only when forced into it, and then only to defend his right to be an individual, to maintain his ambivalence toward mainstream society. His acts of daring were not Murphy's standing on a tank destroyer nor Wayne's charging a bunker, but racing a car toward the edge of a cliff.

Joe Hooper became neither Audie Murphy nor James Dean but instead embodied a lot of both. Like Murphy (and the screen image of John Wayne), Joe performed heroically in war. During times of peace, however, he was closer to Dean, always, always, racing toward the edge of a cliff.

Joe's family was part of the great, restless migration of rural southerners that left for the Northwest during World War II. John Henry Hooper and his wife Maggie first moved their family to Oregon, then back to South Carolina—where Joe had been born on August 8, 1938—then set out for Alaska but only got as far as Moses Lake, Washington.[1]

There they settled, if John Henry's drunken binges and frequent disappearances could be called "settling." From the age of eight or nine he had been riding the rails. Now, even as a father of three (and stepfather of two of Maggie's children by a previous marriage) he would disappear without a word to anyone, hop a train or a bus, and be gone for weeks.[2]

He had a hard time putting down roots—the Hooper family lived in three different houses in town and two small farms out in the country, trying to raise dairy cattle, sheep, and chickens. Neither the farming nor John Henry's series of part-time jobs was enough to make ends meet, so to provide a relatively steady income Maggie worked as a dishwasher at Elmer's Cafe. But the family still struggled financially. As Joe's high school girlfriend recalled, "his parents weren't real wealthy. They were sort of on the poor side. The kids didn't really have a whole lot."[3] And while household life went on all around him, John Henry would barely say a word, sitting quietly in a corner reading the newspaper or western novels, particularly those by Zane Grey and Louis L'Amour.

In 1945 John Henry was thirty-eight, Maggie was forty-two; they had married in July 1935, almost a decade after Maggie's first husband, Raymond Roy Sweatt, died of tuberculosis in 1926. Their family included Joe, his older brother Douglas (born in 1936), a younger sister Audrey (1942), and Frances and Raymond Sweatt Jr., Maggie's children from her first marriage who were already into their twenties; both soon married and moved out of the house. John Henry and Maggie completed their family with another daughter, Kathryn, born in 1948.[4]

John Henry was not much of a role model in an era when the ideal family featured an aggressive, protective, and patriarchal male breadwinner dominating a supportive wife and adoring children. In the Hooper household the kids "never asked Dad for anything. It was Mom. She handled everything. Whatever Mom wanted, she got."[5]

Joe did get one thing from his father that he didn't have to ask for: alcoholism. His drinking would affect his career, his relationships, his marriages; in the end, whether directly or indirectly, it would kill him.

If Joe didn't see much to honor and obey in his father, he also found little to admire in his older brother, Douglas. Tall and thin and with a temperament much like his father's, Doug was an introverted, nonaggressive boy who disliked sports, preferred to back down from a fight, and never married. He did like horses, which have a certain rugged western panache associated with them. Although Joe shared Doug's love of horses, that was their only common interest, and they "never got along too well." Joe considered his brother a "sissy," which in the 1950s was often a veiled reference to homosexuality. Both Audrey and Kathryn believe that Doug probably was gay; if so, his sexual preferences were in stark contrast to the womanizing that became one of his younger brother's trademarks.

While Joe's relationship with his older brother was strained, he got along much better with his little sisters and younger relatives. Even as an adult Joe would have a special affinity for kids, perhaps because he was so impulsively childish himself at times. He used to help Audrey with her homework, made her play baseball "whether I wanted to or not," and taught her how to drive a pickup truck. Unfortunately, he "just didn't teach me how to step on brakes. So I ran into an irrigation ditch." Kathryn considered herself Joe's "pet." And whenever he visited his nephew Jim Gumm, Joe would roughhouse with him and take him bowling.[6]

Moses Lake was a typical American small town. Nestled in the rainshadow of the Cascade Mountains, in 1940 the town was a struggling agricultural patch grafted onto a desert. The few hundred people who hung on did so only in the hope of the so far unfulfilled promise of federally funded, cheap irrigation. The war brought them not water but an army air base that brought a few thousand more people, most of whom left when the war ended. Soon after, the government did begin construction on the long-awaited Columbia Basin Irrigation Project, thus making real the dream of cheap water. With adequate irrigation and a dose of fertilizer the sun-baked landscape turned green with alfalfa, sugar beets, potatoes, and wheat.

The population grew with the crops, from 326 in 1940, to 2,668 a decade later, to over nine thousand just five years later. By 1949 the town had its first hospital and started construction on its first sidewalks and curbs, it began putting in streetlights the next year, and soon a bus service began operating. The *Columbia Basin Herald* went from a semiweekly in 1953 to a daily by 1955.[7]

Despite having a father who was frequently absent or drinking and a brother who was outside the norms of boisterous young male behavior, enjoying a happy childhood in Moses Lake was easy, especially if a kid liked being outdoors, which Joe did. Playing cowboys and Indians or cops and robbers, hunting for ducks and pheasants and rabbits, shooting tin cans with a .22 rifle or blasting away at the azure sky with a .410 pistol or a 12-gauge shotgun (which, said a friend, "just knocked the snot out of us"[8]), tearing up one street and down another on a bike, fishing and swimming during the summer, doing tricks with a yo-yo for hours on end—Joe did them all within the comforting cocoon of a small, friendly community. Like so many boys in Moses Lake, Joe had "a Tom Sawyer–like type of life."[9]

Mischief, of course, always beckoned, but Joe and his boyhood friends generally avoided it. But not always. Joe and Tom Johnson, for example, developed a scam when they discovered that a grocery store kept its empty pop bottles around back. They swiped a few bottles, took them to the front of the store, and turned them in for the deposit, which they promptly spent on peanuts and candy. Unfortunately for the minicriminals the storekeeper caught on after about the third time and called the parents, who "were not happy with us."[10]

Overall, throughout grade school Joe was a fun-loving, happy-go-lucky kid. Redheaded and freckle-faced, he not only enjoyed playing but also participated in extracurricular activities and did his schoolwork. In the sixth grade he received a special certificate "as a reward for achievement in Practical Sales Work," and his eighth grade report card showed him ranked "strong" or "average" (but never "weak") in every subject and aptitude. However, in a prescient comment the teacher noted that Joe's "general attitude could be better."[11]

As Joe grew up his attitude toward school, toward life really, underwent a transformation. According to Joe's sister Audrey, "when he became a teenager everything changed, and I don't know why it changed." His best boyhood friend, Tom Johnson, agreed that Joe changed suddenly and dramatically. Often at odds with both his brother and his father, he taunted Douglas about being a sissy, sassed his father, did little to help out around the farm, and virtually ignored schoolwork. He began socializing with a pack of classmates who considered themselves good guys but admitted they were neither typical nor the nicest kids in school.[12] Others considered them "hoods," or outcasts. These new friends saw a different kid from the one his childhood playmates knew. The maturing Joe Hooper progressively lived at the edge of "ordinary," and his new buddies provided plenty of company out there. Those in the group were not exactly juvenile delinquents since they avoided committing criminal offenses, but they were not model citizens either.

Part of Joe's metamorphosis came from the normal crossing of the Rubicon of puberty, a time of extraordinary change in a child's biology, thinking capacities, and brain functioning that fills a near-adult with internal tumult. Also undoubtedly affecting his attitude was the distinct teen culture that emerged during and after World War II. Adults became deeply worried by the rebellious behavior of their teenagers, by "hot-rods" and rock 'n' roll, rapidly evolving slang and novel hair styles, irresponsibility and juvenile delinquency—according to the *Columbia Basin Herald* the rise in youth crime in the Moses Lake vicinity was "alarming."[13] Nor did parents approve of new teen heroes. Actually, they were existentialist *anti*-heroes. One of the most influential was James Dean, the movie idol whose tragic death in an auto accident in October 1955 sparked a teen cult.

Dean first gained renown in *East of Eden* (1955), in which he played the troubled, misunderstood teenager Cal Trask with such searing conviction that, as a reviewer noted, the role might have led "to his being accepted by young audiences as a sort of symbol of their generation." Fulfilling that prediction was his performance as Jim Stark, the tormented, rebellious loner who respected neither age nor authority in *Rebel without a Cause* (1955), which was released less than a month after Dean's death. When Stark cried "If I had one day when I didn't have to be all confused, when I felt that I belonged some place," he articulated the bewildered anguish that was so much a part of Cold War teenage culture.[14]

But something beyond puberty and teen angst affected Joe, driving him to extraordinary lengths to prove his manhood. Some prominent individuals at midcentury feared that a combination of "momism" (mothers pampering their sons) and aggressive women were undermining male virtues, rendering men weak and meek, and provoking fears about the survival of a neutered society. As the eminent historian Arthur Schlesinger Jr. asked in a 1958 essay, "What has unmanned the American man?" Included in his explanation was a generalized "loss of a sense of identity," which developed out of an increasingly homogenized society that eradicated "all the differences between the individuals who compose it." He also emphasized the new role of women. In language replete with the military metaphors so common in Cold War literature, he argued that it appeared (at least to men) that women represented "an expanding, aggressive force, seizing new domains like a conquering army, while men, more and more on the defensive, are hardly able to hold their own and gratefully accept assignments from their new rulers." The result was "an age of sexual ambiguity" that left "the American male obsessed with his manhood," unsure of his sexual identity and forever worried that, in the words of one eminent doctor, he "will not be man enough."[15]

How did a male prove that he was "man enough"?[16] The answer was never entirely clear since perceptions of how men should act are a product of culture, not genetics. Ideas about manhood vary over time and from society to society. Mid-twentieth-century conceptions of manliness in western civilization arose between the French Revolution and World War I, an epoch that also saw the emergence of strident nationalism. During this era of the "militarization of masculinity," manliness and patriotism became closely linked. Male virtues included honor, aggressiveness, toughness, perseverance, daring, immunity to pain, and a willingness to sacrifice, all of which were especially noble when showcased in pursuit of a higher cause, such as preserving the fatherland. And unlike women, men were unemotional, unwilling, for example, to show fear or pain, which must be mastered and controlled, not displayed. That's why men did not cry readily. As one man put it, men did not weep. They "cry against crying. Their sobbing is distorted by the struggle not to cry out, by grunts and groans uttered only under the exertion of heavy labor."[17] If a man faltered on the emotional front, the failure must be only momentary; men struggled mightily to regain control of their emotions quickly.

Whether or not a man possessed male virtues was never self-evident, so he repeatedly had to prove his manliness, and prove it not so much to women but to other men. Manhood was a relentless series of tests that a man had to pass. Consequently, significant arenas for demonstrating one's manliness were male-dominated activities such as war and competitive sports, where fear could be repressed, pain stifled, and tears rejected. Heterosexual conquests were, of course, a demonstration of manhood, but often collecting sexual "trophies" had less to do with the women involved than it did with impressing other men. Male pleasure-seekers often considered women merely as objects of pleasure or ornamental accessories. Tough, courageous, aggressive, womanizing males were also hard-drinking fellows bent on demonstrating (to themselves and one another) that they could hold their liquor. When it came to male bonding, the barroom was equal to a foxhole or the locker room.

With a dominant mother, a weak father, and a "sissy" for an older brother, Joe may have subconsciously feared becoming "soft" or "feminized," and thus tried doubly hard to compensate for what he considered the failure of his father and brother to act like men. Was it happenstance that Joe relished fighting, excelled at war, concocted legends about himself regarding athletics, and became an inveterate womanizer and heavy drinker?

Entering high school on the cusp of manhood, with rebelliousness surging in his veins, Joe considered school boring and hated following its rules. He increasingly avoided classes. During tenth grade he attended school 126 days but was absent 52 days. If grades are any indication he did not do much studying, either in school or outside of it. All his grades were Cs or worse, except for a lone B in Current World Problems during the second semester of his freshman year.[18] Even when he and his pal Ron Isakson were in detention—and they were in detention a lot—they steadfastly refused to study, preferring to look up "dirty" words in the dictionary.[19]

If Joe did not take academics seriously, what did he enjoy? Not sports. Although Joe was athletic, he "was not one of the 'jocks.'"[20] In high school he showed no interest in running track or playing basketball or baseball and had an abbreviated football career, which consisted of playing on the junior varsity football team in 1955. That year the varsity, who wore white jerseys with maroon numbers and gold stitching, white pants with maroon and gold stripes, and helmets with plastic face masks (the first team in the state to use these protective devices), consisted of eighteen seniors and six underclassmen, but Joe was not good enough to be among the six.[21]

As for the jayvee team, it played five games and won only one of them. A halfback, Joe scored three touchdowns during the season on runs of six, four, and three yards. But his most memorable play was not a touchdown run. It occurred after a defender stopped him at the line of scrimmage and threatened to knock Hooper out of the game if he tried to run his way again. Challenging Joe was never a good idea. Back in the huddle, quarterback Pete Perez called a play for Rusty Cutlip, the other halfback, to carry the ball, but Joe demanded they let him run again. He hit the hole, knees churning high, looking to hurt the opposing player, not heading for the goal line. After the play the unfortunate recipient of Joe's wrath was soon on his way to the hospital with a broken collarbone.[22]

Years later, after Hooper became famous, tales circulated that he had been the Washington state football scoring champion and a track star who was on the verge of being the first American to break the four-minute mile. But, so the story went, he badly injured his leg in an automobile accident, prematurely ending his athletic career. These tales of athletic prowess came directly from Joe, who became an accomplished storyteller, capable of spinning yarns that were humorous, self-deprecating, mesmerizing, believable, and *almost* totally false.[23] As with most great storytellers, a kernel of truth often lay at the center of a web of fabrications. In football he took one season as a jayvee halfback and converted it into gridiron glory. In regard to the four-minute mile, the best he did was to meet some basic Amateur Athletic Union track and field standards as a freshman.[24] And the auto wreck? Joe had been swimming and was driving home without his shoes on when the car left the road, resulting in some minor scrapes not a mangled leg. His former girlfriend said he was lucky to be alive, but Joe told her not to worry. "I was barefoot," he explained. "I won't die barefoot. I'll die with my shoes on."[25] The comment seemed nonsensical to the young woman—and was inaccurate about how he would die.

So Joe was not really interested in high school athletics. Nor was he engaged in other extracurricular activities, not the yearbook or school paper, not the FFA or science club, the speech club or camera club, the band or the glee club, indeed, not anything *in* school.

What interested Joe lurked outside the confines of a classroom. He and Ron Isakson used to do "things we shouldn't have been doing at age 14 and 15." One of their favorite ways to spend the school day was hitchhiking to Spokane ninety miles to the northeast, where they would go to the movies and then hitch back. At least once they thumbed the three-hundred-mile round trip to and from Seattle. Sometimes they put in half a day at school, broke for lunch at the Tastee Freeze, and never made it back for afternoon classes. The lure of the pool tables at Pop's Recreation, next door to the Tastee Freeze, was too strong.

Joe was always hanging out with buddies who liked to smoke, drink, and cruise up and down 3rd Avenue in their hot rods.

Or gambling.

Early on, Joe developed a taste for action, whether shooting pool at Pop's Recreation, bowling for dollars, or rolling the dice.

Joe rarely shot pool for fun; he "played" for money. Roy Wayne Miller, who bummed around with Hooper and Isakson, remembered that Joe "was an exceptionally good pool player" who "made quite a bit of money playing pool as a kid."[26] The same could be said for bowling; he loved to bowl and enjoyed it most when money was riding on the strikes and spares. And Joe enjoyed shooting craps, with one of his regular haunts being the small community of African Americans who lived in Moses Lake, which had the only black church between Spokane and Yakima (the congregation had no more than twenty worshippers).[27] It may be that Joe's ready acceptance of African Americans as equals came from these gambling experiences. Like a professional gambler, Joe always carried a wad of bills in his pocket, sometimes as much as $50 to $100, which was a lot for a teenager in the mid-1950s.

Joe supplemented his gambling income in two ways. First, he often stopped by to say hello to his mom at Elmer's Cafe, and ask her for a dollar. Loving her baby boy, Maggie gave it to him every time. Second, like most of his friends he worked at odd jobs. He applied for his Social Security card on July 3, 1951, when he was not quite thirteen.[28] During the summers he labored for local farmers, changing sprinkler lines, weeding beets, and hoisting hay bales, and hating every moment of it. He did not like farm work, period, not on the family farm and not on anyone else's. More to his liking was setting pins at the Lake Bowling Alley for five cents a line. Joe usually ran four lines simultaneously (most kids could only do three) and received generous tips, so he made quite a bit of money. Since his friends Ron Isakson, Pete Perez, and Al Mason also set pins, he usually had fun, too.

Fun also came in other guises, such as girls, and smoking and drinking. Joe had only one steady girlfriend in high school, Mavis Opp, a cute blonde whose family was comparatively well-to-do; they went steady for less than a year. But Hooper and his pals were always on the chase and, unlike many young men, Joe "wasn't bashful around girls at all."[29] Given the sexually repressive atmosphere of the 1950s, he was surprisingly brazen about sex, a preview of the aggressively open sexuality he displayed as an adult. When most kids signed the annual school yearbook, they wrote some innocuous remarks about friendship and hopes for the future, but not Joe. He made comments about sex. Even though he and Mavis were no longer dating, he inscribed her 1955 yearbook "to the best looking girl in Moses Lake High. A girl who can real[l]y make out." And in his friend Tom Johnson's yearbook he scribbled, perhaps with a mixture of envy and admiration, "Here's to a guy who can really make out with the girls."[30]

When they cruised up and down Third Avenue and Broadway in their cars or stopped in at Harrington's Three-Way Barbecue for a nighttime snack, "cool" teenage males (and Joe was cool) smoked Pall Malls. As for drinking, Joe was for the most part a casual drinker, just like many Moses Lake teenagers who guzzled a few beers at weekend parties. But, ominously, he occasionally showed an unhealthy affinity for alcohol. One night he and Al Mason were watching the high school basketball game when they decided to leave and get some vodka and orange juice. With the makings of a screwdriver in hand, they hopped into the dusty back seat of an abandoned 1941 Chevy coupe sitting behind the school where no one would see them, and proceeded to get plastered. Under the influence of alcohol Joe did what he would continue to do as an adult: he made a spectacle of himself. Returning to the basketball game, he became rowdy, even dashing onto the floor while the game was in progress, and had to be ushered out of the gym.[31]

Such antics, where Joe displayed a craving to be the center of attention, were part of his attraction. Friends understood, instinctively if not intellectually, that Joe was a risk-taker and pleasure-seeker who craved thrills, routinely did things most kids would not dare to do, and would not or could not be embarrassed. Looking back from a distance of fifty years, they speak of him fondly, in part because, as Pete Perez put it, Joe "was just a little different. He just danced to a different piper." Isakson agreed, saying Hooper was "a wild and crazy guy." [32]

Wild and crazy. Also gutsy, adventuresome, and fearless. These were how his buddies described Joe during his last few years in Moses Lake.

And tough.

Joe was a tough kid who knew how to take care of himself in a scrape, and who sometimes went looking for a fight. When he found one he enjoyed it and, once aroused, he had a mean temper. One night he and some friends, bored with nothing to do but drink beer, drove to nearby Ephrata (Moses Lake's foremost rival in high school athletics) "looking for trouble." They went to the basketball game pitting the Ephrata Tigers against a Seattle team, Mount Si. Naturally the Moses Lake contingent sat in the Tiger cheering section—and rooted boisterously for Mount Si. After the game, with tensions already high, Joe and his pals invaded the Tiger Den, a popular hangout for the local kids. "So we went in there, being a bunch of smart asses," recalled Rusty Cutlip, "and I think Joe spit on a guy from Ephrata, and all hell broke loose." The combatants adjourned to a nearby parking lot where Joe squared off against one of Ephrata's star athletes and "beat the shit out of him." [33]

Occasionally Joe even got into a brawl with one of his friends. For example, he and Al Mason got into a fight over a girl. Joe was furious and "by God he just whipped the living dickens out of me, and he wasn't satisfied with that, he grabbed a 2 × 4 and was going to whip me with a 2 × 4 while I was on my back." In his anger would Hooper have really savaged one of his best friends with a board? Al sure thought he would, but no one will ever know because a couple of fellows grabbed Joe and pulled him away. [34]

One thing that helped Hooper in a fight was his high tolerance for pain. Mason marveled that "he never indicated that he ever got hurt in any way," and "if he was hurt, he probably wouldn't tell anybody because it was his problem, no one else's."

His problem, no one else's. In those words lay another key to Hooper's personality. Although he always had friends, Joe was a loner, a guy who did not need anyone to help him and who took "friends" only on his own terms. If you wanted to be around Joe, you did what he wanted to do, and if you did not want to do it, well, fine, just go away. However, he was so personable and his appeal so magnetic, that many people were willing to be Joe's friend on his terms.

The problem was Joe "just didn't know how to show his affection back towards people a lot of times," said Roy Wayne Miller. "I don't think he had the ability to go out of his way and get real involved and real close to a person. He would be with them, but he would never be close." Friendly, yes, but distant. Miller believed something was missing in Hooper's life, something spiritual or psychological, but he did not know what it was. However, he felt certain that "Joe would have a hard time finding his way to a place where he could feel secure and feel happy for the rest of his life."[35]

Rootless and restless, seeking adventure, and bored with school, Joe was never going to be secure and happy in Moses Lake. In late 1955 he and Miller, who wanted to escape his father who "was a pretty tough ol' man," talked about leaving the Columbia River Basin, of asserting their independence by escaping into the wider world. Before acting on their impulses they "waited until after Christmas and New Year's because there were some parties coming up," including one in the Hooper ranch house, which was vacant at the time because the family had moved back into town.

When the Korean War ended in 1953, President Dwight D. Eisenhower warned Americans that they had achieved an armistice on only a single battleground, not worldwide peace. Despite the end of the hot war on the Korean peninsula, the Cold War remained, and Joe Hooper was growing up in the middle of it.

Paradoxically, the Cold War was an era of astonishing affluence and acute anxiety. While the country wallowed in unprecedented wealth, with a burgeoning middle class and rampant consumerism, it also became more fearful and uncertain about its security. Feeling threatened abroad by the lurking Communist menace, and at home by internal subversion, the United States became more militarized, a society preoccupied with security concerns, one in which war was unthinkingly accepted as the prevailing paradigm and metaphor. Americans spoke and thought almost casually about war: cold war and hot war, thermonuclear war and conventional war and limited war, a war on poverty, another on disease, and still another on hunger. From the Interstate and Defense Highway System that Congress authorized in 1956 to help evacuate cities in the event of a war to the space program that commenced a few years later and was modeled after the World War II Manhattan Project that built the atomic bomb, the nation's focus never strayed far from military issues.[36]

In "an eclipse of rationality,"[37] Cold War policymakers not only rejected opportunities to negotiate with the Communists but also exaggerated the external and internal threats. Using rhetoric dripping with imagined perils, sometimes they intentionally over-emphasized Soviet military might and predicted worst-case scenarios for Soviet intentions and behavior, as in the effort to persuade Congress to pass the Marshall Plan. Convinced that the House and the Senate would never respond to mere humanitarian or economic appeals, the State Department presented an inflated picture of the Soviet threat to western Europe. And the new national resolve focused on massive military preparations and hair-trigger readiness, which strategists deemed necessary to prevent more "unprovoked" aggression, as had happened at Pearl Harbor and along Korea's 38th parallel. If deterrence failed, at least the nation would be well armed and prepared to fight.

Still savoring the war-winning performance of American armed forces in World War II and now fearing Armageddon, citizens bestowed unprecedented prestige upon the military. Hooper could hardly miss this since so many military personnel worked at the Moses Lake Army Air Base, which was renamed Larson Air Force Base in May 1950, after Major Donald A. Larson of Yakima, who was killed on a fighter mission over Germany in August 1944.[38] Of course, air base employees sent their children to the local schools where they mingled with the "townies."

Even more than the crops and the weather, the base dominated local news. Improvements to the hangars and barracks, the arrival of the first jet fighters, the death of a test pilot in a crash, a congressional appropriation to build more housing, the arrival of a new air wing for training purposes, indeed, anything associated with the base became front page headlines in the *Columbia Basin Herald*.

One of the most important developments at Larson Air Force Base was the construction of a Boeing Aircraft Company flight center, which was used to test new bombers, initially the B-47 and B-50 and then the B-52. The first B-52, a huge "machine about the size of three high school gymnasiums," arrived for testing in late February 1955, an event the *Columbia Basin Herald* covered on the front page with two pictures and a long story. Four months later when the first B-52 that had been tested at Moses Lake left for its assignment with a combat unit, the newspaper again responded with page one coverage.[39] Years after Joe left Moses Lake he would see B-52s again, this time providing close air support for the Delta Raiders in Vietnam.

Along with the military buildup to confront Communist expansion abroad, Americans fervently pursued domestic Communists or might-be (or even would-be) Communists. Driven by obsessive, highly inflated fears, the public generally supported efforts to quash alleged internal subversion, even if the methods were unsavory and illegal, and even if no threat to domestic tranquility existed. In an ugly, repressive atmosphere, the FBI, CIA, various congressional committees, loyalty boards, and a host of other official agencies went on a witch-hunt against alleged subversives. Bizarrely, FBI director J. Edgar Hoover became so obsessed with hunting presumed Communists that he ignored real criminals, such as members of organized crime, which he denied even existed. He was not the only official during the 1950s and 1960s who behaved irrationally by chasing phantoms while rejecting reality.

In the prevailing mood of militant hyperpatriotism, secrecy became synonymous with security, civil liberties and constitutional safeguards eroded, legitimate dissent was suppressed, and innocent lives were ruined. Novelist Mickey Spillane captured the popular spirit in *One Lonely Night* (1951); the protagonist, Mike Hammer, describes how Communists should be treated: "Don't arrest them, don't treat them with the dignity of the democratic process of the courts of law . . . do the same thing they'd do to you! Treat 'em to the inglorious taste of sudden death."[40] That is, treat 'em exactly the same way the political right accused Communists of treating others.

After conservative Republicans gained control of the legislature in 1946, Washington state was awash in Cold War fears, as exemplified by a 1948 investigation into alleged un-American activities on the University of Washington campus. Headed by state representative Albert F. Canwell, the hearings resulted in three tenured professors being fired for being members of the Communist Party; the University of Washington was the first (but not the last) institution of higher learning to fire professors for their political beliefs. So repressive was the state's political climate that only 103 out of 700 professors on campus dared to defy the mob mentality by signing an open letter critical of the firings.[41]

Nationally, the Red Scare's apex of hysteria came with the outlandish claims—a concoction of innuendo, rumors, slanders, and lies—of the boorish Republican junior senator from Wisconsin, Joseph R. McCarthy. Stunned by President Harry S Truman's victory in the 1948 election, Republicans sought a way to discredit the Democrats and found a splendid avenue of attack in 1949 after the Chinese Communists drove the Nationalist Chinese off the mainland, compelling them to take refuge on Formosa (Taiwan). For right-wing Republicans the explanation for the Communist victory was that Truman's administration was "soft" on Communism, not that the Nationalists were inept, corrupt, and authoritarian. In bitterly partisan attacks, beginning in 1950 McCarthy gained national attention by asserting, without the benefit of proof, that Communists were numerous and influential in the State Department, which helped explain why the Nationalists lost the Chinese civil war.

The televised Army-McCarthy hearings of 1954 discredited the senator by revealing to a broad audience that he was little more than a crude, shameless bully. Censured by the Senate in December 1954, his popularity plummeted, and when he died three years later hardly anyone noticed. Although the senator was gone, "McCarthyism" persisted for decades. The right-wing belief that dissent, nonconformity, or even modest change was disloyal poisoned domestic politics. Some younger conservative Republicans, such as Richard M. Nixon, rose to power by exploiting a McCarthy-like politics of fear, and some government agencies, such as the FBI, persisted in antidemocratic activities, concealing their illegalities behind a veil of secrecy. Lingering McCarthyism warped foreign policy by preventing the government from officially recognizing the People's Republic of China or acting rationally whenever the specter of "losing" territory to the Communists arose.

While abhorring Communism, the nation celebrated "Americanism." What did it mean to be an American? It meant, first of all, being good-hearted and noble, the product of an unsullied past, with a perfect future glistening ahead. Cold War history textbooks portrayed the nation's foreign relations as an unbroken record of disinterested altruism and its domestic affairs as a faultless tale of progress, tranquility, and stability. Students received no hint that the United States might have been an imperial power whose worldwide impact was sometimes less than philanthropic, or that ethnic, racial, and class conflicts historically buffeted the country.[42]

Since Communists were supposedly godless atheists, to be American was to be religious. Or at least a good American *appeared* religious. Although sincere religious beliefs remained widespread, in many cases the self-conscious display of religiosity often seemed more important than genuine devotion. As part of the religious patina, Congress added "under God" to the Pledge of Allegiance in 1954 and two years later adopted "In God We Trust" as the nation's official motto. Formal church memberships soared to unprecedented levels during the 1950s. After all, an individual who belonged to a church was, prima-facie, not godless and therefore could not be a Communist and thus not a subversive.

Religious crusades such as those led by Billy Graham had less to do with piety than they did with combating Satanic Communism. The Devil must be allied with Communism, Graham feared, because only Satan's supernatural power could explain "the tremendous gains of Communism in which they seem to outwit us at every turn." The leading Catholic spokesman, Francis Cardinal Spellman, not only endorsed McCarthy and thereby helped make the Wisconsin senator's excesses respectable but also defined the struggle against Communism as being between "slavery against democracy, evil against good, might against right, Stalinism against God."[43] In the mid-1950s rabidly anti-Communist Catholics were among the most avid supporters of an obscure Vietnamese Catholic politician named Ngo Dien Diem who ruled South Vietnam.

Surprisingly, considering the significance of religion in defining Americanism, the Hooper family was nonreligious. Neither the parents nor the children belonged to a church, though some family members did sporadically attend a Southern Baptist Church. But this was after Joe left home and the family moved to Burbank, California, in the late 1950s. Years later during and after the Vietnam War Joe claimed to believe in God, saying, "not a day goes by when I don't pray three or four times for some reason," but if he really held religious convictions he did so without the benefit of religious training or church membership.[44]

Probably nothing reflected America's self-image better than television, which came of age during the Cold War. In 1955 Americans owned 32 million TV sets, one of which was in the Hooper home. Probably the first TV in Moses Lake belonged to Mavis Opp's parents, who bought it shortly after moving there in the fall of 1952. At that time Moses Lake had only two TV stations, but by late 1955 that number had doubled.[45]

During the Cold War the TV image and the image of the world TV portrayed were identical: black and white. Instead of promoting informed debate about messy international issues, where defining good and bad often resulted in a murky shade of gray, both news programs and entertainment shows were righteously nationalistic, depicting a stark struggle between selfless Americanism and sinister Communism. In a repressive atmosphere where dissent was all too often equated with disloyalty, TV news considered official pronouncements sacrosanct, above challenge or reproach, and reported world events in a relentless us-against-them style. As for entertainment programs, in whatever guise (whether spies, cowboys, or soldiers), fictional TV heroes engaged in an enlightened, brave, and successful *crusade* (note the religious connotation) against a barbarous, dictatorial, and palpably evil foe. For example, in 1955 alone, TV in Moses Lake featured six anti-Communist Cold War spy series: *Passport to Danger, Biff Baker, U.S.A., China Smith, I Led 3 Lives, Secret File, U.S.A.*, and *The Adventures of the Falcon*.

Viewers could also watch military-related programs. Reflecting and nourishing a militarized society throughout the 1950s and well into the 1960s, TV glorified war. It provided live broadcasts of nuclear tests in Nevada (the Advertising Council even sponsored one atomic blast) and allowed the Department of Defense to air its own documentaries, such as the 828 episodes of *The Big Picture* that appeared between 1951 and 1971, and the 26 episodes of *Victory at Sea* that aired in 1952 and 1953 and also appeared on the motion picture screen.[46]

Beautifully produced but chauvinistic, *Victory at Sea* presented what the Defense Department considered timeless "lessons" of war. "War is an act of force," intoned one episode, "and to the application of that force there is no limit, say the philosophers of war." Another segment set forth a mechanistic view of war: "Tarawa, Kwajalein, Eniwetok, *war*. Tarawa, Kwajalein, Eniwetok, *sacrifice*. Tarawa, Kwajalein, Eniwetok, *victory*." That is, War = Sacrifice = Victory. Although military leaders, high-ranking politicians, and the public at large embraced these "lessons," the "lessons" were wrong. The foremost theorist of war, the Prussian Carl von Clausewitz (1780–1831), stressed that all wars have limits, as even a cursory glance at military history demonstrated.[47] And often the seemingly immutable natural law connecting war, sacrifice, and victory came out this way: War = Sacrifice = Defeat.

If it wasn't television, it was the movies.

Kids in Moses Lake went to the movies all the time, if for no other reason than nobody had much else to do in a small town.

In 1949 moviegoers had only one choice: whatever was playing at the Ritz, which had been built three years earlier. By 1955 they could also go to the Lake Theater and, during the summer, the Basin Drive-In and the Sky-line Drive-In, or they could drive the twenty minutes to Ephrata's Lee Theater. Couples out on a date went to comedies, fluffy romantic shows, or those with special appeal to teenagers ranging from entirely forgettable trash such as *Teenage Crime Wave* to classics such as Marlon Brando's *On the Waterfront*, Glenn Ford's *Blackboard Jungle*, and James Dean's *East of Eden*.[48]

But when the boys were out on their own they went to Westerns and, especially, war movies—*The Fighting 69th, Sergeant York, Twelve O'Clock High, Battleground, Beachhead, Strategic Air Command, The Desert Rats, The Fighting Seabees*, and many more. "We saw most of those war movies as they came out," said Pete Perez. "They were a big deal." Rusty Cutlip agreed: "Everybody saw the war movies. I mean, that was the big thing."[49]

For a boy growing up during the Cold War, war movies contained a powerful message regarding the relationship between masculinity and war. No one did more to define manhood in the 1950s and 1960s than Audie Leon Murphy and John Wayne. Murphy, whom Joe Hooper admired to the point of adoration, was the most highly decorated American soldier of World War II and a postwar movie star, while Wayne was strictly a celluloid warrior but no less influential.

Born on June 20, 1925, Murphy came out of rural Texas as poor as the proverbial church mouse, a kid who never had a bike or cowboy boots and never learned to play baseball because he could not afford a glove.[50] His father was a drunken sharecropper who frequently left the family for weeks at a time and then abandoned it altogether when Murphy was fifteen. His mother, who provided the family at least a semblance of stability, died the next year. Given the Murphy's poverty, a lengthy education was out of the question. Before he completed grade school Audie dropped out to work at odd jobs just to survive. Because low-end jobs paid little, survival sometimes depended on hunting skills, and he was a superb outdoorsman and expert marksman, one who could plunk a fleeing rabbit while shooting from a moving car. Whatever despair Murphy may have felt about his condition in life, he could not fall back on religion for comfort since his family, like Hooper's, was nonreligious.

Despite the impoverished childhood, Murphy was spunky, a mean runt of a kid who carried a big chip on his shoulder because of "a psychic need to overcome the sins and embarrassment of [his] father."[51] Audie was always fighting, accepting any challenge just for the thrill of it no matter how big the other boy was—and the other boy was always bigger. Fortunately for Murphy, he found an outlet for his aggression: war. Military matters had long enthralled him. While hoeing cotton under the blazing Texas sun, his uncles, World War I vets, stirred Murphy's imagination by regaling him with stories about their overseas adventure. Poor as he was, Murphy sometimes saved enough money to go to the movies. Only one film was so inspirational that he spent precious pennies to see it twice: *Sergeant York*, starring Gary Cooper as the rural Tennessee pacifist-turned-killer Alvin York, who was America's most highly decorated World War I soldier.

Packing only 112 pounds on a 5 foot 5 1/2 inch frame when he enlisted in 1942 (a statistically average girl in 1941 was 120 pounds and 5 feet 5 inches), the brown-haired, hazel-eyed Murphy looked like a mere boy entering a man's army. The perception was accurate since he lied about his age and was only seventeen, not the mandatory eighteen years old. Small even among infantrymen—who averaged an inch shorter than the rest of the army's average height—Murphy acquired a hated nickname, "Baby," from his top sergeant. Superior officers tried to protect this frail boy, wanting him to become a cook or work at the PX, but he refused, insisting on a front-line assignment. His unit initially saw action on Sicily, then fought its way through Italy and France, and Murphy was invariably in the midst of combat. Even though fear knotted his intestines he repeatedly volunteered for dangerous missions, such as stalking snipers or leading patrols into enemy-controlled territory. Blessed with uncanny woodcraft skills and uncommonly good luck ("Anyway, I'm lucky," Audie said), he displayed a genius for combat and miraculously escaped death time after time. No one knows how many Germans he killed. An army public relations officer estimated the number at 240, but Audie disputed that number. Although he never kept a personal "body count," he was confident that "I didn't kill that many." He simply developed an executioner's mentality, believing that "every Kraut I killed put me a mile or so nearer Texas."[52]

Before the war ended Murphy suffered three wounds, none of them disfiguring, so in that sense his luck held. He received a field promotion from platoon sergeant to second lieutenant in October 1944, and to first lieutenant in February 1945, and earned every medal the army awarded for heroism, including the top three (Medal of Honor, Distinguished Service Cross,

Silver Star). He also lost all romantic notions about combat. The Sicilian campaign knocked "the vinegar out of my spirit," he wrote, and before long he perceived the war as nothing but "an endless series of problems involving the blood and guts of men." Developing a fatalism common to combat soldiers, he believed simply that "we live until we die" and viewed a grave as "merely an open door that divides us from our comrades," so many of whom died in Europe.[53]

Germany's defeat gave him no cause for celebration. By war's end Audie felt nothing but "complete and utter weariness" and was suffering from what medics called "combat fatigue." He feared the bloodletting had stripped away his sense of decency, that he was so ensnared in death that he no longer knew how to live. *Life* magazine made a national hero out of Audie when he appeared on the July 16, 1945 cover, and Murphy eventually resolved "to live again."[54] But coming out of the war with no useful skills (except killing Germans) and churned by internal anxieties, he had no idea what to do with the rest of his life. When Hollywood actor Jimmy Cagney offered him the use of his guesthouse he accepted, staying there in virtual seclusion for months trying to recover his health, both physical and spiritual. "All I wanted," he recalled, "was some peace and time to think things through."[55]

Being in the movie capital of the world and with no other prospects, he tried acting. Surprisingly, he became tolerably good at it—sometimes *too* good. On occasion he exhibited an unnerving intensity, his eyes glaring with such a frightening killer's glare that directors avoided shooting close-ups of his face for fear of scaring the audience.[56] A quick-draw specialist and splendid horseman, Murphy appeared in a number of Westerns; one of his best, *Destry*, showed at the Lake Theater in June 1955, and was so popular it was back for a repeat appearance in January 1956. But he was also a natural for war films. His most significant role was playing himself in *To Hell and Back* (1955), the film version of his autobiography of the same title. The book was an unromantic tale of misery, wild savagery, and brutal, unnatural death; at the end of a battle, when the generals proclaimed victory, it still felt like a defeat to the soldiers. The film sanded off the book's jagged edges, sanitizing and domesticating the war, converting Murphy's terror-filled account into a war story suffused with humor, honor, and glory.

The movie, not the book, taught boys who came of age in the 1950s and served in Vietnam in the 1960s about manhood and war. Following Audie from childhood poverty through his Medal of Honor ceremony, *To Hell and Back* was, in essence, a coming-of-age movie in which war served as a rite of passage from boyhood to manhood. War, courage, and manhood were inseparable. Fortunately, courage was virtually risk-free and the passage into manhood was almost painless—at least in the movie. A single brave man, such as Audie Murphy, could successfully attack machine guns through a hail of lead, or stand atop a burning tank destroyer fending off a concerted enemy attack, and emerge a hero. Those unfortunate few who received mortal wounds expired peacefully, and the occasional soldier who took a non-fatal bullet to the gut or the shoulder lost a mere thimbleful of blood and bore his injuries with quiet dignity, usually with a well-scripted quip on his lips.

Murphy realized the film was a fraud, that he was being a lot braver and more reckless in the staged battles than he had been in the real ones and that the film was far off target in depicting genuine battlefield conditions. But in darkened theaters, eyes wide with amazement and mouths stuffed with hot buttered popcorn, kids did not. Recalling his childhood when he saw Murphy's Medal of Honor action in *To Hell and Back*, a Marine wrote that "he was so brave I had chills running up and down my back, wishing it were me up there." [57]

Despite the hero's welcome, homecoming parades, banquets in his honor, and a Hollywood career, Audie found that living normally again was impossible. His postwar life was "a fight for a long, long time to keep from being bored to death. *That's what two years of combat did to me!*" [58] Beset by a trick stomach, insomnia, and recurring nightmares about the war, Murphy found relaxation impossible even with the aid of tranquilizers, to which he became addicted. A loner who avoided Hollywood's social life, he slept with a light on and a pistol under his pillow—and on three occasions woke up screaming from a nightmare and firing the pistol. Although proud of his medals, "they weren't worth what I went through." [59] So he took no special care of them, losing some, giving others away, and avoiding ceremonies where he needed to display them.

Restless, discontented, and bored, Audie came alive only when he was living on the edge, womanizing, gambling, and doing undercover police work. Obsessive skirt-chasing undermined his marriages to starlet Wanda Hendrix and airline stewardess Pamela Murphy, and compulsive gambling, first exhibited while he was in the army, resulted in chronic indebtedness. Murphy played poker and craps, but his true passion was horse racing. He loved horses—he bought and bred them, enjoyed being around them, and, most of all, liked to bet on them, sometimes losing tens of thousands of dollars during a single afternoon. When not in some woman's bed or placing bets, to dispel his chronic lassitude Murphy hung around the Los Angeles Police Department where he could associate with cops who were men of action, rode on nighttime patrols with Dallas policemen, or even more dangerously, did undercover narcotics work in Tucson. But just living remained a struggle.

John Wayne never wrestled with the traumas that afflicted Audie Murphy because he was never in a war.[60] He had the chance, but when the opportunity came he evaded it. For a decade before World War II, Wayne survived in Hollywood by choking down a diet of bad scripts, but by 1941 he was approaching stardom. Then the war began and Wayne had a choice to make: should he serve his country or himself? With little hesitation and few qualms, he chose the latter. Other actors put their careers on hold and donned uniforms while Wayne maneuvered to avoid either volunteering or being drafted. True, he was in his mid-thirties and had a wife and four young children, but other stars who were as old or older and had children readily volunteered.

With fewer male lead actors available, Wayne's career soared, as did his social life. He deserted his family to pursue his second wife and carried on a delicious affair with Marlene Dietrich on the side (like Audie Murphy, for Wayne one woman was never enough, even if the one was his wife). "It's a damn shame that with a war going on he has to think about his lousy stinking tail," wrote Mary Ford, the wife of Hollywood director John Ford, who had joined the Navy and was serving overseas.[61]

Wayne's single-minded careerism served him well as he became history's most popular actor, with no one else a close second. The idolization of John Wayne was so immense that he was not just a movie star but a cultural icon whose image as a man's man resonated throughout society—or at least among males since he had few female fans. The silver screen Wayne, with his hard-set jaw and growling voice, I-own-the-world swagger, toughness, and bold confidence was a man of action and violence who projected an aura of implacable will, self-reliance, and fierce patriotism. As an actor, dying for his country was such a small price to pay that he did it often. The real man, well, he preferred a safe life of steaks, cigars, and women.

Although Hollywood produced dozens of World War II films every year, *To Hell and Back* and Wayne's role as Sergeant Stryker in *Sands of Iwo Jima* (1949) stirred especially widespread adolescent fantasies of war among the boys who became Vietnam-era soldiers. Arriving in Vietnam, one soldier saw himself "charging up some distant beachhead, like John Wayne in *Sands of Iwo Jima*, and then coming home a suntanned warrior with medals on my chest." [62] This soldier forgot that Stryker did not come home because he died on Iwo Jima, but the mistake is understandable since the fatal bullet wound was so innocuous that a small Band-Aid would have stanched the blood flow. And another combatant admitted that before going to Vietnam he "never talked with anybody about combat experiences. I simply went by what I'd seen in John Wayne movies. I believed it all." [63] Unfortunately, akin to *To Hell and Back*, *Sands of Iwo Jima* presented a sterilized, romanticized war.

Wayne's warless record did not prevent him from wrapping himself in the American flag and calling upon others to make wartime sacrifices during the Vietnam era, and he ridiculed them for being "soft" if they refused. His third wife believed he never wavered from his superpatriotism because he was "trying to atone for staying at home" during his war.[64] Audie Murphy, who had no need to seek atonement, tempered his Vietnam-era patriotism. At times he felt the United States should go all-out for victory even if it took a million troops. Viewing it through a World War II prism, he believed, "we go in, we do the job, then we get out! There's no other way." But at other times he did not think the United States should be in Vietnam, and he worried that his two draft-age sons might be called upon to serve. "I don't want them to try to be what I was. I don't want dead heroes for sons." [65] All too well he knew what real war did to men, even heroes who survived.

If John Wayne represented the ideological rigidity that sent Americans to Vietnam and kept them there beyond any useful purpose, Audie Murphy personified the mixed emotions that most Americans ultimately felt about the conflict. But they both cast a long shadow over that war. Their on-screen personas and their off-screen pronouncements, especially Wayne's, helped militarize the society by ennobling war, by implying that invincible America always won its wars, by persuading a generation of young men that war was painless, and by convincing them that courageous behavior in combat was *the* mark of manhood. For boys reaching military age in the 1960s, the "lesson" they learned from watching Murphy and Wayne movies was simple. Battle tested an individual's courage and character. Those who passed the ordeal-by-combat test by serving bravely and honorably entered the ranks of real men. Those who failed were something less.

A lot of boys went off to Vietnam to be Audie Murphy or John Wayne. To become men.

But one lesson they had not learned by watching the movies was that the dividing line between courage and foolhardiness, between manhood and death, was gossamer thin.

In the quirky 1984 film *Birdy*, Al Columbato (played by Nicholas Cage) is speaking to his near-catatonic friend, Birdy (Matthew Modine), who had been traumatized by the Vietnam War. "They got the best of us; we're totally screwed up," says Al. "In any other war we would have been heroes. We didn't know what we were getting into with this John Wayne shit. Boy, were we dumb."

But in expressing the dislocation of expectations that occurred between reel war fantasies and real war, an experienced combat soldier, not an actor, said it best: "Fuck you, John Wayne." [66]

On January 3, 1956, after completing just the first semester of his junior year, Joe Ronnie Hooper dropped out of high school. Accompanied by his friend Roy Wayne Miller, he walked through the door of the Moses Lake naval recruiting station, beginning a quest to control his fate, to create a comfortable identity at some agreeable midpoint between his view of himself and the world's view of him—and perhaps fearing that the quest would be futile.

Two

Everyone can kiss my ass.

Joe, commenting on his attitude toward life

Joe Hooper had a pair of lips tattooed on his right buttock.

The lips, he said, were a symbol that "everyone can kiss my ass."[1]

Joe and his good friend Gary Foster were in Hong Kong, enjoying shore leave from the USS *Hancock*, and they took a taxi to the skid row area along the Kowloon waterfront, where they walked around, swilled too much cheap beer, and then got "stenciled." Gary got two tattoos on his back, another on his arm.

Joe settled for just one—the lips.

When Joe and Roy Miller appeared at the naval recruiting station in Moses Lake, Joe, of course, had no idea he would end up in exotic Asiatic locales.[2] He just knew he was getting out of Moses Lake, which was triumph enough for a young man with a limited education and no marketable skills. Because Joe was only seventeen, his father signed a parental consent form allowing his son to volunteer. Enlisting at such a young age was not unusual. For example, in December 1955, four Moses Lake boys joined the Navy, and at least two of them were only seventeen.[3]

Joe's enlistment obligated him to serve six years. However, he only needed to remain in the Regular Navy for his minority (that is, until August 7, 1959, which was the day before he turned twenty-one); he could complete his obligation in the Naval Reserve. As with all recruits during the Cold War era of hyperpatriotism, Joe attested that he did not belong to any of a long list of organizations that the attorney general deemed totalitarian, fascist, Communist, or subversive. These ranged from the American Peace Crusade and the Central Council of American Women of Croatian Descent to the Santa Barbara Peace Forum and the Pittsburgh Arts Club—and several hundred more.

Two weeks after being accepted for enlistment at Moses Lake, Joe and Roy received bus tickets to Seattle, spent the night in the YMCA there, and took their physicals at the Armed Forces Examining Station the next morning. The medical examination report indicated Joe was auburn-haired and blue-eyed, thin and wiry with only 148 pounds clinging to his 5 foot 9 1/2 inch frame, and had perfect 20/20 vision.[4]

After passing the physical they took a train, packed with other recruits, to San Diego. Joe enjoyed the train ride, shooting dice almost the entire trip and doing quite well, but neither he nor Roy liked the reception at the U.S. Naval Training Center (the equivalent of "boot camp") at San Diego. No sooner had the recruits stepped off the train than the drill instructors were "in our face like you wouldn't believe. They called us everything but white people. And even the black people they called them white. It was a horrible shock." Followed quickly by another one: a visit to the barber. Proud of his red hair, Joe always carried a comb with him to keep it immaculately neat. With a shaved head he looked terrible, like a cue ball with two big blue eyes staring out of it. And then "we really got the shock when we started through boot camp and all the things they wanted us to do." Boot camp was tough, tougher than either Joe or Roy had imagined. Their drill instructors had "the nastiest mouths" Roy ever encountered, bellowed an unending array of obscenities at the recruits, and oftentimes "were quite brutal." Yet Joe undoubtedly liked boot camp. It brought structure and stability into his life for the first time, and for someone with Joe's temperament, the outdoor physical activity was fun.

Between periods of what seemed to them like verbal and physical abuse, recruits took a battery of occupational tests, which indicated that Joe was average in all categories except for clerical work, where he ranked toward the low end of the spectrum. He typed only fifteen words a minute, a severe handicap. When Joe filled out forms during his military career it confirmed his bottom-rung clerical rating; close attention to paperwork was never among his better attributes.

When Hooper and Miller finally got one day a week off from boot camp they savored the experience, spending those precious days of liberty in San Diego. They went to the movies, strolled up and down Broadway, stopped at local restaurants to get some decent food, and then lingered at the bus stop, basking in those few remaining moments of blissful freedom before catching the last bus back to the base. If they received extended leave time they traveled to Moses Lake where Roy began dating (and eventually married) Mavis Opp, Joe's old girlfriend.

Boot camp ended March 30, 1956. Having endured it together as inseparably as conjoined twins, Joe and Roy suddenly went their separate ways after Roy saw a bulletin board notice calling for tryouts for a naval football team on North Island. He made the team, and as a bonus also made the basketball team. "So basically all I did all the time in the service is play football and basketball over at North Island. I actually had quite an enjoyable life in the service." After boot camp he never saw or heard from Joe again.

While Roy pursued his military athletics, the Navy assigned newly minted Airman Apprentice Joe Ronnie Hooper to an attack squadron (VA-155) on board the USS *Wasp*, an Essex-class aircraft carrier.[5] Since the *Wasp* was at sea in early April 1956, on an Operational Readiness Inspection in preparation for an extended Far Eastern tour, Joe enjoyed two weeks of shore leave after completing boot camp before he walked aboard the ship, which sailed westward on April 23.

The voyage took the crew to Guam, Japan, and the Philippines. Along the way the *Wasp* participated in Operation Sea Horse, a five-day exercise involving both day and night training maneuvers, and searched for a Navy patrol plane that had been shot down off Communist China's coast. Along the way, too, Joe became acquainted with shipboard life by working on the flight deck, checking out planes, pushing them around, and shepherding them off the deck. This was hard, dangerous work what with the noise, the fumes, the planes' folded wings lowering into the flight position, and lots of whirling propellers, each with the potential to maim or kill in a careless nanosecond. Joe also began a three-month tour of Mess Cooking, an almost obligatory task for a junior enlisted man. Overall the young apprentice did well, achieving a perfect 4.0 rating in conduct and 3.8s for professional performance, seamanship, and leadership. By the time the *Wasp* returned to San Diego in mid-October Joe had received his first promotion, to Airman (or E-3).

His family was nearby to greet the returning sailor. Maggie insisted that the family follow Joe, her favorite child, to San Diego. By September the Hoopers had departed Moses Lake—they had not achieved noticeable success in rural living anyhow—and moved to Burbank, California, where they rented an apartment. John Henry worked as a janitor at a company that made stainless steel products and also cleaned up a couple of Burbank bars after hours; the Los Angeles area freeways traumatized him so he refused to drive, either walking or taking the bus to work and anywhere else he needed to go. Maggie did house cleaning at the El Rancho Motel on Burbank Boulevard and, as always, took care of her baby boy. She not only lavished care packages on Joe but, as she had done in Moses Lake, also often gave him money with no questions asked.[6]

While the *Wasp* was back in San Diego the Navy reclassified it as an antisubmarine warfare carrier. After spending three months preparing for this new mission, it left for Cape Horn on January 31, 1957, heading for the East Coast.

By then AV-155, including Joe Hooper, had transferred to another Essex-class carrier, the USS *Hancock*, then based at San Francisco, which became Joe's home port.[7] While there Joe qualified as a Plane Captain for one of the Navy's most successful planes, the *Skyraider*, the Navy's last piston-engine attack plane. The first model flew in 1945 and subsequent versions remained in service as late as 1969. Although seemingly out of place in a jet-propelled era, these slow-moving, low-flying, prop-driven planes performed yeoman duty in Vietnam, delivering bombs, rockets, and napalm with considerable accuracy—and even shooting down a MIG-17 in June 1965. As a plane captain Joe had oversight over the air-readiness of one particular plane.

With Joe Hooper and his new good friend Gary Foster serving in AV-155, the *Hancock* undertook a Far Eastern voyage lasting from early April through mid-September 1957. Originally from Evansville, Indiana, Gary joined the Navy in 1956, the same year as Joe. When he and Joe first met at Moffett Field, "it was like we knew each other forever"; they were equally adept at hell-raising, and they often talked about how they could have been brothers. If so they would have been twins since both were born on August 8, 1938, and were virtually the same height and weight.

Besides Joe getting the tattoo in Hong Kong, he and Gary hot-wired a supply truck in Japan so that they could have their own transportation rather than relying on shuttle buses. Where did they have to go with such urgency? One place was to the brothels. When at sea Joe shot craps, frequently heading down to a weapons locker where a game went on more or less continuously. And Joe and Gary drank. If Joe imbibed only moderately while in high school, he began drinking heavily in the Navy. Booze may have accounted for his increasingly erratic performance record. After late 1956, with only an occasional 3.8 mixed in with a large number of 3.0 and 3.2 ratings, his marks were decidedly lower than his initial sterling performance.

When the *Hancock* returned to San Francisco Joe and Gary got into numerous alcohol-induced scraps, especially with the detachment of Marines at Moffett Field. Fighting between sailors and Marines "really wasn't encouraged, but it wasn't discouraged," even though some of the brawls became vicious. On one occasion Joe had the middle finger of his left hand severely bitten. Although he originally told the medical staff that three civilians attacked him in the alley behind the San Jose bus depot, Joe was lying to protect a fellow serviceman. He had actually been in a fight with a Marine who bit the digit. Since the laceration failed to heal properly and became swollen and painful, a week later Joe reported to sick bay to have the purulence drained and receive a healthy dose of achromycin and streptomycin (Joe was allergic to penicillin) to fight the infection.[8]

Hooper and Foster also engaged in gay-bashing. They would go to "queer parks" and when a homosexual approached one of them they would ambush the man, steal his money and car keys, and then drive around in the stolen vehicle for a while. These were risk-free crimes since the victim could not go to the authorities. Denounced and hounded by politicians, journalists, filmmakers, police agencies, and the armed services, homosexuals had no defenders; anti-gay ideology was so virulent that not even the American Civil Liberties Union, on numerous other occasions the nation's foremost defender of citizens' rights, defended them. For Joe, homophobia was a way of asserting his manhood since "real men" conquered women; gays were soft, effete, womanlike, and real men conquered them, too.[9]

Marines and homosexuals got a reprieve in February 1958, when the *Hancock* departed San Diego for Asia, ultimately becoming part of the powerful naval force that took station off Taiwan to protect the Nationalist Chinese islands of Quemoy and Matsu from a Communist Chinese invasion. The first Quemoy-Matsu crisis occurred in 1953–54 when the Nationalists used the islands as staging areas for raids against the mainland and for infiltrating agents into Communist China, and the Communists threatened to retaliate. When the United States stationed aircraft and artillery with nuclear capabilities on Taiwan and positioned part of the 7th Fleet in the Formosa Straits, tensions eased. Joe may have known something about this crisis since it received considerable attention on both the front and editorial pages of the *Columbia Basin Herald* well into 1955.[10]

Now a war scare over the two small islands flared up again. Nationalist and Communist fighter planes dueled sporadically near Taiwan, and in late

August the Communists hammered Quemoy with a tremendous artillery bombardment, apparently as preparation for an invasion. The 7th Fleet soon had 6 aircraft carriers (including the *Hancock*) and 150 other ships on a war footing in the Formosa Straits. Although the records are unclear, it may be at this time that Joe and Gary volunteered for a group that would rescue downed pilots. Their services were never required since no pilots were shot down; nonetheless, this did not deter Joe from spinning fantastic yarns about his role in a daring rescue.

As the threat of war subsided in the Far East the *Hancock* turned homeward, passing under the Golden Gate Bridge in early October and entering the San Francisco Shipyard six weeks later to undergo a prolonged overhaul. While in San Francisco Joe scored a series of personal triumphs. In early 1959 he received a Good Conduct Medal, demonstrating that his behavior had not strayed too far from the norm. On the last voyage he also began studying to take the test to become an Aviation Storekeeper (or E-4). After failing on the first try he passed the exam the next time and received the promotion, indicating that he was "a pretty good kid, a smart kid."[11] A month later, in mid-July 1959, he passed another exam, the high-school-level General Educational Development (GED) test, giving him the equivalent of a high school diploma. Passing the GED was fairly easy because the Navy had helpful correspondence courses and, as Gary Foster said, "on a ship what else did you have to do when you were at sea but read and two or three guys get together and figure it out."

However, his record in San Francisco was not all on the positive side. While on liberty in mid-November 1958 Joe was attacked between First and Second Streets in San Jose, struck from behind with an object, and knocked unconscious. He received emergency medical treatment at the Santa Clara County Hospital.[12] How did this attack occur? Was it unprovoked? Or did Joe provoke it in a drunken stupor? Was he harassing someone who fought back? The record does not say.

In mid-1959, a personnel officer explained to Joe the advantages of an immediate Regular Navy reenlistment at the end of his minority.

Hooper said he did not intend to reenlist.

After three years and six months of service, on July 16, 1959, he received a $108.60 cash settlement for eighteen days of unused leave, was released from the Regular Navy, and entered the Naval Reserve in Category G, which required no training and no annual active duty so that he could adjust to a civilian occupation.

The same month Joe Hooper left the Navy, a Viet Cong attack near Bien Hoa, South Vietnam, killed Major Dale Buis and Master Sergeant Chester Ovnand.[13]

Americans in Vietnam? *Killed* in Vietnam?

How and why American servicemen were in Southeast Asia in 1959 was a classic Cold War story of ideological rigidity, political timidity, ignorance, and arrogance. From the late 1940s through the early 1970s no president made an accurate appraisal of the nation's vital interests. During the 1950s President Harry S Truman's administration initiated the commitment to Vietnam and President Eisenhower's strengthened it. In the succeeding decade the administration of President John F. Kennedy militarized the commitment, President Lyndon B. Johnson converted it into a full-fledged war, and President Richard M. Nixon stubbornly continued the fighting despite the war's tenuous relationship to America's security interests.

The overarching paradigm for policymakers was a paranoid anti-Communism. They perceived the world as being divided into two spheres. One was the democratic Free World guided by the United States, tolerant of diversity, "generous and constructive" in its impulses, and without "covetousness" in its international relations. The other was the Communist Slave World directed by the Soviet Union, with the Kremlin's "totalitarian dictatorship" at its epicenter.[14] Hooper's hometown newspaper ran a cartoon typical of the day. It showed Abraham Lincoln peering at a globe, sundered in two by an Iron Curtain, with the caption reading "Still half free and half slave."[15]

The Slave World was not only immoral, placing little value on human life and being disdainful of individual rights, but also monolithic and "inescapably militant," an aggressive force bent upon world domination. Again, the *Columbia Basin Herald* vividly portrayed this fear in a political cartoon, this one showing Soviet leader Nikita S. Khrushchev driving a tank dubbed the "Red War Machine." Overhead he had thrown a rope around a star labeled "World Domination." With the Communists always seeking to expand their domain at freedom's expense, the United States and Communism were implacable enemies. As NSC-68, one of the seminal top-secret Cold War state papers, put it, "There is a basic conflict between the idea of freedom under a government of laws, and the idea of slavery under the grim oligarchy of the Kremlin." [16]

First announced in a major address by President Truman in March 1947, "containment" became the unassailable foreign policy lodestar. Like a virulent disease, Communism had to be quarantined before it contaminated the Free World's still-healthy states. Although Communism was such a powerful malignancy that it could not be readily or quickly destroyed, it must not be allowed to expand outside its present boundaries because, again in NSC-68's alarmist language, "a defeat of free institutions anywhere is a defeat everywhere." Any defeat would embolden the Communists and demoralize America's allies, tilting the global struggle in Moscow's favor. The only thing that could frustrate Soviet designs was "if in its forward thrusts it encounters a superior force which halts the expansion and exerts a superior counterpressure." [17] As the words "superior force" denoted, containment relied primarily on military power, not political, economic, and psychological programs.

Reinforcing the containment doctrine were the Munich analogy, a domino theory, a "credibility" mantra, and the fear of reawakening McCarthyism. Policymakers and strategists believed one of World War II's foremost lessons was that democratic nations should never appease an aggressor, as Britain did with Hitler at Munich with such dire consequences. Had Britain, France, and the United States confronted Hitler immediately, so the argument went, World War II would have been averted. Considering Stalin and Communism akin to Hitler and Fascism, policymakers now persuaded themselves and much of the public that the Soviet Union was such a brutal, aggressive foe that it imperiled world peace. To prevent World War III, the Free World must do what it had not done in the 1930s: stand up to threatened aggression forcefully at any time, any place.

The Munich analogy had an almost hypnotic appeal, especially when combined with a domino theory. Although Truman never explicitly used that phrase, the concept had its roots in his administration. President Eisenhower first articulated the principle at a press conference in April 1954, asserting that nations were like a row of dominoes: if the first one fell it inevitably toppled the others. Here was further reason to resist an aggressor immediately, to keep that first domino from falling. Applied to Southeast Asia, the concept implied that if Vietnam "fell" into the Communist camp, then the neighboring dominos of Laos and Cambodia would "fall," followed by Thailand, Burma, Malaya, and Indonesia, and eventually India. Soon dominoes would be toppling in the Middle East. A mechanistic worldview more suited to the neat equations of Newtonian mechanics than to the analytically sloppy world of nation states, the domino theory nonetheless became an unquestioned article of faith, infusing an otherwise insignificant nation such as Vietnam with unwarranted importance.

To make containment work, to avoid a new Munich or a disastrous run of toppling dominoes, the nation had to maintain its credibility. Government officials considered every potential Munich-like challenge or every possible falling domino a test of America's character, of its will and determination, its national honor. The need to maintain credibility became an incessant incantation. The Communists, argued NSC-68, were "seeking to demonstrate to the free world that force and the will to use it are on the side of the Kremlin, that those who lack it are decadent and doomed."[18] To avoid Free World defeatism the United States, as the only nation with sufficient power to stand up to the Communists, must maintain its credibility as freedom's defender. "We have a problem trying to make our power credible," commented President Kennedy, "and Vietnam looks like the place."[19] Consumed by credibility worries, policymakers only rarely asked whether a futile venture in a region of no immediate vital security interest (especially if the rescue effort was on behalf of a nation that was less-than-democratic) might actually harm the nation's standing in the world community by undermining its greatest assets, which were its moral authority and reputation for sensible judgment.

Successive presidents not only worried about preserving credibility abroad but also, after 1954, about preventing a revived McCarthyism at home. The Wisconsin senator cast a long, ugly shadow over domestic political life. Who could forget how "losing" China unleashed a right-wing firestorm that assailed the loyalty of gifted public servants and savaged basic civil liberties? No politician, especially no Democrat, wanted to risk being perceived as "soft" on Communism by "losing" any more territory, especially territory in Asia, no matter how insignificant.

Devotion to a worldview based on an unquestioning anti-Communism

—buttressed by a suspect analogy, an unproved theory, an uncritical concern for credibility, and worries about McCarthy-like domestic politics—negated any need to understand local circumstances or change over time. Ideological rigidity impelled civil and military leaders to overlook a country such as Yugoslavia, which should have punctured the belief in a monolithic Communism because its government represented an independent Communist variant under intensely nationalistic leadership. Prevailing ideology also undervalued the long-standing conflict between the Soviet Union and China for domination in Asia that split those nations into bitterly hostile camps, and ignored the historic enmity between China and Vietnam stretching back several thousand years. More generally, America's staunch anti-Communism caused it to misunderstand the postcolonial upheaval that would have roiled the globe with or without Communism. Unlike in Europe where the line between Communists and non-Communists was comparatively sharp and readily grasped, in Asia the tangled knot of nationalism, anti-imperialism, and Communism was difficult to unravel, sometimes even for native Vietnamese, Laotians, and Cambodians. In North Vietnam most "Communist" soldiers considered their leaders nationalists rather than Communists.[20]

The post–World War II foreign policy paradigm conjured up threats where no threats existed. It prevented policymakers from even attempting to understand Southeast Asian realities, especially in Vietnam where a war between the French and Vietnamese nationalists (known as the Viet Minh) began in 1946.

The French conquered Vietnam during the mid-nineteenth century and ruled it until World War II when the Japanese temporarily replaced them as colonial overlords. Following World War II the Vietnamese desire for independence collided with France's determination to reestablish its colonial empire. Led by the charismatic Ho Chi Minh, the Viet Minh liked neither the French nor the Japanese and fought them both, even receiving weapons and other support from the United States in their struggle against the Japanese. Although a Communist—he founded the Indochinese Communist Party in 1929—Ho was above all else a nationalist whose foremost goal was to free his country from colonialism, and the Communist-dominated Viet Minh attracted nationalists of many different political persuasions.[21]

On the same day as Japan's formal surrender (September 2, 1945), Ho proclaimed the formation of an independent Democratic Republic of Vietnam (DRV), issuing a document that borrowed heavily from the American Declaration of Independence. Unfortunately for Vietnam, *declaring* independence did not automatically *secure* it. Like Britain in North America in the 1770s, France in the 1940s would not willingly leave Vietnam.

The First Indochina War began in November 1946, when the French shelled Haiphong, killing six thousand Vietnamese. The next month the Viet Minh retaliated by sabotaging Hanoi's electric power plant and assassinating a number of French officials there, and the fighting commenced in earnest.

Several months earlier Ho warned the French prime minister, "If we must fight, we will fight. You will kill ten of our men, and we will kill one of yours. Yet, in the end, it is you who will tire."[22] The French government ignored Ho. The Vietnamese leader also had a conversation with a *New York Times* correspondent who expressed incredulity that the Viet Minh, which lacked a large army or modern weapons, could defeat France. With his uncanny ability to peer into the future, Ho responded that although the war would be hard and desperate, "we could win. We have a weapon every bit as powerful as the most modern cannon: nationalism! Do not underestimate its power."

Always ready with an apt metaphor, Ho also argued that the war would be akin to a struggle between an elephant and a tiger. If the tiger stood still, the elephant crushed him. "But the tiger does not stand still. He lurks in the jungle by day and emerges by night. He will leap upon the back of the elephant, tearing huge chunks from his hide, and then he will leap back into the dark jungle. And slowly the elephant will bleed to death."[23]

French General Jacques Philippe Leclerc, who doubted that France was in a position to control Vietnam by force, also issued a metaphorical warning. "Fighting the Viet Minh will be like ridding a dog of its fleas," he said. "We can pick them, drown them, and poison them, but they will be back in a few days."[24] His government paid no more attention to him than to Ho.

Assessing American actions near the end of World War II and Allied war aims as enunciated in the Atlantic Charter and the United Nations, Ho believed the United States supported Vietnamese self-determination. When the war began Ho's faith seemed well placed since the Truman administration initially perceived events in Vietnam correctly, as a colonial war in which an arrogant, greedy France, which had milked Vietnam for a century without noticeable benefit to the Vietnamese, tried to reassert its sovereignty.

As anti-Communist ideology quickly hardened, perceptions changed.

Containing the Soviet Union in Europe required substantial French military participation and France's consent to rearm West Germany so it, too, could contribute to containment. If the United States refused to help France in Vietnam, France might frustrate America's grand strategic design in Europe. Moreover, since American policymakers increasingly considered Ho a Kremlin puppet, not a Vietnamese nationalist, France's struggle looked less like an imperial venture and more like a valiant stand against expansionist Communism. The French nurtured this viewpoint by labeling all Vietnamese who wanted independence as "Communists." By 1947 America was assisting the French.

Wanting to avoid the perception that it was abetting imperialism, at first the Truman administration funneled money and weapons into metropolitan France, arguing that the French used the aid for economic reconstruction and European defense. Of course this was a subterfuge because France diverted much of the assistance to Vietnam. America soon dropped all pretenses. It perceived the problem of containing Communism in Asia as particularly acute after the "loss" of China, especially since the Chinese Communists started providing military assistance to the Viet Minh. In early 1950 the United States began directly supporting the French effort even though it realized Ho was probably "supported by a considerable majority of the Vietnamese people," that he was "the strongest and perhaps ablest figure in Indochina," that his movement "attracted non-communist as well as communist elements," and that the Viet Minh, bubbling with nationalistic fervor, represented "a determined adversary."[25] The outbreak of the Korean War in late June 1950 hardened America's commitment to the French because saving Indochina and South Korea now seemed like a linked pair of anti-Communist crusades.

Despite many optimistic predictions from French generals (victory, said General Henri Navarre in 1953, can be clearly seen, "like light at the end of a tunnel"[26]), despite substantial U.S. military and economic aid, and despite eight years of violence, the fleas were still there and French morale, both at home and in Indochina, plummeted. Utilizing a strategy of protracted war that emphasized the conflict's political and psychological factors instead of its military aspects, the Viet Minh endured unremitting adversity, occasional crushing defeats, and ghastly casualties to outlast the French, as Ho had predicted they would. For the most part French military forces rarely saw enemy soldiers, but nonetheless absorbed constant losses from booby traps, mines, snipers, and ambushes. "If only the Vietnamese would face us in a set battle," wailed a French officer, "how we should crush them!"[27] The Viet Minh tiger rarely obliged the French elephant's preference for high fire-power, set-piece conventional battles.

The last straw for France was the Viet Minh's victory at Dien Bien Phu. In late 1953 General Navarre sent a substantial force into the remote village of Dien Bien Phu hoping to draw the Viet Minh into an open confrontation where they could be massacred by superior firepower. But through Herculean efforts the Viet Minh moved artillery—much of it Chinese-supplied—onto the surrounding hills and settled down for a prolonged siege. The United States rejected a desperate French plea for air strikes to relieve the trapped garrison, which surrendered in May 1954. Out of the original 12,000 defenders, 2,293 were killed, 5,134 wounded, and the remainder endured a long death march to Viet Minh prison camps. Viet Minh losses were greater—8,000 dead and 15,000 wounded—but all that Vietnamese blood paid for a great strategic advantage.

One of the twentieth century's most decisive battles, Dien Bien Phu stunned the French public, causing the ruling coalition to collapse and resulting in the formation of a new government that accepted the inevitable: France could not impose its will on Vietnam. At the Geneva Conference that same month it negotiated a face-saving compromise that allowed it to withdraw with a modest semblance of honor. Twenty years later the United States was in exactly the same unhappy situation.

The Geneva Conference gave the Viet Minh less than the total victory they earned on the battlefield. Pressured by the Soviet Union and China, both of whom wanted to lessen great power tensions and deprive the United States of an excuse to become more deeply involved in Indochina, the Viet Minh accepted an agreement that called for a temporary partition of their country along the 17th parallel. According to the Final Declaration of the Geneva Conference, this demarcation line was "provisional and should not in any way be interpreted as constituting a political or territorial boundary."[28] The line's main purpose was to permit military forces to disengage, the French regrouping to the south and the Viet Minh to the north. Reunification would occur in 1956 through national elections.

The Geneva settlement was replete with danger for the Viet Minh because even before the conference began Washington was searching for a new ruling elite in Vietnam, a "third force" that was both anti-Communist and untainted by the colonial past. Onto the stage stepped Ngo Dinh Diem, an anti-Communist Catholic who had resigned from the French-controlled government when it refused to undertake reforms in order to fight Communism more effectively. Diem's credentials were not perfect compared to the "third force" ideal. A Catholic in a predominately Buddhist country, he negotiated with, rather than fought against, the Japanese, and had not fought the French either; indeed, he lived in Europe and America from 1950 to 1954 during the anticolonial war's most fierce years. Thus, although his anti-Communism was impeccable his nationalist record was suspect, especially when compared to Ho's.

Counterbalancing Diem's less-than-stellar nationalism was a powerful advantage: he knew a number of influential Americans. While in the United States Diem attended Maryknoll Seminary in New Jersey and met many religious and political leaders, including Francis Cardinal Spellman, the leading Catholic anti-Communist, and a Catholic senator from Massachusetts, John F. Kennedy; in turn they introduced him to many other prominent individuals. With substantial U.S. support, Diem returned to Vietnam in 1954 as prime minister of the southern regroupment zone.

In surprisingly short order Diem imposed a superficial stability in the south. He bribed the leaders of two powerful religious sects, the Hoa Hao and the Cao Dai, and incorporated some of their troops into his own army; he also routed the Binh Xuyen, Saigon's foremost criminal organization, which maintained a well-disciplined pseudomilitary force. Most importantly, Diem ruthlessly repressed those Viet Minh who remained in the south after Geneva, urging his military and police forces to consider the Viet Minh less than human and mercilessly wipe them out. And he refused to participate in the elections scheduled for 1956. In all this Diem received the Eisenhower administration's support—the CIA provided bribe money, Americans financed and trained Diem's army, and the government encouraged him to boycott the election.

Diem's apparent success stoked American aspirations for converting the temporary cease-fire line along the 17th parallel into a permanent border by building an anti-Communist country, akin to South Korea, in the southern zone. This would salvage something from the French debacle by containing Communism to the northern half of Vietnam. Eisenhower lavished economic aid on Diem's non-Communist Republic of Vietnam and increased the number of American military personnel advising the Army of the Republic of Vietnam (ARVN). Remembering Korea, these advisers trained ARVN to confront a conventional North Vietnamese invasion across the 17th parallel. Diem was dictatorial rather than democratic and utterly dependent on U.S. economic and military aid, but repression and dependency on behalf of anti-Communism were altogether acceptable to the Eisenhower administration.

A hint of arrogance underlay the supposition that the United States was succeeding where France failed. America's policymakers believed the nation's military might was so awesome, its technological superiority so overwhelming, and its motives so altruistic that it would surely prevail. France had been handicapped by its colonial past and its lack of aggressiveness. No such handicaps afflicted the United States, at least not in its leaders' eyes. Whatever difficulties arose, well, the American "can-do" spirit would overcome them. Overconfidence in American capabilities deceived policymakers and strategists into ignoring Vietnamese history, culture, and ideology. No matter what situation the United States confronted it would not fail because, well, because it was the United States of America, not France.

America was congratulating itself and the Diem government prematurely. The Republic of Vietnam's record in suppressing the Viet Minh in 1955–57 was deceptive because the Viet Minh did not fight back. Ho's government, based in Hanoi, urged restraint on its southern brethren. Having fought an enervating war against France and facing severe reconstruction problems in the war-torn northern half of the country, Ho hoped that somehow the Geneva process would be completed peacefully. He also feared that the Americans might replace the French, so he wanted to avoid any provocation that might serve as a pretext for greater U.S. regional involvement. As a result the first few years of Diem's regime were, as a leading Viet Minh commander put it, "the period of unilateral war because we acted in accordance with the appeal of Ho who called for strict adherence to the Geneva Agreements by waging only political and peaceful struggles in our demand for general elections, and not to resort to armed struggle." [29]

Viet Minh living in the south became increasingly impatient with such passivity, especially after the cancellation of the 1956 election. Killed, imprisoned, and hounded by Diem's security forces, their numbers and morale dropped precipitously, and they complained bitterly about Hanoi's restrictions on using armed force. Despite continued injunctions for caution coming from the north, in mid-1957 some southern Viet Minh, on their own initiative, began fighting back, attacking local garrisons and assassinating Diem government officials. Still the battle remained unequal for the next two years; looking back on the late 1950s, Vietnamese historian Tran Van Giau considered them "the darkest hour" during the entire revolutionary effort.[30]

By 1959 the northern leadership could no longer ignore the mounting casualty toll among the Viet Minh (now called the Viet Cong, or vc). Le Duan, who increasingly replaced Ho as the North's leading policymaker, believed the South's revolutionary flame might be extinguished if the insurgents were not permitted to rebuild their strength and increase their firepower. Consequently, the North took steps to organize and direct the budding rebellion. In doing so it walked a delicate tightrope, trying to nourish the vc without alienating the Soviet Union, which was following a policy of "peaceful coexistence" with the West; without alienating the Chinese who evinced little support for any decision to reunify Vietnam by force; and without provoking the United States into full-scale war. Moreover, some leaders feared that escalating the fighting would divert precious resources from the urgent task of rebuilding the war-torn North. Although moving cautiously, the DRV's leadership realized it risked getting involved in a difficult, protracted struggle to liberate the South.[31]

Meeting in Hanoi in January 1959, the 15th Plenum of the Central Committee sanctioned using armed force in support of political actions, establishing base camps in South Vietnam's Central Highlands, and returning a limited number of Viet Minh (vc) who had regrouped to the north after Geneva. The "years of political struggle," as the official history of the North Vietnamese Army labeled 1954–59, were over.[32]

During the spring and summer of 1959 the Central Committee's Military Commission set up three special logistical units: Group 559 to move troops, weapons, and supplies south through Laos; Group 759 to provide for seaborne infiltration; and Group 959 to support the Laotian People's Liberation Army. In September 1960 the Central Committee authorized creation of an overt coalition organization to mobilize the political opposition to Diem's regime, resulting in the formation of the National Liberation Front (NLF) several months later. In early 1961 the Hanoi government ordered all armed units in the South to unite in the People's Liberation Armed Force (PLAF), the NLF's military arm.

Once authorized to use force the vc demonstrated that Diem's success had been an illusion. Now countering violence with violence, the vc exploded in numbers, finding thousands of willing recruits who seethed at Diem's elitist, dictatorial rule. By the end of 1961 the PLAF numbered 15,000, a fivefold increase in the vc since the spring of 1959.[33] Government agents who swaggered through the countryside with impunity only weeks before soon found sanctuary only behind barbed wire at local military outposts. Much of the countryside rapidly came under vc control.

Deprived of the fruits of their victory over the French, in 1959 Vietnamese nationalists/Communists again reluctantly resorted to war on behalf of liberation and unification, this time against an American-sponsored "puppet" regime that quickly proved incapable of self-defense. Progressively the war was less against Diem's forces and more against the United States, which poured vast resources and hundreds of thousands of troops into South Vietnam to shore up its dependent client state—and to contain Communism.

Many individuals warned the United States not to assume the mantle of French colonialism by getting too deeply involved in Indochina.

Take the Joint Chiefs of Staff position paper 1992/4 of July 1949, which asserted that the "widening political consciousness and the rise of militant nationalism among the subject people cannot be reversed." Trying to do so would be "an anti-historical act likely in the long run to create more problems than it solves and cause more damage than benefit."[34]

Take General Matthew B. Ridgway, the Army's Chief of Staff at the time of Dien Bien Phu. As pressure built for U.S. intervention, General Ridgway commissioned a study of the problem. Fighting in Indochina would entail a misapplication of limited resources that were better employed in more important theaters (such as Europe), disruption on the home front resulting from increased draft calls, activating reservists, and extending terms of service for active duty personnel, and 28,000 casualties per month because the Viet Minh represented a formidable foe.[35]

Take British Foreign Minister Anthony Eden. When American Secretary of State John Foster Dulles predicted an apocalyptic run of toppling dominoes if Dien Bien Phu fell, Eden calmly responded that ideological rigidity was blinding the United States. Even if the Viet Minh controlled all of Vietnam, few dominoes would topple, not Thailand, India, Burma, Malaya, Pakistan, Indonesia, not the Philippines nor Japan.[36]

Or take British novelist Graham Greene's 1955 novel *The Quiet American*, which predicted tragic results if America became the new France.[37] Greene set the novel in 1951–52 when it began to look like France might lose the First Indochina War. One of the main characters was Alden Pyle, a Harvard-educated member of the American Economic Aid Mission who was really a CIA operative trying to find that elusive "third force." To erode Communist support he supplied explosives to terrorists who killed innocent women and children, then blamed the slaughter on the Viet Minh.

Greene chose the name "Pyle" on purpose—a pile is a hemorrhoid, a pain in the ass, and that is what Pyle (America) was. Pyle told another character, British journalist Thomas Fowler, that he could call him Alden, but Fowler replied that "I'd rather stick to Pyle. I think of you as Pyle." From Fowler's perspective Pyle was a dangerous innocent abroad. He "had pronounced and aggravating views on what the United States was doing for the world," was "young and ignorant and silly" with no notion of "what the whole affair's about," paid "no attention to words he didn't like," and was "as incapable of imagining pain or danger to himself as he was incapable of conceiving the pain he might cause others." In short, Pyle was "impregnably armoured by his good intentions and his ignorance."

Fowler tried to educate Pyle, explaining that the West had "no business here. It's their country," and they "don't want our white skins around telling them what they want." Only the Communist political commissars, not the French or the Americans, really "cared about the individuality of the man in the paddy field" and treated him "like a man, like someone of value."

Unlike the commissars, Pyle believed the Vietnamese were uncomplicated, childlike, not men and women at all. "These people are so friendly when you treat them right," he exudes. "The French don't seem to know how to handle them." The Vietnamese would respond much better to the United States because Americans "came in now with clean hands," untainted by European colonialism.

Realizing that Pyle was the type who "comes blundering in and people have to die for his mistakes," Fowler plaintively asks, "Why don't you just go away, Pyle, without causing trouble?"

One reviewer's response to *The Quiet American* was to dismiss it as "icily anti-American" and pro-Communist.[38] Like Pyle, the United States would neither be educated nor go away.

Pyle—played in the book's movie version by none other than Audie Murphy—died at the hands of a vc assassin.

During the 1950s Joe Hooper had no interest in developments in Indochina, which would eventually suck him into the vortex.

But he was very much interested in Sandra Nell Schultz, a pretty, though not ravishing, teenager.[39] Delicate, almost fragile looking, she was considered quiet but classy, "a real nice sweet, super sweet, person . . . a real gentle type person."[40] Which is very much how she described herself: very quiet, very shy, meek, gullible, and naive. She enjoyed a sheltered life, so protected by her father and brothers that though she was twenty years old chronologically she had the maturity level of a budding teenager.

Born in 1938, she lived in the family home in San Bernardino until, after briefly attending a nearby junior college, she enrolled at San Jose State College (now University) where she lived on campus. Shortly thereafter her father, a self-taught metallurgical engineer, was transferred by his company to the San Francisco area. With her parents now living in nearby Campbell, and unsure of what she wanted to do with her life, Sandra dropped out of school and moved into her parents' new home. Needing a job while she sorted things out, Sandra became a clerk-typist at Moffett Field where her mother worked in the supply section of the Air Force Liaison Office. Sandra began working at Moffett Field in December 1958 and almost immediately met Joe.

She was everything the brash, boisterous, worldly Joe Hooper was not.

As Joe Hooper matured, women found him irresistibly alluring. Not only did he have "a way with words with women," but he also became the master—literally—of the flowery gesture. While stationed at Moffett Field he and Gary Foster would sneak over to the officers' quarters after dark and cut red roses, then take them to the lady who operated the base laundry. They never paid for laundry. A few years later when Joe visited Gary and his wife Arlene after the birth of their first child he quickly got distracted by a woman standing in the window of a nearby apartment. Grabbing some flowers off the Fosters' table he set out on a mission. Within moments Gary and Arlene saw him inside the woman's apartment, with her holding the flowers and Joe's back to the window. Behind his back he was waving to them as a signal of success.[41]

Joe may have been just a country boy, a bit rough around the edges, but with women his words and actions were pure honey. Arlene Foster spoke for a lot of females when she said that "Joe was the kind of person I don't think you could know without loving him."[42]

When Joe met Sandra another sailor was already dating her. Joe embraced the challenge, attacking forcefully on two fronts. "He snowed me. He just overpowered me," Sandra recalled. "Actually," she continued, "I think he got along with my mother better than me." Mrs. Schultz agreed that she had a fine relationship with Joe, who "could charm the skin off a snake if he wanted to. He had charisma. He could be a son-of-a-gun also, but if he wanted to be charming he could." Although he snowed Sandra and charmed her mother, Mr. Schultz took Joe's measure and was never fooled by him. He disliked the young man.

Sandra, however, was in love, or at least so she thought. Since the lovebirds had little money, about the most expensive thing they did was go bowling. With his muster-out money from the Navy, Joe even bought her a bowling ball and bowling shoes. Joe did not own a car, so if they needed to go somewhere they borrowed Gary Foster's, or the car that Sandra's brother Larry owned. But they spent much of their time strolling through the orchards near Campbell, which was still quite rural, and having sex, which was a new experience for Sandra but not for Joe. They had sex "everywhere. I mean Joe was very talented," and he "was totally shocking me all the time with things I didn't want to know."

Although Joe brought home some fancy condoms from Asia they did not use them and by mid-March Sandra was pregnant. What were their options? "An abortion?" asked Sandra. "I didn't even know that word." Rarely in the 1950s did couples with children live as husband and wife without benefit of marriage. Thus marriage was the only answer, which necessitated a trip to the Hoopers in Burbank so Sandra could meet her future in-laws. She perceptively assessed the Hooper family even though the visit was brief. John Henry was not there, nobody knew where he was, and nobody talked about him. Maggie was "a kind, good-hearted woman" who "worked really, really hard" and "took care of the whole family." Joe "adored his mother" and "felt protective of her," and was closer to his sisters than he was to Douglas, who still lived at home. Being from the South, the Hoopers ate "strange" food. Joe's favorite sandwich consisted of peanut butter and mashed bananas, though he also wolfed down grated cheese, mayonnaise, and pimento sandwiches. For variety, he loved butter beans.

Sandra and Joe were married on May 17, 1959, in a small Baptist church in Reno, Nevada.[43] The bride wore a lovely white lace dress at the ceremony witnessed by her mother Ruby and her brother Dana. After the shotgun marriage Sandra's parents drove the newlyweds to San Francisco and paid for a hotel so they could enjoy a brief honeymoon. The next morning they walked to the Greyhound bus depot, took the bus back to Campbell, and moved into Sandra's bedroom in the Schultz's home on Virginia Avenue. Temporarily, Sandra thought.

The marriage was a disaster.

After Joe mustered out of the Navy he took a job selling Cory cookware door-to-door, but he barely earned enough to make payments on the wedding ring he bought Sandra. Worse, "he would go out selling the pots and pans and he would come back with lipstick on his shirt." Equally bad, Joe was getting too comfortable in the Schultz home, content to have Sandra's parents provide free room and board and transportation. While he was still in the Navy he would ride to work at Moffett Field with Mrs. Schultz, and he sometimes borrowed the Schultz car (a big green Lincoln) to attend the horse races in San Francisco. About the only contribution Joe made to the household was to accompany Mrs. Schultz to the market, when he would wear big clog shoes he purchased in the Orient "so that people would notice him."

Sandra objected to this freeloading. She felt that they "needed to get out of my folks' house, but he was perfectly happy there. He even told me I should go to work after [the baby] was born because I was qualified to get a job, and he would stay home with the baby."

By August 1959, when her grandfather died, Sandra was desperate. "I wanted us to go somewhere," she said, "and start our own life." Hoping to jolt Joe into action, as she and her parents left for the funeral in San Bernardino she left him a note saying he needed to move out of the house, find a new place, and then she would move in with him. When they returned three days later Joe was gone. He and a friend moved into an apartment complex near San Jose State populated with college students, not all of them males. Joe "was having a good time." When Sandra mentioned divorce, he intimidated her with the note she had left, saying he would fight for the custody of their child, that "he was going to use [the note] against me, and he would take the baby and I would never see him. He would have the baby totally." Naively, "I believed him. I believed him!" She packed her clothes, put them in the car, and her parents delivered her to the apartment.

Sandra stayed less than a week, but in one sense the week was liberating. Unknown to Joe she found the note and flushed it down the toilet. Then she asked Joe to take her to her parents' house, which he did. A week later he was out on the front lawn making a spectacle, screaming that he wanted his wife back. Attempting to salvage the marriage, Sandra's father arranged for counseling. She went; Joe did not. Based on his conversations with Sandra, the marriage counselor believed she and Joe were so different that the marriage would never work. Sandra filed for divorce.

On December 8, 1959, the divorce case came to trial. Joe did not appear, while Sandra was represented by counsel. Since the defendant "failed to answer the complaint within the time allowed by law, or at all," the judge granted the divorce, giving Sandra full custody "of the parties' minor child when born." Joe was to have reasonable visitation rights and was ordered to pay $100 per month alimony and another $50 per month for child support.[44]

Six days after the trial Sandra started out the door for work, but suddenly turned around and told her mother, "I think we better go." They hurried to the hospital—at least as fast as rush hour traffic permitted—and later that day Robert Jay Hooper was born. Sandra chose the name Robert because it sounded "manly" and Jay after the blue jay, a bird she liked. When Joe heard about the baby's birth he showed up at the hospital, carrying a dozen red roses and causing "such an uproar around there wanting to see *his* son." Joe held Robert briefly, becoming so emotional he cried. Not wanting to endure any more of Joe's spectacles at the hospital, Sandra went home the next day. Soon Joe was camped on the Schultz's front yard, yelling that he was going to stay there. Finally, Sandra called the police, who forced him to leave.

After that Joe had only a few sporadic contacts with Sandra and Robert, in part because in January 1960 he moved to Burbank where he lived close to Maggie, John Henry, and his siblings. On one of his rare visits back north he was fortunate enough to see Robert take his first steps in the Schultz's front room. When Joe became a paratrooper he sent a framed picture of himself jumping out of an airplane, but Sandra did not put it on display. And he called twice. Once was from Korea in the early 1960s when he asked if Sandra's second husband wanted to adopt Robert; if so, Joe's legal obligation to pay child support would cease. In the late 1960s, after learning he would receive the Medal of Honor, he phoned again to let Sandra know that Robert, as the son of an MOH recipient, could automatically go to West Point. But when he reached college age Robert preferred majoring in English at the University of California at Santa Barbara to the Military Academy.

Sandra emphasized that Joe "did not mistreat me." He slapped her once, but "I deserved it." The problem was that Joe was not ready for marriage. The wedding occurred only because she became pregnant, not because Joe *wanted* to be married.

Summing up her daughter's failed marriage, Mrs. Schultz noted, in an understatement eloquent in its simplicity, "These were trying times."

All that remained from the marriage were remnants—and lies.

A big cooking pot. When Joe was selling Cory ware he gave the Schultz family a set of pots and pans, and when the marriage ended he wanted it back. Sandra returned it all except for one pot, the one she was using to heat Robert's bottles.

A wedding ring. Joe hounded Sandra to return it so he could stop making payments on it, but she refused. Years later when Robert got married his mother gave him the ring, and he had the diamonds removed and rearranged on a new gold setting for his wife. Later they divorced and his wife kept the ring. So only the original setting remained.

An old Navy jacket. Somehow Mr. Schultz kept Joe's Navy jacket and eventually gave it to Robert. The brother of a friend stole the jacket and used it as a work coat, spattering it with paint before Robert recovered it.

A few dollars. Joe never followed the judge's orders regarding alimony and child support. For a while he sent $50 savings bonds (which he could buy for much less than that), but Sandra could not afford to wait until they matured and cashed them immediately. Soon he stopped sending the bonds, claiming his mother needed the money more than Robert. That, of course, was a lie. The money flow was always from Maggie to Joe, not vice versa.

But Joe told worse lies, hurtful, vicious lies.

For example, the kernel of *truth* was that Joe had an ex-wife and a son. The big lie that Joe told one of his future wives was that Sandra died giving birth to Robert, and that the baby died a few days later.

Three

Student was involved in various infractions and was
preoccupied, apparently, with his social life off post.

*Official explanation in Joe's Personnel File for his
dismissal from the Army's Primary Helicopter School in 1966*

Joe Hooper got into the Army by accident.

After leaving Sandra and Robert, he moved to Burbank and spent four
months doing low-end factory work in nearby Glendale. By May of 1960, he
later told his childhood friend Tom Johnson, "he was bored and he didn't
have a good job and he didn't know what he wanted to do."

He decided to reenlist in the Navy.

He arrived at the recruiting office just about quitting time and the Navy
recruiter was already gone. But a nearby Army recruiting station was still
open, so Joe became a soldier rather than a sailor.[1]

After attesting that he had no record as a juvenile delinquent, passing
the medical exam, and filling out enlistment papers, Joe received an honorable discharge from the U.S. Navy Reserve on May 30; the next day he enlisted as an E-3 (Private First Class) in the Regular Army for three years.[2]

Joe entered an institution that was stridently anti-Communist. In 1959
the Army adopted a new political indoctrination program to help young soldiers distinguish Americanism from Communism. Centered on ten pamphlets that comprised the *Democracy versus Communism* series, the program
represented an unrelenting attack on Communists, accusing them of innate
violence, perfidy, hypocrisy, and heavy-handed oppression. Communism
resulted in a sheeplike population huddled behind the Iron Curtain, deprived of all those marvelous attributes, such as freedom of speech and press,
that defined America. Reading the pamphlets, an individual learned that
Communists were just like Nazis, only worse.[3]

After completing basic training at Fort Ord, California, Joe volunteered
for airborne training. Considering his risk-taking and hypermanliness, this

decision was not surprising. In mid-July he departed for the 82nd Airborne Division at Fort Bragg, North Carolina, where he made his first "practice" jump from a tower on August 8 (his twenty-second birthday) and his first real jump from a plane three weeks later.[4]

One can imagine the tense would-be paratroopers on the tarmac awaiting their turn that hot, humid August morning, running in place, going through equipment checks, being harangued by drill sergeants about the fatal consequences of even the slightest mistake, and getting one last opportunity to "chicken out," which some invariably did.

Not Joe.

He boarded the plane, took his seat across the aisle facing some other excited (or scared) young man, then sprang to life when the jumpmaster ordered the men to stand and hook up their static lines. A green light came on, signaling "Go!" Down the cargo bay, clumsily, to the open door. Then hurtling backward, driven by a blast of cold air, plunging toward earth, and suddenly, viciously, snapping to a near-stop as the parachute opened, driving "your nuts into your belly if you didn't have the harness set right, snatching you hard even if you did. The pain was welcome, considering the alternative. It was life itself grabbing hold of you."[5] Giddy relief, and perhaps a few moments to admire the world at your feet before gravity took hold with a vengeance and trees, rocks, and bone-breaking hard ground leaped out of the earth directly at *you*. Touchdown, a quick rolling fall, a gathering of the silk, a glance skyward as other 'chutes billowed above, a wave of exultation at being alive.

It wasn't Joe's only thrill.

He also found a willing sex partner in North Carolina, and in September 1960 was arrested for "cohabitation," although the charge was later dismissed in court.

After being with the 82nd Airborne for thirteen months, the Army sent Joe to Korea, where he joined Company E, 20th Infantry Regiment, activated there in June 1960 as an "orphan" since no other units from the 20th Infantry were in Korea.[6] Stationed at Sihung-ni, a village of mud huts with dirt floors nestled in the barren hills south of Seoul, it provided security for the nearby 83rd Ordnance Battalion.[7]

Company E's Sihung-ni compound was four or five square blocks, enclosed by a fence topped with barbed wire. The ammo depot E Company guarded was in an isolated location approximately ten miles farther south so a steady stream of vehicles trucked the guards back and forth along the embanked roadways jutting above the rice paddies. Driving this route could be harrowing. Not only were the roads "rustic," that is, just dirt and gravel, but they also were "*so* narrow. You wonder sometimes how you can pass vehicles on the other side." Sometimes you did not. With civilian pedestrians, bicycles, oxcarts, and military vehicles from jeeps to large trucks all trying to use the same space simultaneously, "accidents happened constantly."[8]

The ammo depot consisted of a few small buildings and many underground ammunition bunkers surrounded by a horseshoe-shaped ridge. The soldiers in E Company did not know what the bunkers contained, but they knew it took two men turning keys simultaneously to open the doorway to the main underground tunnel, and rumors abounded that nuclear weapons were stored there.[9] On the level ground at the mouth of the horseshoe and running along the entire ridge was a barbed-wire tipped fence, punctuated at intervals by guard towers. Soldiers from E Company guarded the fenced area; some manned the towers while others walked the perimeter with guard dogs.

Joe served in the dog platoon; his canine companion was a huge, dark-furred German shepherd named Bo Bo.[10] The dogs weighed as much as 140 pounds and were vicious; when attacking they went for the groin or the throat and could easily knock a large man to the ground. Each dog had only one handler and responded only to that soldier. Men like Kenneth K. Sugarawa, who was in charge of the company's motor pool, feared that if one of the animals got loose it could be extremely dangerous for anyone in the area. Watching the dog platoon members practice defending themselves from an attack by another handler's dog drove the point home. The dogs wore collars and muzzles, but they were operated by a quick release system that might be *too* quickly released.

Guard duty at the ammo depot could be tedious and unpleasant. Repeatedly the same comment appeared in Company E's morning reports: "Record of events section: Usual organizational duties." While the summer heat was miserable, winter was a climatic ordeal. More than one soldier was frostbitten; with their thick, well-groomed fur, the dogs endured the cold better than their handlers.

As did many GIs, Joe alleviated the tedium in many ways. He drank and fought, the two usually going together. One night he and a black soldier both had too much to drink and got testy. The noncommissioned officer in charge of the club, Sergeant Benjamin F. Dansby, was Joe's friend and de-fused the fracas before it became serious, then had a few more drinks with Joe. When Hooper left the club, five black soldiers jumped him, but Joe grabbed a broken 2 × 4 and clubbed several of them to the ground before other soldiers broke up the fight. On his days off Joe frequently played chess, rarely losing. And he regularly visited a combined orphanage and leper colony run by an elderly Catholic priest, where he delivered powdered milk. Ordinarily dog handlers mixed powdered milk with the dog chow, but Joe evidently decided that children had a more urgent need for it.[11]

Hooper and Sergeant Dansby also hustled Korean women. One pitch-black night they took two women skinny-dipping in a lake miles from the compound. An old Korean farmer warned them not to go swimming, but Joe and Ben both manfully attested they were unafraid of snakes. When they got out of the water, Ben's pickup truck was stuck. Although "it was so dark you could only see a few feet," Joe took off alone, going overland rather than following the road, toward the compound. Within an astoundingly short time he returned with a truck and rescued the pickup truck. Joe, Ben, and the women then went back to the club (which was closed but Ben had the key), where the lights showed them why they should have listened to the farmer. Leeches ruined whatever sexual escapades Ben and Joe had in mind for the evening.[12]

Most of all, Joe made life more bearable for much of the time he was in Korea by living with a Korean woman he called "Mama-san." Joe's friends knew her as "Diane," an attractive, well-educated woman who allegedly had some Japanese blood. She had rounded rather than slanted eyes, and "in comparison to other village girls she carried herself more like a model than a prostitute. She looked good in either Korean or Western style clothes." The relationship between Joe and Diane was not always calm—a common theme with women and Hooper. At one point she threw him out of the hooch they shared, leaving Joe sitting in the cold, comforted only by Sergeant Dansby and a bottle of Jim Beam.[13] According to members of Joe's family, he had at least one, and maybe two, children with her. His sister Audrey recalled that "he was going to bring her back with him, but for some reason it never happened, and I never asked."[14]

The woman may have been a *kijich'on* (military camptown) prostitute. One unsavory aspect of stationing American forces in Korea was the emergence of widespread prostitution near military bases (including the one at Sihung-ni), an activity that the American and South Korean governments sponsored and regulated as a way to promote "friendly relations" between the two nations. Between the end of the Korean War and the mid-1990s, more than one million women worked as kijich'on prostitutes. By 1961 the gonorrhea rate among active duty Army personnel in Korea was approximately seven times higher than the worldwide Army rate, and it stayed outlandishly high into the 1970s.[15]

A kijich'on was usually young, undereducated, lower class, and the victim of previous sexual or emotional abuse. Having had sexual relations with foreigners, these women were pariahs in Korean society, which had been racially and culturally homogenous for centuries. Rejected by their country, camptown prostitutes hoped to marry a serviceman and move to the United States, leaving their degraded status behind. At the least they sought a nonbinding "contract cohabitation" relationship in which the kijich'on and a GI lived together for an agreed upon period of time, often the length of the soldier's duty tour. Then the woman did not have to sell her body nightly in the bars surrounding U.S. bases.

Perhaps Hooper set up a contract cohabitation arrangement with Diane. Or maybe he promised to marry her but changed his mind. Since a mountain of red tape made it difficult to get a woman out of the country—after all, the South Korean and American governments had a stake in maintaining camptown prostitution—soldiers routinely abandoned their Korean families. And Joe never had any patience with paperwork, or any trouble finding a new woman somewhere else.

Overall, Joe enjoyed Army life, so much so that while in Korea he received an early honorable discharge from his original enlistment and immediately reenlisted for a six-year hitch ending May 31, 1968. He stood an even 6 feet, weighed 175 pounds, and still had red hair and perfect vision.[16] Airborne qualified and with a Military Occupational Specialty (MOS) as a Light Weapons Infantryman, he arrived in Korea as an E-4 (Corporal), but soon entered the noncommissioned officers' ranks with a promotion to E-5 (Sergeant). Joe was no Hawkeye (the incredibly good marksman in James Fenimore Cooper's novels about the American frontier). When seventy-five men from Company E qualified on the rifle range with the M-1, forty-seven of them shot better than he did.

As a sergeant Joe could command and control light infantry weapons at the squad level, understood the capabilities and limitations of the unit's crew-served and individual weapons, and knew how to observe and adjust fire, collect local military intelligence, lay mine fields, prepare simple demolitions, and construct minor combat fortifications. A sergeant needed a "natural or acquired aggressive nature," which suited Joe perfectly. Unfortunately for the long run, according to the *Manual of Enlisted Military Occupational Specialties* the list of "Related Civilian Occupations" was short: "None."[17]

Hints that Joe was less than an ideal garrison soldier first appeared in Korea.

Although he received a Good Conduct Medal in June 1963, his conduct was not always good. In June 1962 Joe returned almost twelve hours late from a temporary duty assignment. In April 1963 he left his post without being properly relieved, and the next day an Article 15 proceeding (known in the ranks as a "Fifteen Fucker") restricted him to the company area for a week. More Article 15s loomed in the future.

On October 16, 1963, Hooper departed Company E for thirty days' leave, going home to spend time with the Hooper clan in California before reporting to the 2nd Armored Division at Fort Hood, Texas.[18] Often working on the training ranges, which was hard, active, outdoor duty (just the kind Joe enjoyed), he performed so well that the noncommissioned officer in charge wrote a special letter praising Joe's alacrity and tenacity in executing assignments, recommending that he be promoted, and suggesting that he receive a three-day pass as a token of appreciation.

Joe's next assignment would take him to the 101st Airborne.

President Johnson wanted two minutes, just two minutes, to say something about Vietnam.

He was talking to Secretary of Defense Robert S. McNamara in late February 1964. The secretary had contributed some ideas for a speech the president would soon deliver in Miami Beach, and surprisingly, the draft speech did not mention Vietnam, where the American-supported war against the Viet Cong was not going well. President Johnson thought this omission was a mistake.

McNamara was not so sure. The difficulty, he said, was deciding exactly what to say about Vietnam.

The president had some thoughts on the matter embodying a number of Cold War pieties. The United States had a commitment to defend freedom; if it pulled out of Vietnam the dominoes would start falling; appeasement was unacceptable. Yet, Johnson continued, the country had no commitment to *fight* in Vietnam and it did not want to "get tied down in a Third World War or another Korean action." So the best option was to do what America was already doing, giving the South Vietnamese advice, training, and equipment so they could win their own war.

Johnson's approach contained a fundamental weakness. What if the South Vietnamese, despite ample American support, would not or could not defend themselves? Then the United States either had to go to war or withdraw, permitting the Communists to tear a ragged hole in the containment policy. South Vietnam was so obviously losing the war that McNamara feared, "we're right at that point" where the United States had to choose between fighting the war itself or leaving South Vietnam to its fate—that is, to its extinction.[19]

By 1964 the central fact that bedeviled U.S. participation in Vietnam was distressingly obvious: South Vietnam had neither the skills nor the will to preserve its artificially created independence. Thus it repeatedly lost the war, only to be resuscitated by ever-greater American intervention. Although trying to nourish an independent South Vietnam, the United States was simply keeping an utterly dependent client state alive through desperate life support measures. "Without the United States," said President John F. Kennedy in November 1963, "South Vietnam would collapse overnight."[20]

The Viet Minh originally defeated the French, only to see their victory snatched from them by the Eisenhower administration's intervention on Diem's behalf. By early 1961, when President Kennedy assumed office, Diem was losing the war against the vc. Rather than accept South Vietnam's defeat the Kennedy administration intervened more dramatically, waging what the Communists called a "Special War," which was a U.S.–sponsored war effort by local client forces but without direct large-scale American participation in combat.

During the Kennedy years the United States indirectly attacked the vc on multiple fronts: economic, military, and political. The administration funneled almost a billion dollars to Diem. Militarily, it increased the number of advisors from 900 to 16,000 and allowed them to undertake a limited combat role; inaugurated a counterinsurgency effort by dispatching Special Forces, primarily to South Vietnam's Central Highlands; commenced Operation Ranch Hand, an aerial herbicide spraying program to deny the VC cover and kill their crops; and equipped ARVN with napalm, helicopters, fixed wing aircraft, armored personnel carriers, and other new weapons. On the political front, the United States supported the Strategic Hamlet Program, a pacification plan designed to deny the National Liberation Front (NLF) access to the rural population and win "the hearts and minds" of South Vietnam's peasants by improving their standard of living.

All this and more. To little avail.

The transfusion of financial aid and military largess only temporarily revived South Vietnam. By 1963 ARVN was performing so pitifully that the VC sent messages north saying that capturing U.S. weapons from the South Vietnamese was easier than bringing Soviet or Chinese arms down the Ho Chi Minh Trail. Americans derisively referred to some ARVN outposts as "Vietcong PXs." [21] In addition the Strategic Hamlet Program was a disaster. It forcibly removed villagers from their ancestral homes and confined them in unfamiliar locations behind barbed wire and moats, where they experienced degraded, not improved, living conditions. Actually, Colonel "Albert" Pham Ngoc Thao, who ran the program, probably considered it an incredible success since he was a VC agent and the wrong-headed, ruthless program impelled large numbers of alienated South Vietnamese to join the VC. [22]

By late 1963 the "Special War" was obviously failing. Although the U.S. government was unwilling to admit it, the problems were fundamental. Diem's support came almost exclusively from a thin slice of society: the urban elite and wealthy landowners who despised the peasantry, Vietnamese Catholics, and the armed forces. His army staggered under the double burden of low morale and a soaring desertion rate. Compared to Diem government officials, villagers perceived the NLF as honest, efficient, and sympathetic to their concerns. Not the least of Diem's difficulties was a tough, resourceful, and determined adversary. [23]

Choosing to believe the flagging war effort resulted from President Diem's ineptitude rather than an unwise and unpopular cause, the Kennedy administration sanctioned a coup that resulted in Diem's murder in early November 1963.

The coup was a crucial turning point, prompting the United States to escalate the war. In consenting to Diem's overthrow the United States made a de facto pledge of continued, even enhanced, support for the conflict.[24] Of course, it hoped new leadership would inspire the South Vietnamese to defend themselves, but instead the result was chaos bordering on anarchy as coups, counter-coups, and potential coups convulsed the body politic, further undermining the war.

The United States was no innocent in some of these affairs. It particularly supported General Nguyen Khanh's coup against General Duong Van Minh, who committed a cardinal sin: he explored peace prospects, proposing negotiations with the NLF to establish a "government of reconciliation."[25] Viewing any neutralization project as tantamount to a Communist victory, the Johnson administration rejected any diplomatic solution, whether proposed by South Vietnamese, Americans, Charles de Gaulle of France, United Nations Secretary General U Thant, or North Vietnam, which earnestly tried to open negotiations. "Has Hanoi shown any [serious] interest in negotiations?" asked a State Department intelligence report. "Yes, repeatedly." But the United States was willing to negotiate only if the VC and North Vietnam wanted to surrender by foregoing their goal of a unified Vietnam.[26]

To compensate for South Vietnam's ever-greater weakness the United States undertook a number of escalatory measures throughout 1964 and the first half of 1965, staving off unequivocal defeat—and leading steadily toward full-scale war. In March 1964, President Johnson, who assumed the presidency following Kennedy's assassination in late November 1963, approved National Security Action Memorandum 288, the first explicit statement of U.S. policy. It decreed that the United States sought "an independent non-Communist South Vietnam"; unless it succeeded Southeast Asia would fall under Communist domination and the rest of the world would be demoralized by America's inability "to help a nation meet a Communist 'war of liberation.'" The United States was still trying to help South Vietnam defeat the VC, who received support from the North, "by means short of the unqualified use of U.S. combat forces," but "it is vital that we continue to take every reasonable measure to assure success in South Vietnam."[27]

Among the "reasonable" measures was increasing the number of U.S. military personnel in South Vietnam from 16,300 to 23,300 in 1964, and implementing Oplan 34A, a covert operations program against North Vietnam that included espionage, sabotage, guerrilla raids, and intelligence gathering.[28] The Navy's Desoto Missions did much of the intelligence work with specially equipped destroyers that collected information about North Vietnam's radar, charted and photographed the coastline, and intercepted radio communications. By late May the administration had drafted a congressional resolution (in essence a declaration of war) asserting that the United States would "use all measures, including the commitment of armed forces" to maintain an independent South Vietnam.[29] Officials believed the resolution might not pass if presented to Congress simply in response to the current situation. However, they agreed "that in the event of a dramatic event in Southeast Asia we would go promptly for a Congressional resolution."[30] Using Canadian diplomat James Blair Seaborn as the messenger, in June the United States threatened North Vietnam with devastation from air and naval attacks unless it stopped the war—soon.[31]

Responding to events in the Tonkin Gulf in early August, which the administration chose to interpret as the dramatic pretext it was awaiting, the United States launched Operation Pierce Arrow, the first air attack on North Vietnam, and Congress passed the Gulf of Tonkin Resolution supporting the president's determination "to take all necessary measures to repel any armed attack against the forces of the United States and to prevent further aggression."[32] Soon Johnson was invoking this resolution as if Congress had passed an explicit declaration of war, justifying the spiraling violence in Vietnam.

In the administration's version of events, presented to the public when Congress debated the Gulf of Tonkin Resolution, North Vietnam launched a mini–Pearl Harbor, conducting two unprovoked assaults against Navy patrols in international waters. On August 2, North Vietnam attacked the destroyer *Maddox*, and on August 4 it struck at the *Maddox* and another destroyer, the *Turner Joy*.

Johnson and his spokesmen were being deceitful. They knew the August 2 attack was not unprovoked, but was a response to Oplan 34A attacks in the area. They also knew the *Maddox* was not an innocent victim, but instead participated in Desoto activities. And they had good reason to believe the second attack did not happen. Several hours after the alleged event, the head of the *Maddox*'s Desoto mission cabled the Pentagon that no attack took place; jittery sailors misconstrued radar and sonar readings as torpedoes. Despite doubts and contradictory reports, Washington insisted an attack occurred on August 4. Nor did the North Vietnam leadership author-ize the August 2 attack; the Thanh Hoa naval base commander ordered it on his own initiative.[33]

Two senators, Democrats Wayne Morse of Oregon and Ernest Gruening of Alaska, perceived the administration's falsehoods. "If the Senators want my opinion, a snow job is being done on us by the Pentagon and the State Department," said Morse during the debate on the resolution. He warned that "history will render a final verdict in opposition to the resolution."[34] However, the administration lied so convincingly and waved the patriotic flag so gloriously that only Morse and Gruening voted "No."

Incredibly, both in the congressional debates and to the North Viet-namese, the administration emphasized the fictitious events of August 4 rather than the real August 2 attack. Again using Mr. Seaborn as an emissary, the United States told Hanoi that "Americans were and are at a complete loss to understand the motive" for the August 4 attack. "They had decided to absorb the August 2 attack on the grounds that it very well might have been the result of some . . . mistake or miscalculation." But the August 4 attack was "obviously deliberate and planned and ordered in advance." The only logical conclusion was that "North Vietnam was intent either upon making it appear that the United States was a 'paper tiger' or upon provoking the United States."[35]

To the North Vietnamese, Seaborn's message must have seemed prepos-terous. They knew the August 2 attack was not unprovoked, that the *Maddox* was not an innocent victim, and that no attack occurred on August 4. Was the United States deliberately manufacturing a provocative incident? From the enemy's perspective, the only reasonable explanation for such duplicity was that the United States was looking for a pretext to escalate.

Lying. Deceit. Secrecy. Subterfuge. On a wholesale scale by both civil and military officials.

These hallmarks of the Vietnam War neither began nor ended with the Gulf of Tonkin Resolution. Dissimulation began in earnest during Kennedy's presidency and persisted for the duration, reaching a crescendo in the Nixon administration. The purpose behind most of this deception was to keep the truth not from the enemy but from the American public because, as the BDM Corporation concluded in a postwar "Lessons Learned" study for the De-fense Department, "each administration feared the public would not support the President's policies if the full outline of those policies and the means employed toward their attainment became known."[36]

To keep up "reasonable" pressure in the aftermath of the Gulf of Tonkin Resolution, Operation Barrel Roll, a *covert* bombing campaign against the Pathet Lao and North Vietnamese forces in Laos, commenced on December 14. (The Pathet Lao was the front group for Communist forces in Laos and was heavily dependent on Vietnamese Communist support.) "Covert" meant secret from Americans, not enemy forces who knew bombs were falling on them. In early 1965 the United States conducted two publicly announced "retaliatory" air raids against North Vietnam—Operation Flaming Dart in response to a VC attack on American installations at Pleiku and Flaming Dart II as revenge for a VC bomb that shattered a U.S. billet in Qui Nhon. Then in early March it launched Operation Rolling Thunder, which was no tit-for-tat operation but a sustained bombing campaign against North Vietnam. Shortly after Rolling Thunder began the first U.S. combat troops (two Marine battalions) went ashore at Da Nang to guard the air base there. Others Marines soon followed, and in May the first Army ground combat unit (the 173rd Airborne Brigade) arrived. Meanwhile, in National Security Action Memorandum 328, signed on April 6, the troops received authorization to conduct offensive operations in support of ARVN.[37]

In explaining most of these escalatory actions the Johnson administration was less than candid. For example, the Pentagon press release announcing the initial deployment of Marines said the South Vietnamese government requested them, but Saigon had neither been consulted nor notified in advance. And although the April 6 memorandum was a fundamental change in policy, committing the United States to ground combat rather than just an advisory role, the president directed that these "changes should be understood as being gradual and wholly consistent with existing policy."[38]

In May 1965, newspaperman David Wise coined the phrase "credibility gap" to describe the abyss between what civil and military spokesmen said about the war, and what was in fact happening.[39] Repeatedly officials who emphasized the nation's credibility put their personal credibility at risk by being so dishonest so often.

More deceitful was Johnson's critical decision in late July not just to support ARVN, but also to expand and Americanize the war by committing large numbers of combat forces. As of June 1, the number of ground forces approved for Vietnam totaled approximately 77,250 (including 7,250 South Koreans). On June 7, however, the commander of Military Assistance Command, Vietnam (MACV), William C. Westmoreland, asked for massive reinforcements "as rapidly as possible" to give him "a substantial and hard-hitting offensive capability on the ground to convince the VC that they cannot win." [40]

Westmoreland's message ignited a debate lasting nearly two months. The Joint Chiefs of Staff (JCS) supported the general's request, stating that the expanded forces would destroy the enemy's main force battalions and major base areas.[41] The president's military advisers also gave lots of advice, much of it wrong. For example, Johnson asked, "If we put in 100,000 [troops] won't they put in an equal number?" The "weight of judgment," JCS Chairman General Earle Wheeler responded, was that the enemy "can't match us on a buildup." As it turned out, this opinion had the weight of helium. Civilian advisers also chimed in with militant advice. The president assembled a bipartisan group of elder statesmen, known as the "Wise Men," who recommended expanding the war to preserve America's worldwide security. McNamara told Johnson he had three options: withdraw and be humiliated; continue with the same policy, which was not working; or substantially expand the U.S. military presence. The third option, he said in another helium-filled prognostication, presented "the best odds of the best outcome with the most acceptable cost to the United States." [42]

The president also received contrary advice. Unlike General Wheeler the U.S. Intelligence Board's Special Intelligence Estimate concluded the enemy could not only match a U.S. buildup but also could hide in the mountains and jungles to avoid a direct confrontation with American forces.[43] Under Secretary of State George Ball told the Wise Men they reminded him of "a bunch of buzzards sitting on a fence and letting the young men die. You don't know a goddamned thing about what you're talking about." [44] Ball argued that Johnson's hawkish advisers grossly exaggerated the costs of a compromise settlement and that the alternative to a negotiated peace was "a protracted war involving an open-ended commitment of U.S. forces, mounting U.S. casualties, no assurance of a satisfactory solution, and a serious danger of escalation at the end of the road." He also highlighted the relationship between mounting casualties and declining public support, as the Korean War demonstrated.[45]

The critics' access to Johnson did not equate with influence, and the president listened only to the advice he wanted. He *chose* war, authorizing 50,000 men immediately, another 50,000 by year's end, and, implicitly, more after that as Westmoreland needed them. As with the decision for Rolling Thunder, Johnson neither revealed the full extent of what he had approved to the American public, nor consulted with South Vietnam about the decision.

Both the enemy and White House aide Horace Busby captured the significance of what happened in July.

From the enemy's perspective, the Americans' "special war" strategy had been bankrupted. Now, with ARVN confronting "the prospect of annihilation and disintegration," the imperialists were sending "their own expeditionary army to the battlefield to rescue the puppet army." [46]

Busby also realized that the United States was not continuing an old war but starting a new one. "The 1954–1964 premises, principles and pretexts no longer apply," he wrote in a memo for the president. "This is no longer South Vietnam's war. We are no longer advisers. The stakes are no longer South Vietnam's. We are participants. The stakes are ours—and the West's." [47]

Sloppily, unsteadily, with no tidy beginning event like Fort Sumter or Pearl Harbor, the United States was involved in a big war.

But the public did not know it yet.

"Cognitive dissonance" is what psychologists call a theory that explains much of the seemingly irrational and self-defeating behavior civil and military leaders displayed during Vietnam. [48]

Just as a person who is thirsty feels physical discomfort, an individual who perceives contradictory information experiences psychological discomfort. In both cases the person tries to alleviate or reduce the discomfort. A thirsty person takes a drink of water. An individual who knows things that are psychologically inconsistent will try to make them more consistent, thereby reducing the dissonance.

Political and military leaders knew both domestic and international support for the war was lukewarm and tentative. "I don't think the American people are for it," President Johnson told Senator Richard Russell. "I don't think the people of the country know much about Vietnam and I think they care a hell of a lot less." His national security adviser, McGeorge Bundy, agreed, telling Johnson that 90 percent of the people wanted nothing to do with the war.[49] If the public had full knowledge of what the administration was doing and why, of how corrupt and despotic the South Vietnamese government was, and of how badly the war was going, even the modest level of support might evaporate.

Moreover, by 1965 the United States had not generated foreign support for its warlike position. Of the world's 126 nations, exactly 1 (Australia) gave its unequivocal assent; 3 others (Thailand, the Philippines, and South Korea) were lukewarm, and were essentially mercenaries rather than allies since they demanded substantial payments to contribute manpower to Vietnam.[50] Even most Asian countries, those most likely to become falling dominoes, rejected America's policy. As a CIA report put it, antiwar sentiment "permeated" Asia.

Yet knowing all this, Kennedy and Johnson took the nation to war rather than accept peace, even if on less-than-ideal terms. To reduce the resulting dissonance, the government engaged in "effort justification," exuded false optimism, and discounted bad news, figuratively shooting the messengers who brought it.

Constantly exaggerating the positive benefits of fighting in Southeast Asia and overstating the negative effects of withdrawing was one way Kennedy, Johnson, and Nixon justified their decisions.[51] As the escalating war yielded little or no success despite rising taxes and mounting casualties, three administrations defended the decision to fight more stridently rather than reassess their policies. Unwilling to admit they acted unwisely and were wasting the nation's resources, they reduced their dissonance by attempting to make the decision for war seem wise and just, and the potential results of not fighting catastrophic. For example, they engaged in hyperbole regarding the potential for a Communist-inflicted bloodbath on the South Vietnamese and the dire prospects for a Communist-dominated world after all the dominoes fell. Each president seemed to believe that if he found the right way to massage the English language, then everything would turn out fine.

Flowing from effort justification was an excessive optimism, which began in earnest during the Kennedy administration. General Paul Harkins, the original MACV commander, was so excessively optimistic (and so unfailingly wrong) that among young officers the phrase "pulling a Harkins" meant making a poor decision or misunderstanding a situation. He issued daily "Headway Reports" in which the United States and ARVN were, of course, always making headway against the VC.[52] One classic example of his astounding optimism was the Battle of Ap Bac in January 1963. Although an outnumbered and outgunned Viet Cong force inflicted a stunning defeat on ARVN, revealing to all open-minded observers that backing South Vietnam was a risky proposition, Harkins refused to acknowledge the defeat. Instead he predicted imminent success for the Diem government. His March 1963 "Summary of Highlights" claimed that "barring greatly increased resupply and reinforcement of the Viet Cong by 'infiltration,' the military phase of the war can be virtually won in 1963."[53] At that time "infiltration" was virtually nil because the VC's manpower pool was entirely *inside* South Vietnam, and Harkins had received strongly worded negative assessments of the war from at least five senior Army advisers. With good reason a fellow general noted that Harkins was not regarded "as an intellectual giant."[54]

Effort justification also entailed avoiding dissonant information by eliminating or belittling data that punctured the comforting optimism. Bad news was unwelcome in the White House or MACV headquarters, and those who insisted on presenting pessimistic assessments suffered banishment. Johnson barred Vice President Hubert H. Humphrey from the inner circle of decision makers because he questioned the war's wisdom. When Secretary of Defense McNamara turned "dovish" Johnson replaced him with Clark Clifford, a former "dove" whom Johnson believed had turned into a "hawk." Surrounding himself with sycophants, a president reduced his dissonance because his advisers reinforced the original (disastrous) decision, thus giving it added validity.

When newspaper or TV reporters sniffed out the pessimistic truth behind the official optimistic smokescreen, policymakers attacked them with a vengeance, challenging their scruples, patriotism, and intelligence—they were only sensation-seekers angling for a Pulitzer Prize not *true* Americans, and were pathetically young and naive. None of this was true—reporters ferreted out reliable information, oftentimes from soldiers who were in the field and understood how badly the war was going, and subjected it to objective analysis. But the truth made no difference. David Halberstam's reporting in the *New York Times*, which was far more accurate than Harkins's fairy tales of progress, so offended President Kennedy that he tried to pressure his publisher into removing him from Vietnam.[55] And here is how Johnson described reporters: "They're little chickenshits. . . . They're a pretty bunch of chickenshits. . . . They're just chickenshits."[56] Nixon's hatred of the media was so pathological he considered the press an archenemy.

Like the nation's political leadership, the military high command did not tolerate unpleasantness. Harkins censored and suppressed the reports of Lieutenant Colonel John Paul Vann, an experienced adviser who believed the United States was losing the war. Nonetheless Vann was invited to brief the JCS, but at the last moment the chairman removed Vann from the agenda.[57] During the war the Defense Department's Office of Systems Analysis produced "The Southeast Asia Analysis Report," which was often critical of the military in Vietnam; the JCS tried to restrict its circulation to senior Pentagon leaders, who could keep its contents secret. A Pentagon study conducted by some of the Army's best young officers, known as the PROVN report, demonstrated that America's strategy was self-defeating but MACV ignored or dismissed its findings.[58]

Having made bad decisions, civil and military leaders lost their objectivity. Struggling to justify their actions, their comments about Vietnam and future wartime plans were often illusionary and delusionary.

Rather than engaging in self-deception, the antiwar movement that emerged in 1964–65 embraced an alternative method for reducing dissonance. Having no stake in the decision for war, peace advocates assessed the situation differently. They compared the stated goal of an independent, non-Communist South Vietnam against the war's human and monetary costs for the United States and Vietnam, against South Vietnam's corrupt despotism, against ARVN's ineptitude, against the near-universal international condemnation of America's role in Southeast Asia, and against the enemy's dedicated nationalism.

They eliminated potential dissonance by urging the United States to withdraw from Vietnam.

In 1965 rival Black Muslims assassinated Malcolm X, southern rednecks were murdering civil rights workers, a race riot in Watts left thirty-five dead, several biographies of the late John F. Kennedy by administration insiders hit the bookstores, Mariner 4 flew within 5,700 miles of Mars and transmitted pictures of the red planet back to earth, Major Edward White left the confines of Gemini 4 to conduct the first U.S. space walk, two Americans shared the Nobel Prize for Physics, and the bodies were piling up by the hundreds in Vietnam.

Joe was at the 101st's home station in Fort Campbell, Kentucky, where he completed the Air Delivery Course, the Jumpmaster Course, and the division's Recondo School. In the Air Delivery Course he learned how to be the Army's representative for an Air Force plane that was going to parachute supplies to an Army unit on the ground—that is, how to rig the load, put it on a pallet, load it on the plane, and then make sure the Air Force dropped it properly. A jumpmaster was the man in charge of a parachute jump, controlling everything from the preflight briefing to the actual jump, including the authority to halt the jump at any time if something went wrong. A shorter and less intensive version of the Army's Ranger School, Recondo School provided training in patrolling, rappelling, hand-to-hand combat, escape and evasion techniques, and field survival.[59]

From the 101st Airborne Joe was assigned to the Army's Primary Helicopter School at Fort Wolters, Texas, where he suffered a significant setback, being dismissed from the Warrant Officer Rotary Wing Aviation Course in February 1966. Joe "was involved in various infractions and was preoccupied, apparently with his social life off post," read the dismissal recommendation, which concluded by saying Hooper showed an "overall lack of motivation and immaturity."

Reassigned to the 82nd Airborne at Fort Bragg, Hooper completed a course for noncommissioned officers on nuclear, chemical, and biological warfare, and took special training on how to perceive the presence of a riot control agent known as CS. Considering the frequent upheavals in U.S. cities during the 1960s and America's self-proclaimed role as a global policeman, this was important knowledge since the Army frequently used CS. Joe again performed well in duties that required action, such as conducting training in both day and night patrolling during the Fort Bragg ROTC Summer Camp. In September 1966 the Army promoted him to E-6 (Staff Sergeant).

Staff Sergeant Joe Ronnie Hooper soon moved again, heading to the Canal Zone in Panama for his fifth duty assignment since leaving Korea three years earlier. Four days before Christmas he reported to the Headquarters and Headquarters Company, 3rd Battalion, 508th Infantry Regiment, an airborne unit stationed at Fort Kobbe, nestled next to the Pacific Ocean near Panama City. In July 1967 Joe was reassigned from the 3rd Battalion's Headquarters Company to Company B.

The 508th was the alert unit for the Army Forces Southern Command, providing it "with the rapid reaction force and mobility of an airborne unit." [60] Consequently the regiment engaged in numerous training exercises that included airdrops and jungle warfare, much of it taking place in a dense jungle nicknamed "Zone D" because it resembled Vietnam's infamous War Zone D. Although much of Zone D was so well-trod it made the training seem less than realistic, some of the conditions were ideal preparation for Vietnam—for instance, coping with the hot, humid, rainy weather and with the leeches, mosquitoes, and other biting and stinging creatures that flourish in jungles.

In addition to jungle training, the 508th had several other important missions. One was riot control. Anti-American riots rocked Panama in 1959 and again in 1964 when four U.S. soldiers and twenty-four Panamanians died and hundreds more were wounded. Considering the nationalistic resentment Panamanians felt about their country's neocolonial status and the ongoing American exploitation of their economy, planning for future riots was wise. Another significant mission was providing troop and equipment support for the U.S. Army School of the Americas, founded in 1949 to fight insurgents throughout the Western Hemisphere. The school taught counterinsurgency warfare to Central and South American armed forces and internal security agencies, including Panama's hated National Guard. By the mid-1970s, 34,000 students had graduated, some of them eventually becoming dictators in their home countries. [61]

Joe Hooper's initial assignment was as a Platoon Sergeant in the Headquarters Company's communications unit. How, when, or why Joe became involved in communications is unknown, but in March 1967 he received an MOS in Field Communications, meaning he could install and maintain field wire systems, operate a field telephone switchboard, find and fix damaged wires and connections, and receive and process messages in an operations center, including a limited amount of encryption and decryption. If Joe was looking beyond military life, the new MOS had a great advantage over being a Light Weapons Infantryman: related civilian occupations were numerous in a society dependent upon televisions and telephones. [62]

Joe did not keep the new MOS. By September 1967 his Army career was spiraling downward, rapidly.

At 6:00 a.m. on May 1 Joe missed reveille formation, resulting in a Fifteen Fucker that sentenced him to forfeit $163 for one month (his monthly salary was $360.50), restricted him to the battalion area for thirty days, and reduced him in grade from an E-6 to an E-5, though the latter penalty was suspended for ninety days. If he behaved for three months he would remain an E-6. However, Joe could not maintain good behavior that long and on June 10 the Battalion's commanding officer vacated the suspension and the reduction in rank took effect immediately. In mid-July Joe was AWOL for two days. Another Article 15 ensued, resulting in the forfeiture of $73 for one month, restriction to Company B's limits for two weeks, and extra duties for those two weeks.

A month later Hooper was AWOL again, this time from 6:00 a.m. on August 11 until 9:00 a.m. on August 12 and from 6:00 a.m. August 14 until 12:30 p.m. on August 16. The result was not just another Article 15 but a Summary Court-Martial that restricted Joe to the battalion area for sixty days, took another $177 in pay, and reduced him to an E-4. In the midst of all these proceedings Hooper lost his communications MOS, reverting to a Light Weapons Infantryman. He also stopped writing home, which so worried Maggie that she wrote to the company commander asking about her son's welfare.[63]

What was at the root of this troubling behavior? Joe later told yarns about being court-martialed for punching an officer, which was patently false, though Joe spun it so convincingly that most people believed it. Apparently the real problem was that Joe found the brothels and bars in Panama City so alluring that he would sometimes sneak off base; even if he had a pass he would not leave the loose women and cheap booze in time to fulfill his military obligations.

If Joe—now Corporal Hooper rather than Staff Sergeant Hooper— continued on his current path he would soon be an E-3, exactly where he was when he enlisted in May 1960.

What rescued him was the Vietnam War.

In a monumental miscalculation, U.S. policymakers assumed (or at least hoped) that at some point along the escalatory ladder they climbed between

1961 and 1965 the Communists would realize they could not defeat the world's greatest superpower.

Convinced they could not succeed, the Communists would—logically, rationally—abandon the struggle for unification.

But instead of buckling under to American threats, the Communists followed their own escalatory path. Although neither the vc nor the North Vietnamese wanted a war with the United States, they were not intimidated. "The U.S. imperialists are not invincible," asserted a Communist strategist. "Compared with imperialists of other countries, they are mightier. . . . We do not underestimate our opponent—the strong and cunning U.S. imperialism. But we are not afraid of the United States." [64]

Initially the Communists had not been eager to see Diem overthrown since his "intolerance and brutality had alienated whole segments of South Vietnamese society and were daily contributing to NLF strength." They also feared that a "coup would likely bring to power a group of generals completely beholden to the U.S., presaging a more effective cooperation between Washington and Saigon." [65] But as South Vietnam's post-coup instability further crippled an already losing war effort, in December 1963 enemy leadership boldly decided to strengthen the vc to win the war as soon as possible. [66]

To support the NLF, North Vietnam sent troops to the South from its regular army (formally known as the People's Army of Vietnam, or PAVN, but also called the North Vietnamese Army, or NVA). Initially these soldiers were "regroupees," native Southerners who moved north of the 17th parallel during the Geneva Convention's military disengagement phase. But Oplan 34A operations, the Gulf of Tonkin Resolution, and Flaming Dart bombing raids convinced the Communist leadership that the United States was shifting from a "Special War" to "Limited War," signifying direct American participation in combat. To counter this threat in late 1964 North Vietnam dispatched the first Northern-born regulars, three complete regiments, to the South. [67] At approximately the same time the NLF formed its first division-size unit, the 9th vc Division located northwest of Saigon. Early in 1965 the Politburo approved an even greater effort, trying to destroy ARVN and present the United States with a fait accompli before it could intervene in great strength.

Hanoi reconsidered its options after Johnson's July decision for large-scale war. Although now recognizing it lacked the ability to achieve victory in the near future, Hanoi again refused to kowtow to intimidation, deciding to match America's escalation stride for stride, to engage in a dangerous, difficult, and inevitably protracted war against an adversary of awesome military power, hoping ultimately to erode the superpower's will and determination.

Communist leadership escalated the war despite profound misgivings about the ultimate results. The prospect of a direct confrontation with the United States, wrote a vc leader, "filled us with sick anticipation of prolonged and vastly more brutal war" in which "the scale of violence would increase geometrically."[68] Escalation might also alienate a vital ally, the Soviet Union, which was following a policy of "peaceful coexistence" toward the United States and opposed an expanded Southeast Asian war. Finally, some leaders feared that an aggressive war in the South virtually invited destructive American bombing of the North. Better to preserve the gains made in the North since the end of the French war, they argued, than to risk everything on the South's behalf.

But Communist "hawks" prevailed against the "doves," in part because they miscalculated America's intentions, but primarily because they considered unification a sacred goal. The U.S. decision to fight was, from Hanoi's perspective, perplexing. After all, America watched the Communists win the Chinese civil war without intervening militarily, refused to save France in 1954, allowed a Communist regime to remain in Cuba after a half-hearted invasion scheme went awry, agreed to neutralize Laos, and had no vital interest in Vietnam.[69] Presidential politics in 1964 were also heartening. On the campaign trail Johnson was a peace candidate, scourging Americans who were "eager to enlarge the conflict," and who called "upon us to supply American boys to do the job that Asian boys should do. They ask us to take reckless action which might risk the lives of millions and engulf much of Asia."[70] But when the peace candidate won he almost immediately became a war president. One can excuse the Communists for being mystified.

Even had they realized Johnson would go to war the North Vietnamese and vc would not have backed down from fighting "the war against the Americans to save the nation." They understood that "the American imperialists were by nature aggressive and warmongers," and that they "possessed enormous economic and military power."[71] Still, they would never accept the American fabrication that North and South Vietnam were separate nations. From their perspective the North was simply, in the words of one of

Vietnam's foremost strategists, Vo Nguyen Giap, "the revolutionary base for the whole country."[72] U.S. leaders spoke of Northern "aggression," but this was a fiction. It did not make good press to tell the truth, which was that the United States was propping up a corrupt, authoritarian regime that created the conditions inspiring the insurgency in the first place. No, it sounded better to save freedom-loving South Vietnamese from brutal Northern invaders. Charges of Northern aggression were also fictitious considering that Communist leaders came from all over Vietnam, not just the North.[73]

For the VC and the North Vietnamese, not only national survival, but also a social transformation and Vietnamese cultural values were at stake, and they were prepared to wage total war to achieve them. In unifying Vietnam the nationalists would destroy the French- and American-based regime, replacing it with a new economic, social, and political order embodying a fundamental redistribution of wealth and power. A social revolution was occurring, wrote John Paul Vann, one of the most knowledgeable Americans regarding Vietnamese affairs, "and the principles, goals, and desires of the *other* side are much closer to what Americans believe in than those of the Government of Vietnam." The vast majority of people supported the NLF "because it is their only hope to change and improve their living conditions and opportunities."[74] As one nineteen-year-old VC woman prisoner told her interrogators, NLF members "are those who stand up to fight the evil in order to protect the people."[75]

Along with advocating nationalism and social revolution, Communist propaganda appealed to cultural values. Americans and their South Vietnamese puppets, proclaimed the "Manifesto and Program of the National Liberation Front of South Vietnam," "poison the minds of our people with a depraved foreign culture, thus degrading our national culture, traditions, and ethics." The NLF's goal was to "eliminate the enslaving and gangster-style American culture and education; to build a national, progressive culture and education serving the fatherland and the people."[76] Compared to the rampant moral debauchery—prostitution, pornography, drug abuse, bribery—wherever the United States and South Vietnam held sway, the NLF seemed virtuous.

National unification. Revolutionary societal transformation. The preservation of a distinctive Vietnamese culture. These were the enemy's goals.

For the United States the war never meant as much since its vital interests, much less its survival, were not at stake.

Like the Communists, the United States engaged in escalation despite trepidations and internal disagreements. The Johnson administration received a staccato of accurate assessments regarding its ally's weakness and its foe's strength, America's limited security interest in Southeast Asia, and its vulnerabilities when fighting in a far-off country ill-suited to conventional warfare. The warnings came from influential individuals, the intelligence community, and war games.

Three of the most pessimistic and prophetic insiders in 1965 were Vice President Humphrey, Clark Clifford, and George Ball. In early 1965 Humphrey argued against deepening involvement in what was a civil war. "People can't understand," he wrote, "why we would run grave risks to support a country which is totally unable to put its own house in order." The United States should cut its losses and get out now.[77] Clifford did not believe the United States could win a war in Vietnam. "If we send in 100,000 troops," he noted in late July 1965, "the North Vietnamese will match us. And when they run out of troops, the Chinese will send in 'volunteers.' Russia and China don't intend for us to win this war. If we lose 50,000 men there, it will be catastrophic in this country. Five years, billions of dollars, hundreds of thousands of men—this is not for us. . . . I cannot see anything but catastrophe for our nation in this area." Having made similar arguments, Ball sent Clifford an approving note: "I'm glad to have such an eloquent and persuasive comrade bleeding on the same barricade."[78] Neither Humphrey nor Clifford nor Ball was persuasive enough.

The administration also had high-level warnings that the domino theory was flawed—that Johnson was wrong when he insisted that if the Communists "take South Vietnam, they take Thailand, they take Indonesia, they take Burma, they come right on back to the Philippines."[79] The president asked the CIA whether all Southeast Asia would fall under Communist dominion if North Vietnam controlled Laos and South Vietnam. "With the possible exception of Cambodia," concluded the CIA report, "it is likely that no nation in the area would quickly succumb to Communism as a result of the fall of Laos and South Vietnam. Furthermore, a continuation of the spread of Communism in the area would not be inexorable, and any spread which did occur would take time—time in which the total situation might change in any number of ways unfavorable to the Communist cause." As long as the United States retained island bases fringing the Asian mainland, such as the Philippines and Okinawa, it could still deter both North Vietnam and China. Two years later the CIA still came to the same conclusion: the effects of losing the war "are probably more limited and controllable than most previous argument has indicated."[80]

Although the phrase "war games" seems like an oxymoron, the military "plays" them seriously. The JCS's Joint War Games Control Group war-gamed Vietnam four times between 1962 and 1965 in games codenamed Sigma I-62, Sigma I-64, Sigma II-64, and Sigma II-65, and the results always revealed the dismal prospects for fighting successfully in Southeast Asia.[81]

Thus President Johnson and other high-level policymakers heard about the risks they were taking, and they developed privately expressed doubts. "A man can fight if he can see daylight down the road somewhere," Johnson told Senator Richard Russell. "But there ain't no daylight in Vietnam. Not a bit." "There's no end to the road," agreed Russell. "There's just nothing." The president believed the enemy was *never* going to quit, and consequently saw no diplomatic or military plan that could achieve victory.[82] Yet the administration followed a strategically reckless course without ever systematically examining such basic questions as "what U.S. force would ultimately be required, what our chances of success could be, or what the political, financial, and human costs would be if we provided it."[83]

The explanation as to why Kennedy and Johnson, at every step, when confronted with the choice of escalating or accepting defeat in a region where success was problematic, chose escalation flowed from a reflexive anti-Communist ideology reinforced by a concern for credibility, domestic political considerations, hawkish military advice, and the presidents' personalities.

In typically overwrought language, "hawks" claimed leaving Vietnam would be "worse than a victory for the Kaiser or Hitler in the two World Wars," and that "The road to appeasement was the road to war."[84] Kennedy and Johnson shared these views, uncritically accepting the idea that Communists were striving for global hegemony. As McNamara put it, in regard to Vietnam "there was such determination to do something, anything, to stop the Communists that discouraging reports were often ignored."[85] So were *encouraging* reports about events elsewhere, such as those in the early and mid-1960s by the CIA and the American embassy in Moscow demonstrating that the Sino-Soviet rift bordered on open warfare and that the

Communist world faced "spectacular" problems. Such studies should have undermined the belief in a monolithic Communist conspiracy and encouraged a more flexible policy.[86] But they did not.

As for credibility, Bundy told the president that the "international prestige of the U.S., and a substantial part of our influence, are directly at risk in Vietnam." In March 1965 a subordinate wrote a memo for McNamara breaking down American war aims into percentages. "To permit the people of SVN [South Vietnam] to enjoy a better, freer way of life," a goal trumpeted in public, constituted merely 10 percent of the nation's objective. Another 20 percent concerned keeping South Vietnam and adjacent territory out of Chinese hands. The foremost objective, 70 percent, was "to avoid a humiliating U.S. defeat (to our reputation as a guarantor)."[87]

Presidential decision-making often had little to do with Vietnam per se, and much to do with domestic politics. Foreign policy and domestic politics have often been inseparable,[88] but never more so than during Vietnam. As Democrats living under the double shadow of Truman's "loss" of China and Republican-driven McCarthyism, Kennedy and Johnson feared being "soft" on Communism. If they failed to escalate and the Communists gained control of South Vietnam, a right-wing backlash might sweep them from office. Johnson insisted "he was not going to be the President who saw Southeast Asia go the way China did." If the dominoes started falling there, "God Almighty, what they said about us leaving China would just be warming up, compared to what they'd say now." Republican leaders such as Richard Nixon were already "raising hell about it today."[89] Thus he would not withdraw even if he truly believed, as he once said, that the United States could not fight successfully ten thousand miles from home and, in any event, Vietnam was not worth fighting for.[90]

Yet both presidents also worried about escalating too dramatically. For one thing, they might lose their traditional liberal constituency, which increasingly opposed the war in Vietnam. That was one reason Johnson played the charade of peacemaker during the 1964 campaign and kept his aggressive decisions secret by always acting imprecisely and incrementally; he did not want "to give any indications that we're getting involved in a war." For Johnson, a second factor inhibiting an aggressive approach to the war was his grave concern for the "Great Society," which was his ambitious (and costly) domestic reform program aimed at eliminating social, economic, and racial injustice. An expanding war with skyrocketing costs, he feared, would siphon off the Great Society's funding, destroying his dream of an equitable society. A third restraint on aggressive action was fear of making a bad situation worse by provoking China (or the Soviet Union). After talking with some of his hawkish advisers, Johnson told Senator Richard Russell, "they don't believe that the Chinese Communists will come into this thing. But they don't know and nobody can really be sure." Personally, to Johnson it looked "like we're getting into another Korea. It just worries the hell out of me. . . . I believe that the Chinese Communists are coming in."[91]

Heightening the prospect of renewed war with China was the hawkish advise the military provided after 1960–61. Throughout the 1950s most military officials doubted the necessity or wisdom of fighting in Southeast Asia. In 1959, for example, the JCS understood that Asian upheavals resulted from indigenous problems, not externally directed subversion. Both Communist and non-Communist areas were "characterized by inter- and intra-national stresses and strains that almost defy solution by orderly processes." The root cause of these difficulties was an acute nationalism "fed by residual resentments against European colonialism."[92]

Military officials failed to act on these realities by advising disengagement from Vietnam, which might have permitted the president to withdraw without igniting a conservative fury. High-ranking officers advocated the early commitment of the largest possible force, thereby keeping the escalatory pressure on Kennedy and then Johnson. Army leaders deplored Kennedy's preference for counterinsurgency, preferring a full-scale, high firepower, conventional war. General Paul D. Harkins, the first MACV commander, based his strategy on destroying the enemy army, and General Lyman L. Lemnitzer, Chairman of the JCS, urged Kennedy to "grind up the Vietcong with 40,000 American ground troops . . . grab 'em by the balls and their hearts and minds will follow."[93]

The JCS advocated defeating North Vietnam even if China intervened and nuclear weapons were necessary. "Some of them are awfully irresponsible," Johnson said about his military advisers. "They'll just scare you. They're ready to put a million men in right quick." "Bomb, bomb, bomb. That's all you know. Well, I want to know why there's nothing else," a frustrated president told Army Chief of Staff Harold K. Johnson. "You generals have all been educated at taxpayers' expense, and you're not giving me any ideas and any solutions for this damn little piss-ant country. Now, I don't need ten generals to come in here ten times and tell me to bomb. I want some solutions." [94]

But the armed forces had few innovative ideas. In one way or another, the high command always wanted *more:* more bombs, more troops, more firepower, and more freedom to enlarge the war, even at the risk of igniting a worldwide conflagration. The JCS unanimously agreed that "if we should lose South Vietnam, we would lose Southeast Asia. Country after country on the periphery would give way and look toward Communist China as the rising power of the area." Therefore temporizing or expedient measures would no longer suffice. More military power, much more, was necessary. [95]

Caught among the conflicting pressures not to "lose" Vietnam, to avoid war with China or the Soviet Union, and to win in the next election, successive presidents managed the war politically but never resolved the fundamental issues. Instead Kennedy and Johnson finessed them, sidestepping the difficult decisions whenever possible. They played to the political center, taking a middle-of-the-road approach between the "fanatics" on either side, between those advocating unilateral withdrawal and those supporting all-out war. Gradual escalation, an incremental approach, had substantial domestic benefits. It permitted the president to postpone a difficult decision between all-out war or an unattractive peace. Going forward a step at a time pleased neither the rabid hawks nor dedicated doves—for the former the step was too short, for the latter too long—but appeased the majority of those Americans who were paying attention to the escalating war. Johnson acted as if he was still in the Senate where a majority of the votes could always be secured on an issue, no matter how contentious. And he was positive every individual could be bought, including Ho Chi Minh. The war, Johnson said, was "like a filibuster—enormous resistance at first, then a steady whittling away, then Ho hurrying to get it over with." [96] Had Vietnam been an appropriations bill, or Ho a congressman, that strategy might have worked. Since this was war and Ho had no selling price, it did not. Each step, no matter how seemingly moderate, resulted in an expanded commitment. [97]

In not backing down from the war, Kennedy, Johnson, and Nixon also met contemporary conceptions of manhood, which centered around being tough, demonstrating willpower, enduring pain, avoiding humiliation, and winning, winning, winning. In American political life, power and manhood had long been linked: those in authority acted manly to retain political legitimacy. A leader who was not bellicose and militant risked being perceived as soft, feminine, homosexual, and cowardly.[98] Consequently, testosterone sometimes overrode judgment as war-making became a form of masculine display. As one historian asserted, the presidents did not really fear Communism, which was increasingly fragmented, or the Soviet Union with its commitment to détente, or even China, which, despite its vast manpower reservoir was comparatively weak. No, what frightened them was the prospect of embarrassment, humiliation, weakness.[99]

Emotionally immature and intellectually mediocre, Kennedy needed to prove his manhood to measure up to his predecessor's military credentials, and to compensate for his frail health, which was far worse than voters realized,[100] and less-than-sterling record in World War II when a Japanese warship rammed and sank the torpedo boat he commanded, in part because of Kennedy's negligence. Three factors helped convert this incident into a heroic success. First, naval censorship prevented an accurate depiction of events in the initial newspaper accounts. A second was Kennedy's fortuitous friendship with John Hersey, a gifted young writer who extolled his friend's exploits in print. And finally his wealthy father's vast public relations resources kept a distorted, pro-Kennedy version of events in the public eye. As president, Kennedy projected a cult of toughness, a macho image, not only by conquering women through incessant affairs but also by deriding others as weak.[101] The State Department, he said, was "a bowl of jelly. It's got all those people over there who are constantly smiling. I think we need to smile less and be tougher."[102]

When it came to projecting machismo, Johnson surpassed Kennedy, who he considered "a scrawny man with a bad back, a weak and indecisive politician, a nice man, a gentle man, but not a man's man."[103] Deeply troubled, obsessively fearful of being dominated, intensely competitive, intemperate, self-pitying, petulant, and so paranoid it raised questions about his mental capacity to govern, Johnson had good reason to worry about his manhood.[104]

During World War II he, like John Wayne, ducked when the bullets were flying. Holding a Naval Reserve commission, he flew as an observer on one mission in the South Pacific before resigning his commission and returning to Congress. In an obvious ploy to curry favor with a congressman, the Navy awarded him a Silver Star. The citation said that shortly after eight Japanese fighters intercepted the mission the plane Johnson was in developed mechanical difficulties and turned back alone, yet the future president "evidenced coolness in spite of the hazard involved." In truth Johnson's plane aborted just half an hour after takeoff and never got within sight of the enemy. Yet Johnson made splendid political use out of his fabricated heroism, repeatedly having the medal "awarded" to him while on the campaign trail and wearing a silver lapel pin for the rest of his life.[105]

Perhaps to compensate for this less-than-manly behavior, he *would not* be the first president to lose a war. "I have the choice to go in with great casualty lists," Johnson said in July 1965, "or to get out with disgrace."[106] Whether the United States should be in Vietnam or not was irrelevant, he insisted. The fact is "we're there. And being there, we've got to conduct ourselves like men." If South Vietnam became Communist his opponents would claim "I was a coward. An unmanly man. A man without a spine." When a group of reporters badgered him about why the United States was in Vietnam, the president reportedly "unzipped his fly, drew out his substantial organ, and declared, 'This is why!'" That is, the United States was there because the president was a man. Because the country had to be tough, fight, get bloodied, Johnson despised the "doves." "Hell," he said about one of them, "he has to squat to piss," and another he called a "frustrated old woman."[107]

Johnson constantly used gendered language. In his view of international relations, "If you let a bully come in and chase you out of your front yard, tomorrow he'll be on your porch, and the next day, he'll rape your wife in your own bed," which would be the ultimate personal humiliation for a man. Hence, never appease the bully by letting him into the yard. Johnson also equated gradual escalation with seduction rather than rape, emphasizing he would go up North Vietnam's "leg an inch at a time. . . . I'll get to the snatch before they know what's happening, you see." Following the Gulf of Tonkin Resolution the president exalted that "I didn't just screw Ho Chi Minh. I cut his pecker off."[108] Much of Johnson's language bristled with homophobia. Regarding Vietnam, he feared that "If I don't go in now and they show later I should have gone, then they'll be all over me in Congress. . . . they'll push Vietnam up my ass every time. Vietnam. Vietnam. Vietnam. Right up my ass." "I'll tell you what happens when there's a bombing halt," he said on another occasion. "I halt and then Ho Chi Minh shoves trucks right up my ass." [109]

Nixon was equally obsessive about manhood, going through his presidency consumed with showing the world (and himself?) "who's really tough." When he said, "We will not be humiliated. We will not be defeated," he meant, "I" rather than "we." [110]

Put in starkest terms, three presidents, blinkered by anti-Communism, trapped by domestic political constraints and aggressive military advice, and imprisoned by their sense of masculinity, opted to have young American males killed and maimed rather than "lose" Vietnam, the next election, and their personal reputations.

On the positive side, they kept the war limited, thereby preventing casualties on a more massive scale.

President Johnson got chills thinking about one of his valets, Sergeant Kenneth Gaddis who had six children. To Johnson the sergeant symbolized all the armed forces, and as he contemplated going to war he thought "about sending that father of those six kids in there. And what the hell are we going to get out of his doing it?" [111]

Johnson did not get enough chills.

Consequently he found himself as a wartime commander-in-chief who learned by hard firsthand experience what any military historian could have told him in advance: war is unlike any other endeavor; it generates its own momentum and follows its own logic, which is discernible only in retrospect; luck, chance, and uncertainty exert more "control" over it than does the human will; war is suffused with irony, paradox, and contradictions; its consequences are almost always unanticipated, and usually worse than expected.

On September 9, 1967, Joe and three other soldiers departed Panama and Company B of the 3rd Battalion en route to Fort Campbell, where the 101st Airborne was undergoing a dramatic expansion to meet Vietnam's rising manpower demands.

His new unit would soon get a nickname.

The Delta Raiders.

Four

He'd have been in the stockade,
probably still sitting there,
or in Fort Leavenworth.

*Captain Charles Wayne McMenamy, on Joe's probable fate
if he'd been assigned to any company other than
the Delta Raiders in 1967*

"He just had that charisma," said Artillery Forward Observer Mike Watson. "Everybody just trusted him. You felt good around him. I believe if he told those guys to lay down their weapons and attack with their bare hands, they would have done it. Captain Mac was the best military leader I've ever seen, bar none, before or since."[1]

Captain Mac.

Officially, Captain Charles Wayne McMenamy. He stamped his zestful personality—his energy, passion, endurance, and bravery—on the original Delta Raiders, and the unit never lost this aspect of its heritage during four years in Vietnam.

Born on the last day of 1940, McMenamy enlisted at age nineteen, became an army mechanic, rose through the noncommissioned ranks until 1964 when he accepted a Regular Army commission, and ended up in the Special Forces (sometimes called the Green Berets) in Vietnam, serving as the Executive Officer of Detachment A-502 from January through mid-September 1966. Then he transferred to Detachment A-503 where he organized a company of Rhade Montagnards, one of the twenty-five or so indigenous, seminomadic tribal groups in Vietnam's Central Highlands.[2]

In the Green Berets McMenamy demonstrated extraordinary leadership abilities, accepting problems as challenges and invariably producing logical, workable solutions. During numerous combat operations he remained confident no matter how intense the fatigue and stress, was always cool under fire, mission-oriented, and led by example, which created "an unhesitating willingness to follow his lead and direction." With such inspirational leadership the Rhade unit became the battalion's best company and it lived on after his departure "as one of the finest, indigenous fighting units in the Republic of Vietnam."

McMenamy's departure came after a harrowing experience in support of Project Omega, a Special Forces intelligence-gathering operation that supplemented Project Delta, which conducted long-range reconnaissance missions. Six-man Omega teams (two Special Forces and four indigenous personnel) operated behind enemy lines, not just in South Vietnam but also, despite numerous official denials, in Laos and Cambodia. In early 1967, near the rugged, mountainous intersection of the three nations, an Omega team discovered an enemy tunnel complex running from Cambodia into South Vietnam. The plan was for McMenamy to lead a reinforced Rhade platoon to the tunnel exits to act as "bait," hoping to lure the NVA out of their tunnels and into the open where American firepower could slaughter them.

As happened with many "secret" missions, this one was compromised, probably by lax security procedures, or possibly by ARVN who secretly worked for the VC. When the six helicopters, each carrying seven men, arrived at the landing zone (LZ) at last light, the enemy was waiting. Mc-Menamy was in the first chopper, which was hovering over a small grassy area when gunfire erupted. The bird shuddered as bullets tore through its thin skin. Only two men got out before the landing was aborted: "Jimmy," McMenamy's Montagnard bodyguard, was shot through the shoulder and fell to the ground while McMenamy, fearing the helicopter was about to explode, leaped out. Unfortunately he misjudged the distance, hitting the ground so hard it knocked his breath out. Gasping for air, he saw the helicopter struggling away in the gloom—and heard the enemy approaching. He resolved to count to three, then jump up shooting and kill as many of them as he could before they killed him.

Counting: one . . . two . . . two-and-a-half. . . . Recounting: one, two, two-and-a-half. Again. And again. He stalled any heroically suicidal action just long enough for several helicopter gunships to arrive. As they sprayed the area with machine gun bullets McMenamy and Jimmy took advantage of the diversion to escape. "With the adrenaline going and heart beating, you run and run and run and break contact." The bottom line was that Mc-Menamy "was so scared that I just wasn't going to get caught. It was clearly in my mind that if I got caught I would get tortured and killed, no doubt whatsoever."

Four days later, with the enemy in dogged pursuit, they were still on the run—literally *running* all night and much of day, only occasionally holing up for a few hours. On this fourth day they found a hiding place, put out two claymore mines and camouflaged their position, and then McMenamy made a quick recon of the area. Spotting six NVA heading toward the hideout, he circled back to alert Jimmy, arriving just moments before the enemy. McMenamy detonated the claymores and fired a full clip from his M-16, killing four NVA, but the other two slipped around his right flank and threw a grenade. The explosion knocked him down. Instantly an NVA was on him, just about to stab him with a bayonet, when Jimmy opened fire from his camouflaged position. Both NVA fired back, killing Jimmy. But the Montagnard saved McMenamy, killing one NVA and severely wounding the other, whom the captain dispatched with his knife.

On the fifth day McMenamy spotted a small reconnaissance plane. Using a signal mirror and praying the pilot would not mistake it for muzzle flashes and call in a tactical air strike that would incinerate him, he summoned help. Delivered to a medical facility, Captain Mac slept for twenty-six hours and when he awoke he could not move. Sleeping twenty hours a day for the next week, his body slowly recuperated. Eventually McMenamy hobbled out of bed but needed crutches for another week until his legs fully recovered.

Then he left Vietnam for Fort Sill, Oklahoma, becoming an instructor at the Army Artillery and Missile School. Immersing himself in the new assignment with typical vigor, McMenamy "rewrote instructional manuals incorporating imaginative training aids and clever skits, thus enhancing and stimulating classroom presentations," took eight credit hours of college classes in his spare time, and impressed everyone with his dynamic manner.

In late summer 1967 he received an offer. Did McMenamy want to return to Vietnam? As the commander of a rifle company? And, by the way, could he form the company from scratch and have it ready for combat in just ninety days?

The man and the challenge embraced.

Captain Mac headed for Fort Campbell to command D Company, 2nd Battalion, 501st Regiment, 2nd Brigade, 101st Airborne Division. His opportunity arose for two reasons. First was General Westmoreland's relentless requests for more troops. In early August, the Pentagon alerted the 101st's 2nd and 3rd Brigades for deployment to Vietnam (the 1st Brigade deployed there in 1965), with an arrival date of February 10, 1968. However, with more soldiers urgently needed in an escalating, stalemated war, Westmoreland pressured Washington to advance the arrival date to December 13, 1967.[3]

Second, in mid-1967 the Pentagon authorized adding a fourth rifle company to each battalion. A traditional three-company configuration was adequate for linear warfare in which a battalion typically deployed two companies on line and held one in reserve. But in Vietnam, where battalions not only searched huge areas in all directions for an elusive enemy but also provided security for sprawling base areas, the Army needed more infantrymen. With four companies a battalion commander could use three in the field while keeping a fourth for base security. The original companies were A (Alpha), B (Bravo), and C (Charlie); each new company was D (Delta, the "bastard child").[4]

Rapidly bringing two brigades up to authorized strength while simultaneously forming the Delta companies, each consisting of approximately 160 officers and men, created an immense need for a scarce resource: deployable paratroopers. Being an airborne division the 101st could not utilize ordinary "leg" infantrymen, and some airborne-qualified men could not leave because their enlistments soon expired, they were slated for West Point or Officer Candidate School (OCS), or had already served in Vietnam. Even though 1,000 "nondeployables" (primarily Vietnam vets) volunteered to deploy, the manpower situation remained dire, resulting in a worldwide quest for airborne troopers. In August and September 4,500 jump-trained soldiers poured into Fort Campbell. The strength of Joe Hooper's 508th Infantry in Panama dropped from 755 in early August to 520 in late December.[5]

McMenamy built D Company from the ground up. To "help" him inaugurate it, Alpha, Bravo, and Charlie each provided five men. Naturally company commanders used this opportunity to rid themselves of their least desirable soldiers; Captain Mac fetched a few of them directly from the stockade. "The others," he said, "had one foot in jail and one foot out. They all had disciplinary problems of one sort or another."

Good troops were not the only shortage: McMenamy began with exactly four empty offices and two empty company bays. Requisitions went out quickly, and equipment flowed in slowly; inspired scrounging filled some of the gaps. The first "training" some men did was assembling office furniture, wall lockers, and bunk beds, cursing all the while that someone could not invent a wall locker with fewer than fifty-eight nuts and bolts, or bunk beds that did not resemble erector sets. With his unit activated McMenamy had the same paperwork requirements as any other company commander, such as daily morning reports to type and various files to maintain, but he had no morning report forms, no typewriter, no manila folders, and no file cabinet. Some of the unit's vital equipment, such as field radios, arrived just in time to be packed in Conex containers for shipment to Vietnam.

As airborne troopers arrived from the 82nd Airborne Division and XVIII Airborne Corps at Fort Bragg, the 509th Infantry in Germany, and the 508th in Panama,[6] a less enthusiastic commander than McMenamy might have despaired. Since he was forming an infantry unit he needed troopers with an 11B (Light Weapons Infantryman) MOS. He received some of them, such as Joe Hooper, Edward J. Pettit Jr., Richard L. Buzzini, Lonnie Nale Jr., Noah R. Rockel, and Bobby L. Rakestraw. A few others, such as Salvator Bongiorno whose training was in long-range reconnaissance, were close to an 11B. But the newcomers included Military Policeman Robert L. Rainwater, electronic and repair parts specialist Alfred M. Mount, clerks Tex W. Gray, Eugene E. Robertson, and Richard Ryan, Signal School graduate Dale A. Urban, cryptographer Roy L. Barber, truck mechanic Wayne A. Horne, and dozens of others without any advanced individual infantry training.[7]

When some of them learned they were in an infantry unit they believed the Army made a *terrible* mistake that would be remedied as soon as they brought it to the attention of the proper authority. After explaining he was a cryptographer with classified information who did not belong in a unit where he might be captured, Barber watched Company D's First Sergeant Arthur Scott Jr. scratch his chin for a moment. "Cryptographer? That's Signal Corps isn't it?" Scott asked. Yes, replied Barber. "OK, perfect. Now you're an RTO [radio telephone operator]," which was one of a company's more onerous and dangerous duties. Hoping to be a "base camp warrior," Al Mount endured the same shock when Sergeant Scott told him, "You'll make a good automatic rifleman, son."[8]

How did Captain Mac meld this disparate group into a cohesive company? For one thing, collectively the men were smarter than an average infantry unit since the Army usually placed its most intelligent soldiers in noninfantry MOS's. Being intelligent the newcomers learned quickly and were easy to train. Military Policeman Robert Rainwater became an instant mortarman. After just four weeks of training his mortar squad won three out the four battalion firing competitions, "and the reason we didn't win the fourth one is because they wouldn't let my tube participate." Also, the men were not misfits. "We had spit shined boots," said Sal Bongiorno. "We had starched uniforms. We could look like a poster. And we were airborne. We had pride in that."[9]

McMenamy also benefited from splendid subordinates. For weeks he eyed the battalion s-1, Lieutenant Cleo C. Hogan Jr., hoping to snare him as the company's executive officer (xo) because "I had a responsibility to the men to ensure they got the best, for the xo is just a heartbeat from commanding the unit." In November McMenamy got his man. Three months later in the midst of a crisis, Hogan provided indispensable leadership for D Company, validating McMenamy's selection. A longtime 101st Airborne Division veteran who had already served in Vietnam, First Sergeant Scott was beloved because he really "took care of his people. We were kind of like his kids, and he mothered us, took care of us."[10] For platoon leaders McMenamy received Lieutenants Robert L. Brulte, a college graduate who was also an ocs honor graduate, Lee E. Grimsley, an honor graduate from Tuskegee University's ROTC program, and William D. ("Dave") Loftin, a quietly confident ROTC graduate from Henderson State College. These subordinates "were remarkable people. They were not so exceptional as to be supermen, these were just good, solid American citizens, and fortunately for us all of them were trained and very capable."[11]

Most important in creating the company was Captain Mac's inspirational leadership and innate understanding of soldiers. He set out to build a special esprit de corps, to give the men "a central focus that they can all relate to, and make that so dominant in their day-to-day activities that it overrides personal feelings."

That focus was being a Delta Raider.

The name came from the battalion commander, Lieutenant Colonel Richard J. Tallman who, like McMenamy, came up through the ranks, beginning his military career as a World War II machine gunner. Like Captain Mac, Tallman also served a previous tour in Vietnam, as the Deputy Senior Advisor to the ARVN 22nd Infantry Division.[12] Now he was chiding McMenamy (though not too vigorously since he considered the former enlisted man a kindred soul) about the raiding of another company's supply rooms, allegedly by Delta Company. Such a reputation, Tallman said, was unbecoming. Keeping a straight face, Captain Mac assured Tallman that it had to be a case of mistaken identification. Or, just possibly, it might be an over-zealous dedication to company's needs by some of his men.

Raiding. Raider. The Delta Raiders!

McMenamy instilled the new identity at every opportunity so that "there was nothing else. Even your rank was second to being a Raider." In the 82nd and 101st Airborne Divisions, a soldier saluted an officer and said, "All the way!" Returning the salute, the officer replied, "Airborne!" Not D Company, where men shouted, "Raider, Sir!" and the officer echoed with, "Raider!" Officers outside the company were initially befuddled when D Company men saluted and cried, "Raider, Sir!" but they accepted it and replied with the normal, "Airborne!" When in formation and called to attention, the men shouted in unison, "Raider, Sir!" Doing pushups they counted them off: One Raider, Sir! Two Raider, Sir! Three Raider, Sir! Raider, Raider, Raider, everywhere, all the time. D Company troopers were not just airborne, they were special, they were Raiders.

Being special, they always did more. If other companies ran a mile, Raiders ran two, or five.[13] Captain Mac did not just order the extra effort, he did it with the men. Rank did not count, being a Raider did.

He also developed cohesion by mitigating racial issues. In the mid-1960s race riots were annual urban events; indeed, in late July 1967, elements of the 82nd and 101st Airborne Divisions helped quell an upheaval in Detroit.[14] With perhaps half of the Delta Raiders being African American, McMenamy recognized the potential for racial turmoil. Not everyone was like Joe Hooper who made no race-based distinctions and never "saw any color" when looking at an individual.[15] Consequently Captain Mac monitored each platoon's racial mixture, keeping a balance.

Looking at the platoon leadership positions, Dave Loftin was white, as was his Platoon Sergeant Bernard Z. Hines; Bob Brulte was white, but Platoon Sergeant James Deland was African American; Lee Grimsley and Platoon Sergeant George R. Parker Jr. were both African Americans. Captain Mac assigned Parker to Grimsley's platoon because the platoon sergeant was overweight (his nicknames were "Stocky Duty" and "Heavy Duty"), was ancient compared to most Raiders (he was thirty-five), and had been away from infantry duties for a long time working in a vehicle maintenance unit. So McMenamy "wanted a lieutenant who would really put the pressure on George, and I felt that Lee, another African American, could do it. They could all do it, but George might interpret the same thing being said by Dave or Bob as maybe being racially motivated. You took out that factor by putting him with Lee Grimsley." As it turned out Parker needed no pressure. He performed his duties well and despite the excess poundage kept up with even the youngest Raiders.[16] In part because of Captain Mac's sensitivity, racial tension was virtually absent. As Raider Samuel Ayala summed it up, McMenamy was very caring about his men and "didn't care whether you were black, white, or brown."[17]

Mac also avoided "papering" a soldier, white or black, whenever possible. The Fifteen Fuckers and Summary Courts-Martial littering other commands were absent from the Raiders because Captain Mac handled disciplinary matters without any official paperwork. "I wouldn't say that a Raider never did anything to warrant an Article 15 or worse," he said, but having been an enlisted man he knew that even an excellent soldier sometimes strayed. After all he was "dealing with a fairly rambunctious group of guys. Anybody that was crazy enough to jump out of a perfectly good airplane has something lacking somewhere. The possibility for some other character deficiency is much higher than for somebody who rationally said 'I'm *not* jumping out of a perfectly good airplane.'"

No one benefited more from the captain's empathy for occasional character defects than George Parker and Joe Hooper.

Sergeant Parker committed the (usually) unforgivable sin of punching one of his men, but no official record of this transgression appeared.[18] Hooper's wayward behavior in Panama did not miss a beat at Fort Campbell.

All the Raiders remembered their first encounter with Joe. The corporal had that distinctive red hair, was more knowledgeable about the Army than they were, seemed so old they thought of him in a fatherly sense,[19] and was obviously missing two stripes on his sleeve. "He seemed like a quiet guy, shy guy," said Tex Gray, "and then I saw all those stripes missing and I said 'Uh oh, watch out for this guy.'"[20] Of course Joe loved regaling the youngsters with wild tales about the missing stripes.[21]

Hooper was also "more gung-ho than Captain Mac was, and that was saying a lot."[22] Former Raiders remember the details differently, but on one occasion someone in authority—Sergeant Scott, Captain Mac, or the division commander, depending on who tells the story—assembled the company and began "this mean guy attitude, he's telling everybody how mean he is. . . . You could hear a pin drop. And he's up there saying I am the meanest man in the 101st Airborne Division and if there's anybody—*anybody*—out there who thinks they're meaner than me, I'd like to hear you."[23] Hooper leaped up before anyone else could even take a breath, avowing he was not afraid of the speaker or of anybody or anything else. With such bravado, no wonder he reminded Raiders of the comic book hero Sergeant Rock.

He reminded Captain Mac of a pain-in-the-ass. Thirty years later the Raider captain maintained that "Joe Hooper would have never gotten out of Fort Campbell if he'd have been in any other company. He'd have been in the stockade, probably still sitting there, or in Fort Leavenworth." On Joe's first weekend pass he went AWOL, reportedly drinking heavily and spending too much time with a lady in nearby Hopkinsville. Instead of papering Joe, Captain Mac made a gentleman's agreement that he would voluntarily restrict himself to the company area for two weeks. For fourteen days Hooper was a model soldier, but the next weekend he was AWOL again. Another agreement. Then the cycle repeated itself one more time. However, as the departure date for Vietnam neared, Hooper, always thriving on action, became a serious soldier.

By October the personnel turbulence from the departure of nondeployables and the arrival of replacements subsided, leaving ten weeks for training. But during the last four weeks half the brigade at a time received two weeks leave, really leaving only six weeks. How to use the limited training time most effectively was the question confronting Colonel John H. Cushman, the 2nd Brigade commander. A cerebral West Pointer (class of 1944) who was the Senior Advisor to the ARVN 21st Infantry Division in 1963–64, he opposed committing U.S. forces to Vietnam's populated lowlands, "where, unable to tell friend from foe, they could do grave harm; fighting in the countryside was properly a task of Vietnamese troops." Working to improve the South Vietnamese armed forces should be America's guiding principle. Alas, he realized Westmoreland favored an attrition strategy employing U.S. troops to do the nasty work of killing off the enemy, not a pacification strategy permitting the South Vietnamese to control the countryside on their own.[24]

Although fearing attrition would be self-defeating, Cushman prepared his men for battle, even in the populated countryside if necessary. He decided to use three weeks for squad training, two for platoon training, and then the sixth week for a brigade exercise. For five weeks squads and platoons learned how to attack, defend, and patrol in what seemed like nonstop organized chaos as the men made parachute jumps, attended booby-trap school, went through a gas chamber, set ambushes, and heard live rounds cracking close overhead. Centered in Stewart State Forest south of Dover, Tennessee, the brigade exercise lasted from November 6 to 10. Although some troopers wondered at the anomaly of conducting jungle warfare training in the freezing cold, the exercise was a success, particularly for Joe Hooper whose conduct was so exemplary that McMenamy gave him one of his stripes back.[25]

Naturally the Raiders trained harder than other companies. While others slept Captain Mac's men practiced night operations. James R. Kearns later joined the Special Forces and when that training got tough "what would get me through was just remembering that I was a Delta Raider. I thought everything after that is downhill and nothing else could be that hard, and there's no sense in quitting because you never did then."[26]

Still, as Raider Tex Gray knew, "it wasn't a whole lot of training to be ready to go over there." Even Battalion Chaplain William Erbach realized that "none of what we did really prepared us for what we had to face in Vietnam. They just couldn't duplicate the circumstances. But at least we got into the mental mode that we were going to war." Brigade Commander Cushman agreed. "Our limited time to get ready reflected Westmoreland's urgent need for reinforcements and so we were not fully trained," he wrote. "But we were good and we felt good about ourselves."[27]

Nobody felt better about themselves than the Raiders. Battalion Commander Tallman emphasized that McMenamy's company set the performance standards for the entire battalion, not only in training, but also later in combat. Its reputation "as the most outstanding company in the battalion was due almost entirely to the fine start which resulted from Captain McMenamy's tenure as its commander."[28]

Mac loved his men, and they knew it. But he also had that other attribute of a gifted combat leader. If necessary he would unhesitatingly give the orders that got some of his beloved soldiers killed. He understood that "Violence goes with war. War is violent. The most dangerous thing is to close your eyes to that fact. You can't have a nice war."[29]

William C. Westmoreland was the embodiment of American military leadership in Vietnam.

Known as Westy to his friends, he was a consummate careerist who never missed an opportunity for self-promotion and assiduously cultivated his public image as a dynamic, successful officer. In projecting this aura he had several advantages, one being that he looked like a recruiting poster for generals, what with his handsome, craggy features, ramrod-stiff posture, and faultless attire. Westy was always ready to be photographed, especially from a low angle so that he looked taller and more imposing than he was. Nor did it hurt that his South Carolina–born wife, who was much younger than he, bubbled with gracious beauty. Moreover, Westy performed admirably in combat roles in World War II and Korea, displaying a hyperaggressiveness that caught the attention of several important superiors, especially Maxwell Taylor, who commanded the 101st Airborne Division at Normandy, became Army Chief of Staff in the 1950s and the JCS Chairman during the Kennedy administration, and then served as ambassador to South Vietnam in 1964–65. With such an influential mentor Westy's star soared and in mid-1964 he replaced General Harkins as MACV commander.[30]

His unbroken record of success and rapid ascent up the chain of command convinced Westy he could overcome any obstacle, especially since he was "lucky."[31] George Armstrong Custer felt the same way.

Westmoreland's career stamped him as a man of action, not of intellect. After graduating from West Point in 1936 he made only four forays into an educational environment: a brief mess management school for second lieutenants that he did not take seriously; the parachutist school; a three-month management course at Harvard's Graduate School of Business where he learned statistical techniques; and a stint as Superintendent of West Point, which was an administrative, not intellectual, position. Westy was almost proudly anti-intellectual. Men liked action above all else, he told the West Point class of 1964. "Speculation, knowledge, is not the chief aim of man— it is action." Consequently soldiers wanted leaders who displayed boldness, decision, and energy. "He, then, who will command among his fellows," Westy asserted, "must tell them more in energy of will than in power of intellect."[32]

He lived by this motto. In the late 1950s when he commanded the 101st Airborne Division a training exercise went fatally awry when violent winds hammered the second wave of paratroopers, killing five and injuring dozens more. High over the drop zone with his command group, Westy learned of the dreadful conditions and the tragedy unfolding below—then jumped. As he hit the rough, rocky ground the wind billowed his parachute, dragging him one hundred yards toward some dangerous gullies before troopers rescued him. Westy's fawning biographer wrote that this jump was the "very sort of action Taylor would have wanted him to take. It showed that he had the requisite bravado, bravery, and reckless daring of an airborne commander."[33] Perhaps. But one might question the judgment of a commander who so carelessly risked his life and the lives of his men, who chose aggressive, image-building action in a situation where the stakes were so low. After all, this was a training exercise, not Normandy.

As MACV commander Westy's penchant for action remained intact; indeed, he personified the typical workaholic general who had "little time or inclination for reflective philosophical thinking."[34] He kept several books by his bed, including some of Mao Zedong's writings on revolutionary warfare and several volumes by Bernard Fall, who wrote extensively on the French experience in Indochina and understood the enemy's methods better than almost any other westerner. But Westy did not much benefit from these volumes because he "was usually too tired in late evening to give the books more than occasional attention."[35] He preferred to expend his energy visiting the battlefield where he sometimes gathered soldiers around in a tight cluster to deliver a victory speech extolling the troopers' bravery. Occasionally these pep talks were absurdly misplaced; one time the soldiers knew the enemy had been victorious and wondered, in a sardonic way, whether Westy was smoking illegal drugs.[36]

Westy's intellectual deficiencies were well known in the Army. General Phillip Davidson, his G-2 in Vietnam, wrote several pages defending Westmoreland's intellect, insisting he was "no dummy." But Davidson admitted that many of Westy's subordinate generals doubted whether he met the "towering mental standards" his position required. One was Bruce Palmer Jr., Westy's deputy in Vietnam. Although his boss was "thoughtful, sensitive, and very shrewd," no one accused him "of being overly endowed with intellect."[37] Unfortunately, as Clausewitz observed, although war may seem uncomplicated it "cannot be waged with distinction except by men of outstanding intellect." Being "no dummy" was not enough. Success demanded "brilliance and exceptional ability."[38]

Reflecting his lack of intellectual curiosity, Westmoreland knew little about Vietnam's culture and history; neither did any other high-ranking commander. Thus they did not know that Vietnam's martial past elevated military qualities to primary cultural values. Early in their history in a movement akin to America's westward expansion, the Vietnamese fought their way down the Indochinese peninsula, defeating the Cham, the Khmer, and numerous tribes in the Central Highlands. The Vietnamese were also intrepid defenders. "Our history through the centuries," said Pham Van Dong, "is perpetual struggle with nature and invaders." Vietnam fought the Chinese for hundreds of years before expelling them, repelled Kublai Khan's Mongols three times, and sent the French scurrying back to Europe like a whipped cur.[39] The Americans' disdain for France's experience was especially egregious since they were fighting the same enemy on the same terrain. But the only "lesson" Westmoreland and other commanders learned from the French debacle was to avoid another Dien Bien Phu. They cared little about the preceding eight years, preferring to believe, on the basis of only cursory knowledge, that the French failed because they were inept and too defensive-minded, mistakes Americans would not replicate.[40]

The Vietnamese gloried in their giant-killer role. Through patience, guile, and astounding self-sacrifice, they killed one giant after another. Now another behemoth was astride their land, but this did not scare them. "The United States Army, strong as it is," noted Dong, "is not as terrifying as [Kublai] Khan."[41]

The military leaders' ignorance about Vietnam's militant past nourished their arrogance. Collectively they were self-confident to the point of self-worship. As junior officers they helped America extirpate the Nazis and Japanese militarists, and as senior officers they compelled the Russians to back down during the Cuban Missile Crisis. Now the nation's awesome military power was in their hands. Why bother to learn about the Vietnamese? Such knowledge was irrelevant since "those raggedy-ass little bastards" (as senior officers in Saigon called them) stood no chance against the world's Goliath.[42] Thus, for example, the United States never systematically studied such vital matters as the enemy's officer corps and strategy.[43]

A postwar study commissioned by the armed forces reminded them of what it dramatically labeled an "*OVERALL LESSON*": "Incomplete, inaccurate, or untimely knowledge of one's enemies (his history, goals, organiza-

tion, leadership, habits, strengths and weaknesses, and above all, his character and will), results in inferior policies and strategies; raises the cost in time,
treasure, anguish and blood; and increases the possibility of the ultimate defeat of one's initial objectives. KNOW YOUR ENEMY!!!"[44] That military professionals ignored such an elementary lesson in the first place was a tribute
to their hubris.

In a powerful example of cognitive dissonance, when facts threatened to
prick the high command's optimistic bubble, it ignored them. One example
was the Army's unwillingness to admit a single defeat, as if losing even one
battle was shameful, a sign of weakness and moral degradation. Although the
enemy frequently defeated American forces the Army insisted it never lost a
battle, winning by pretense what it did not win on the ground. In the early
spring of 1967 official reports depicted Operation Paul Revere IV as a great
success, but an officer who participated in the operation realized that "we
did *not* win and we were *not* brilliant. In fact, we were stupid, lethally so,
and Charles [the VC] won the day." Later that year after the battle at Dak To,
MACV issued a victory declaration, but the men who fought there knew better as they prepared 376 bodies for shipment home and worried about another 1,441 wounded comrades. In May 1968, U.S. forces suffered a sharp
defeat at Kham Duc, and a soldier remembered that in 1971, "every time we
went out we got our ass kicked."[45] And so on—many times over.

The United States, concluded the same postwar report that alerted the
military leadership to elementary lessons, "lost more battles, both large and
small, than it admitted or possibly even comprehended."[46] By calling defeats
victories—that is, by lying to themselves—commanders deprived themselves of the opportunity to engage in constructive self-criticism and make
appropriate adjustments.

In January 1967 the Southeast Asia Office under the Assistant Secretary of Defense (Systems Analysis) began publishing the "Southeast Asia
Analysis Report," which repeatedly exposed flaws in MACV's conduct of the
war. Rather than grapple with the criticism the JCS twice tried to stop the
"Report's" distribution and Westmoreland railed against systems analysts
who "constantly sought to alter strategy and tactics with naive, gratuitous
advice."[47]

The high command's reluctance to admit errors produced mortal results. The "Report" demonstrated, for instance, that when battalion commanders held their command for more than six months their battalions

"suffered battle deaths 'in sizable skirmishes' at only two-thirds the rate of units under battalion commanders with less than six months' experience. Increased command experience of a rifle company commander also led to fewer battle deaths, but the effect was not as great." In short, Westmoreland's policy of a six-month duty tour for battalion and company commanders generated needless deaths.[48]

MACV was unimpressed. Its response to the "Report" distorted the data, thereby "proving" that the systems analysts were wrong, and argued that commanders were burned-out after six months, an assertion that much evidence contradicted. Battalion Commander Otis Livingston, speaking for many of his peers, thought the six-month rotation policy was about the worst thing that happened to a commander because "just about the time you get your feet on the ground and begin to know who the people are and their capabilities and that sort of thing you were out of there."[49] Incredibly, MACV also admitted the "Report" was correct, saying, "it is a truism that experience in battle will lead to fewer friendly losses from the point of view of a 'learning curve.'"

Driven by a corrosive careerism, the six-month duty tour remained, constantly renewing command inexperience, with young men paying a sanguinary surcharge. Nothing guaranteed rapid promotion more than combat command; since the number of combat leadership positions was finite, Westy limited command to six months so that more officers got their "combat command" ticket punched. "Current policy is fine for training more commanders for the next war," wrote one general, "but there is [a] question in my mind if it would not be more advantageous to concentrate on this war and the reduction of casualties in it." Another officer believed that Westy "couldn't have found a better way if he had tried, of guaranteeing that our troops would be led by a bunch of amateurs.[50]

An astonishing 87 percent of generals considered careerism a problem. Blaming poor-quality soldiers or inadequate home front support for the Army's collapse in the late 1960s was easy, observed a perceptive general, but the real problem "was one of ineffective leadership, in large part because many leaders made a career out of their own careers rather than a career out of leading their own units."[51] The system, noted a lieutenant colonel, "gets quite a few professional West Point officers promoted. It also gets more draftees killed than need be." Those in the ranks understood this all too well. "I have no respect for any general officer," said Medal of Honor recipient

Staff Sergeant Kenneth E. Stumpf. "Priority number one is promotion; priority number two is their social status. They could care less about that young private down there. If there is any blame at all for defeat in Vietnam, it was our general officer leadership."[52]

Enemy battalion-size and larger-size attacks required special massaging to keep the truth from piercing the Army's optimistic paradigm. MACV's preliminary estimates indicated the enemy launched a modest forty-five major attacks during 1966, a figure the JCS used when briefing the president, Congress, and the media to "prove" Westy was making progress. However, revised numbers showed the enemy actually made 174 large attacks in 1966. Indeed, while the VC/NVA conducted only ten such attacks in January 1966, it launched twenty-five in January 1967. JCS Chairman Army General Earle Wheeler correctly surmised that the United States was, at best, stalemated. The new figures meant that "despite the force build up, despite our many successful spoiling attacks and base area searches, and despite the heavy interdiction campaign in North Vietnam and Laos, [enemy] combat capability and offensive activity throughout 1966 and now in 1967 has been increasing steadily."[53]

Alarmed, Wheeler urged Westy to "do whatever is necessary to insure these figures are not released to news media or otherwise exposed to public knowledge," because if "these figures should reach the public domain, they would, literally, blow the lid off of Washington." Two days later Wheeler explained that "I cannot go to the President and tell him that, contrary to my reports and those of the other chiefs as to progress of the war in which we have laid great stress upon the thesis you have seized the initiative from the enemy, the situation is such that we are not sure who has the initiative in South Vietnam." Urgent action was necessary to contain the truth, so Wheeler dispatched a special team to Saigon "to sit down with your people and review criteria, inputs, procedures etc."[54] The result was that the initial figure of forty-five attacks remained intact; the real number of 174 large attacks—the inconvenient fact—disappeared.

"Our senior officers knew the war was going badly," wrote Colin Powell, a junior officer in Vietnam who eventually became Chairman of the JCS and then Secretary of State. "Yet they bowed to group think and kept up pretenses. . . . As a corporate entity, the military failed to talk straight to its political superiors and to itself."[55]

Overestimating themselves, underestimating the enemy, and shielding themselves and their political superiors from unpleasantries, military leaders relied on wishful thinking, not wisdom. Westy, for example, believed victory was *inevitable* because Americans had greater firepower and mobility, were smarter, had more endurance and guts, and had a better cause.[56]

Only the arrogant could misconstrue reality so bizarrely.

Many Americans in Vietnam, including General Westmoreland, were bigots, and their racism contributed to their overweening self-assurance. They equated poverty and technological backwardness with stupidity, believing those little brown-skinned Vietnamese were childlike, that figuratively speaking Americans must teach them to walk before they could run.

And the Vietnamese had no reverence for life, the way Americans did. As Westy put it, "the Oriental does not put the same high value on human life as does the Westerner. Life is plentiful, life is cheap in the Orient. And, as the philosophy of the Orient expresses it, life is not important."[57]

He was wrong.

The Oriental valued life, but Westmoreland did not value Oriental life. Consequently he devised a strategy that emphasized killing Orientals.

The conflict in Vietnam was a *revolutionary* war, not a guerrilla war, and certainly not a conventional one, though it incorporated features of both since guerrilla and conventional warfare were techniques, or tactics, the revolutionaries employed.[58]

How could colonial peoples overthrow powerful imperial overlords and their indigenous allies, seize political power for themselves, and transform their societies? Answering that question generated revolutionary (or people's) war. The most prominent practitioner was China's Mao Zedong. Diverging from western thought and experience, Mao emphasized political rather than military concerns by eliminating the distinction between peace and war, noncombatant and combatant, and the political and military spheres. A second brilliant strategic insight concerned space and time. Since nationalists initially lacked sufficient military power to hold territory or win quickly, Mao made a virtue out of necessity by refusing to fight for "vital" terrain and by protracting the war.

The Maoist model for successful revolutionary war embodied a linear three-stage progression. At first the revolutionary forces were on the defensive and in the shadows, retreating and hiding to survive while building political support; military activity consisted of guerrilla raids, ambushes, and subversion. As they became stronger and approached equality with the imperialist army the revolutionaries moved into phase two (called mobile warfare) when guerrilla bands coalesced into regular units and fought larger, more conventional battles. In the last stage they launched a conventional counteroffensive, overwhelming the imperialists who, with only a limited interest at stake, gradually lost the political will to continue the struggle.

The Vietnamese accepted some aspects of Mao's theories. However, based on their historical experience and understanding that every war has unique circumstances resulting from ideas, emotions, and conditions prevailing at a particular time and place, they modified the Chinese model. From Mao they adopted the idea that no dichotomy existed between the political and military spheres, that both political and military *dau tranh* (struggle) were necessary. Indeed, their relationship was symbiotic; metaphorically, armed dau tranh was the hammer, political dau tranh the anvil. The former embodied violence at all levels, from a lone gunman assassinating a village leader to full-scale conventional warfare; the latter incorporated three interrelated programs: *dich van* subverted the enemy-controlled population; *binh van* undermined the enemy's military forces and civil servants; and *dan van* maintained support in "liberated" areas.

Because Ho and his followers believed political strength, not military power, was decisive, they were less concerned with winning battles than in retaining access to the population. Dedicated followers were a necessity. "A revolution is like the rising tide," said Ho, "and the reliable elements are like the pilings sunk in a riverbed; it is they who will maintain the soil at low tide."[59] Diverting U.S. attention into remote areas away from populated areas allowed Communist cadres to operate with relative impunity in the villages where they served as examples of self-sacrificing revolutionary virtue, spread class hatred against the urban elite dominating the South Vietnamese government, and decried America's imperialism and decadent culture. If all else failed they kept the population submissive through sheer terror. Revolutionary forces did not need to occupy a village physically since they believed a lone guerrilla could hold it if the people supported him (or in some cases, her) but a battalion could not control a hostile village.[60]

Revolutionary cadres enlisted the whole population, obliterating the distinction between civilian and combatant by recruiting women, old folks, and children, truly making the conflict a *people's* war. For very good reasons U.S. and South Vietnamese interrogators invariably asked defectors and prisoners of war about the Women's Liberation Association, a Communist/ nationalist organization in South Vietnam that mobilized females for the struggle. In the VC women fought as guerrillas, served in militias and self-defense forces, and conducted an array of auxiliary duties from carrying out assassinations and acting as guides to providing food and bandaging the wounded. One study concluded that women commanded 40 percent of all PLAF regiments. In North Vietnam few women served in PAVN, but they carried a heavy burden for local defense, manning anti-aircraft batteries, providing up to 30 percent of the personnel in village self-defense units, defusing bombs, and capturing downed American pilots.[61]

Kids as young as seven or eight served as lookouts, carried messages, built booby-traps, and flung grenades. "Children were trained to throw grenades," said a VC, "not only for the terror factor, but so the government or American soldiers would have to shoot them. Then the Americans feel very ashamed. And they blame themselves and call their soldiers war criminals."[62] With women and children playing such important roles the concept of a "noncombatant" became hazy.

Along with the paramount importance of political factors, including the militarization of the civilian population, the Vietnamese accepted Mao's emphasis on protraction. The war's political nature and protraction were reciprocal: nurturing political support took time, and high morale sustained a long war. Astutely perceiving that the United States had neither the patience nor a compelling national interest to fight in Indochina forever, especially on behalf of a corrupt, inept ally, the Communists considered time a weapon. Against America's technological superiority and vast military power, the VC/ NVA fought back with patience and an extraordinary willingness to endure casualties, denying the U.S. victory while inflicting casualties until America reached a political crossover point where the home front no longer supported an interminable war. Giap predicted that as the number of dead Americans increased, "their mothers will want to know why. The war will not long survive their questions."[63] In an age of mass politics, when popular opinion was a dominant force in warfare, the administration could provide no convincing raison d'être for young Americans to die in Indochina. Avoid losing long enough and inflict enough casualties, and the United States would accept defeat and go home.

Because the United States was so formidable that a successful escalation to the third stage was problematic, the Vietnamese *theoretically* accepted Mao's linear three-stage progression from guerrilla to mobile to conventional warfare, but they *practiced* a more pragmatic, flexible approach. Rather than being concerned about a mechanistic formula, enemy strategists did not consider progression from one stage to the next as automatic or regard any of the three stages as irreversible. If they escalated into the mobile or conventional stage and suffered a defeat, even a seemingly catastrophic one, they felt no compunction about reverting to guerrilla warfare and re-emphasizing political dau tranh while rebuilding their strength. Thus no defeat was decisive.

Drawing on historical experience in which they waged conventional warfare in their expansionist offensives and guerrilla warfare in defending against powerful aggressors, the Vietnamese embraced what military theorist Truong Chinh called a "war of interlocking" whereby "the regular army, militia, and guerrilla forces combine and fight together." While American military leaders considered guerrilla and regular forces distinct, Chinh argued they were complementary in the Taoist sense of yin and yang, a union of opposites that had a synergistic effect, making their combined power greater than either form of warfare operating alone.[64] Historians refer to the blending of multiple military forces as compound warfare.

The Communists also considered the cities, densely populated ricelands, and mountainous jungles as distinct battlefields, each calling for a separate approach.[65] In a province like Thua Thien they simultaneously utilized political dau tranh in Hue, combined political dau tranh and guerrilla warfare in the villages, and fought in a more conventional style in the mountains. The flexibility resulting from the enemy's seamless interweaving of political and military dau tranh amazed an American general who asserted that the VC/NVA carried "on a different kind of war in each of South Vietnam's forty-four provinces." While one province endured simultaneous mobile attacks and guerrilla harassment, a neighboring province might be completely peaceful. "Even more unusual," he marveled, "was the fact that the level of conflict in each province varied surprisingly."[66]

Based upon their experience during August 1945 when the Vietnamese population rose in a mighty anti-French demonstration, Communist leaders modified Mao's third stage to include a "general uprising" as well as a conventional offensive. Central to the uprising was *thoi co,* or the opportune moment when the government was weak, the population alienated, and the revolutionary forces strong. Through the dau tranh strategy the Communists would heighten the people's revolutionary consciousness until, sparked by a general offensive, it ignited in a conflagration that "like a forest fire, consumes all before it," shattering the imperialist army and seizing power.[67]

In the early 1960s Communist leaders expected a general uprising to collapse the South Vietnamese government, but they adapted the concept after the United States became deeply involved. Although their propaganda still talked about an apocalyptic victory the revolutionaries had scant expectation of driving a superpower into the sea. Instead they anticipated a general offensive–general uprising to undermine the South Vietnamese government and deflate America's "aggressive will," which was a psychological, not military, objective. The goal was not to render the United States *incapable* of continuing the war—that was physically an impossible task—but to make it *unwilling* to do so.[68]

Intensely political and psychological. Deliberately protracted. Total in the sense that it enlisted all of society. Complex and ambiguous because of the multiple levels and ever-shifting stages of military dau tranh and the constantly changing relationship between the military struggle and the three types of political dau tranh. That was the enemy's way of war.

Two factors made the VC/NVA's strategy especially effective. One was that their interlocking warfare was "fortified."[69] Nearby sanctuaries and powerful allies shielded their conventional units from destruction, and the regular forces in turn protected the ubiquitous local and irregular forces. When hard pressed, main force units fled to safe havens in Cambodia, Laos, and North Vietnam that were for the most part off limits for U.S. ground forces, though not for air power.

Westmoreland and the JCS hated the politically imposed restrictions that kept them from invading the sanctuaries and the North. But they were disingenuous about the issue, building an alibi in case they lost the war. They lied to the president, never telling him the war was unwinnable if the limitations remained in place. To the contrary, they implied they were winning, even within the restrictions; removing them would simply achieve victory more quickly.[70]

Instead of directly confronting their civilian superiors, military leaders adopted what General Wheeler called a "foot in the door" approach. With the fighting underway they confidently expected to whittle away the restrictions and so repeatedly pressed for a bigger, wider war. Rather than devise a strategy that fit within the political constraints they weaseled to have the constraints removed, refusing to accept the president's decision.[71] At a White House discussion in April 1967, Westy proposed operations in North Vietnam, even though Johnson had religiously rejected such plans for two years. Yet the general seemed surprised when "No one around the table, to include the President, expressed any great enthusiasm for the operation, and the discussion died." However, he continued, "I will proceed to work out alternative courses of action in the event the administration decides to pursue a different strategy."[72]

President Johnson was determined not "to let some military idiots talk him into World War III." Believing that military leaders "need battles and bombs and bullets in order to be heroic," he was suspicious of their advice and worried by their recklessness. According to Secretary of Defense McNamara, Johnson was shocked by the "almost cavalier way" that the JCS talked "about the possible use of nuclear weapons." "They see everything in military terms," he complained. As president, he could ill afford to be so tunnellike in his vision.[73]

Military leaders assumed widening the war would ease their task, but expansion might not have made any difference, or might have transformed a difficult war into a more difficult one. Depriving the enemy of their Cambodian sanctuaries, a CIA report argued, would complicate the war for VC/NVA but "would not constitute a decisive element in their ability to conduct military operations in South Vietnam." In regard to invading Laos, plans "might look attractive on the maps they print in the newspapers," said PAVN General Nguyen Van Vinh. "Perhaps it is of comfort to the U.S. public. But in fact they cannot do it." As one high-ranking Communist leader explained, "an attack on central and lower Laos would mean opening another front nearer to North Vietnam, and then the U.S. troops would have to clash with the North Vietnamese main force" on ground ill-suited for America's high firepower style of war. If nothing else the logistical problems would be nightmarish at best, insoluble at worst.[74]

As for North Vietnam, a high-level presidential advisor noted that substantial PAVN forces remained there. "If we cannot deal satisfactorily with the forces now in South Vietnam," he wrote, "I do not see how we could improve the position by taking on more than 300,000 additional forces in North Vietnam."[75] Enemy leaders agreed. While certainly not welcoming an invasion, they anticipated one and did not fear it. "As for an American strike into the North," said a PAVN colonel, "this would have taken place in an area that had been well prepared to wage people's war and where our ability to provide material support to the main forces was much greater than anywhere else." Throughout the North the Communists dug bunkers and trenches in every hamlet, organized self-defense militias in every village and district, and armed the populace with Soviet and Chinese weapons, expecting every man, woman, and child to fight to the death. Looking back, a U.S. general admitted that while PAVN would fight the main battles, the enemy's "mobilization of the peasants guaranteed a long, bitter, no-front war of attrition." He was glad the United States never tested the North.[76]

Would widening the war render the enemy less dedicated, tenacious, or clever? Would it improve the climate and terrain, which negated much of America's technological superiority? Could expansion occur without employing forces dedicated to other worldwide commitments, such as NATO and South Korea? Could it be done without increasing casualties and expenditures, thereby further disquieting a home front already uneasy over the war's spiraling cost in blood and treasure?

Expanding the war might also provoke Chinese or Soviet entry into the war or, as Secretary of State Rusk feared, perhaps incite them "to give us problems in Berlin or Korea."[77] No one knew what their flash point was, but Korean War nightmares reminded the political leadership that China, at least, had a flash point. Relations between China and the Soviet Union deteriorated dramatically during the 1960s, culminating in a military buildup along their common border, battles along the Ussuri River, and Soviet inquiries as to whether the United States would support a preemptive strike against China's budding nuclear facilities. Neither Communist nation favored an escalating war in Indochina since each feared an open confrontation with the United States, but neither wanted to appear dilatory in supporting the Vietnamese revolution. Consequently the Sino-Soviet rivalry was a godsend for Hanoi, which adroitly maneuvered between the Communist powers, exploiting both for substantial aid.[78]

The relationship between North Vietnam and China contained both converging and diverging interests. On the one hand, their ideological outlook was similar and they both feared deeper American intervention in Indochina. On the other hand, anxious to avoid being dependent on their much bigger neighbor, North Vietnamese leaders zealously guarded against becoming Chinese surrogates (which, of course, was exactly what American policymakers erroneously argued they were). At the same time, China was wary about Vietnamese expansionism throughout Indochina. Hence, Chinese policy toward North Vietnam wavered between cooperation and containment, with the former prevailing up through 1968. After that Beijing was less concerned about the United States and more worried about an anti-Chinese alliance between a Vietnamese-dominated Indochina and the Soviet Union. Consequently, the containment aspect of Chinese policy became paramount.

Along with economic assistance China provided massive amounts of military equipment and sent 320,000 troops to North Vietnam between 1965 and 1969, primarily engineering units that built and maintained defensive works, air fields, and transportation networks, or anti-aircraft troops that defended strategic targets and protected the engineers. By undertaking these vital tasks the Chinese freed PAVN forces to fight in the South. Beijing also assured North Vietnam that China would enter the war if the Americans invaded, and periodically warned the United States to that effect. Preparation for war against the United States became the dominant national theme and included a wrenching economic dislocation as China constructed a new industrial base deep in the interior, far removed from the vulnerable coast. "No question about it," said one administration insider. "China was in an assertive, to put it mildly, pose in those years."[79]

Soviet military assistance to North Vietnam ranged from medical supplies to jet fighters and grew steadily until by 1969 it replaced China as the North's principal supporter. The Kremlin also dispatched 3,000 technicians, some of whom manned anti-aircraft batteries and surface-to-air missile (SAM) sites that shot down American planes. Even worse, it threatened to send "volunteers," an issue Soviet leader Leonid Brezhnev raised in March 1965 when he announced that many Soviet citizens had volunteered to fight in Vietnam. A month later a joint Soviet–North Vietnamese communiqué revealed that the Soviets would permit volunteers to leave for the front if

American aggression continued, and a year after that the Warsaw Pact issued a joint declaration about volunteers joining the Vietnamese in their struggle against the United States. Perhaps the threat of volunteers was a bluff, a smokescreen to make the Soviet technicians appear less threatening. But Washington could never be sure.[80]

Meeting with Westmoreland and Wheeler in April 1967, Johnson asked, "At what point does the enemy ask for volunteers?" "That is a good question," responded Westmoreland, a response that simply stated the obvious. The question *was* a good one, one the President could ill afford to ignore despite the military's incessant demands for expansion in a war that involved no compelling national interest. Fortunately Johnson understood that the enemy has "two big brothers that have more weight and people than I have. They are very dangerous."[81]

Realizing the war was being lost, military leaders belittled the difficulties and dangers that expansion entailed and chanted "our hands were tied," absolving themselves for the debacle. Although some generals and admirals never deviated from this alibi, at least Westmoreland ultimately perceived the truth. Twenty-five years too late, after having done so much to poison civil-military relations, Westy achieved at least temporary retrospective wisdom, admitting that "we have to give President Johnson credit for *not* allowing the war to expand geographically."[82]

The second factor enhancing the enemy's strategy was that Westmoreland devised an unsuccessful strategy. In this endeavor he relied not only on his own instincts but also on his operations chief, General William DePuy, who simplistically believed in more and more bombs, shells, and napalm until the enemy surrendered.[83] Westy's task was to implement a strategy that achieved the war's political objective, which was gin clear: the creation of an independent, viable, non-Communist South Vietnam. In pursuing the ground war, President Johnson "never tried to tell me how to run the war," said Westy. "He deferred to my judgment, let me run the war . . . as I saw fit, he backed me and supported me without exception." With excellent reason people in the Pentagon called Vietnam "Westy's war."[84]

Blinded by his conventional war experience in World War II and Korea, lacking humility and the capacity for constructive self-criticism, devoted to peripatetic action not tempered by intellectual analysis, leading with his fists rather than his brain, and convinced that the enemy had irreversibly escalated into the second or third stage of a Maoist people's war, the MACV commander failed the foremost test of generalship by misconstruing the war. He was not alone. Collectively American generalship ignored the war's decisive political aspects and local circumstances, only vaguely perceived the nuances and flexibility that characterized the enemy's strategy, and stubbornly considered the Army's doctrine akin to dogma.[85]

Because Westy believed it was "always the basic objective of military operations to seek and destroy the enemy and his military resources" (the enemy disproved this daily), he embraced an aggressive attrition strategy employing massive firepower in search and destroy operations. He wanted a "substantial and hard-hitting offensive capability" so that "United States troops with their energy, mobility, and firepower can successfully take the fight" to the enemy.[86]

The goal of Westmoreland's brute force attrition strategy was, in DePuy's words, "to stomp" the VC/NVA to death until the United States reached the "crossover point" when it inflicted more casualties than the enemy could replace, thereby compelling the Communists to surrender.[87] Success meant counting bodies, lots of them, not controlling territory, so the primary measurement of progress was the body count. To rack up bodies the most important thing "was to fight—to engage the enemy and create casualties. It mattered little that you accepted combat in regions with certain advantages for the enemy—the prime objective was to engage and to kill him."[88]

Westmoreland hoped to impose something akin to World War II on Vietnam because it fit his inflexible mentality and the Army's preexisting doctrine, equipment, training, and force structure. When asked what the answer to insurgency was, Westmoreland answered "Firepower," a single crisp word that encapsulated the Army's preferred modus operandi: use America's technological virtuosity and industrial genius to generate more than enough firepower to stomp the enemy, just like the United States stomped the Germans in 1944–45. Rather than adjust to Vietnam's singular circumstances the Army played out its institutional repertoire, whether or not doing so was wise or relevant.[89] "I'll be damned if I permit the United States Army, its institutions, its doctrine, and its traditions, to be destroyed just to win this lousy war," commented one general.[90]

In adopting an attrition strategy Westmoreland rejected two alternatives. Rather than destroying the enemy, some observers suggested denying the vc victory through an enclave strategy. Recognizing the war's political nature, the Marines in particular wanted to establish coastal enclaves in the populated areas, protecting the people, encouraging loyalty to the South Vietnamese government, and training the South's armed forces, which would bear the brunt of battle. U.S. forces would reinforce ARVN if Communist units ventured out of the wild mountainous regions to threaten the lowlands. But if the vc/NVA wanted to stay in the uninhabited highlands, fine, let them sit there and rot. Enclave advocates realized they were yielding the initiative but believed the initiative was less important than outlasting the enemy at the lowest cost to the United States. Supported by the JCS, Westmoreland rejected enclaves as inglorious. Glory—even if it entailed a higher cost, demanded fighting battles, not sitting in static positions.[91]

Another rejected strategic approach was pacification, the process of winning the peasants' hearts and minds and providing them with long-term security. While MACV and the JCS gave pacification rhetorical support, all the real effort went into destroying the enemy. Summing up the Army's position, Lieutenant General Julian J. Ewell said he had two rules. One, he tried to mesh pacification efforts with military operations, and two, "*military operations would be given first priority in every case.*" Lieutenant Generals Stanley R. Larson and William B. Rosson echoed their colleague.[92] Reflective of this attitude, in fiscal 1969 only 4 percent of America's expenditures in South Vietnam went for civil programs, including pacification.[93]

Because Westy had so little interest in pacification—he considered it a boring distraction and unduly defensive[94]—he gladly left this "other war" to ARVN. But if the United States was disinterested, ARVN was ineffective. Beset by poor leadership, low morale, apathy, and corruption, all too often ARVN victimized rather than protected the population.[95] The result was that while Americans chased the enemy's large units out in the boondocks the vc's village infrastructure remained virtually unscathed. The South Vietnamese population never felt secure, or worse, felt more threatened by ARVN than by the vc. This was a fundamental problem since people were unlikely to transfer their loyalty from the vc to Saigon if they felt insecure.

With enclaves rejected and pacification shunted onto the far back burner, American firepower drenched Vietnam, delivered primarily by tactical aircraft, armed helicopters, and artillery rather than small arms. Brigade Commander Colonel Sidney B. Berry Jr. wrote an influential pamphlet embodying the Army's philosophy. A successful officer "spends firepower as if he is a millionaire and husbands his men's lives as if he is a pauper. . . . During search and destroy operations, commanders should look upon infantry as the principal combat reconnaissance force and supporting fire the principle destructive force." In a later essay he emphasized that success depended on "the massive use of supporting firepower." Or as Brigadier General Glenn D. Walker put it, "You don't fight this fellow rifle to rifle. You locate him and back away. Blow the hell out of him and then police up." [96]

The firepower disparity between the United States and its enemies was extraordinary. America's peak munitions expenditure was 128,400 tons per month in 1969. By contrast, the VC/NVA reached their maximum in 1972: 1,000 tons per month.[97]

Much American firepower was wasted or, worse, counterproductive. In 1966 the Army fired only 15 percent of its artillery rounds in direct support of troops, with the remainder devoted to "harassment and interdiction," that is, against targets where the enemy might be—or might not. With an inexhaustible ammunition supply, officers "used to dream up missions just to keep the guns hot." Army Chief of Staff Johnson questioned whether this unobserved fire, though staggering in volume, did much good. One estimate was that 350,000 tons of harassment and interdiction fire in 1967 killed only fifty to a hundred enemy soldiers.[98]

In some ways firepower was worse than useless. It increased *American* casualties when artillery rounds or bombs fell short or long, as some inevitably did. Or when they were duds, which was the case with approximately 2 percent of all shells and 5 percent of the bombs dropped by B-52s. The enemy converted duds into booby-traps and mines, which helped kill 539 Americans and wound 5,532 more in the first half of 1967 alone.[99] Firepower excesses also rendered infantry units less effective. By relying on externally provided firepower, lamented General Palmer, infantrymen lost the "skillful use of fire and maneuver on their own." Lieutenant General Arthur S. Collins Jr. realized that "unbridled firepower has not made us a better or more effective army. . . . I am not impressed with our use of firepower, which has been wasteful, inefficient, and lacking the stamp of the true professional." To him, having infantrymen locate an enemy soldier or two, then fall back and call for artillery, helicopter gunships, and bombs rather than relying on rifles and grenades, was absurd.[100]

Equally serious, the Army's big unit war and wanton firepower played into the Communists' hands, as captured enemy records often indicated. Since the VC/NVA needed access to the population, they wanted to prevent U.S. forces from engaging in a serious pacification effort in the coastal plains where most South Vietnamese lived. They hoped to lure American forces into the mountainous jungles, and since Westy's strategy demanded fighting to generate a high body count the enemy never waved a red flag out there very long before the Americans charged. Battles in the Central Highlands provided Communists a double bonus, not only distracting the United States from pacification but also allowing the VC and NVA to fight under favorable conditions. Out on the frontiers they had short supply lines and nearby sanctuaries and could spring ambushes in the dense foliage; in addition, the jungle canopy and foul weather hampered American firepower.[101]

Westmoreland's strategy also aided the Communists by alienating the South Vietnamese population—killing and maiming citizens, destroying property, and forcing people to flee the war-soaked farmlands. American soldiers, wrote a North Vietnamese colonel, "were just like easygoing tourists with guns" who perpetrated mindless destruction.[102] South Vietnamese civilians fled not only the bombs, shells, and napalm, but also the million of gallons of chemical defoliants (Agents Orange, Blue, White, Purple, Pink, and Green) that poisoned the landscape. How many civilians died, suffered wounds, or became refugees? Numbers are imprecise since the United States was reluctant to keep accurate statistics revealing the brutal consequences of its policies. A reasonable estimate was that between 1965 and 1972 more than 400,000 civilians died, while another 1 million were wounded.[103] Between 1964 and 1969, at least 3.5 million South Vietnamese (20 percent of the population) became refugees, a figure that excluded 1 million more whom the war temporarily displaced.[104] Shattered villages pimpled the landscape, so many rice fields went untended that Vietnam imported rice, and a once-thriving agricultural land became urbanized as people huddled in squalid refugee camps that clung, like festering scabs, to every city; in just ten years urban-dwellers increased from 15 percent to 65 percent of the population.[105]

"You're no different from the Nazis," a drunken ARVN colonel told an American officer. "Look at you. Blue eyes, blond hair, all of you. The Super Race. For you it is a game of power and killing and glory. . . . You make our villages just disappear as you please. You're just like the Nazis."[106] The comparison was extreme, but the colonel's anti-American sentiments were widespread.

Numerous reports and independent observers discussed the irony of devastating the country the United States was supposedly protecting. "We can assume our unobserved fire alienates the local peasants in most cases," said one study, "thus harming our efforts to break down their loyalty to the support of the Viet Cong." American doctrine, noted the British counter-insurgency expert Sir Robert Thompson, was stupid because "It doubles the firepower and squares the error. Every artillery shell the United States fires into South Vietnam might kill a Vietcong but will surely alienate a Vietnamese peasant." The disruption, destruction, and death resulting from America's firepower, wrote Jonathan Schell, was so immense that it created "an indelible bitterness that no new program—unless it were a program to raise the dead—could hope to overcome."[107]

Yet the high command continued pursuing a depopulation policy, hoping to eliminate the enemy's support in the countryside. It considered a flood of refugees a sign of progress, and as for the dead and maimed, when journalist Neil Sheehan asked Westy if civilian casualties bothered him, he replied, "Yes, Neil, it is a problem, but it does deprive the enemy of the population doesn't it?"[108] And, he might have added, they were only Asians.

Bombs. Shells. Rockets. Napalm. Defoliants.

They rained on South Vietnam, turning that small nation "into a crucible of suffering—a nation that was finding out, in its flesh, what it means to be a pawn in a world of great powers."[109]

Yet the United States made little progress toward "victory."

"Soldierly virtues such as integrity, courage, loyalty, and steadfastness are valuable indeed," wrote John H. Cushman, who was a major general by 1972, "but they are often not accompanied by insight."

As Cushman phrased it, insight came "from a willing openness to a variety of stimuli, from intellectual curiosity, from observation and reflection, from continuous evaluations and testing, from conversations and discussions, from review of assumptions, from listening to the views of outsiders, and from the indispensable ingredient of humility. Self-doubt is essential equipment for a responsible officer in this environment; the man who believes he has the situation entirely figured out is a danger to himself and to his mission."

Unfortunately, in Vietnam, with all its nuances and complexities, insight often came too late, and only "through adverse experience. I believe that great costs could have been saved in the Vietnam experience if our individual and collective insight had been better as things were developing."[110]

North Vietnam's General Giap understood that acquiring insight was the antithesis of relying on mathematical calculations. "The United States has a strategy based on arithmetic," he said in 1969, referring to such things as the body count and the number of artillery shells expended. "They question the computers, add and subtract, extract square roots, and then go into action. But arithmetical strategy doesn't work here. . . . If it did, they'd already have exterminated us."[111]

Being young, predominately working class, only modestly educated, and true believers in America's cause, the Raiders' enlisted men (including noncommissioned officers) personified the Army from 1965 to 1968.

With most of them born in the late 1940s, many Raiders were either teenagers or in their early twenties. The average age of Vietnam War draftees and volunteers was nineteen; by contrast the average World War II soldier was twenty-six. "I spent my childhood growing up in Southeast Asia," said Noah Rockel, birth class of 1948, "which was a very quick time to grow up."[112]

Primarily as a result of the Selective Service System's class bias, few enlisted men came from society's elite. While middle- and upper-class youth received deferments by going to college or exploited draft law loopholes to avoid serving, the system "channeled" lower- and working-class men into the military. A reasonable estimate was that 25 percent of enlisted men were poor, 55 percent were working class, 20 percent were middle class, and only a negligible number came from the upper class.[113] As with most infantry units the Raiders' enlisted personnel overwhelmingly came from the first two categories. They often perceived military service as a step up in social status and economic security, while middle- and upper-class contemporaries viewed it as a step down.

Between 1966 and 1971, 19.4 percent of Vietnam veterans who were enlisted men had less than a high school education, 60.3 percent were high school graduates, 13.2 percent had one to three years of college (including community college), and only 7.2 percent were college graduates.[114] The Raiders fit this collective profile. Samuel Ayala, Ed Petitt, and Jodey Gravett were typical high school dropouts. Born in McAllen, Texas, in 1947, Ayala enlisted before graduating from high school when his dad died "and things got pretty bad for us." Pettit made it through the tenth grade and tried to get a GED in the service, but "I failed that, too. Hell, I was worried about partying." Gravett was born in Japan in 1947 and raised in a small Catholic orphanage near Yokohama until age twelve when an American Navy man, Jack Gravett, and his wife adopted him. He dropped out of the eleventh grade "because I heard that a war was going to start in Vietnam, and I don't know why, but for one reason or another I wanted the action." [115] Others, such as Tex Gray, Roy Barber, and Richard L. Buzzini, were high school graduates, while a handful, including Sal Bongiorno, Ava G. James, Craig Sturges, and Al Mount, sampled college before entering the Army.

Officers fit a different profile. Although few college graduates served as privates, corporals, or sergeants, they predominated in the officer corps. Approximately 13 percent of all Americans who died in Vietnam were officers, many of them college-educated graduates of the service academies, ROTC, and OCS. Since many of these officers served in hazardous roles such as pilots and infantry lieutenants and captains, it meant that privileged, suburban males did not escape the war's harshest consequences. Indeed, men from affluent communities were actually about 10 percent *more likely* to die than were other servicemen. [116] Out of the Raiders' four original lieutenants —Hogan, Brulte, Grimsley, and Loftin—all were college graduates, three received commissions through ROTC and the fourth through OCS, and two were killed in action.

Interestingly, in North Vietnam the sons of higher-status groups bore a disproportionately heavy wartime burden, including diminished chances of survival. Rather than angling to get their sons a deferment or a rear area military position, many Communist Party leaders and better-educated men nurtured such a strong ideological commitment to independence that they willingly sent their male offspring off to war, often in the most dangerous positions. [117]

Collectively the Raiders were proud Americans, "bright eyed young men that really believed we were in Vietnam to stop communism and help the [South] Vietnamese government gain control of their country." [118] They saw themselves standing in a succession of freedom's defenders, from their Doughboy grandfathers in World War I to their GI fathers in World War II, and now to themselves, the Grunts of Vietnam. American culture told them that what they were doing was right. Hyperpatriotic parents applauded their military service, John Wayne and Audie Murphy revealed the path to manhood, and their government proclaimed Communism a security threat. Noah Rockel spoke for many Raiders when he assured his high school sweetheart Joyce, "that Freedom isn't cheap. I'm going over there to fight to make this world we live in a better place. So my little brown eyed [future] wife I'll fight just so that when we're married we'll have a better place in which to let our children grow."[119]

The war that Joe Hooper and the other Raiders envisioned for themselves was a close facsimile to World War II, good guys in a noble cause against evil foes, with righteousness prevailing in the end. It never dawned on him or them that the political leadership committed the country to a questionable cause or that high-ranking commanders futilely expended their blood in pursuit of a flawed strategy.

Joe Hooper deserved a better war.

So did the rest of the Delta Raiders.

So did they all.

Five

Some day you're going to marry me, Blonde Mama-san.

*Joe's reaction upon meeting Hollywood
actress Carollyn DeVore for the first time.*

When it comes to showmanship, Hollywood has no advantage over the armed forces, and the Army choreographed Operation Eagle Thrust with all the precision of a silver screen musical.

History's largest and longest military airlift into a combat zone, Eagle Thrust moved the 101st Airborne Division's 2nd and 3rd Brigades—10,000 men and 5,300 tons of equipment—from Fort Campbell to Vietnam.[1]

One of these men was Joe Hooper.

The intercontinental movement began in mid-November 1967, when advance teams began base camp preparations at Phuoc Vinh north of Saigon for the 3rd Brigade and at Cu Chi to the northwest of the capital for the 2nd Brigade. The 25th Infantry Division, which occupied the sprawling 1,500-acre Cu Chi base since the spring of 1966, not only provided space within its perimeter for the 2nd Brigade but also gave the newcomers access to its ice plants, walk-in refrigerators, sports fields, swimming pools, clubs, PXs, and miniature golf course. Now new latrines, barracks, showers, mess halls, and tactical operations centers (TOCs) sprouted from the earth in a feverish sweat of activity, making the base livable for the 2nd Brigade, at least from the U.S. Army's extravagant logistical viewpoint.

A month later, amid below-freezing temperatures, huge C-141 Starlifters and C-133 Cargomasters began ferrying the 2nd Brigade's men and material westward via Washington state, Alaska, and Japan, before dropping south to Bien Hoa, which, like Cu Chi, was one of many massive U.S. bases pimpling the landscape.

At 9:45 a.m. on December 13 a well-rehearsed arrival ceremony began when a military band and honor guard moved into position at the Bien Hoa airfield. Ten minutes later the 101st Airborne Division commander's plane landed, and precisely five minutes after that Major General Olinto M. Barsanti deplaned, followed by his General Staff and Special Staff, all attired in the designated uniform of the day. The honor guard came to "Present Arms" and the band blared the "Screaming Eagle March" as Barsanti moved to a premarked position five feet from the speaker's microphone where General Westmoreland, a former 101st commanding general, awaited the much-needed reinforcements. With a crisp salute Barsanti pronounced the 101st Division "Ready for combat," listened to a few welcoming remarks from his superior, made a brief reply, and then the entire ceremonial group retired to the vip lounge for refreshments.

Although the 101st was now in what stateside drill instructors called "the land of the two-way firing range," Major General Barsanti's claim that the division was prepared for combat was a magnificent exaggeration. For one thing, not all the division was in Vietnam yet. The Delta Raiders, for example, did not leave Fort Campbell until December 16 and landed at Bien Hoa on the 18th (crossing the International Date Line, they lost December 17). Even after arriving, men needed acclimatization to Vietnam's conditions, sounds, sights, and smells. And having rushed to Vietnam with only minimal training, the two brigades required thirty days of in-country training.

What immediately struck nearly everyone were the heat and humidity, the noise, the filth, and the less-than-enthusiastic welcome from the South Vietnamese. "I won't lie to you and say how pretty it is or how nice it is because it isn't," wrote Lieutenant William Fred Aronow (who joined the Raiders in February 1968) to his wife. "It's muggy as hell, very hot & damp and its only spring here. The hot season hasn't started yet!" Artillery pieces, including huge 8-inch and 155 mm guns, fired all night, jolting the sensibilities and making sleep nearly impossible. As the 2nd Brigade moved from Bien Hoa to Cu Chi it passed through Saigon. "Oh yes," Aronow explained, "some parts are truly lovely, but most of it isn't 'quaint' or 'rustic,' Honey, it's just plain filthy!" The capital was "a hellhole of stinking shops with the craziest damned drivers (motorbikes and tiny cars) you ever saw." The pervasive squalor in Saigon and the surrounding area, with hogs, cattle, chickens, and people running in and out of ramshackle one room houses appalled Lieutenant Hogan: "Civilized people could not live in this filth." [2]

The four-hour bus ride to Cu Chi raised a dust-speck of doubt about

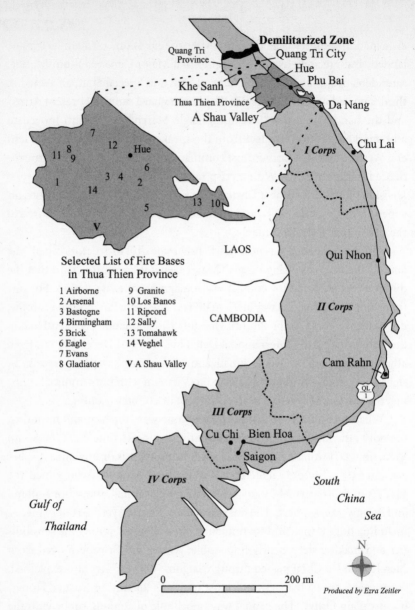

Demilitarized Zone

Quang Tri
Province

Quang Tri City

Hue

Khe Sanh

Phu Bai

Thua Thien Province

V

A Shau Valley

Da Nang

I Corps

Chu Lai

7

12

8

11

9

Hue

6

1

3

4

2

14

5

13

10

LAOS

Qui Nhon

Selected List of Fire Bases
in Thua Thien Province

1 Airborne   9 Granite
2 Arsenal   10 Los Banos
3 Bastogne   11 Ripcord
4 Birmingham 12 Sally
5 Brick   13 Tomahawk
6 Eagle   14 Veghel
7 Evans
8 Gladiator   **V** A Shau Valley

CAMBODIA

II Corps

Cam Rahn

QL 1

V

III Corps

Cu Chi   Bien Hoa

Saigon

IV Corps

Gulf of

Thailand

South

China

Sea

N

0   200 mi

Produced by Ezra Zeitler

Map 1: Corps Tactical Zones in South Vietnam and Fire Bases in Thua Thien Province

America's cause among some men. No one greeted them like saviors. In Saigon little kids ran into the streets and yelled, "Fuck You!" while "adults were hardly overcome with joy at our arrival. Most of them looked on in very solemn respect OR CONTEMPT. Some flashed 'the bird,' others the 'V' for victory sign, but MOST were VERY quiet, not committing themselves one bit." Adding to the tense situation, "we were just waiting for someone to toss a grenade in one of our trucks." Once beyond Saigon's teeming slums the rice paddies were lovely, "but something about it all seems forbidding."[3]

Lieutenant Christopher C. Straub, a platoon leader in the 25th Division who later commanded the Delta Raiders, was at Cu Chi when the 2nd Brigade arrived. It consisted of a Headquarters and Headquarters Company and three battalions: the 1st of the 501st Regiment (or 1-501 in military shorthand), the 2nd of the 501st (2-501), and the 1st of the 502nd (1-502). Out of the Brigade's strength of 2,900 officers and men, the Delta Raiders numbered 154, including six cooks and four medics. To Straub the troopers looked like typical newcomers to the war zone, what with their spiffy uniforms, short haircuts, hair-trigger edge, and eagerness to win the war. "Their attitude," said Straub, "was, well, this war's over now that we're here." All in all they seemed STRAC, meaning they displayed a highly professional appearance and demeanor.[4]

They may have looked STRAC but that sheen concealed various levels of anxiety. Sergeant Parker heard that some men said they were not scared about the prospect of combat, but he thought, "there's something wrong" with those people; he started getting scared as soon as he learned he was going to Vietnam. Noah Rockel shared Parker's anxieties, admitting, "I've got Butterflies."[5] Most Raiders agreed.

An exception may have been Bobby Rakestraw who was feeling "pretty brave" and was more curious than anxious about how he would perform in combat. Of course, Rakestraw was a tad different. Ever since the sixth grade his ambition was to be a paratrooper. Upon enlisting he made the recruiting officer promise that he could go airborne. "Son," said the recruiter as he took a long, satisfying puff from a big cigar, "I can guaran-damn-tee it!" The recruiting officer understood the pressing demand for combat soldiers and could not believe his good fortune in finding a high school graduate so eager to become one. For Rakestraw going to Vietnam to do his patriotic duty was a dream come true, not a cause for concern.[6]

As the 2nd Brigade moved into "hooches" the troopers scrounged for material to make them comfortable and got blisters and sunburns filling sandbags to make them safe. In an indication of how poorly the war was going, after two years of fighting around Cu Chi security was still an urgent concern. The day after the 2nd Brigade arrived the radio propagandist known as Hanoi Hannah welcomed the unit, promising it would soon get mortared. The threat was disquieting because the VC were seemingly omnipresent. Men sat in their hooches watching the fireworks display from the nightly war that went on right outside the perimeter and listening for the sound of that first incoming mortar round—and taking some comfort in knowing their furious sandbagging made their bunkers "relatively safe from anything short of a nuclear war." [7]

While settling in the men pulled nighttime bunker duty along the brigade's sector of the six-mile-long perimeter. Several bands of barbed wire seeded with claymore antipersonnel mines were the first line of defense, supported by bunkers spaced about every thirty to thirty-five feet. Two riflemen or a machine gunner and his assistant manned each bunker, with a telephone link to the battalion TOC. Mortars were preregistered to provide close-in support, and artillery batteries reached farther out. Troops often had a first-generation Starlight scope, a night vision device that, unfortunately, often gave the illusion of movement when none existed. "Nights on the bunker line," dryly noted the brigade commander, "were rarely quiet." [8]

Almost immediately the 2nd Brigade began a two-stage training regimen under the 25th Division's tutelage. The first phase concentrated on the "lessons learned and combat techniques peculiar to III Corps Tactical Zone," which consisted of the provinces surrounding Saigon. Training teams from the 25th Division taught the paratroopers about detecting and destroying mines and booby traps, maintaining weapons in the corrosive climate, clearing roads, patrolling, and search and clear operations. Company commanders and platoon leaders made helicopter reconnaissance flights, and platoon leaders and platoon sergeants accompanied 25th Division units on brief, local operations. Phase two began with small units from the 2nd Brigade undertaking short-range patrols by themselves. These solo missions quickly evolved into longer and larger exercises, including company-sized combat assaults and even battalion-sized search and clear operations. [9]

For good reason Captain Mac called this second phase "training with a bit of realism attached to it," because when troopers moved even a few yards beyond the Cu Chi perimeter they entered treacherous territory.[10] The 25th Division's base camp stood on strategic ground, straddling the primary land and water routes into Saigon from the north and west. Nearby were the Fil Hol Plantation, Ho Bo Woods, Boi Loi Woods, Iron Triangle, War Zone C, and War Zone D, all areas the Viet Minh, and now the vc, dominated. Not only was the surface terrain difficult, but the Communists also dug tunnels by hand—hundreds of miles of them, a pauper's subway system connecting villages and strongholds and stretching from Cambodia almost to Saigon. So cleverly camouflaged were tunnel entrances and exits that they were nearly impossible to detect.

During daylight the Viet Cong were human moles, staying in their belowground living areas to avoid American tanks, bombs, artillery, and chemicals. In those subterranean chambers they waged a constant battle against claustrophobic panic, insufficient oxygen, the sewerlike conditions caused by inadequate human waste disposal, and other creatures who found haven in the tunnels—bats, huge spiders, poisonous snakes, easily riled hornets and bees, fire ants that delivered vicious bites, and rats, both rodent and human. "Tunnel rats," small American soldiers with a pistol in one hand and a flashlight in the other, sometimes ventured into the underground mazes where the fighting was done blindly, savagely, and at close quarters with handguns, knives, spears, and ear-drum shattering grenades.[11]

At night the moles emerged, gratefully, to fight in wholesome air.

Beginning with Operation Crimp in January 1966, U.S. forces swept through the enemy strongholds, and one commander after another proclaimed victory. The Army also declared much of the region a free fire zone —that is, the Americans pulverized the area at random with bombs and artillery. Free fire zones were supposedly devoid of noncombatants; sometimes they were. Once vibrant with rice paddies, orchards, and rubber plantations, by the time the Delta Raiders arrived Cu Chi was fast becoming the "most bombed, shelled, gassed, defoliated, and generally devastated area in the history of warfare." From the air, wrote an officer, "the ground resembled [a] lunar landscape for miles on end, so close together were the shell holes." On American military maps one word replaced numerous village and plantation names: "Destroyed."[12]

Although villages and plantations disappeared under a firepower deluge the United States neither destroyed nor depopulated the tunnels. Resilient and dedicated, the vc were still plentiful when 2nd Brigade troopers made their initial excursions outside the wire. "The more the Americans tried to drive us away from our land," a VC major said, "the more we burrowed into it." As late as February 1969, three VC squads achieved a remarkable little victory. At the cost of only thirteen men, they penetrated the Cu Chi perimeter, blowing up fourteen Chinook helicopters and killing thirty-eight Americans.[13]

Unsurprisingly, then, "training" exercises were often indistinguishable from actual operations, and the 2nd Brigade immediately suffered casualties. On December 27, 1-502 made the brigade's first training excursion outside the perimeter. No one expected trouble in the area of operations only about two miles east of Cu Chi since the 25th Division's 2nd and 3rd Brigades and a squadron from the 4th Cavalry recently scoured the region, and none had contact. But 1-502 stumbled into an area infested with mines and booby traps, then blundered into an ambush that resulted in a nasty firefight. The enemy shot down a rescue helicopter, killing all four on board. Commanders wanted to call in air and artillery support, but the enemy forces were so close to the U.S. lines that heavy firepower might have done more damage than good. Nor could the Americans retreat since that meant leaving wounded men behind. So they stayed and fought until early evening, when the enemy withdrew. 1-502 recovered its dead and wounded, hunkered down in a night defensive position (NDP), and bloodied and beaten returned to Cu Chi the next day.[14]

Two days later another disaster occurred, resulting in friendly fire casualties, or what the Department of Defense called "misadventure," as if the family trip to grandmother's house for Thanksgiving dinner became a misadventure when the station wagon had a flat tire. A-2-501 (Company A, 2nd Battalion, 501st Regiment) was on patrol when a mortar round fell short, killing four and wounding ten.[15] Bad luck, but bad luck, like good luck, is an integral part of warfare. Unfortunately A-2-501 had more than its share of grim fortune. Although they called themselves "The Alpha Avengers," others eventually knew the unit as "Hard Luck Alpha" because it suffered an ongoing series of catastrophes, which was not good news for Joe Hooper who became a platoon leader in that company in 1971.

Meanwhile Hooper's current unit, D-2-501, was also afield. When the Raiders arrived in Vietnam, Joe was an RTO in the headquarters group carrying a field radio, a PRC-25 (or as the troops called it, a Prick-25). When the xo Cleo Hogan joined the unit in the field, which was not often, Hooper carried his radio, which is how Hogan first met Joe.[16] But normally Hooper, like the other RTOs, was close to Captain Mac who depended on multiple radios, each attuned to a different frequency—one for his platoons, another for the battalion commander, a third for artillery support, a fourth for the unit's 4.2-inch mortars, and still another as a backup, perhaps to talk to a helicopter gunship pilot, arrange a medevac, or communicate with brigade headquarters. Since the company commander often needed to communicate with different elements simultaneously, one radio was insufficient no matter how rapidly an RTO changed frequencies.

Normally a captain did not carry a radio, but Captain Mac was not normal and he shouldered the one on the company net so he could talk with his platoon leaders. RTOs carried the others, staying close to the captain, at his beck and call. At least that was the theory. But Joe Hooper could not resist the sounds of battle. As soon as firing began he dropped the Prick-25 and headed for the front, leaving Captain Mac or another RTO to hoist two radios. After this happened twice McMenamy bowed to the inevitable, detailing another soldier as an RTO and assigning Hooper as a 1st Platoon squad leader.[17]

Thus Joe was at the front during a vicious firefight within sight of Cu Chi, one that some Raiders considered the worst combat they experienced. The 1st Platoon established a nighttime ambush on a slight rise, with Cu Chi visible in the background, hoping to surprise the VC who regularly lobbed mortar shells into the base. Once the platoon set up its position, including claymores and booby-trapped grenades all along the perimeter, Hooper disappeared alone into the jungle. Soon he was back, having spotted a couple of VC setting up a mortar tube. When they fired the first projectile, Joe's platoon called in illumination rounds from Cu Chi so they could see the VC and kill them. Alas, the rounds burst directly over the Americans, revealing the ambush. Instantly the VC started shooting, and 1st Platoon fired back.

At Cu Chi the incoming mortar rounds and the muzzle flashes from the nearby small arms fire ignited a response, catching 1st Platoon in a crossfire between the VC and the 25th Infantry. Fortunately tracked vehicles had worn trenches more than a foot deep near the ambush site, providing shelter for a number of paratroopers. Ava James was even luckier, flopping into a six-foot-deep hole, safe from flying lead. But not from falling bodies. Other soldiers piled on top of him, including Hooper and bulky George Parker, knocking James's breath away. One panicked soldier just raced around inside the ambush perimeter; although flying metal shredded his uniform the man was not wounded. Eventually the firefight died out as the VC mortarmen vanished and the 25th Division realized it was shooting at other Americans.[18]

The enormous firepower the 25th Division spewed out during the firefight convinced Roy Barber, who was on the receiving end of all that flying metal, that "I would never volunteer for Viet Cong work."[19] Barber overlooked an important point, however. Although impressive, the firepower display was innocuous, hurting no one, friend or foe.

As D Company gained experience men discovered that war was "not like it is on TV or the movies."[20] Fear was pervasive, and battling the elements was often worse than fighting the enemy. The 100-degree heat was enervating, made more so by the hard work of patrolling while burdened with backpacks that weighed up to eighty pounds. To mitigate the searing heat men left their flak jackets at the base camp, preferring to risk death rather than make the ovenlike conditions worse.[21] Each soldier also carried at least three-quarters of a gallon of water and gobbled salt tablets like jelly beans, but nothing eased the pain of fighting the bomber-sized mosquitoes, sloshing through swamps and rice paddies, or hacking through jungles. "We had a wonderful time out in the boonies, my feet! Ouch! Do they ever hurt," Noah Rockel informed his sweetheart after one operation. "I'm so tired & sore all over that I can hardly move."[22]

Conditions, not the enemy, caused the Delta Raiders' first casualty when a soldier collapsed from heat exhaustion on December 29.[23] Nonbattle casualties such as heat exhaustion, malaria, and FUOs (fevers of unknown origin) constantly sapped the Raiders' "foxhole strength"—and that of every other rifle company.

The next day, around 2:00 a.m. while the company was in its NDP, the Raiders experienced their initial action when the enemy tripped a couple of flares, some men thought they saw movement in the inky blackness, and several soldiers responded with grenades and M-79 rounds (an M-79 was a riflelike grenade launcher that hurled grenades farther than the human arm could). After daylight D Company searched the area for bodies or blood trails, but found none.[24]

For the next several weeks the Raiders conducted numerous patrols without seeing the enemy. Typical was the Raiders' helicopter-borne assault into an area where military intelligence pinpointed a vc battalion. The information was either wrong or compromised; all Captain Mac's men found in three hours of diligent searching was a tunnel system that connected nearby villages, fields, and roads. The tunnels complex impressed Joe Hooper, who described it as "about the size of a small city. They had a hospital, mess eara [area], sleeping quarters and the works. Boy do they dig tunnels all over the place." [25] But no vc were defending the tunnels. The operation became exciting only after the Raiders returned to Cu Chi and discovered they inadvertently left one soldier behind. Everyone from Colonel Cushman on down feared the vc killed or captured the man. But the private had merely fallen asleep and snoozed right through the roar of departing helicopters. Three choppers returned on a frantic search and rescue mission and found him cowering in some bushes. [26]

At other times the Raiders had limited contact—a few sniper shots, some harassing fire from a handful of vc, or a quick mortar barrage. But they did not kill any vc—at least none they could prove. Take the Raiders' three-day, two-night operation along the Saigon River in early January. "The bugs almost carried us away," Hooper told his parents, and "we lived in water up to our chest most of the time." At one point they were setting up an ambush on the river's edge when Joe stumbled into a camouflaged hole, went into water over his head, and came out in the river, gasping. The Raiders found a punji pit of green bamboo stakes, several bunkers, a small tunnel complex, and four mortar casings. They also sank two sampans floating down the river. Hogan believed four vc died in the water but Hooper was not sure. "How many vc were on then [them] we dont know," he informed his mother and father. "Some got away—the rest swept down stream." [27] In fact, since III Corps' area of operations was heavily populated, D Company could not be sure the people on the sampans were vc, not innocents.

Not until January 15, 1968, near the end of the training period, did the Raiders definitely contribute to Westmoreland's beloved body count. Because Captain McMenamy was on a helicopter reconnaissance with Lieutenant Colonel Tallman, Lieutenant Hogan led the company that day. The Raiders landed in a fifty-acre rice paddy and began a futile four-hour search for five vc spotted earlier by a helicopter pilot. After the company was loaded back on the choppers and returning to Cu Chi, a helicopter escort reported seeing the vc "running away from near where we had just been. So we sent three helicopter loads in there. As soon as we got on the ground we opened fire. We went up about fifty yards and we had killed 2 vc." One was young, the other middle aged, and between them they had one AK-47 (the superb Soviet-built automatic weapon most vc and NVA carried). Although the other three vc escaped, the bodies were "a big occasion" for the battalion because D Company had killed 2-501's first enemy soldiers.[28]

When the thirty-day training period ended in mid-January, the 2nd Brigade's record was not impressive as the training phase revealed "growing pains." Airmobile operations were not precisely timed and NDPs had poorly constructed fighting positions and inadequately cleared fields of fire. Major General Barsanti issued detailed instructions to remedy such defects. His "Combat Notes #1. Defense Discipline" instituted uniform procedures for establishing "defense positions without exception. Defense will include bunkers with low silhouettes, overhead cover, and forty-five degree firing ports, warning devices, barbed wire obstacles, claymore mines, primary and alternate communications, and a thoroughly integrated fire plan." And so on.[29] If troops followed these instructions, they would be relatively safe from an enemy mortar attack. But three other things would be certain. They would begin preparing their positions well before dark, reducing their time on patrol; they would be exhausted after "humping" the boonies and then doing the digging and cutting necessary to comply with Barsanti's dictates; and because of all the noise and movement the enemy would know exactly where they were.

Adding to the lackluster record was, as Colonel Cushman admitted, the lack of contact "unless the enemy sought it. The advantage was with the enemy."

And while casualties were relatively light during the sporadic contacts, they "were not outnumbered all that much by 'body count.'" When Westy asked about the casualty ratio he "frowned when he heard the numbers."[30] The 2nd Brigade was not doing much to win the race to the crossover point, that point in time when the Americans began killing more vc/NVA than could be replaced.

After a month of training/operations Cu Chi was no more secure than when the 2nd Brigade arrived. On January 18, for instance, the vc sent twenty-three mortar rounds crashing into the base, and two nights later they launched a ground attack that penetrated the perimeter, leaving eleven GIs dead and thirty-five wounded.[31]

While adjusting to the tactical rhythm during their in-country training the 2nd Brigade also gained confidence. Men now knew what getting shot at was like. Although no one ever got used to it, the troopers at least survived the initial shock and the profound wonder that somebody was trying to kill them, thereby reducing future anxiety. As the 2nd Brigade commenced post-training operations Cleo Hogan spoke for many Raiders when he wrote, "Somehow I don't have the fears and apprehensions I had before."[32]

Men became accustomed to the rhythm of operations. A unit went into the field for a set period, from several days to several weeks, and then returned to a base camp to refit, recover, and unwind, enjoying steaks and chicken for dinner, bacon and eggs and pancakes for breakfast, plentiful beer (and soft drinks for the oddballs), refrigerators and folding cots, TV and first-run movies, and athletic events ranging from football to horseshoes. Along with heavy drinking, one other diversion especially appealed to Joe Hooper. A soldier "could get laid right there within 100 yards of camp." Joe did.[33]

Special occasions brought special efforts. The Delta Raiders put up Christmas decorations; unfortunately, "they look as out of place as snow in the desert," wrote Cleo Hogan. "I don't think Santa Claus could find this place."[34]

But a USO show did, bringing to Cu Chi a lighthearted touch and a bevy of beautiful women.

One of them was Carollyn DeVore.

The Hollywood actress was blonde, busty, and beautiful.

Born and raised in Los Angeles, 5 feet 8 inches with an eye-catching 40-24-36 figure, and bearing "a certain resemblance, both in looks and style, to the late Marilyn Monroe," she personified the "California Girl" popularized in a Beach Boys song.[35]

She began modeling at age eleven, won more than 100 beauty contests, and appeared in numerous TV shows, commercials, and feature films, often playing the dumb blonde role, "which made me a lot of money in those days," at least enough to live on comfortably in Hollywood. Having attended summer school religiously, Carollyn graduated from high school at sixteen, got married immediately, was soon pregnant—her son Rolly DeVore II was born in 1964 when Carollyn was only seventeen—and within three or four years was divorced.

In December 1967, Carollyn did her first of three consecutive Christmastime visits to Vietnam as a USO entertainer, a role she eagerly sought because she was promilitary despite Hollywood's alleged liberal bias. Moreover, she was previously married to her high school sweetheart, Rolly De-Vore, who served as a helicopter pilot with the 4th Division during the war. So she wanted to see for herself what Vietnam was like. With her adventurous spirit, once there she participated in "handshake tours," which involved a whiff of danger. A small group of lovely young women climbed aboard an open-door helicopter and "combat assaulted" into base camps and fire bases where they smiled, signed autographs, looked ravishing, and shook hands, bolstering morale.

Carollyn was particularly enthusiastic about visiting the 101st Airborne Division and the airborne troopers were exceptionally excited about her because, like them, she was "airborne." For a Lilt Home Permanent commercial she did three practice jumps, then jumped three or four more times while they shot the commercial, and for the fun of it eventually parachuted another dozen times.

When she and a small group arrived via helicopter at Cu Chi—"a scary place," said Carollyn—a handful of officers and a few enlisted men were waiting to help them out. One of the latter was Joe Hooper. "He looked at me, and he's a very intense person, with this crazy grin," she recalled, "and he said 'Oh, Blonde Mama-san is here, and she's Airborne!' And I don't know what it was. The light bulbs went off, the magic, whatever Hollywood things you want to say about it." She met thousands of soldiers in Vietnam and "I never really paid any attention to anybody. And I get off this helicopter and here's this guy and I'm just going 'Wow! Who is this!' So he had that kind of charisma."

While she and the other women served chow in the mess hall, Joe hovered nearby, approaching her a couple of times. "Are you a Yankee?" he asked on his first approach. No, her parents were from Georgia, good news for a South Carolina–born boy. "Some day you're going to marry me, Blonde Mama-san," he informed her when he sallied forth a second time. This nervy soldier unnerved her, but she was also attracted to him. The other women began teasing her, wanting to know "What's going on with you and the redhead?"

Suddenly word arrived that VC were in the vicinity, so the USO troupe hastened to the chopper. Just before she boarded Joe gave Carollyn his camouflage poncho, saying, "Blonde Mama-san, this will keep you warm. Thanks for coming to Eagle Country. Stay Airborne!" As the bird eased upward Joe waved, then slid from view.

She immediately regretted not exchanging addresses with him.

Soldiers in each significant Army unit wear distinctive shoulder patches, or insignia, and wear them proudly.

Many are colorful, dramatic, and readily identifiable. The 1st Cavalry Division (Airmobile) has a patch of black and gold featuring a broad stripe and a horse's head, the 25th Division sports one that is red and yellow with a lightning bolt zigzagging down the center, and the 11th Armored Cavalry Regiment's is red, white, and black with a horse majestically rearing on its hind legs.

But nothing compares with the 101st Airborne Division patch, which consists of a bald eagle's white head superimposed on a black shield. The eagle has a bright yellow beak that is open as if the bird is screaming, revealing a flaming red tongue. Over the shield is a black arch with the word AIR-BORNE emblazoned in a brilliant yellow that matches the bird's beak.

Although the 101st's nickname was the Screaming Eagles, others derisively—perhaps jealously—called it the "One-oh-worst" or the "Puking Buzzards" or the "Screaming Chickens." But unit members lionized the insignia, considering it a symbol of the division's heritage, made sacred by its airdrop behind German lines on D-Day, participation in Operation Market Garden, and the heroic stand at Bastogne in December 1944. Vietnam was a different war but the men in the 101st were still volunteers, still airborne qualified, and (at least so their leaders asserted) determined to live up to the division's epic past. Cleo Hogan believed that compared to regular "leg" units, airborne soldiers were "a little better cut of individual, black or white. We got higher class individuals than just Joe Schmoe off the street because they were volunteers." Noah Rockel's grammar was poor but his sentiments were excellent. His division was "the most proudest fighting unit the U.S. has, the 101st Airborne Division, the Screaming Eagles. They're the most proudest paratroopers there are. And we were asked to do a job here. So we're doing it."[36]

Pride, of course, can be carried too far. Because those bright shoulder patches were easy to see out in the boonies the Army wisely mandated that units adopt camouflaged, or subdued, insignia for combat operations.

With the bravado so typical of the 101st's leadership, Major General Barsanti refused to subdue the Screaming Eagle patch.[37]

A small man with a "high-toned squeaky, woman's-type voice," Barsanti was a veteran of the hedgerow fighting in Normandy during World War II and the Inchon operation during Korea, and had a well-deserved reputation as a hard-charging officer with a mercurial temperament. In three wars his hard charging resulted in seven purple hearts for himself (two of them in Vietnam), and many, many more for the men he commanded. Working for Barsanti was never a pleasure because his explosive volatility and bullying inspired disgust and fear more than respect. A shrewd judge of character, Cleo Hogan "never had any use for Barsanti" because he thought the general was literally crazy.[38]

A true believer in Westmoreland's style of war, Barsanti advocated relentless offensive operations conducted under an umbrella of supporting firepower. In a missive on the "Fundamentals of Infantry Tactics" he emphasized using the infantry to locate the enemy and fix it in place "and then using all available firepower to finish him off." Infantry, he wrote, "finds the enemy, but firepower destroys him." Barsanti wanted the "maximum effective use of artillery and air firepower for combat operations, using all supporting weapons first, then committing our manpower." His motto was "firepower before maneuver," and when he enumerated the hallmarks of good tactical leadership the first was utilizing firepower swiftly and massively.[39]

Everyone in the division knew Barsanti wanted contact with the enemy so that the 101st Airborne could do its fair share—*more* than its share—of the killing. William Erbach, battalion chaplain for the 2-501st, overheard a conversation in which Barsanti ordered Cushman to "Get me more bodies!" The chaplain considered this a "terrible, terrible line" because Barsanti was saying that "I don't care about people, I don't care what it costs, just the honor, glory, etc. to the 101st is important. Raise that body count."[40]

Of course what offended Chaplain Erbach pleased General Westmoreland.

Second to none when it came to hard charging, Captain McMenamy applauded Barsanti's decision regarding the full-color patch. Wearing a subdued insignia "was like robbing a soldier of his soul, his identification, his respect," and would dissolve the mystic esprit de corps that sustained a unit's fighting power. As if to doubly prove his point, McMenamy added more of the rainbow to the Raiders. He wanted to send a clear message to the enemy that the Raiders were a unit to be respected, and to everyone else that this was a special company. On Christmas Eve he and First Sergeant Scott drew a rough sketch of the Raider Patch. The finished product was light blue and diamond-shaped with black edges, a black bow drawn taut in the center, with a black arrow ready to speed toward its prey. Along the arrow's shaft, in bright red, was RAIDERS. Whether tucked into a helmet headband or pinned to a uniform shirt, the Raider Patch was another of Captain Mac's ploys to make his company feel distinctive.[41]

And no one could order the Raider Patch subdued because it was not authorized in the first place.

In a "Concept of Operations" formalized in August 1965, Westmoreland outlined a three-phase victory plan.

U.S. and other Free World Military Forces would halt the losing trend by the end of 1965. Then in Phase II, spanning the first half of 1966, they would assume the offensive, destroying enemy forces in high priority areas. Lasting another twelve to eighteen months, Phase III would complete the enemy's destruction and allow U.S. forces to begin withdrawing. Under the plan the war would be all but won no later than New Year's Eve, 1967.[42]

Things had not gone according to plan.

Instead of deploying to Vietnam to help mop up a nearly defeated foe, the Delta Raiders arrived in the midst of a stalemated war, akin to World War I but without the trenches. Presidential adviser William Bundy aptly called it "an all-out limited war" as, step-for-step, the VC/NVA expanded their forces to counter the increasingly impressive U.S. order of battle in Southeast Asia.[43] By late 1967, after two and a half years of escalating war, neither side had a clear advantage.

The United States failed to achieve a quick victory because the enemy frustrated Westmoreland's attrition strategy, which relied on helicopter-borne mobility and awesome firepower—and flawed assumptions. The general assumed that Americans could find and pulverize enemy main force units beyond the crossover point, but his massive search and destroy operations often did a lot of searching and comparatively little destroying. Simply stated, the vc/nva refused to be found—except when they wanted to be, and then the contact was usually an ambush or a brief firefight involving a squad, a platoon, or at most a company, not some World War II style encounter. When in contact with their adversaries, the vc/nva cleverly negated much of America's *apparent* superiority in mobility and firepower.[44]

A government official identified a major problem with an attrition strategy when he observed, "I see no reason to suppose that the Viet Cong will accommodate us by fighting the kind of war we desire." A Joint Staff war game completed in August 1965 agreed, concluding that if the enemy units adopted a strategy of avoiding major engagements, U.S. troops would have grave difficulty finding them.[45] As usual, when confronted with concepts that did not conform to its modus operandi, macv ignored the warnings and learned the hard way. Its chief intelligence officer from 1967 to 1969 admitted that finding vc/nva units "turned out to be an almost impossible task," and even when enemy forces were inside South Vietnam they "could not be brought to major battle." More than a few officers shared the frustration of a general who complained that "Goddamnmit, they won't come out and fight."[46]

Realizing their best hope was a protracted war requiring patience and tenacity, the vc/nva saw nothing "cowardly" about avoiding battle, about remaining elusive and sacrificing territory for time. "I can imagine that you think I'm in firefights, ambushes and assaults about twenty-four hours a day," a Delta Raider wrote his wife. "It's not that way. Some units may be a month without any contact at all. Others may have three days of light contact and then a couple of weeks without any. Most of the time is spent trying to locate and fix the enemy."[47]

The enemy hid by dispersing into small units, scattering like a covey of quail amidst the hamlets in the populated lowlands or under the triple canopy jungle in the Central Highland's inaccessible ridges and valleys. They were also highly mobile, expert diggers, magicians with camouflage and deception, and refused to fight even for seemingly vital base areas. A vc or nva main force battalion might disperse over a dozen or more miles, staying in platoon- and company-sized sectors until they needed to reassemble at the critical time and place.[48] Finding them was not quite as bad as looking for a needle in a haystack, but it was close, particularly since they exploited the established patterns that guided American operations. U.S. infantrymen, for example, rarely operated outside the range of supporting artillery. Enemy soldiers drew a 10,000-meter radius circle around any fire base with 105 mm howitzers and then remained outside the circle, knowing the grunts stayed inside it. Also, GIs usually did not operate close to the boundaries of their area of operations, fearing friendly fire incidents. Learning this, the VC/NVA lurked in the wide crease between two areas of operation.[49]

With no large logistical requirements tying them to fixed bases, enemy units remained mobile, avoiding detection by rarely staying in one place for more than a few days, and by moving at night or during rainy or foggy weather, which grounded reconnaissance planes and helicopters. "Charlie just thrived on nighttime," marveled a grunt. "He could move through the dark and never make a sound. He knew exactly where he was going; he was good." As soon as the VC and NVA stopped moving they began digging—they "could dig a hole from here to Mississippi overnight," said the Raiders' George Parker. "They can dig in. They can dig *in*."[50]

To an army without air cover, camouflage and deception took on special urgency. Employing strict camouflage discipline, the VC/NVA concealed their tunnels, holes, and bunkers so well they were invisible from just few feet away. In battle they entwined their uniforms and helmets with branches and twigs so that they were nearly impossible to see. To draw interest away from where they really were they resorted to deception, such as building dummy positions with less-than-perfect camouflage, often in areas the VC or NVA never intended to occupy. When Americans spotted these false positions they hammered them with artillery and air attacks, or sent ground units into the wilderness on futile operations.[51]

Even if U.S. forces discovered a base area out in the jungle the enemy often abandoned it rather than fight, hoping the grunts would miss some concealed caches, and when the Americans left (as they always did) the VC or NVA salvaged what remained. The same was true in the villages. Rather than risk heavy casualties by opposing a search and destroy operation, guerrillas and political cadre fled until the GIs departed, then returned, keeping the revolutionary infrastructure intact.[52]

Although Army Chief of Staff Harold Johnson exalted that helicopters gave soldiers a victory over three of their oldest foes—time, terrain, and fatigue—helicopter mobility was often only an *apparent* advantage.[53] Not only were choppers limited in where they could land, but helicopter-borne operations were also so "noisy" they guaranteed U.S. forces lost the initiative. Moreover, the VC/NVA developed superb military intelligence assets that revealed many operations in advance.

In theory airmobility allowed infantrymen to achieve surprise by striking unexpectedly whenever and wherever they wanted. But in practice helicopter warfare had many disadvantages, starting with daunting maintenance problems. It took approximately ten hours of maintenance for every hour of flight, which in turn required an enormous logistical base that demanded protection, thus soaking up manpower that might otherwise be searching for the enemy. Because of maintenance difficulties, rarely were enough "birds" available, which meant too few men made an assault or that the troopers arrived in shifts; those landing first were extremely vulnerable.[54]

Choppers also had a limited range; after delivering an assault force to a landing zone (LZ) they still needed enough fuel to return to the nearest refueling point. As early as 1962 the enemy recognized that "the starting point for heliborne operations is usually near the objective and thus the enemy's element of surprise can be compromised."[55] Operations in bad weather or at night were perilous. To mitigate weather problems, Army Pathfinders often became glorified meteorologists, providing real-time weather reports from fire bases and LZs.[56] Wherever they reported that the fog was dense, the clouds low, the winds high, or the rains torrential, helicopters could not go —and they could not go a lot of places much of the time. "After action reports" from the 101st Airborne Division noted that airmobile units often waited several days for a break in the weather to make a combat assault. Troopers conducted operations only when the weather cooperated, not necessarily when and where the enemy was vulnerable.[57]

While airmobility advocates crowed that "Terrain obstacles are now only the enemy's problem, not ours," the terrain was often a limitation, especially in mountainous jungles where LZs were at a premium. Relatively flat open areas were so scarce that units created small teams armed with chain saws and axes to rappel into the jungle to hack helicopter-size holes through the canopy, the loud buzzing and whacking telling nearby VC or NVA exactly where the LZ was. Since finding or creating new LZs was difficult, Americans frequently reused the old ones, which were often deathtraps as the enemy laced them with booby traps (BBTs) and mines, preregistered mortar fire on them, and set ambushes there.[58]

And helicopters were vulnerable, not only to bullets but to accidents. Within 1,500 feet of the ground, choppers were within effective small arms range. "If we aim at their nose," noted an enemy document, "we will hit either the engine or the pilot. If we aim at two-thirds from the nose of the aircraft, we will hit the gas tank and set the aircraft on fire." Knowing how effective rifles and machine guns could be against a chopper, one pilot declared he "was always happy to be flying high. Even higher would have been fine with me. Very few pilots were killed by staying away from the ground." Rumor had it enemy soldiers who shot down a chopper received immediate promotions. "If so," deadpanned an infantryman, "the helicopters helped quite a few enemy soldiers along in their careers." Before the war ended the United States lost 2,587 helicopters in combat and another 2,282 in accidents, killing 5,289 servicemen.[59]

As a means of reducing the vulnerability of both men and machines before making an assault, units "prepped" the LZ in advance with artillery fire (if for no other reason than to detonate mines and BBTs). But this also alerted enemy forces that they were coming. Of course the "wop-wop-wop" of approaching helicopters gave warning of an impending attack. As one chopper pilot bluntly asked, "How could anyone be taken by surprise by a flight of Hueys?" Once a unit was on the ground, helicopters regularly delivered hot chow and supplies, pinpointing the patrol's location. In addition, a patrol frequently road-mapped its route by conducting "recon by fire" as it moved, calling in artillery fire overhead to flush out the enemy. Rather than being flushed, the VC and the NVA simply hid.[60]

Evading the Americans was also easy because the VC/NVA excelled at military intelligence. "The enemy knew everything there was to know about us," grumbled one general. "They knew when we were going to strike, where we were going to strike, under what conditions—ground, air, or naval. That permitted him to make do with but a fraction of the assets and resources we required to operate."[61] Although U.S. forces justifiably blamed the South Vietnamese for many intelligence leaks, the Americans were far from blameless when it came to compromising security.

The VC's A3 technical reconnaissance unit, for instance, had great success exploiting radio security lapses. Its personnel understood the communications of local American and ARVN units better than U.S. and South Vietnamese personnel did. "Having heard the confusion on American and South

Vietnamese nets when frequencies and calls signs were changed," wrote a historian who studied the unit's activities, "they learned to adjust to new Signal Operating Instructions more quickly than the communicators in the nets."[62] Sometimes Americans made the job almost too easy. When allied operators became confused by the changes (as they often did), headquarters broadcast the new frequencies and call signs in the clear—that is, without encoding them!

A3 often focused on the 1st Cavalry Division's air nets, listening to the nightly transmission of the division's helicopter support unit. These intercepts told the VC which units would be airlifted into battle the next day and their destination. A3 also listened to the Air Liaison and Air Warning Nets. Concerned with medical and special aviation support, the former broadcast in the clear so stations without security equipment could still request assistance. The latter "broadcast information concerning air strikes [including B-52 strikes], artillery barrages, and impending enemy attacks to every fire base and to all aircraft flying through the area. Besides receiving prior warning of maneuver and fire support plans, the Viet Cong also learned from the Air Warning Net whether their own attack plans had been compromised and whether American and South Vietnamese units were being alerted."[63]

Not only did the VC and NVA intercept messages but they also utilized their knowledge of American communications to "jam" frequencies to prevent transmissions, or to engage in "imitative deception," entering the radio nets to send bogus messages canceling attacks or artillery bombardments, or to redirect artillery fire and air strikes—sometimes onto American positions.[64]

Officers understood that communications security problems were widespread, yet seemed incapable of enforcing security procedures. General W. B. Rosson complained of the "consistent violation of security within virtually all voice nets, particularly those utilized for command and fire support coordination," resulting in many abortive operations. Another general lamented that "we never achieved even a reasonably good posture" in communications security. Field reports consistently identified lax procedures in handling classified material, including Signal Operating Instructions.[65]

The enemy, Westmoreland complained, was "uncommonly adept at slithering away."[66] Considering the limitations on airmobility, the "noise" operations generated, and the systemic intelligence failures, slithering away did not take much skill.

Forewarned, sometimes the enemy decided not to slither and hide but to fight, though rarely in the pitched battles Westy sought. Vietnam was an atomized war of incessant small unit actions with remarkably few large battles. Indicative of the enemy's unconventional style of war, by 1967 more than 96 percent of all engagements with the VC/NVA occurred at the company level or lower; the battalion-size attacks that so concerned Westmoreland and the JCS were exceptions compared to the several *thousand* other enemy actions *per month*.[67] Most combat veterans experienced firefights, ambushes, sniper fire, a low-tech, high-fear war of BBTS and mines, and standoff attacks by rockets and mortars. But few fought in a battle that bought all of America's high-tech arsenal to bear.

Characteristic of the war was the firefight, a vicious, quick exchange of gunfire at close range, often ignited by an ambush. In most firefights the enemy held the initial advantage, fighting at its chosen time and on carefully selected terrain. The VC/NVA preferred fighting under the triple canopy, which provided cover for ambushes, contained few LZs for American reinforcements, and minimized the effect of artillery and air strikes. Shells detonated in the treetops, helicopters and tactical aircraft could see neither friendly nor enemy forces, and the colored smoke Americans used to mark positions often dissipated before it burst through the canopy—or worse, blew behind American lines resulting in friendly fire casualties. The VC/NVA also stayed close to Cambodia and Laos where they found sanctuary if the situation became desperate. For good reasons George Parker believed that fighting on the enemy's turf gave the adversary a 25 to 30 percent advantage.[68]

Many firefights began with a shattering burst of small arms fire from well constructed and well concealed ambush positions—though Westmoreland could not accept that his units were being ambushed so he insisted on calling these affairs "meeting engagements."[69] Day after day of tedious, futile searching suddenly erupted in terror and near chaos. "Enemy contact in the jungle usually occurs at point blank range," wrote Major General Barsanti, "and more often than not the enemy will enjoy the advantages of fortifications, snipers in trees, communication trenches, and minefields to the front and flanks."[70] Firing from only a few yards away, the enemy's fusillade momentarily stunned those still alive in the ambush zone. Return fire was initially ragged and scattered, lacking direction and purpose since the VC or NVA positions were so beautifully camouflaged that even the muzzle flashes were invisible. In the resulting "mass hysteria," a soldier recalled, all he could do was *hear* the enemy firing. "No one knew what was going on. I didn't know what we were supposed to do. I just dropped down and gave supporting fire." A Raider platoon leader admitted that a firefight was "really quite hectic," happening so fast he felt useless as he hugged the ground, and from that unenviable position tried to organize his men.[71]

Patrols often blundered into ambushes because of inexperience. "They walk into traps that wouldn't fool a baby," wrote Giap.[72] At one level U.S. forces remained novices because of the one-year rotation policy. A popular adage maintained that the United States did not fight in Vietnam for ten years, but fought in Vietnam one year ten times over. Westmoreland adopted the one-year policy to keep morale high but the unfortunate results were lowered combat proficiency and a higher death rate. Units suffered from constantly renewed inexperience as the tour of combat-tested veterans expired and untested replacements assumed their place. The newcomers invariably fought against experienced enemy soldiers who served for the duration, so the failure to capitalize on hard-won expertise had mortal consequences. Twice as many Americans died during the first six months of their tour as in the second six months. "Thus, the longer one stayed alive after arriving in Vietnam, the better one's chances for survival, presumably as a result of a learning curve, which had to be repeated for each new arrival." Longer tours might have cut the death toll. Not only were the increased fatalities detrimental to morale, but so also was the emphasis on personal survival that the one-year tour nourished. Living through 365 days rather than defeating the enemy often became an all-consuming concern.[73]

Heightening the Americans' inexperience were the hyperkinetic operations that sent a unit careening from place to place. "Every time we were getting familiar with an area, we moved to a new one," wrote a platoon leader. "The enemy always knew the territory. We were strangers wherever we went." And because headquarters jealously guarded information, often refusing to share it with tactical commanders, the ground-pounders rarely had adequate intelligence. "Thus, each unit entering an area of operations re-discovers evidence of the enemy on its own, which tends to prevent an accurate assessment of recent enemy activity," concluded a "lessons learned" report from the 2nd Brigade, 101st Airborne. "In addition, valuable time and manpower is wasted searching the same areas repetitiously." Equally bad, intelligence that reached the tactical level was often unreliable. One soldier believed the intelligence branch either read its maps upside down or got "information from smuggled Chinese fortune cookies."[74]

In theory the good news about an ambush was that Americans now knew where enemy soldiers were, so they could call in artillery, tactical air, and aerial rocket artillery (ARA) and add cadavers to the body count. Since virtually the only way troops "found" enemy forces was to stumble into an ambush, the infantry became little more than "bait." Commanders sent out squad-, platoon-, or company-sized patrols hoping the lure of such a small unit would entice the VC or NVA to take the bait. The ambushed unit then formed a defensive perimeter and called for fire support. In essence, the Army adage about the infantry finding, fixing, fighting, and finishing the enemy was no longer relevant. Now the infantry found and fixed, but firepower did the fighting and finishing. Of course this was dangerous for the bait, but high-ranking officers believed the potential for a high body count was worth the risk. Those being ambushed probably disagreed; one platoon leader referred to his unit as a SLIP, or Sacrificial Lamb Infantry Platoon.[75]

All too often the baited hook was barbless. Rather than let themselves be slaughtered, the enemy "avoided initiating actions which might result in large and unacceptable casualties from the firepower of allied forces," and devised tactics that nullified much of their adversary's firepower.[76] They sprang ambushes in dense foliage, during bad weather, and near nightfall (all of which curtailed externally supplied firepower), and along narrow ridges that were hard to hit with distant artillery fire or bombs dropped from fast-moving aircraft. If some or all of these conditions did not prevail the enemy preferred not to fight, waiting for more opportune times and targets.

When they initiated contact the VC/NVA invariably fought from well-fortified positions capable of surviving all but direct hits from artillery shells, rockets, and bombs. A Delta Raider was astounded that firepower "seemed like it had no effect on them. They would hollow out mountains and hollow out big hills and use them as safe havens." Another soldier watched a village disappear from tactical air strikes. No one, he believed, survived the savage attack, but as the last plane roared away "several enemy soldiers resumed well-aimed shots at our heads as we peered over the banks of a canal."[77]

Enemy soldiers knew it took several minutes for an ambushed unit to receive its initial fire support, that firepower arrived sequentially not simultaneously, and that Americans avoided bringing shells, bombs, and rockets too close to their own lines. To get support, the ambushed unit's commander called to the rear by radio. But sometimes radio reception was poor, or the officer delayed calling because he could not see where he needed the support as he peered through the vegetation. Even after the call went through getting clearance to fire artillery caused a further delay while the area was checked to make sure no other friendly units were nearby.[78] Air support was invariably slower to arrive than artillery support. On average, it took twenty minutes for an airplane diverted from another mission to begin dropping bombs, and twice that long if a plane had to "scramble" from its base.[79] When artillery shells and then bombs finally landed they often provided a colorful pyrotechnics display and rearranged the jungle but killed few VC/NVA, who were in fortified positions or had already "exfiltrated" the battle zone.

Many firefights were over quickly—about a third of them lasted less than fifteen minutes—because the enemy wanted to "retreat" before American firepower arrived. Captured enemy documents and prisoners never spoke of "retreat" but instead of a well-rehearsed "withdrawal phase" that was integral to the battle plan. With remarkable discipline, they frequently took their dead, wounded, and weapons with them. "Got away clean. No bodies. No blood trails," marveled a grunt who had just survived a firefight. "They drifted off like ghosts, and we had to ask, where had they gone?"[80] After most firefights Americans held the battlefield and were thus technically victorious, at least according to western concepts of battle. They also cradled their dead and wounded, which robbed the "victory" of much satisfaction.

Even if trapped the VC/NVA rarely endured firepower's concentrated fury. As a brigade report put it, "Experience has demonstrated the difficulty in employing simultaneous fire support assets. In most cases aircraft are wary of operating in the same area that tube artillery is being fired." Ground commanders understood that coordinating support elements was a challenge. "I had a number of occasions when I had to stop artillery, bring in air support, and start the artillery again," read one typical account, "and about that time the helicopter gunships would arrive and tell me they were there to support me, and then again I would stop the artillery and use the gunships."[81]

If they did not withdraw, enemy tactics emphasized fighting at close quarters, "hugging" the Americans or "grabbing their belt," especially during daylight. When grunts fell back into a defensive perimeter the VC/NVA pressed them hard, knowing they were often safest when close to U.S. positions since artillerymen and pilots were reluctant to make a fatal mistake by firing shells or dropping bombs too near American lines. As Major General Barsanti complained, too many friendly fire incidents were occurring as "a result of supporting fires being too close to friendly positions. The enemy's tactic of hugging the friendly positions complicates the task of delivering supporting fires with a margin of risk in inflicting friendly casualties." Barsanti and others insisted that forward observers, artillerymen, air crews, and combat unit leaders "must exercise a higher degree of coordination and judgment, and exercise strict adherence to safety procedures." Consequently firepower, though stupendous in quantity, was often cautiously applied, staying well away from U.S. positions. The heavy ordnance shuddering the earth often killed comparatively few enemy soldiers who remained close to U.S. forces until darkness or bad weather allowed them to break contact and slip away. Sometimes instead of escaping at nightfall the NVA bedded down for a few hours' sleep within sixty or seventy feet from an NDP, knowing they were safe there.[82]

Typical of the enemy's ability to survive firepower displays was the firefight Raider Lieutenant John Frick's platoon endured in August 1968: "About 25 meters down the trail the [scout] dog alerted us. We brought up a machine gun to recon by fire. We also brought up a squad on the left trail to fire into the area. When the squad on the left opened up, the NVA opened up on them. . . . We just kept firing, got our wounded out, then withdrew and called in artillery, [helicopter] gunships, and jets. So that describes my first firefight. In the afternoon 3rd platoon led out down the trail and 5 meters beyond where we got hit, the gooks opened up on them. . . . We pulled back again and artillery, gunships, and air strikes went over the area again. Today we by-passed the area to get to a LZ for log [logistical resupply]."[83] Despite the firepower, rather than risk being ambushed, re-ambushed, and then re-ambushed again, the Raiders avoided the area. Similar examples of units being re-ambushed after saturating an area with firepower were legion.[84]

The VC and NVA also avoided firepower's devastating effects by relying on "economy of force" measures such as snipers, BBTs and mines, and standoff attacks and harassment. Snipers constantly badgered patrols, firing a few shots, killing or wounding a man here and there, then disappearing before the GIs reacted. Nor could grunts respond to the BBTs and mines that produced sudden explosions, pained screams, dead and maimed comrades, and no visible target for revenge. "U.S. forces continue to suffer excessive casualties from enemy BBTs," complained an official report. "Positive command action must be taken at all levels to minimize these unacceptable losses."[85] But nothing eliminated casualties from mines and BBTs, in part because the explosives "were so well concealed that they were like plastic surgery on the earth." "They hang from the trees," lamented one soldier. "They nestle in shrubbery. They lie under the sand. They wait beneath the mud floors of huts. They haunted us." From January 1967 through September 1968, almost 25 percent of all soldiers and Marines killed in action (KIA) died from BBTs and mines.[86]

Every time a mine or BBT detonated morale sagged because GIS recognized the enemy "could hurt us like that and we couldn't hit back." In a typical example, during one month a company lost four men killed and approximately thirty wounded from BBTs and mines, yet had not seen "a single verified dink the whole time, nor have we even shot a single round at anything."[87] Knowing the enemy's explosives often came from dud American ordnance made the anguish run deeper.

Standoff (or indirect) attacks and harassment by mortars and rockets added to the fear and frustration. In a standoff *attack* perhaps thirty rounds came crashing into an American installation, exerting military pressure against a target the VC/NVA did not intend to assault. For every fifty to sixty rounds fired in these attacks, the enemy killed one of its adversaries. The Communists also conducted standoff *harassment,* unleashing perhaps half a dozen mortar rounds almost at random at an isolated target. Indicative of their ability to hide, the VC/NVA often moved mortars so close to the target that GIS heard the distinctive "ploomp" as projectiles left the tubes. They heard the sound often, enduring 16,494 standoff incidents in 1967, 15,845 in 1968, and 16,049 in 1969.[88]

Indirect attacks and harassment cost the VC/NVA little more than the ammunition since the soldiers themselves were usually gone before Americans responded with artillery shells or other firepower displays. For such minimal costs they secured maximum gains, not only in U.S. dead and wounded but also in lowered morale. A Delta Raider who endured twelve days of mortaring atop Fire Base Gladiator became "frustrated that there was nothing for us to shoot back at. We were helpless against the mortar. We could watch for flashes from the tubes and [call] Artillery in on suspected locations, but of course the enemy had already moved by then."[89]

Broadly speaking, the vc/nva retained the initiative even during the most intense years of America's military buildup. With nearby sanctuaries in North Vietnam, Cambodia, and Laos, and with their uncanny ability to hide inside South Vietnam, they determined their own losses by dictating the number, size, duration, and intensity of combat operations and by devising tactics that minimized firepower's killing effects. Secretary McNamara understood the situation as early as November 1966. No matter what the United States did—no matter how many more troops it sent to South Vietnam or how peripatetic its forces were—it could never kill the Communists beyond the crossover point.[90]

True, the U.S. army's "steamroller approach to war" killed and maimed hundreds of thousands of enemy troops but this massive bloodletting did not translate into permanent strategic or political success.[91] The Communists absorbed the losses, which were beyond what Americans considered "reasonable," and kept fighting, serene in the justice of their cause, certain that American and international opinion would turn against an unjust war, and confident that without outside support South Vietnam would soon collapse.

At the least, their doggedness frustrated America's expectations of a quick victory.

Few Americans fought the vc/nva without granting them a measure of respect, without admitting that though small in stature, they had big hearts.

More by necessity than by choice Communists steeled themselves for a difficult war by embracing the belief that men were more important than materiel, that ideology and an indomitable spirit could prevail over wealth and technology. Inferior in firepower and logistics, they compensated by stressing political motivation and the gut determination to endure unendurable hardship and losses. In September 1966, for example, the enemy launched an "Emulation Campaign of Troop Training, Combat Competition and Determination to Defeat the U.S. Aggressors" designed to eliminate pessimism, a dread of violence and hardship, hesitation and dejection, and "desertion, rallying, surrender and suicide."[92] Political commissars accompanied units at the company level and above, and soldiers spent much of their training time receiving political education and indoctrination about Vietnam's heroic past, the sacred nature of their cause, and the inevitability of victory.

The enemy's three-man military cell organization also helped sustain morale since it provided a ready-made "buddy" system. "During fighting," said an enemy corporal, "everybody had the duty to take care of his wounded cell members or move his dead cell members out of the battlefield. During a mission, people in a cell should stay close together and help one another in their joint duty." After an engagement a cell leader reported on the morale of his two comrades to his squad leader, who forwarded it to his platoon leader, and so on up the chain of command. Through this reporting and surveillance system commanders had a "snapshot" of a unit's morale, and could provide remedial political education/indoctrination when and where necessary.[93]

Serving for the duration rather than a year, men developed an intense fatalism; not only were they willing to die, they *expected* to die in the patriotic effort to expel the invaders. "They were more patient than we were," Raider Jodey Gravett admitted. "They had all the time in the world to die."[94]

While waiting to fight (and die) they suffered Spartan conditions, living on a diet deficient in proteins and vitamins, afflicted with intestinal parasites that caused chronic anemia, and suffering from malaria and other diseases that weakened the body's ability to withstand wounds. If wounded, medical care was primitive: no immediate intravenous fluids to prevent death from bleeding and shock; no helicopters to whisk them to a medical facility in minutes; no anesthetics to relieve pain during amputations; and in many cases no modern surgical equipment. Ministering to the vc in the Cu Chi tunnels, Dr. Vo Hoang Le performed brain surgery with a mechanic's drill.[95]

Enemy soldiers seemed immune to despair and doubt, to fear and grief, to normal needs and wants. They were not.[96] But so many of them overcame their doubts and fears that one scholar believed the vc/nva prevailed because of their "quixotic disregard for the impossible, a quality I came to think of as 'ordinary heroism.' So many apparently normal human beings had demonstrated in one way or another a damn-the-consequences approach to life that it began to seem like a national trait."[97]

The enemy's performance humbled some American generals who initially exuded an arrogant self-confidence. "My biggest surprise, and this was a surprise in which I have lots of company," said General DePuy, "was that the North Vietnamese and Viet Cong would continue the war despite the punishment they were taking. I really thought that the kind of pressure they were under would cause them to perhaps knock off the war for awhile, at a minimum, or even give up and go back north. But I was completely wrong on that." General Rosson admitted that "One came to admire, possibly envy, the vc and nva for their stealth, mastery of camouflage, ability to move and operate at night, noise and light discipline, and removal of bodies and weapons from the battlefield." The enemy, he continued, "demonstrated convincingly their ability to withstand the physical and psychological hardships of campaigning 'for the duration' in an environment of uncommon severity and danger."[98]

Lower ranking officers and enlisted men shared the generals' sentiments. "The North Vietnamese was probably the most determined little individual that you could ever imagine," said Cleo Hogan. "He's up against an American force that has airplanes, artillery, armor, and the latest weaponry and gadgetry. With all these things against him, and with almost no communication to Hanoi, or probably even to his next higher headquarters, this little individual is out there fighting the United States Army."[99]

Many other Raiders praised the enemy. James Kearns perhaps summed up the collective attitude, saying, "I hated them, but I learned to respect them." But some, including Joe Hooper, said little or nothing about hate. Joe considered the nva excellent soldiers, highly disciplined and tough. He claimed he made friends with some nva prisoners, telling a reporter that his happiest moment during his first tour was "when I walked out in the middle of a field, unarmed, and talked thirteen of the enemy into surrendering. I gave them cigarettes and food and we just sat down together and cried. When you get right down to it, we have a real human brotherhood relationship for the North Vietnamese—a real feeling of respect for them."[100]

As so often, Hooper's tale was an embellishment of what happened. In April 1968, the Raiders—not Joe alone, much less Joe alone unarmed—captured seventeen nva. Joe was happy they surrendered, "so we dint have to kill them, or them us." He talked to half a dozen of the prisoners and he and other Raiders gave them food and cigarettes, but they hardly became friends as Joe claimed. To the amazement of the nva the Americans did not kill them because, as Joe wrote, "even we are kind at times."[101] Kind. At times. What this meant was that at other times Americans did not treat prisoners kindly. Executing them was not unknown as ample evidence indicates. Murdering prisoners mortified intelligence officers since dead soldiers could not reveal vital information.[102]

In this case Hooper's comment about "a real human brotherhood" held firm and the enemy prisoners lived. Many Raiders shared his admiration for the adversary. To give one example, Craig Sturges considered the adversary "really tough. I mean we pounded the living crap out of them on a number of occasions, I mean gunships, artillery, aircraft—B-52s, jets, napalm. They lived off the land, they lived on very little, they didn't ask for much, and they gave you everything you wanted [in battle]." He believed that "if they'd had all the resources on their side of the fence that we had, it wouldn't have been a fair fight." [103]

Admiration for the enemy affected morale as grunts began asking questions, often the first step toward enlightenment. "Such firepower, yet they keep coming," wrote Raider Ray Blackman about the Battle for Hill 805 in July 1970. "What drives these men that we call gooks?" A colonel who marveled at the enemy's dedication wondered, "Am I right? Should we be killing them?" And a junior officer realized that no matter how many NVA and VC the Americans killed, they were still going to be there again the next day. "And so the more you did this, you kept wondering, what the hell am I doing here?" [104]

Nor did it help that GIs respected the VC/NVA more than ARVN, almost unanimously considering South Vietnamese soldiers inept and cowardly.

The Delta Raiders headed north from III Corps to I Corps.

For administrative purposes the United States divided South Vietnam into four Corps Tactical Zones: IV Corps in the Mekong Delta, III Corps surrounding Saigon, II Corps in the Central Highlands, and I (pronounced "eye") Corps, which comprised South Vietnam's five northernmost provinces.

Since its in-country training occurred in III Corps, the 2nd Brigade believed it would spend its combat time there, too. As soon as training ended it began search and destroy operations, commencing Operation Casey in mid-January in the jungled terrain sixty miles north of Saigon. Troopers did a lot of hacking through the jungle and received a few sniper shots but had no real contact, despite military intelligence indicating a VC regiment was there. The brigade did find a base camp and called in artillery and air strikes to destroy it. "There was nothing left of the jungle for a square mile," observed Cleo Hogan, "except toothpicks and splinters. If anyone was in there he was blown into ten million pieces." [105]

Suddenly on January 22 Colonel Cushman received orders to move to I Corps, which was not a complete surprise because he knew an enemy buildup in the far north deeply concerned Westmoreland. He particularly worried that the NVA would "liberate" the northernmost provinces of Quang Tri and Thua Thien, which were isolated from the rest of the country by a long ridge from the Annamite Mountains that struck the South China Sea at Thua Thien's southern border. QL-1, which was the main north-south highway from Saigon to the demilitarized zone (DMZ) and South Vietnam's only high-speed surface road, followed the narrow, winding Hai Van Pass across the ridge. Making the situation in the two provinces even more precarious was the absence of an all-weather port. Pumping logistical support into northern I Corps would be difficult at best.

Initially the III Marine Amphibious Force, headquartered at Da Nang, had responsibility for I Corps, but the Marines were spread thinly across five provinces. Moreover, Westmoreland doubted they were up to the task of protecting such vital terrain. "The military professionalism of the Marines falls far short of the standards that should be demanded of our armed forces," he wrote. Although brave, "their standards, tactics, and lack of command supervision throughout their ranks requires improvement in the national interest . . . many lives would be saved if their tactical professionalism were enhanced." [106]

In April 1967, Westy sent Task Force Oregon (a provisional infantry division) into southern I Corps, allowing the Marines to concentrate along the DMZ and the Laotian border. In September 1967, Task Force Oregon morphed into the Americal (23rd Infantry) Division, with its headquarters at Chu Lai. To provide additional fighting strength MACV upgraded the 1st ARVN Division in northern I Corps, arming it with modern weaponry. [107]

The situation, however, grew bleaker, especially at Khe Sanh, a base camp six miles from Laos and fourteen miles from the DMZ that Westmoreland ordered the Marines to hold despite their strenuous objections. Unlike the army's leaders they saw little utility in fighting the NVA in primitive border regions. "When you're at Khe Sanh," said a Marine officer, "you're really not anywhere. It's far from everything. You could lose it, and you really haven't lost a damn thing." [108] But Westmoreland believed the position blocked infiltration from Laos, served as a base for long-range patrols into that country, anchored the western end of the DMZ defensive line, and provided an eventual jump-off point for a Laotian invasion, a project he advocated despite the president's objections.

From April through October 1967, the Marines fought a vicious battle at Khe Sanh, and by the end of the affair Westmoreland was obsessed with the base, believing the NVA were intent on taking it and that its loss would be an American Dien Bien Phu. As he often did, the MACV commander was arguing by analogy, but historical analogies are fraught with peril. Convinced the NVA was striving for a new Dien Bien Phu, he ignored alternative explanations—for example, that the enemy was putting pressure on northern I Corps to entice him to move troops away from South Vietnam's populous regions.

An NVA buildup around Khe Sanh beginning in the fall of 1967 unsettled Westy, and when fighting erupted there on January 21, 1968, he responded quickly, not only ordering the 101st's 2nd and 3rd Brigades northward but also the 1st Cavalry Division (Airmobile), previously based at An Khe in II Corps. To command the burgeoning army forces in I Corps, as well as the Marines, he created a Forward Command Post under General Creighton W. Abrams. Westy also established a secret MACV working group to study the use of tactical nuclear weapons, which was no academic exercise; he was more than willing to use those weapons, or chemical agents, to save Khe Sanh.[109]

Perhaps sensing Westmoreland's urgency, Cushman headed north with alacrity. Once in I Corps the 2nd Brigade would participate in Operation Jeb Stuart under the operational control of the 1st Cavalry Division, meaning the brigade was under the Cav commander's tactical control and depended on him for consumable supplies such as rations, ammunition, and fuel. Designed to destroy enemy bases and units in the coastal plain between Hue and Quang Tri City, Jeb Stuart began on January 22. A day later one of Cushman's battalions (1-501) arrived in Phu Bai just south of Hue. The Delta Raiders' battalion, 2-501, pulled out of Operation Casey on January 24, returned to Cu Chi by helicopter, and arrived at Phu Bai two days later. The brigade's other battalion, 1-502, flew directly from Cu Chi to Quang Tri City.[110]

The Raiders believed 2-501 was going to Phu Bai as the first step toward rescuing the Marines trapped at Khe Sanh. According to Captain McMenamy, the plan was to move from Phu Bai to Quang Tri by chopper, then overland to Khe Sanh. Lieutenant Aronow also believed the Marines needed rescuing. "The damn Marines just sit on their butts up here and don't chase or attack the NVA" the way the army did, so the 1st Cav and the 101st Airborne were going to "show them that with a little initiative and daring, what you CAN do!"[111]

When 1-501 and 2-501 arrived at Phu Bai they immediately deployed about three miles north to LZ El Paso, which was literally a huge graveyard. The Raiders first saw it the afternoon of January 26. Although admitting that the locale "had a bad feeling" about it, Captain Mac was not altogether displeased since "the many concrete headstones and tombs offered excellent natural (or in this case, un-natural) cover." He set up his headquarters near a tomb that had a three-foot-high concrete fence around it. Meanwhile, other Raiders dug in near individual graves. "I hope whoever's buried here won't mind," Noah Rockel wrote his girlfriend.[112]

Even if the deceased did mind, the aggravation was brief because El Paso was a staging area for the brigade to move farther north. By January 30 it was scattered along a fifty-mile line running northwest to southeast: 1-502 was at Quang Tri City and 1-501 was at LZ Jane (about six miles south of Quang Tri City), leaving only 2-501 at El Paso, waiting to move to Camp Evans ten miles south of LZ Jane.[113]

As units pulled out of El Paso, those remaining tightened the perimeter, which was getting precariously small. Fortunately the situation seemed routine, with the Raiders conducting short patrols during the day and then hunkering down in NDPs. On the night of the 27th the company heard movement to its right front and somebody (or something) tripped a flare, but nobody saw anything. The next day the Raiders' artillery forward observer saw some armed men in the distance, a tracked vehicle hit a mine resulting in minor damage, and the company detonated a dud enemy mortar round. A sniper fired a few shots on January 29, and the next day the Raiders saw two people on a far-off hill. That was it for action.[114]

Until the night of January 30–31.

That evening El Paso received at least fifty mortar rounds, which killed four and wounded nine, none of them Raiders. That same night the enemy also hammered the Raiders' old base at Cu Chi with a standoff attack. Cleo Hogan and a handful of men who stayed behind to pack the company's gear endured the crashing mortar and rocket fire. Thankfully 2-501 was gone;

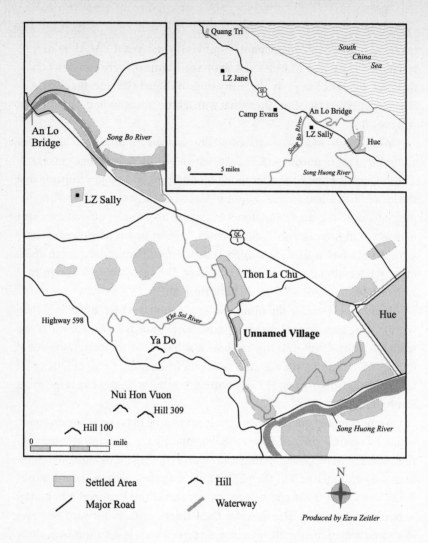

Map 2: The Delta Raiders' Area of Operation

otherwise casualties would have been heavy. In response Cleo wished the United States "would bomb Hanoi until there was nothing left but a hole in the ground."[115]

Simultaneous attacks on El Paso and Cu Chi, hundreds of miles apart. Was that a coincidence?

In 1968, the Tet holiday marking the start of the lunar New Year began on January 30, and predictions filled the air. Based on what happened in previous years during Tet, Cleo Hogan expected a truce. "Its a time of reunion and friendship so all hostilities cease during this period," Cleo informed his wife Glynna.[116]

The CIA's Saigon station was not so sanguine, anticipating something important, perhaps decisive. In November 1967, Joseph Hovey and other station analysts predicted a three-phase campaign with grandiose military and political goals surpassing anything the VC/NVA previously attempted. Captured documents, Hovey wrote, foretold sustained attacks in phase one from October through December. A series of bloody border battles in which the enemy displayed unusual aggressiveness—at Con Thien near the DMZ in September, Loc Ninh in III Corps in October, and Dak To in II Corps in November—showed a close correlation between what the documents predicted and what actually happened. The enemy, Hovey surmised, hoped these battles would "force the redeployment of major Allied military units to the border areas where the VC/NVA enjoy sanctuary and will be able to inflict heavy casualties upon them." Tying down U.S. forces along the borders would "relieve the pressure on the VC/NVA activities in the populated areas."

In the second phase, January through March 1968, Hovey predicted the enemy would launch a long-promised "general uprising" with guerrillas attacking heavily populated areas, expecting to occupy some urban centers and isolate many others. Follow-up attacks would characterize a third phase from April through June. Hovey believed the Communists were unduly optimistic, that they had "committed themselves to unattainable ends within a very specific and short period of time." But even if they failed to achieve their maximum goals they could still do grave harm. They might "inflict unacceptable military and political losses on the Allies regardless of VC casualties during a U.S. election year, in the hopes that the U.S. will be forced to yield to resulting domestic and international political pressure and withdraw from South Vietnam." Also, the vc/nva could revert "to a relatively low-intensity stage of warfare after having inflicted maximum casualties on the Allies and pre-empting any major allied offensive campaign."[117]

Westmoreland agreed with neither Hogan nor Hovey; in particular, he was more confident than the cia's spooks. The general did not expect a nationwide Tet truce, and certainly not a "general uprising" involving a concerted attack on South Vietnam's cities. Instead he anticipated a concerted effort against Khe Sanh, perhaps involving some *diversionary* urban assaults. The enemy, he believed, no longer had the capability to launch a broad-based offensive, much less a successful one, because U.S. forces had reached the crossover point during the spring. That was why Khe Sanh obsessed him. He did not want the enemy achieving a strategically insignificant but spectacular victory now that the vc/nva were sliding irreversibly downhill.

Westy exemplified what presidential confidant Harry McPherson referred to as "the hungry optimism that is a part of the military personality." The military had a "natural tendency" to "feel that things are going pretty well, and will go much better if we only have a few more bodies [troops] and bombs," which was exactly the macv commander's attitude, as well as that of Chairman of the jcs, Army Chief of Staff, and the jcs as a whole.[118]

"The vc/nva forces no longer have the capability of achieving a military victory," Westy confidently asserted in his "Command Guidance" of January 1967. "We must make 1967 the year during which it will become evident to the enemy and the world that we can and will achieve our military objectives." His goal was to "increase the momentum of our successes" by maintaining the offensive on a seven-day-a-week, round-the-clock basis, decimating enemy units and destroying their base areas, interdicting their communications both by land and sea, and last (always last in Westmoreland's mind) supporting pacification.[119]

By March macv suspected the crossover point was close, that attrition from battle, disease, and desertion was exceeding recruitment and infiltration. In April Westy informed Wheeler that his suspicion was correct: "It appears that last month we reached the crossover point in areas excluding the two northern provinces," Quang Tri and Thua Thien. In June macv concluded the United States had reached the crossover point throughout South Vietnam.[120]

Westy's optimism glistened in November, the same month Hovey and his colleagues completed their pessimistic assessment. "I am very encouraged," he told newspaper reporters during a visit to the United States. "I have never been more encouraged in the four years I've been in Vietnam. We are making real progress." In a subsequent address to the National Press Club he announced that "the end begins to come into view." Enemy forces were steadily declining, they could no longer recruit in South Vietnam to any significant extent, their recent offensives in the border regions failed, and their hopes were bankrupt. "With your support," he intoned for the public's benefit, "we will give you a success that will impact not only on South Viet-Nam but on every emerging nation in the world." [121]

Westy's meaning was clear: victory was near! Although also optimistic, General Johnson was not so certain. "I only hope that he has not dug a hole for himself with regard to his prognostications," he wrote General Abrams. "The platform of false prophets is crowded!" [122]

In a paradoxical cycle that prevailed throughout the war, although proclaiming success Westmoreland needed reinforcements, asking for them in April and again a few months later. "The situation is not a stalemate," he explained to Secretary McNamara in July; "we are winning slowly but steadily, and this pace can accelerate if we reinforce our successes" with 200,000 more troops. And invade Laos. Also disquieting was MACV's campaign plan for 1968, which differed little from the previous year's. If things were going so well, why did Westy need to do in 1968 what he supposedly did in 1967? [123]

Still, as 1968 began Westy looked back on a successful year, one with a few disappointments, of course, but one characterized by genuine progress. [124]

The general's optimism flowed from delusions: an inflated body count, a flawed estimate of enemy strength, and wishful thinking.

Many cadaver counts were fiction, not fact. Getting a precise body count under combat conditions was difficult, and in any event headquarters rarely questioned the figures, unless they were too low, in which case, one way or another, they became higher. So officers and men in the field frequently made up a figure or greatly exaggerated the number of bodies. An intelligence officer in the 1st Cav helped falsify body counts—always to the high side—because "It was easier to fake it than to count." And William Erbach, 2-501's chaplain, recalled that often the count "was just a bold-faced, pure, unadulterated lie." [125]

Soldiers were not eager to try for an accurate count since doing so was dangerous. Learning that Americans scoured battlefields in an Easter egg–like hunt for corpses, the VC/NVA planted mines and BBTS, posted snipers, and set stay-behind ambushes. So many GIS got killed or wounded this way that the Department of the Army published a pamphlet alerting officers to the problem. "I shudder to think," wrote one general, "how many of our soldiers were killed on a body-counting mission—what a waste." [126]

Anecdotal evidence revealed how inflated some body counts were. An after action report for the Battle of the Slopes in June 1967, claimed 513 bodies, 106 by actual count and 407 by artillery called in on likely enemy avenues of movement, even though GIS did not find a single body in those areas. The soldiers who did the fighting estimated the real count was between fifty and seventy-five. That same month, after a battle near Ap Bac the ground commander was unable to produce a body count immediately, but division headquarters reported 256 bodies anyway. The next morning a battlefield search found seventy. Headquarters often refused to accept a figure that was not high enough because "Good commanders scored high body counts. And good commanders got promoted." One field officer who tried to be honest called in a body count of seventy. For this low number he received so much grief from his superior that he finally shouted "Jesus Christ, Colonel, what the hell do you want? My men are out there digging up fucking graves. Tell me what you want. What figure do you want? I'll tell you whatever you want to hear." They settled on 175.[127]

The body count was also inflated because it routinely included civilians. All too often GIS followed the "Mere Gook Rule" that "If it's dead and Vietnamese, it's VC." Harry McPherson advised the president that MACV's figures were highly suspicious because "nobody seemed to know how many innocent bystanders, impressed baggage carriers and others have been included in the VC 'body counts.'" [128]

During the war several studies extrapolated enemy losses from captured documents. Based on seventy documents, the first showed that enemy killed in 1966 were 20 percent below MACV's estimate. Another effort examined eighty-four documents for enemy dead from 1965 through 1968, deriving a figure 30 percent lower than official estimates. Finally, in a highly refined analysis, 136 documents revealed 231,940 total enemy losses (killed in action, died of wounds or disease, missing in action, prisoners of war, and deserters) from 1965 through June 1968, which was only about *half* of MACV's figure.[129]

More than 60 percent of the generals who responded to a postwar survey considered the body count a fraud. "Often blatant lies," said one. "A fake —totally worthless," commented another. A third called the false reporting a blot on the Army's honor. A postwar "Study on Military Professionalism" agreed.[130]

Westy's estimate of how many VC/NVA he was fighting was as dubious as the body count. Estimating an enemy's order of battle (OB) is always difficult, but was especially so in Vietnam because the VC/NVA structured their forces differently from westernized armies, the rate of recruitment and infiltration was ambiguous, and most importantly, the attrition strategy made the number of enemy troops the prime measure of success. Only if force levels fell could the United States reach the crossover point.[131]

During 1966–67 some intelligence analysts discovered discrepancies in MACV's information regarding the PLAF. Its organization was complex but in general terms contained four categories, beginning with the insurgent political infrastructure, which MACV little understood and never tried to count accurately. A second category was the militia, which MACV divided into three subgroups: guerrilla squads or platoons were permanent hamlet- or village-based organizations composed of part-time soldiers; self-defense forces included older people, youths, and women; and secret self-defense forces were akin to self-defense forces except they lived in hamlets controlled by South Vietnam. Better armed and trained than guerrillas were Local Forces, organized in companies and operating at the province level. At the apex stood Main Force battalions, regiments, and even divisions.

Because MACV believed the war was conventional, it concentrated on the NVA and the VC Local and Main Forces, paying significantly less attention to guerrillas, political cadres, and self-defense forces. However, these irregulars were indispensable: they set mines and BBTs, planted punji stakes, conducted terrorist and sabotage missions, harassed patrols and convoys, secured military intelligence, and provided a recruiting base.

One of the first analysts to question MACV's OB was the CIA's Samuel Adams, descended from the Adams family that produced two presidents. In August 1966 he read a captured document indicating 50,255 militia were in Binh Dinh Province, broken down into guerrillas, self-defense, and secret self-defense forces. But MACV's OB listed only 1,466 guerrillas in that province, with no breakdown by type. Checking another province, Adams found

MACV's total was 3,210 guerrillas and self-defense militia, but captured documents indicated 20,407 in both categories. Other documents revealed similar discrepancies. And while MACV listed all the VC's regiments and divisions, it listed no support units, which might total 50,000 soldiers. The implication was obvious: the VC was a lot more numerous than MACV believed, and far from being decimated the PLAF was expanding.

As an institution the CIA initially accepted Adams's analysis. In January 1967, its special assistant for Vietnamese affairs agreed that MACV's estimate of 277,150 confirmed VC was "far too low and should be raised, perhaps doubled. A raising of the OB figure to a more realistic level would allow the intelligence community to make a better informed appraisal of what we are up against." [132]

When Westy's intelligence chief General Joseph A. McChristian grasped the OB problems he took corrected higher figures to Westy, who in essence ordered him to lower them. McChristian refused. For his integrity Westy fired him, replacing him with General Philip Davidson, who was more amenable to manipulating the OB numbers to keep them low. Although it previously included all the irregular forces in the enemy's OB, in October 1967, MACV arbitrarily omitted the self-defense forces, secret self-defense forces, and the infrastructure, retaining only the guerrillas and the Local and Main Forces. It did this even though it added the dead from the eliminated categories in the body count, and even though the militia put grunts in daily peril. Although the irregulars did not assault the core of American military might, they nibbled pretty ferociously at its edges.

Elements within the CIA opposed the arbitrary reduction but MACV remained steadfast and the CIA capitulated in what one official called "the mistake of the century." [133] The net result was that when 1967 ended, MACV listed VC strength at 224,651, down substantially from the previous year. Had that figure been accurate, then Westy was winning the war, just as he claimed. But the doctored number undercounted the VC by at least half; the real number indicated the war was stalemated at best.

The OB controversy was not just about numbers but also about the nature of the war. Convinced they were in a conventional conflict, army commanders wanted to count only regular forces such as the NVA and the VC Local and Main Forces. To accept irregulars and paramilitary forces required a broader, more complicated definition of "the enemy," one indicating that the problem was more complex than killing uniformed soldiers. To acknowledge the political cadre, self-defense forces, and secret self-defense forces meant the conflict was exactly what the enemy said: a revolutionary war with widespread popular support.[134]

MACV's OB chicanery led Americans in Vietnam to underestimate the NLF, persuaded many citizens at home that the war was nearing an end, and supported Westy's wishful thinking. Having demonstrated to his own satisfaction that the body count was up and the enemy's OB was down, as 1968 began Westy assumed the VC/NVA were operating from a position of weakness, perhaps desperation. Thus MACV rejected information indicating the border battles might be a diversion. While Hovey perceived them as the first phase in a tremendous offensive campaign, Westy interpreted them as defensive responses to his aggressive operations. At most the enemy hoped for a psychological victory, probably by a conventional assault on Khe Sanh *after* the Tet holidays.[135]

Westy was determined the NVA would achieve no victory, psychological or otherwise. The MACV commander was ready to inflict a Dien Bien Phu in reverse, or soon would be as the 1st Cav and 101st Airborne rushed north.

Hogan, Hovey, Westmoreland. Three different expectations. Somebody's prediction was wrong, as Hooper, Captain Mac, and the rest of the Delta Raiders soon found out.

Six

It was just a matter of time.
There's going to be somebody hurt.

*Captain McMenamy's laconic comment about
the inevitability of casualties among the Delta Raiders*

Vietnam's national flower, wrote a grunt serving in I Corps, "should be an immense thorn."

Another GI had a similar thought. After humping the boonies for dreary hours, he suddenly stopped and called to his lieutenant. With a hand encrusted in scabs, scratches, and sores, the soldier pointed to a delicate flower with soft red petals, saying, "That is the first plant I have seen today which didn't have thorns."[1]

So beautiful from afar, so thorny up close and at war.

That was Vietnam.

Superficially, I Corps was a sightseer's delight. Bluish tints marked its eastern edge, where the South China Sea caressed a thin waist of white sand covered with scraggly vegetation. The hues ebbed and flowed together in a dramatic display—not just blue, but sapphire, turquoise, indigo, cerulean, azure. West of the beach was a coastal strip, perhaps ten miles wide and dominated by rice agriculture, the paddies attired in emerald during the growing season and delicate yellows as the harvest neared. Floating like enchanted islands in a sea of rice were dark green havens, each representing a hamlet, with individual homes tucked amidst hedgerows, bamboo, bananas, and palm trees. Then came an undulating piedmont region with hills up to 350 feet high and sparsely wooded. Stretching from the hills into Laos were mountains, verdant, multihued, dazzling, almost hypnotic in their brilliance when sunlight struck them at the right angle. Some peaks were 7,000 to 8,000 feet high with slopes so steep they seemed vertical, a bewildering land of razorback ridges, hidden ravines, gushing streams, and double or triple canopy jungle.

From a soldier's perspective the external beauty was deceptive, marred by the climate, the alien nature of the primeval rain forests, and the fact that someone was trying to kill him.

Technically, South Vietnam had a dry season and a rainy season, depending on the southwest and northeast monsoons. However, regional variations were so pronounced a USO information pamphlet warned that both a rainy and dry season occurred "somewhere in the country at all times." [2]

In general terms, the dry season in I and II Corps lasted from March to October, broiling people and things with relentless heat, the temperatures climbing to 100 degrees (or more) day-after-day, sparking an unquenchable thirst. A typical grunt carried up to half a dozen one-quart canteens, and gulped down all the water by midmorning. So he also carried iodine tablets to purify puddle water, and Kool-Aid to smother the vile taste. [3] From October through February the northeast monsoon brought chilly temperatures (into the 40s at night) and entombed the region in low clouds, dense fog, and drizzle, or what the French collectively called "crachin." To the south in III and IV Corps, the weather pattern was almost exactly the reverse. There the dry season was from November through May while the southwest monsoon delivered drenching downpours from June through October.

The Delta Raiders arrived in I Corps toward the end of the crachin season, which had a certain irony to it. They left Fort Campbell's cold and dampness for Cu Chi's heat. After they were acclimatized there, "they put us on a plane and sent us to I Corps where it was cold and rainy just like Fort Campbell." As Captain Mac laughed, "This is about right for the army!" [4]

Four points about the weather. First, the climate played a decisive role in operations. Because the monsoons were despotic, dominating everything and everybody, the only reasonably good campaigning weather was from February through May when a dry season prevailed nationwide. Not surprisingly, the enemy's three major offensives—in 1968, 1972, and 1975—occurred during those crucial months. Second, I Corps was the country's wettest region: annual precipitation was seventy-two inches in Hanoi, eighty in Saigon, but 128 in Hue. Third, the weather pattern was a mystery to grunts. "I could never figure out whether we were in the dry season or rainy season," one wrote. "The mixture of alternating rain and sun made me wonder if the distinction was a figment of someone's imagination." Another complained that "Even in the dry season nothing ever dried in the bush, it only became less wet."[5] Finally, no matter what the season, grunts were always uncomfortable. As Raider Bob Saal put it, "I don't think this country has got any nice weather. Either it is cold, rainy, and miserable or it's hot, dry, and miserable."[6] But forever miserable.

Few grunts had anything nice to say about the triple canopy jungles, either. At ground level was a profusion of vines, ferns, brush, and small trees struggling for sunlight; this underbrush was so thick it cut visibility to a few yards. A second stratum consisted of adolescent trees, densely packed and reaching twenty-five to thirty feet skyward, and the top canopy consisted of mature hardwoods, some of them one hundred feet tall. Interspersed throughout the rain forests were bamboo stands, their shoots densely packed and six inches in diameter, and patches of elephant grass, which grew higher than a tall man's head and had razor sharp edges. Sunlight rarely reached the ground, so even at high noon the jungle floor was gloomy; at night the darkness was so densely black a man felt blind. Soldiers wished they could lose their sense of smell, too; rotting vegetation, unwashed bodies, and sweat-soaked uniforms yielded a sewerlike stench.[7]

An inexhaustible supply of repugnant, sucking, and biting creatures inhabited the jungles. Slimy black leeches "were everywhere—like a horror movie and you're in it," wrote a Marine. Malaria-carrying mosquitoes were vicious and swarming. In the war's perverse way, army-issued mosquito repellent did not "work worth a damn on bugs, but it's hell on leeches." A few drops on a leech and it withdrew instantly. The worst thing was to pull a leech off because it left an ugly round hole that bled profusely. Flies, wrote Lieutenant Frick, worked in concert with the mosquitoes. The former "relieve the mosquitoes promptly at 0630, and work right up to quitting time at 1830 hours when the mosquitoes come out for their nightly harassing mission." Red ants nested in vines and trees and when disturbed they bit—hard. If red ants were twice as big, remarked an officer, no one, American or Vietnamese, could survive in the jungle.[8] Worst of all were the poisonous reptiles—Asiatic cobras, Malayan and brown kraits, Russell's and bamboo vipers, paradise flying snakes, and others.

"You had all those distractions to deal with," noted a Raider, "besides watching for booby traps and gooks."[9] Out in the boonies a patrol had two choices, neither of them good. It could walk the well-worn trails, but the enemy sowed them with mines and BBTs, posted snipers and trail-watchers,

and planted ambushes. Or it could cut an archway through the dense un-
dergrowth using "a human chain saw," which was a machete-wielding GI.
When a patrol came upon bamboo or elephant grass, it often zigzagged,
which made land navigation difficult. Cutting through the tough bamboo
was next to impossible, and the elephant grass, well, Dale Urban recalled his
first encounter with it: "I always wore my shirt undone in front, my chest
was always exposed. I remember hitting that elephant grass. Wow! I've got
all sorts of cuts and the sweat was starting to burn the cuts, so I had to shut
my shirt back up. Yeah, elephant grass was tough to move through." Another
soldier believed anyone who "walks more than fifty feet through elephant
grass should automatically get a Purple Heart." [10] Hacking and zigzagging,
climbing the precipitous slopes, traversing the fast-flowing streams, suffering in the enervating heat, and keeping alert for ambushes, a patrol was fortunate to move four or five hundred yards a day.

Conditions were only slightly better in the ricelands. Narrow dikes
sliced through the paddies but troops hesitated to use them because they
were frequently booby-trapped. Walking on a dike was an ordeal, every step
carefully measured, the placement of each foot calculated, eyes glued downward looking for BBTs. So grunts usually went through the paddies, which
was arduous work in the growing season, the muck sucking at their boots,
clinging to each step like a brownish, soft concrete. Moreover, prolonged
immersion in water resulted in trench foot, a painful malady in which the
skin peeled off in huge strips, leaving raw sores that turned septic and became
festering red welts that refused to heal—as did virtually any cut, rash, or boil.

And those island-hamlets, so enticing from afar like a desert oasis, were
dangerous. Since much of I Corps had been a Viet Minh stronghold and was
now dominated by the VC/NVA, a defensive labyrinth usually lay hidden in
the hedgerows, treestands, and bushes, a warren of spider holes, fortified
bunkers with thick overhead cover, and connecting trenches and tunnels.
Peering across acres of rice, enemy soldiers had excellent fields of observation and fire. "Fifty meters across a rice paddy is a long march," wrote a
platoon leader. "It was like walking through a minefield. At any moment the
enemy may open up on you and tear your unit apart." [11] GIs had no place to
hide, and because of the muck they could not run very far very fast.

Grunts really waged two wars, one against the elements and the other
against the VC/NVA, and the latter was often the easier conflict since nature

seemed more malevolent and belligerent than enemy soldiers. Joe Hooper thought a paragraph in the 101st Airborne's 1968 Vietnam yearbook summed up a soldier's life: "Here a soldier fights a difficult war against many enemies. He fights the heat and exhaustion of clawing his way up a forested ridge line under full ruck and he fights the shivering cold of the monsoon rains under the flimsy protection of a hastily erected poncho. He fights insects, dirt and discomfort. And, of course, he fights against death." [12]

No wonder grunts referred to the United States as "the World." In Vietnam, said Richard Ryan, "it was like you were completely somewhere else," but nowhere on planet earth. [13]

These alien conditions now ensnared the Delta Raiders.

To make things worse, they collided head-on with the Tet Offensive, the war's most decisive campaign, one that made virtually every Raider a combat veteran.

Vietnam veterans with extensive combat experience were a rare breed because the likelihood of intense fighting depended on four factors.

Location was paramount since combat was not evenly distributed. Ten of Vietnam's forty-four provinces accounted for half the American combat deaths, and all five I Corps provinces were in the top ten. During 1967–68, out of 23,851 Americans KIA, 12,732 (53 percent) died in I Corps. In 1968, 33.6 percent of KIAS occurred in the northernmost provinces of Quang Tri and Thua Thien. [14]

Being in a maneuver battalion was also important. In 1968, 88 percent of U.S. personnel were in support or administrative positions—these "combatants" were what ground troops called REMFs (Rear Echelon Mother Fuckers). The REMFs, were relatively safe. Ground-pounders like the Delta Raiders were not. Grunts in maneuver battalions averaged about fifteen times the KIA rate of all other forces. [15] With good reason soldiers called a light weapons infantryman (whose MOS was an 11-B) an 11-Bullet-stopper.

Also influential was the annual combat cycle, determined primarily by the weather. The heaviest fighting always occurred from February through June during the countrywide dry season; a lull occurred in July, followed by a combat spike in August and September, and then relative quiet from October through January. Year after year, on average May produced the highest number of combat deaths, October the fewest. [16] A captain who began his six-month combat tour in July might see very little action, but one who started in January probably endured frequent contact.

Finally, combat intensity varied from year to year, with 1968 being the worst. In round numbers, between 1964 and 1967, fifteen thousand Americans died in combat; in 1968 another fifteen thousand died; then in the rest of the war fifteen thousand more were KIA.

In a sense the Raiders were unlucky. Moving north, they arrived in the region with the most intense combat, on the eve of the combat cycle's peak months, and in the year of the most ferocious fighting.

In another sense they were among the war's most fortunate units.

During the first four months of 1968 the Raiders waged a "good" war, akin to what their father's fought against the Germans and Japanese. As a kid Cleo Hogan saw all the World War II movies including *To Hell and Back* and *Sands of Iwo Jima,* which "more accurately portrayed what I saw in 1968" than did Vietnam movies such as *Platoon* and *Hamburger Hill.*[17] His perception was not altogether skewed.

The Raiders could not imagine losing the war. After all, they represented The United States of America. And they believed the cause was wise and just. "We chose to be there," said Craig Sturges. Hogan "thought the cause was worth it, no question," that Vietnam was the time and place to stop Communist expansion. Lieutenant Aronow agreed: "The core of us were right where we wanted to be doing right what we were doing." History, he wrote his wife, "will make us both proud that we sacrificed to come here and fight."[18] Although admitting the war seemed strange from afar, Hooper believed once you were there "you realize the job you have to do and go about doing it as best you can."[19] True, not all Americans embraced the war, and the antiwar movement was escalating by the time the Raiders mobilized at Fort Campbell. But Vietnam still remained tolerably popular and in late 1967 and early 1968 public support rebounded considerably in response to a massive "we are winning the war" campaign the Johnson administration conducted. So the sons were optimistic they would duplicate their fathers' victory.

Moreover, from February through May of 1968 the Raiders fought conventional warfare, well suited to U.S. tactics, training, and weapons. In Quang Tri and Thua Thien provinces, tucked against North Vietnam and isolated from the rest of South Vietnam, North Vietnamese regulars, not the vc, predominated. Now the NVA concentrated in large units, came out from under the triple canopy, and fought toe-to-toe with their adversaries. Temporarily the war ceased being a series of disconnected incidents, a formless and fragmented struggle, but instead involved a definite campaign with well-defined battle lines that could be followed on a map. Down in III Corps, wrote Hogan, the Americans "had to look for the vc and didn't find them very often," but when the Raiders arrived in I Corps the NVA were "looking for us and we found them every day."[20]

When the combatants found one another they did not have to worry too much about civilians getting caught in a crossfire. Civilians and their concomitant militia forces were virtually nonexistent in Quang Tri and Thua Thien because the fighting there had already depopulated the countryside. Hundreds of thousands of people in I Corps were refugees and the only place where villages remained intact and inhabited was bordering QL-1, where women, children, and old folks were relatively safe.[21] Joe Hooper, for one, was proud he never killed a civilian. "In every fight I was in," he said, "we fought only North Vietnamese regulars."[22]

The civilian's absence meant the Raiders rarely grappled with the confounding problem of distinguishing combatants from noncombatants. Nor did they confront angry, sullen villagers who seemed to have little interest in being "saved." Areas saturated with mines and BBTs, where "you're constantly finding yourself being over-cautious just to survive," were comparatively rare because the NVA did not set many of them, except along QL-1. Only infrequently did the Raiders experience the sickening ordeal of having men maimed by an unseen enemy. Twice wounded by BBTs, Platoon Sergeant George "Stocky Duty" Parker was almost uniquely unlucky among the Raiders.[23]

The war was also "good" because the original Raiders were an elite unit with exceptionally high esprit de corps. Without exaggeration RTO Lonnie Nale proclaimed the Raiders "the most elite company that the 2nd Brigade had." As with the rest of the brigade's companies, Delta Company deployed as a *unit* at a time when most men went to Vietnam as *individual* replacements. Since almost all Raiders were airborne-qualified volunteers, unit cohesion was extraordinary, not yet diluted by often-reluctant draftees who were regular "leg" infantry.[24]

Primarily because of Captain Mac's special morale-building measures, the Raiders exhibited a special camaraderie. "There was a *genuine* bonding of guys from all different areas of the country," insisted Sal Bongiorno, "and from all different makings—city guys, country guys, north and south—but there was a *genuine* bonding."[25] The bonding crossed racial lines; Sergeant Parker, an African American, insisted the Raiders had no race problems and whites such as Hooper mingled easily with black comrades, whom he considered brave, tough fighters.[26] Drug problems were also nonexistent during the first half of 1968, though their poisonous influence was already seeping into other units. One Raider admitted trying marijuana but his experiment began and ended with two joints.[27]

And just as their fathers liberated Paris and Manila so, too, would the Raiders help liberate a city, South Vietnam's third largest and most beautiful city, the old imperial capital of Hue.

"A miasma of trouble hangs over everything," wrote the president's wife in her diary, January 5, 1967. Fighting a limited war, she continued, "is unbearably hard."[28]

In the year since her diary entry the poisonous vapor thickened rather than dissipating.

Euphemistically called "civil disturbances," urban race riots threatened social stability. They began in Watts in August 1965 and escalated in parallel with the war. By the end of 1967, hundreds of additional racial disturbances occurred, killing and wounding thousands and doing $112 billion in property damage. Repeatedly the Johnson administration relied on the Army and the National Guard to occupy various cities and restore order. But the resulting "peace" was tenuous and everyone expected another violent summer in 1968.[29]

Simultaneously the economy foundered. Refusing to cut social programs or raise taxes while fighting an ever-bigger war, the administration used deficit financing to pay for much of the conflict, which was costing more than $20 billion a year by 1967. The result was inflation, a soaring international trade deficit, and rocketing interest rates. Concerning the war's economic impact, as early as January 1966, the staunchly anti-Communist *Wall Street Journal* questioned whether "the U.S. is inflicting more injury on the Communists or on itself." Nearly six hundred worried businessmen, including a former Federal Reserve Board Chairperson, signed an open letter the next year asking the president to stop the war for "moral" and "practical" (that is, economic) reasons. Finally in August 1967, the government imposed a 10 percent surcharge on individual and corporate income taxes, but the war's costs continued outstripping federal income and both citizens and companies loathed paying more taxes.[30]

The flow of caskets from Southeast Asia increased dramatically, from an average of 477 per month in 1966 to 816 per month in the first half of 1967. More than anything else, war deaths dismayed the public, especially when coupled with Westmoreland's requests for more and more troops in a war that seemed stalemated. The Army knew that deaths, far more than antiwar protests, eroded public support. In mid-1966 Chief of Staff Johnson told a division commander, who just fought a battle in which one of his units suffered thirty KIA and one hundred wounded in action (WIA), that if casualties of that magnitude continued "the American people won't support this war." Also understanding the correlation between battle deaths and public morale, the VC/NVA targeted Americans to keep the KIA rate high. The deaths often occurred one or two at a time, but they added up quickly.[31]

Reinforced by the fear of social disintegration, the economic malaise, and especially the prospect of an interminable war that seemingly served no clear-cut vital national interest, the antiwar movement became larger, more active, and more boisterous. Wartime dissent was an American tradition—in all of its wars dating back to the Revolution, only World War II lacked significant dissent—but opposition to Vietnam became unusually virile and widespread, primarily because the public became so disenchanted and frustrated with the war.

"The American people," noted Secretary of State Rusk within weeks after the Gulf of Tonkin Resolution, "are already beginning to ask what are we supporting and why."[32] The administration had no good answers to those questions. To argue that the United States was supporting freedom in Southeast Asia seemed absurd considering South Vietnam's corrupt, despotic regime. Nguyen Cao Ky, the government's prime minister and then vice president, had only one hero, Adolph Hitler. "But the situation here is so desperate," he said, "that one man would not be enough. We need four or five Hitlers for Vietnam."[33] And mindlessly reiterating the old shibboleths and homilies about Communism made less and less sense as the Communist world's complexity, diversity, and mutual antagonisms became increasingly evident.

By late 1965 the president, as yet unaware of how profoundly misguided Westmoreland's strategy was, argued that "the weakest link in our armor is public opinion." The key difficulty, as Under Secretary of State Nicholas Katzenbach stated in the summer of 1967, was "that if we were winning the war, we were not winning it very quickly." Could "the tortoise of progress in Vietnam stay ahead of the hare of dissent at home?" In November 1967 a group of eminent former political and military officials warned the president "that the prospect of endless inconclusive fighting is the most serious single cause of domestic disquiet about the war." Former national security adviser McGeorge Bundy concurred; what really hurt the administration was not the antiwar movement per se, "but the cost of the war in lives and money, coupled with lack of light at the end of the tunnel." [34]

Disaffection was diffuse and hydra-headed. Initially Johnson most feared the "hawks" who wanted to go all-out to defeat North Vietnam even if it involved fighting the Chinese and Soviets, and bitterly opposed restrictions on the bombing campaign and force levels. By mid-1967 the doves, whose growth was strikingly gradual, concerned him as much, if not more. [35] Those who wanted out of the war were amorphous, diverse, fragmented. At the most basic level a division existed between those comparative few who aggressively protested and that much larger contingent who opposed the war without actively protesting. [36]

Protesters themselves were splintered among principled pacifists, liberals who supported the capitalist system but challenged the war on ethical and practical grounds, and New Left radicals who considered Vietnam a textbook example of how the ruling capitalist class exploited "Third World" peoples and wanted to build a new society devoid of racism and capitalism. These differences rent the antiwar movement in noisy, angry disputes over tactics and personalities, insuring that it had neither a national organization nor unified leadership. Sometimes it seemed that antiwar groups opposed each other more than they did the war. No unified antiwar movement existed. By 1969 it consisted of approximately seventeen thousand national, regional, and local organizations, and these multiple smaller movements only occasionally overcame their differences to participate in nationwide events.

Protests began as a rivulet in 1964–65 but two years later assumed riverlike proportions. The pacifist War Resisters League sponsored a New York City demonstration in May 1964, at which a dozen young men burned their draft cards, and protested again in December. Two months later a few hundred stalwarts from the Women Strike for Peace and the Women's International League for Peace and Freedom picketed the White House. In the spring of 1965 the movement broadened in two directions. The radical Students for a Democratic Society staged the first major demonstration against the war in Washington, and professors began conducting college and university "teach-ins" challenging the administration's interpretation of Southeast Asian events. A turning point occurred in January 1966, when Senator William J. Fulbright's Senate Foreign Relations Committee held televised hearings on the war, publicly exposing the administration's numerous delusions and falsehoods.

Many subsequent protests were small and local but a few were enormous, with national significance. In May 1966, for example, four ordinary middle-class housewives from San Jose stood in a street for seven hours blocking trucks loaded with napalm bombs, and then later protested outside a huge napalm bomb storage facility in nearby Alviso. Less than a year later the Spring Mobilization to End the War in Vietnam attracted two hundred thousand people in New York City and another fifty thousand in San Francisco. The government considered an antiwar march on the Pentagon in October 1967 so serious it mobilized federal troops to protect the symbol of American military supremacy from its own citizens.

The activists' critique of Johnson's Vietnam policy was multifaceted, revolving around questions of necessity, wisdom, and justice. Many perceived the conflict as a civil war in an insignificant nation involving no security threat. Only the government's paranoid anti-Communism and unwillingness to acknowledge Vietnamese nationalism impelled the country into the war, which harmed great power relations, destabilized the international order, alienated America's allies (especially in NATO), undermined social reforms at home, and destroyed domestic tranquility. With their country unleashing furious destruction on an agricultural peasant society, protesters also criticized the war as immoral. Of course, Americans had no conscious intent to devastate South Vietnam, but the devastation was nonetheless immense. There might be, McNamara told the president, "a limit beyond which many Americans and much of the world will not permit the United States to go. The picture of the world's greatest superpower killing or seriously injuring 1,000 noncombatants a week, while trying to pound a tiny backward nation into submission on an issue whose merits are hotly disputed, is not a pretty one." [37]

In spreading their messages activists faced two grave problems. The World War II generation equated government criticism with disloyalty. Most citizens considered the president's pronouncements akin to royal decrees or papal bulls. Because the presidency assumed virtually unchallenged authority on security matters during the 1940s and 1950s, those who questioned Johnson and the foreign policy elite's Cold War paradigm were especially suspect. And the president draped himself in the flag, accusing his critics of near-treason, of prolonging the war by encouraging Hanoi and by polarizing and dividing society. Johnson's charge exemplified the delusion of omnipotence, as if the only people who mattered in the war's outcome were Americans, that if only they were united the enemy's defeat was inevitable. The vc/nva acknowledged the antiwar movement and were grateful for it, but as North Vietnam's Premier Pham Van Dong told an American reporter, "in the final analysis we know we must count mainly on ourselves."[38] Which they did. As for polarization and divisions, cia Director Richard Helms realized that "These are just words to describe the fact that the country is not with you."[39] Yet the president's accusations had a reflexive appeal to millions of citizens.

The other difficulty was the media's inaccurate portrayal of antiwar activities before 1968. Some protests were dramatic theater indeed: Norman Morrison immolated himself outside McNamara's Pentagon office and the Catholic pacifist Roger LaPorte burned himself alive outside the United Nations building in New York;[40] agitators poured blood on Selective Service files and burned draft cards; others sided openly with the enemy by carrying Viet Cong flags; more than a few were smug wiseasses—when asked at his draft board hearing whether he was willing to fight in Vietnam, the former national secretary of the Students for a Democratic Society responded, "Sure I am—just not on your side."[41] But most dissidents avoided such dramatics, working phone banks, praying, petitioning, writing letters, picketing, and peacefully marching, trying to spread their message through persuasion.

Overwhelmingly prowar before 1968, the media had little interest in conveying antiwar arguments. Shunning the issues, their coverage was negative, undercounting the crowds, emphasizing the trivial or the bizarre such as the protesters' "hippie" attire and hirsute appearance, portraying activists as unrepresentative and deviant, and emphasizing the violence that accompanied protests. Watching television news and reading the newspapers, it seemed axiomatic that protests and violence went hand-in-glove. Disruptions did mar many demonstrations but usually when *prowar* counter-demonstrators initiated and provoked it. Between 1965 and 1968 virtually all unruly behavior flowed from right-wing hecklers and thugs (though beginning in 1969 fringe elements in the antiwar movement became very violent). As the *Christian Century* put it, by 1966 it was "open season on dissenters." Prowar militants even killed a few protesters.[42]

The image of antiwar activists as unpatriotic and violent was a double-edged sword not easily dulled. Overall, the population despised and reviled antiwar protesters.

Nonetheless, many ordinary citizens, their instinctive patriotism corroding and dismayed by the war's futility, increasingly shared the activists' sentiments, even though they were unwilling to take their discontent from their kitchens and dens into the streets.

Who were these silent citizens whose sentiments, if not their actions, turned progressively antiwar? According to the opinion polls they were predominantly older Americans, the under-educated, women, African Americans, and Jews, in contrast to the war's most avid supporters: the young, the highly educated, males, whites, and Republicans.

Prowar support was strongest among those under thirty, weakest among those fifty and older. Although the media created the popular image that colleges and universities were antiwar breeding grounds, this was wrong. In August 1965, Gallup reported that 69 percent of the college-educated favored the war, compared to only 50 percent of those with a high school education; three years later the respective figures were 42 percent and 26 percent. Out of the nation's 2,500 institutions of higher learning, antiwar sentiment was noticeably strong only in the 150 to 200 most prestigious schools. A minority of college students opposed the war, and only a small fraction of them actively protested. Within every category, women were probably more antiwar than men. African Americans disliked Vietnam in greater than average numbers, especially after Dr. Martin Luther King Jr. denounced the war in April 1967, criticizing his government as "the greatest purveyor of violence in the world today." If King's eloquence did not persuade, then Muhammad Ali's more earthy explanation did: "No Viet Cong ever called me nigger." Led by Rabbi Abraham Joshua Heschel, a revered theologian and teacher who gave a famous speech on "The Moral Outrage of Vietnam," Jews consistently opposed the war. The Republican Party, ever-willing to use the Communist expansion bugaboo for political advantage, steadfastly supported it.[43]

In general, as fall temperatures began dissipating the summer heat in 1967, escalating antiwar sentiment deepened the national malaise, threatening to undermine President Johnson's Vietnam policy. The war tormented him, but never enough to give it up, never enough to choose peace rather than a larger war. He spoke often of peace and made several attempts to begin negotiations, but these never amounted to anything more than a flurry of diplomatic activity, excited newspaper headlines, and domestic propaganda points for the White House. In truth, Johnson was not interested in a negotiated settlement—only in an agreement that insured a non-Communist South Vietnam, which is to say only in an agreement that was tantamount to the enemy's unconditional surrender. Since the Communists were no more interested in a negotiated settlement than the president (unless it resulted in South Vietnam's immediate death), the war continued.

"I don't know what the fuck to do about Vietnam," the president moaned. "I wish someone would tell me."[44] Many dissenters told him; he just did not like their advice.

In October 1967, Army Chief of Staff Johnson gave an anguished speech to the Association of the United States Army's annual meeting, asking whether "freedom and stable government for a diverse group of warring Asians" were worth the life of thousands, a hundred, or even a single American soldier. "This thought tears mercilessly at the heart and soul of every thinking person."

General Johnson thought spending the lives was worthwhile.[45]

General David Shoup, a Medal of Honor recipient in World War II, the Marine Corps Commandant under Eisenhower and Kennedy, and the embodiment of a tough, fighting Marine, disagreed: "I don't think the whole of Southeast Asia, as related to the present future safety and freedom of the people of this country is worth the life or limb of a single American."[46]

Millions of others, as loyal to the United States as General Johnson or President Johnson, agreed with General Shoup, particularly those whose sons, fathers, brothers, husbands, uncles, and boyfriends were doing the dying.

The same month General Johnson spoke to the Association of the United States Army, the Gallup poll showed that for the first time a plurality believed the United States made a mistake in sending troops to Vietnam.[47]

In the fall of 1967 the American government launched one of the war's most important campaigns, the "Success Offensive."

The resulting action took place not in Southeast Asia but within the United States as the Johnson administration tried to discredit the antiwar movement and shore up public opinion with optimistic predictions about the war.

The president viewed antiwar activists with disdain. "Why should I listen to all those student peaceniks marching up and down the streets?" he asked. Then he answered his own question; he should not. "They were barely in their cradles in the dark days of World War II; they never experienced the ravages of Adolph Hitler; they were only in nursery school during the Korean War; they wouldn't know a Communist if they tripped over one. They simply don't understand the world the way I do."[48] True. Free from a World War II perspective and an unthinking anti-Communism, they understood the world of the 1960s better than Johnson.

Unwilling to consider his critics as intelligent men and women of good will who disagreed with his policy, the president perceived them as personal enemies. Determined to suppress them, he unleashed a vast domestic intelligence network against antiwar leaders and organizations, and ordered the CIA and FBI to uncover evidence that activists were Communists, or at least Communist financed and dominated. The CIA's Operation Chaos, a clear violation of its charter prohibiting domestic surveillance, the FBI's Operation Cointelpro, and an Army illegal domestic Intelligence Command all used an array of "dirty tricks" to tarnish and undermine the movement. They employed illicit wiretaps, opened mail, forged inflammatory letters and literature, carried out burglaries, framed protesters on drug charges, acted as agents provocateurs to incite violence, spread disinformation, and through a vast network of informants kept authorities well-versed on the protesters' plans.[49]

As for Communists and Communist connections, neither the FBI nor CIA found any. "On the basis of what we now know," concluded an October 1967 CIA report, "we see no significant evidence that would prove Communist control or direction of the U.S. peace movement or its leaders." Another report noted that some antiwar leaders "have close Communist associations but they do not appear to be under Communist direction," and the CIA again found no evidence linking Moscow to the peace movement. A year later the CIA repeated the exercise but discovered "no convincing evidence of Communist control, manipulation, or support of student dissidents."

Rusk and Johnson were incredulous. "I just don't believe this business that there is no support," said the president. Under intense pressure to do better the CIA tried a fourth time, but with the same result.[50]

Johnson was incapable of understanding that his flawed policies, duplicity, and deceit, and the protesters' genuine concern for the national welfare, motivated the antiwar movement, not Communism. Undeterred by the investigations' negative results, the president and his spokespeople leaked word about secret information connecting antiwar activities to Communists.

The president was more successful in shoring up public opinion than in destroying the antiwar movement. Rather than confront disconcerting facts and ideas, he tried to finesse the deteriorating situation in Vietnam and at home through a public relations campaign based on deceptions. He ordered the Saigon embassy and the military brass to "search urgently for occasions to present sound evidence of progress in Viet Nam," and they dutifully complied with a barrage of optimistic data. Guided by a newly established Vietnam Information Group, the PR effort centered on the assertion that the war was not stalemated, that success was on the horizon if the country just stayed the course a while longer—this even though Johnson admitted in early November that the war had "been on dead center for the last year."[51]

The campaign's biggest guns were the Wise Men (the elder statesmen who periodically advised Johnson on Vietnam) and General Westmoreland. Since Johnson assembled the Wise Men "strictly as a validation exercise" for his policy, former members of the group who now opposed the war were not invited. After receiving a series of carefully screened briefings, including an intelligence assessment containing the woefully low figures regarding VC strength, the true believers, Pavlovian-like, concluded the United States should continue the war to "save" South Vietnam, which was vital to American security. Believing the war was going well, the men urged Johnson to de-emphasize "battles and deaths and dangers" and emphasize that the war's end was near.[52]

Had they received more honest briefings the Wise Men might have given different advice. They did not have access to CIA director Richard Helms's recent memo assessing the consequences of defeat. While admitting that "if the U.S. accepts failure in Vietnam, it will pay *some* price in the form of new risks," those risks were far more limited than the administration's apocalyptic rhetoric indicated.[53] Nor did the Wise Men receive retired Admiral

Gene R. La Rocque's devastating report, the result of six months of study by ten admirals and a Marine brigadier general, demonstrating that victory was highly unlikely. Also absent was McNamara's memo asserting the United States would be no closer to victory by the end of 1968 even though another 10,900 to 15,000 Americans would die. Even if implemented, the JCS's recommendations for expanding the ground war and intensifying the air war would not end the conflict quickly, but carried extreme risks of a wider conflict. The only sensible course, the secretary argued, was to get out of Vietnam.[54]

The Success Offensive's second big cannon was Westmoreland, who first visited the home front in April 1967, to rally support. Now in late November he returned, expressing exuberant optimism, promising victory in the near future. Although later arguing he made these public appearances reluctantly, at the time he was enthusiastic. In fact, in a cable to General Wheeler he discussed the virtues of a public relations blitz. "Of course," he cautioned, "we must make haste carefully in order to avoid charges that the military establishment is conducting an organized propaganda campaign, either overt or covert."[55]

The PR campaign stanched the hemorrhage in public support. In July 1967, pollsters asked, "Just your impression, do you think the U.S. and its allies are losing ground in Vietnam, standing still, or making progress?" Ten percent thought the United States was losing, 46 percent considered the war a stalemate, and only 34 percent believed America was winning (the other 10 percent of the respondents, undoubtedly living under a large rock somewhere, had no opinion). In late November the answers were: 8 percent losing ground, 33 percent standing still, and 51 percent making progress (8 percent had no opinion). Those who thought the United States was winning jumped from a third to half.[56]

Incredibly, President Johnson did not use Westmoreland's visit to discuss the war's strategy even though an increasing number of officials were losing confidence in attrition.

As soon as Westy began Americanizing the war and going after the enemy's main force units, doubts arose. The general's strategy caused U.S. troops to do the bulk of the fighting, resulting in high casualties, the perception that South Vietnam contributed little to its own defense, and an attenuated pacification effort. In October 1966, McNamara saw "no reasonable way to bring the war to an end soon" because VC/NVA morale remained unbroken and they adjusted to their losses by adopting "a strategy of keeping us busy and waiting us out (a strategy of attriting our national will)." If anything, pacification was going backward. The United States must improve its position "by getting ourselves into a military posture that we credibly would maintain indefinitely—a posture that makes trying to 'wait us out' less attractive." The American people needed assurances that the war's costs and risks were "acceptably limited, that the formula for success has been found, and that the end of the war is merely a matter of time." Doing this required stabilizing force levels and the bombing of North Vietnam, which would minimize casualties and limit the horrific image of a mighty superpower savaging a primitive nation. It also demanded vigorous pacification.[57]

None of this occurred. As the war became more costly, yet remained barren of tangible progress, as the illusion of quick victory evaporated, discontent with Westy's operations festered. "It is most difficult to hold the line," Walt Rostow told the president in April 1967, "if the picture of the Vietnamese forces in the U.S. is one of lethargy, incompetence, corruption, inaction, while U.S. forces and casualties expand." Early in 1967 some people, with the president's approval, began exploring ways to remove Westmoreland gracefully, such as making him ambassador to South Vietnam.[58]

That fall several Wise Men, as McGeorge Bundy noted, "raised important questions about the military tactics now being followed." Perhaps a high level review was necessary, though questioning a field commander's tactical judgment was "obviously a highly sensitive matter." However, "If the battles near the borders are not wise, or if search and destroy operations in heavily populated areas are likely to be politically destructive, then the plans of the field commander must be seriously questioned." Bundy suggested holding carefully prepared discussions with General Westmoreland, emphasizing "that what I am suggesting here is something that really has not been done in this war so far, to the best of my knowledge." So far the administration had refrained from discussing tactics and strategy, and instead exercised control by limiting both the force levels in South Vietnam and the bombing of North Vietnam. "But now that the principal battleground is domestic opinion, I believe the Commander-in-Chief has both the right and the duty to go further."[59]

Convinced, on December 18, 1967, the president wrote, "we should review the conduct of military operations in South Vietnam with a view to reducing U.S. casualties, accelerating the turnover of responsibility to the

GVN, and working toward less destruction and fewer casualties in South Vietnam."[60]

Astoundingly, Bundy was right. Westmoreland's attrition strategy existed in a vacuum. From 1965 to 1968 the government undertook no systematic discussion of how the war should be fought. One explanation for this initially was an outmoded tradition of a field commander's autonomy, another was the over-confident belief that no matter what the United States did it would win, and still a third was Johnson's leadership style, which dampened intergovernmental controversy by seeking a consensus. The war's conduct pleased neither hawks nor doves, but the president appeased both by choosing a middle course. "There have been no divisions in this government," Johnson told the National Security Council. "We may have been wrong but we have not been divided." As renowned Vietnam scholar George Herring observed, Johnson's comment was a delusion since the administration was wrong *and* divided.[61]

More than anything else, strained civil-military relations prevented a coherent strategic discussion.[62] An adversarial civil-military relationship developed quickly after World War II and by the mid-1960s high-level officials and high-ranking officers seemed incapable of talking to each other honestly. Both sides were disingenuous and dealt with each other through indirection. Because Johnson and McNamara wanted military acquiescence for their decisions, not forthright advice, they maintained a facade of consulting with the JCS to protect themselves from a right-wing backlash. Before making any final decision on Vietnam, presidential advisor Jack Valenti had suggested in late 1964, the president should "sign on" the JCS "either by having the Chairman present at the decision-making meeting—or one meeting with the entire Joint Chiefs present." If "something should go wrong later and investigations begin in Congress, it would be beneficial to have the Chiefs definitely a part of the Presidential decision so there can be no recriminations."[63] The administration also bought the Chiefs' support by hinting at more aggressive future actions and by promising selected JCS members concessions for their particular service or for themselves.

For their part, the military chiefs believed graduated escalation was fundamentally flawed but they offered no effective alternative, in part because interservice rivalries, which often degenerated into childish squabbles, were so paralyzing they could not agree on strategic issues. The Air Force advocated strategic bombing as a war-winner, the Army and MACV put faith in attrition, the Navy emphasized a blockade, mining harbors, and Mekong Delta riverine patrols, and the Marines wanted to settle into enclaves and engage in pacification. Yet they lied to the president by forwarding unanimous recommendations. Take the air war over North Vietnam. Only the Air Force and Marines fully endorsed it, the Navy had reservations, and the Army did not believe it would produce significant results. Nonetheless, when communicating with their civilian superiors the Chiefs buried their disagreements. Concealing such basic differences was a disservice, observed General Palmer. "Differing views must be surfaced to the highest level—the president—in order that no false sense of security is engendered through what appears to be unanimity."[64]

Instead of confronting McNamara and Johnson with reasoned objections to graduated pressure, the JCS maneuvered to increase the tempo and scale of the escalation, hoping it eventually evolved into a full-scale war to destroy North Vietnam. They repeatedly chanted their mantra of more troops, more bombing, a naval blockade, full national mobilization, geographical expansion of the war, and the Chinese and Soviets be damned—or nuked.

By recycling these requests the Joint Chiefs engaged in a cynical ploy. They understood the political realities constraining the president and knew he could not approve these measures, but by forcing him to say "No" they manufactured an excuse for their failures. Do not blame us. We had to fight with one hand tied behind our back. By 1967, "preserving their own and the armed forces' reputation, not the Republic of Vietnam, had become the principal goal of American generals."[65]

They repeatedly argued that Johnson had fatally slowed the force buildup, especially by refusing to mobilize the Reserves. The buildup was actually quite rapid, and Johnson could do little about most of the factors constraining it. He could not ignore the cruel paradox that a military effort vigorous enough to topple Hanoi would probably provoke war with China or the Soviet Union. Even if they did not go to war the Chinese and Soviets could cause trouble elsewhere, such as Berlin or Korea, and the United States might be unable to respond. A JCS evaluation of the country's worldwide military posture and the effect large deployments to South Vietnam had on it, painted a grim picture.[66]

South Vietnam's economy and logistical base were too fragile to support the lavish American way of war instantly. Policymakers understood that "a reasonably stable economy in South Vietnam is essential to unite the population behind the Government of Vietnam—indeed to avoid disintegration of the SVN society. Runaway inflation can undo what our military operations accomplish." Force-feeding too many Americans into the country too quickly threatened to ignite an inflationary spiral.[67]

As for logistics, in 1965 Saigon and Cam Ranh Bay were the only deepwater ports, and they had but five deep-draft berths between them; airfield facilities were virtually nonexistent; only one railroad ran from the capital to the DMZ and it was a single track; QL-1 was incapable of carrying heavy military traffic; no barracks or other essential structures existed; Vietnam had only a limited lumber industry; and basic construction materials were not readily available. Remedying these problems was difficult because the Army was critically short of essential skills. For instance, it contained just one port construction engineering company. Not until July 1967 did Westmoreland report that he could support more troops than he had.[68] The training base in the United States was also inadequate to sustain a rapid buildup. Chief of Staff Johnson expanded the number of basic training companies and OCS so rapidly that standards deteriorated. "OCS has not lowered its standards," went a wry joke, "they just no longer require the candidates to meet them."[69]

The Reserve issue was particularly thorny, but military leaders showed little understanding of how the prickliness affected the president. All the Pentagon's war plans were contingent upon calling up Reserves to bridge the gap between the active-duty forces and newly minted draftees, so the decision not to mobilize caused temporary disarray. While the Regular Army was structured toward combat, the Reserves contained many combat support units with critical logistical and engineering skills. Without the Reserves, the Army depleted the strategic reserve and cannibalized NATO to sustain the war, leading to a deteriorating worldwide posture. Mobilizing the Reserves was also a dramatic political act, one the JCS thought signaled to the populace that the United States was in a war and not engaged in some insignificant military adventure. More than 90 percent of the generals responding to a postwar survey considered not mobilizing a serious error.[70]

The president was not unaware of these factors but dealt with countervailing pressures. Reserve mobilizations during the Korean War and the 1961

Berlin crisis went poorly, particularly during the latter event when reservists, their families, and their employers saw no clear and present danger justifying the call-up. A public outcry sapped national morale. Johnson feared repeating that mistake. He also believed a Reserve call-up would wreck his Great Society programs by focusing national attention squarely on Vietnam rather than important domestic issues. In short, as CIA director Richard Helms recalled, the president understood that mobilizing the Reserves would cause a ruckus "because it was going to take people away from their jobs and that causes all kinds of domestic turmoil. These things fan out immediately." The JCS believed that "mobilization had traditionally unified the country," an assertion that revealed their ignorance of history.[71]

Two ways existed for the president to mobilize Reserves, either requesting a congressional resolution or declaring a national emergency. The former might provoke an acrimonious debate about the war itself, not the Reserves, and make *any* commitment to South Vietnam more difficult. As for a national emergency, it permitted only a one-year mobilization and since Westmoreland expected the war to last longer than that a call-up was of limited utility. Speaking of one-year mobilizations, the military could have alleviated some of its manpower crunch by modifying its one-year tour policy—if not for draftees then at least for career soldiers—which it refused to do.

Johnson also recognized that while mobilizing the Reserves alerted the public to the war's seriousness it also signaled the Chinese and Soviets, thus increasing international tensions. Calling up the Reserves, he said, was "too dramatic. And it puts me out there further than I want to get right at the moment." In particular, he feared the North Vietnamese would immediately begin pressuring the Soviet Union for aid that they were not presently getting.[72]

In any event, the military sent contradictory messages about the issue. Westmoreland assured the president that "We're going to win this war for you without mobilization." "I was not in favor of calling up reserves until after Tet," recalled Westy after the war. "The President talked to me about this at great length." Despite their clamor for Reserves, in December 1966, when McNamara asked the JCS whether any of them favored a Reserve call-up, each replied "No." And when the president asked JCS Chairman Wheeler about the Reserves in October 1967, he responded that "We certainly do not need them at the current level of operations," which the military believed was already winning the war.[73]

For men who supposedly placed such a high value on honor, the JCS's hypocrisy was monumental. Chief of Staff Johnson thought the Defense Department's civilian leaders "were intellectual prostitutes whom I cared little for, or respected, because they simply were not prepared to assume the responsibility for their actions." [74] This from a man who believed pacification advocates were right and Westy was wrong but kept quiet, who favored sharp limitations on the air war yet agreed to JCS papers advocating its expansion, who vigorously disagreed with the war's conduct but lacked the courage to resign in protest.

Whether Westmoreland was capable of engaging in an earnest strategic and tactical review was doubtful. With his concept of doctrine embedded in concrete and his grandiose self-delusions, he ignored previous opportunities to rethink his strategy. One example was the March 1966 PROVN study, commissioned by Chief of Staff Johnson and compiled by ten stellar young officers. After eight months of debriefing officers returning from Vietnam, studying that nation's history, and drawing parallels with other countries, the group raised grave questions about attrition. Noting that the situation in South Vietnam was deteriorating and that "1966 may well be the last chance to ensure eventual success," PROVN suggested that U.S. forces were waging the wrong war. Victory lay not in great battles, mass slaughter, and indiscriminate destruction but "through bringing the individual Vietnamese, typically a rural peasant, to support willingly the GVN." Pacification "must be designated unequivocally as the major U.S./Government of Vietnam effort." For Westy to accept PROVN meant admitting his strategy was flawed, so he killed it through a bureaucratic ploy, praising it while recommending it be reduced to a "conceptual document" and forwarded it to the National Security Council for further study—never to be seen again.[75]

A remarkably cogent strategic critique emerged from the Office of Systems Analysis, which assessed Westy's spring 1967 request for 200,000 more soldiers. In a prescient rejoinder, the Office noted additional troops entailed greater costs, more blood, and another step in an endless escalation—in short, further problems in areas already alienating the public. Reinforcements would not ensure victory anytime soon; driven by fervent nationalism rather than Communism, the enemy was willing to wait until domestic discontent compelled the United States to leave. America needed patience, too, if it hoped to win the race between South Vietnam's glacial development and the "gradual loss in public support, or even tolerance, for the war." The document explained that MACV already had *more* than enough troops if it used them effectively, implying, of course, that Westy was misusing his army. A subsequent Draft Presidential Memorandum incorporated these arguments because its author worried about the "fatal flaw" of giving Westy troops "while only *praying* for their proper use." Responding to the Memorandum the JCS, reflecting MACV, expressed vigorous objections to its basic orientation and recommendations.[76]

Still another challenge to Westmoreland came from the Marines, who opposed his quest for a conventional victory through decisive battles, especially in the mountains.[77] Why not let the North Vietnamese have them? All they gained were fetid jungles, a few thousand Montagnards, rotting skin and uniforms, and rampant malaria. "The rationale that ceaseless U.S. operations in the hills could keep the enemy from the people," wrote a Marine officer, "was an operational denial of the fact that in large measure the war was a revolution which started in the hamlets and that therefore the Viet Cong were already among the people when we went to the hills."[78]

Marine Lieutenant General Victor Krulak, Commanding General of the Fleet Marine Force, Pacific, initially supported attrition but quickly perceived Westy's strategy as misguided because "the Vietnamese people are the prize." The MACV commander's self-declared victories in search and destroy operations were irrelevant since the big unit war "could move to another planet today, and we would still not have won the war." Marines fought enemy units if they ventured from the mountains into the ricelands, but saw no purpose in sending "battalions thrashing around in the green hills against vanishing targets." Every Marine chasing the NVA, Krulak declared, was wasted. Commandant Wallace Greene and Lieutenant General Lewis W. Walt, the III Marine Amphibious Force commander from 1965 to 1967, shared Krulak's views.[79]

Instead of pursuing attrition, the Marines wanted to establish Combined Action Platoons (CAPs) and conduct Stingray operations. A CAP consisted of a rifle squad working with a Popular Force platoon to provide continuous security—day and *night*—for a hamlet. Unlike the Army's search and destroy operations, CAPs waged war *in* the villages rather than *on* them. Wherever a CAP was functioning, election turnouts increased, terrorism declined, and movement on rural roads became safer. Security assessments revealed that hamlets with CAPs were almost twice as safe as those without them, and the CAP casualty rate was significantly lower than among troops on search and destroy operations.

Small long-range reconnaissance (or strike) teams, generically called Stingray because they stung and fled, were the Marines' preferred modus operandi. Unlike MACV the Corps viewed small units as an alternative, not an adjunct, to large unit operations. A Stingray force, usually four to six men, was stealthy, often operated in enemy territory, relied on surprise, and emphasized inflicting damage without absorbing any. "Whereas a large unit often endeavors to inflict as many casualties as possible regardless of the cost to itself," wrote one expert, "a strike team endeavors to inflict as many casualties as it can on the enemy at no cost to itself. Like the Viet Cong, strike teams will try to refuse contact when they don't like the situation." Strike teams had a higher rate of enemy contact and suffered proportionately fewer casualties than maneuver battalions. And the ongoing trickle of casualties they inflicted eroded enemy morale in the same way BBTs and mines afflicted Americans.[80]

Practicing pacification, working with Vietnamese paramilitary forces to provide long-term village security, utilizing small unit tactics that avoided unnecessary destruction and excessive casualties, the Marines irked the Army from the highest level down to Joe Hooper. Despising the Marines' seeming timidity and the way they coddled the peasantry, Westy pressed General Walt to forget pacification, get into the mountains, and start killing North Vietnamese. Major General DePuy ranted that "the Marines came in and just sat down and didn't do anything. They were involved in counterinsurgency of the deliberate, mild sort."[81]

The anti-Marine attitude permeated the lower ranks. "We have brought smoke on the emeny [sic]," Hooper wrote his parents three months after the Raiders arrived in Thua Thien. "Killing Hundreds and Hundreds, dont know how many. We are doing our part. But we are a small group and can't carry the ball our own self. The mariens [Marines] could help, but they are useless."[82]

In any event, no strategic review occurred before the Tet Offensive compelled it.

Cleo Hogan was wrong.

Tet was a time of fighting, not peace.

Westmoreland was wrong.

Khe Sanh was not the enemy's objective, but one of history's most successful deceptions. "I believe the enemy sees a similarity between our base at Khe Sanh and Dien Bien Phu," he wrote in a late January 1968 cable, "and hopes, by following a pattern of activity similar to that used against the French, to gain similar military and political ends." For another month, despite all evidence to the contrary, Westmoreland believed Khe Sanh was the Communists' ultimate prize. Even his foremost defenders acknowledge that Westy looked foolish focusing on Khe Sanh while considering a nationwide offensive by tens of thousands of enemy troops a diversion.[83]

Hovey was right.

The attacks on El Paso and Cu Chi were not isolated, but part of the Communists' General Offensive-General Uprising, a concerted effort against the urban areas that exploded across South Vietnam the night of January 30–31. By day's end the VC/NVA assaulted twenty-seven of South Vietnam's forty-four provincial capitals, five of its six autonomous cities, fifty-eight of its 245 district towns, and more than fifty hamlets. Although a few attacks occurred prematurely on January 29–30 because some forces used an outdated lunar calendar, different from the new one in Hanoi, the Tet Offensive still surprised MACV.[84]

Neither MACV headquarters nor the embassy evinced any particular urgency on January 30, continuing business as usual. All over Saigon officers who went home for the evening awoke, startled by gunfire, shocked that VC were in the capital. Marine guards hastily shepherded Ambassador Bunker, clad in pajamas and a bath robe, to safety in an armored personnel carrier.[85] Westy misjudged everything about the enemy offensive: he assumed a post-Tet assault, thought the target would be Khe Sanh not the cities, and could not envision an intense, coordinated, nationwide offensive. How could an adversary nearing defeat do something like that? "Even had I known exactly what was to take place," commented General Davidson, Westy's intelligence chief, "it was so preposterous that I probably would have been unable to sell it to anybody. Why would the enemy give away his major advantage, which was his ability to be elusive and avoid heavy casualties?"[86]

Why indeed.

Western scholars have such limited access to Vietnamese archives that a complete answer remains speculative. But three factors seem certain.

First, the Tet Offensive was the culmination of a complex strategic debate centering on whether *thoi co* (the opportune moment) had arrived, when a dramatic shift from political to military *dau tranh* and from guerrilla to conventional warfare might radically alter the strategic balance. Communist strategists, like revolutionary leaders historically, were fractured between those advocating aggressive military action and those who favored postponing it, fearing a premature attack would be counterproductive, alerting the enemy and provoking counterattacks.[87]

Judging the time was appropriate for a grand strategic risk during the forthcoming dry season, enemy forces began stockpiling logistical support and rallying supporters for a supreme effort. "The people's historic hour has struck!" exhorted a propaganda leaflet. "All of you, take arms! All of you, take to the streets!" "The bugle call of the Fatherland ordering the assault has sounded over mountains and rivers," it continued. "Let the entire army and people surge forward simultaneously to destroy the enemy and liberate the country!" Another pre-Tet leaflet spoke of a "new era, a real revolutionary period, an offensive and uprising period" in which victory was near. "If we miss this opportunity, we will never be able to complete the mission of liberating the Fatherland with which the people have entrusted us."[88]

A second certainty was that the VC/NVA primarily targeted South Vietnamese forces and installations, not Americans, during Tet. Perceiving the inherent tension between the United States and South Vietnam and hoping to sow further discord, General Giap targeted the weaker partner, knowing he could not possibly deliver a knockout punch against the United States. The goal, wrote General Tran Van Tra, one of the commanders entrusted with implementing the offensive, was to annihilate ARVN and overthrow GVN by igniting a rebellion in the cities, thereby "wresting the government into the hands of the people."[89] That was why Giap ordered the costly border battles (including Khe Sanh) as a deception. Luring the Americans into remote border regions presumably left South Vietnamese forces and government officials isolated and vulnerable in the urban areas. Of course, success depended on whether the urban population was seething with revolt, how well ARVN fought, and how quickly U.S. forces reacted.

Third, the Politburo foresaw a range of possible outcomes. On the optimistic side, the Communists might achieve "a major victory in all the important battlefields, the offensive and uprising would succeed in all the big cities, the aggressive will of the enemy would be crushed forcing them to agree to negotiations to end the war in accordance with our demands." Note that the enemy had no expectation of a total victory over the United States, of driving it into the South China Sea, but only aimed at defeating its "aggressive will." Less hopefully, even if the VC/NVA won important victories "the enemy might still have many forces supported by big bases and would continue to fight." A third possibility was unlikely but nonetheless required "active precautions": the United States might pour in more troops and invade North Vietnam, Laos, and Cambodia.[90]

Hanoi doubted the United States would escalate. With only a rump South Vietnamese government and an emasculated ARVN remaining, with its illusions of success shattered and its Limited War exposed as a failure, with increasing domestic antiwar pressure, and with American resources already stretched thin meeting its worldwide commitments, the Johnson administration would probably opt for negotiations.

So the enemy struck, nowhere harder than Hue. Concealed by the northeast monsoon's foul weather, early on January 31, the 4th and 6th NVA Regiments launched a coordinated mortar, rocket, and ground assault, quickly gaining control of the city except for MACV's compound, the 1st ARVN Division's headquarters, and a few other scattered positions. Local VC aided the attack. Although short of trained personnel, weapons, ammunition, and food, the Hue City Party Committee joined in the effort "to bring the war into the enemy's rear cities, spoil the pacification scheme, develop the Revolutionary strength and consolidate and expand our areas of activity," thus creating a favorable strategic position. The VC 12th and Hue City Sapper Battalions both slipped into the city in advance and contributed to the initial success. In the nearby countryside the NVA consolidated positions that held open a route for reinforcements and supplies and blocked the arrival of American and ARVN reinforcements. The enemy also severed QL-1 in many places.[91]

In Hue a savage battle occurred, with ARVN forces trying to clear the city north of the Perfume River, which bisected Hue, and the Marines fighting south of it. In this fierce combat the NVA and VC had several advantages. Fighting from room-to-room, house-to-house, and street-to-street negated American mobility and the dismal weather hindered external firepower support, as did the desire to minimize damage to one of South Vietnam's largest and most beautiful cities. Perhaps most importantly, for several weeks Westy remained focused on Khe Sanh, underestimating the enemy forces in Hue and the strength of their blocking positions to the north and west. He kept a tight leash on the area's reserve forces, fearing to use them somewhere other than Khe Sanh.

But at least some help was on the way.

As part of Operation Jeb Stuart, the 1st Air Cavalry Division's 3rd Brigade undertook the relief mission, which began on February 2. The 1st Cav's commander, Major General John J. Tolson III, had virtually no information about the enemy situation but assumed the NVA expended its strength against Hue so the path to the city should be relatively open. He expected the 3rd Brigade's 2nd Battalion, 12th Cavalry Regiment (2-12) to move southeast paralleling QL-1, close the enemy's back door to the city, and link up with ARVN and the Marines, all without much difficulty.[92]

"Unconfirmed reports of enemy activity in the hamlet of Thon La Chu," cautioned an intelligence assessment. But Tolson and others ignored the warning, which was unfortunate since the NVA's main blocking position centered on the village, just three miles northwest of Hue. Wooded and heavily fortified, La Chu was the tactical headquarters directing the battle for Hue. A lesser but still important position was just to the south at Bon Tri. Elements from at least three NVA regiments and several Local Force companies and militia units were in the area.[93]

Pushing through La Chu to Hue was too great a task for one battalion. When 2-12 entered the village on February 3 a trooper rhetorically asked, "How are we goin' to get outta This Fucking Place?"[94] The answer was "Not easily." During the night of February 3–4, 2-12 was surrounded, desperately fighting to stave off annihilation, which it avoided only through a precarious night withdrawal. It left behind eleven hastily buried American bodies.

The 5th Battalion, 7th Cav then joined with 2-12 and for more than a week they tried to crack La Chu, but without success and with heavy losses.

In mid-February the 1st Battalion, 7th Cav and the 101st Airborne's 2-501, which was assigned to the Cav's 3rd Brigade, further reinforced the effort.

"It was just a matter of time," said Captain McMenamy about the inevitability of the Raiders' first battle casualty. "There's going to be somebody hurt."[95]

But when 2-501 withdrew from El Paso to the Phu Bai airfield on February 2 and then deployed northward to Camp Evans some fifteen miles northwest of Hue, no one knew the battalion would be "up to our butts in North Vietnamese" for the next four months, resulting in a bloodletting that lasted until the annual June lull provided relief.[96]

Camp Evans was just off QL-1 a few miles north of the An Lo Bridge spanning the Song Bo River. "It was just a mud hillside," recalled Cleo Hogan, "with very, very primitive infantry conditions." The place was a dump, an ugly empty spot in the middle of nowhere, devoid of showers, electricity, supplies—short of everything except mud, a numbing chill, and nearby NVA anti-aircraft defenses. Precipitation fell on twenty-five days in February, with a trace recorded on a twenty-sixth day, and temperatures averaged ten degrees below the expected minimum, meaning it fell into the 40s at night and climbed only into the 60s by day. As for airmobility, the NVA "are death on helicopters," wrote Hogan. "Every time we send them up they get shot down."[97]

At Camp Evans the Raiders pulled perimeter guard duty, picked up air-delivered supplies (since the VC/NVA cut QL-1, the only way to supply Evans was by air drops), and conducted short patrols on which they received sniper shots and found signs of the enemy, but only occasionally spotted enemy soldiers. They also tried to stay dry and warm.[98]

On February 7 Delta Company suffered its first battle casualty when Bradford Gagne, an expert skydiver, stepped on a booby-trapped anti-personnel mine, blowing off his left leg and permanently injuring the right one. Captain Mac was distraught. During his first tour many of his Special Forces buddies were killed or wounded, and he did not want to endure the pain of losing more friends. Upon joining the Raiders he was "determined not to let anyone or thing get too close, to tune out any feeling of emotion in order to maintain some form of sanity." But it did not work because the Raiders "were a part of me and I of them." Somewhat easing the anguish were Gagne's parting words. "Don't forget to forward my CIB," he implored the men loading him onto a medevac, "and my Raider patch." Mac loved that unit pride. Incredibly, Gagne resumed skydiving after rehabilitation.[99]

Five days after Gagne's injury the Delta Raiders were ordered southward to PK-17, an ARVN regimental headquarters about the size of a football field and surrounded by a minefield. Originally a French outpost, PK-17 was just south of the An Lo Bridge and stood at a cement post adjacent to QL-1 that was exactly seventeen kilometers from the center of Hue. Joe Hooper's platoon (1st Platoon) guarded the bridge. Early in Tet enemy sappers blew out two of its sections but army engineers soon cobbled together a passable span. 1st Platoon's job was to insure it remained intact. Meanwhile 2nd and 3rd Platoons conducted patrols to intercept NVA reinforcements. The day after arriving at PK-17 they swept through a small village in the morning, killing one VC. That afternoon the Raiders suffered their second battle casualty when a BBT wounded Frank Wingo.[100]

On Valentine's Day, late in the afternoon, things got worse. Deployed in two lines ten to fifteen feet apart, 2nd and 3rd Platoons patrolled east of the An Lo Bridge. The first line crossed a three-foot-high berm separating two rice paddies, hopped across a ditch surrounding the far one, and stepped forward, heading across the open rice land toward a distant tree line "when all of a sudden the enemy opened up on us from the far side of the rice paddy." Al Mount dove into the ditch, where Sergeant Parker also sought shelter "so it had to be a pretty good sized ditch." Hunkered down, the Raiders returned fire for a few seconds when Mount "heard an explosion and it got black, and it dawned on me that it was dirt coming down on my head." Firing continued briefly and then the enemy broke contact. When Mount looked around he saw Harold Begody, a quiet man, a Navajo Native American who was in the second line directly behind him, sprawled in the dirt, face down, dead, a burnt circle singed into the ground between them. Mount realized the explosion raining earth on him killed Begody. Sergeant Parker and others were certain an M-79 round fired from a captured American weapon was the culprit. During the firefight another Raider, Richard L. Buzzini, was WIA when two punji stakes punctured his left calf as he took cover. These wounds were not only painful but also became infected because the enemy tipped the stakes with excrement; Buzzini was out of the field for about a week while antibiotics worked their magic.[101]

That same day Joe Hooper, undoubtedly restless guarding a bridge while others were on patrol, manufactured a little action. When artillery fire hit a nearby area he and an artillery communications sergeant made their own damage assessment, without asking permission. They conducted a mini-patrol into the area even though it was "known to be infested with bad guys." "This was fairly typical of Joe," according to Captain Mac. "He didn't ask anybody and nobody said he couldn't."[102]

Also on February 14, Lieutenant Aronow, soon to leave his position as the battalion intelligence officer to become Delta Company's executive officer, wrote to his wife half in disgust. "I just wish the President and Government would level with the public about what is REALLY going on over here. We're taking it on the chin up here in I Corps and the NVA are really doing well in their plans." [103]

Toward evening the Raiders carried Begody's body—"the heaviest thing I ever carried in my life," said Mount—in a poncho back to PK-17, where it took hours before a helicopter evacuated the cadaver. Laying there in the dark, the shrouded body spooked more than one Raider. [104]

First a bloody drizzle—Gagne, Wingo, then Buzzini and Begody.

The next day a sanguinary flood began.

Seven

I swore up and down this guy was nuts.
He wasn't afraid of anybody.

The Delta Raiders' Bobby Rakestraw,
expressing an opinion that many soldiers had about Joe

What with the bright orange hunting-style vest he was wearing, Eugene "Raider Rob" Robertson looked out of place on a battlefield. But there he was on February 15 in a nasty firefight, plunking away with his M-79 grenade launcher just about as fast as he could load and aim.

For Robertson and other Raiders the arrival of long-delayed mail on February 14 dissipated some of the gloom Harold Begody's death caused. Henry Tabet received a picture of his wife and their children, which he proudly showed to his good friends. Tabet was doubly fortunate that night since a few mortar rounds crashed into D Company's position and one of them scored a direct hit on his bunker. Tabet was unhurt, causing more than a few comments about what a lucky man he was.

Raider Rob received an especially welcome package. He had previously written his mother showing her a picture of an M-79 round and giving its dimensions, asking her to make a vest to carry the ammo. Opening the package, he saw that the vest was great, just perfect—except for the color. Robertson normally humped several bandoleers of M-79 rounds, plus four old World War II field packs (two slung over each shoulder) crammed with more ammo. The weight rubbed his shoulders raw. Now he unloaded the packs, loaded up the vest, and slipped it on.

The evenly distributed weight "felt so damn good," he recalled twenty-five years later with a delicious savoring in his voice. So he wore the vest when the 2nd and 3rd Platoons conducted a search and destroy mission the next morning. "I looked like a bloomin' idiot out there in orange. But it felt so good!" [1]

The two platoons, approximately sixty men, "saddled up" at first light and headed due south from PK-17. They first encountered a graveyard with freshly dug enemy positions that were extensive enough to hold a reinforced company, a disquieting discovery since military intelligence said no more than a platoon was in that area. A few minutes later when the Raiders received sporadic sniper fire, Captain McMenamy maneuvered to get behind the snipers, 3rd Platoon commanded by Lieutenant Bob Brulte on the left with 2nd Platoon under Lieutenant Dave Loftin on the right and slightly ahead of 3rd Platoon, swinging around like a gate.

As 3rd Platoon's scouts reached a sparse treeline and peered across a paddy, they spotted several NVA in an island-hamlet, a group of houses entangled in dense vegetation approximately fifty yards away. The scouts reported their discovery to Lieutenant Brulte who relayed the information to Captain Mac. Just as he arrived at Brulte's position the enemy fired on the scouts who had ventured well into the rice paddy, hitting Sergeant David Cash.

No one could tell whether Cash was dead or alive, but either way the Raiders had no intention of abandoning him. Like many units with high esprit de corps, they refused as a matter of principle to abandon anyone, dead or wounded. "We didn't believe in leaving a dead man behind or waiting two or three days to retrieve his body," said Joe Hooper. "We always went back —even against orders—to get the men. We never had an MIA." [2] Moreover, medical care was so excellent that soldiers survived even monstrous injuries if they got to a hospital quickly, so a sense of urgency attended the retrieval of a wounded man. The unwritten policy was for another soldier or soldiers to sprint into the open, grab the body (which might be alive or dead), and haul it back to safety.

Deleterious consequences flowed from this policy. The NVA and VC took advantage of the Americans' dogged practice of never leaving anybody behind, often shooting to wound rather than kill, using the wounded man as "bait," knowing another soldier would rush to the injured man and stoop to pick him up, thus making an easy target. All too often the sprinter got shot, meaning the number of bodies needing recovery *increased*. Not only did the number of dead and wounded escalate, sometimes in a cascade that depleted a unit's fighting strength, but also the attack stalled as men became preoccupied with getting casualties medevaced and virtually forgot about the enemy.

Higher headquarters frowned on what they considered a misplaced concern for casualties; they wanted soldiers to press the attack, arguing that the best way to assist dead or wounded men was "to maintain pressure on the enemy so that medevac operations can be conducted in a safe environment."[3] But for field soldiers, well, the attack be damned! They were going to save their buddies. Raider Rob spoke for all the Raiders. It never bothered him to risk getting shot trying to retrieve a body because "I knew someone would do it for me."

In any event, the Raiders had marched into an ambush, "a hellacious scrap" as Lieutenant Loftin called it. In classic style, the NVA sprang the trap at close quarters, "hugging" the Raiders.

The NVA's initial fusillade was a prelude to a rocketing volume of fire —"the most God-awful automatic weapons and rifle fire," said Robert L. Rainwater, who received four wounds before the day was over, a "shocking amount of noise that was just overwhelming." Several other Raiders besides Sergeant Cash were hit out in the paddy, including John Wheat, Richard Ryan, and Henry Tabet. The latter was killed—never to see his wife and children again, his luck extinguished. The other two were wounded, Wheat much more seriously than Ryan. The rest of 3rd Platoon took refuge in a little wooded finger jutting into the paddy, pinned down by an enemy force much larger than the platoon McMenamy expected to encounter.

When the NVA began working around 3rd Platoon's left flank, Captain Mac ordered Loftin to shift 2nd Platoon from the right front to the threatened flank, where most of his men deployed along a paddy dike and near the edge of a small woodlot. But Loftin also left a few soldiers on 3rd Platoon's right flank in case the NVA moved in that direction, a wise decision since the NVA were soon inching that way, trying to surround the Raiders. Loftin also stationed a fire team to watch the rear and directed Staff Sergeant Clifford C. Sims's squad to set up an LZ in an abandoned rice field not more than fifty or sixty yards behind the front.

Born in June 1942 in southern Florida and a 1961 high school graduate, Sims got married shortly after enlisting for six years in October of that year. He received his Parachutist Badge at Fort Benning in 1962, reenlisted early for six years in 1964, and as a member of the 82nd Airborne deployed to the Dominican Republic in 1965. Responding with his typical machismo to what he perceived as a threat of a Communist takeover there, President Johnson first dispatched the Marines and then part of the 82nd. When a few wild shots were fired, Sims and many others qualified for a Combat Infantryman's Badge (CIB). Since no one was really in grave danger, many people considered those CIBs suspect.

As part of the worldwide levy to flesh out the 101st Airborne, Sims arrived at Fort Campbell in September, joined Delta Company, and was soon promoted to Staff Sergeant. Like Joe Hooper, Sims had a less-than-perfect record. In December 1964, he missed a company formation and received an Article 15 and while in the Dominican Republic he fell asleep on guard duty, earning another Fifteen Fucker.[4]

Lieutenant Loftin considered Sims "a very average guy," thoroughly unremarkable, neither a Rambo nor a wimp, but dependable. Sims's men liked him. "Just a good ol' country boy, a nice human being" who talked about getting out of the service after twenty years so he could go hunting and fishing, said Craig Sturges. "Very, very straightforward" and "very, very well respected" was how Raider Rob described his squad leader.

Robertson received a stiff dose of straightforward-ness as Sims established the LZ. So hard pressed was 3rd Platoon that Sims ordered Raider Rob to report to Lieutenant Brulte with his fire team. Robertson asked him how to get there. "Go where the shooting is!" Following those straightforward directions, he found the lieutenant who began pointing out enemy machine gun positions. Kneeling next to a little bush but without any other cover and attired in bright orange, Raider Rob emptied his bandoleers and vest and then scrounged ammo from the dead and wounded, firing at least 100 M-79 rounds. "I had bullets zinging everywhere. It didn't faze me," he recalled. "I'm just a lucky man to be here to tell you this."

As 2nd Platoon got into the fight Captain Mac sought external help. He thought about calling in tactical air, but Loftin advised against it because the enemy was so close. No one wanted a napalm bomb accidentally charring American soldiers. Working through his Artillery Forward Observer Mike Watson, McMenamy did call to PK-17 for artillery support. As a safety measure the first rounds purposefully hit long and then Watson radioed adjustments, "walking" the shells toward the enemy lines, which were precariously near the American position. When the rounds finally "walked" onto the NVA positions, Watson ordered the artillery to "fire for effect," that is, to fire away.

Almost immediately McMenamy, who had completed artillery school, sensed something was wrong. "You know what a battery sounds like when it fires. The battery was only a mile away, back at PK-17, so you could hear the guns. The sound of the guns in the distance sort of triggered something and my sixth sense said something doesn't sound right." Five rounds hit on target almost simultaneously. But the powder bag for the last round "cooked off" for a split second before firing, which meant less explosive force to push the projectile out of the gun tube.

Which meant the round hit short.

It exploded in the midst of 3rd Platoon, close to Bob Brulte, a piece of shrapnel hitting him in the head. He screamed McMenamy's call name into the radio: "Raider Six, Raider Six! Short round, Raider Six! Short round, cease fire!" His voice faded, "Short round, cease fire. . . . Short round, cease fire." Then a bare whisper. "Raider Six, Raider Six," a dozen times or more, slower and lower until death stilled his voice.

No one else died from the friendly fire incident, but it injured half a dozen other Raiders, several of them badly, a jaw blown off here, a foot severed above the ankle there. Brulte's RTO, Ron Hendricks, had a hole bigger than a fist torn out of his back. Raider Rob was fortunate, taking only a few small shrapnel chunks in the back, which was his third friendly fire wound since errant M-79s twice hit him when the unit was in the Cu Chi area.

Although the short round caused an immediate loss in fighting strength and rattled the survivors, the Raiders recovered quickly. Still, they confronted critical problems. One was to recover the increasing number of dead and wounded as men tried to retrieve those wounded in the initial ambush and by the short round and got shot themselves; included among the fresh casualties were platoon medics David H. McKieghan and Alex D. ("Doc") Spivey. The PK-17 Command Post recommended that Captain Mac withdraw and cut his losses, but he refused to leave any of his men on the battlefield because they "weren't just soldiers, they were family, Raiders. I had brought them here and I was damn well not going to leave them wounded and dying, for the enemy." Nobody considered the additional casualties incurred while saving downed comrades or recovering their limp bodies unnecessary.

Another difficulty was simply holding their positions, especially since no one was eager for more artillery "support," thus giving the enemy more freedom of movement than usual. "The bad guys ended up being all around us," remembered Captain Mac. "It didn't make much difference where you shot. There were bad guys everywhere." Many Raiders worried the NVA would overwhelm them in one concerted surge. Expressing a common fear, Mike Watson was "pretty sure we were all going to die that day."

The commander of the Air Cav's 3rd Brigade ordered two companies of 5-7 Cav to rescue the trapped platoons, but they retreated before they got within half a mile of the Raiders' position. An official report said they "relieved some of the pressure" on the Raiders; if so, McMenamy and his men were unaware of it. The Air Cav also dispatched helicopter gunships and ARA but they were few in number, did not stay on station long, and did little to suppress the NVA.

No artillery. No cavalry dramatically riding to the rescue in Hollywood fashion. Feeble gunship support. Captain Mac summed up the situation: "We were still bogged down, nobody else was around, nobody else was coming." And "we started running out of ammo."

"When you're in a firefight," Raider Richard Buzzini observed, "you're trained to expend a lot of your ammo because you think there's always more available. You don't just use it intermittently, you just fire it all up."[5] Normally this worked well. Ammo *was* plentiful because as soon as a battle began U.S. troops cleared an LZ for medevacs and resupply choppers. The problem on February 15 was that the LZ was by necessity close to the front lines, subjected to hostile fire from three sides as the NVA lapped at the Raiders' flanks. Neither medevacs nor resupply birds got in or out easily.

Two risky resupply missions, one by air the other by land, alleviated the ammo crisis. Back at PK-17, First Sergeant Scott and XO Lieutenant Fred Aronow were sipping coffee and discussing administrative problems when they heard the firefight erupt in the distance. Monitoring the battle over the radio, they listened to the urgent pleas for ammo and desperately wanted to help. Unfortunately, the 101st Airborne's helicopters had not arrived in I Corps yet, so they turned to the Air Cav for assistance. But that division's supply system temporarily collapsed during Tet and its units in contact with the enemy demanded whatever helicopter support was available, so spare birds were scarce.[6]

Details are vague, but somehow Scott and Aronow commandeered a helicopter and stuffed it with ammunition. Legend has it that Scottie pulled a pistol on the reluctant pilot, giving him a "fly or die" order. He flew, though he did not land, instead hovering three or four feet above the Raiders' fire-swept LZ while Sergeant Scott kicked ammo boxes out the door. The hover lasted little more than a minute before the empty bird soared away, wearing new bullet holes in its plumage.

Aronow had become D Company's XO when Cleo Hogan assumed command of the battalion Headquarters Company on February 10. Needing a new XO, McMenamy requested Lieutenant Aronow, a Distinguished

Military Graduate from Gonzaga University's ROTC Detachment. Originally deploying to Vietnam with C Company, Aronow became the battalion civil affairs officer and then its intelligence officer before transferring to the Raiders. The XO assignment disappointed and frustrated him. As a budding career soldier he wanted to command a platoon, see some action, and earn some medals, not sit in the rear handling administrative and logistical duties.

Aronow's first full day in his new position was February 15, so he knew virtually none of the Raiders.[7] He tried to persuade McMenamy to let him accompany the search and destroy operation, but the captain said no, the XO had too many administrative duties to go into the field. Anxious to find a way into the battle, by mid-afternoon Aronow could restrain himself no longer. Assembling a fifteen-man relief force burdened with ammo, donning a few extra bandoleers, and toting a box of M-60 ammo in each hand, he led the ad hoc band southward on the run.

One man in the relief column was Joe Hooper, though how he got there nobody knows. 1st Platoon was still guarding the An Lo Bridge where, said RTO Ava James, "Hooper always kept contact with me because I knew everything before anybody else because of the radio."[8] On the 15th James was monitoring the desperate fight. Perhaps Joe sidled up to his position, heard the unfolding crisis on the radio, ambled down to PK-17, and linked up with the XO's relief column. Heading toward the action was, of course, typical of Hooper.

Upon reaching the battlefield Aronow reported to Captain Mac who directed him toward Loftin's position on the left. "My people arrived with extra machine gun ammo and we laid down a hell of a volume of fire that stopped the gooks' attempt to flank us," Aronow wrote his wife two days later. With the crisis on the left averted, Mac radioed Aronow to assume command of 3rd Platoon. By the time he circled back to 3rd Platoon's position, the NVA's fire abated to sporadic sniper shots and all of Delta's dead and wounded "were accounted for but one and someone said he was out in the open rice paddy to our front between us and the Gooks." This, of course, was Sergeant Cash.

The XO "didn't have the nerve" to ask the men of 3rd Platoon, who had already repeatedly exposed themselves to danger in recovering the dead and wounded, to go out there again. "So I went, with another sergeant, and we

ran into the field under covering fire from our people and found Sgt. Cash
—dead—and we loaded him on a stretcher, grabbed his weapon, and ran
like hell for the bushes." For these actions, Hooper, with some input from
Sergeant John B. Gingery, wrote an eyewitness statement supporting a Silver
Star for Aronow.[9]

Recovering the last body brought "a big sigh of relief" to Captain Mac.
With a clear conscience and intact honor, he ordered a withdrawal to PK-17.
Aronow and 3rd Platoon led the retreat while 2nd Platoon provided covering fire, with McMenamy, Loftin, and Watson being among the last to evacuate the battlefield. Fortunately for the Raiders, the NVA had broken contact
so the flanks were clear; only a few snipers took parting shots. "It seemed like
after an all-day battle," Loftin recalled, "it just got quiet and they quit shooting." As the Raiders cleared the area Watson called in artillery fire on the
enemy's positions, but one wonders how much damage this fireworks display did.

That night the Raiders tallied their casualties: six dead, twenty-two
wounded, seventeen of them requiring medical evacuation. In two days the
company lost seven men killed and twenty-three wounded, thus leaving it
with the strength of approximately two platoons. One of those with a minor
wound was Captain Mac who had a grenade fragment graze his scalp. As
for the enemy body count, nobody knew. "We're not sitting there taking a
count," snarled McMenamy. But higher-ups wanted a figure. So D Company
estimated it killed eight, somebody hypothesized that ARA killed twenty-
four, artillery another twenty-two, and the Cav's rescue mission two, for a
total of fifty-six, which was pretty much a WAG (wild-ass guess).

Unlike Westmoreland who was incapable of admitting a defeat, D Company knew "*we got our butts kicked.*"[10] Morale sagged. The sight of all those
casualties was "devastating to some of us," according to Craig Sturges. For
the first time he questioned whether he would return "with a chestful of
medals, and the bands would be playing, and I'd come home and run for
Congress or something." Noah Rockel did not "feel like doing much any
more. I [am] tired of this ole War. It stinks."[11] Later he recalled that "We
were probably on rock bottom. Our hearts were taken from us. I didn't
know what defeat was. The United States Army doesn't get defeated against
a bunch of peasants with little pistols and old guns and stuff like that. You
just don't get *defeated*. And we felt like we got defeated that day." Of course,

Rockel's supposition was wrong. The NVA were not peasants with anti-quated firearms but highly motivated professionals equipped with modern weapons, including AK-47s, light and heavy machine guns, B-40 rocket-propelled grenades, and various sized mortars.[12]

Particularly sad duties devolved upon Hogan, Aronow, and McMenamy. Temporarily whisked from his new position as Headquarters Company commander, Cleo reported to Graves Registration to identify the dead, a gruesome but important task. Sometimes the NVA switched dog tags on American corpses, creating additional misery for grieving families back home. And then sometimes a KIA's face was so disfigured that identification was difficult. Indeed, Cleo had difficulty identifying one body, necessitating that D Company hold a 100 percent muster on February 16 and prepare a roster of all its personnel so that the "missing" man could be identified.[13]

Having "grown five years older over here already," Aronow returned to Camp Evans where he refitted the company, took care of the personal effects of the dead and wounded, and wrote condolence letters. "Seeing the men die and bleed from terrible wounds, then come back and sort through their gear and send it to their families, etc., takes a hell of a drain on a guy," he admitted.[14]

Grieving over the empty foxholes the night of February 15, Captain Mac could not sleep despite his utter exhaustion. He kept replaying the battle in his mind, questioning what he did wrong, and what he did right. In a small lined note pad he compiled a list of the dead and wounded, a stark reminder that much had gone terribly wrong. Reflecting the immense strain he was under, Mac's scrawled printing was nearly illegible and he misspelled the names of men he knew well, such as "Bute" for Brulte.

That evening McMenamy also sketched an elegy to his Raiders, which in part read:

> With your blood you have forged a tradition of valor and pride and through this a brotherhood is born.
>
> Thus, you are bound forever, one to another, by this, your baptism of fire.

The next morning Lieutenant Colonel Tallman and other officers swarmed in to question Captain Mac about the battle and to insist that he write medal citations immediately. That was "probably the last thing on my list of things to do," but the brass insisted so he spent part of the day compiling the names of those who performed most heroically. Medics McKieghan and Spivey disregarded their own safety to treat the wounded; Billy R. Barnett, Glenn P. Williamson, and Lorin W. Johnson pulled injured men off the battlefield; Staff Sergeant Eulas F. Gregory rallied his men at a critical moment.

On and on the list went.[15]

"War is Hell," grunts scrawled on latrine walls, cloth helmet covers, and everywhere else from Saigon to Quang Tri, "but actual combat is a motherfucker."[16]

Many Raiders learned this fundamental truth, and in learning this they learned some other things that combat veterans, at least those who were contemplative, understood.

One. Although fighting was the central military act—a major battle, wrote Clausewitz, was "concentrated war"—they could not explain what combat was *really* like. "When a soldier moves forward against fire," noted Professor Roger Spiller, one of America's finest military historians, "he steps beyond the boundaries of anything we understand." Noncombatants can nibble around a battle's edges but they can never pierce its dark heart because in no other human activity was the infliction of large-scale death and suffering the pronounced goal. "When you go into combat the most important thing, in my opinion," said Craig Sturges, "is to make sure that the enemy gives his life for his country."[17]

Metaphors, analogies, logic, rational analysis, artful and eloquent prose, none of these adequately revealed the essence of combat. "It was an experience you can never explain in a million words," wrote a 1st Cav sergeant.[18] Combat-tested veterans usually talked so little about the actual fighting because words could not describe what they endured. Indeed, to make sense of it for themselves, or perhaps to ward off unwelcome inquiries, or maybe just to shield themselves from thinking too deeply about what they saw and did, many soldiers relied on a misleading analogy: they were just doing their job. "Danger?" wrote Fred Aronow. "It's funny, but you don't worry about that. Your job comes first, and all of us feel that way, I guess." "It was just one of those jobs that had to be done, and I was there to do it," said Lonnie Nale, who as an RTO was in a high-mortality position because the enemy knew the importance of radio communications. "I was just doing my job as a squad leader," commented Joe Hooper after one of his battlefield exploits. [19] But what Aronow, Nale, and Hooper did was not akin to stocking shelves at the local supermarket or brokering stocks or teaching history.

Two. High-ranking officers and historians may write about a "minor" action with "light" casualties but every firefight was a major action for those involved, and no matter how "light" the casualties they weighed heavily if the dead and wounded were your friends.

Three. Random and capricious, combat eluded all efforts to control it. Expertise and experience counted for something, but not enough. Raider Bobby Rakestraw noted that fighting "is not something you can train for." A platoon leader acknowledged that "Rational decision making or technical and physical skills may save you once or twice. But a man in combat is exposed a thousand times." "Sometimes you make right decisions and everybody comes out great," said Steve Hawk, who served with Hooper during his second tour, "and sometimes you make right decisions and somebody gets killed." Good soldiers died as readily as slackers, and why one man lived and another did not—why a short round landed beside Lieutenant Brulte and not somebody else—was an inscrutable mystery. The "Big Referee in the Sky," a grunt wrote, "makes the rules and takes out players and sends in subs. Nothing else really counts." [20]

Four. Words such as glorious and romantic might apply to Hollywood-style war but not to Vietnam-style combat, where filth, fatigue, and fear reigned. "I'd seen enough blood, dead bodies and suffering to understand there was damn little glory in what we were doing," wrote one veteran. "To be more specific, there may have been some glory for the battalion commander, but for the guy getting shot at, forget it. There's no glory in that at all." Or as Cleo Hogan observed, you do not charge machine gun nests like Audie Murphy did in *To Hell and Back* without dying. [21]

Five. Battle was the ultimate test. "You don't get a fail or pass mark," said Captain Mac, "you live or die." [22]

On his birth certificate it says Cleo C. Hogan Jr., but his nickname was Whimpy.

Cleo was anything but wimpy, as he demonstrated for five months as the Delta Raiders' commander, a position he assumed on February 20.

The Raiders spent two days after their defeat reshuffling personnel to bolster battered 3rd Platoon, providing perimeter security at PK-17, and conducting nearby patrols. Although Aronow hoped to retain command of 3rd Platoon, it went to a Lieutenant Dave Bischoff. In the field everybody was edgy and cautious. On one patrol they received sniper shots from a hooch about five hundred feet away. In response Captain Mac leveled it with artillery fire. "Somebody says, what happens if there are friendlies in there?" he recalled. "I'm not in the frame of mind to risk anybody trying to maneuver to take out that sniper and get some more people killed. We know the bad guys are there. We've been fired upon. So we level it." [23]

Meanwhile military intelligence intercepted enemy messages revealing that the commander in Hue had been killed. His successor wanted to withdraw but received orders to continue fighting. As ferocious combat devastated the city, the 1st Air Cav organized a four-battalion relief effort to help drive the NVA out. The 101st Airborne's 2-501 joined the Cav's 1-7, 5-7, and 2-12 for this campaign. [24]

The Delta Raiders concentrated at PK-17 as a first step in assembling 2-501. 1st Platoon came in from the An Lo Bridge and then the reunited Company provided security at LZ Sally, a new LZ that the unit hastily established just west of PK-17. The rest of the battalion arrived at Sally from Camp Evans on February 19 and, minus Company B (which assumed guard duty at the An Lo Bridge, provided security for LZ Sally, and served as a ready reaction force), headed southeast toward La Chu. Artillery shells led the way, with each wooded village receiving a heavy dose. Directly behind the artillery barrages came A and C Companies, with the Raiders trudging behind them. [25]

A small wooded hamlet that seemed to float in an ocean of rice paddies received an intense preparatory bombardment, and the lead companies passed through it without incident. Somehow they missed a camouflaged NVA force with snipers hiding up in the trees and soldiers burrowed down in spider holes. As Delta Company approached the hamlet the enemy struck, first hitting A and C Companies from the rear and then the Raiders from the front. Before the fighting ended several hours later, 2-501 absorbed five KIAS and nineteen WIAS, eighteen of them requiring medevacs. Although officially estimated as a reinforced company, Lieutenant Loftin thought the enemy force was much smaller than that, but seemed larger because the NVA fought so skillfully from carefully selected positions. [26]

The Raiders were simultaneously lucky and unlucky, lucky because they suffered only one of the twenty-four casualties but unlucky because that one was Captain Mac.

As the company's scouts entered the woods McMenamy and his small command group were still walking across a paddy. Suddenly the enemy opened up on A and C Companies, and in moments the battalion commander was on the radio to McMenamy. A sniper must have been watching intently. McMenamy carried one radio and now huddled with an RTO carrying the Prick-25 set to the battalion net. This had to be someone important! Just as Captain Mac began talking to Lieutenant Colonel Tallman a bullet ripped through his knee, knocking him flat on his back "like somebody takes a 2 × 4 and hits you." Craig Sturges killed that sniper. Having just entered the tree line, he heard the shot almost directly overhead, saw Mac go down, and then emptied a full M-16 clip into the tree. Tied into the branches, the sniper and his rifle only fell about three feet. Shocked to see that the "soldier" was about fourteen years old, Sturges felt "like I had just shot a kid, not a man." A sergeant pointed out that the kid had a rifle, and the guilt eased.

Soon bullets were flying everywhere. McMenamy began to get up, seeking protection behind a small dike about twenty-five feet away, but bullets kicked up dirt next to his helmet. So he lay there and bandaged his knee, then again tried moving, with the same result. Snipers were pinning him down, waiting for others to come racing to the rescue, but Mac shouted at his men to stay away, to remain in protected positions. Gathering his courage and ignoring the bullets snapping all around, the captain finally reached the dike on his third try.

Fearful that D Company's rifle and machine gun fire was passing through the village into the other two companies, Captain Mac ordered his men to break contact. An RTO dropped his radio, raced out and grabbed Mac, and carried him to safety as the Raiders fell back and called in a medevac.

When the Raiders put their beloved captain on the chopper he turned the company over to Lieutenant Loftin but also informed the battalion commander that Cleo Hogan should assume permanent command. Then the bird arced off, McMenamy its only passenger, strapped to a stretcher, which itself was strapped down. No sooner were they airborne than the pilot, learning of casualties in the other companies, asked his passenger if it would be all right to pick them up. The solicitude was false since the pilot already made up his mind. Within moments McMenamy was again in the battle, this time tied down inside a helicopter.

Battalion chaplain William Erbach, who habitually appeared near the front, carried a wounded man to the medevac. Erbach knew that McMenamy believed he was invincible and had warned him that he was as vulnerable as anybody else. Now the chaplain grinned at the captain, saying, "I told you so!" Feeling utterly helpless as bullets and grenade fragments punctured the helicopter, Captain Mac panicked but "couldn't get the damn straps off the litter. I would have dragged myself outside the helicopter." Fortuitously he glanced at the pilot, though he could only see the back of his helmet, which was bouncing up and down to the idling chopper's rhythm and swiveling from side to side as the pilot surveyed the situation. "All of a sudden it just impressed me that he was so cool sitting under fire. Here he is, like, 'Ah, just another day at the office.'" The panic attack subsided and in moments they were heading for emergency medical treatment at Camp Evans.

Captain Mac was out of the war—but not permanently. Wheelchairbound for a month, graduating to crutches, and finally walking again, he endured such a grueling rehabilitation that by Christmas he passed the physical to go to flight school. Becoming a Cobra pilot, he returned to Vietnam in the early 1970s as commander of an Air Cav Troop in the 1st Cavalry Division and flew 621 combat missions, which included one memorable day when he was shot down three times; by day's end he considered crashing to be just another way of landing.

When McMenamy was medevaced Mike Watson "was scared to death. And I'm sure the other people who knew he'd been wounded were scared to death. We're in major trouble now because Captain Mac's gone. He was a guy we trusted, but who knows what we're getting now."

They need not have worried.

Captain Mac chose his successor wisely.

Kentucky born and raised, Cleo Hogan entered Western Kentucky University intent upon becoming a doctor. During the first two years he had to take physical education courses or ROTC; he chose the latter and discovered he preferred the military to medicine. A Distinguished Military Graduate, he accepted a Regular Army commission as a 2nd Lieutenant, completed airborne training at Fort Benning, and finished number two in his Ranger

School class. Assigned to the 101st Airborne at Fort Campbell, he saw riot duty in Detroit and joined Delta Company as xo the day before the unit left for Vietnam, making him the last of the Original Raiders. He remained as the xo until February 10 when he went to the Headquarters Company.[27]

Cleo was doubly surprised the morning of February 20 to learn he was taking command of D Company. Not only had he commanded the Headquarters Company for only nine days but also he was a lieutenant while company command was a captain's slot. Nonetheless within an hour he arrived in a rice paddy almost four miles north of Hue where Lieutenant Colonel Tallman met him, explaining that "The past few days D Company has taken it on the chin and I thought you could help to pull them together since you had been with them at Cu Chi." Tallman also emphasized that the assignment was temporary "until a captain comes in, then you go back to Headquarters Company."

Three weeks later Tallman brought a new captain out to the Raiders, sending Hogan back to LZ Sally where Colonel Cushman saw him alight from the helicopter. The brigade commander asked him what he was doing in the rear. Informed that Tallman had reassigned him to the Headquarters Company, Cushman "became raving mad," ordered Cleo to return to the Raiders immediately, and then followed him out to the field. None too politely he informed Tallman that Cleo was the company commander even if he was only a lieutenant. The battalion and brigade commanders exchanged harsh words—after all, Tallman was technically correct since he had the authority to appoint his subordinates and a captain should command a company. But Cushman was insistent. The new captain departed. Cleo stayed.

Hogan's three weeks in command had convinced Cushman and the Raiders that though deficient in rank, he was an exceptional leader. Although not as openly aggressive or overtly charismatic as Captain Mac, he was conscientious, professional in demeanor, tactically sound, not inclined to rash judgments. According to Fred Aronow, Hogan "was the right guy for us at the right time, just like Chuck McMenamy was the right guy for us at the time the unit was born." [28]

"It didn't take Hogan long to really gain the men's confidence," recalled Mike Watson. "We weren't scared long." [29]

It may be that the only place Joe Hooper was really at peace was at war.

Genuine war lovers, natural warriors who thrive in war's climate of danger, hardship, chance, and uncertainty, are rare. A World War II study suggested that 2 percent of combat soldiers were predisposed to be "aggressive psychopathic personalities," that is, men who were comfortable in combat, who found a sense of personal freedom there, a liberation of the soul they never enjoyed in the responsible world of rules and bureaucracy, suburban homes and rush hour traffic, wives and children.[30] Unencumbered by a pretentious patriotism or ideology and ever-ready to tempt fate, these few men never reacted like ordinary mortals to battle's frightening din, chaos, and suffering. In novelist John M. Del Vecchio's *The 13th Valley*, the 101st Airborne's Sergeant Daniel Egan represented such a soldier. "War. It's wonderful," he marveled. "It don't make a gnat's ass difference who the enemy is. Every man, once in his life, should go to WAR. . . . Beautiful WAR."[31]

Egan-esque soldiers such as Joe Hooper were trouble in the peacetime army, invaluable in war. "There are parade ground soldiers," said Fred Aronow, "and then there's the guys you want to saddle up and go to war with, and they're not always the same guys."[32] Joe was no parade ground soldier. He could not endure the peacetime Army's banalities, its inspections and work details, its deadening routine and silly rituals.

But war, that was his element.

Being in the field energized him, as everyone who served with Joe recognized.

Cleo Hogan: "When a battle was going on, he wanted to be there. He loved it. . . . Hooper just thrived on shooting at the enemy, being shot at, moving from one place to another, helping this guy, helping do this, and loved it. Every minute of it."[33]

Richard Ryan: "We're here in a goddamn country that we don't know anything about, we've never been there, and we're kind of just muddling our way through and hope to get the hell out of there alive. But it seemed like with Hooper that he was really born and raised there, that this was his niche. I think war was his niche. . . . Truthfully, I think he loved it. There's no doubt in my mind he loved it. You could tell. He's there like a kid in a candy store. . . . I always thought he was a little touched anyway, because he enjoyed war. There was something that wasn't natural about him."[34]

Richard Buzzini: "Wartime was his time to shine, that was his forte. I think he actually liked it a lot. He was very good at it. . . . I think Hooper thrived on that environment. He was in his element when he was in war. . . .

He enjoyed himself in Vietnam. That was his command performance. Leadership under those kinds of stressful situations was his forte."[35]

Noah Rockel: "Joe was a leader. He really was a leader. He just knew what to do, and was kind of a take-charge type person. To me he was gung-ho. He liked what he did."[36]

Aronow: Hooper was "the finest field soldier I've ever met."[37]

Joe was so at ease in a combat environment that it surprised some of those who knew him that he served only two tours or that he did not become a mercenary.[38]

Why was he so good at war?

Splendid woodcraft skills and a "kind of a sixth sense about fighting," as fellow Medal of Honor recipient Patrick Brady phrased it, were important.[39] That sixth sense included acute senses of smell, sight, and hearing. Hooper claimed he could smell the enemy, which was probably true; the vc/nva ate a lot of fish and *nuoc mam,* a pungent sauce made from rotten fish that left campsites and trails reeking, so a sensitive nose discerned enemy soldiers in the vicinity. He was also "a very keen-eyed person at night," claimed Platoon Sergeant George Parker. "He had eyes like a cat. He could see at night." Joe bragged about his hearing, how he could hear the smallest twig snap, and about how he remained perfectly still for long periods, listening.[40] His superior ability to smell, see, and hear, and to remain as still as a marble statue made Hooper especially valuable on night ambushes.

Wiry and strong, Joe was also tireless. Active campaigning never exhausted him the way it did other men. Hooper's energy astounded Craig Sturges. When the Raiders were at a base camp Joe partied "basically with an anger, because he never stopped. Never stopped partying, never stopped fighting, never stopped being angry, always on the move. I can honestly tell you I don't think I ever saw him sleep." Unsurprisingly, when 1st Platoon was guarding the An Lo Bridge, while other soldiers rested Hooper set up trip-wires and explosives along the perimeter each night.[41]

Like Audie Murphy, Joe thought he was lucky, was grateful for it, and talked about his good luck in "self-amazed kind of terms." Others spoke with awe about his incredible luck, about how he had a guardian angel on his shoulder. "The Good Lord had to watch out for him over there," observed Richard Ryan.[42] Luck is an immense consideration in warfare. "No other human activity is so continuously or universally bound up with chance," Clausewitz believed. "And through the element of chance, guesswork and luck come to play a great part in war." Luck, of course, is not just a part of war but also a formidable and ubiquitous aspect of human existence. But luck is not spread evenly across the human race; as one philosopher wrote, "Good luck seems to accompany some people and bad luck to haunt others in more or less systematic ways."[43] Joe was one of the fortunate ones and to insure continuing good luck he doubly propitiated the Good Luck Gods, always carrying the pocket-sized Bible he received from Chaplain Erbach at Fort Campbell and a St. Christopher's medal—strange charms indeed for a nonreligious person.

"First in, first to fight," was Hooper's motto, which encapsulated his aggressiveness, eagerness to close with the enemy, and love of risks. Perhaps a fatalistic attitude liberated him from ordinary concerns. "You can't worry about dying," he told Mark Hawk. "When the time comes, it comes. If you worry about it day in and day out, that's going to affect your performance. Don't worry about it."[44] Because he did not worry about life or limb, many men who served with Hooper (and did worry about life and limb) considered him invaluable. "If you were in a brawl you wanted to be with him," said James Kearns. "If you had to fight, you'd like to be with Hooper." According to Craig Sturges, there was something "electric about him." Joe "went out of his way to find the action, and I never saw him back down from any of it." Most importantly, "he always had the upper hand." Joe just did "crazy things," said Lieutenant Aronow. "Crazy only in the sense that they were extremely audacious. And he always seemed to know when he could get away with it."[45]

Aggressiveness melds into courage. People considered aggressive are often those "who simply do not scare easily or who seem to thrill to fear or who just get mad as hell or who just don't give a damn."[46] Individuals such as Joe Hooper often seemed fearless. "I swore up and down this guy was nuts," recalled Bobby Rakestraw. "He wasn't afraid of anybody. *Nobody* on this earth, or any other earth, he wasn't afraid of them. The man was afraid of nothing." Wayne "Bear" Anderson, who served with Hooper during his second tour, thought he "was fearless. He had to have a screw loose."[47]

One other thing helped Hooper in soldiering. He had a high tolerance for pain, which perhaps facilitated his aggressive, seemingly fearless approach to combat. Being courageous might be easier if getting injured does not hurt much.

Summing up the prevalent attitude, Medic Brian Oak stated that "I never knew a braver man." Or as Richard Ryan put it, Hooper "was a John Wayne kind of guy."[48]

How does God differentiate between cowards and heroes?

That was what Civil War veteran Robert J. Burdette asked in "The Coward," a chapter in his memoirs. Based on his extensive combat experience, Burdette agonized over questions having no easy answer because "courage" can be enigmatic and malleable.

One of Burdette's fellow soldiers repeatedly ran away from combat but whenever the next battle occurred he moved forward with his unit, intent on performing courageously, only to flee once again in terror. Was this man a coward because he fled? Or was he courageous because he kept trying despite the demons that made him quail in the face of danger and the personal disgrace he experienced as he sped from the fighting?[49]

Other questions concerning courage are equally difficult to answer. Was Audie Murphy courageous? In the sense of doing incredible battlefield deeds, of exhibiting physical courage, the answer was obviously yes. But Murphy admitted he was deficient in moral courage. Sometimes he refused to act sensibly because "I lack[ed] the guts to take being thought a coward." He was so fearful of cowardice, of being shamed, that he did "brave" things. Vietnam veteran and novelist Tim O'Brien knew he went to war only "because I was embarrassed not to"; not going meant shame for himself, his family and friends.[50] Acting bravely because an individual feared disgrace or ridicule hardly fulfilled the heroic image of valor; Aristotle thought shame-inspired courage was far less commendable than pure courage, of being courageous because it was a wonderful thing to do. On the other hand it took guts for a man to reject society's pressure to conform, to say, "No, I will not go to Vietnam. Consider me a coward, call me a sissy and a faggot. Send me to federal prison. But I will not go." Here you had a fearless coward. Perhaps more men would have been "cowardly" if they had had more courage.

What distinguishes courage from rashness, madness, stupidity, and a host of other less desirable traits? Does passionate impulsiveness count, or must courage be cold, calculating, deliberate, dispassionate? His fellow soldiers often said Hooper was nuts, that he had a screw loose. Joe was certainly not crazy, but what if someone on the edge of insanity performed heroic deeds. Was he loony or courageous? Where was the dividing line between courage and what Vietnam combat vets called "John Wayne fever," that is, a bout of stupidity?[51] If a dim-witted (or iron-willed) individual did not perceive the danger realistically, were his actions valorous? "There's a hell of a difference between courage and bravery and foolhardiness and stupidity and that difference is no fine line," Aronow wrote his wife.[52] Perhaps, but the lieutenant did not indicate where to draw the dividing line.

Was courage always gloriously assertive—single combat in the Homeric mode, the gallant charge, the grand gesture in the nature of Pickett's Charge—or could it be endurance and fortitude, simply doing one's duty? General Dwight D. Eisenhower, for example, considered "real heroism" to be nothing more than "the uncomplaining acceptance of unendurable conditions." "I could say every man in the Raiders was a hero," said Raider Grady Towns. "Every man in that company performed his duty."[53] Can something as mundane as not complaining be heroic? Is every soldier who does his duty equally courageous?

What about a person who quivered uncontrollably at the prospect of offensive operations, but fought furiously on defense? Coward, hero, or both?

Were courage and character synonymous? Was courage a character trait, like being an introvert or extrovert? Before the twentieth century the formula was simple: character = bravery. Men of upstanding character, embodying virtuous self-discipline, made a conscious choice to act courageously. A deficiency in courage indicated a fundamental character flaw; cowards lacked character. Some modern observers suggested a different model, one indicating that every man, no matter how sound his character or how self-controlled, had a breaking point because courage was an exhaustible resource. A man's courage, like his bank account, was expendable. He might be very courageous one week, acceptably courageous the next, then marginally so, and finally, his account depleted, a coward. Thus the same individual exhibited courage and cowardice.

Does weaponry affect the definition of courage? In an era of short-range, man-powered weapons such as spears, swords, and arrows, unrestrained aggressiveness made sense. Similar "courageous" behavior against chemical-energy weapons such as machine guns, artillery, and tanks, was all too often not bravery but suicide.[54]

Although most questions about courage resist definitive answers—as Joe once said, "It's hard to define bravery, courage, valor"[55]—two things seem certain.

In American culture courage and manhood were inseparable. Proving one's courage by surmounting physical danger and hardship was a rite of passage for males. As one Vietnam veteran put it, he feared society's censure if he did not go to war, feared weakness, and feared "that to avoid war is to avoid manhood." Another vet "wanted to prove to myself that I was a brave man. . . . No matter what happened out there, I thought to myself, I could never retreat. I had to be courageous." [56] Boys both longed for and dreaded the combat test, being eager to prove they were tough and manly but also anxious that they might fail the test, revealing themselves as unmanly, soft, womanish. Research indicated soldiers entering combat for the first time worried more about acting disgracefully than they did about death or maiming; however, after their initial exposure to battle they feared death and mutilation more and being a coward less. [57]

The compulsion not to display cowardice was especially imperative in the presence of a soldier's buddies. One of the most compelling answers as to why men fought so willingly was comradeship. [58] Ideology, patriotism, training, leadership, even personal character exerted some influence, but they were husks concealing the meaty kernel of comradeship, that special bonding among young soldiers intent on proving their manhood, each one determined to obtain and retain the respect of the others. A platoon leader recalled one of his soldiers who was scared of being killed, but "was more scared of letting his friends down than of getting hurt." When this soldier was KIA the platoon leader asked, "What could I say? That he was brave because he was afraid to be afraid?" [59] Yes. And that was true for many boys who died trying to display their manhood.

Male camaraderie in combat units was intense, accidental, fragile, and at times emotionally draining. "Vietnam," wrote Raider Paul Grelle, "can best be described as 'lack of.' The lack of sleep, the lack of clean cloths and lack of water and food. However, the one thing that was never lacking was the 'bonding' between grunts." Another Raider, Dave Gray, recalled the furious monsoons, the leeches, and the onerous humping in the boonies, but would happily "do it again, just to be with such good warriors." And Captain Mac never recalled "anyone seriously wounded or dying saying, in essence, in their last words 'God bless America.' The final words before being medevaced, or dying, always expressed concern for their fellow Raider, and the unit as a whole." [60]

The intense bonding occurred even though a soldier had no influence over whom higher authority assigned to his squad, platoon, or company, so his buddies were accidental, with no common heritage. Nonetheless these accidental "brothers," sharing a quest for mutual survival, created a brotherhood, a family with its siblings knitted together as tightly as the Hatfields or the McCoys. Capturing the family-like atmosphere that prevailed in his squad, Joe Hooper wrote his parents thanking them for a package of food, adding that "It dint last long, because we share everthing we get but It filled us up for one night and really tasted good after C Rations." The day Raider Ray Blackman went to the field he "was instantly taken to a very primitive state of mind. The only thing that mattered at all was the ground I was standing on and those standing there with me. It was the basic tribal instinct of survival." [61] He did not yet know a single soldier standing there with him, but the combat environment automatically made them his tribe.

However, as Chaplain Erbach recognized, the combat family was often short-lived, "broken up by bullets, by booby traps, by rotation." When someone in the family died, a soldier felt the loss acutely. "You feel it more, you'll remember it more than anything else that might happen in your life," according to Captain Mac. [62] At the same time, a soldier developed a callused attitude toward anyone outside his small brotherhood. When the Germans killed Audie Murphy's best friend he did not care if the next hill was corpse-strewn as "long as I do not have to turn over the bodies and find the . . . face of a friend." Hooper shared Murphy's attitude. As his first tour ended he wrote that he would "miss my buddies. When the new guys get it, it dosent quite bother me as much but when one of my guys who I came over with gets killed, it really hurts. Lost one of my best buddies the other day. His dying words, were tell Hoop to hang in there and give him my pistol. Well enough of that befere [sic] I get carried away." [63] The last thoughts of Hooper's buddy (Sergeant John B. Gingery) were not for his country or parents, but for his pal. And Hooper did not want to show emotion, to reveal weakness, by explaining how devastating the sergeant's death was.

Considering the brotherhood's battlefield intensity, the bonds could be surprisingly transient. Grief for a dead comrade was often excruciating. But the sorrowing could not last long because wartime demands left little time for grieving; all too soon another comrade was dead, if not tomorrow then the next day. Despite rosy postwar reminiscences about the allures of comradeship, soldiers often engaged in "ghosting" (staying in a rear area longer than necessary), or rejoiced about getting out of the bush and into some safe rear area position, "deserting" their brothers in pursuit of personal well-being. Moreover, many wartime buddies, very different in personality and interests, would not have been pals in peacetime and when they returned home the once-inseparable friendships quickly withered away. Joe Hooper, for example, made no effort to maintain contact with the men he met during either of his tours.

The second certainty about courage was that at its core it involved *fear,* "the fear of violent death, pain, and mutilation, the fear of being killed and at times, too, the fear of having to kill." [64] A courageous soldier must recognize danger and risks, and then overcome his fear. Although others considered Audie Murphy and Hooper fearless, these were external perceptions; what they indicated was that both men acted *as if* they were fearless. For themselves, they admitted fear. "Fear is moving up with us," Murphy acknowledged in his autobiography. "It always does. . . . I am well acquainted with fear. It strikes first in the stomach like the disemboweling hand that is thrust into the carcass of a chicken." Sitting around a campfire one night, Chris Luther asked Hooper how he felt during his Medal of Honor action. "Well, I was scared to death." One way or another the courageous person overcame or managed fear. "I just felt comfortable knowing this guy had fear like everybody else but knew how to control it," commented Luther. "That really is the mark of a great soldier regardless of your rank. He could just control fear. Even if he was scared to death you would never know it." [65] The key was not denying fear, but to function even when in its grip.

"Anybody who says they aren't scared is a goddamn liar!" Steve Hawk insisted.[66] And correctly so since fear is instinctual. Because all animals need to escape from danger to survive, the brain has a mechanism to detect danger that compels the body to respond to a threat quickly and automatically. In humans this watchdog mechanism is the amygdala, an almond-sized structure buried deep in the brain.[67]

The amygdala is part of the limbic system, a ring of structures encircling the brainstem and forming the border between it and the cerebral hemispheres, that is, between the brain's primitive and "intellectual" levels.[68] Evolutionarily ancient, the brainstem controls basic physiological functions such as heartbeat and respiration. Covered with the cerebral cortex and incorporating the most recent evolutionary brain tissue, the cerebral hemispheres are where "thinking" occurs. Emotions and reason (or thought) meet in the limbic system.

The "hub in the wheel of fear," the amygdala receives inputs from two sources, one quick and crude the other slower but more refined. A stimulus such as the sight of a snake speeds directly to the amygdala from the sensory thalamus by leaping across a single synapse, but also reaches the amygdala indirectly via the cortex, a route that is slower because it involves multiple links. The short, fast thalamic pathway cannot make fine distinctions— was it a snake or just a stick?—but screams "Snake!" and ignites the body's responses to potential danger before the slow, indirect route differentiates between a snake and a stick.

Fear is involuntary. Because the amygdala operates outside of consciousness, an individual is afraid before he or she knows it. Fear and the body's reaction to danger comes first, the recognition that you are afraid arrives later. This system is quite sensible. When survival is at stake, reacting to a potentially dangerous stimulus even if it turned out to be innocuous is better than not responding. Reacting inappropriately to a stick by leaping away is wiser than not responding to a rattlesnake.

The amygdala is akin to a police communications center that can simultaneously send urgent messages to many locations. The operator (amygdala) scans incoming sensory signals, searching for trouble signs, constantly asking, "Is this something that can cause harm?" When the answer is "Yes!" the amygdala, in conjunction with the hypothalamus and several other brain structures, dispatches crisis signals throughout the brain and body.

One set of signals arouses the autonomic nervous system, consisting of the sympathetic and parasympathetic branches, which are antagonistic to each other. The former directs activities that involve expending energy, preparing the body to meet danger, while the latter controls quiet activities such as digestion. They operate much like a water faucet. Under normal conditions the two branches remain in balance, the water being lukewarm because the hot (sympathetic) and cold (parasympathetic) taps are running equally. But when one runs wide open and the other is closed, the water is hot or cold. That is why soldiers often feel utterly drained after a battle, to the point of being psychologically and physiologically incapacitated. In reaction to the body's previous total arousal for combat via the wide open hot water tap, which is now closing down, the parasympathetic backlash has the cold water running at full force.[69] It often takes considerable time before the two taps are again in balance.

When the brain urgently summons the sympathetic nervous system to action, the body undertakes a number of unconscious, spontaneous activities: the heartbeat speeds up; blood pressure rises; the bronchial passageways dilate so that more air can reach the lungs more quickly; all unnecessary body movements freeze at least temporarily, but often for extended periods (since many predators respond to movement, freezing is often the best thing to do when danger is near); nonessential functions such as bladder and sphincter control shut down, which is why many soldiers soil themselves by involuntarily urinating or defecating; the liver secretes glucose for a quick energy supply; profuse sweating reduces elevated body temperatures; eye pupils dilate for better vision; and the adrenal glands release a flood of the hormones adrenaline, which generates an enormous pulse of energy, and nonadrenaline, which makes the senses even more alert, setting the brain on edge and permitting a more rapid response to danger.

Other alert signals unleash endorphins, which are the brain's natural painkillers and act much like morphine or opium. Because of their opiate-like qualities they deaden sensitivity to pain, which is helpful since the probability of injury is great in a dangerous situation; being undistracted or undeterred by pain helps insure survival. Also, a cascade of dopamine, the brain's natural thrill-seeking and pleasure drug—it creates pleasurable sensations—results from the warning messages.

Without any conscious thought, then, the body prepared itself to confront a fearful situation.

Exactly how a person manifests his or her fear is determined in part by "display rules," which are the conventions, norms, and habits people develop to manage their emotions, and which can vary not only among individuals but also across cultures. But the amygdala is capable of executing an "emotional hijacking," impulsively overwhelming the rational brain so completely that a person does not know what he or she is doing, becoming delirious with rage or fear, unable to hear, speak, or think clearly. An emotional hijacking can be so powerful that the heart rate jumps thirty beats per minute within a single heartbeat! Emotions dominate rationality because the direct route from the sensory thalamus is far stronger than the indirect route through the sensory cortex. Once the body begins cruising on emotional autopilot, gaining rational control by consciously deactivating the amygdala is extremely difficult.[70]

When confronted with danger one soldier might fight back, another may try to hide by freezing, and still a third will flee. Whether fighting, freezing, or fleeing, each response was natural, instinctive. Influenced by surging brain chemicals and perhaps gripped by an overpowering emotional reaction seated in the amygdala, quite possibly none of the men was thinking or consciously chose which protective method to employ. All three actions were responses to the same stimulus, and each could potentially achieve the goal of reducing fear.

Neurobiology may trump character, determining who was a "coward" and who was a "hero." As twice-wounded Vietnam veteran and Hollywood director Oliver Stone understood, "Cowardice and heroism are the same emotion—fear—expressed differently."[71]

Not a physical, but a *neurobiological* profile may explain much of a soldier's behavior.

Different people confronting the same stressful environment do not react the same way since no two brains have the same neural circuits, chemical soup, or genetic composition. A soldier's genome, for instance, predisposes him to act in certain ways because basic temperament is genetically determined. An eminent developmental psychologist, Jerome Kagaan, identified four basic temperaments—bold, timid, upbeat, melancholy—each dependent upon differences in the brain's neural circuitry. Timid, dour adults were born timid, dour infants; bold, ebullient adults were bold, ebullient children.[72]

Genes, of course, are not destiny; an individual is not the absolute prisoner of his or her genes. They are important, but so is the environment—that is, who and what an individual is derives from the interplay between genetics and life experiences, ranging from exercise, sleep, and diet to goal-setting. Nonetheless, genetic heritage influences an individual to be adept at some tasks, inept at others; it predisposes some men and women to be "courageous," to not scare easily, and others to be "cowardly." Thrill-seekers, who often seem courageous, have a longer version of the D4DR "thrill-seeking" gene than do reflective, mild-mannered personalities. This gene facilitates the brain's absorption of dopamine. Another gene, the so-called anxiety gene, affects the absorption of serotonin, a neurotransmitter that inhibits aggressive behavior.[73]

And the pain gene, called the mu (μ) opiate receptor gene, influences an individual's perception of pain by determining how many mu opiate receptors he or she has. Mu receptors absorb the endorphins that diminish pain. If an individual has few receptors and therefore cannot absorb sufficient endorphins, even a small wound can be excruciating. In short, in large part pain is a genetically regulated problem, with some people being innately and acutely sensitive to it and others much less so.[74]

What was Joe Hooper's profile? The answer must be speculative and incomplete at best, but he was certainly born with a bold temperament and probably with more than ample testosterone since high levels foster aggressive, excessive, impatient, and often antisocial behavior.[75] He undoubtedly had the longer version of the D4DR gene and a plentiful dopamine supply, thereby enhancing his sensation-seeking and risk-taking. And he must have been blessed with an active mu opiate receptor gene and with endorphins spewing from his synaptic vesicles, making him unusually oblivious to pain. He also probably had a low serotonin level so that little or nothing dampened his aggressiveness. It may also be that he excreted large amounts of 17-OHCS (cortisol), an adrenal steroid released in response to a stressful environment. Individuals with high cortisol levels are predisposed to handle stress effectively; they are consistently successful competitors, perceive their situation in a way that minimizes danger, and feel invulnerable and omnipotent.[76]

Finally, Joe's adrenal glands probably gushed adrenaline in abnormally high amounts. He told his sister Audrey about the "rush" he got before going into battle, about how he could *hear* the adrenaline roaring in his bloodstream, about how clear everything was and how focused he became when the fighting began, about how nothing in the world compared to the exhilaration and euphoria of combat. He may well have been an adrenaline junkie, addicted to the rush. As he once said, he could not help himself, he just got "high" during a fight.[77]

Exactly what Hooper meant by getting "high" remains unknown but it might have involved a trancelike state, an out-of-body experience induced by adrenaline, dopamine, endorphins, and other body chemicals, in which a soldier perceives himself both as an actor and a spectator in an unfolding drama. A Civil War soldier perhaps best described this phenomenon: "Amid the roar and din of musketry and the horrible swish and shriek of shells, the intellect seemed to be disembodied, and, while conscious of the danger of being hurled headlong into eternity at any moment, the pressure upon the brain seemed to deaden the physical senses—fear among them," wrote Lewis M. Hosea of the 16th United States Infantry. "Fear came later when the fight was over, just as in the waiting moments before it began; but throughout the day while the battle was on I remember having a singular feeling of curiosity about personal experiences. I seemed to be looking down upon my bodily self with a sense of impersonality and wondering why I was not afraid in the midst of all this horrible uproar and danger."[78]

Whatever sensations the "high" encompassed, like a drug addict Hooper was always searching for the next one. When the action slowed he became "a little down in the dumps." But "As long as we are on the move and fighting things aren't so bad."[79]

He would be on the move soon, to the biggest battle of his life.

Eight

The next thing I knew they were
patting me on the back and calling me a hero.

*Joe, telling another soldier that he
did not remember much about his Medal of Honor battle*

*The President of the United States of America, authorized by Act of
Congress, March 3, 1863, has awarded in the name of The Congress
the Medal of Honor to*

STAFF SERGEANT JOE R. HOOPER, UNITED STATES ARMY

*for conspicuous gallantry and intrepidity in action at the risk of his
life above and beyond the call of duty:*

*Staff Sergeant (then Sergeant) Joe R. Hooper, United States
Army, distinguished himself by conspicuous gallantry and intrepidity on 21 February 1968, while serving as squad leader with Company D, 2nd Battalion (Airborne), 501st Infantry, 101st Airborne
Division, near Hue, Republic of Vietnam. Company D was assaulting a heavily defended enemy position along a river bank when
it encountered a withering hail of fire from rockets, machine guns
and automatic weapons. Staff Sergeant Hooper rallied several men
and stormed across the river, overrunning several bunkers on the
opposite shore. Thus inspired, the rest of the company moved to
the attack. With utter disregard for his own safety, he moved out
under the intense fire again and pulled back the wounded, moving
them to safety. During this act Staff Sergeant Hooper was seriously
wounded, but he refused medical aid and returned to his men. With
the relentless enemy fire disrupting the attack, he singlehandedly
stormed three enemy bunkers, destroying them with hand grenades
and rifle fire, and shot two enemy soldiers who had attacked and
wounded the chaplain. Leading his men forward in a sweep of the
area, Staff Sergeant Hooper destroyed three buildings housing enemy riflemen. At this point he was attacked by a North Vietnamese*

officer whom he fatally wounded with his bayonet. Finding his men under heavy fire from a house to the front, he proceeded alone to the building, killing its occupants with rifle fire and grenades. By now his initial body wound had been compounded by grenade fragments, yet despite the multiple wounds and loss of blood, he continued to lead his men against the intense enemy fire. As his squad reached the final line of enemy resistance, it received devastating fire from four bunkers in line on its left flank. Staff Sergeant Hooper gathered several hand grenades and raced down a small trench which ran the length of the bunker line, tossing grenades into each bunker as he passed by, killing all but two of the occupants. With these positions destroyed, he concentrated on the last bunkers facing his men, destroying the first with an incendiary grenade and neutralizing two more by rifle fire. He then raced across an open field, still under enemy fire, to rescue a wounded man who was trapped in a trench. Upon reaching the man, he was faced by an armed enemy soldier whom he killed with a pistol. Moving his comrade to safety and returning to his men, he neutralized the final pocket of enemy resistance by fatally wounding three North Vietnamese officers with rifle fire. Staff Sergeant Hooper then established a final line and reorganized his men, not accepting treatment until this was accomplished and not consenting to evacuation until the following morning. His supreme valor, inspiring leadership and heroic self-sacrifice were directly responsible for the company's success and provided a lasting example in personal courage for every man on the field. Staff Sergeant Hooper's actions were in keeping with the highest traditions of the military service and reflect great credit upon himself and the United States Army.

Thus read Joe's Medal of Honor citation.

It was based on eight eyewitness accounts, which contained many additional details about Joe's heroics; a postbattle study of the battlefield's terrain and enemy defenses; and a set of maps depicting Hooper's movements during the fighting.

America's first "medal" for bravery was a purple cloth patch, heart-shaped with a lace fringe or binding. General George Washington created it in

August 1782, to inspire "virtuous ambition" and "unusual gallantry" among his soldiers. Wanting the "road to glory in a patriot army and a free country" to be open to all regardless of their social and economic standing, officers and enlisted men alike qualified for the award. But before granting the medal General Washington demanded documentation attesting to the individual's heroic performance.[1] Since the Revolution ended the next year, only three men received the "Purple Heart" before it went out of existence.

A complex system of military awards and decorations evolved from the Revolution's simple cloth swath.[2] Not until the Mexican War, when Congress created a Certificate of Merit, did the country have another method of distinguishing courageous service, this time with a special document and an extra $2 per month salary. But like the Purple Heart, the Certificate of Merit lasted only for the war's duration.

Early in the Civil War Congress created a Navy Medal of Honor (MOH) to reward sailors who "most distinguish themselves by their gallantry in action and other seamanlike qualities during the present war." Commissioned officers were ineligible on the assumption that they were honored for heroic displays by being promoted. An almost identical Army MOH soon followed. In 1863 Congress awarded the first MOHS, established the medal as a permanent decoration rather than being limited to the current war, and made officers eligible to receive it. Although the MOH rapidly acquired a special mystique, abuses abounded because no explicit criteria indicated what actions qualified for the award. President Abraham Lincoln distributed some MOHS with so little gravitas that they seemed like tokens or souvenirs. For example, he authorized the medal for all 864 members of the 27th Maine Regiment for simply reenlisting.

Concern over ongoing abuses prompted the government to reform the system. In 1904 Congress mandated official documentation describing the valorous deed before an MOH could be awarded. The next year President Theodore Roosevelt insured that considerable pomp accompanied an MOH presentation. Until then bestowing the medal was often an informal procedure—in some cases officials sent MOHS by registered mail and if the recipient was not home the medal ended back at the War or Navy Department. To transform receiving an MOH into a memorable occasion, Roosevelt decreed that the award "will always be made with formal and impressive ceremonial" and that whenever possible the president (or his designated representative) would make the presentation.

As the MOH acquired more dignity, a desire to correct previous abuses prompted formation of a special review board. Meeting in 1916 the board studied all 2,625 MOHs awarded up to that time, rescinding 910 of them (including those of the 27th Maine). It also recommended creating additional medals to reward different levels of courage, reserving the MOH for the bravest of the brave.

Landmark legislation in 1918 was the genesis for the "Pyramid of Honor," a hierarchy of decorations for heroism and meritorious service. At the pinnacle stood the MOH, which conferred special benefits on the recipient: if space was available, he received free military transportation; he also received a modest monthly stipend (initially only $10 but raised to $100 in 1961 and to $200 in 1978); and if otherwise qualified a recipient's children were automatically admitted to a service academy without regard to regional quotas. Below the MOH in descending order were newly created decorations: the Distinguished Service Cross (DSC) for bravery slightly below the level meriting an MOH; the Distinguished Service Medal for particularly meritorious service; and a Silver Star Citation, which became the Silver Star Medal in 1932. That same year Congress also revived the Purple Heart, which became the pyramid's base; any member of the armed forces killed or wounded in action received it.

The new Silver Star and resurrected Purple Heart reflected the post–World War I trend, which was to create more medals and to bestow awards more liberally. Congress added an array of decorations to the pyramid between the Silver Star and the Purple Heart, including the Distinguished Flying Cross (1926), Bronze Star Medal (1944), and Army Commendation Medal (1945, retroactive to 1941). Within this medal hierarchy, the most important ones were the top three for heroism, which the Army defined as "Specific acts of bravery or outstanding courage, or a closely related series of heroic acts performed within a short period of time."[3] These were the Silver Star, the DSC, and especially the MOH.[4]

During World War I the Army and Navy granted comparatively few medals, and presented them so slowly and reluctantly that the high command seemed mean-spirited. Determined to rectify that mistake, the services awarded medals more generously and quickly during World War II. Some generals even carried Silver Stars in their pockets to decorate men in the field within an hour or so after they performed heroic feats.[5] By Vietnam such "impact awards" were routine—perhaps too routine; as Colonel

Cushman noted, the practice of making impact awards could "perhaps lead to abuses, but I know of none in the 101st Airborne Division."[6] He must not have looked very hard. Especially after 1968 when the armed forces were trying to sustain morale in a lost war, officers conferred medals with such little discrimination that troops derisively called them "gongs," mere baubles or trinkets.

A potential problem with impact awards, whether deserved or not, was that officers presented them before anyone collected eyewitness statements or wrote the citations. If a staff officer did not file the requisite paperwork retroactively, no record of the award existed in a soldier's personnel file. And staff officers were sometimes too lazy, too forgetful, or too overwhelmed by events to do the paperwork. Raider Dale Urban, for example, received a Bronze Star with V device (that is, for valor rather than meritorious service) as an impact award in April 1968, but his official records contain no mention of it.[7]

Combat troops often viewed medals for courage cynically, even contemptuously. By institutionalizing valor, medals exploited their bravery, encouraging heroic displays, often at the cost of life and limb. By publicly recognizing and rewarding an individual's heroic acts, the high command hoped others would emulate him, thereby cloning courage.[8] "Awards and decorations," said Army Regulation Number 672-1, "are an effective means of fostering high morale, incentive, esprit de corps, and a sense of accomplishment through public recognition of heroism, achievement, or meritorious service."[9] From the Army's perspective, a medal-draped hero such as Audie Murphy was a model of approved behavior, a representative of the organization's most cherished values; the goal was to have an Army of Audie Murphy-like replicas. One of the 101st Airborne's commanding generals insisted that his aggressive awards program "provided the impetus" for the unit's high performance level.[10] Recounting the heroism of several fellow Raiders, Roy Barber said, "this is what I'm supposed to be like . . . this is what is expected of me."[11]

The armed forces realized that medal granting not only encouraged battlefield heroics but also sustained home front morale, making parents and local communities proud of their boys. "Proud of you for the medals," wrote Dale Urban's father, who was boasting to all his friends and neighbors about his "wonderful brave Son." His parents wanted to know more about a

Bronze Star he recently received "so we can tell about it OK." Another grunt even envisioned the hometown newspaper's story announcing his bravery: "A Chicago-area Marine has been awarded a Silver Star in Vietnam, it was announced today." [12]

Grunts also viewed medals with suspicion because they did not have to serve at the front very long before they realized that *everyone* up there deserved them. But determining who actually received medals seemed akin to a lottery with only a handful holding the winning number. World War II Marine James W. Johnston, who saw more than his fair share of fighting, asserted that the awarding of medals for valor was "an unqualified miscarriage of justice and a spurious practice. It implies that men with medals for valor are valorous and men without them are not. Nothing could be further from the truth. . . . Day after day I have watched countless line company Marines and infantry soldiers commit deeds of great courage and sacrifice and receive nothing for their efforts." A careful postwar study confirmed this, asserting that medals undermined rather than sustained morale because too many heroic acts went unrewarded. [13]

Medal awarding remained erratic in Vietnam. Although Army regulations decreed that "it is the responsibility and privilege" of any individual with personal knowledge of a heroic act to submit a medal recommendation, many injustices occurred because no one took the trouble to initiate an award action. Captain McMenamy believed "it's guaranteed that there's a lot more [heroic acts] that aren't recognized than are." Chaplain Erbach agreed, asserting that hundreds of heroic actions went unreported every day. Another Vietnam veteran insisted that for every soldier who received an MOH "there were thousands that did things as equally deserving that never got it." [14] Joe Hooper also understood that medals did not always go to those who deserved them. After the war he told his old Navy buddy Gary Foster that "the real heroes are still over there with their face down in the mud." [15]

As front line soldiers realized, one of the gravest injustices was that officers and rear area personnel routinely acquired the lion's share of medals, which were such important symbols that when professional soldiers met they instantly "read" the decorations on each other's chest. To have an impressive chest officers aggressively pursued medals, especially those for heroism, and sometimes without a great concern for their validity.

During World War II, one rifle company in the 84th Division received about 120 medals, including 100 Purple Hearts and four Silver Stars. However, the fifty-eight officers in Division Headquarters received about four times as many medals; even the division's rear echelon enlisted men garnered twice as many medals as those who did the fighting. The division's MPS and quartermaster troops also outdid the combat soldiers in the medal count. Yet the front line troopers endured several one-hour periods when they suffered more killed and wounded "than the total casualties sustained during the entire war by all of these rear-echelon outfits lumped together, but that was the way it was." [16]

In Vietnam medal-mania continued to afflict the officer corps, which cynically exploited medals. As one soldier wrote, "it's a fact of army life that colonels get the medals and privates clean the latrine." Another grunt concurred, observing that "To a significant number of career officers, their raison d'être for being in Vietnam was to survive their one year tour, gain combat command for their military records, and amass as many medals and commendations as possible." [17]

Some officers received medals even when they did not deserve them, though that sometimes required hyperbole bordering on lying to create worthy citations. Future Chairman of the JCS Colin Powell recalled watching a departing commander receive three Silver Stars and a handful of other medals and thinking that "this is insane" since the officer's performance had not been particularly noteworthy. Powell also realized the wholesale awards granted to officers "diminished the achievements of real heroes—privates or colonels—who had performed extraordinary acts of valor." Like Powell, Lieutenant Colonel Otis Livingston, commander of 2-501 in the early 1970s, believed the high command so over-used decorations that they devalued all medals, even those that were truly deserved.[18]

Writing medal citations was often an act of creative fiction, not fact-telling. One of a unit's most valuable officers was a citation writer, a man with a gilded pen who transformed an inconsequential act into something marvelous. Many times medal granting became a prose competition contest, and woe to those outfits lacking a gifted writer. As a battalion executive officer, former Raider platoon leader John E. Frick had orders from the battalion commander that every one of his company commanders was to have a Silver Star. So Frick always found *something* that at least remotely justified a medal, then dressed it up in the appropriate verbiage adorned with brilliantly composed hyperbole. "You should read some of the masterpieces

I turn out," he wrote his wife. "My knowledge of adjectives and a vivid imagination really comes in handy for writing up awards."[19] Officers sometimes recognized their citations were less than honest. Colonel Cushman, for example, referred to the "typical hyperbole" that garnished his Silver Star citations.[20]

The Silver Star suffered special abuse from the officer corps. "Officers were more likely to get a Silver Star for less action than an enlisted man, no question," said Cleo Hogan. "Officers didn't deserve the Silver Stars as often as they were given them." One officer admitted he received a Silver Star for "an act I did not perform, during an action that occurred *after* I left [the unit]."[21] What saved the MOH and DSC from similar perversion was that they needed more than one eyewitness, which was all a Silver Star required.

High-ranking officers were also concerned that their subordinates and enlisted men get medals, and lots of them. Their reasoning was that if a combat unit did not receive many medals then it must not be aggressive and, therefore, was not contributing to a high body count. This in turn indicated that the commanding officer was not successful. Major General Julian Ewell, commander of the 9th Infantry Division, had a formula: he wanted one medal for heroism issued for every enemy eliminated. The 101st Airborne also stressed the connection between medals and enemy bodies. Next to the body count, Chaplain Erbach noted, nothing "showed the great, grand, and glorious heroism being exhibited by the paratroopers" more than medals.[22]

So commanders ensured that both they and their men had chests worthy of notice. John Frick went home with several medals for bravery, but questioned their validity. Sending one of his Bronze Star citations to his wife, he implored her not to believe a word of it; the allegedly courageous actions it detailed were simply "what's necessary to write to make it sound like I'm a hero. . . . Some time in private I'll tell you in greater detail what really happened and you'll make me give the medal back." Raider Dave Loftin received an Army Commendation Medal for valor, but thought he "received it because I just happened to be in the area. I didn't do anything heroic that day."[23]

All told the armed forces in Vietnam issued more than 1.25 million medals for bravery, which was approximately 1.2 million more than they awarded during the Korean War.[24]

"Look at how many people got a Medal of Honor," said Raider Jodey Gravett, "but yet they're dead."[25]

Gravett had a point. Doing what was necessary to receive an MOH was often fatal.

During World War II Congress awarded 433 MOHS, but 243 of the recipients died and only 190 of them lived to have the medal placed around their neck. In Vietnam receiving an MOH was even more deadly: out of the 238 MOHS, 151 men received it posthumously with only eighty-seven surviving. Looking at just the Army in Vietnam, out its 155 MOH recipients, ninety-seven were posthumous awards and only fifty-eight went to individuals who lived.[26] Soldiers in Hooper's division, the 101st Airborne, received nineteen of the Army's MOHS, eleven of them posthumously.[27] Those who survived their heroic actions were often wounded, sometimes grievously; an unhurt MOH recipient was indeed a rarity.

Hooper was one of the Army's fifty-eight survivors, and the wounds he received on February 21, 1968, were neither crippling nor disfiguring.

At the heart of battle is killing.

And the Delta Raiders were approaching a killing ground as part of the four-battalion drive toward Hue, with Thon La Chu, the doorway to the old imperial capital, the initial target. D-Day for the renewed assault was February 21, 1968.

The advance began with the three battalions from the 1st Air Cavalry Division aiming directly at the village. Positioned on the Air Cav's right flank, 2-501 would pass near an unnamed village just south of La Chu, a couple of dozen houses loosely grouped in a dark green island jutting up from the surrounding paddies (the Raiders called the place La Chu because that was the closest named village). As 2-501 moved forward, C Company was on the left, D Company on the right, A Company was in reserve, and B Company was still guarding LZ Sally. Thus the Delta Raiders were on the operation's right flank. Lieutenant Hogan had ninety-two soldiers—the equivalent of two full-strength platoons; less than a week later the company had only half that many men.[28]

By midmorning on the 21st the Raiders knew that the enemy, which military intelligence indicated was the 90th NVA Regiment, was nearby. They found discarded NVA equipment, passed through a recently occupied bivouac big enough to hold at least 100 men, and discovered two large cooking fires with pots of rice that were still warm. Shortly after 11:00 a.m.

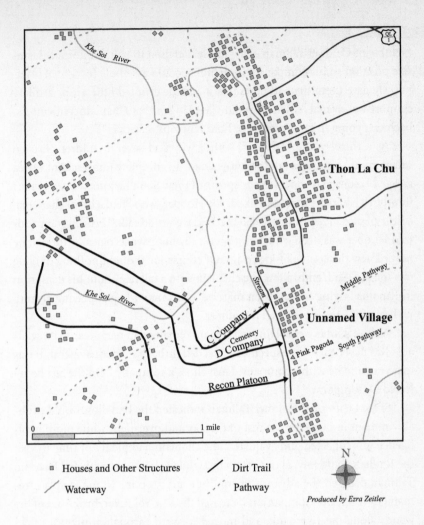

Map 3: Route to the February 21, 1968 Battlefield

Lieutenant Colonel Tallman ordered the battalion to halt and form a defensive position so his company commanders could assemble for a final briefing. He gave them the bad news that if a battle erupted little air or artillery support was available. He also told Cleo Hogan that Chaplain William Erbach was going to D Company to hold religious services.[29]

As a thirty-year-old "softy" with a wife and several children, Erbach called upon "resources I didn't know I had" to complete jump school with a gaggle of teenage troopers in the spring of 1967. Soon he joined 2-501 at Fort Campbell where he met (and liked) Joe Hooper, who "had a bit of charisma, a little pizzazz. He just interested me, and we would talk." Erbach soon realized Hooper was deeply hurt, not physically but psychologically, though he never knew the source of Joe's pain. Of course Joe thought nothing of lying to a man of God, enthralling the chaplain with a tall tale about his demotion in Panama, saying he had been married and a major began playing around with his wife, so he punched the officer.

Although many chaplains in Vietnam remained in rear areas to be available whenever they were specifically needed, Erbach's "modus operandi was to go out and be with a company. I just chose a company." On the 21st he selected D Company.[30]

Since Lieutenant Colonel Tallman indicated the battalion would probably remain in place for the rest of the day and overnight while more intelligence was collected and evaluated, the chaplain had plenty of time to visit the Raiders. Suddenly, about 1:15 p.m., while Erbach was with 3rd Platoon, Tallman ordered the advance to continue at 1:30 p.m. So the chaplain remained with Delta Company as it crossed the Khe Soi River, broke out of the woods along the riverbank, and moved forward through a huge rice field crisscrossed by small dikes and containing an elevated graveyard. Off to their left front was a stream, and beyond it was the unnamed village, with a North Vietnamese flag flying above it. "Oh, shit!" thought Al Mount. "This isn't good when they're that bold, flying the NVA flag."[31]

As the Raiders headed southeast through the stubble of the harvested paddy, 1st Platoon was on the left and 3rd Platoon on the right, with the company headquarters element behind them, followed by 2nd Platoon. Suddenly a soldier in 3rd Platoon fell backwards and began thrashing violently. Thinking the trooper was having an epileptic seizure, Cleo and a medic ran forward.

Instead of a seizure the man had a bullet wound through his left shoulder.

No one heard the shot.

The company halted while Hogan called in a medevac. Lieutenant Colonel Tallman was soon on the radio, urging him to get the Raiders moving again, which he did as soon as the medevac departed. 1st and 3rd Platoons trudged no more than 100 to 150 yards before gunfire erupted from the treeline along the western edge of the unnamed village. It looked like every tree was firing at them. The men sought shelter in the graveyard while Hogan radioed Tallman with the news. When the battalion commander ordered the Raiders to attack, 1st and 3rd Platoons crossed the rice paddy toward the village. 1st Platoon splashed through the stream, scaled the far bank, which was ten or fifteen feet high in places, and disappeared amidst the village's thick foliage. 3rd Platoon almost immediately took shelter along the stream and did not enter the village.[32]

From this point on what the Raiders called the "Battle of La Chu" can be reconstructed only in broad outline.

Everyone remembered vignettes, a few bits and pieces of information, but they were disconnected in time and space. No one presented a coherent, chronologically accurate account of what happened or what any individual did. "Unless you had an overhead camera to watch it develop, it would probably be well nigh impossible from first-hand reports to get an honest picture," Chaplain Erbach explained. "You could get a modicum, you may come close, but. . . . I don't know whether you will *ever* legitimately be able to reconstruct the whole thing."[33]

One problem in reconstructing the battle was that no one saw more than a small part of the battlefield at any one time. With angry metal whirling across the battlefield, few soldiers stuck their heads up to peer around. "I was trying to cover my ass," said Edward J. Petitt Jr., "When those AK-47s start firing over your head, you try to get down low . . . you're down there kissing the ground . . . you get as low as an ant."[34] Even if a man did momentarily look around he did not see much. The day was gloomy because of the crachin, and the low clouds and fog created a foreboding darkness even at midday. Further restricting an individual's vision was the smoke from buildings that were soon ablaze and, as Joe Hooper's MOH file emphasized, the dense vegetation. In a sense the Raiders fought blindly, often unable to see more than twenty or thirty feet and moving and shooting as much by ear as by eye.[35]

Secondly, the battle degenerated into fragmented chaos. Historians often superimpose neat battle lines on a map but these are only abstract representations of what happened because combat is never neat. At La Chu men from the various platoons became intermingled. As Platoon Sergeant Parker noted, in combat "you get all mixed up on the line." "Once you get in initial contact," he continued, "you can't sit up and draw a diagram, no kind of form or fashion, you just have to act, and things are happening so fast!"[36]

According to Roy Barber the battle was "kind of a free-form thing in which everybody kind of gets tangled up and you end up in these odd places." With a sense of wonderment he described the action as a "frenzy." Combat that day was primarily "an individual person against the rest of the world rather than an organized assault. It was a lot of people being alone, or two or three people together. It was a very individual thing." One moment you were by yourself, the next moment a fellow Raider was at your side, and a few minutes later you were with somebody else, though you were often unsure as to exactly who it was. The "only deciding factors in determining what you did were whether somebody was shooting at you, whether you had ammunition, and whether someone was wounded and needed immediate aid." If somebody shot at you, you fired back; if you ran low on ammunition, you searched for more; if somebody was wounded, you rendered aid. As men fired and maneuvered, went looking for ammunition, and moved back and forth between the medevac area and the front line they inevitably lost some of their unit organization.[37]

Others agreed with Barber's assessment. To Jodey Gravett everything suddenly "went berserk and nobody knows which end is up and which way to go or nothing." Most Raiders "were all confused, much as I was, as to exactly what was going on." "It was hard to know what somebody else was doing twenty feet away from you," observed Sal Bongiorno, "because you were content with what was going on in front of you. Fifty yards away from you was a whole other [world]." Craig Sturges agreed. "As an individual you're only concerned about your sphere of influence" he recalled, "and you don't know what the hell is going on behind you and to the side of you." Remembering the chaos, Richard Buzzini admitted that "everything is pretty vague" so "it's hard to say exactly what I did."[38]

At first glance Hooper's MOH file, as recapitulated in the Prologue, compensated for the blurry vagueness of so many Raiders. However, despite the file's thickness the evidence it contained was thin. What the file said about enemy defenses, the terrain, and the weather was accurate, but the key parts, such as the citation and the eyewitness statements, were problematic. As for the citation, no reputable historian accepts a medal citation as "the truth." The policy at the Army's Center of Military History, for example, is not to use medal citations as evidence because, as the Center's Chief Historian said, usually no one *knows* what happened during a combat action; citations are often largely fictitious, or filled with half-truths at best.[39]

With a Medal of Honor citation, however, the eyewitness statements seemingly negate this problem. Unfortunately, all the "eyewitness" accounts in Hooper's file that can be verified were flawed. Those by 1st Platoon Leader Grimsley and Staff Sergeant Lonnie Thomas cannot be verified because the former died later in the war and Sergeant Thomas cannot be located.

Hogan and his executive officer, Fred Aronow, compiled a joint two-paragraph statement that spoke in generalities about how Hooper "was conspicuous, charging bunkers, braving intense fire, and leading his men over position after position. . . ." Three specific points were that Joe *evacuated* (not necessarily *rescued*) some of the wounded, suffered multiple wounds, and killed an enemy soldier with his bayonet.

But Aronow was not, and never claimed to be, an eyewitness. On February 21 he wrote his wife from Camp Evans, saying he would return to Company D the next day, and that "the day passed with no more casualties, thank God." In fact, the Raiders suffered one dead and twenty-two wounded that day.[40]

The joint statement, said Hogan, "is essentially what I wrote, but that is not my signature."[41] Forged signatures on eyewitness statements were apparently not unusual since witnesses were often in the field, on R and R or sick leave, recovering from wounds in a distant hospital, or dead when documents were ready for their signatures. So someone else signed them. "I imagine that's happened more than once," said Roger C. Donlon, who received the Vietnam War's first MOH, "especially when they get upgraded" from, say, a Silver Star to a DSC, or a DSC to an MOH.[42] All the verifiable "eyewitness" signatures in Hooper's file were forgeries. More significantly, Cleo's initial account of the battle, contained in a letter on February 27, mentioned no individual as being exceptionally heroic. And a "diary" he compiled shortly after the war based upon his almost-daily letters to his wife and other documents noted only that "Joe Hooper and Sgt Urban killed about 5 or 10 NVA." Whether Hooper or Urban did the killing was unclear, how they killed them was unstated, and whether they killed five or twice that many was uncertain—and even ten dead NVA were only half as many as the MOH file attributed to Hooper alone.[43]

In subsequent accounts Hogan elaborated on what he saw. He encountered Hooper several times during the battle, usually as Joe was coming back from the front line carrying wounded soldiers and looking for more ammunition. At one point Hogan saw Hooper shoot an NVA, but he did not see him stab an enemy soldier with a bayonet, though he "was told pretty reliably that he did." Based on what he witnessed Cleo did not think Hooper merited an MOH. Only after collating his limited first-hand knowledge with that of other "eyewitness" statements did he believe Joe deserved the medal.[44]

Platoon Sergeant Parker's eyewitness account was the most detailed—four double-spaced pages that were at the core of the MOH file. Parker's account provided much crucial information, such as how Hooper, supported by Dale Urban, destroyed the enemy's last bunker line. However, Parker neither wrote nor signed the statement. Although he knew Joe was heavily engaged in the fighting, he did not explicitly recall seeing him until the Raiders were setting up their postbattle NDP. During the battle he was too busy to notice any particular individual. "A Platoon Sergeant doesn't know anything until it's actually over with because you have so many [men] to protect and so much to do. You have to make sure everybody stays on line. You have to control the firepower as to where it's going, to shift your fire and all that kind of stuff." As for who did all the killing, "In an area like this you don't know who killed who. The only thing you know is that you're just shooting."[45]

According to Chaplain Erbach's eyewitness statement, he was "wounded by a gunshot at close range. Sgt Hooper prevented the enemy from killing me by rushing to my position and shooting the enemy. He then helped carry me to the rear. . . . As I was trying to inspire the men on the field I found that Sgt Hooper's amazing bravery was the greatest inspiration possible and made hero[es] out of timid men as they attempted to follow his example." A map in the MOH file showed the exact spot inside the village where Hooper rescued the chaplain. Apparently reinforcing this account was a newspaper clipping glued inside the Bible that Erbach presented to Joe at Fort Campbell, where the chaplain gave a Bible to every man in the battalion. The story quoted Erbach as saying, "If I hadn't seen God preserve him so many times, for the sake of the rest of us, I'd have to believe that Joe isn't human."

When asked in 1996 if he wrote a testimonial for the MOH file, Erbach said, "No, I did not," and when told that the file contained an account written in his name he laughed in amazement. After hearing the statement attributed to him in the clipping, he again responded with peals of laughter. "I wonder where that came from?" he asked. "Lord of Mercy! Oh, gosh, the fiction grows, eh?" The truth was that he never got into the village and that Hooper neither rescued him nor carried him to safety. As soon as the shooting began Erbach and Hooper temporarily huddled behind a mound, probably a grave. Looking off to the right Erbach saw that 3rd Platoon, commanded by Lieutenant David Bischoff who had replaced Brulte two days earlier, had stopped advancing. So "I stood up, literally stood up on the battlefield and screamed at him to get his people out of there. Here I was, the stupid chaplain playing battalion commander. And Joe's laughing! He thinks this is funny." When Joe and the chaplain advanced from their haven a bullet grazed Erbach's stomach. Joe "took his combat dressing and wrapped it around my gut" and they began walking forward again. Before they reached the stream the wound started hurting so Erbach left Joe and walked back to an aid station. Whatever "heroics that Joe participated in were after I left the battlefield—on my own steam. My wounds were neither grave nor debilitating so I had no need of assistance."

Erbach believed someone fictionalized an eyewitness account for him because he was with Joe when he got wounded, and that "became a very easy handle to inflate. To save the Savior, and that's kind of the way the guys looked at the chaplain. He was their good luck charm or whatever, and if we could put in there that Joe saved the Savior, boy, that would make it even look better." [46]

Tex Gray's statement was brief but dramatic, describing how Hooper rescued him from what seemed certain death. But like Erbach, Gray neither wrote nor signed a statement. He was with Hooper when they entered the village but soon parted ways and "I never did see Hooper again after that. I don't know where he went after that." A machine gunner, Gray quickly ran out of ammunition and "started playing John Wayne. I walked up through there with a .45 pistol in my hand. That .45 couldn't hit the broad side of a barn."

When Gray took a bullet in the shoulder and fell into an enemy trench, Ava James saved him from a grenade explosion by flinging himself on top of Tex, protecting everything but his head. Grenade fragments tore into Gray's skull, causing permanent optic nerve damage, and severely injured James. Tex does not know who pulled him out of the trench. He was floating in and out of consciousness, and when he was conscious he "didn't see anything. I was hugging that trench." No matter who rescued him from the trench, Tex was certain Emanuel Burroughs carried him back to safety. But his memory was inaccurate since Burroughs was KIA six days earlier.[47]

When interviewed in 1998 Edward J. Petitt Jr. recalled writing and signing an eyewitness statement but, like Tex Gray, his memory was flawed. At the most basic level his last name was Petitt, but the statement has it typed and signed as Pettit. Moreover, his statement noted that Joe was wounded early in the fighting, that he "blew up a couple hooches with LAWs and stabbed one NVA when the gook's rifle misfired," that Dale Urban followed "right behind him with his rifle to get what he missed," and that after the battle "he made sure everybody else was taken care of and then he prepared the men for the next day's fight." However, in 1998 Petitt had no idea when Joe was wounded. When asked what weapons Hooper used he mentioned only fragmentation grenades and an M-16. Questioned specifically about LAWs, he did not remember Joe using them. Nor did he recall Hooper stabbing an enemy soldier, know who Dale Urban was, or remember seeing Joe at the end of the battle. Petitt undoubtedly saw Hooper that day, but only intermittently. Like most soldiers he kept low to the ground and primarily watched his immediate front. "If you'd have been there," Petitt said, "you'd have been worried about what the hell was in front of you!" And in any event "Everything happened so damn fast it makes you kind of wonder what you did see."[48]

Finally, the file contained an eyewitness statement from Dale Urban who supposedly accompanied Hooper during the battle's climactic phase. Urban did not write or sign the statement. For several reasons linking Dale and Joe made sense to whoever wrote the account. Initially both men served in 1st Platoon, though due to 3rd Platoon's heavy casualties on February 15th

Urban was reassigned to it. Despite vastly different personalities they were good friends. While Hooper was wild, craved attention, and an outrageous storyteller, Urban was quiet, unassuming, and a man of rock solid integrity. According to Craig Sturges, Dale was "the most unassuming person you're going to meet." But "he's bad news. He's a fightin' guy. If Dale was on my left I knew I didn't have to worry about my left, or if he was on my right I knew I didn't have to worry about my right." Fred Aronow considered Dale "the strong silent type" who "speaks absolutely straight. No question about that."[49]

On February 21, 1968, Urban was with Hooper as they started across the rice paddy but then Dale veered to the right. "I never saw Joe again until after we got done," he insisted. "It must have been someone else with Hooper. It wasn't me. I was not with Joe and Joe was not with me."[50]

A final problem hindering an accurate battle account was the frailty of memory.[51] Because of memory's fundamental nature, at some point almost every veteran trying to recount what happened became frustrated, saying, "I don't remember," "I wish I could remember," or "It's so hard to explain." Bright and articulate, these men were honest and were not afflicted by abnormally poor memories about other aspects of their lives. But when it came to combat their memories were fragile. They truly forgot (or *never* remembered in the first place) much of what happened. What they did recall was often no more than a few isolated fragments, which they often could not place in chronological sequence or explain where they occurred on the battlefield.

Memory, which like fear is dependent on neurobiology, is not a unitary phenomenon or process; no single memory is stored in a single location in the brain. Instead memory consists of interconnecting systems and subsystems, each regulated by different brain structures and processes. A single memory is scattered throughout the brain in many different networks of neurons, and the pieces come together only when it is time to recall the memory.

At the most basic level, scientists distinguish between implicit and explicit memory; although these continually interact they operate on separate systems. In large part controlled by the amygdala (the brain structure so intimately involved with fear), implicit memory exerts a pervasive influence on thoughts, actions, and perceptions but operates outside the realm of conscious awareness. On the other hand the hippocampus, a seahorse-shaped structure located near the amygdala, performs the leading role in explicit memory, that is, in conscious recollections that can be brought to mind and described verbally, such as names, faces, things, and events.

Within explicit memory researchers have identified immediate, working, and long-term memory. Often called a sensory register, immediate memory absorbs vast amounts of information, but holds it for less than a second. Only a small amount of the information entering the sensory register filters into working (or short-term) memory. The rest vanishes, wrote one authority, "like breath on a windowpane."[52]

Unless an individual makes a conscious effort to remember it, the information transferred to working memory exists for less than a minute before it, too, disappears. Short-term memory holds the material an individual is thinking about or paying attention to at the present moment. However, it only retains about seven items at a time—for example, the seven digits in a telephone number—and as new items are added older ones evaporate. An individual can look at a phone number, perhaps mentally repeat it once, and then dial it without looking at it again. While concentrating on the seven numbers, however, no other information can enter working memory. Moreover, once the individual begins talking on the phone (thus breaking his or her concentration) the number evaporates from short-term memory. If someone wants to retain something in short-term memory for more than a moment and transfer it to long-term memory the information must be rehearsed. Only by rehearsing the number multiple times (perhaps by thinking or talking about it) can the phone number enter long-term memory—after a while an individual no longer has to look up the number of his or her best friends.

Thus only a small percentage of the information entering immediate memory makes it into short-term memory, and then only a fraction of that data moves into long-term memory. Long-term memory actually contains three separate types of memory: semantic, which deals with factual and conceptual knowledge; procedural, which permits people to learn skills and acquire habits; and most importantly for reconstructing a battle, episodic, which allows an individual to recall specific incidents. Of course, the information that avoids extinction and reaches long-term episodic memory is merely a hazy, shadowy representation of the information that originally entered the sensory register since many of the details have been winnowed out by the functioning of immediate and short-term memory.

Memory problems can be especially acute in a combat environment. With so much life-or-death information swamping the sensory register and short-term memory, sometimes the brain has difficulty absorbing *anything*. Because memories are consolidated during sleep, particularly during the rapid eye movement stage when the brain "replays" many of the day's events, inadequate sleep disrupts the formation of new memories.[53] Collectively the Raiders had not been getting enough rest and would not get a good night's sleep for another five days. Acute stress and trauma also afflict explicit memory formation. For example, they often result in "absorption," a narrowing of one's focus of attention, such as a mugging victim's "weapons focus." The unfortunate individual provides a detailed description of the assailant's gun—the center of attention—but recalls little about the periphery, such as what the assailant looked like and wore. Such "tunnel vision" explains why soldiers often remember so little of what went on around them.

Furthermore, hormones released during traumatic experiences can interfere with the hippocampus, the key brain structure in explicit memory. One scientist wrote about the "stress-induced breakdown in hippocampal memory function," and how severe stress can "devastate explicit memory."[54] A flood of stress-released hormones can produce irreversible changes in the hippocampus, actually causing it to shrink, and therefore not only hindering the formation of new memories but also eradicating old ones. Repeated exposure to stress can also blur or merge the memories of each specific traumatic event, so that veterans who experienced multiple combat situations will have sketchy and incomplete memories about any particular episode.

Finally, stress can induce a "dissociative state," which occurs as a defense against trauma. Among other things dissociation creates a sense of detachment and depersonalization, and alters the perception of time and distance. Combat veterans frequently report a sense of unreality or an out-of-body experience. A soldier feels dissociated from the battle, as if he was in a dream or trance floating above the fray, looking down upon that poor soul (himself) enduring such mayhem and misery. No combatant stated this more succinctly than Tadayoshi Sakurai, who wrote about a battle during the Russo-Japanese War: "I turned to my right and went forward as in a dream." "Everything," he said, "passed through my mind as in a dream, so my story must be something like picking out things from the dark."[55] Many soldiers before and since have reported the same phenomenon.

Dissociation also disrupts the well-ordered chronology and concise measurements that dominate civilian life, which are irrelevant in combat. During peace, time is monotonously regular. Seconds build rhythmically to minutes, minutes accumulate with mathematical precision to hours, and so on. But in battle, time advances irregularly, moving forward by fits and starts, now standing almost still and then hurtling forward at an accelerated speed. Battlefield time may be compressed or it may be expanded, but it rarely matches civilian time. Consequently, reconstructing a chronologically reliable sequence of events during a battle is difficult. Even if events actually happened simultaneously on different parts of the battlefield, the combatants' varied perspective on time generally makes it impossible to correlate them precisely.

During the battle Dale Urban "just lost all track of time. It seemed like it was twenty to thirty minutes, but I have no idea." Bobby Rakestraw was also unsure about February 21: "I couldn't even tell you how long the battle lasted. It seemed like it lasted an eternity." What seemed like less than half an hour to Urban was an eternity for Rakestraw. Neither Roy Barber, Richard Buzzini, nor Dave Bischoff could be more specific. All Barber knew was that "the sun was up when it started, and the sun was still up when it was over," by which he meant the battle began and ended during daylight. For Buzzini the battle "didn't last a long time. Or, then, I really don't know whether it lasted a long time or not. It seemed like a few hours, but maybe it was just an hour." Lieutenant Bischoff did not "think it was any more than two or three hours, but it could have been all day. Honestly, for a million dollars I couldn't tell you what time the battle began, or how long that battle went." In short, a battle began when it began and ended when it ended, and nothing else mattered.[56]

As for distance, it became a psychological condition rather than a measurable element. Whether a soldier had to move a meter or a mile was immaterial. What counted was whether he could traverse the distance, however great it might be, and still be alive when he reached his destination. The stream the Raiders crossed to get into the village, observed Barber, "seemed much bigger and much wider crossing it under fire than it did in the movie [a postwar video showing the stream]. Assaulting across it under fire, yeah,

I guess an inch would seem like a mile." After veering off to his right away from Hooper, Urban ran south along the stream before crossing, but how far? "I just ran to get out of the line of fire, and then I got across as quickly as I could." That is, how far he ran was of no concern. He ran far enough to avoid the enemy's immediate gunfire, which meant he was going to live at least a few minutes more. Toward the end of the battle Rakestraw remembered Hooper "right over there on my left." How far to the left? He could not say. Ava James also recalled seeing Hooper. Trying to estimate how far away Joe was, James grew frustrated, saying "I don't know. I'm trying to visualize distances and it's not coming to me at all." How far was it from one side of the village to the other? Rakestraw had "no idea. I couldn't tell you." Nor could anyone else.[57]

Despite the problems created by sensory overload, sleep deprivation, and stress, some data enters long-term episodic memory. But this does not mean the information can be accurately recalled. Quite the opposite; the "explicit memory system is notoriously forgetful and inaccurate."[58] The "subjective experience of remembering can be simultaneously compelling and dead wrong," wrote another authority, because people can have "elaborate false recollections."[59] That is, sometimes even vivid memories are wildly inaccurate. The problem is that a memory's output rarely equals its input. Unlike a camera, copying machine, or computer, memory does not record perfect replicas of events, people, places, or documents, or retrieve precise data stored on some brainlike equivalent of a hard drive. The inability to recall the past accurately does not result from a brain deficiency; memory is *naturally* subject to distortion and decay. Here are some of the reasons why.

An "encoding process" transforms what a person sees, hears, feels, or thinks into a memory. Encoding is selective in the sense that what a person already knows shapes what he or she encodes. "We remember only what we have encoded," wrote one neuroscientist, "and what we encode depends on who we are—our past experiences, knowledge, and needs all have a powerful influence on what we retain."[60] Witnesses often have different recollections of an event because preexisting information seeps into new memories and corrupts them during encoding. Knowing what was likely to happen in a certain situation can also be incorporated into a new memory even if it did *not* happen. Realizing that Joe Hooper loved combat, for instance, some Raiders may have expected him to behave like a hero and therefore "remembered" that he acted bravely, even if they did not see him perform heroic acts.

The result of encoding is an engram. When a memory is being encoded an action potential fires along a neuron's axon to its terminal region, releasing packets of the neurotransmitter glutamate, which binds to specialized receptors (known as AMPA and NMDA receptors) on the dendrites of adjoining neurons. The resulting molecular changes strengthen and stabilize the connections among all the neurons that have fired. These new connections represent an engram. But a memory is not instantly fixed at the time of learning. It may take several years to develop its permanent form through a consolidation process in which the memory becomes less resistant to forgetting through repeated rehearsals—through repeated firing of the engram's neurons—either by talking, thinking, or writing about the experience. Neuroscientists have slang expressions for this phenomenon. One is "neurons that fire together wire together," which means that the more often an act or thought is repeated the stronger and more resilient the connections become; each time the neurons fire their electrochemical volleys they strengthen the connections. Another slogan is "use it or lose it," implying that if the brain circuits are not used, the connections will undergo "disuse atrophy," slowly withering and perhaps eventually dying.[61]

During consolidation a memory is malleable, subject to various disruptions and distortions. One potential corruption is filling in the blanks in a memory from a preexisting script, which is "a kind of mental repository containing and representing information abstracted from a class of similar events but excluding concrete details about specific occurrences."[62] If only a partial memory is available a script may taint it by filling in gaps with generic knowledge about probable behavior. Accretions from different scripts can transform an anemic memory into a dazzling recollection, in part because rehearsing incorrect information from a script makes it seem real. A second potential vulnerability is "source amnesia," or remembering something without being able to recall exactly where or when the information was acquired or what the accompanying sights and sounds were. So a memory becomes a mixture, incorporating a name from this memory, sounds from another, and sights from still a third. According to one authority, "source memory is extremely fallible, and the failures to remember the correct source of acquired information are responsible for various kinds of errors and distortions in eyewitness recollections."[63]

Instead of reproducing an event memory *reconstructs* it. Every memory is the result of both the past and the present. Fundamentally, memories are subjective, imaginative reconstructions not exact reproductions. Indeed, the distinction between memory and imagination is often blurry at best. Although a memory usually retains some "truth"— or at least a warped, edited version of it—memories sometimes more closely resemble creative fiction than what "really" happened in the past.[64] A memory (the subjective experience of recollecting an event) and its engram (the stored fragments of an episode) are not identical because a memory can be retrieved only through a process that alters the memory. In particular, "The way you remember an event depends on your purposes and goals at the time you attempt to recall it. You help to paint its picture during the act of remembering." That is, a memory depends as much on the present moment as it does on the past. The emotions a memory ascribes to a past event, for example, "may sometimes arise from the way in which you set out to retrieve a memory in the present."[65] Thus the retrieval process reconfigures even the most dramatic memories, so that every memory symbolizes rather than replicates the past. As one scholar starkly put it, "a memory changes each time you think about it," losing clarity and specificity as it undergoes what experts refer to as "graceful degradation."[66]

The "retrieval cue" is of crucial importance. An engram remains dormant until "awakened" by a cue, which works only if a similarity or affinity exists between the encoded memory and the cue. A broad range of retrieval cues will awaken a deeply consolidated memory, but a shallow engram requires a precise cue before it can be remembered. Parts of an individual's past remain dormant because the right cue never triggers the appropriate engrams. If an interrogator does not use the proper cues, an eyewitness will provide an incomplete recollection. And the way a question is worded or what a person is told by others affects what a person *believes* he or she remembers. Such "suggestions" exert a powerful influence on retrieval. The memories evoked by "Did you see someone with Joe Hooper?" or "Did you see Dale Urban with Joe Hooper?" will be quite different. And a Raider who was unsure of exactly what he saw could develop a robust memory if, for example, one of his buddies told him that "you must have seen Hooper doing that."

Mood congruence also influences memory. An individual is more likely to recall a memory established in one mood if he or she is in the same mood during the retrieval process. Being sad makes it easier to recall negative experiences, being happy prompts happy memories. Memories formed during intense fear may be especially difficult to retrieve if the individual is no longer afraid.

And, of course, time and memory are enemies. Over time, memories are subject to simple forgetting. If an engram remains unrehearsed (unused), the original synaptic connections may progressively weaken until the engram fades away. Finding a retrieval cue that elicits an engram made increasingly shadowy by the passage of time becomes more and more difficult. Moreover, over time the brain encodes and stores new engrams on top of old ones. Not only do the old and the new memories inevitably alter each other by becoming intermixed but also new memories interfere with the ability to recall older ones. Sometimes the forgetfulness is astounding. In one study researchers interviewed 590 people who were in automobile accidents during the previous year. More than a fourth forgot the accident![67]

Four concluding points about memory.

Just because someone engaged in fabrication does not necessarily prove he or she was lying. Instead, perhaps the person's memory was false.

To compensate for memory's innate limitations, corroboration is vital. If two or more people confirm an event, confidence in each individual's memory increases.

Depending on their genetic makeup and life experiences, individuals exhibit an astounding diversity in their memory capabilities. Occasionally a person seems immune to memory's normal frailties.

Had eyewitnesses for Joe Hooper's MOH been interviewed immediately after the battle their recollections inevitably would have been flawed and partial. But such factors as scripts, source amnesia, and suggestion would not yet have seriously distorted them. Nor would they have decayed because of passing time.

Unfortunately, no one went looking for witnesses until many weeks later.

Joe Hooper's MOH file was the culmination of a lengthy chain of elaboration.

Heroes are often created by a crass sort of supply and demand. As one expert on MOH recipients put it, "There are many instances where the morale of the Nation or the morale of a division require reinforcement and stimulation." So officials found and exalted heroes. Chaplain Erbach said much the same thing: "There was a *need* on the part of the upper echelon, going all the way up to the division level, there was a need to make heroes. So there was a certain amount of pressure to create documents that told of heroic tales and deeds."[68] It reflected favorably upon commanders such as Colonel Cushman and General Barsanti if their units received lots of medals. Valorous awards implied their men were fighting with high morale and killing lots of the enemy, thus contributing to the attrition strategy. The body count and medals became the standards by which a unit measured its prowess.

Like Captain McMenamy before him, Lieutenant Hogan felt the pressure to award medals and make heroes. In Cleo's case the pressure came from Lieutenant Colonel Tallman. Approximately a week after the Battle of La Chu when the Raiders reached Hue and settled into temporary quarters, the battalion commander told Hogan that "a battle of that significance should be rewarded. He told me to put the word out to the troops, and to take some time the first chance I got and submit some people for awards." Up to that point, "in the course of everyday war, medals just didn't come to mind. Most of us thought that what we did was part of our job and we didn't expect awards for our actions." Prodded by Tallman, Cleo asked the platoon sergeants and others for recommendations.[69]

As a result of his investigations Hogan submitted Hooper, Urban, and Parker for Silver Stars and Sergeant Clifford Sims and four others for Bronze Stars.[70] A new commander in a company where no one had received any medals yet, Cleo had "no 'yardstick' to measure what awards should be recommended." At "this time a SILVER STAR was like the moon to me. I could not even fathom what a DSC or Medal of Honor would be like to receive or recommend." With only slight modifications the Hogan-Aronow eyewitness statement in Hooper's MOH file was what Cleo originally submitted for the Silver Star.

Sometime in mid-April the Silver Star recommendations for Hooper and Urban came back to company headquarters. Cleo learned that higher headquarters wanted the awards upgraded to DSCs. The higher award carried a higher standard of documentation. After substantial reworking, including gathering "eyewitness" statements for both men, company headquarters resubmitted the files in early May. "Within just a few days," Hogan recalled, "the recommendations were returned and we were told to submit them as a Medal of Honor for Hooper and Urban." Tallman had approved the DSCs but the brigade commander, Colonel Cushman, wanted them upgraded.

Since standards were higher for an MOH than a DSC, the files underwent another revision. An MOH required more and better eyewitness statements and a more elaborate citation. For example, Hooper's MOH citation contained crucial embellishments compared to the DSC. The DSC had Hooper rescuing only one man, while in the MOH he saved several soldiers, supposedly including the chaplain. That Hooper's MOH citation emphasized rescuing the wounded was no accident. Under conditions prevailing in modern warfare, with long-range weapons and mass armies imposing a numbing dehumanization, few opportunities for a glorious charge or heroic single combat arise. Dashing onto the battlefield to save a wounded comrade was an opportunity for the heroic gesture, to manifest courage and manhood dramatically, to demonstrate individual, charismatic, affective bravery. A study of MOH citations from the Civil War through Vietnam revealed that battlefield rescue was one of the most common themes.[71]

The DSC also referred only to Hooper's "wounds"; the MOH added hyperbole by inserting the phrase "multiple wounds and loss of blood." Another addition was that the DSC citation ended with Hooper rescuing a wounded man, but the MOH asserted that he then "neutralized the final pocket of enemy resistance by fatally wounding three North Vietnamese officers with rifle fire."[72] As explained later, Dale Urban, not Joe Hooper, shot those officers.

What happened next puzzled Cleo Hogan. Although he "thought that the statements submitted for Urban were more outstanding than those submitted for Hooper," the latter's went forward as an MOH while Urban's remained a DSC. Why this happened was a mystery. In any event, Colonel Cushman recommended approval of Hooper's MOH and forwarded the file to higher headquarters.

By May 6, Hooper knew he was being recommended for the MOH. "Mom you and Dad," he wrote, "will probably take a trip with me sometime next year to Washington D.C. and meet the new President of the United States. I have been recommended for the nation's highest military award. The Medal of Honor. Well, what do you think of that?" In one sense the probability of receiving the award concerned Joe. Should he stay in the Army? With his six-year enlistment expiring in May, he gave considerable thought to life after the army, especially about going to civilian flight school. He thought he would enjoy civilian life, particularly if he had "a wife and kids of my own." "I was so dead set on getting out," he told his parents, "but know [now] I feel as though I should stay in."[73]

The time lag between the battle and the need to acquire eyewitness statements for a DSC and then an MOH was at least six weeks, which made finding reliable witnesses difficult. By then many of the battle's participants were no longer available. Tex Gray and Ava James, for example, were back in the United States receiving medical treatment. More significant was the problem of individuals recalling who had done what during the battle. To most participants February 21 was "just another day at the office," not all that different from February 15 or 19, or from much of the fighting the Raiders endured after February 21. Living in the field and engaged in numerous combat operations, not much differentiated yesterday from today or today from tomorrow, so memories became blurred, incapable of distinguishing one killing field from another.[74]

Memory distortion also occurred in the weeks after the battle. For instance, during the fighting James Kearns, who was on 3rd Platoon's right flank, looked to his left front and saw a lone American amidst "a lot of activity, a lot of NVA running all over. . . . I couldn't believe that one of our people was in there running around like that." At the time Kearns did not know who the soldier was but about a week later someone told him he must have seen Joe—a classic example of suggestion.[75] Had he been asked to write an eyewitness account in May he would have attested to Joe's fabulous heroism. But Hooper and Kearns were widely separated during the battle and a thick veil of vegetation lay between them. Kearns actually saw Dale Urban not Joe Hooper.

Furthermore, since no one knew Joe would become a celebrity nobody paid particular attention to him. "Joe Hooper was just another trooper to me," said Hogan. Bobby Rakestraw saw Hooper during the battle, "but I wasn't thinking 'I gotta remember this because this man's going to be famous some day.' It was just like he was one of the guys."[76] *Everyone* was moving and firing. Perhaps what ultimately drew special attention to Hooper was that by dint of his personality many Raiders knew who he was, as opposed to a quiet person such as Urban.[77]

Hooper was lucky to live through the battle, lucky some people realized he played an important role in the fighting, lucky the high command exerted pressure to exalt and reward heroism, lucky his file went forward instead of Urban's, and lucky Fred Aronow was the company's executive officer. As everyone knew, "The awards business was commonly determined by how articulate the individual was who was writing up an incident."[78] An awards board more readily accepted recommendations with polished prose than those with poor grammar, punctuation, and spelling. An accomplished wordsmith who became a lawyer after the war, Aronow did most of the work to compile the file because, as he wrote, "one of the major functions as xo [executive officer] was to process awards and decorations."

Nearly three decades later Aronow's recollection was understandably vague as to exactly how Hooper's MOH file was compiled. He recalled doing a lot of paperwork, interviewing witnesses and polishing their statements, visiting the battlefield to make maps, and talking with Hooper. In particular Joe explained how he and Urban cleared the last bunker line. Since Dale was not there perhaps Joe was the source of the confusion about who was with him that day.

Aronow was not at the battle and had no firsthand knowledge as to what anyone saw or did. Therefore he acknowledged that corruptions may have entered the process regarding who witnessed what.

However, he knew two things for certain.

Upgrading the medals from Silver Stars to the more prestigious awards required "an awful lot of work." And compiling the files "was difficult because of the time [lag]," with all it implied for locating reliable witnesses and for memory's potential distortions.

So, in broad outline what happened that day?[79]

When the firing began the Raiders were in the middle of a vast rice paddy. While 3rd Platoon provided covering fire, 1st Platoon, which included Joe Hooper, crossed the paddy, forded the stream, ascended the far riverbank, crossed a road (which was an eight-foot-wide dirt trail suitable for bicycles and wagons but not motor vehicles), and plunged into "La Chu." When a soldier was near the stream he was in "dead ground," safe because enemy gunfire coming from the elevated village passed over his head. 1st Platoon then provided covering fire while 3rd Platoon crossed the stream, but Lieutenant Bischoff and his men were pinned down before they entered the village.

Meanwhile the headquarters element and 2nd Platoon took refuge in the cemetery, which was on raised ground and filled with small tombs. "If you're looking for a place to get some cover," said 2nd Platoon's Lieu-

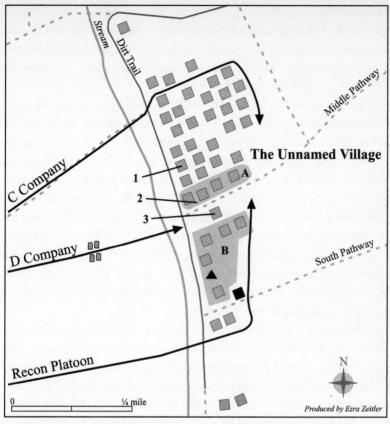

The Unnamed Village

Produced by Ezra Zeitler

0   ¼ mile

A	Main area of Hooper's actions
B	Main area of Urban's actions
1	Building with the red roof
2	Sims killed here
3	House that exploded

▲   Pink Pagoda

■   The final large bunker

▨   Houses and other structures

▦▦   Cemetery

Map 4: The Battle on February 21, 1968

tenant Loftin, "a cemetery's not a bad place to go because there's all these little nooks and crannies you can hide in." Or as Hooper put it, a graveyard was often the Raiders' favorite position because it was at least "half way safe" there, with the dead sheltering the living.[80]

Two narrow footpaths sliced through the village from east to west, one in the middle and the other on the south edge. 1st Platoon's axis of advance followed the middle path. Because the stream bank near this path was high and steep, an earthen ramp led from the stream to the trail and then through a wooden archway marking the footpath's entrance into the village. Along both sides of the path and to its north the vegetation was dense and houses were plentiful. Between the middle and south footpaths the terrain was more open with comparatively few hedges, trees, gardens, or houses. A religious shrine (the Raiders called it the pink pagoda because of its pinkish hue) was in an open field about halfway between the middle and south footpaths. 3rd Platoon, the unit Dale Urban was in that day, attacked in the vicinity of the pink pagoda and the south footpath.

As the battle began a tremendous volume of machine gun fire came from a substantial building with a red roof located north of the middle path, not only threatening 1st Platoon's attack but also endangering the headquarters element and 2nd Platoon at the cemetery. Platoon Sergeant Parker radioed Hogan from the village suggesting that 1st Platoon pull back and call in aerial and artillery support because it was confronting a large force that was well concealed in fortified positions. Knowing the Raiders would receive little external fire support that day, Hogan reported the grim situation to Tallman, who may not have believed Cleo's dire assessment. After all, C Company was walking through the northern third of the village without encountering *any* resistance. He directed Hogan to continue the attack.

Complying with Tallman's order, Hogan told Parker to neutralize the red-roofed building. At that moment Tallman broke into the radio net saying a helicopter gunship with ARA (aerial rocket artillery) was overhead and gave Cleo the necessary call sign and frequency. Contacting the pilot, Cleo asked him to destroy the building with the red roof. Responding that he could see fifty buildings with red roofs, the pilot asked which one was the target. Trying to inject a humorous touch, Cleo told him to "just pick out one and we'll sort 'em out later." The pilot did not laugh. So Cleo popped a yellow smoke grenade, gave him a magnetic heading and a distance from it, and asked him to fire a marker round, which hit within twenty-five yards of the target. Radioing the adjustment, Cleo watched with satisfaction as rockets blasted the building, ending the threat from that location.

The Raiders received no further external support either from the air or artillery. The engagement became a pure grunt battle, one of men against men instead of machines against men. Even had artillery support been available the Raiders could not have used it. With the Raiders and the NVA intermixed, no clear battle line existed. Sometimes the enemy even emerged from bunkers and spider holes behind the Raiders. "We were mixed right in with them [the NVA]," recalled Mike Watson, the artillery observer serving with the Raiders, "so you couldn't really get artillery support where you needed it because we were so close to them, without wiping out half your own unit."[81]

With a premium on rifles, machine guns, and grenades, a key concern was ammunition. Roy Barber remembered that because the Raiders expected a battle "half these guys looked like Mexican bandits with all the ammo they carried" in bandoleers draped across their chests.[82] But they fired a lot in a hurry and more than one soldier found himself in danger because he ran out of ammo. To solve the ammunition problem men scrounged from the packs and pockets of wounded comrades, or filtered to the rear, grabbed extra ammo, and returned to the front. In desperation some used enemy weapons, but this was quite dangerous because an AK-47 and an M-16 made distinct sounds. In a battle fought as much by sound as by sight, an American firing an AK-47 might draw friendly fire.

Soon Hogan lost radio contact with Lieutenant Grimsley and Sergeant Parker in 1st Platoon. He remained in communication with Lieutenant Bischoff, but also lost contact with 3rd Platoon's platoon sergeant, James Deland. A communications failure sometimes occurred when a radio got damaged, or when an RTO wanted to play John Wayne, or both. When a grenade went off in a nearby tree, RTO Ava James was unhurt but his radio was not. Fixing it through inspired tinkering was a possibility, but "I just kind of dumped it. I was tired of it. I couldn't get into the action having to stay back with the radio all the time. I wanted to get in a little bit of action."[83] While an admirable fighting spirit, it left Cleo uncertain about what was happening inside the village.

To find out, he ordered the headquarters element to spread out, dash across the paddy, then reassemble in the dead ground along the stream. While Staff Sergeant Clifford Sims's squad of 2nd Platoon provided covering fire, the headquarters group (twelve men) sprinted from the cemetery. Bullets whizzed by them at every step but all made it to the sheltering stream bank. Then Cleo led them up the earthen ramp, through the archway, and into Hell.

As Cleo's group took cover among some fallen bamboo trees just inside the village and a dozen yards north of the middle footpath, the gunfire in front of them was deafening. Hogan radioed Tallman, saying he thought major portions of 1st and 3rd Platoons were being annihilated. Cleo then confided to Mike Watson "that D Company may well end up like Custer at the Little Big Horn."

Fearing his headquarters element might be isolated and anxious to discern the fate of 1st and 3rd Platoons, Hogan radioed Loftin to send him a squad. Before it arrived, Platoon Sergeant Parker materialized out of the vegetation and reported, to Hogan's immense relief, that the battle was going well even though he had several slightly wounded men and his soldiers needed more ammo. He did not, however, know whether a gap existed between 1st and 3rd Platoons. Several men in the headquarters gave him their ammunition and then Parker plunged back into the brush. Then Joe Hooper arrived, half carrying a wounded soldier and with two less severely wounded men following him. Like Parker, Joe was looking for more ammo and knew nothing about 3rd Platoon. Parker and Hooper alleviated Cleo's worries about 1st Platoon but he was increasingly concerned about 3rd Platoon.

Hogan directed Hooper to take the casualties down the ramp and back to the graveyard where Loftin had established a medevac position, and to bring back more ammunition. Just as he was about to depart Sergeant Sims's squad from 2nd Platoon arrived, lugging extra ammunition that a medevac helicopter delivered at the cemetery. Sims's men dropped to the ground near the command group. "Nobody was standing up," said Cleo, "because bullets were flying everywhere." Hooper now pointed out the medevac area to the wounded men, grabbed some ammo, and headed to the front, keeping to the left (north) of the middle footpath. No one knows how the wounded got to Loftin's medevac position.

Hogan ordered Sims's squad to find 3rd Platoon. The sergeant led his men south across the middle footpath, toward what was becoming a yawning gap between 1st and 3rd Platoons. As 1st Platoon fought its way forward near the middle footpath, Bischoff's platoon remained bogged down, the men standing or crouching behind the stream bank, secure in the dead ground. Although Bischoff eventually became a first-rate platoon leader, he did not perform well on February 21. Bischoff "just wasn't doing his job," explained Erbach, which is why the chaplain foolishly stood up and screamed at him. "He was not leading by example, he wasn't giving anybody orders, he was just there." [84]

The son of a World War II infantry officer, Bischoff grew up in Woodland Hills, California, a typical All-American Cold War boy who enjoyed Little League baseball and loved being in the Boy Scouts, which "was kind of para-military" with its uniforms, inspections, drills, and badges. After being drafted in 1966 he went through OCS and jump school at Fort Benning, then headed to Fort Campbell where he became the leader of 2-501's Recon Platoon.

When the 101st Airborne deployed to Vietnam, Bischoff wanted "to just do whatever it took to win the war right when we arrived." But after long discussions with disillusioned junior officers from the 25th Infantry Division at Cu Chi and with CIA operatives at Ben Cat, he developed doubts about the war, deciding that "my mission was to keep everybody alive and I didn't care if nobody got killed." By "nobody" he meant American or Vietnamese. "Now, if we had to kill to protect our guys, we did without hesitation. But I wasn't looking for trouble." This attitude became commonplace after the Tet Offensive, but in early 1968 Bischoff's outlook was unusual in the 101st Airborne.

To Bishoff the stream bank "seemed like a thousand feet high," an immense obstacle. With "everybody scared shitless" and mass confusion all around, he could not summon the courage to lead his men over the bank. In his defense, he confronted a difficult situation. Despite having no previous battle experience, after the artillery shell killed Brulte he inherited 3rd Platoon, a decimated unit that had been hastily reorganized and was not in the highest morale. Assuming command just two days before the battle, he knew virtually no one in his platoon, much less the rest of the company. The terrain ahead was relatively flat and open, providing little protective cover, and with enemy gunfire raking the lip of the stream bank "it would have been a shooting gallery" if his men tried to advance. Still, he admitted, "in this whole battle, I was the less effective force of everybody. I did the least. I probably could have been a lot more aggressive." [85]

As Sims moved into the gap created by Bischoff's leadership failure, he glanced into a burning building filled with ammunition and about to explode. Sims hastily moved his men back toward the headquarters element.

When the building blew up it "didn't leave a crater or anything, but it was dangerous" as bricks, concrete, and shrapnel hurtled through the air, wounding two troopers.[86]

Following the explosion Sims resumed his search for 3rd Platoon. He had just begun moving when an NVA popped out of a hole and fired a quick burst. One bullet hit a bamboo limb, bounced into the air, and fell right between Hogan and Sims, lying there in the dirt glowing red hot. Suddenly Hooper appeared and shot the NVA. As Hogan recalled the scene, Joe was intensely excited. "Joe Hooper was loving every minute of what he was doing. I can't quite understand how a guy could love to shoot and be shot at, but in all honesty Joe was having a good time, or at least he sure wanted to get back up there and mix it up. He just needed a little more ammo."

As soon as Hooper killed the enemy soldier Sims again moved forward. He took a few steps when another NVA threw a hand grenade that landed amidst Hogan, Sims, and other Raiders. Sims screamed, "Get back! Get back!" As everyone dove for cover the sergeant jumped on the grenade, which detonated almost instantly. It blew him into the air, turning his stomach and groin into jelly, leaving him alive but unconscious and bleeding badly. Using a poncho as a stretcher four men carried him to the medevac area, but his wounds were mortal.

When Hogan later submitted Sims's name for a Bronze Star he did not realize the sergeant jumped on the grenade intentionally, but thought he accidentally fell on it while leaping for cover. Several days later Lieutenant Colonel Tallman expressed irritation with the Bronze Star recommendation, informing Cleo that many Raiders believed Sims deliberately sacrificed his life to save others. "Hell," said Tallman, "this is Medal of Honor stuff." He told Hogan to start collecting data, see what eyewitnesses said, and then reevaluate the situation. Cleo soon reported to the battalion commander that so many men were certain Sims smothered the grenade on purpose that he was going to submit an MOH recommendation.

Fred Aronow quickly gathered the necessary material and sent the paperwork to battalion headquarters. Less than three weeks after the battle Tallman forwarded Sims's MOH file to Colonel Cushman, commencing its journey toward the White House. Although the file began moving through the bureaucracy two months before Hooper's, a clerical error—failure to submit the citation, eyewitness statements, and other enclosures in the requisite number of copies—delayed final approval until seven months *after* Hooper's MOH received President Nixon's signature.

Despite Aronow's efforts, errors crept into Sims's file. The maps locate 1st Platoon too far north and 3rd Platoon too far inside the village, and mislocate the site of Sims's self-sacrifice, putting it south (instead of north) of the exploding house. And the file says Sims threw himself on a booby trap, when it was a grenade. Some of the eyewitness reports contain unreliable information. For example, Cleo Hogan's claimed that "SSG Sims started to move forward when a North Vietnamese lunged from a bunker. With a fierce blast from his M-16 SSG Sims killed the North Vietnamese." Hogan later stated he did *not* see Sims kill an NVA, although he acknowledged that the sergeant might have. Watson's statement observed that Sims's squad "launched a furious attack on the enemy that probably saved 1st Platoon from annihilation. During this attack SSG Sims could be seen easily enough at all times because he never took cover, so busy was he directing his men and adjusting their fire." Watson's account also stated that when Sims moved out in search of 3rd Platoon, the headquarters element went with him. According to Hogan's recollections, Sims did not launch a "furious attack" to save 1st Platoon, and the headquarters group remained in place when his squad went looking for 3rd Platoon. And, of course, no one saw much for very long.

Unknown to Hogan, who anguished over the gunfire coming from the direction of the pink pagoda, the NVA were unable to exploit the gap between 1st and 3rd Platoons because a one-man American army, Dale Urban, plugged it.[87] When Urban and Hooper approached the village, Dale veered to the right and ran south along the stream, staying in dead ground. Alone, he crossed the creek near the south footpath. A sparse treeline bordered the path for a short distance before the trail emptied into a vast rice paddy. As soon as Urban climbed the stream bank he attacked a two-man bunker near the treeline and close to the stream, killing one NVA while the other escaped. He moved a few steps north when an enemy soldier (perhaps the one who fled the bunker) stepped from behind an obstacle, "pointed his rifle, and pulled the trigger, and his gun didn't go off. Misfired. I shot him with my M-16."

Continuing north along the stream because he heard AK-47s firing from that direction, he knocked out a bunker complex, though he cannot recall how many bunkers were in it. From the complex he saw dense vegetation to his north, which was the tangle of trees and brush along the middle footpath, and heard a tremendous amount of gunfire in that direction, which was from 1st Platoon's battle. Moving toward the sound of the guns, he attacked a bunker in the thick vegetation just south of the middle footpath. Two NVA staggered out, badly hurt. Fearful they might shoot him if he left them, he slit their throats using a double-edged Gerber knife with a six-inch blade that his girlfriend's parents sent him. Later in the war someone stole the knife, but after the war he married the girl, which was undoubtedly better than keeping the knife and losing the woman.

Then Dale turned east, staying in the heavy cover where he felt some-what safe until he encountered another bunker, which he destroyed. From there he moved to the pink pagoda, a small cement building with an open doorway. Setting his M-16 down against one side of the doorframe and lean-ing against the other side, Urban lit a cigarette. Having been a high school athlete, he never smoked until arriving in Vietnam, where he became a butt-to-butt minifurnace. Seeing no one in front of him, he thought the battle was over in his immediate vicinity. He was also "waiting for the rest of the guys to get caught up with me because I'm getting too far ahead." He "was worried about getting shot in the back, which is why it took me so long to move from one place to another. I had to make sure there wasn't somebody directly behind me who might mistake me for the enemy."

Halfway through the cigarette, gunfire erupted from a bunker to his left front in the treeline along the village's east edge. The sudden fusillade startled Dale—and left him shaking uncontrollably after the battle as he contemplated how easily he could have been killed when he crossed in front of that bunker while walking to the pagoda or while he stood framed in the doorway. Crawling forward across the open terrain, he threw an incendiary grenade into the bunker, then lay on top of it. From there he looked back toward the stream and saw American soldiers advancing. Bischoff had his men moving now that Urban had eliminated most enemy resistance on 3rd Platoon's front.

Another unexpected fusillade erupted from a huge bunker at the vil-lage's far southeast corner, where the trees lining the south pathway met the treeline on the village's east side. The NVA were firing at Bischoff's men mov-ing up from the stream, not at Dale. As 3rd Platoon hit the ground, Urban rolled to his right but could not see any enemy soldiers. Nonetheless he fired at the bottom of the treeline, then scrambled back onto the bunker. After waiting several moments he peeked out through the trees on his left, looked down the treeline, and saw three dead NVA officers right where he shot. As he continued watching in that direction, American soldiers approached from the south and threw grenades in the massive bunker. When several wounded NVA stumbled out of it, "They were killed right there. Everybody just opened up, though I didn't."

Although Dale did not know it, those Americans were from Recon Platoon, Bischoff's old outfit. About the time Sims's body arrived at the medevac area, Tallman had asked Hogan if he could use Recon, which contained approximately thirty men. Yes! The Recon commander, Lieutenant Ken Buch, contacted Cleo, saying he was about a quarter of a mile behind the medevac area. Could Buch see the archway? No. Cleo walked back out to the earthen ramp, looked south, and noticed the pink pagoda. Could Buch see it? He could, so Hogan directed him to move south of the shrine and then attack north until he linked up with 3rd Platoon.

Immediately after the conversation with Buch the commander of C Company radioed Hogan and urged him to keep attacking. Having crossed the village north of 1st Platoon without any opposition, his men were in the rice field on the village's far side, shooting NVA trying to flee eastward. The troopers were eager for more easy killing. Unfortunately for the Raiders, rather than engage in suicidal flight, the surviving NVA stayed put, forcing D Company to root them out one at a time.

Before 1st Platoon assaulted the enemy's final pocket of resistance in its front, Hooper appeared for a third time at Hogan's position, carrying a wounded man and, as usual, needing ammunition. The wounded soldier— no one knows who he was—told Cleo that "Sgt Hooper seemed to be everywhere . . . charging bunkers, throwing grenades and generally inspiring all the men around him."

After Recon Platoon hurled grenades into the massive bunker at the village's southeast corner, it continued northward and helped 1st Platoon eliminate the last enemy bunkers in its area. The Raiders then linked up with C Company in the rice field, ending the battle.

As quiet descended on the battlefield Urban stepped into the rice on the village's far side and encountered his buddy Joe Hooper. Dale believed Joe arrived in the group that came from the south, but this was erroneous. Joe came from the north.

Dale Urban's DSC file was as mysterious as Hooper's Medal of Honor. It contained "eyewitness" statements by none other than Joe Hooper, as well as Parker, Jodey Gravett, and Ronald D. Scott. As with Hooper's eyewitness accounts, the signatures were forgeries and the statements contained inaccurate information.[88] All erroneously claimed Hooper and Urban acted together. Joe stated that Urban led "the first attack across the stream where we knocked out six bunkers" and "was with me most of the way afterward, attacking bunkers, and leading attack after attack with great courage." According to Parker "SGT Urban and SGT Hooper were always in front, storming bunkers and knocking our fortified houses." Gravett and Scott concurred that Hooper and Urban acted as a team. Scott also allegedly saw Urban "help move three of his wounded men to the rear," which did not happen since no other troopers were with Dale.

A fascinating aspect of the two files concerned the three NVA officers killed by unaimed fire near the battle's end. Both files claimed Hooper and Urban fired together. Joe's file asserted he moved forward alone to investigate the results, while Dale's maintained that he "courageously crawled forward and found three North Vietnamese officers, killed by rifle fire behind the concealing underbrush." Both men received credit for the act, but the deed was Urban's, and his *alone*.

With good reason Dale never understood his DSC citation, though he certainly deserved the medal even if the eyewitness accounts and citation were fabrications. Indeed, perhaps he, as much as Hooper, deserved a Medal of Honor.

Joe Hooper's situation was more than a little ironic.

Although his MOH file was virtually worthless as evidence, Hooper played a paramount role in 1st Platoon's struggle—perhaps *the* paramount role. Hogan, for example, saw Hooper at least three times. Twice he carried wounded men, although whether he actually *rescued* them was unclear. All three times Hooper was looking for ammunition; having acquired it he headed back to the front.

Other soldiers, none of whom wrote eyewitness statements, observed Hooper in the thick of the battle. Ava James, the RTO who ditched his radio, spent a lot of time with Hooper at Fort Campbell and considered him a mentor. He recalled that Hooper led the initial assault. Later, after James crossed the stream with Grimsley and Parker, Joe came back to them. "He's got his hand on his dick and an M-16 in his other hand and he's swearing up a storm, I mean he's cussing!" A small piece of shrapnel had hit Hooper's penis. When he asked the platoon medic to take a look at it, the medic declined. "I'm not going to touch that thing," he insisted. "There's no telling where it's been." Joe bandaged his own penis, rounded up some ammo, and went back to the battle. Moments later James threw his damaged radio down, grabbed a machine gun and ammunition from a wounded Raider, and went to find Hooper.

Before locating his mentor James fired all his M-60 ammo, so he worked his way back to Hogan's command element, reloaded, and again went searching for Joe. James was on the south side of the middle path when he saw Hooper on the north side. He "was working his way down the bunker line. We were nodding back and forth. We got about half way [through the village] and I ran out of ammo again, and I think he made a trip back in the meantime and got ammo, too. We were kind of taking turns. And we were the only two guys that I saw up there. There was nobody else up there at all."

When James returned from his second resupply mission he spotted Hooper again, still north of the middle pathway. Intermittently James stuck his head up, squinted through the burning haze, and saw Joe assaulting buildings and bunkers. At one point, he recalled, "Hooper was down in this trench stabbing this guy." James and Hooper signaled back and forth, maneuvering from building to building, fighting farther into the village, providing mutual support as they advanced, before James made a third ammo trip to the rear.

Relocating Hooper, they were still alone when they encountered the final bunker line. Several other troopers joined them there, including Tex Gray who was almost immediately shot in the shoulder and became wedged in a trench. As James struggled to lift Gray out of the trench, more Americans arrived. Just then the grenade went off that re-wounded Gray and blew a hole in one of James's lungs and injured his legs and spine. Being a young male James quickly "checked my package [groin and testicles] to make sure I was all there. First things first. I had holes in me as big as a fist." Medic Terry Loucks "basically told me that I was OK. Of course he was lying."

In James's estimation Joe was not just the spearhead of the assault, he "*was* the attack because there's nobody up there with us until the very end."[89]

Note that Ava James played the role ascribed to Urban in Hooper's MOH file. In the chaotic haze perhaps Joe mistook Ava for Dale.

Samuel Ayala also knew Hooper was at the battle's forefront. Three decades later Ayala still became choked with emotion talking about Joe. When Sam reached the dead ground along the stream embankment he and several other Raiders initially stayed there, but not because they were afraid. "You know something crazy is that we couldn't hear [anything]. We didn't believe that the enemy was just in front of us. In fact, I did something really stupid. I jumped up the embankment, walked a little bit toward the village, and took a leak." Eventually he and the others realized a battle was in progress and fought their way into the village.

Carrying an M-79 grenade launcher, Ayala suddenly found himself out of grenades, alone, and armed only with a bayonet. An NVA popped up and aimed at him, but his AK-47 misfired when a round jammed in the breach. Sam lunged at his adversary with a bayonet, believing he was going to die. To his surprise he killed the enemy soldier. But before he died the NVA clubbed Ayala with his rifle above the nose and on his knee and also stabbed him in the side. Sam was alive but wounded, and still alone with enemy soldiers in the immediate vicinity. Suddenly Hooper appeared, draped with bandoleers of M-16 ammo and accompanied by several other soldiers. "He and his men took care of the situation, completely took care of the situation. He just took over, and they kept on fighting to clear the area and then set up a perimeter. Had he not come I definitely would have been dead."[90]

Like Samuel Ayala, Noah Rockel, who was in 3rd Platoon, found shelter behind the stream bank and initially could not hear the raging battle. He and two other soldiers had their backs against the embankment, facing the rice paddy, and saw a helicopter land at the cemetery. Just then Hooper came out of nowhere, walking fast, bent slightly forward at the waist, saying, "I need some volunteers *now!*" Only nineteen, Rockel thought Hooper "looked like an old man." Incredibly, Noah thought the helicopter had delivered hot chow and did not realize it was a medevac. He believed Hooper wanted men to go get the food, so of course he volunteered. "And that's how I ended up with Joe Hooper that day," not going for chow but into "one hell of a fire-fight." For a while Joe threw grenades into hooches, bunkers, and trenches, moving quickly for an old man, while Rockel provided support with an M-79. But Noah did not witness everything Hooper did, first because "my ass was gettin' on the ground," and second because he eventually lost contact with Joe inside the village.[91]

Richard Ryan, Al Mount, Bobby Rakestraw, Roy Barber, and Richard Buzzini also witnessed some of Hooper's actions. "I don't know how we got in the village, I don't know at what point we advanced in there, but I know that Hooper was responsible for getting us in," Ryan recalled. "Hooper kind of launched his own offensive, and he was able to break down enough of their defense that we were able to go into the village. If it wasn't for him, we'd have never got in there." Mount moved forward with Hooper on his right, and a couple of Raiders to his left. He did not remember anyone in front of them as they leapfrogged from position to position. When Hooper gave him a "move out" hand signal he "got up and went toward the next point of cover," but he took a bullet in the leg, which felt like someone hit him with a baseball bat. "From that point on I can't tell you what anybody else did." [92]

Like everyone else, Rakestraw "didn't see everything Hoop did. I was too busy keeping my butt going. . . . I can't remember every detail or exactly what he did or didn't do. But I know that every time you looked up it seemed like he was there." In particular Bobby knew that "Just before Ava James got hit Hooper was right over to my left, advancing." Barber and Buzzini also saw Hooper during the battle's final stage. Barber encountered him just to the south of the middle footpath, in the direction of Dale Urban. "He was out of breath and wild-eyed, but then, just about everybody else was, too. It was intense." Buzzini, who was right next to Barber for a while, saw Hooper "running back and forth doing all kinds of things. He was in one place and then he was in another." [93]

Perhaps more important than what fellow Raiders saw was what Hooper wrote about February 21 in an undated two-page document.[94] Its origins remain unknown, but when resubmitting either the Silver Star as a DSC or the DSC as an MOH, Hogan or Aronow probably asked Joe to describe in writing what he did that day. "As a general rule," said Hogan, "when I would write up awards and decorations on individuals I gave them to the men and said, 'Is this accurate? Is what I'm saying about you true?' I might have asked them to put it into a form that we could send back for typing at the first opportunity." Upon reading Hooper's account thirty years later, Cleo thought it looked like one of these documents, suitable for typing after someone in the rear corrected the spelling and fleshed out the sentences.[95]

Here was what Joe wrote, with all his typical misspellings and erratic punctuation:

On 21st Feb [19]68, Co D 2/501 Abn [Airborne] was on a search and destroy mission two miles west of Hue, Vietnam.

As SSG Hooper's platoon advanced into a wood line, a pitched battle ensued. A well organized complex of enemy bunkers, designed to bring devasting [devastating] flanking fire on the friendly forces, had the company at a stand still.

Disregar[d]ing his own saftey, SSG Hooper took six men and charged the bunkers wiping out part of their forward element, forcing them to leave behind large amounts of weapons and ammunition.

Then seeing one of his men get hit, and pinned down, SSG Hooper crawled forward under heavey enemy fire, and took the wounded man to saftey. Returning to battle, two more men were wounded and traped by grenade fire. Hooper repeatedly exposing himself to enemy fire he went forward and brought one man out. On returning for the seccund [second] SSG Hooper was wounded by grenade fire, disregar[d]ing his own wound he crawled forward and brought the man out. At this time SSG Hooper refused to be evacuated, insisting that he remain with his platoon.

Reorganizing his platoon to press the attack forward, SSG Hooper saw a fellow paratrooper, pinned down behind a burning hut, going to his aid SSG Hooper knocked out three enemy bunkers making it possible for the traped man to pull back.

As the battle neared the finish six hours later, SSG Hooper's paltoon encounted [encountered] the enemy's final line of bunkers. The enemy stubborney [stubbornly] refused to give up their postions. Running out of ammunition, SSG Hooper inspired his men by attacking the enemy with grenades and engaging them in hand to hand combat. Again seeing one of his men get hit and traped in a trench, SSG Hooper crawled forward, got the wounded trooper on his back, and shot the last NVA solider with a 45 cal[iber] pistol as he tossed a hand grenade, wounding SSG Hooper a seccund time.

SSG Hooper's personnal courage and bravy [bravery] did a great deal in accomplishing the Co[mpany] mission, completely destroying a North Vietnam regimental headquarters which was controlling the NVA offense [offensive] at Hue, Vietnam.

Much of Joe's account accords with his MOH file. For example, he led the charge against the enemy's first bunker line; rescued a number of wounded men, including one trapped in a trench near the battle's end (probably Tex Gray); reorganized his men and led them forward, pressing the attack; received several wounds but refused to be evacuated; and killed an NVA with a pistol.

Substantial differences remain between what Joe wrote and the MOH file, which is more precisely detailed and elaborate. For instance, it provided the names of the men Joe rescued—whether the names were accurate cannot be proven. Instead of repeating a vague reference to "wiping out part of their forward element" the file claimed he eliminated exactly five enemy bunkers. Joe wrote of "the enemy's final line of bunkers," but the file asserted he destroyed exactly seven bunkers. Not only was the MOH file more precise, it also contained episodes missing in Hooper's account. Although Joe said he engaged in hand-to-hand combat, the file dramatically described how Joe killed the NVA officer with his bayonet. Another dramatic incident, where Joe maneuvered behind a building, burst through the back door, and had enemy bullets missing his head by an inch, was absent from Joe's statement. Nor did his account say anything about rescuing Chaplain Erbach, firing LAWS, capturing two NVA, being on top of a bunker and hearing enemy soldiers whispering below, or operating in tandem with Dale Urban to destroy bunkers and kill three enemy officers.

In addition to his written account, Joe occasionally talked to journalists and friends about that day. Sometimes he exuded humility, admitting he was scared and proclaiming he did not do anything exceptional, that he was just doing his *job*, that "it wasn't so much a matter of bravery as saving your ass." Whatever he did was motivated by comradeship. "I was," he said, "primarily interested in the safety of the men." He also emphasized that he saw men die who did braver things than he did.[96]

But Joe's propensity for storytelling usually got the better of him. "I eliminated 85 enemy in the six-hour battle and rescued six of our trapped and wounded men," he regaled one reporter, with typical exaggeration. "I captured thirteen enemy soldiers and was wounded seven times. We were out of ammunition in the first ten minutes," so he resorted to "sticks, stones, enemy weapons and anything I could get my hands on."[97]

Joe especially enjoyed recounting the incident, detailed in his MOH file, about the time when the AK-47 he was carrying was out of ammunition, the

NVA officer's M-16 misfired, and he killed the man with a bayonet. Hooper related that story to Aronow when he was compiling the MOH file, just like Joe told him about being with Dale Urban, which was not true.[98] The only eyewitness who remembered actually seeing Joe stab an NVA was Ava James, but perhaps his memory was faulty in one of the many ways that memory can be unfaithful. At the least the story's colorful details were probably untrue. Perhaps Joe did not remember much more than engaging in some generalized "hand to hand combat." When talking with Aronow, who was expressly looking for material justifying an MOH, maybe Joe converted this amorphous incident lurking vaguely in his brain into something better, into a *great* war story, replete with imaginative details.

The story's details varied every time Joe told it, often a sign of fabrication. In some versions the NVA officer had a pistol not an M-16, the AK-47 Joe was using was not out of ammunition, and he used a bowie knife instead of a bayonet. "I thought I was dead," Joe told one writer, as he explained how he stared into the barrel of a pistol, "but when he finally fired, the gun jammed! He threw it down and ran. I should have stayed where I was and simply shot him. But I was mad. He'd *laughed* at me. So I ran after him and threw him on the ground. But the guy was a karate expert. I took a bad licking. I might have been killed. Luckily I carried a bowie knife, and when I got an opening, I drew it and slit his throat." In another retelling Joe used a Russian bayonet. In still another he was carrying Chaplain Erbach and had to put the chaplain down before he killed the officer. Instead of slitting the NVA's throat he stabbed the man, with the blade getting so tightly stuck in the chest bone and the handle becoming so slippery with blood that he had a hard time withdrawing it. Whatever version Joe used, he told the story with such conviction that listeners believed it.[99]

Joe undoubtedly had his most honest conversation about February 21 with Platoon Sergeant Mark S. Hawk, who served with Joe during his second tour and had a Hooper-like love of combat. They were alone that night on a desolate fire base. Once the battle started, Joe told him, he really did not "remember a whole lot about it because there were some 'empty spaces' in his mind." He recalled starting toward the village, blowing up some bunkers, and getting wounded, but not much more than that. "But some of the stuff they say I did, I guess I did it" because so many people said he did.

"The next thing I knew," Joe continued, "they were patting me on the back and calling me a hero."[100]

Nine

Into every life a little steel must fall.

William Fred Aronow,
the Delta Raiders' executive officer, providing
a fatalistic explanation for the company's numerous casualties

Victorious armies rarely sleep easily on the battlefield, and the Raiders were no exception as a deep gloom enveloped them the night of February 21.

No joy, no jubilation, not even any sense of victory pervaded the Raiders' NDP. Dazed, trembling, and exhausted as their collective parasympathetic nervous system kicked in with a vengeance, the Raiders endured a miserable night. A light drizzle fell and the temperature dipped into the upper 40s so everybody was cold and wet. Emanating from the shattered NVA bodies stacked nearby, a repugnant fresh-kill odor of blood and entrails assailed the nostrils.

To some, those shattered bodies were gratifying. Cleo believed his company killed at least twenty-five NVA, which made him "the proudest man around of my company. We had overrun an enemy company and wiped them out." Arriving at the site of the battle, Aronow was euphoric. "The Delta Raiders are the greatest!" he exalted to his wife. "Lt. Hogan did a great job yesterday!" The Raiders had "scored a MAJOR victory!" In tallying up the day, the Battalion Daily Journal noted that at the cost of one man killed and approximately thirty wounded, 2-501 racked up "50 BODY COUNT!"[1]

The bodies that were such a fulsome addition to Westmoreland's attrition strategy spooked some of the men. Samuel Ayala stared at the human cordwood all night, fearful that "one of the gooks might just get up and kill me." To others the bodies were a mangled reminder that the day had been costly for the Raiders as well. "I figured half the guys we evacuated would die," recalled Cleo Hogan. "Some of the guys they were carrying back were severely, *severely* wounded and I figured that within a week I would hear that half of them had died."[2] Remarkably, only Clifford Sims died; all the other wounded Raiders lived. Thinking of their medevaced comrades generated

conflicting emotions among the survivors. The sudden loss of so many injured buddies hurt deeply. Yet the survivors were also relieved, glad the casualty quota for that day had not included them. But—another conflicting
sentiment—what about tomorrow's quota?

Just before nightfall 2-501 established an ad hoc cordon around the unnamed village, with the Raiders to the east and south, C Company to the
north, A Company to the west, and B Company providing security at Battalion Headquarters. During the night intermittent shots came from NVA
still hiding inside the perimeter, nearly igniting a firefight between A Company and the Raiders. A few NVA sniper shots prompted A Company troopers to return fire, but some of their bullets passed through the village and
hit in D Company's sector. Thinking they were under attack, the Raiders
shot back. Quickly grasping the situation, Hogan ordered his men to stop
shooting unless they had a definite target, and soon A Company ceased firing, too. The budding friendly firefight ended "but everyone was so tense
that no one slept."[3]

One of the most amazing things Joe Hooper did on February 21 was
to help prepare the Raiders' NDP. He not only warded off the depressive
effect, the overpowering urge to do nothing, of the parasympathetic backlash, but also ignored his wounds. "We're exhausted. We're preparing to
settle down for the night," Sal Bongiorno recalled. "And Hooper's still making sure everybody's taken care of." Ayala and Bobby Rakestraw also marveled that Hooper remained so calm that evening and acted so efficiently and
professionally.[4] At one point during the night Joe hunkered down for a few
minutes with Dale Urban and they engaged in some black-humor teasing.
The object of their dark humor? Who had the worst wound. Although he did
not recall being shot, Dale had a nick about four inches from his heart,
which he patched up in the field.[5] Joe had wounds to his left hand, left leg,
and groin area. Although he did not feel too much pain, certainly the shrapnel in his penis was bothersome for such an aggressively sexual man.

By daylight Joe was much more concerned. Walking over to Company
Headquarters, he asked Hogan if he could be evacuated. Several other soldiers had already requested a medevac that morning "basically because they
wanted to get out of the war," so Cleo was suspicious. Joe initially showed
him his hand, which Hogan said did not warrant evacuation since the Raiders now had a foxhole strength of about sixty men, and Cleo needed every

trooper he had. Then Joe said he had been hit "down here" and pointed to his groin. Cleo asked to see the wound, but Joe was reluctant to lower his trousers until ordered to do so. His badly infected groin was swollen to the size of a large grapefruit. When Cleo touched the area "the pus just spurted out of it. I said, 'My God, Joe, you should have been sent in yesterday. Why didn't you tell me?' And he said, 'Well, we were so short handed I didn't want to leave you all.' I said, 'Well, you're got to get out of here now.'"[6]

Joe later exaggerated the nature of his wounds. He told one newspaper reporter he had "little hope for his recovery" when he entered the hospital because he lost so much blood. But official medical records listed his wounds as "Not Serious" and his prognosis as "good."[7] Even with his comparatively minor wounds, Joe was temporarily out of the war.

About the time Joe was medevaced, the Delta Raiders captured two cold, wet, and scared NVA soldiers. They belonged to a communications and ammunition unit with the 90th NVA Regiment, which explained why the Raiders found so much communications equipment and ammunition in the village. "The POWs [prisoners of war] fell to their knees, begging for mercy," wrote Hogan, "and when they did not respond to my statement for them to stand, one of my men hit one of them with his M-16. I reminded the men of the importance of prisoners, and ordered the men to stop mistreating them." This would not be the last time that at least some Raiders abused captured enemy soldiers.[8]

With the POWs on their way to Battalion Headquarters, 2-501 swept back through the unnamed village. While A and D Companies acted as blocking forces to the west and east respectively, C Company entered the village from the north and Recon Platoon searched the south edge before heading north. C Company got about half way through the village when a camouflaged sniper killed two men and wounded three more. A furious manhunt ensued involving C Company and the Recon Platoon, bringing the entire operation to a halt for more than two hours. Finally Lieutenant Buch, the Recon Platoon commander, spotted the man and killed him. Clearing the village cost C Company four KIA and twice that number WIA, three more dead but many fewer wounded than the Raiders suffered the previous day.[9]

Having cleared the village, 2-501 turned east, heading for Hue. For the next several days the battalion maneuvered toward the city, a miserable experience in the chilly, damp weather and with the NVA putting up sporadic resistance, never engaging in a pitched battle but fighting a delaying action that cost the battalion at least a few dead and wounded every day. Fred Aronow caught the flavor of the advance. "I wish I had something cheery to say," he wrote his wife, "but there isn't. . . . This war is a horrible experience but certainly a maturing and aging one." [10]

Two incidents on February 23 shocked Cleo Hogan, one revealing the NVA's brutality, the other ARVN's cowardice (at least from the American perspective). That morning the Raiders discovered a massacre, with approximately thirty Vietnamese civilians dead, each with a bullet wound to the head. Toward evening the Raiders entered an ARVN compound where the South Vietnamese soldiers "were all wearing laundered uniforms; the camp was well supplied; the men were laughing and joking about how badly the men of the 2-501st looked." Even when combat erupted in the vicinity, these ARVN had not ventured out of their compound, which left Cleo angrily wondering why Americans were doing so much of the fighting.[11]

On that same day the enemy high command ordered its forces in Hue to escape. Capturing La Chu and the immediate vicinity was a turning point in the Battle of Hue, not only disrupting a regimental headquarters but also severing a crucial enemy logistics route.[12] As the Raiders neared the city they encountered dozens of young Vietnamese males with short haircuts, all claiming to be members of the South Vietnamese air force trying to get back to their base. "And we bought that," Aronow lamented. "I'm sure I must have personally talked to 15 or 20 or 25 NVA soldiers, because that's how they got the hell out. . . . They walked right out through us in the confusion, a lot of them on bicycles." The Raiders also discovered the enemy's well-constructed trenches and bunkers, which made some of them happy the NVA fled. As Fred Aronow informed his wife, "We'd have lost a lot of men if they'd stayed to fight."[13]

Late in the afternoon of February 25 the Raiders reached Hue. By then they did not look like an American airborne company. Instead, they resembled a small, bedraggled guerrilla band—or even an NVA unit. D Company was down to forty-six filthy, unshaven men, which was basically the size of a full-strength platoon.[14] The depleted ranks were stark evidence that the Raiders were living by their new motto: "Into every life a little steel must fall." [15] Moreover, the survivors wore and carried a lot of NVA equipment. "I myself carry a North Vietnamese bayonet and wear a brown NVA officer's belt with a Communist star on the buckle," reported Aronow. "A lot of guys sleep in NVA hammocks and carry NVA rucksacks. We have to search bodies anyway and can keep anything we want." One grunt sported a Star of Lenin medal, Cleo Hogan donned the insignia of an NVA company commander, and many men carried Chinese-made pistols.[16]

Although grimy and cross-uniformed, the Raiders received a warm welcome from many of Hue's residents, especially the 500 people who hid in a Catholic Church and orphanage while the NVA occupied Hue. "These people were really jubilant!" exalted Aronow. "The Yankee liberators!" [17]

That night the Raiders hunkered down in several ravaged buildings, their sleep disturbed only by an occasional sniper shot. The next morning First Sergeant Scott became a momentary hero when he helicoptered in, bringing eggs, spam, biscuits, and coffee, which was the first hot meal the Raiders had in a week.

The luxurious life lasted less than twenty-four hours. On the 26th Hogan received orders to sweep back through the area of the previous week's fighting to look for enemy equipment and bodies. By the 28th the Raiders were at the unnamed village, sickened by the vile odors from the still-smoldering fires, from the rotting NVA bodies that no one had bothered to bury, and from the decaying pigs, water buffalo, and other animals killed on February 21.[18]

Intelligence reports indicated that the North Vietnamese "could not mount large scale attacks because of the large number of losses incurred during the TET Offensive" and that most NVA units had retreated into the mountains to obtain replacements and new equipment.[19] Local Forces were reportedly well-armed, well-supplied and in high morale, but were not expected to launch many major ground attacks, though they might increase their efforts at interdiction and harassment with mortars and rockets.[20] As a result the Raiders suddenly could not find any enemy units. Search and destroy operations continued, but were generally uneventful (or in military lingo, had "negative contacts"). The Raiders also provided security for mine sweeping teams on Highway 1, and on March 1 a convoy made it from Phu Bai to Camp Evans for the first time since the Tet Offensive began, thus reopening a key logistics line.[21]

A welcome respite from field operations came in mid-March when D Company pulled six days of "palace guard" duty, serving as the security force for Battalion Headquarters at Fire Base Pinky, 2-501's recently established base camp situated midway between Hue and LZ Sally. The 101st Airborne was rapidly developing the latter into its base camp, something akin to the 25th Division's sprawling complex at Cu Chi.

During the battlefield lull from late February through mid-March, Operation Jeb Stuart ended. 2-501 left the 1st Air Cavalry's operational control and returned to the 101st Airborne's 2nd Brigade. Almost simultaneously the 101st Airborne Division launched Operation Carentan I, which blended seamlessly into Operation Carentan II on April 1. Combined, the two operations lasted until May 17. Their primary purpose was to destroy enemy forces and base areas in the foothills east and south of Hue, in the mountainous jungles along Route 547 leading from that city to the A Shau Valley, and in the coastal plains northwest of Hue. Division headquarters assigned the 2nd Brigade the task of clearing the coastal lowlands, where the paddy dikes and villages were elaborately fortified, graphic proof that the area had been an enemy stronghold for many years.[22]

As the fighting temporarily ebbed, D Company regained some its strength as wounded soldiers trickled in from the hospitals, including Joe Hooper, who spent more than a week in an Air Force hospital at Cam Ranh Bay. When Raider Lonnie Nale visited him, Hooper "was up walking around and goofing off. His wound wasn't that serious, it was just where it was." Joe's nephew, James Gumm, who was stationed at Cam Ranh Bay, also discovered Joe in a lighthearted mood. So did Chaplain Erbach, who was in the same hospital. When they saw each other they embraced, laughed, and strolled around outside, talking "about the weather, the women, wine, you know, the typical things that you talk about. We did not talk about the battle, nothing, it never came up." Joe sought out other wounded Raiders. He found Ava James and regaled him with a fantastic yarn about how the Raiders used stacked up NVA bodies as a shield during an enemy human wave attack the night of February 21. Not until 1996 did James learn this was a fable.[23]

For soldiers whose wounds were not serious, a hospital stay was a pleasurable interlude—decent food, a bed with clean sheets, indoor plumbing, friendly visitors, and female nurses being among the amenities. Raider Eugene Robertson, who was still recovering from the wounds he suffered on February 15, was "living like a king. I got a bed with sheets and does that feel a lot better than the wet ground and a poncho. I get three hot meals a day and you don't know how much better that is than C-rations. These people at Cam Ranh Bay don't even know a war is going on."[24] Hooper actually had fun with one of his wounds, showing nurses an X-ray of his swollen penis with the shrapnel fragment in it and joking that he hoped they took the shrapnel out but left the swelling in. Or perhaps they could leave the metal in and it would serve as a French tickler.[25]

Despite the niceties of hospital life, Joe was so eager to return to the combat zone, where he was always so comfortable, that he went AWOL, simply walking away from the hospital without being officially discharged. Sometime around March 5 he rejoined the unit, still wearing a hospital gown.[26] No one knows how he got from the hospital back to the Raiders.

On the 11th he wrote his parents from Fire Base Pinky, informing them that he was fine, but seeing Hue saddened him. "What use to be a beautiful city is nothing but a big pile of rumble [rubble]. This war is terriable. I am so sick of destroying these beauitful homes and killing anything that moves. I wish to hell we would pull out. These people are happy. They have 4 or 5 kids, a few acers [acres] [and] 4 or 5 water bafflo [buffalo]. They dont want nothing else. The V.C. come in and kill them if they dont hide them, and then we kill them getting charlie out. It really effects you, to see women and kids on there knees begging you not to go in there village, because they know their homes will be destroyed and faliny [family] killed. But thats war."[27]

Joe contemplated leaving the army, but did not have enough money to attend civilian flight school so he would stay in Vietnam and save money, "or until charlie gets me good." Four days later he changed his mind, as he revealed in a letter headed "60 days left"—that is, he had sixty days remaining before his six-year enlistment expired. Despite money problems he was "going to get back in June. I am getting out."[28]

Just before the Raiders' palace guard duty ended late on March 14, Joe captured a VC. He and his men "turned him in for qu[e]stioning instead of killing him"—the implication being that other prisoners were not always so fortunate. As the Raiders departed Fire Base Pinky less than an hour later, Hooper was not expecting much combat because, "We killed most of the NVA. Whats left we drove into the mountains." In the past three weeks the only noteworthy excitement came from ambushes, not battles. "We have been sitting [setting] up ambush[e]s at night," Joe told his parents, "and getting 5 or 6 a night that try to sneak back into the mountains." Joe exaggerated;

the Raiders were not adding to the body count with such nocturnal regularity. Their first successful ambush was on March 3, killing one NVA. Four nights later, by which time Joe rejoined the unit, another six enemy soldiers died. Not for another two weeks did the Raiders execute another successful ambush.[29]

Although night operations were difficult and dangerous, an American general lamented that the army handicapped itself by not conducting them more vigorously. The general stated one of the war's truisms: the enemy controlled the night, in large part because the Americans conceded it without a fight. As foxhole wisdom acknowledged, the "Night belongs to he who claims it. It is a friend to weak armies because strong armies are usually lazy."[30] Collectively Westmoreland's forces were too lazy to seize the night, but General Barsanti was an exception. Demonstrating that a truism does not always embody the whole truth, he ordered his division to deny the enemy its freedom of movement between sundown and sunup. The 2nd Brigade commander, Colonel Cushman, embraced that challenge.[31] Almost every evening each rifle company in his command established at least one ambush. Cleo Hogan normally sent out four, each about squad sized (eight to twelve men).

An ambush required special preparation and techniques. As a unit patrolled during the day, it looked for suitable ambush sites. When night fell the ambushers moved into these predetermined positions, always leaving an escape route and having a prearranged rally point. After springing an ambush, the men fired for no more than a minute or two before sprinting to the rally point. There they paused until everyone was accounted for before returning to the company NDP.[32]

Peering into the darkness on ambush duty, men knew not to stare directly at an object but to look off center. The reason for this was that the human eye has both cones and rods. Grouped only in the eye's center, cones are used to see during the day; clustered on the periphery, rods are vital for night vision. If a person looks directly at an object at night, it can literally disappear; only by looking fifteen or twenty degrees to the side will it reappear.[33] Also, when the firing began a soldier was supposed to keep one eye closed to save some night vision, but in the excitement few soldiers remembered to do this.[34] One great technological advantage the Americans had was the starlight scope, which was far superior to human rods; it yielded a green-tinged image that approximated daylight.

Ideally when the Raiders (or anybody else) sprang an ambush they relied on claymore mines and grenades because these did not reveal a soldier's exact location the way a muzzle flash did.[35] However, once the squad leader detonated the claymores everybody usually blazed away, generating maximum firepower to inflict maximum damage in minimum time. The trick was to fire low since "you can hurt or maim somebody with flying rocks but you're not going to shoot too many guys in the trees at night!"[36]

Most soldiers abhorred ambush duty. After humping the boonies all day, staying alert most of the night was an ordeal. When not on their two-hour watch, some men faded into an agitated half-sleep despite distant artillery fire and the chirps, growls, and whistles of night animals. But most could not sleep—nor could they talk, smoke, or swat at swarming mosquitoes for fear of alerting the enemy. Suffering in miserable silence, soaked in sweat and drizzle, hands and face blackened with camouflage grease, each man wrestled with the "anxiety, the agony, and the fear that tonight may be the last night that you will ever see the sunset."[37]

Ambushes often came up "dry" or, worse, went awry. Despite all the security precautions, occasionally the enemy ambushed the ambushers. At other times the ambushers encountered too many enemy soldiers and allowed them to pass through the kill zone unhindered. George Parker recalled his first ambush, when neither he nor anyone else even twitched as a company-sized enemy unit walked right past them because "There were too many of them for us to handle."[38]

And sometimes, such as the night of March 18, an ambush was FUBAR (a World War II acronym that stood for "Fucked Up Beyond All Recognition").[39] Four squads departed the NDP for their preselected ambush locations. One element had a new RTO, a Private First Class named Hanna, a replacement who recently joined the company and who was going on his first ambush. A half hour later Hanna's voice came up on Hogan's radio, choked with fear, saying, "They're all dead, they're all dead." The NVA had attacked his squad with knives, machetes, and axes, and hacked the men to death; Hanna claimed that everyone but himself was KIA. Cleo reported this catastrophe to battalion headquarters, but soon all the "dead" men straggled back into the NDP, all perfectly healthy. Now the only remaining task was to retrieve the RTO, who was hiding in the bushes, so paralyzed with fear it took several hours to get him back to the company position.

Exactly what happened that night remained unclear. Initially Hogan believed that two of the ambush squads "ran into each other in the dark and scared both of them to death." Fred Aronow and George Parker agreed, and were thankful that nobody started blasting away.[40] In later years Cleo became convinced that the squad encountered an NVA patrol, but in the darkness the troopers initially thought it was another Raider ambush element. Only when they were within arms length did the Americans and NVA grasp the situation. Each side bolted in opposite directions without firing a shot.

The next morning, as Hogan briefed his platoon leaders and platoon sergeants about the day's mission, somebody tapped him on the shoulder. When Cleo turned and saw that Private Hanna had interrupted him, he was livid, and became even more livid when the private informed him that he was not going with the company any more. Hanna insisted that Cleo call him a helicopter. "O.K., Hanna, you're a helicopter," Hogan replied. "Now do you feel better?" The humor eluded the sullen man, who only reluctantly accompanied the unit that day. Toward dusk he purposely shot himself in the foot; in military terminology he had a Self Inflicted Wound (SIW). Boarding the medevac chopper that Cleo requested, Hanna yelled, "I told you, you were going to call me a helicopter."

Aronow and others raged at Hanna's unmanly conduct. Everyone else was petrified, too, but they mastered their fear and had little sympathy for "cowards." "We damned near had a lynching here tonight," Aronow wrote his wife shortly after "the spineless bastard" shot himself. "Now that spineless wimp will occupy space in a hospital that a REAL man needs to have." The only consolation, the executive officer believed, was that Hanna would be court-martialed, spend six months in jail, and then serve twelve months in the field before being discharged.[41] Maybe Hanna was a coward, but perhaps his amygdala-based fear system was defective and he could not tolerate fear as well as most men, using the self-inflicted wound as a way to "flee" danger.

If the ambush duty psychologically crippled some soldiers, it energized a small handful of others, none more so than Hooper. According to Aronow the Raiders "became masters of the night ambush and Joe Hooper was one of the 'professors.'" Joe was "electric," said Craig Sturges, because "when you went out on any ambush, or anything, with him you *knew* you were going to find something."[42]

Joe demonstrated his professorial skills two nights after Hanna's fiasco when he set an ambush along a narrow trail at the base of Ya Do, a mountain one and a half miles west of the unnamed village.[43] In his squad that night were Dale Urban, Richard Buzzini, Bobby Rakestraw, Harry Longbottom, and four or five others. Fighting off fatigue, the men got out a starlight scope, placed claymores along the trail, then took up positions parallel to it, with every other man sitting up and the others lying down. A piece of detonating cord ran from man to man; a tug on one end alerted everyone. Shortly after 11:00 p.m. twenty to twenty-five NVA walked down the trail, so many that only half of them fit in the kill zone; maybe more were still behind them but in the darkness no one could tell. Prudence might have dictated not triggering the ambush or else the Raiders might find themselves in a firefight, thus threatening the foremost goal of an ambush, which was to "keep from getting anybody killed. Kill as many of them as you can, but definitely none of us." Such a one-sided killing match ideally required both surprise and numerical superiority, or at least near-equality. Even after achieving surprise, a night firefight with a larger force risked getting some of "us" killed.

Having little patience with prudence, Joe detonated the first claymore and all hell broke loose. Claymores and grenades exploded while rifle and machine gun fire rippled the night air. Some NVA died in the initial firestorm, and a few more were killed trying to rescue their downed comrades. When the survivors regrouped and began shooting back, Hooper's squad broke contact, raced across a small stream, and reassembled on a dirt road, which was the preassigned rendezvous point. From there they trudged back to the company NDP. Two Raiders suffered wounds. A machine gunner took a glancing blow to the head, and Dale Urban had shrapnel in his left wrist and "a lot of dirt and sticks and little bitty rocks and stuff stuck in the gums of my mouth, and I had little cuts on my face where a grenade went off."

Official records claimed a body count of eight, but no one stayed around to count bodies that night and the NVA undoubtedly policed the battlefield after the ambush element retreated. Returning to the site the next day the Raiders found one body and some body parts, though not enough to estimate exactly how many enemy were KIA.

Whatever the enemy toll, Hooper received a Silver Star for the ambush. With wild hyperbole the citation explained that when the Raiders fell back, the enemy pursued and Hooper provided a desperate one-man rear guard, "firing magazine after magazine into the awesome hostile force, ignoring the lethal rounds hitting all around him." Although Joe later claimed that he "only held them off for fifteen minutes, but I guess that was long enough," in truth no such heroic delaying action occurred. The citation also credited the ambush with a body count of *at least* fifteen. Although clearly an exaggeration, even that number was small compared to Joe's fabrications. In the Hooper version, his ten men confronted 300 NVA and killed 154 of them, or, in another account, only 152.[44]

By late March the Delta Raiders had such a superb reputation for ambushes that higher headquarters ordered Cleo to Da Nang to provide a briefing on his company's success. "We were out there to seek and destroy the enemy," he explained, "but a lot of other companies were out there to seek and avoid 'em. . . . If you just go out there and make enough noise, they'll avoid you because the NVA were not looking for a fight. They were trying to survive."[45]

On March 20, the day of Hooper's ambush, the Raiders left the populated rice lands, heading into the uncharted, primeval wilderness straddling the Vietnamese-Laotian border.

Their initial objective was Nui Hon Vuon, otherwise known as Hill 309, steep and barren, with a peak that was not much more than fifty yards across. Since the hill dominated the surrounding terrain, the idea was to establish a fire base there so that 2-501 would have artillery support when it plunged into the jungle, which began on Hill 309's back slope. The Raiders' movement was part of an assault by both 2-501 and 1-502 that had enemy Base Area 114 as its ultimate objective.[46]

Taking Hill 309 ignited more than a week of nearly continuous combat. In mid-afternoon of March 21 Lieutenant Bischoff's 3rd Platoon was two-thirds of the way up the hill when gunfire erupted from the hilltop, driving the platoon back. Four Air Force jets pounded the well-camouflaged NVA positions for nearly an hour, as did some distant artillery. Then 3rd Platoon, now reinforced by 1st Platoon, launched a second attack, which was also unsuccessful. More bombing, a third attempt, and a third failure was the final proof that becoming "King of the Hill" was not going to be easy.

During the night and throughout much of the next morning the hilltop received a thorough pounding from artillery and mortars, from two .50 cali-

Maggie Hooper with Douglas, Audrey, and Joe, in South Carolina in 1944 or 1945, before the Hooper family moved to Moses Lake, Washington. Photo courtesy of Audrey Hooper.

Grade school portrait of Joe. Photo courtesy of Faye and Joey Hooper.

A snapshot of Joe as a teenager in Moses Lake. Photo courtesy of Faye and Joey Hooper.

Joe in the Navy, where he began his military career in 1956 after dropping out of high school midway through his junior year. Photo courtesy of Faye and Joey Hooper.

Joe and his first wife, Sandra. They married in May 1959, after she became pregnant and were divorced seven months later, even before their son Robert was born. Photo courtesy of Sandra Horwege.

Joe and his guard dog Bo Bo, in Korea in the early 1960s. Photo courtesy of Audrey Hooper.

MOST HIGHLY DECORATED GROUP IN VIETNAM

[HANDWRITTEN LABEL ON FLAG/IMAGE] CPT. ORGANISED UNIT

Group portrait of the Delta Raiders before departing Fort Campbell for Vietnam. Captain Charles W. McMenamy, the officer who organized the unit, is standing just behind the soldier holding the company flag. Joe Hooper is on the far right in the top row. Platoon Sergeant George ("Heavy Duty") Parker is fourth from the left in the bottom row. Photo courtesy of Charles W. McMenamy.

Captain McMenamy at Cu Chi in Vietnam, December 1967. Photo courtesy of Cleo C. Hogan Jr.

The page from Captain McMenamy's note book in which he listed those killed and wounded on February 15, 1968. Photo courtesy of Charles W. McMenamy.

The earthen ramp leading up to the archway that marked the middle pathway through the unnamed village where the battle of February 21, 1968, occurred. Hooper received the Medal of Honor for his actions that day. Photo courtesy of Cleo C. Hogan Jr.

Standing to the front of the building with the red roof, looking back over 1st Platoon's attack route into the unnamed village. Note the stream in the foreground that the Raiders had to cross. Photo courtesy of Cleo C. Hogan Jr.

Joe Hooper taking a nap in the field shortly after he "escaped" from the hospital and returned to the Raiders. He is still wearing the top half of his hospital gown and has wrapped himself in a sheet of plastic. Photo courtesy of Richard L. Buzzini.

A candid shot of the Raiders' attacking near Phuoc Dien in April 1968. Cleo Hogan carried a 35 mm camera with him and sometimes handed it to one of his RTOs to take action shots like this. Photo courtesy of Cleo C. Hogan Jr.

The Delta Raiders' second commander, Captain Cleo C. Hogan Jr. receiving his Combat Infantryman's Badge from Lieutenant Colonel Richard J. Tallman. In the background reading the order is the company's executive officer, William F. Aronow. Photo courtesy of Cleo C. Hogan Jr.

The Medal of Honor ceremony at the White House on March 7, 1969. Left to right: Joe, Fred W. Zabitosky, President Nixon, and Clarence E. Sasser. Photo courtesy of Faye and Joey Hooper.

The Medal of Honor ceremony. Left to right: Joe; Balbine's son Peter from a previous marriage; Joe's second wife Balbine; President Nixon; unidentified; Maggie and John Hooper, Joe's parents. Photo courtesy of Faye and Joey Hooper.

Hollywood starlet Carollyn DeVore (wh
was promilitary despite Hollywood's a
leged liberal bias) in January 1969, shor
after she returned from Vietnam a
Thailand where she had been on a US
tour. Photo by PFC Terry Walpole. Pho
courtesy of Carollyn DeVore.

Joe and Carollyn and her son Rolly from a previous marriage. Joe liked wearing h
dress white uniform. Photo courtesy of Carollyn DeVore.

Joe Hooper's Medal of Honor attached beneath the pelican on the Joe Mann Monument in Best, Holland. PFC Joe E. Mann, from Reardan, Washington, received a posthumous Medal of Honor while fighting to liberate Best in World War II. In high school Joe wrote a brief paper about PFC Mann. In his typical impetuous way, Joe climbed the monument and placed his medal there. He later climbed back up and retrieved it, but left the medal with city officials. It is now on display in the Airborne Museum in Best. Photo courtesy of Irene Bennett.

Joe and some of his men in camouflage during his second tour. Joe is in the lower right. He sent this photo to Carollyn, with the inscription reading, "Love you forever Carollyn. Please don't give up. We will allways [*sic*] be togeth[e]r. Take care of our wond[e]rful son. Love, Joe 'The King of Vietnam in Exile.'" Photo courtesy of Carollyn DeVore.

Hooper receiving his second Silver Star for bravery during a firefight in early April 1971, just days before he finished his second tour in Vietnam. Photo courtesy of Audrey Hooper.

A formal military portrait of Joe taken on June 8, 1971, following his second tour, showing all of his medals. U.S. Army Photograph #PC-188777, courtesy of the National Archives.

Joe and Faye at O'Hare Airport in December 1971. They were on their way to visit Joe's family for the holidays. Faye is holding an angel ornament that Joe had given her for Christmas. Photo courtesy of Faye and Joey Hooper.

Joe working at the Veterans Administration in Seattle. Note the stylish side-burns and longer hair. Photo courtesy of Faye and Joey Hooper.

Joe and Faye with their daughter Joey. Photo courtesy of Faye and Joey Hooper.

Joe holding Joey. Note that Joe was no longer trim and lean. Photo courtesy of Faye and Joey Hooper.

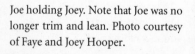

The flag being folded at Joe's burial in Arlington National Cemetery in 1979. Photo courtesy of Audrey Hooper.

Joe Ronnie Hooper's headstone at Arlington National Cemetery. Photo courtesy of the authors.

ber machine guns (which had a longer range than standard .30 caliber machine guns), from several 90 mm recoilless rifles, and from Navy and Air Force warplanes. "I loved to have the bombers bomb for us," said Hogan, who unquestionably accepted the Army's way of war. "It's the way to fight a war. You don't get as many guys hurt when they're bombing." Still, the NVA drove back a fourth attack, this one by 2nd Platoon with 3rd Platoon providing support. "It's unbelievable how brave they were," wrote Cleo regarding the NVA. When the Raiders withdrew about 800 yards away, enemy soldiers crawled out of their bunkers and waved at them, "just like they were daring us to come up again. By this time I was furious. I had been kicked off the hill four times and decided that hill was going to belong to me."

So Hogan sent 3rd Platoon forward again, but this time as a diversion while Dave Loftin's 2nd Platoon executed a flanking maneuver to the north that took the defenders by surprise. As Loftin's men reached the peak they assailed the NVA positions with grenades and small arms fire. Shortly after noon 2nd Platoon had Cleo's hill for him.

Hogan had no time to savor the victory before the high command descended on him to bask in the reflected glory—and make his life miserable. Still on an adjacent hill from where he directed the battle, Cleo and 1st Platoon were preparing to deploy to Hill 309 when he received word that "Dinner Plate" (the code name for Lieutenant General William B. Rosson, who was the overall Army commander in I Corps) was coming to his location. Almost immediately, Hogan recalled, "my position looked a little like Chicago's O'Hare airport." Rosson arrived with his two helicopters, Barsanti was not far behind with two more choppers, and then Colonel Cushman and Lieutenant Colonel Tallman, reflecting their impoverished rank, arrived with only one chopper each. "Here they are on top of the hill," Hogan related, his voice still tinged with disbelief, "wanting a briefing on what's happening and we're still fighting a war."

They all eventually departed, but Barsanti promised to return in an hour to award impact medals. When the general asked Cleo how many medals he wanted, Hogan started to say what he would like to have. Barsanti cut him off, yelling in his high squeaky voice, "DAMN IT Lieutenant, don't bargain with me. Tell me what you want, not what you would like to have." Almost speechless because of this childish tantrum, and unsure of who had done what over on Hill 309, Hogan sucked in his breath and responded, "Sir,

I want 3 Silver Stars; 10 Bronze Stars with V; and 5 Army Commendation Medals with V device." He was still at the naive stage where he "thought asking for a Silver Star was going overboard. Hell, that's a tremendous medal. They don't come in crackerjack boxes." "Now that's more like it," Barsanti replied.

For the next hour Cleo put the war on hold as he tried to sort out who deserved medals, and got those men from Hill 309 to his position. Under the hurried circumstances no one was sure that the most deserving soldiers actually received the awards, but Hogan did the best he could. The impromptu medal ceremony turned ugly because Barsanti's aide apparently had only two Silver Stars, provoking the general into another tirade. To remedy the aide's "error" the general took the Silver Star off the second recipient, whispering that he would get the man a new one, and pinned the medal on the third recipient. Then he pulled another Silver Star out of his pocket and pinned it on Hogan, who, as he told his wife, spent most of the battle ducking bullets. Cleo deserved a Silver Star, but for La Chu, not Hill 309. When Hogan reflected on this affair, he "realized that the aide had the 3 Silver Stars that I had requested, but since MG Barsanti had taken one to pin on me, the aide was one medal short." A classic bully, Barsanti blamed his helpless subordinate.

Because of the delay for Barsanti's medal ceremony, Hogan no longer had time to deploy the Company Headquarters and 1st Platoon to Hill 309 before darkness descended. During the night the NVA mounted a furious counterattack against 2nd Platoon. All Cleo could do was call in artillery support and hope that Loftin's platoon beat off the attack, which it did, killing a handful of NVA and, remarkably, suffering no casualties. During the morning of March 23, Cleo finally arrived atop Hill 309 with the Headquarters element; later that afternoon 1st Platoon joined the rest of the unit.

While the Raiders dug in, an unfortunate incident occurred. The previous day an NVA mortar round killed Walter H. Anslow. His brothers-in-arms wrapped the dead man in a poncho, awaiting an opportunity to medevac the body. Fortunately, six replacements were helicoptering to D Company and Anslow's body could be removed on the chopper. As it touched down, the NVA fired a mortar barrage. Hit by shrapnel, the helicopter lurched upward and the new men hurriedly jumped to the ground, one of them landing on the poncho-wrapped body. "When the smoke cleared, the man was covered with blood and went berserk," wrote Hogan. "For more than 30 minutes I tried to snap the man out of it, but it was no use and I finally called a Medevac for the man." The grim introduction to the combat zone transformed the soldier into a neuropsychiatric casualty, taking him out of the war just as surely as if he was shot.

Replacements began changing D Company's character, diluting its original esprit de corps because they did not share the enthusiasm for the war exuded by Captain McMenamy and Cleo Hogan and the soldiers who initially deployed to Vietnam with them. One of the new men was Dale Stengel, born in Kearney, Nebraska, in 1947. He flunked out of Kearney State College, was drafted, and trained as a rifleman. Flying into Vietnam in early March, Stengel thought the place looked like a prairie dog town. "I couldn't figure out what in the heck all these little mounds were. They ended up being bomb craters!"

Like many replacements who arrived beginning in late March, Stengel was different from the Original Raiders. He was a "leg," a regular infantryman trained to conduct combat assaults from helicopters but not airborne qualified, and viewed those who were with disdain. "I always told these paratroopers that only two things fell out of the sky. One was birdshit and the other was fools, and I was neither." Unlike the Original Raiders, Dale did not like Cleo Hogan's leadership style. "The military was very important to him. But the military was not at the top of my priority list by a long ways." Never very good at taking orders, Stengel thought the company commander was too gung-ho, gave too many orders, and put too much emphasis on spit-and-shine.[47]

Nonetheless, like most reluctant draftees he performed his duty—until August 18 when a piece of shrapnel caved in his skull at the right temple and lodged between his eyes, where it remained permanently, leaving him with a dent in the side of his head and imperfect vision and hearing. Aronow believed men like Dale Stengel were "the real heroes of the war." Sent to Vietnam involuntarily, they served honorably, without excessive bitching and moaning, and increasingly carried the combat load. In 1965 only 16 percent of battle deaths were draftees, but by 1970 that percentage escalated to 43 percent.[48]

Reinforced by a few less-than-enthusiastic replacements, the Raiders spent several uncomfortable, dangerous days and nights on Hill 309 while

Tallman established Fire Base T-Bone on a three-hill complex that incorporated Hill 309, and began concentrating the battalion there. After dark the NVA probed and mortared, often evoking knee-rattling terror among the defenders. When they tested the perimeter the night of March 23, the Americans hurled grenades down the hill and called in illumination rounds that created an eerie half-light. At a critical moment Hooper, who was with a few men on an observation post, rolled a massive explosive charge down the hill. When it detonated the entire hill shook. The next morning revealed a charred array of "uniform parts, weapons parts, and body parts."[49]

Having captured and held the mountain, the Raiders expected to become the battalion reserve force for a few days while C Company attacked westward toward a smaller peak, Hill 100. But while D Company captured Nui Hon Vuon, C Company sustained devastating losses securing a nearby peak, Hill 285. By the time C Company assembled on T-Bone, it was at less than one-third authorized strength, incapable of further sustained combat. Tallman gave Cleo the bad news: his unit would continue the attack. "I wasn't prepared for this," Hogan wrote. "D Company was getting the call for all the action."[50] In this case, *too much* action.

On March 26 the Raiders departed Hill 309's bare knob and descended into the jungle, which was wet, damp, and so thick that at midday it seemed like midnight, so thick that "you can't even move. You can't maneuver a company, you can't get around."[51] As the descent began Hooper was optimistic. True, it seemed like the Raiders were fighting twenty-four hours a day, but that was because they were "right in the N.V.A. strong point, [and] we have them on the run now. So we may end this operation soon. In a couple more days." Although the fighting did not bother Joe, he had other concerns, such as wanting more letters and care packages from home. Moreover, he reluctantly had to stop taking pictures. His film at the PX at Cu Chi was destroyed during the Tet Offensive and, even more aggravating, he recently lost his camera.[52]

Joe's optimism, like American optimism regarding Vietnam as a whole, was misplaced. With 2nd Platoon leading, the Raiders moved no more than 1,500 yards when the NVA sprang an ambush.[53] Hogan pulled the company back into a tight perimeter and called in artillery and mortar fire, which continued for the rest of the day and through the night. The firepower had little effect. When the attack resumed the next morning the Raiders immediately made contact. In a battle as fierce as La Chu, "D Company was engulfed in a hail of automatic weapons and small arms fire. The battle was hand to hand, in very thick vegetation. Artillery, 4.2 [inch] mortar, aerial rocket artillery, and TAC AIR strikes were used, but the NVA were so close that the supporting weapons were largely ineffective."[54]

Cleo soon learned that his best platoon leader and good friend, Dave Loftin, was severely wounded when a bullet hit him in the chest, broke two ribs, passed through the right lung, and lodged just above the sternum. Amazingly, Loftin started walking back to a small landing zone that Hooper's squad was furiously hacking out of the jungle. Seeing him wobbling down the trail, Joe grabbed his arm to provide assistance. But feeling faint, Loftin sat down. "Hooper was right there and he bent down over me, telling me I was going to be all right, don't pass out. I kept saying 'I can't breathe, I'm not able to breathe,'" Loftin recalled. With a chuckle he continued, "And that's when the ugliest man I've ever kissed bent down and plugged my nose, and gave me mouth-to-mouth resuscitation!" Joe probably saved his life, though no one knew it at the time. As a medevac chopper whisked the platoon leader away, Hogan was sure Loftin would die and said a final prayer for him.[55]

Moments later Cleo got more bad news. At least half a dozen other Raiders were wounded, including George Parker. Worse, the NVA's initial fusillade killed Clifford L. Williams, one of the recent replacements who had been 2nd Platoon's point man that day. His death especially angered Stengel, who believed an inexperienced man had no business walking point.[56] Although Hogan had orders to pull back, Williams's body was still on the battlefield. Hogan knew "his Soul was in the hands of a just God," but "simply could not leave the body to the ravages of the jungle."

Among those volunteering to retrieve the body were First Sergeant Scott and Staff Sergeant Ronald H. Bowman, who quietly made their way to the body. Just as they bent down to pick it up, an enemy soldier appeared about twenty-five yards away, a machine gun cradled on his hip. Instead of shooting, he smiled. Overcoming their terror, Scott and Bowman hefted the body, turned away, and walked back toward the company, expecting to be shot. They were not. Like the 101st Airborne, the NVA always tried to retrieve their dead so the Communist soldier understood the paratroopers' merciful mission. In his ongoing quest to be the center of attention, Hooper reconfigured this event, telling friends that he accompanied Scott during this episode, leaving Sergeant Bowman out of the story.

As Cleo Hogan recognized, in this "gesture of good faith from an enemy we so often curse and despise and never really understand," the NVA displayed the common humanity shared by the Raiders and the Communists. The Raiders did not always reciprocate such goodwill gestures. For example, they evidently felt no compunction about shooting VC who were asleep, that is, who were as defenseless as Scott and Bowman had been.[57]

Amid these events—Loftin presumed dead, Williams dead, others wounded, and the firefight still blazing—Cleo experienced a moment of stunning clarity, wondering "if all of Vietnam was worth the lives of these men." Another usually enthusiastic soldier also expressed doubts. "I don't really understand just what we're trying to prove by being in there [the jungle]," Aronow wrote his wife. "I really don't. When we leave, the gooks will move right back in." He could hardly wait for his upcoming R and R to "get away from this horrible war."[58]

Cleo Hogan quickly snapped out of his lethargy. "It wasn't whether it was worth a life, it was that we still have to get out of here. We ain't out of this jungle yet." Four air strikes between noon and 4:30 p.m. resulted in several spectacular secondary explosions and paved the way for the Raiders to advance—those "bombs sure do come in handy," Cleo informed his wife.[59] After hunkering down for the night and receiving only sporadic mortar fire, March 28 dawned quietly. Without encountering any resistance, the Raiders climbed Hill 100 and were counting NVA bodies when they received an urgent message to prepare for immediate extraction. Within two hours D Company was in a rice paddy north of Ya Do.

That night distant rumbling and an earthquakelike sensation told the Raiders why they left Hill 100 so hastily. B-52s pulverized the area. Although D Company was several miles away, "you could hardly walk because the ground was shaking so violently."[60]

Expressing a widely held view, Hooper was relieved "to get down from those terrible hills." While in the mountains he "got two more purple hearts but the wounds were small. Bits of scrappel [shrapnel] in the right arm and left hand." Along with leaving the jungle and his wounds being minor, a third tidbit of good news was that "we are getting a break. After 86 days of steady fighting we are going to Utah Beach. A place just like Cam Rhan [Ranh] Bay. So we should have it made."[61]

A month after the Tet Offensive began, Walt Rostow, the Special Assistant for National Security Affairs, advised President Johnson that 1968 was undoubtedly the "year of decision."

Rostow and other advisers did not necessarily expect the war to end soon, "but its outcome will be foreshadowed by the events of this year."[62]

When the Raiders emerged from the mountains in late March, the effects of the Tet Offensive were not yet entirely clear, nor would they be for months. As with most battles, Tet was no hairpin "turning point"; its immediate effects were ambiguous. But its long-term implications were decisive, and they signaled an American defeat.

Taking place against the backdrop of the Success Offensive, Tet eroded the public's confidence in the competence and credibility of its civilian and military leaders, and convinced a vast number of Americans that not only was the war being lost but also the United States could never win it at an acceptable cost. Despite repeated promises of imminent victory, the enemy was neither appreciably weakened nor noticeably less resolute after enduring three years of stupendous firepower. Westmoreland's strategy, costly in American resources and lives, was revealed as bankrupt. America, it seemed, was dumping its resources down a bottomless sinkhole. As the *New Republic* summed it up, the government's "prophecies are as discredited as the policies they serve."[63]

Consequently, Tet compelled the Johnson administration to reexamine its approach to the war. An especially important aspect of the reassessment was the military high command's bleak outlook during February and March. The military later tried to absolve itself from any blame for its less-than-stellar performance in Vietnam by concocting a myth that the United States won the Tet Offensive, and that only a weak-willed commander-in-chief and the media's portrayal of the battle as a defeat subverted public opinion. But at the time many high-ranking officers and the CIA agreed with the media. As Secretary of Defense Clark Clifford (who replaced McNamara on March 1) put it, "despite their retrospective claims to the contrary, at the time of the initial attacks the reaction of some of our most senior military leaders approached panic."[64]

Few generals were as blunt as Army Chief of Staff Harold K. Johnson, who stated that "We suffered a loss, there can be no doubt about it." But the unrelenting pre-Tet optimism was no longer visible, even in Westmoreland. While publicly proclaiming victory, Westy officially revealed a litany of difficulties and fears. Realistically, he cabled General Wheeler, "we must accept the fact that the enemy has dealt the Government of Vietnam a severe blow." In bringing the war to the cities, the VC/NVA inflicted great damage and disrupted the economy, so that the "people have felt directly the impact of war."[65]

Although correctly recognizing that the South Vietnamese suffered acutely during Tet, Westy blamed the wrong combatant for most of the damage. Indiscriminate firepower from American and South Vietnamese units caused most of the devastation in Hue (where South Vietnamese and American "information" agencies accused the VC/NVA of massacring 3,000 people, a number that was undoubtedly inflated) and elsewhere. Can Tho, Ben Tre, Saigon's Cholon district, and dozens of other places were little more than dead-filled rubble when Tet ended. As one officer warned, the destruction might "exceed our capability for recovery and battles we win may add up to losing the war" because of the increased hatred among South Vietnamese.[66]

While contending that the Communists suffered a military failure, Westmoreland acknowledged that the enemy's military goals were secondary, that its objectives "were primarily psychological and political." He did not, of course, comprehend the importance of this insight because he proclaimed victory on the basis of a huge (and, as usual, inflated) body count and the Communists' inability to capture any cities permanently. Having never understood the war, he continued measuring "success" on the basis of short-term conventional American standards. He never assessed the situation from the enemy's longer-range perspective, which paid greater attention to political and psychological factors, shifts in momentum, and the regional and international balance of forces. And in any event, even in raw military terms the enemy retained considerable staying power; even at the unprecedentedly high loss rates for early 1968 the VC/NVA could fight for another dozen years![67]

Additional communications from Westy revealed that although ARVN fought well, MACV questioned whether the South Vietnamese could survive another round of attacks. Westy "would welcome reinforcements" not only to "prevent ARVN from falling apart" but also as a reserve force. Sharing Westy's concern about a depleted, demoralized ARVN, Wheeler told the president that "The Joint Chiefs feel that we have taken several hard knocks. The situation can get worse. We do not know the ability of the North

Vietnamese and the Viet Cong to recycle and come back to attack." The JCS Chairman emphasized that "we are not better off than we were on January 15." [68]

The next day Westmoreland's tone became urgent. Based on a more complete assessment, he believed "we are now in a new ballgame where we face a determined, highly disciplined enemy, fully mobilized to achieve a quick victory." ARVN's status remained precarious and the logistical situation in I Corps was tenuous. Without more troops the United States could not regain the initiative, and "a setback is fully possible." Thus he *desperately* needed reinforcements.

Based on this unsettling message, President Johnson's advisors unanimously agreed to send emergency reinforcements, approximately 11,000 men. But Wheeler raised a key issue, one he knew the president adamantly opposed. "The Joint Chiefs," he said, "feel that if you deploy these men there should be a call-up of the reserves." The JCS believed that sending even this modest reinforcement without a reserve call-up would so deplete the strategic reserve that it imperiled America's worldwide commitments. As a result, for the first time, the JCS rejected MACV's request for more troops, perhaps hoping to force Johnson into calling up the reserves. "At long last," noted the *Pentagon Papers,* "the resources were beginning to be drawn too thin, the assets became unavailable, the support base too small." [69]

Despite the JCS's recommendation against deployment without a reserve call-up, McNamara ordered the emergency reinforcement to Vietnam. But this squabble was a mere foretaste of what was to come. Profoundly worried by the military's pessimistic assessments of ARVN, the reports of widespread damage, the prospect of renewed enemy assaults, and possible battlefield defeats, Johnson dispatched General Wheeler to Saigon on February 23.

Wheeler's candid report based on his consultations with Westmoreland was unnerving. Although the enemy suffered heavy losses and "failed to achieve his initial objective," it nearly succeeded in a dozen places. Tet "was a near run thing," and more Tet-like offensives were in the offing. Whether the South Vietnamese could withstand additional sustained pressure was problematic. If Wheeler had doubts about America's ally, he had none about the Communists. They had "the will and the capability to continue," their "determination appears to be unshaken," and they were freely roaming the countryside, dealing a severe blow to pacification efforts. With its resources already stretched too thin, MACV would "be hard pressed to meet adequately all threats. Under these circumstances, we must be prepared to accept some reverses." To avert this potentially disastrous situation, Wheeler forwarded Westmoreland's new request for reinforcements: 206,756 men, which would raise the number of troops in South Vietnam to 731,756. Filling this request entailed a further Americanization of the war, required mobilization of 280,000 reserves, and demanded enormous expenditures. Rejecting it signified "that an upper limit to the U.S. military commitment had been reached." [70]

Secretary of Defense Clifford recalled that Wheeler's report was somber, discouraging, and shocking. Its gist "was not only that the recent offensive was a colossal disaster for us, but that another one was on the way. It is not possible to overestimate the degree of concern and even fear that possessed the heads of our government when Wheeler returned. He said we were in an emergency situation—that we were in real peril." [71]

CIA estimates reinforced Wheeler's report. South Vietnam's leadership was so problematic it might lose control over some provinces, especially in I and IV Corps. Expecting the Communists to sustain a high level of activity, the CIA predicted that the enemy offensives would be contained, but only after severe losses, followed by continued stalemate. Even if the United States sent massive reinforcements, the Communists would not capitulate because they had ample resources to increase their troop strength. As they had done in the past, the VC/NVA could match another American escalation. [72]

In this crisis atmosphere, Johnson asked Clifford to undertake an "A to Z Reassessment," undoubtedly expecting hawkish advice since Clifford was a known prowar advocate. Indeed, as McNamara lost faith in the war Johnson was determined to replace him with a true believer. The new Secretary of Defense, however, quickly traveled McNamara's path from hawk to dove. During February and early March, as he attended White House meetings as an interested observer and then replaced McNamara, he lost his talons. Among other things he discovered that former Secretary of State Dean Acheson was right when he told Johnson that "With all due respect, Mr. President, the Joint Chiefs of Staff don't know what they're talking about." [73]

After a few frantic days of intensive briefings, Clifford's study group recommended sending 22,000 additional troops to meet the immediate crisis and undertaking a very limited reserve mobilization. But the fundamental decision on whether to meet the full request should be contingent upon an improved performance by ARVN and on a comprehensive strategic review. No strategy could succeed unless the South Vietnamese government dramatically reformed and ARVN played a larger, more important role in the fighting. As for Westy's plea for reinforcements, that was just more of the same on an ever-grander scale. Thus it embodied the non sequitur the armed forces had employed since 1964–65: What we are doing is not working, so we need to do more of it. Reinforcements committed to continued attrition would not "bring about a quick solution in Vietnam and, in the absence of better performance by the Government of Vietnam and the ARVN, the increased destruction and increased Americanization of the war could, in fact, be counterproductive." The NVA and VC were so strong that no quick military solution was possible.[74]

Clifford told Johnson that following the well-rutted road of "more troops, more guns, more planes, more ships" would simply continue the war at a higher intensity, resulting in more dead VC and NVA—and "significantly higher" American deaths (which were already exceeding the KIA rate in the Pacific Theater during World War II).[75] If the government met this request, in another year Westmoreland "may want another 200,000 to 300,000 men with no end in sight." Meanwhile the devastation inflicted upon the country the United States was trying to save would intensify. Doubting "that a conventional military victory, as commonly defined, can be had," the president's advisers emphasized that "*there should be a comprehensive study of the strategic guidance to be given General Westmoreland in the future.*" Although not included in the final memo, the study group's thinking focused on shifting from attrition to a strategy of population security, with the goal being a negotiated settlement rather than a World War II–style victory.[76]

Johnson's advisers also reminded him that Vietnam did not exist in a vacuum. Economic instability, worldwide security problems, and the potential for domestic upheavals were all cause for profound concern. The additional cost for Westy's reinforcements would be $2.5 billion in 1968, $10 billion in 1969, and $15 billion in 1970. These huge figures came against the backdrop of a faltering national economy beset by soaring deficits, rising inflation, surging interest rates, and higher taxes, and against an international gold and dollar crisis that, as the president wrote, could "set in motion forces like those which disintegrated the Western world between 1929 and 1933."

"Our fiscal situation is abominable," lamented Johnson. Sending reinforcements would make it more abominable.[77]

As for other security concerns, the American army in Europe was disintegrating, leaving NATO less capable of defending itself. But in 1968 the foremost concern was Korea, where it seemed the war of 1950–53 might reignite, especially after North Korea tried to assassinate the South Korean president and then on January 23 captured the *Pueblo*, an American spy ship. Deliberations about the *Pueblo* reminded McNamara of the Cuban Missile Crisis. Several thousand soldiers destined for Vietnam went to Korea instead, aircraft in Vietnam were sent to Korea, and men serving close to the Korean DMZ received authorization to wear the Combat Infantryman's Badge.[78]

Domestic security was also worrisome. In considering reinforcements, the JCS had to examine "the capacity to meet the possibility of widespread civil disorder in the United States," and Johnson hesitated to send the 82nd Airborne Division, the only combat ready division in the strategic reserve, "because of the possibility of civil disturbances here in the U.S."[79]

While the administration was still pondering Westmoreland's request and Clifford's reassessment, the *New York Times* published an account of Westmoreland's request for massive reinforcements. Because the article mirrored the sentiments that high-ranking military and civilian leaders privately expressed, its tone was gloomy.[80] Reasonable people began asking, "If the U.S. just won a great military victory, as General Westmoreland and President Johnson claimed, why does Westmoreland need more than 200,000 more troops to stave off defeat?" As with the Success Offensive's deceit, the official optimism about Tet was exposed as a fraud.

The *Times* article accelerated the erosion of public support in middle America, which judged the war for itself, not at the behest of antiwar activists. Tet shocked people because they had believed the United States was doing well militarily. Obviously it was not, so "Everyone has turned into a dove." Citizens ceased supporting the war, said presidential adviser McGeorge Bundy, "not because our people are quitters," but because "a great many people—even very determined and loyal people—have begun to think that Vietnam really is a bottomless pit." The war, they believed, was futile and the nation should cut its losses *now*. With good reason General Wheeler feared that if the trend remained unchecked public support would soon be too frail to sustain the war effort. The president agreed, saying that "The country is demoralized. . . . We have no support for the war."[81]

Symbolic of the public decline was Walter Cronkite's TV report on February 27, when the revered CBS anchorman, whom Johnson considered a responsible journalist, gave his assessment of Vietnam. "To say that we are closer to victory today is to believe, in the face of the evidence, the optimists who have been wrong in the past," Cronkite said. "To suggest we are on the edge of defeat is to yield to unreasonable pessimism. To say that we are mired in stalemate seems the only realistic, yet unsatisfactory, conclusion." Cronkite was not alone in veering from the war. The media, as usual following public opinion rather than creating it, began chugging along in middle America's wake. Between January and March seven major newspapers and four major magazines (*Life, Look, Newsweek, Time*), all previously prowar, became antiwar.[82]

Undoubtedly seeking *some* prowar advice other than from the JCS, Johnson assembled the Wise Men, a hawkish group that vigorously supported the war in late 1967. He asked them to receive high-level briefings and then provide recommendations. One exchange during an intelligence briefing demonstrated the military's continuing inability to perceive reality. The briefer claimed the enemy lost 45,000 dead in February. One of the Wise Men, United Nations ambassador Arthur Goldberg, asked what enemy troops strength was when Tet began. Between 160,000 and 175,000. And what was the ratio between killed and wounded? Three-and-a-half to one. The briefer did not grasp that by these calculations the number of Communists killed and wounded was approximately 20,000 *more* than their alleged total strength! But Goldberg did. If those figures were correct, he observed, the Communists "have no effective forces left in the field." Why, then, were reinforcements needed?[83]

To the president's dismay, the Wise Men gave a Clifford-like appraisal. Almost all agreed that no military victory was in sight, and some insisted that South Vietnam must do more. Speaking for the group, McGeorge Bundy explained that the United States "can no longer do the job we set out to do in the time we have left and we must begin to takes steps to disengage. . . . We all felt there should not be an extension of the conflict. This would be against our national interest."[84]

Responding to the unsettling events of February and March, a worried president addressed the nation on March 31.[85] Although claiming that the Tet Offensive failed, he acknowledged that the Communists might soon renew their attacks in an attempt to make 1968 a turning point. But four key aspects of the speech demonstrated, perhaps inadvertently, that the enemy won Tet because the offensive changed America's approach to the war.

First, wrapping himself in the peacemaker's mantle, the president proclaimed he was "taking the first step to de-escalate the conflict," immediately and unilaterally reducing the present level of hostilities by curtailing the bombing over much of North Vietnam. Moreover, instead of 200,000 reinforcements, the United States was sending only 13,500, all of them support troops. "We have no intention of widening this war" by attacking North Vietnam or Laos, said the president, restating the position he steadfastly maintained.

The upper limit of America's commitment had been reached. Rejecting the military's "more of the same" approach and further escalation, the United States took the first step toward de-escalation and de-Americanization. Once begun, the process became irreversible. Just as surely as America's "Special War" failed by late 1963, Tet and its aftermath revealed that its "Limited War" to win militarily inside South Vietnam was also a failure. The decisive moment had arrived. The United States either had to escalate dramatically by going beyond South Vietnam's boundaries with ground troops, or it had to disengage. Rejecting geographical escalation, Johnson began the disengagement.

Second, reflecting a persistent theme among his advisers, the president insisted that the South Vietnamese must do more for themselves. America could "help provide a shield" to nurture South Vietnam's development, but the ultimate outcome depended upon its determination and resourcefulness.

Here Johnson shifted the war to the South Vietnamese in a process later called Vietnamization. Following up on his speech, in mid-April the JCS announced that it was gradually turning the war over to the South Vietnamese. But hoping that ARVN could succeed where the American Army failed was wishful thinking. The United States intervened in the first place because South Vietnam could not defeat the Communists, and few Americans thought they could do so now, though exactly why they remained so weak seemed a mystery. "What is the real difference?" Johnson asked his advisers. "What makes the North Vietnamese fight so well, with so much more determination than the South Vietnamese?" In response, CIA director Richard Helms resorted to a Cold War cliché, attributing North Vietnam's superior fighting to "a combination of good training and good brain washing." [86] No one was willing to acknowledge that a superior cause, one worth dying for, not "brain washing," sustained the enemy.

Third, the United States was "ready to send its representatives to any forum, at any time, to discuss the means of bringing this ugly war to an end."

Here the president hoped the peace gesture, even if rejected, would stem the erosion of home front support. *However,* nothing in the speech indicated that his policy of achieving an independent, non-Communist South Vietnam changed; as General Abrams emphasized, "The President, despite political pressures, remains solidly and unshaken behind the allied effort to ensure a free Republic of Vietnam." [87] By shifting to gradual de-escalation and Vietnamization, Johnson tried to salvage a policy that was under relentless attack. Having fought without any serious negotiations for nearly four years, the United States would now fight while negotiating, so the war continued at a high level of violence. But, the mere fact of negotiations softened U.S. resolve and limited the administration's ability to prosecute the war. [88]

Finally, to further heal the divisiveness afflicting American society and to undercut the antiwar movement, Johnson withdrew from the presidential race.

Here he hoped to gain nine more months to pursue his policy, to inject some backbone into the South Vietnamese, and to insure that the war at least remained a stalemate so that no matter how many more dead it cost, he would not be the first president to lose a war.

Leave that ignominy to his successor.

Less than a week into the Tet Offensive, McNamara observed that "half the enemy units in Tet were not in [MACV's] order of battle." [89]

Yet MACV subtracted *all* bodies from the order of battle, thus inflating the percentage of enemy soldiers killed.

And Westy's headquarters continued juggling the order of battle to prove that the United States won Tet because of the immense slaughter it inflicted on enemy forces. "Tomorrow will be a sort of day of truth," Navy Commander James Meacham, a high-ranking MACV intelligence officer, wrote his wife on March 2. "We shall then see if I can make the computer sort out the losses since the Tet Offensive began in such a manner as to prove that we are winning the war. If I can't we shall of course jack the figures around until we *do* show progress." Ten days later Meacham wrote again. "You should have seen the antics my people and I had to go through . . . to make the February enemy strength calculations come out the way the general wanted them. We started with the answer and plugged in all sorts of figures until we found a combination the machine could digest, and then we wrote all sorts of estimates showing why the figures were right which we had to use. And we continue to win the war." A week later he wrote a third letter. "We had a crash project to prepare a briefing for the press on enemy strength as of 29 February—complete with viewgraphs. . . . I have never in my life assembled such a pack of truly gargantuan falsehoods."[90]

The Wheeler-Westmoreland request for 206,000 reinforcements and the consequent mobilization of 280,000 reserves was disingenuous.

Military leaders knew they were losing the war, that attrition was a failure; they knew they had frittered away the public's support, that Johnson steadfastly opposed a reserve call-up, and that the enemy could match any new American buildup. Yet instead of developing new strategic approaches they sent in a massive request for more of the same.

When the president rejected their request, as they assumed he would, he immunized the armed forces against greater culpability for defeat by providing them with an alibi for losing the war: the president did not give them what they needed to win.[91]

Johnson was aware that the military might resort to this ploy. "I don't want them to ask for something, not get it, and then have all of this placed on me," he said at the height of the Tet crisis.[92]

They did.

They did not.

It was.

Claims of a great Tet victory by the Johnson administration and the military high command evoked ridicule.

"If this is a failure," deadpanned Senator George Aiken, "I hope the Viet Cong never have a major success."

"If taking over a section of the American embassy, a good part of Hue, Dalat, and major cities in the 4th Corps area constitutes failure," quipped Senator Eugene McCarthy, "I suppose by this logic that if the Viet Cong captured the entire country, the administration would be claiming their total collapse."

Even the long dead George Armstrong Custer chimed in through the voice of humorist Art Buchwald. "'We have the enemy on the run,' says General Custer at Big Horn. 'It's a desperation move on the part of Sitting Bull and his last death rattle.'"[93]

The ridicule exposed the truth, which the citizenry understood. A Gallup poll in June 1968 revealed Tet's impact. After the Success Offensive's euphoria, when 51 percent believed the United States was winning and only 8 percent thought it was losing (33 percent thought the war was a stalemate, and 8 percent had no opinion), now only 18 percent believed the United States was winning and 25 percent thought the United States was losing (47 percent thought the war was stalemated and 10 percent had no opinion).[94]

In compelling the United States to break the pattern of escalation, embrace the chimera of Vietnamization, and extend the olive branch, the Tet Offensive virtually guaranteed the enemy's ultimate success. Much hard fighting lay ahead, but if the VC/NVA remained patient, victory would be theirs.

"Now we're going to Utah Beach for a little rest," Cleo Hogan wrote his wife. "We certainly deserve it."[95]

Utah Beach was a critical supply point, an over-the-beach logistical facility on the South China Sea east of Quang Tri. Arriving there on March 31, the same day as Johnson's speech, the Raiders stayed a little more than two weeks. "Utah Beach is not much," Joe wrote his parents. "A bunch of sand and a lot of ocean. 13,000 miles across which is home." For much of the time the Raiders walked in the white sand that was so dazzling it looked like snow, went swimming, body surfing, and fishing, and played full-speed tackle football without pads, using a canteen for a pigskin and causing nearby "legs" to stare in disbelief. Compared to their recent string of battles, the duty was easy. The men built bunkers, strung barbed wire, manned the perimeter at night, set ambushes, and conducted a few local reconnaissance-in-force operations. They also provided security for mine-clearing teams, who provided an essential but not always successful task. Mines regularly destroyed trucks and other vehicles, as Hooper attested. "We had three trucks blowed up carr[y]ing mail," he informed Maggie and John.[96]

The mine explosions, combined with frequent encounters with booby traps, snipers, and mortar fire, were reminders that the VC/NVA were nearby. Joe wondered "how long the quiet will last." For the Raiders' fellow company, A-2-501 (which Joe served in during his second tour), not long enough. In another of a long series of misfortunes, on April 6 the Alpha Avengers lost eleven killed and ten wounded in a vicious firefight. "Had a couple [of] good buddies from Panama killed" in that encounter, Joe told his parents. While saddened by A Company's losses, especially the men he knew personally, Joe was proud that D Company had "the best record over here in our Division. So far we have had only 11 killed—maney [sic] many wounded but only two or three bad. We have bought smoke on the emeny. Killing Hundreds and Hundreds, dont know how meney [sic]." When talking to some enemy prisoners, he "asked them what they feared most. They said Bombs, art[illery], and then Paratroops. We have really did a good job here."[97]

Only eleven killed. Few as that seemed compared to the number of enemy bodies, those dead Raiders were a poignant reminder of mortality. On April 7 the Raiders held a memorial service for them, which "was real nice, considering the place and faccialties [facilities]." The place was a small sand knoll, with the ocean not far in the distance. In front of a large wooden cross and waving flags were eleven upturned rifles, each one with a helmet on the butt and a pair of boots at attention in front. The Raiders sat in the sand while Chaplain Erbach conducted religious services.[98]

With only "about fifty days left in this hell hole," Hooper was not planning on being in Vietnam much longer. Although combat pay allowed him to send money home, the extra money was "not worth being here," that is, in hell. The nether world took a toll on him. He was down to "190 lbs of soild [solid] rock. Would only weigh 180 if I could only get off the dirt and filth thats caked on me. At least the sand has got the green clorer [color] off my feet thats been there since Cu Chi." He reminded his parents to write flight schools for information because he wanted "to get my commerical license and instrument rating in fixed wing & Hello [helicopter]. Will plan on a mounth off and start school arou[n]d 1st of July."[99]

Quite unexpectedly a battle interrupted the Raiders' rest. In midmorning of April 10, as many Raiders were relaxing and swimming, they suddenly received orders to shed their swimming trunks, don battle gear, and prepare for a combat assault at Phuoc Dien, a village about six miles southeast of

Utah Beach.[100] The previous day, a patrol from A Company encountered a few NVA near Phuoc Dien. Early on the 10th, battalion headquarters sent a platoon from A Company to investigate. As it approached the village, the NVA opened fire, inflicting multiple casualties. The rest of A Company was soon on its way to rescue the beleaguered platoon, and so were the Raiders.

Combat assaults were common, but never routine. The men assembled at the pickup zone where they waited for the helicopters to arrive, checking and cleaning their equipment and fidgeting nervously, sitting, then standing, then sitting again, the anxious minutes dragging by far more slowly than in civilian time. Heavily laden with gear, they waddled to the birds. After takeoff, they climbed high into the air, above 2,500 feet to avoid small arms and machine gun fire. For fifteen or twenty minutes a trooper enjoyed the ride, perhaps falling into a near-trance, awestruck by Vietnam's physical beauty, cooled by the air rushing through the open doors, savoring every delicious moment because he knew he could not ride the sky forever.

At the first hint of the descent "you come back to reality," said Fred Aronow, "and your rectum starts sucking wind because you never know what's going to be there when you get on the ground." Having already been "prepped" by jets, artillery, and ARA, the LZ received a final raking when the door gunners fire into likely enemy hiding places. As the earth sprinted up at them, heliborne soldiers felt unbearably trapped in the grip of uncontrollable forces, human meat being hauled to the battle in a fragile machine that, if hit, "has the flying characteristics of a falling safe." In these final fast moments "your spine gets quivering," said George Parker, who admitted that some times he was so scared his nickname should have been "Shakey Duty," not "Stocky Duty."[101]

Relief flooded over everyone if the LZ was "cold," but Phuoc Dien was "hot." As the choppers neared the ground, three of them were too close to the woodline surrounding the village and the NVA opened up. When RTO Lawrence Eller jumped out he took a round in the head, dead instantly; two other men were wounded. Caught in an open rice paddy, the company charged toward the wooded village, receiving fire support from gunships. As the Raiders entered the first hedgerow they discovered a well-constructed system of bunkers and trenches reminiscent of La Chu, and signs of a large NVA force. Relaying this information to Tallman, Cleo was ordered to withdraw and call for tactical air and artillery support. Hogan did not have to be ordered twice since he "really believe[d] in bombing a place before I go into it." His preferred method was simply to "withdraw a safe distance and bomb and artillery the place until there is nothing left then we go in and gather up weapons and equipment." [102]

Shells, bombs, and ARA saturated Phuoc Dien, followed by a liberal application of the riot control gas, CS, which irritated eyes and throats and caused chest pains, nausea, and choking. General Barsanti advocated using CS to reduce American casualties because it penetrated fortifications, forcing enemy troops into the open or incapacitating them. Other elements of the 101st Airborne employed CS extensively during Operation Carentan, but this was the Raiders' first experience with it. Delivered by specially designed E8 Tactical CS Launchers and by CS grenades dropped from helicopters, the gas attack was the immediate prelude to an assault by A and D Companies. [103]

Unfortunately for the Americans, stiff winds quickly blew much of the gas through the village. Also unfortunately, neither the firepower nor the CS dislodged or incapacitated the enemy. The paratroopers again made it to the first hedgerow, but then met heavy resistance, not only from the NVA but also from lingering CS. After ten minutes Hogan realized that communicating with his men through a gas mask was too difficult, so he removed it and cried his way through the attack with a burning throat and eyes. His men did the same. Through his tears Hogan realized the Raiders "were about to be chopped up." Fortunately Cushman "ordered us to pull back, and use more tactical air and artillery. This we did."

With darkness approaching, Cushman decided to encircle the village, or in the parlance of the day, establish a cordon. Ordering B Company to reinforce Alpha and Delta, the three companies spread out around Phuoc Dien, which was no bigger than two or three city blocks and surrounded by hundreds of acres of rice paddies. All night the Americans hammered the trapped NVA with artillery and bombs, and to insure the enemy did not escape under the blanket of darkness kept the area illuminated with flares dropped from aircraft or fired from artillery, lighting up an isolated Vietnamese village like Times Square. The Communists attempted numerous breakouts, most notably about 4:15 a.m. when they struck Bischoff's 3rd Platoon. Several Raiders were wounded, but they beat back the attempt with only a few NVA escaping.

External firepower, supplemented by two 106 mm recoilless rifles that were ideal for blasting bunkers too stout for LAWs to eliminate, continued pounding the village throughout the morning. Meanwhile, using a portable loudspeaker, a psychological operations team that Colonel Cushman sent to D Company broadcast surrender pleas. Around noon a lone NVA carrying a white flag stepped out of the woods. He told Hogan that if the Americans stopped firing the remaining NVA would surrender, and when the bombardment ceased approximately twenty NVA filed out of the village, "stopped, formed a platoon formation, stacked arms just like a parade and then marched to the 3rd Platoon area with their hands on their heads." Many of those surrendering expected the Americans might kill them. Instead, the Raiders gave them food and cigarettes before the prisoners were airlifted to Utah Beach. Hooper was glad "to see them come out and give up. So we dint have to kill them, or them us." [104]

As usual, when Joe later embellished his role in this incident, telling reporters that *he* "had the good idea" that the NVA were scared to death, that *he* persuaded Hogan to call for a psychological operations unit, and that *he* stepped into an open field, armed only with cigarettes and C-rations, and enticed the NVA to surrender. At first, he said, only a lone Communist soldier warily approached him. "We were both shaking. I've never been so scared in my life, as we shared a cigarette. Then he turned and called his friends out of the woods. That was the greatest feeling in the world." [105]

In another tribute to the enemy's ability to endure lavish firepower, resistance in Phuoc Dien was still not ended. When Companies B and D swept the village, diehard survivors among the rubble, many of them severely wounded, fought back. Not until almost 5:00 p.m. was the village finally cleared. Two hours later the Raiders were back at Utah Beach. At a cost of one Raider KIA and another fifteen WIA, Cleo's company racked up a body count of at least sixty-five, plus the prisoners, thus helping to destroy a company-sized NVA unit.

"[T]he Raiders brought smoke as we allways do," Hooper informed his parents, but the battle was tough and "for a while I had my doubts." He received a Bronze Star Medal with V device (that is, for valor) for April 10. According to the citation—questionable evidence at best—Hooper led "a fierce attack on the enemy" and "repeatedly exposed himself to deadly sniper and mortar fire as he carried the wounded men out of the impact area. Again and again he made the dangerous trip, treating the wounded after he had evacuated them, until all the casualties had been moved to safety."[106] Aside from this account, the historical record is silent on what Joe did that day.

His Bronze Star must have been an impact award because he mentioned it in an April 12 letter. "I haven't did two much," he modestly wrote. "Earn[ed] the Silver Star, Bronze Star w/ V, Vietnam Cross of Gallantry, Amy Commendation with Valor, 3 Purple hearts and a bunch of other junk, you cant [wear?] on civil[i]an clothes."[107]

Phuoc Dien was Colonel Cushman's second major cordon operation, following one by 1-501 in March 26–28 that was not entirely successful since some of the enemy escaped during the night.[108] U.S. forces had been using cordons for three years, but most were partially successful at best as the enemy invariably slipped away. An officer who carefully analyzed his unit's experiences, Cushman sought methods to overcome the problem of making the VC/NVA stand and fight so that superior external firepower could be massed against them.

Although the first few cordons were improvised, including Phuoc Dien, Cushman soon developed tactics that guaranteed success. After locating an enemy force, he surrounded it before nightfall. All units not in contact with the enemy elsewhere hastened to the battlefield by trucks, helicopters, or forced marches to strengthen the encirclement. Continuous nighttime illumination was necessary since the enemy exploited even ten minutes of darkness. Foxholes had to be no more than ten meters apart; the VC/NVA slithered through gaps wider than that. Maximum firepower, including special equipment such as the 106 mm recoilless rifle and CS, descended on the trapped enemy. Grunts loved these cordons. "We were getting a lot of NVA, not from small arms but the air strikes and artillery," said Raider Eugene Robertson. "We were weeding them out, we were getting rid of them, and we weren't taking casualties. That's why I liked them."[109]

"If you make contact with the airborne, get away," said a captured enemy document. "They will surround and destroy you."[110] That was certainly true in Cushman's command, which conducted a dozen successful cordons in the coastal lowlands during the spring of 1968.[111] But his methods were not universally applicable. They worked as long as the enemy massed in lowland villages surrounded by oceans of rice so that the battlefield could be isolated. Virtually the only time enemy units did this was from February through May of 1968. Moreover, though causing few American casualties, Cushman's cordons were costly to the South Vietnamese, whose homes were reduced to rubble. They were so destructive that subsequent commanders used "refined" methods: "soft cordons" that, at least in theory, depended on selective air and artillery strikes against carefully identified targets.[112]

Before that change, however, the Raiders, having departed Utah Beach on April 17, engaged in two other cordons in which Fred Aronow commanded the company because Hogan was on R and R. Hogan and Aronow had an uneasy relationship. An airborne Ranger, the latter "much preferred to be in the field with the guys than in the rear sorting out the equally important mail, paperwork, beans and bullets at LZ Sally. I tried to split time back and forth and I think I spent more time in the field." He certainly spent more time there than Hogan wanted; and from Cleo's perspective, even when in the rear Aronow did not adequately perform essential tasks there. Aronow actually agreed with Hogan's assessment. "I guess I haven't been doing a very good job in my administrative duties," he admitted to his wife; detesting paperwork he left too much of it undone.[113]

On the surface Aronow was confident and aggressive but, as he confided to his wife, this exterior masked deep concerns: "It really hurts me to show any weaknesses to anyone (reason: insecurity and inferiority complex)." Perhaps to prove his toughness and competence, he aspired to command an airborne rifle company, so when he got to "borrow" Hogan's company he was elated. In part he relished the opportunity to "participate in armed combat against an enemy of our country" because it was "a matter of Male Pride and Honor, something which for the rest of my life I can always hold dear, that I tried to do my best for my country." Moreover, "command time is the thing for promotions." Intending to make the Army his career, Aronow craved not only male glory and promotions, but also medals. Although he assured his father that he was "not medal-hunting," he was "damned proud" to learn he had been recommended for a Silver Star for racing onto the February 15th battlefield to recover a body. He was especially pleased because Joe Hooper wrote a supporting letter, and because a Silver Star looked "nice on the record and on the dress blues!"[114]

Aronow's first cordon was at the adjacent villages of Kim Doi and Thanh Trung, just five miles north of Hue. Lasting from April 21 through April 23 and involving all of 2-501's companies, it resulted in a dozen wounded Americans (only a few of them Raiders) but seventy dead NVA and another thirteen captured. What Joe Hooper did during these three days is unknown.[115]

The Kim Doi–Thanh Trung cordon was particularly noteworthy because it included the ARVN 1st Division's Black Panther Company (an all-volunteer unit that served as the division's reaction force), the 222nd Regional Force Company, and five Popular Forces platoons. Both Barsanti and Cushman advocated cooperating with the South Vietnamese armed forces, perhaps because the ARVN 1st Division, stationed in I Corps, was commanded by General Ngo Quang Truong who was a relentless fighter. As early as February 8 unit commanders were ordered to "effect immediate liaison/coordination with ARVN, Regional Forces, Popular Forces, and other advisory elements," and the high command insisted that the "terms Little People or Gooks will not be used. Use Popular Forces, Regional Forces, ARVN, civilians, indigenous personnel." [116]

Cooperation with South Vietnamese armed forces became another principle in Cushman's cordons because they "could tell friend from foe far better than we could. They were far more familiar with the area than we could be. Vietnamese authorities had access to intelligence through the villages and hamlets where we had little. And [they] had numbers to augment our own." Another benefit was their superior ability to locate BBTs. [117]

No matter what benefits Colonel Cushman thought the South Vietnamese brought, few subordinate commanders enjoyed working with them. "In all honesty," said Cleo, "I was more scared of Popular and Regional Forces than I was of the NVA" because they were incompetent, lacked motivation, and, worst of all, were not dependable. Many times he "was forced to take them when I would rather have been without them." [118] Aronow was even more vehement, truly detesting "the worthless, begging, slovenly, *spineless*, characterless Vietnamese. *South Vietnamese*," who "have no national pride at all!" Although developing nagging doubts about whether the United States was winning the war, and even whether the war was worth fighting, he still hated Communism. "*But*, if these spineless wimps don't start showing a general trend toward nationalism and concern for their country, I don't want to risk my neck for them." [119] Almost all Raiders agreed with these assessments. To George Parker working with Popular and Regional Forces "was a headache because half of those jokers were VC." ARVN soldiers were "chickenshits" said Bobby Rakestraw, and Richard Ryan discovered that they "weren't the crack troops that the North had." [120]

Few Raiders asked *why* the South Vietnamese fought so poorly. To contemplate that question might lead to uncomfortable conclusions about the wisdom of America's role in the war, especially since racial or cultural explanations were self-evidently flawed. While *our* Vietnamese seemed sheep-like, *their* Vietnamese fought like tigers—but they were all Vietnamese.

Aronow's second cordon was the war's most successful cordon operation. It occurred at Phuoc Yen and Dung Son, nestled in a bend in the Song Bo River three miles from Hue, between April 28 and May 3. A big operation, it involved eight companies from four battalions (though not all were at the battlefield simultaneously), the Black Panther Company, three Popular Force platoons, and fifty local militiamen. The Raiders arrived about 6:30 p.m. on April 29, when Aronow incurred Cushman's wrath because he seemed slow getting the company into the proper blocking position, and departed during the afternoon of May 2.[121] "That was no fun," said Dale Stengel, summing up the operation. "There was no way I slept for three days and three nights through that battle because it was so tense." Thirty years later Bobby Rakestraw still remembered the sights and smells of shattered and charred NVA bodies, which "was the worst of anything I saw over there in terms of blood and guts. It was really upsetting."[122]

When the cordon ended, total friendly casualties were ten dead and fifty-six wounded, but according to official accounts (which should always be taken with the proverbial grain of salt) more than 425 NVA were KIA and another 107 were prisoners. A few NVA escaped during brief lapses in illumination, but for all practical purposes the 8th Battalion, 90th NVA Regiment was rendered combat ineffective. Subsequent prisoners of war and captured documents indicated that the battalion's destruction disrupted the enemy's plan to attack Hue on May 2.

Hooper was not at the Phuoc Dien–Dung Son cordon, nor was he in the field when the enemy's "mini-Tet" exploded across Vietnam beginning at midnight on May 4. Although this offensive lacked the intensity of Tet and consisted of more indirect fire attacks and fewer ground assaults, May 5 to 18 were *the* two most costly weeks of the war for Americans; 1,168 died and 2,479 were so badly wounded they required hospitalization, as opposed to 1,120 KIA and 1,909 hospitalized during Tet's two bloodiest weeks. And the devastation the United States inflicted on South Vietnam was again immense. "When you must use these tactics (referring to bombing, napalming, and heavy artillery fire into the urban areas)," a South Vietnamese official told an American visitor, "I know you are losing the war." In many places the number of homes destroyed and civilians killed was greater than during Tet. "Someone," the official insisted, "should be tried for this murder and destruction." [123]

Hooper wrote his parents from LZ Sally on April 27, May 3, and May 6, revealing that he had been in the rear since at least April 27 and would remain there. In the May 3 letter he informed Maggie and John that he was "Tired, been traveling all w[ee]k." [124] He had been to Cam Ranh Bay to see his cousin James Gumm, but "he left two days before I got there. So I stayed there two days and took in a little sun. Then back here." He wanted to tell Jim to "keep that pistol I gave him. Don want him selling it. I went thru hell to get that." Hooper had given Jim the Chinese Communist–made .45 pistol, which he took from the February 21 battlefield, while he was at the hospital in Cam Ranh Bay. Soon he would be leaving for Bien Hoa and "then my last plane ride which is to the USA."

As a potential MOH recipient, Joe spent his last month in Vietnam virtually under house arrest. "The Bn. Co. [Battalion commanding officer] wont let me go back out in Battle. They want to keep me alive," Joe wrote. "He has more or less put me under lock and key. Anytime I go any where I have to let him know and then its by helecoptor only. Because of the snipers and mines on the roads."

Preparing to depart Vietnam because his six-year enlistment was expiring, Joe was ambivalent. "Will be glad to get home," he mused, "but will miss my buddies." Also, he had been "so dead set on getting out" to attend flight school, "but know [now] I feel as though I should stay in." If he received the MOH "it will be in memory of my buddies who fell on the battlefield and I feel as though I owe it to them to remain in. So I [have] been laying awake nights trying to make a decision. So far nothing." But he was going to check into the possibilities.

After leaving I Corps Joe spent a few days in Saigon drinking and whoring. He left Vietnam soon after being promoted from E-5 to E-6, and left the Army shortly after arriving home. [125] "I havent saved a million [dollars]," he wrote "but I have the merrious [memories] that you never could buy for all the money in the World."

By the time Hooper departed Vietnam, the original Delta Raiders were just about gone.

Of the 154 men on the Raiders' original roster, only sixty-three remained with the company in early June.[126]

Some Originals left through an "infusion" program in which Raiders went to other units and men from other units joined the Raiders. The purpose was to avoid having all the men in a particular company go home at one time when their one-year tour ended.

Others had had enough combat and sought rear echelon duties, even with another unit, as self-preservation trumped comradeship. "Everyone is trying to get out of the field," wrote Eugene Robertson in mid-May. "All the old guys that came over with the division, that is. We have been told that we have seen more action in two months than other units see in their whole tour." He favored an officer-like six-month tour (or less) for grunts. Ironically, when he first arrived in Vietnam, he thought about extending, "but that was before I knew what a gook was."[127]

Still other troopers were recovering from wounds, never to return to the war, or at least to the Raiders. Tex Gray never sufficiently recovered to go back to Vietnam. On the other hand Richard Buzzini, who recuperated at Camp Zama in Japan, did return but found a relatively safe position serving on a harbor patrol boat. He felt guilty for not rejoining the Raiders, but at the time he "didn't want to go back into combat. I thought I had used up all my nine lives."[128]

Seventeen Raiders died between January and June, sixteen of them in battle and one in a truck accident.[129]

The replacements were still Raiders, but they were not Originals, not airborne qualified, and not volunteers. Eugene Robertson "served with more replacements than Originals for my year. I can probably name you maybe eighty Original Raiders, but I couldn't name five replacements. . . . There was no attachment to the replacements."[130]

By late May the Raiders' had so many new men they held a training exercise by "attacking" fortified villages just to the northwest of La Chu.[131]

"For there is a fundamental difference between the sort of sporadic, small-scale fighting which is the small change of soldiering and the sort we characterize as a battle," wrote the eminent British military historian John Keegan.[132]

Battles get publicity, the small change does not.

But small change has its own agony.

Take Robert E. Terrell and Noah Rockel. As the Raiders were hunkering down in a cemetery in the late afternoon of April 26, a booby trap detonated, literally blowing Terrell in two and gruesomely injuring Rockel. When the explosion occurred, Rockel recalled, "everything in my life went in slow motion, from the clang, to the blast. It all came in stages, it seemed like minutes apart." As the metal fragments hit him he "just felt my body being twisted, the M-16 coming out of my arms, and then I remember laying there and hearing somebody yelling 'Medic!'" Then it started getting dark, "and I started thinking 'Ah, God, I'm going to die out here.'" But a medevac soon arrived and in moments Rockel was on his way to eighteen months in hospitals.[133]

Initially Noah had no idea how badly he was hurt. In one hospital he was in a room with several mirrors. Not knowing they were mirrors, he looked over to "see this poor guy beside me over there in the other bed and he's bandaged from his knees all the way up so you couldn't even see his face, which was all covered. I thought, 'Man, I really feel sorry for him.' The nurse came in and she'd be working on me, and I'd look over there and there'd be a nurse working on him. She'd leave, my nurse would leave. It took a while before I caught on: That's me!" That poor guy in the other bed had 1,380 wire sutures—he was so torn up that regular stitches would not work—holding him together. The prognosis was so critical that authorities sent a telegram to his family saying that if anyone wanted to see him alive, they had better get to his bedside *now*.

Before leaving for Vietnam, Rockel and his high school sweetheart, Joyce, were engaged. Red-haired and brown-eyed, she wrote at least one letter to him every day. "Only God and I know how much I love you," read a typical missive. She said her prayers "each night for God to bring you back so I can give you some of the love I've stored up for you. I'll never be able to show you just how much I love you because I could love you 2 life times and still have love left over." Rockel expressed reciprocal sentiments.[134] Convinced that in his condition his life would never amount to much, Noah tried to drive her away when he arrived at an Ohio hospital near their hometown. Joyce would not leave. She worked split shifts and between shifts rushed to the hospital, where she sat "by his bed and he wouldn't talk to me for anything. He was really mean to me." But her persistence and their love prevailed. In September he got a three-day "pass" from the hospital so they could be married.

Initially they did not see much of each other because Noah remained hospitalized for another year, being transferred from Ohio to Ireland Army Hospital at Fort Knox and then to another hospital at Fort Bragg. Incredibly, at Fort Bragg the Army returned him to active duty even though he was so badly scarred he could not lift his duffel bag. Only intervention by his congressman stopped the Army from shipping him to Korea.

Life has not always been easy for the Rockels because Noah's wounds, even when "healed," limited what he could do. And he has always felt cheated in life by that booby trap since he loved the Army and had planned to make it a career.

Still, more than three decades later he and Joyce were still married, still in love, they had a daughter and a grandson, a comfortable home, and a dog —named Army. Despite all the difficulties Noah Rockel created a stable life for himself.

Joe Hooper did not.

Ten

He was just a wild man.
The wildest person.
A real free spirit. Crazy.
Just a wild man. Not boring!

Carollyn DeVore, describing Joe's personality.

Carollyn DeVore was at home on Rowena Avenue in Hollywood when the phone rang.

The USO wanted her to be one of four young women to greet four soldiers flying into Los Angeles to help celebrate the fiftieth anniversary of Junior ROTC. Standing last in line because she was the tallest of the four women, and wearing high boots and a tight miniskirt, Carollyn watched as the first three girls paired off with the first three deplaning soldiers. Peering at the fourth solider she thought her eyes were deceiving her. "I didn't have my glasses on and I'm *very* nearsighted—and I thought 'No way. It couldn't be that redheaded guy.'" [1]

The redheaded guy who'd flirted with her so outrageously in Vietnam in December of 1967.

As TV cameras recorded Joe Hooper's arrival, with typical brazen impulsiveness he grabbed Carollyn and "[he] kissed me like I have never been kissed." For Carollyn "the world stopped again." "Who was that man mauling you on TV," her mother wanted to know. "It was pretty disgusting."

Not to them. From that moment on they were together, obsessed with each other, living, as Carollyn put it, "about twenty years in two years."

They first made love after a social function honoring John Wayne held at the Biltmore Hotel where Joe lived for several months. After sitting across the table from each other during dinner, "without saying a word, we both mingled and worked our way through the crowd and went up to his room." Although Carollyn lived in a big two story white house with a marble staircase, Joe's beautiful, romantic hotel room remained their love nest for many weeks because she did not want "to bring some man home, and have my son there." Her son was Rolly DeVore II, who was born in 1964. Carollyn divorced Rolly's father several years later, but she deeply loved her son. Raised in a strict Baptist home, Carollyn also worried about offending her parents.

Carollyn didn't know about another problem.

Joe Hooper was married.

His wife's maiden name was Balbine Pauline Starte, though most people called her Sabina. Born in Germany in 1921, she married Anton Boenigk, who served in a German panzer unit during World War II. They had three children, two in the old country and one in the United States. The oldest was Christa, born in 1942. Reflecting her mother's beauty and using the name Christa Speck, she was *Playboy*'s Playmate of the Month in September 1961, and ultimately Playmate of the Year.[2] Four years after Christa came Rainer, and then after the family moved to America in 1956, Peter was born on January 20, 1957, in Los Angeles. The Boenigks briefly lived in Pasadena before moving to an apartment on Garfield Street in Glendale. Anton worked as a welder in an aerospace company until he died of cancer in 1965.

To support the family after Anton's death, Sabina worked two jobs. She managed the Garfield Street apartment building; the owners did not want the hassles of cleaning up, showing apartments, and doing the paperwork, so they hired her.

And she worked in a bar.

Which is where she met Joe.[3]

Exactly how this happened is uncertain, though Joe told his old Navy buddy Gary Foster they met by accident when he was driving a big Honda motorcycle and went into the bar to escape a rainstorm.[4] After that Joe began hustling Sabina, who was fun-loving, gregarious, and still beautiful despite being in her mid-forties. Because she was seventeen years older than Joe, she resisted his advances. Then one night, Peter later learned from his mother, "some guy at the bar was drunk, and he was trying to give my mother a hard time and I think Joe threw the guy out of the bar." After this display of conspicuous gallantry Balbine quickly succumbed to Joe's charms. They married in July 1968, in Las Vegas.[5]

At the time Joe was a civilian. After being retained in service seven extra days for the government's convenience, on June 11 he received an honorable discharge. Joe claimed he was "self-employed" for the next six months, but was actually unemployed, leaving him plenty of time to visit family and friends, from whom (like most GIs) he received a warm homecoming.[6]

Maggie and John Henry now lived on a small farm near Zillah, Washington. There Joe regaled his kin with his Vietnam experiences and, remarkably, reconciled with John Henry. "When he's around you've got to talk Army, or you might as well forget it," said Maggie, who was confident Joe was going to become a commercial pilot. "He's all for his men and his buddies." As for his father, Joe's sisters agreed that they developed a good relationship. "They were two peas in a pod. Exactly. They were so much alike it was like they were twins," recalled Kathy. "The way they looked, the way they acted, their thinking, their drinking." Often they got into bar fights, returning home drunk and bedraggled. Joe not only went drinking with John Henry, but also with Audrey's husband, which she resented. "There used to be a lot of conflict with me and Joe because he would take my husband out drinking, and leading him astray. I used to get really mad at Joe about doing that."[7]

Joe also visited his cousin James Gumm, then stationed at the Presidio. Jim deposited the pistol Joe gave him at Cam Ranh Bay with his mother for safekeeping, so Joe later stopped by the Gumm family home to pick it up.[8]

Some of his Moses Lake boyhood friends received a surprise visit. Married and living about ninety miles south of Moses Lake, Ron Isakson was already in bed when Joe called one night in August or September. Excited at the prospect of seeing his schoolboy chum, Ron put on his clothes, drove to Moses Lake, bought a case of beer, and went to Ron and Don Schieble's house where they "just sat there and talked all night and heard war stories." Joe "just mesmerized me with the stories that he had," said Ron. "Each and every one of them were absolutely the truth. These weren't made for TV. It was true, real life war stories." No doubt the tales were mesmerizing but given Joe's penchant for fabrication and embellishment, they were probably not all true.

Emerging from the (tall) tales was the impression "that there was just something about war, or being involved in a conflict, that he just couldn't stay away from it." Joe was thinking about reenlisting in part because the MOH conferred special status. More importantly, as he explained to his pals over too many beers, "he really wasn't fit for civilian life because he'd been trained to kill and that's all that he knew how to do. He said 'It's really pathetic but I don't know how to do anything but kill. That's what I am, and that's how I think. Just an absolute trained killer.'"[9]

Six feet tall and weighing 185 pounds, Joe reenlisted for three years on January 10, 1969, in Los Angeles. At that point he had eleven years, six months, and seven days of active service. Surprisingly, along with Balbine and Peter, Joe listed Robert Jay Hooper (the son he had with his first wife Sandra in late 1959) as a dependent even though he was doing nothing to help support the boy.[10] Shortly after he reenlisted Joe, Balbine, Peter, and Rainer, moved out of Balbine's Garfield Street apartment and into military housing on Baker Street in Saugus, California. Shortly afterward Rainer, then in his early twenties, left home to be on his own.

The Army assigned Joe to the San Fernando recruiting station where he did some recruiting, though the results were somewhat mixed. One day, or at least so he told Gary Foster, he signed four recruits, but two were convicted felons and two were illegal immigrants. The Army primarily gave Hooper public relations duties, in part to counteract the burgeoning antiwar movement. Joe was a surprisingly good public spokesman. For one thing, he looked the part of a hero. "With the manners of a Boy Scout, the clean cut looks of the astronauts and a very genuine smile," wrote one journalist, "Master Sergeant Joe Hooper of Saugus looks more like a war hero than even John Wayne."[11]

Along with his striking military presence, Hooper could be an effective speaker. The news director for Public Relations International considered Joe "the finest PR man I have had the pleasure to meet" in his thirty years in the business. When Joe spoke to the Braille Institute of America, the more than two hundred blind members of the audience "were all impressed with the patriotism and courage of this young American, and they expressed their feelings through enthusiastic applause." The members of Fullerton Lodge No. 1993 considered Hooper "our 'Never to be Forgotten' guest speaker." And the public affairs officer for the Beverly Hills Council of the Navy League of the United States had high praise for Hooper's public appearances; indeed, he was "also motivating many of us who as professional public relations people tend to become jaded with discouragement from time to time."[12]

An unfortunate aspect of Joe's PR duties was that they took him away from Peter. One of the reasons Balbine married Joe was that she thought he would be a wonderful father for her youngest son, who liked Joe very much and called him "Dad." Joe talked about adopting the lad because he "was definitely very attached to the kid."[13] "It was a time in Joe's life when he wasn't a father yet and he wanted to be a father, and I needed a father," recalled Peter, who did not know about Robert Jay Hooper but sensed that he was just the perfect age boy for Joe. Peter may have been a substitute for Robert since they were born within a year of each other. Joe provided discipline for Peter, took him to Dodgers baseball games, and got him involved in the Boy Scouts. "We had a lot of fun," said Peter, especially before Joe's Army duties became extremely time-consuming.

Newly wed, newly enlisted, and newly settled, Joe Ronnie Hooper received the Medal of Honor from newly elected President Richard M. Nixon at a glittering White House ceremony on March 7, 1969.

If the American people wanted a president who was bigoted, paranoid, and power hungry, and who had the morals of a petty criminal, and for good measure was a kleptomaniac, Richard Nixon was their man.

"That white sonavabitch Nixon," exclaimed Jax, one of the main characters in John Del Vecchio's novel *The 13th Valley*, "he aint nothin but a plague on mankind. Man, that dude sly. He one cagey mothafucka."[14]

More succinctly, as *Newsweek* put it, Nixon was "a whack job."[15]

"It wasn't easy to keep hold of your integrity or honor or pride when you worked for Richard Nixon," concluded Chief of Naval Operations Elmo Zumwalt. How could you when the president cheated on his taxes, underpaying by $400,000? How could you when the president often spiced discussions with vulgarities and anti-Semitism? How could you when Nixon's White House conversations almost routinely discussed blackmail, obstruction of justice, burglary, stealing sealed documents from the National Archives, and repressive activities such as misusing the FBI and IRS to harass or, better, destroy perceived enemies? The concern in the White House was rarely with illegality, but about getting caught.[16]

"Nobody is a friend of ours," Nixon insisted in a typical display of paranoia, and on another occasion he told an aide not to "be too damn sure about anybody!" The concept of a *loyal political* opposition resulting from the two party system eluded him; everyone was his *personal* enemy. Nixon was so poisoned with grudge-laden hate that he could never consider polit-

ical opponents simply as individuals who disagreed with him about issues. To Nixon, policy *debates* were absurd; every issue was *war*, a battle for
survival. "We're going to screw them another way," threatened the president when talking about the *Washington Post*. "They don't really realize how
rough I can play . . . when I start, I will kill them."[17]

The president preferred secrecy and lying instead of open government,
instead of dealing with the Congress, the public, the cabinet, and even the
JCS. So compulsive was Nixon's deceitfulness and deviousness that the Joint
Chiefs actually spied on the White House to discover the administration's
national security policy. Republican senator Barry Goldwater considered
the president "the most dishonest individual I have ever met in my life. . . .
Nixon lied to his wife, his family, his friends . . . his political party, the American people, and the world."[18]

Along with his mendacity, Nixon was also narcissistic, holding a grandiose self-image, and was obsessed "by some kind of mystic machismo."
Perhaps because he was actually weak and indecisive, the president prided
himself on being tough, rough, and mean, fortifying his courage with war
movies and alcohol. His favorite film was *Patton*, a World War II saga that
nourished his heroic fantasies. Even comparatively small amounts of alcohol intensified his truculence or, worse, rendered him incoherent. Behind
his back National Security Adviser Henry Kissinger referred to the president
as "that drunken lunatic," "the meatball mind," and "the basket case." Booze
may have contributed to the president's violent mood swings from excessive
passivity to hyperactivism that resulted in such erratic governance.[19]

Kissinger realized that Nixon feared being perceived as weak, and when
he wanted to goad the president he accused him of being "a weakling."
"Goddamn, you['ve] *got to fight*," Nixon told his press secretary. "That's the
trouble with our people. They don't know how to fight." But like his hero
Patton, the president was tough and knew how to fight! He could not "have
a high minded lawyer" because he wanted "somebody as tough as I am for
a change." When assessing an individual a key question was always "Is he
tough?" One man was fine because "He's mean, tough, ruthless. He'll lie, do
anything. That's what you need." But another was suspect because "He may
not be tough enough."[20]

Not surprisingly, the president surrounded himself with men of similar ilk. Vice President Spiro Agnew was a crook who resigned his office in

October 1973. Nixon's campaign manager and subsequently his Attorney General was John Mitchell, who became prisoner number 24171-157 at Maxwell Air Force Base prison, gaining the ignominy of being the highest-ranking government official ever imprisoned. A case can be made that Henry Kissinger was guilty of war crimes.

Kissinger and Nixon were such kindred souls that historians write about "Nixinger" when discussing the administration. Like the president, Kissinger had little respect for democratic government and was contemptuous of the truth. Speaking about Argentina, a pluralistic democracy, he saw no reason why it should be allowed to "go Communist due to the irresponsibility of its own people"—that is, due to a free and open election. "Kissinger doesn't lie because it's in his interest," said one of his associates. "He lies because it's in his nature." The president's adviser was also subject to obsessive insecurity, paranoia, violent mood swings, and erratic behavior. Indeed, Nixon—no paragon of rationality himself—sometimes considered his subordinate's behavior "not very rational" and thought he needed psychiatric help dealing with a persecution complex.[21]

Lustful for power, Nixon achieved the presidency partly as a result of near-traitorous behavior. After months of difficult negotiations in Paris, just before the 1968 election, real progress occurred in the peace talks including, among other arrangements, a bombing halt over all of North Vietnam and the inclusion of the NLF in the negotiating process. Johnson consulted directly with General Creighton W. Abrams, who replaced Westy as MACV commander after the Tet Offensive, about the bombing halt, and the general supported it with "no reservations" because he believed the enemy would respond positively.[22]

One reason the negotiations suddenly leaped forward was that the North Vietnamese preferred to deal with Democratic candidate Hubert Humphrey after the election rather than the certified Cold Warrior Richard Nixon. On the other hand, South Vietnamese President Thieu wanted Humphrey defeated, and wanted nothing to do with any sort of coalition government that included the NLF. As Johnson put it, "Thieu and the others are voting for a man they see as one who will stick with [the war]—Nixon."[23]

Johnson feared—rightly, as it turned out—that Thieu might sabotage the negotiations. Indeed, secret contacts occurred between Thieu and the Nixon campaign to prevent a premature peace, at least from their perspective. The key contact was Anna Chennault, widow of the famous American commander of the World War II Flying Tigers. Speaking for the Nixon campaign she assured Thieu that the Republican candidate would vigorously support South Vietnam, so he should resist pressures from Johnson to cooperate in the peace process. Encouraged, Thieu duplicitously sandbagged Johnson and Humphrey. After privately hinting that he supported negotiations, Thieu publicly proclaimed his opposition shortly after Johnson announced the bombing halt, and then deliberately stalled the negotiating process. The Humphrey campaign, which had been rapidly gaining support, quickly lost momentum.

The Nixon-Thieu skullduggery bound the two presidents together in continued war. Nixon promised Thieu support, and Thieu helped deliver the presidency to him. Although Johnson knew of the illegal contacts, he learned about them through illegal wiretaps and so could not reveal the information. "Can you imagine," the president said, "what people would say if it were to be known that Hanoi has met all these conditions [for peace] and then Nixon's conniving with [South Vietnam] kept us from getting it." American boys, Johnson complained, were going to die because of Nixon's political ambitions, though he really had little reason to criticize others in this regard.[24]

Four years later Thieu sabotaged another peace effort, one based on many of the terms being proposed in the fall of 1968, and which Nixon ultimately accepted in January 1973.

When he was in the Navy during World War II, Nixon bragged, he "played a little poker."

From that card game he learned that "when a guy didn't have the cards, he talked awfully big. But when he had the cards, he just sat there—had that cold look in his eyes." Now Nixon believed he had the cards.[25]

To win the game all he had to do was play the hand right, which meant heeding the public's voice by liquidating the Vietnam imbroglio. Protected by his impeccable, militant anti-Communist record from renewed McCarthyism, he could label the conflict "Mr. Johnson's War," blame the whole sorry mess on the Democrats, and extol the Republicans' virtue for ending the tragedy.

It appeared he might do exactly that. During the election campaign he stressed that "we can't have a foreign policy with Vietnam hanging around our necks. I will deal with it within six months." "I'm going to stop that war," he boasted, "Fast." Sharing the president's optimism, Kissinger told a group of Quakers to "Give us six months, and if we haven't ended the war by then, you can come back and tear down the White House fence." Nixon believed "there's no way to win the war. But we can't say that, of course. In fact, we have to seem to say the opposite, just to keep some degree of bargaining leverage." Attacking the Democrats for failing to make peace, the Republican candidate claimed he had a "secret plan" to end the war.[26]

However, trapped by the twin Cold War bugaboos of national credibility and virulent manhood Nixon played his cards poorly. Yes, he wanted the war to end, but only if the enemy surrendered. "For the United States, the first defeat in our nation's history," he intoned, "would result in a collapse of confidence in American leadership, not only in Asia, but throughout the world." Defeat for such a "tough" man was a humiliating prospect. Echoing his predecessor, he insisted that "I will not be the first President of the United States to lose a war."[27]

Determined to preserve an independent, non-Communist South Vietnam Nixon fought for what he called "peace with honor," which was the war's greatest euphemism. Under that diehard policy men died hard in the paddies and jungles of Southeast Asia. More than 15,000 names that would be engraved on the Vietnam Memorial piled up to keep a South Vietnamese tyrant in power, to quench Nixon's thirst for high office, to satisfy his inflated sense of manhood, and to achieve defeat with dishonor.

Nixon had no secret plan. As Kissinger told the president and the National Security Council eight months after the administration assumed office, "We need a plan to end the war." Nor did Nixon and Kissinger understand revolutionary warfare any better than their predecessors. "Along with their political forebears, both Nixon and Kissinger suffered from a fundamental inability to enter into the mental world of their enemy," wrote a Viet Cong leader, "and so to formulate policies that would effectively frustrate the strategies arrayed against them, the strategies of people's war."[28]

For men who prided themselves on being shrewd realists, they compiled a stunning record of misjudgments regarding Vietnam, overestimating themselves, Vietnam's importance to America's credibility, and the influence of the Soviet Union and China on North Vietnam, while underestimating the enemy's skill and determination. Typical of their initial disdain for the enemy was Kissinger's comment: "I refuse to believe that a little fourth-rate power like North Vietnam does not have a breaking point."[29]

Without a plan but with sublime (and naive) self-confidence, Nixon ordered General Abrams to exert maximum military pressure to improve America's negotiating position. Meanwhile, Kissinger issued National Security Study Memorandum #1 ordering a survey of government agencies to assess the war's status. The resulting document provided a snapshot of the war from the government's perspective, but the picture was blurry. All agencies agreed that South Vietnam's position was improved, but questioned whether the government could "survive a peaceful competition with the NLF for political power in South Vietnam." Its armed forces "alone cannot now, or in the foreseeable future, stand up to the current North Vietnamese–Viet Cong forces." Although suffering heavy recent losses, the Communists had "not changed their essential objectives and they have sufficient strength to pursue these objectives." They could "outlast allied attrition efforts indefinitely," in large part because they controlled the casualty rates for *both* sides, and could still launch offensives, though not as dramatic as Tet. The North Vietnamese, believing they could "persist long enough to obtain a relatively favorable negotiated compromise" despite their heavy losses during Tet, were "not in Paris primarily out of weakness."

Beyond these points, the agencies divided along a major fault line. Group A (MACV, CINCPAC [Commander in Chief, Pacific Command], the JCS, and the embassy in Saigon) was optimistic about the future. One reason MACV's assessment was so positive was the military's ongoing inability to be honest with itself. Abrams suppressed negative analyses that came in from the field.[30] Group B (the Office of the Secretary of Defense, the CIA, and to some extent the State Department) was skeptical about South Vietnam's prospects. The optimists gave "greater relative weight to allied military pressures" than did Group B. They also stressed recent improvements in ARVN and the pacification program, but Group B thought the "improvements" were insignificant or illusory. While MACV and the JCS thought South Vietnam controlled 75 to 90 percent of the population, the Office of the Secretary of Defense, the CIA, and the State Department asserted that between 50 and 66 percent of the rural population was "subject to significant VC presence and influence." Compared to Group B, Group A's estimate of the enemy order of battle was quite low.

Group B agreed with a recent National Intelligence Estimate downgrading the "domino theory." The estimate concluded that if the Communists took over South Vietnam, then Laos and Cambodia might enter Hanoi's orbit but the rest of Asia would not be unhinged. Group A vigorously disagreed.[31]

In the past the Group A agencies were consistently optimistic and consistently wrong.

With no plan and no government-wide consensus, but determined to win the war, the administration improvised a two-track policy. One was "linkage." In exchange for arms limitation talks, economic cooperation, and other benefits, the United States wanted the Soviet Union to exert pressure on North Vietnam to agree to an "honorable" compromise, something akin to what the Communists superpowers did to the Viet Minh in 1954 at Geneva. An astounding misperception, this forlorn hope ignored the belief by North Vietnam and the Viet Cong that their so-called allies sold them out at Geneva. They were determined not to repeat history.

At least ten times during 1969 the administration asked the Soviets for help, always getting an evasive reply because, although embarrassed to admit it, Moscow was unable to translate its material support for Hanoi into political influence. The Soviets viewed their ally much like the United States perceived South Vietnam: as stubborn, unreliable, and self-serving. Nixon also tried to establish linkage through China, but that, too, failed. The Chinese were not inclined to help the Americans, and in any event they exerted no more control over the independent-minded North Vietnamese than the Soviets did.[32]

Since linkage was unproductive Nixon resorted to bluster, employing what he called the "madman theory," which relied on the threat of excessive force and irrational unpredictability. "I want the North Vietnamese to believe I've reached the point where I might do *anything* to stop the war," he told his aide H. R. Haldeman. "We'll just slip the word to them that 'for God's sake, you know Nixon is obsessed about Communists. We can't restrain him when he's angry—and he has his hand on the nuclear button'—and Ho Chi Minh himself will be in Paris in two days begging for peace." Nixon ordered the National Security Council to plan for massive blows against North Vietnam in an operation code-named Duck Hook, which, according to an administration insider, was "designed to achieve maximum political, military, and psychological shock, while reducing North Vietnam's over-all war-making and economic capacity to the extent feasible." The administration then leaked the order so that Hanoi knew about it. Through French and Soviet intermediaries the president also informed North Vietnam that if no substantive negotiations occurred before November 1, 1969, the United States would resort to "measures of great consequence and force."[33]

Three things happened. The October 15 Moratorium to End the War in Vietnam, the largest national antiwar protest, caused Nixon to fear that radically escalating the war would further undercut public support, which increasingly agreed with the title of ex-Beatle John Lennon's song "Give Peace a Chance." Second, Secretary of State William P. Rogers and Secretary of Defense Melvin R. Laird, along with important members of Kissinger's staff, opposed Duck Hook, arguing that it would only make the situation worse. Finally, though expecting the United States to unleash the bombers and perhaps invade, North Vietnam did not blink.[34] Although infuriated by the domestic protests, advice from "weak" subordinates, and the Communists' refusal to bow to America's will, Nixon let November 1 pass without unleashing Duck Hook; indeed, he had decided against it several weeks earlier.

Trying to salvage his reputation for being both tough and mad, Nixon substituted a Joint Chiefs of Staff Readiness Test for Duck Hook. The test was a nuclear alert designed to remind the Soviets and the North Vietnamese of the president's unpredictability and of the awesome power at his disposal, and thereby jar the Soviets into pressuring Hanoi into making concessions at the bargaining table. Like Hanoi's reaction to the Duck Hook threat, the Soviets ignored the nuclear alert.[35]

With linkage a failure and Ho Chi Minh remaining in Hanoi rather than scurrying to Paris, Nixon found himself with essentially the same policy Johnson enunciated on March 31, 1968: to buy time to win the war domestic dissent must be quelled, the United States must lessen its commitment, and South Vietnam must do more to help itself.

Because nothing generated dissent and dismay more than casualties, reducing the number of Americans KIA was urgent, especially on the heels of mini-mini Tet, the Communists' February 1969 offensive, and a disaster called Hamburger Hill. Occurring from August 18 to 24, 1968, mini-mini Tet was a feeble replica of the February and May offensives, but the eighty-one ground assaults and 103 standoff attacks killed 308 U.S. soldiers. A major enemy offensive began on February 23, 1969, and lasted for six weeks. Specifically trying to kill Americans without exposing their own main units to destruction, the VC/NVA sent another 1,740 U.S. soldiers home in caskets, fueling antiwar sentiment.[36]

Although the attacks that began in February represented a normal dry season offensive, planned months in advance because of logistical difficulties, they came only a month after Nixon's inauguration. In his typical combative way and with no understanding of the combat cycle, he considered the offensive a personal affront, "a deliberate test, clearly designed to take the measure of me and my administration at the outset." When challenged, Nixon retaliated. In March he initiated Operation Breakfast, the secret bombing of enemy bases in Cambodia, hastening that country's decent into mass misery, mayhem, and murder. The operation was not a secret to enemy forces, who knew bombs were falling on them. "Secret," as mentioned previously, meant that neither the American Congress nor the public knew about it. In undertaking the Cambodian bombing campaign, Nixon hoped to signal Hanoi (and Moscow) that he was *tougher* than the previous president and was therefore both willing and able to escalate the war in unpredictable ways.[37]

The battle for Dong Ap Bia, nicknamed Hamburger Hill by the troops who were in the meat-grinder, lasted for ten days in mid-May and involved units from the 101st Airborne, then commanded by Major General Melvin Zais. U.S. forces repeatedly launched uphill frontal assaults against a solidly entrenched NVA force. After killing fifty-six Americans and wounding 420, the NVA withdrew into Laos, and Zais became king of the hill—briefly. One week later the United States abandoned Dong Ap Bia and the NVA returned.

Maybe enemy losses at Hamburger Hill were, as Zais crowed, "awesome in comparison to his known strength." But having Americans die for real estate and then abandoning it reinforced the public's profound sense of the war's absurdity and futility. Zais believed that "obviously the enemy had to be engaged where he was found," but many citizens and soldiers wondered why. Why engage the enemy on its chosen ground? Having driven the enemy from a position, why abandon it? "The *absolute, absolute* ridiculousness of Hamburger Hill," said Chaplain Erbach. "The waste of people, for what? To possess a hill. We did that every day. You go up and possess a hill, and then you give it up. You just move on, you leave it there, and it becomes overrun by vc again." Bobby Rakestraw shared Erbach's dismay. "Waste all that ammunition, and time, and life, and just leave it! Why? You never could get an answer from anybody." Expressing their disgust, disgruntled GIs offered a $10,000 reward for anyone who assassinated Zais.[38]

Responding to the public outcry against Hamburger Hill and more senseless deaths—polls indicated a steady decline among all political, age, and educational groups for the president's handling of the war—Nixon ordered Abrams to make reducing American casualties a foremost objective. And the president was going to make that task easier. One way to avoid casualties and thereby placate public opinion was to reduce the number of Americans engaged in battle. On June 8, 1969, Nixon ordered the withdrawal of 25,000 soldiers, not just halting the Americanization of the war but reversing it.

Once begun, troop withdrawals became irreversible, especially since Secretary of Defense Laird, initially an avowed hawk, became dovish, as had McNamara and Clifford before him. Like a movie running in reverse after the U.S. buildup hit its highpoint of 543,500 troops in April 1969, the American presence gradually declined. By the end of 1970, troop strength was down to 344,000, and when 1972 ended only 24,000 Americans remained (all support troops, not combat units), which was essentially the number in South Vietnam in 1964. These withdrawals were unilateral; no agreement mandated that North Vietnamese troops also redeploy from South Vietnam.[39]

To compensate for the declining American presence, the United States sought to strengthen South Vietnam through the dual policies of Vietnamization and pacification so that it could ultimately defend itself without massive external assistance. Even if the Communists refused to negotiate, a refurbished, reinvigorated South Vietnam would confront them with the prospect of perpetual war. A "MACV Objective Plan" insisted that getting South Vietnam to do more was "the heart of the matter." Reducing American forces was essential not simply as "a ploy to 'buy time,' but also as a necessary method of compelling the South Vietnamese to take over the war. They must!"[40]

Crassly stated, Vietnamization (the Communists called it "puppetization"[41]) meant changing the color of the corpses from white to brown by shifting the combat burden to South Vietnam's armed forces. Having intervened massively in 1964–65 when South Vietnam proved unable to defend itself, and having wreaked stupendous damage without making that would-be nation any more secure, the United States was now returning the war to the South Vietnamese. Everyone understood that strengthening ARVN and the Regional and Popular Forces (collectively known as the Territorial Forces) was a difficult, long-term process—if it was possible at all.

Although officials publicly extolled Vietnamization, soldiers in the field and the high command had grave private doubts. Lieutenant Frank M. Campagne, for example, knew "that the South Vietnamese would never, ever be ready to fight the North Vietnamese or the Viet Cong. They could never be ready." Too many ARVN units were like the 5th ARVN Division, which, observed Secretary of the Army Resor, "could *not* go backwards. It was as far back as it could go except for *disbanding*." Kissinger provided Nixon numerous memos showing why Vietnamization would not work, and Abrams felt it was nothing but a "slow surrender," a fig leaf covering America's retreat. MACV believed that "unless the North Vietnamese return to North Vietnam, there is little chance that *any* improvement in the Republic of Vietnam's Armed Forces or *any* degree of progress in pacification, no matter how significant, could justify significant reductions in U.S. forces from their present level." General Wheeler agreed "that we will have to maintain a residual support force in South Vietnam for some years to come unless and until the withdrawal of the North Vietnamese is achieved."[42]

Nonetheless the delicate balancing act began without mutual troop withdrawals: reducing U.S. troops and casualties fast enough to appease the public and Congress, but not so fast that South Vietnam collapsed before Vietnamization and pacification could succeed. The idea was to expand and modernize ARVN to take over the big unit war against the VC/NVA regulars while upgrading the Territorial Forces, supplemented by the National Police and a newly created People's Self Defense Force, to assume the local population security mission. Meanwhile remaining U.S. forces would progressively become advisers rather than combatants, reverting to their status of the early 1960s.

The growth in South Vietnam's armed forces was impressive. In 1968 ARVN totaled 380,000, but two years later the figure stood at 416,000. The Air Force, Navy, and Marine Corps underwent similar expansion, as did the Territorial Forces, which numbered 392,000 in 1968 and 534,000 in 1970. Although often overlooked, the Territorials bore more of the war's brunt than ARVN. Because they provided local security and were the troops closest to the people, the enemy often targeted the Territorials to retain access to the rural population. Except for 1968, the chances of getting killed in the Territorials was higher than in ARVN. As part of Vietnamization the United States armed both ARVN and the Territorials with M-16s and provided ARVN with a massive infusion of heavy firepower weapons. By 1971 the National Police was 114,000 strong and the People's Self Defense Force, a lightly armed and minimally trained militia, contained 4,429,000.[43]

In one aspect Vietnamization was resoundingly successful: by shrinking the number of U.S. troops, American casualty figures declined dramatically. Not only that, Vietnamization also reduced the probability that any remaining individual U.S. serviceman would die in combat.[44]

Still, Americans continued dying.

As for the South Vietnamese armed forces, the question remained whether quantitative growth translated into qualitative improvements. Very much *wanting* success, many generals discerned success. According to Major General John M. Wright Jr., progress was palpable. The 1st ARVN Division in I Corps was an "outstanding combat division," the Territorials were becoming more aggressive, and the "development of the previously non-existent People's Self Defense forces is encouraging." Another general wrote that progress in improving and modernizing ARVN forces in I Corps was impressive, "and prospects for continued improvement in combat proficiency and increased self-sufficiency are very encouraging." A "lessons learned" report claimed that an intensified training program for the Territorials was "extremely successful. It has substantially improved the capability of local forces and, more importantly, has established a cadre that can continue its own development."[45]

Enemy documents indicated that Vietnamization worried the VC/NVA, especially the strengthening of the Territorial Forces and the People's Self Defense Force. These organizations seemed to be intensifying their activities, increasing their patrolling, laying ambushes, searching for tunnels and caches, gathering intelligence, capturing and killing agents, and more effectively using psychological warfare. As a result, South Vietnamese forces had "encroached upon land in many areas causing us many difficulties, especially in holding on to densely populated areas."[46]

Still, Vietnamization remained untested in a major campaign.

The concomitant of Vietnamization was pacification, the effort to break the clandestine vc infrastructure's grip on the countryside and convert the population into loyal supporters of President Thieu's government, thereby allowing it to compete successfully in the political realm with the Communists. The enemy's highly structured bureaucracy inside South Vietnam, the infrastructure commanded most Communist operations, conducted terrorist and subversive activities, and provided men, money, supplies, and intelligence to local forces. Although infrastructure members were technically "civilians," these were hard-core vc, so skilled at covert operations that scores of them successfully posed as loyal South Vietnamese officials for many years. As long as the infrastructure survived, the rural population was never secure.[47]

Long the war's unwanted stepchild, pacification became a high profile concern in the waning months of Johnson's administration, as demonstrated by an Accelerated Pacification Program that began on November 1, 1968. Now that protecting the population was suddenly a high priority, the U.S. Army ordered some of its units to provide direct support for the pacification effort, although fighting the conventional war remained its highest priority. Under the new pacification program and its follow-on efforts, the South Vietnamese government returned to many rural areas recently under vc control.

Four elements integral to pacification warrant special mention. One was the controversial Phoenix Program, which eliminated specifically identified infrastructure members. Although news reports labeled Phoenix an assassination program and ugly abuses unquestionably occurred, assassinations per se were rare. Yet some 26,369 vc were "neutralized," killed in the battlefield's shadows when the suspects fought rather than surrender. Phoenix operatives also apprehended 33,358 men and women. One way or another, the infrastructure suffered.[48]

Another way to attack the infrastructure was to persuade the vc to "rally," that is, to change sides. Designed to attract defectors by offering a monetary reward and lenient treatment, the Chieu Hoi (Open Arms) Program potentially paid huge dividends by weakening the enemy while saving allied lives. Individual ralliers (called Hoi Chanh) sometimes brought their weapons with them, provided intelligence about supply caches, persuaded other vc to surrender, worked in interrogation centers, and served as "Kit Carson" scouts for American units, locating mines and bbts and guiding them through unfamiliar terrain. The program peaked in 1969 when

47,000 people rallied; the next year the number was 33,000 and in 1971 it was 20,000. Despite the decline, these were still substantial numbers.[49]

Once back in the countryside following the Tet disaster, South Vietnam and the U.S. Army undertook numerous civic action campaigns; from the American perspective, they served two purposes. One was to improve living conditions to alleviate the underlying causes of the insurgency, which, the United States erroneously presumed, flowed from a low standard of living. The other was to enhance the South Vietnamese government's image in the eyes of the local population. With great pride the Army tallied up the number of roads, bridges, canals, dikes, schools, dispensaries, and market places built or rebuilt; of wells dug; of medial assistance and health training provided.[50]

And finally, in early 1970 the South Vietnamese government addressed a contentious issue that undermined its popularity since the 1950s. It undertook serious land reform through a Land-to-the-Tiller program, intending to create a nation of independent landowners. Within three years the program distributed 2.5 million acres to 800,000 tenant farmer families, dropping the farm tenancy rate from 60 percent to 10 percent, which was a remarkable achievement.[51]

As with Vietnamization, American commanders were sanguine about pacification. General Zais believed the 101st Airborne's civic actions "were extremely effective" and noted a "very evident resurgence of confidence in the Government of Vietnam by the people." Another general also extolled pacification's success and the population's improved attitude, asserting that people were less complacent and more determined to resist the VC. Devised to measure pacification's progress, the Hamlet Evaluation System indicated that between 1967 and 1972 some 8.2 million South Vietnamese became secure.[52] To an extent the enemy agreed with these assessments. "Our side," wrote a North Vietnamese colonel who was recalling the post-Tet situation, "suffered seriously from the subsequent pacification plans dreamed up by the Americans, such as Operation Phoenix and the Chieu Hoi campaign."[53]

Still, until South Vietnam stood alone against a resurgent adversary, no one knew whether the gains were solid and permanent or fragile and reversible.

Joe was hung-over when he received his Medal of Honor on March 7, 1969. President Richard Nixon's first MOH presentation recognized three *living* recipients: Hooper, Specialist Five Clarence E. Sasser, and Sergeant First Class Fred W. Zabitosky.

Approximately 300 invited guests assembled in the East Room for the occasion. Among them were two senators, four congressmen, six brigadier generals, thirteen major generals, and four lieutenant generals, not to mention a plethora of lesser military brass. The chain of command for 2-501 when the Battle of La Chu occurred was present: Tallman (now a colonel), Cushman (now a brigadier general), and Barsanti. Each MOH recipient also invited a small personal party. Among those in Joe's group were Sabina, Rainer, and Peter; Maggie and John Henry; Captain McMenamy, Lieutenant Grimsley, Platoon Sergeant Parker, and Chaplain Erbach.[54]

The Hooper family's schedule was hectic, with visits to Arlington Cemetery, the Lincoln Memorial, and other national shrines. "We were treated like royalty, even though we were kept so busy with receptions and visiting monuments that we hardly had time to notice anything else," said Joe. Fortunately he got some relief from the sightseeing tour. Captain Mac, Grimsley, and Parker "rescued" him the night before the ceremony. "We got down to the bar," said McMenamy, "and took it over, had some serious discussions and drinking." The conversation, of course, focused on "The Raiders. It's always the unit."[55]

After a late night of heavy drinking Joe was frazzled and nervous the morning of the ceremony. As he, Balbine, Peter, and Rainer prepared to depart for the White House, Joe was in a panic. During a pickup basketball game in Korea an errant elbow knocked out his upper right central incisor, and now he could not find his false tooth. They frantically tore apart the room looking for it, when Balbine suddenly asked, "Did you check your mouth?" Sure enough, the false tooth was already in place. Always on the prowl for an outrageous story, Joe later told people he "showed up for that ceremony a bit smashed. My breath damn near blew Mr. Nixon over." Joe was not drunk, just unnerved.[56]

After being escorted from the Oval Office to the Red Room, Nixon mingled with the three recipients and their families, who had been briefed on proper behavior such as addressing Nixon as Mr. President. But when Balbine met him she said, in her thick German accent, "Oh, so you're Richie!" Nonplused, Mr. President responded "Oh, so you're a kraut!" After approximately ten minutes of socializing, the families walked to the East Room and a few minutes later, with "Hail to the Chief" playing in the background, Nixon entered down the center aisle, followed by Secretary of the Army Stanley R. Resor, General Westmoreland (now the Army Chief of Staff), and the recipients.

Approaching a double stand-up microphone, Nixon asked the audience to be seated and began his remarks, immediately departing from his prepared text, which was mistitled as "*Medal of Honor Winners.*" Those who wear the medal refer to themselves not as "winners"—they were not engaged in some athletic contest—but as "recipients." The prepared speech was also uninspiring, filled with clichés about "the bravest of the brave" and their eagerness "to help make the world a better place." The president cribbed concepts from the speech, but used his own words. One theme concerned honor. "We cannot honor these men," he said. "But they have honored America. They have added to the honor of the nation by what they have done." Another stressed the recipients' willingness to risk their lives. "They are men who faced death," noted Nixon, "and instead of losing their courage they gave courage to the men around them."

Most importantly, Nixon latched onto the prepared text's emphasis on youthfulness. Unfortunately, he became confused, getting Zabitosky's age correct (twenty-six) but saying Sasser was thirty and Hooper was twenty-one. In fact, Sasser was twenty-one and Hooper was still only twenty-nine. Both Sasser and Hooper flashed quick smiles but, realizing that laughing at the commander-in-chief was ill advised, snapped back to a stern-faced demeanor. Taking a backhanded slap at hippies and student antiwar protesters, the president observed that "When we think of America's younger generation, we sometimes have a tendency to emphasize what's wrong with them, and sometimes young people do get into trouble, sometimes they do not follow the patterns that older people think they ought to follow." However, the three "magnificent men" by his side demonstrated "that we can be very proud of our younger generation."

Secretary Resor then read the MOH citation for each man. As he read Hooper's, Joe stood ramrod stiff, looking straight ahead, blinking furiously, sometimes several times a second. After each citation, Nixon draped a Medal of Honor around the recipient's neck, firmly shook the man's hand, and whispered a few congratulatory words.

A group picture of the president and the recipients followed, and then

Nixon suggested that the audience "would like to see their families. We'll have a picture with each one of the families." Balbine, Peter, Rainer, Maggie, and John Henry stepped onto the platform, joining Joe and the president. Nixon evoked a laugh from the Hoopers and the audience when, correcting at least part of his earlier error, he asked Joe, "How do you feel being thirty, and these other fellows so young?"

In the postceremony receiving line Chaplain Erbach shook hands, including the president's, until he reached Joe. "I stood in front of Joe. I couldn't shake his hand. We fell, literally, into each other's arms," Erbach recalled, his voice choking. "There in the midst of all of that pomp and circumstance and all of the dignitaries, here were two guys who knew something special. And for us, we were back, we were just us, the way we were two years before that. And I had not even spoken to the man. We just hugged. Tears were coming down our eyes." Then the chaplain moved down the line. "That's the last I ever saw of Sergeant Hooper."[57]

Joe was tremendously proud of his MOH. He occasionally made self-effacing comments about the medal, saying, for instance, that it was "representative of tradition, of history. I wear it for what it represents." "I especially feel proud and honored to wear the medal," he commented on another occasion, "for the servicemen who did not return from Vietnam."[58] But most of all Joe wore the medal for himself and was not reticent about letting other people know he had it. He accepted the $100 a month pension the medal brought with it, and told Peter that as the son of an MOH recipient he was eligible for automatic appointment to West Point. Soon he had new business cards printed reading "Joe R. Hooper, Congressional Medal of Honor," and had ballpoint pens produced that bore a symbol of the MOH and his signature. Joe gave a handful of the pens to Gary Foster but often distributed them to people at random. For example, he sometimes walked into a bank and gave one to each of the tellers. Joe also sent pictures of the ceremony to 101st Airborne Division in Vietnam, where they were soon reproduced for "conspicuous display throughout the Division in the Medal of Honor Display; at the Division Museum, Division Briefing room, and other conspicuous places."[59]

Clifford Chester Sims never had the opportunity to display his pride because the MOH he received for his actions on February 21, 1968, was awarded to him posthumously. Although his paperwork started through bureaucratic channels long before Hooper's, his award was not presented until December 2, 1969. Vice President Spiro T. Agnew presided at the ceremony.[60]

The Army had a hard time identifying the immediate family because Sims, like Hooper, was not always accurate and complete in filling out Army forms. Locating his widow Mary and "daughter" Gina was easy, but beyond that things got complicated. Clifford and Mary had no children of their own but were in the process of adopting Gina when he left for Vietnam. Even though formal adoption never occurred because of Sims's death, Gina continued living with Mary Sims and considered Mary and Clifford her mother and father.[61] Another complication was that in his paperwork Sims said his mother was killed in a traffic accident and his father died in World War II. However, the Army's effort to locate all the next of kin revealed that his father, James Sims, "was very much alive. He took the military representative to the police station to prove he was the father." His mother, Irene Sims, was also alive, though she was separated from her husband.

Why did Sims consider his parents dead? Because they were, or at least his biological mother and stepfather were. No one knew who Clifford's biological father was, though his last name was probably Pittman since that was Clifford's last name during his youth. Thirty years after Sims's death, no one remembered his biological mother's name, but while Clifford was still a baby she married a Mr. Bythwood, who became his stepfather. His biological mother was killed in an accident before Clifford was four years old, and Mr. Bythwood died in Korea (not World War II), leaving Sims an orphan.

Several families cared for Clifford after his mother's death, but by the time he was a teenager he was homeless. The local police became involved when he began stealing food to survive. Rather than incarcerate the young man, a white police officer went to the black community in Port Saint Joe, Florida, and urged someone to adopt the youngster. James and Irene Sims stepped forward, adopting Clifford when he was thirteen and changing his last name from Pittman to Sims.

Sims's widow barely knew his parents. Mary and Clifford met in the hallway of George Washington High School during the 1958–59 academic year and were married on December 25, 1961. But much of their courtship was formal and long distance. Although Mary, whose mother was *very* strict, lived only a few blocks from Clifford, they often wrote letters to each other and she was not allowed to step foot inside the Sims's home until after they were married. Shortly thereafter she moved to Fort Bragg with her husband, which meant developing a relationship with James and Irene Sims became even more difficult.

Cleo Hogan was stationed at Fort Lee, Virginia, when he received word to go to Washington for Sims's MOH ceremony. At a Pentagon briefing he learned that the event might be unpleasant because Sims's widow and parents had argued over whether she or they would receive the Medal of Honor and any money owed to Sims's estate.

Taking place on the second floor of the White House, the ceremony honored four posthumous recipients. The room was arranged in a square, with the family, relatives, and military friends of each recipient on one of the four sides. Because of the rift in the Sims retinue, Mary and Clifford's parents stayed about twenty feet apart. Standing in the center of the room were Agnew, dressed in a beautiful suit that changed colors from light green to burgundy whenever he turned, and General Westmoreland. Speaking flawlessly and without notes, the vice president made remarks about each recipient, looking directly at Mary as he spoke about Sims's heroism. Then Westmoreland presented the medal to her, not to James and Irene.

Immediately after the ceremony Cleo headed for the reception and refreshments, but an aide pulled him aside saying Westmoreland wanted to see him. "Come in, Captain," the general said from behind a big mahogany desk, "I want to talk to you about Vietnam." They chatted briefly about Sims, then about how the Raiders ran patrols and conducted ambushes, and about the NVA. After forty-five minutes an aide reminded Westy that he was late for an appointment. "Well," he replied, "they're not going to start without me," and kept talking with Cleo. After waiting a few respectful minutes the aide spoke up again. "Sir," he implored, "we've got to go."

Arriving at the reception almost an hour late, Cleo found the refreshments depleted and the situation "very strained" with the widow and parents still avoiding each other. He tried to talk with Mary and then with the parents, but getting a conversation going was impossible.[62]

Along with the MOH, Clifford Sims posthumously received a Purple Heart, a Silver Star for gallantry in action on February 15, a Bronze Star for meritorious service, and from the South Vietnamese government the Military Merit Medal and the Gallantry Cross with Palm. Remounted and reframed by their daughter Gina in the early twenty-first century, Mary still proudly displayed Clifford's medals. And in 2002 the Florida Legislature passed a bill naming a new 120-bed Bay County facility the Clifford Chester Sims State Veterans' Nursing Home.[63]

Until the Battle of the Black Sea in Mogadishu, Somalia, on October 3, 1993—a battle made famous in the movie *Black Hawk Down* (which was based on a book with the same title)—when two Delta Force snipers received MOHS, the Delta Raiders were the only company to have two MOH recipients from the same company in the same battle. As with Clifford Sims, Sergeant First Class Randall D. Shughart and Master Sergeant Gary L. Gordon received their awards posthumously.

More than a quarter century later Peter Boenigk still recalled how much fun the Washington trip was. His only complaint was that "we were really getting sick of steaks. We were eating steaks every night we were there. We just wanted a hamburger."

Unfortunately, the MOH ceremony was virtually the last happy moment that Joe, Balbine, and Peter had together.

Shortly afterward Joe left the Baker Street house after physically abusing Balbine for the second time. Joe had hit her on at least two occasions. Peter didn't see the first incident, which occurred after Joe had been drinking heavily and while they still lived in the Garfield Street apartment. A day or so afterward, when they all met for dinner and a tense effort at reconciliation, the boy asked his mother to give Joe a second chance. Since he apologized profusely, blamed the incident on the alcohol, and promised to stop drinking, she consented.

He didn't keep his promise. Not long after they returned from Washington, Peter heard noises coming from his parents' bedroom. When he peeked in the door Joe had his mother pinned down on the bed and was slapping her as she screamed, "Stop it! Stop it!" Bravely, the lad pushed Joe off his mom and they fled to another room—the one where Joe kept a pistol—and locked the door. Joe was soon knocking at the door, crying and saying he was sorry. Balbine went out to talk with him but "then he started getting mean again" and she quickly retreated to the safe haven. Locating the gun, she gave it to Peter, told him to sneak out the window, and take the weapon to Joe's superior who lived a few houses away. The master sergeant came running, took Sabina to his home where she and Peter spent the night, then returned to calm Joe down.

Balbine had no interest in attempting a second reconciliation. Within a day or so she and Peter moved back to an apartment in Glendale, and Joe moved to the Biltmore.[64]

Either Carollyn never asked why he was living there or Joe lied because for months after they met she did not know about Sabina.

Carollyn quickly discovered what many other women did, that Joe had a soft, almost "feminine" side that was wonderfully charming. "Everyone," Joe once told her, "has male and female qualities," and she certainly thought he was androgynous. He seemed to love children. One time he spoke at a Scoutarama at the Anaheim Convention Center where he spent hours signing autographs for kids, and he participated in the Los Angeles Big Brothers organization. Most importantly, he loved Rolly. By the summer of 1969 Joe had not only won Carollyn's heart but also her son's, so she allowed him to move into her house, which was soon militarized. They christened it the "Hollywood Bunker," painted the door black with a big white Screaming Eagle on it, and hung Joe's dog tags on Carollyn's antique iron bed. Over the fireplace they kept a framed photo of Joe and President Nixon at the MOH ceremony, and on the wall they kept a map of Vietnam. Rank in the Bunker flowed from Sergeant Joe to Corporal Rolly to Private Carollyn.

As he did with Peter, Joe treated Rolly as an instant son and Carollyn referred to him as "your boy."[65] Joe's sister Audrey thought her brother picked "women because of their children. I don't know if it was because of losing [Robert] or what, but he seemed to always have women with children."[66] In fact, when Joe picked up Carollyn for their first date, he asked, "Don't you have a little boy?" Yes. Well bring him along. So they all went to a restaurant at the corner of Hollywood Boulevard and Western Avenue for Chinese food, which, said Carollyn, "was great because that's probably the only time I've dated anyone who said bring your child with you."

Rolly attended Page Military Academy and "Joe taught him to shine his shoes, shine his brass, loved taking Rolly to school, and often spoke to the school." Joe also took him to Dodgers baseball games where they visited the dugout and met the players, and to auto races such as the Riverside Grand Prix where Joe was the Grand Marshall and he and Rolly rode in the pace car. He taught the boy how to spin a yo-yo, and when traveling on Army PR duties mailed him a stream of postcards. During a brief trip to Holland he sent at least five, all showing windmills since they fascinated the boy. "Hi Son—another windmill. You will get tired of them I bet," read a typical card. "Wish you and your mother were over here to see this beautiful country. Sure is great. The people [are] so good and nice. Well I will keep sending these. You will have a nice collection. Take care of Mommy. L[ove]. Joe."[67]

Not only did he display a paternal instinct, but Joe was also tender with a paraplegic friend, Mark Aubel. "Joe would take him out of his wheel chair and help him get into the swimming pool and swim with him," Carollyn said. "Joe had a heart of gold. He was very giving." Another way he gave was by constantly surprising Carollyn, which "was a big deal with him." He showered her with yellow roses—one of his trademark romantic gestures —and gifts, including two ao dais (one green, the other fuchsia) like those worn by Vietnamese women, a block of stamps commemorating the first moonwalk, a pair of hand-made deerskin moccasins, and beautiful dresses. Sometimes Carollyn came home to find that not only had Joe picked up Rolly from school and washed the car, but also cleaned the house. "This man could clean a house better than ten maids," she exclaimed, and he could also sew a mean stitch.

One surprise was inadvertent. Filling out a school form for Rolly, Joe had an epiphany. Carollyn's given name was Carolyn, with only one "l," but he discerned that if she added a second "l" it would have "rolly," her son's name, in it. With childlike glee he showed Carollyn his discovery. From that moment on she used the double "l."

Like many lovers they had affectionate nicknames, "their" songs, favorite clothes, and secret codes. Carollyn was always the Blonde Mama-san. Joe was her GI Joe, or later the Boy Hero, "because sometimes I didn't think he was quite as grown up as he should be." Songs such as "Leaving on a Jet Plane" by Peter, Paul, and Mary, John Denver's "Country Roads," Glenn Campbell's "Gentle on My Mind," Elvis Presley's "Kentucky Rain," and a handful of others transported them to a blissful state, as did the phrase "yummy-yummy." Whispered discreetly or scrawled on a letter, that was their codeword for sex. Joe and Carollyn bought matching Navy jeans at a Melrose Avenue Army Surplus Store and wore them everywhere, looking like "military hippies." "We were kind of like the love children except we were very military," recalled Carollyn. They rode horses at the Burbank Equestrian Center (Joe was the better rider), frequently went dancing (they were both fantastic dancers), and loved walking along the beach (where they sometimes engaged in yummy-yummy in the morning's wee hours).

During his spare time Joe often settled down with a book about Patton or Rommel, his heroes. Perhaps, if Carollyn was out of sight, he thumbed through pornographic magazines. When she discovered these "gross" publications she threw them out in disgust.

But idle moments were scarce because, as a relatively high profile Hollywood couple, they lived a hectic social schedule. They went to the Third Annual Salute to the Armed Forces on Friday evening, June 6, held at the Beverly Hilton Hotel and sponsored by VIVA (Voices in Vital America), an organization dedicated to supporting "our American form of government and our military in their stand against aggression." Joe called the occasion "a great success—So great in fact—that they received a bomb threat and were picketed."[68]

The next night they were at the annual meeting of the Southern California Chapter of the 101st Airborne Division Association, with Weldon "Red" Combs serving as master of ceremonies. A Senior Project Engineer for Hughes Aircraft, Red had been a World War II airborne trooper, though he arrived in the European Theater as a replacement late in the conflict and never made a combat jump.[69] Also in attendance was General Thomas L. Sherburne, who jumped with the 101st on D-Day, was an artillery officer during the Battle of the Bulge, and later commanded the 101st. Joe and General Sherburne sat with Red at the head table and gave speeches. The general spoke on "The Way It Was," while "to help bridge the generation gap" Joe "was honored to 'Tell the way it is Today.' It was a great night to visit with those warriors of past and present, for they have been 'Born' of the great events which have shaped our destiny. New periods of national enthusiasm and fervor will come . . . but there will always remain a deeper reverence for the older."[70] Without much formal education Joe could "get up, and with reasonably good grammatical ability, convey, in sort of a homespun way, the message. He was quite effective, very good. And he seemed to be at ease."

As soon as the formal ceremonies ended they "got down to our serious partying. It turned out both Sherburne and Hooper would drink just as fast as somebody would put a drink in their hand." Always surrounded by people who wanted to talk with them, "they never had a chance to go to the bar and order drinks," said Red, "so I made sure they had drinks coming."

Sharing many attributes—red hair, a passion for the 101st, heavy drinking—Red and Joe were instant friends. "From then on," said Red, "we just seemed to be a twosome, or a threesome or a foursome," depending on whether Carollyn and Red's wife Anna were with them. Although everyone else called Weldon "Red," Joe called him "Redhead." Joe often went to Red's and Anna's home where he "became like a member of the family. He meant an awful lot to our daughter Diane, too." One time after an earthquake trembled the house, frightening Diane, Joe "sat down with her, which is one side of Joe, being sensitive to somebody's feeling and sitting down with the younger person and talking with them in a very casual way, alleviating their concern or fear."

Redhead and Joe often swapped war stories, which sometimes became tedious for others. They could talk forever, complained Carollyn. "I think I fell asleep when they started telling war stories at a party over there." One particular discussion stuck with Red. He asked his friend about the My Lai Massacre. Joe responded vehemently saying that Lieutenant William L. Calley Jr., who was an active participant with his men in perpetrating the atrocity, "should have been shot. That's how strongly Joe conveyed to me that he disagreed with Calley." Professional soldiers, Joe insisted, did not do things like that. They "had certain standards that you had to uphold," standards that Calley failed.

A week after the 101st Airborne dinner Joe and Carollyn were at the Army Ball at the Beverly Hilton, where they sat with General and Mrs. Omar Bradley. This was a special evening. Carollyn wore a gorgeous white gown Joe bought for her and they danced, holding each other tight, especially when Neil Diamond crooned "You're Just Too Good To Be True." And for the first time Joe asked Carollyn to marry him. Soon he bought matching mesh-style gold wedding bands and they began talking seriously about the future, about having children (the first two would be Joe Jr., and Sara), about adopting several Vietnamese children, about moving to the Fort Campbell area near the home of his beloved 101st Airborne and not far from some of the nation's premier horse-raising and horse-racing locations, for Joe was displaying an affinity for horseflesh and the track.

In September they went to the Hollywood Bowl where Bob Hope was presenting a star-studded show. Learning that they were in audience, Hope announced that "I have a Sergeant Joe Hooper, Medal of Honor winner, out in the audience, and he has Carollyn DeVore, one of our entertainers, held hostage, and could he let her come up on stage?" They raced onto the stage together to a standing ovation. When the performance was over Hope asked them to appear in a show he would be taping in November. During mid-October Joe and Carollyn were in Houston attending a Medal of Honor Convention, where he showered her with yellow roses, a gold watch with a burgundy face from Nieman Marcus, and a black nightgown, also probably from Nieman Marcus since Joe and another MOH recipient spent considerable time studying the live models in that store's negligee department.

And so it went, a seemingly endless round of high profile public appearances by an increasingly well-known Hollywood duo.

Between major social engagements they enjoyed less visible dates, though unlike ordinary people in a big city they were never anonymous. On some occasions Joe dressed in civilian clothes—he wore a lot of brown since it went well with his red hair—but preferred to wear his white dress uniform. One of their favorite places to dine was the Los Angeles Press Club, an exclusive restaurant for news people, in part because "Joe loved all the attention from the press. He loved being a celebrity." Redhead and Anna Combs agreed that Joe loved the attention and adulation he received.[71]

Wherever they went together Carollyn was behind the wheel because Joe hated to drive; one of the few things he feared was dying in an auto accident.[72] Riding shotgun, Joe invariably gently rested his left hand on her right leg. Like most individuals who drink and drive, especially those who are thrill-seekers, Joe was not a good driver. One time after drinking too much he borrowed Carollyn's car to go the Beverly Hills Hotel. Going too fast into the hotel entrance, he rolled it. The car was virtually unscratched but Joe got a nasty cut on his forearm. "Lady," he told the female doctor who was going to give him a painkiller before sewing it up, "I don't need Novocain. Just stitch it up." Which she did.

In a potentially more dangerous crash, Joe flipped another car, pinning himself inside; the vehicle spewed gas and leaked oil, the ignition still running. While most onlookers hesitated, fearing an explosion and fire, a man named John Zecca stepped forward, turned off the ignition, and freed Joe. Ironically, in January 1969, Joe had rescued two people from a burning car. "I was driving on the freeway [near Saugus] when I came upon an accident that had just occurred," he told a reporter afterward. "There were people all around just looking at a car on fire with two people inside of it. It must have been a reflex of my combat days but before I knew it I was running toward the car and pulling people out." The military-hero-turned-civilian-hero also rendered first aid to one of the victims, who was badly hurt.[73]

Only rarely did Joe travel without Carollyn, and that was normally by plane. On July 4, 1969, he flew to Daytona Beach to attend the Firecracker 400 stock car race, renamed the "Medal of Honor 400" that year. Roger C. Donlon, the Vietnam's War first MOH recipient, was there too. They rode in the pace car and spent time in the crew pits where a lot of "pinup" girls were milling around. Roger's wife Norma was not happy. "I didn't like my husband to hang around with Joe because Joe was single and the pretty girls were always there, all the girls down there in the pit were hanging all over him, and of course I was up in the stands."[74] Norma was partly wrong. Joe was not single, but being married never deterred him from being with other women.

Joe also flew to Washington State alone, first in May (less than a month after he re-met Carollyn) to participate in Zillah's Community Day celebration and then in August to serve as the Grand Marshall for the Moses Lake Grand Parade. During the Zillah trip he was still basking in his newfound glory. Awaiting him were Maggie and John, the mayor, the Eisenhower High School band, veterans from the Zillah and Yakima American Legions Posts and the Yakima VFW, gifts from local merchants, tickets to the Fireman's Ball with music provided by Jim Parker's Western Playboys, and the thanks of a grateful population to whom Joe Hooper was a hero. He was Grand Marshall of the Community Day Parade, which glistened with patriotism, including color guards from the American Legion and VFW, floats sparkling with red, white, and blue, and five Gold Star mothers.[75]

When Joe went to Moses Lake three months later his parents joined him there and he visited old friends, including Tom Johnson, Pete Perez, and his former girlfriend Mavis Opp. When he related some of his exploits to Mavis she "thought he was feeding me just a bunch of crap." Given Joe's storytelling, some of what he said was undoubtedly inflated or concocted. Reflecting his changing attitude toward his current Army responsibilities, he also told Mavis he wanted to return to Vietnam, "but they wouldn't let me because he was a hero." This rang of truth, confirmed by Johnson and Perez who both recalled that Joe was drinking *very* heavily, did not like his Army PR and recruiting duties, and missed Vietnam. He "could not function in our society, in a civilian society," Tom realized. "He enjoyed being in Vietnam, he enjoyed taking care of his people—that's the way he put it, 'his people,' which was his squad. He took a lot of pride in the fact that he took good care of his people." When Joe indicated to Pete that his military duties were boring, Pete suggested he go to school. "I don't think I'm school material," Joe replied. "The military showed me one thing: how to kill as many as I could so silently it was unbelievable."[76]

After several months of PR duties Joe was tired of the "sometimes dull and routine jobs required of a hero, like speaking engagements, television appearances and interviews with newspapers throughout the country." He later estimated that he averaged twenty speeches a week while touring for the Army. Attending such functions as the Navy League dinner, the Anaheim Kiwanis breakfast at the Disneyland Hotel, the Dwight David Eisenhower Memorial Services, the San Fernando Valley Loyalty Parade, and the swearing in of 669 new Americans became tedious obligations. Appearing on TV ceased being exhilarating. The *Tonight Show,* the *Joey Bishop Show,* the *Lucille Ball Show,* the *Doris Day Show,* and *Hollywood Squares* (where he won $17,000 including a piano he gave to Carollyn) were no longer fun. Recruiting was equally onerous. Not only was the quality of men who were enlisting distressingly low, but Joe also "hated rules, hated regulations, hated all the crap that went with them."[77]

And despite the appearances on television, Joe's real Hollywood ambition—to become the next Audie Murphy—eluded him.

Joe couldn't understand why.

After all, he and Murphy shared many similarities. They came from humble beginnings and were undereducated, excelled in war but had difficulty adjusting to peace, received field commissions, loved guns and always slept with one nearby, sought adrenaline highs by associating with law enforcement personnel, were dreadfully poor at managing money, loved horses and horse racing, abused alcohol, and shamelessly chased women. Audie had married actress Wanda Hendricks (who later divorced him) and, if he had his way, Joe would marry Carollyn. The news media proclaimed Joe and Audie the most highly decorated soldiers of their respective wars. They even had paraplegic friends. Murphy befriended Perry Pitt, a badly wounded lieutenant who wallowed in near-suicidal despair until Audie encouraged him to live, while Joe was friends with Mark Aubel. Joe also claimed that he and

Audie had fathers who "gave us their love and guidance," which was non-sense since Audie's father deserted the family and Joe's played a minimal role in his upbringing.[78]

As a kid in Moses Lake, Joe loved Audie Murphy and John Wayne movies and by his teenage years he was so obsessed with becoming a movie star that his Navy buddy Gary Foster called him "Hollywood Hoop." Joe and Carollyn talked about writing a book about his life and having Hollywood produce a film akin to *Sergeant York* or *To Hell and Back,* revealing his military exploits and their love to the theater-going public. Considering a book-and-movie deal likely, Joe mentioned it in a will he later signed at Camp Eagle. And why not? National news outlets extolled him "as authentic an American hero as that legendary World War I sergeant, York, or an equally famous World War II sergeant named Audie Murphy." Although they fantasized about Joe starring in his cinematic autobiography, Joe and Carollyn also thought Steve McQueen, famous for his tough-man roles, might make a good onscreen Hooper. At one point they met with Robert Evans at Paramount Studios who was interested, but considering the growing anti-Vietnam sentiment the timing wasn't right.[79]

Hollywood wasn't going to make a film about a Vietnam hero.

And now the hero was languishing in the Hollywood Bunker—bored, restless, and increasingly unhappy.

Salvation lay back in Vietnam where he could regain a sense of brotherhood, take care of his people, utilize his killing skills, escape red tape, and do something he was good at—being a combat soldier.

If Carollyn was obsessively in love with Joe, why didn't she marry him?

One problem was that Balbine and Joe were still married. Divorce was a possibility, though after a divorce an individual had a one-year waiting period before he or she could remarry. An annulment left both parties immediately free to remarry. On December 12, 1969, Balbine filed for an annulment or divorce on the grounds of mental cruelty, a commonly stated cause for divorce or annulment that often shielded the real cause. The court document asserted that Balbine and Joe separated two weeks after their marriage, that Joe never consummated the marriage, and that they never "cohabited as husband and wife." These assertions were false, but based on them Balbine asked for an annulment, or if not entitled to that, a divorce. To hasten the proceedings Joe, then in Panama, waived his rights to respond to Balbine's petition. Joe probably did not understand the different consequences of a divorce versus an annulment. But he waived his rights on the assumptions that Balbine was asking for a divorce, not an annulment, and that she would continue on expeditiously with the court proceedings.[80]

"I don't think I was told what was really going on" between Joe and Balbine, said Joe's attorney David Darr, who did not know Joe was an MOH recipient. According to Darr, Hooper was a "close-mouthed type of gentleman." "You could not be dragged into a long conversation with this man." Joe told his lawyer only what he absolutely needed to know and not a word more. But Darr recognized that the nonconsummation story was absurd.

When Balbine took no action by September 1970, Joe became anxious because he wanted to marry Carollyn. Darr contacted Sabina's attorney, Phil. H. Jackson, who explained that "his client had not responded to his various requests to bring this matter to a conclusion." After consulting with Joe, Darr notified the court he was going to file a motion to withdraw Hooper's waiver of his rights. Joe was especially aggravated because he learned for the first time of Balbine's claim that he never consummated the marriage; aside from being untrue this was humiliating. Moreover, Balbine had assured Joe that if he gave her money and paid her attorney fees "she would have the day set for the hearing of our case." He gave her $1,000 and paid $350 to Mr. Jackson—"We bought her off," said Carollyn. But Balbine continued stalling.

Darr's motion to withdraw Joe's waiver jolted Balbine into action. In early October 1970, the case went to trial before the Honorable Lester E. Olson. Darr withdrew the motion to withdraw Joe's waiver of his rights, and Joe swallowed his manly pride and let the nonconsummation lie stand.

On November 4 Judge Olson nullified the marriage, leaving Joe and Carollyn free to marry.

By then, however, Carollyn recognized Joe's dark side. While predominantly warm and wonderful, their relationship was also tempestuous and ugly. That is, their relationship was much like Joe who was, as one of his friends remarked, "a man of extremes," a veritable split personality with a tendency to be either very good or dreadfully bad.[81] Joe understood his dual nature, sometimes signing letters and cards to Carollyn as "GI #1 Joe," but at other times using "GI #10 Joe." In the vernacular, #1 meant angelic, the best, while #10 was devilishly bad.

Fifteen years of maturation and several months of field duty in Vietnam did little to domesticate Joe's wild streak; his personality remained rooted in his Moses Lake teenage years. He "would beg me to stay with him until he was forty," Carollyn wrote. "He even cried about it. Maybe that is why he was so wild—he knew his life would end too early and he needed all the love and excitement he could get." "He lived in the fast lane," she observed on another occasion, "he was wild, he knew he would die at a young age." Again: "He was just a wild man. The wildest person. A real free spirit. Crazy. Just a wild man. Not boring! Never boring for a second!" And again: "I always had a feeling he knew he was on a tight schedule, and that's another reason for the erratic, or just *insane,* behavior." At times Anna Combs, who knew him less well than Carollyn, felt like grabbing him and screaming "Joe! Behave yourself. Calm down." [82]

Joe's impetuous, damn-the-world attitude had a primal charm but was also wearing and worrisome, especially for someone wanting a reasonably stable life. Joe was so intense he rarely slept. If he did drift off for few hours, he kept a gun on his side of the bed and held Carollyn so tightly she could not break his "grip" without waking him. She often awoke alone. Joe would be downstairs, squatting, staring off into space, and smoking cigarettes, either Pall Malls or Camels, which were his favorite brands.

Among Joe's faults were a jealous streak and a nasty temper, oftentimes alcohol fueled. When he was out of town he had Los Angeles Police Department friends follow Carollyn; she "couldn't go anywhere without him knowing where I was, who I talked to, and what I did." As for Joe's temper, his police department friends told her that when ordinary people got angry they had "a little switch that says 'Stop.' But he didn't have the 'Stop' switch." Joe's jealous anger could boil over into a frightening, destructive rage. "I have never met anyone as mean as him in my life," said Carollyn. One time she came home from working on a TV show and Joe had kicked in the front door, shot holes in the fireplace, and threw her framed celebrity pictures against the walls, showering glass everywhere. She never knew what ignited this tantrum. [83]

In retrospect, said Carollyn, she was stupid for not immediately recognizing that Joe was an alcoholic. Friends like Redhead Combs who plied Joe with liquor were doing him no favors. Wanting to help Joe beat the alcoholism, Carollyn studied books on the subject and talked to Joe's friends and to Joe, who acknowledged he had a drinking problem since his youth.

Because she loved him intensely, blamed Vietnam for his erratic behavior, and did not want anyone thinking badly of him, Carollyn overlooked the excessive drinking and boorish behavior and "covered his ass." Joe lost his false tooth so often in his drunken stupors that Carollyn finally began carrying a spare. When he was too drunk to make scheduled public appearances she made excuses, saying "he was sick or whatever." She "didn't want people to see this person who was sometimes weak when he was supposed to be so strong" and "didn't want our country to know their Hero was tarnished." Sometimes, however, Carollyn was not there to protect him. Former Raider platoon leader David Bischoff was attending a two-year college when he learned Joe was coming to campus as a recruiter. Resplendent in his uniform and MOH, Hooper was so drunk he did not even recognize Dave.[84]

Wounding Carollyn more deeply than the alcoholism was Joe's womanizing. Soaking up attention from women like a sponge, he was "a chronic womanizer," guilty of "military womanizing above and beyond the call of duty." Many times Joe was not the aggressor, but he never mounted a strong defense either. Carollyn was unaware that women hustled men until she went on publicity tours with him when "women were just after him. I've never seen anything like it." Returning from an overseas trip he had a stewardess on each arm, and Carollyn was sure he had their phone numbers in his pocket. Another time he came home from a cocktail party *two days* late reeking of booze and with earrings in his uniform pocket.

The most hurtful escapade occurred when Joe was in Holland in September 1969, the trip when he sent Rolly all the windmill postcards and when he had an affair with a woman named Renee. He went to Holland to represent the Army, especially the 101st Airborne, in ceremonies celebrating that country's liberation during World War II. One of his stops was at Best where Private First Class Joe E. Mann, who served in the 101st Airborne Division, died in a fierce battle, receiving a posthumous MOH. Joe Mann was from Reardan, Washington, ninety miles from Moses Lake. After the war Best erected the Joe Mann Monument in a quiet wooded area, with a tri-paneled base depicting parts of the battle, including Mann's death. Atop the monument was a highly symbolic sculpture: a mother pelican sacrificing her own flesh so that her babies could live.[85]

Joe felt a special kinship to Mann: they were both from Washington, served in the 101st Airborne, and shared the same first name. He told Irene Bennett, Mann's sister who was in Best for the ceremonies, that her brother was his hero. Reciting her conversation with him, she wrote that as a boy Hooper "read about Joe Mann and how he won his Medal of Honor. His interest led him to write a theme in high school about the Medal of Honor, honoring my brother by using his story." Joe also "made pilgrimages to Reardan to try to imagine young Mann's life there. He further related that he had saved clippings from periodicals about my brother."

Early in the day Joe went to the monument to spend some time alone. By afternoon a special buzz hummed around the town, something about the Joe Mann Monument. In a testimonial to combat brotherhood across the generations, Joe Hooper shinnied up one of the monument's three tall supports and attached his own MOH just below the pelican. "This valiant gesture was the cause of the hubbub in town where the story had spread rapidly."

Having been warned that the MOH was not safe atop the monument, after the ceremony Joe climbed back up to retrieve his medal. At the request of Queen Julia of Holland he left it with Best officials who gave it a revered spot in the Airborne Museum in their city. After returning to the United States Joe requested a replacement. Concerned with his MOH down to the smallest detail, Joe noted that the new medal lacked the green enamel in the rays of the star and soon requested a replacement for the replacement.[86]

At some point during the Holland trip Joe met Renee. He gave her his recruiting office address, but the men there, being helpful, brought his mail to the Hollywood Bunker while Joe was out of town. After opening the three or four letters from Renee, some of which included her picture, Carollyn was devastated and furious. "So I took the letters, took a knife, and put them in the front door. So when he came home they were in the front door." Joe denied the self-evident affair. "Loving a man with *no* morals is frustrating," said Carollyn.

They had a huge fight over Renee, and Carollyn asked Joe to move out. The next morning she came downstairs and heard Joe moaning in the bathroom. She kicked in the locked door to find him on the floor, a whiskey bottle by his side. Joe had vomited, losing his false tooth in the process, and had "slit his wrists—not real deeply, but enough there was blood all over." Fortunately, Rolly was not home because he usually stayed with Carollyn's parents on weekends so did not witness this ugly scene. Carollyn bandaged Joe up and sobered him up, and then he threatened to kill himself if she ever left him, a threat he uttered often.

Even worse than the womanizing was the physical abuse "because it was really scary." A major incident occurred shortly after they reconnected. Carollyn threw a big party at her Rowena Street home, mixing her Hollywood friends with Joe's Army and police department buddies. Joe became exceptionally drunk, and for some unknown reason got angry at Carollyn. Grabbing her wrist, he took her into a spare bedroom where she kept an ironing board. "He pulled a huge knife, the one he always carried, and laid it on the ironing board and hit me in the face so hard I flew across the room," she recalled. "I hit him back as hard as I could. I knocked him to the floor. His medals were bouncing off his uniform all over. He was shocked. He was wild." Joe started screaming incoherently—Carollyn thought maybe he was yelling in Vietnamese—and she yelled right back at him.

The guttural sounds from the small bedroom could be heard above the blaring music, and her cousin, Norman White, then the president of the Hollywood Stuntman's Association, and a couple of other men grabbed Joe and escorted him from the house. "I was sporting a huge black eye, bruised face, and broken heart. He called me, I would hang up on him. He finally came and slept on my front porch, cried, begging me to trust him again, saying he would never hit me again." Carollyn took him back.

No matter what Joe did—the jealousy, the rages, the drinking, the womanizing, the abuse—Carollyn knew that "he loved me more than anything." Still, it was "terrible to love someone as much as I loved Joe and be abused, and be scared."

One of Joe and Carollyn's best mutual friends was Martin Barsky, who had a local radio program and was the managing editor of a small weekly Los Angeles paper, the *Downtowner*.

Because of Barsky Joe wrote a "Screaming Eagle" column for the *Downtowner*. The paper announced that Hooper's column would "answer questions sent in by Downtowner readers along with questions most frequently asked of him during his hundreds of public appearances." Joe wrote an editorial introducing himself. "As long as men love liberty, more than life itself, as long as they treasure the priceless privileges bought with the blood of our forefathers, there will be men like me," he wrote, or at least *allegedly* wrote.[87] Joe and Marty usually huddled together, often at the Hollywood Bunker, with Marty interviewing Hooper while both men smoked and drank. Barsky then turned the interview into a column by polishing up Joe's thoughts and putting Joe's name to it. So even if Joe did not write the columns, they reflected his perspective, though Barsky may have occasionally put words in his mouth. In any case, none of the seven columns soared above the mundane.[88]

Hooper and Barsky were superhawks, squarely in the Nixon administration's camp. "What do you think of President Nixon's Peace Formula?" a reader supposedly asked. The president's peace plan, responded Hoopsky, "was generous in its terms. . . . I would like to remind every American that it is you who vote and elect our leaders. These people have a far greater knowledge on world affairs, than you or I. It is your duty as citizens to unite behind and support your nation."

Another question was, "Why don't we bring all the boys home from Vietnam?" "Because 90 percent of our servicemen don't want to come home!" Once there they "see the violence and terror inflicted by the North on the people of the South" and want to help the South Vietnamese gain freedom. Are not the lives lost in Vietnam being wasted? No! But to insure that their sacrifice was not in vain the country must "safeguard the freedom for which they paid so dearly." Only cynics believed "our men went away blindly and fought blindly," with no conception of the issues at stake. No true American "can accept this cynical counsel of despair." "Is morale low in Vietnam?" "Definitely not! The morale is very high. "How are the anti-war demonstrators doing in combat after they are finally drafted?" Just great! To prove the point Hooper/Barsky told about Nicholas Schoch, a medic, "a skinny, freckle-faced 21 year old who talks like a philosopher, hates war and worked like a demon taking care of wounded buddies on Ap Bia Mountain [Hamburger Hill]."

A Fourth of July column lamented that Americans "used to show our patriotism on a greater scale than we do today. Then, flag waving was not considered corny or unsophisticated." Those who prized freedom and loved their country should be less self-conscious about showing patriotism. "I should like to see an outward show of patriotism once again. . . . This is the day for you to express your pride in America—and take your stand unflinchingly for the Cause of Freedom."

Peter Boenigk had a few parting glances of Joe, whom he considered "the next closest thing to a father that I had" after his biological father died.

When Peter and Balbine moved into an apartment after the separation,

Joe stopped by to get a photo album from the MOH trip. "When we were in Washington," said Peter, "we had a photographer follow us around to everything that we did. He wanted those pictures just as a memory."

During his first tour Joe carried a Saint Christopher's medallion as a talisman. Of course he told tales about it. He kissed it every night as he said a prayer, Joe told a reporter. "One night I reached for it to pray and it was gone—I had lost it." That night enemy mortars and rockets thumped the ground all around him. "The next morning at daylight I saw this big rocket sticking in the ground about three feet from me. It was a dud. It didn't explode. And laying about an inch from the rocket was my St. Christopher's medal." When he and Balbine married he gave it to Peter, showing him a dent in it, saying it saved his life by stopping a bullet. The boy believed the medallion was indeed a good luck charm. As Joe prepared to return to Vietnam in the spring of 1970 he wanted the medallion back. Peter gave it to him.

In November 1970 when the judge granted the annulment Peter saw Joe at the courthouse.

He never saw him again.[89]

Eleven

It's not the same war.

*Joe's reaction upon returning to
Vietnam in the spring of 1970 for a second tour*

Carollyn was asleep in her Saigon hotel room when a hand clamped over her mouth, hard, smothering her scream.

It was Christmas of 1969, and she was on her third USO tour, rediscovering that the information packet she received was correct: the "welcome you receive from troops in the field will more than compensate for any undue hardship endured by you . . . thousands of men eagerly await your arrival." And "the troops like seeing girls in skirts." [1]

No matter how soft and sensual they were, the women sponsored by the USO could not be prima donnas, said Johnny Grant who pioneered the practice of taking lovely women to Vietnam for no other reason than to look sexy and say hello to soldiers. They worked six days a week, often in areas where combat operations were underway; they could use little technical equipment since they often performed on a flatbed truck or in the open under a parachute; dressing rooms, toilet facilities, hair spray, soap, and other amenities were minimal or nonexistent; Vietnam's tap water was not potable; and transportation was limited, subject to being diverted to combat missions at the last moment, and dangerous. During her Christmas 1968 tour Carollyn flew over the Delta in a small fixed-wing airplane that received ground fire. Bullets hit the reserve tank, spewing fuel all over the baggage but doing no other damage. [2]

Prima donnas were also excluded because the actresses and models saw war's ugliness up close visiting hospitals. Carollyn visited men with malaria, amputated limbs and other nasty wounds, and terrible burns, always keeping a brave public face but often weeping when no one was looking. She especially remembered a patient with a tube down his throat who initially neither smiled nor spoke. "He wrote me a note and said I looked like his sister. So I got my pen and wrote him saying, 'I'm sorry that she is so ugly.' He smiled and laughed and that made me the happiest person in the world." [3]

Carollyn and three other lovelies were in the boonies for most of the two-week 1969 tour. She mailed Joe, who was now stationed in Panama, a steady stream of Polaroid snapshots with handwritten captions. On December 17th, for example, she sent a photo from Cu Chi, showing a GI wiping mud off her midcalf boots. Four days later, looking "so grubby," she was at a fire base near Ban Me Thout with her first husband's old unit, the 4th Division. [4]

And four days after that, on Christmas, Carollyn and her three companions were in Saigon enjoying a sumptuous dinner featuring shrimp cocktails, roast turkey with all the traditional trimmings, and the favorite holiday desserts—fruitcake, mincemeat pie, and pumpkin pie with whipped topping. Dressed in a stunning purple miniskirt, Carollyn dined with MACV commander Creighton Abrams and her escort officer who was a West Point graduate. Afterward the West Pointer escorted her to the hotel in time to beat her 10:00 p.m. curfew. [5]

On Christmas day she had sent Joe a card and a photo. On the card, which featured the churches of Saigon, Carollyn wrote, "To Joe—Love Mama San. I prayed we would be together—I love you Joe!" The photo showed a miniskirted Carollyn standing in a doorway at the Saigon Heliport Flight Operations Center, giving a thumbs-up sign. "Merry Christmas My GI Joe," she wrote on the front. "I love you Sweet. Happy New Year. From Siagon Christmas Day." On the back she added "Joe—Right after this was taken I got a letter from you—its Christmas—I love you." [6]

A good thing, because the hand clamped over her mouth belonged to her GI Joe, whispering to her to keep quiet.

How did he get to Saigon? Into her room? Have a jeep parked outside the hotel? She never knew the answers to these questions.

What she did know was that she "was so excited he was there I couldn't even believe it." Joe motioned her to put something on, and she slipped into the purple dress she wore at dinner. They sneaked out of the hotel using the stairs rather than the old elevator, which made a lot of noise, climbed into the jeep, and drove to a tiny white building in a gated yard. Inside the building a "real cheesy looking guy who looked like a Vietnamese pimp" greeted them. Giving Carollyn a velvet box with a two-karat diamond in it, Joe said they were going to get married (even though he was still married to Balbine), and he would get the diamond set in a ring later. The Vietnamese man conducted a brief ceremony and gave them a piece of paper to sign. Joe put the paper in his pocket, they drove back to the hotel, made love, and then he was gone as mysteriously as he had appeared.

"I got night ambushed," Carollyn recalled. She never considered the Saigon wedding an official ceremony, though she thought the episode was recklessly romantic. For Joe the sojourn was certainly reckless since the company morning reports do not indicate that he had official leave time.[7]

Considering his stateside duties intolerable, by mid-1969 Joe was pushing to return to Vietnam. Fearing for his life, neither Carollyn nor the Army wanted that. As a compromise the Army had reassigned Joe to Panama to teach jungle warfare techniques, perhaps hoping this would be warlike enough to appease him. Before departing for the Canal Zone his friends threw a farewell party at the Stake Out Restaurant hosted by Robert Hill, a real estate agent, and Marty Barsky; among the many guests were John Zecca, the man who pulled Joe from the white Fiat, Los Angeles Police Department officer J. D. Smith, and former wrestling great Les (Don Eagle) Neeley. More quietly, Joe, Carollyn, and Rolly drove to Zillah so he could say goodbye to Maggie and John Henry.[8]

Joe boarded the plane for Panama thoroughly drunk and with Rolly pouting because his "dad" was leaving. After arriving at Fort Kobbe on October 20, he joined Company A, 3rd Battalion, 5th Infantry (which had replaced the 3rd Battalion, 508th Infantry in June 1968) the next day. Consisting of two regular rifle companies and one airborne company, the battalion trained primarily in heliborne assaults, but the one company also practiced parachute drops at both high and low altitudes. Serving in the airborne company Joe rappelled down cliffs and hacked through dense jungles, but also made a number of jumps. "Well the jump came off fine," he wrote Carollyn after his first leap. "Just like I [had] never been away." Aside from training for war, the 3rd Battalion also assisted the Panamanian government in riot control.[9]

While in Panama Joe showered Carollyn with notes and cards, drank excessively, and took two trips, apparently only one of them authorized. The relationship with Carollyn was showing strains. "Love you as much this morning as I did last night," read one note, "Will be away until Friday. Then make a jump into Ft. Kobbe. Hope things are working out there for us. Love you Carollyn." Part of the problem was Balbine's failure to move quickly for an annulment/divorce. "Have not heard from the Witch's lawyer," complained Joe. But Joe also knew he had not been a model partner, signing a postcard, "Love you forever #10 Boy-san." He tried appealing to their mutual tender concerns. On a postcard showing the Santa Clara Beach he scrawled, "Wish you and I were here on this lovely beach. What we could do—yummy." And he wrote about his "son" Rolly and "our dear Sarah," the baby girl they talked about having.[10] In between training and obsessing about Carollyn, Joe drank. For his thirty-first birthday (August 8, 1969) Carollyn gave him a gold Rolex, but he became so drunk he got hit by a bus, shattering the watch.[11]

On November 12 Hooper received ten days administrative absence to attend the November 14 launch of Apollo 12 from Cape Kennedy. Launched in rainy weather—"God we were soaked," Joe wrote—the spacecraft suffered a near disaster 36.5 seconds into the flight when lightning temporarily knocked out power in the spacecraft, though fortunately not in the rocket. On the 19th two of the crewmen became the third and fourth humans to walk on the moon when they stepped out of the Lunar Excursion Module onto the Ocean of Storms. While at Cape Kennedy Joe chatted with President Nixon for a few moments, went out drinking, and called Carollyn. Evidently they had a loving conversation about Carollyn's upcoming trip to Vietnam and a trip to Panama that she and Rolly were contemplating. Joe signed his next postcard "I Love You. #1 Boy San."[12]

The boy-san abused his administrative absence, returning to Fort Kobbe two days late, which was not the only time he was derelict in returning to duty. On January 22 he received seven days ordinary leave; he was gone an extra day. Unlike his earlier Panama tour, no Article 15 or court martial followed these transgressions.[13]

And at least in these instances his commander knew he was gone.

Back at the Hollywood Bunker for New Year's Eve, Carollyn received flowers ordered through the La Cienega Flower Shop and a telegram sent from the El Panama Hotel reading, "May this be the last one we are apart happy new year No. 1 boy hero."[14]

Hoping they could be together soon, Joe received permission for Carollyn and Rolly to visit the Canal Zone for two weeks, arriving on or about March 20. Since his last duty day in Panama was March 19, he was planning to use fourteen days (out of his thirty-seven days of accumulated leave) vacationing there. Expecting to travel, Carollyn and Rolly got the requisite shots. But then she thought, "I'm going to be in Panama with this *crazy* person, in a foreign country, not in the middle of Hollywood where I could escape a little." Also, she knew he was drinking heavily and feared he might be abusive. When they did not come to Panama, Joe departed immediately for the Hollywood Bunker.[15]

California was not his ultimate destination. As the morning report noted, he was released from Company A, 3rd Battalion, 5th Infantry "for future assignment to [the] 101st Airborne Division," which was in Vietnam.[16]

Joe and Carollyn were soon on a whirlwind social circuit, dining on Cantonese cuisine at Ho Toy's restaurant, sipping "apple shots" (made from vodka and California apple juice) at Mattero's in Westwood, and attending the Academy Awards on April 7. For that august ceremony Joe was attired in his white dress uniform and Carollyn, with a dark tan, wore a white, two-piece silk pants suit trimmed in gold. Joe had surprised her by ordering the outfit from Thailand. Aside from one lady mistaking Joe for a doorman, the evening went well, especially when they went backstage and Joe, a real combat hero, got to meet the tinseltown pretend hero John Wayne. Joe was thrilled.[17]

But by the Academy Awards their relationship was in serious trouble because of what happened in Zillah during a week-long visit at Easter, a trip that started out so well and ended so badly.[18]

During their previous trip to the Hooper farmstead Carollyn "fell in love with Joe's mom," calling her Grandma Hooper almost from the moment they met. Maggie felt the same about Carollyn. "My mother just loved her to death," Joe's sister Audrey recalled. "Probably her favorite one [of Joe's women]. I think she liked Carollyn the best. And I think it was because Carollyn was sort of 'country.' Easy going. She was real glamorous, but she was really a nice person." Kathy agreed with her sister's assessment. Carollyn, she said, "was just sweet, just plain, down to earth sweet."[19]

Carollyn also loved the way John Henry "welcomed me with open arms," and found Douglas (who still lived with his parents) to be "a quiet man, shy, nice." Zillah was a special haven because Joe, who was never comfortable in a city, "seemed to be at peace while on the farm and around horses." Rolly too enjoyed the visit since he ran wild all over the farm and the Hoopers spoiled him. So as they drove to Zillah in Carollyn's 1969 red Volkswagen beetle, they anticipated a wonderful vacation.

Most of all Carollyn and Joe were giddy because, thanks to the Saigon wedding night, she was three months pregnant. Although Carollyn was not "showing," Maggie intuitively knew even before they told her. "When is my grandchild going to be born?" she asked as she stepped out of the house to embrace Carollyn, Joe, and Rolly upon their arrival.

On Easter they attended the 11:00 a.m. services at the Church of the Nazarene, where Pastor G. D. Craker read scriptures from Matthew 28 and the congregation sang hymns, including "All That Thrills My Soul," a title with special meaning for Joe and Carollyn that Sunday. Afterward they feasted on a huge family dinner cooked by Maggie.

Sitting at the head of the dinner table, at one point Joe quietly excused himself. Carollyn found him outside, alone, leaning against a fence, looking at the horses, sobbing. "I feel so guilty," he told her as she cradled his head, "because I am here, I have this great dinner, but my troops are in Vietnam and they probably don't have nice food today. I'm with my family and the girl I love, and these guys are over there suffering. I have to go back there." Although inwardly fearing he might be killed, she assured him that she supported his decision. That night they slept in an antique bed, the window open, a breeze cooling the room. "You could smell the freshness of the air," recalled Carollyn. "Joe fell asleep peacefully."

While in Zillah Joe and Douglas "worked with the horses, and there was like no care in the world," though Carollyn recognized that Douglas was "the total opposite of Joe" and that the brothers did not really like each other. They "were kind of like brothers, but there wasn't that bond between them." Joe and Carollyn went down to the river and fired shotguns, having a great time blasting away at cans they threw into the current. And they were guests of the Zillah American Legion and Auxiliary where they showed colored slides Carollyn took in Vietnam and answered questions.[20]

They also went to the Squeeze Inn, a tiny bar where Joe was a big hero. He drank too much and something—who knew exactly what—ignited his volatile temper. When he and Carollyn came out of the bar Joe slammed her against the Volkswagen, then hurled her against a wall. Back at the farm they went to the barn, where Joe continued manhandling Carollyn, leaving her shaking with rage and fright.

Carollyn miscarried.

The trip back to California "was just a nightmare." Joe was horribly upset not only because he had an affinity for children but also having a baby with Carollyn would bind her to him. As for Carollyn, not only was she suffering from the miscarriage but also Joe kept a Bowie knife on the car floor and she feared he might use it on her. Looking back on it, she realized how sad the situation was "because I always just loved him. You know me, I look at the world through rose-colored glasses, and kept thinking 'Oh, it's Vietnam, it's something, and he'll change.' He didn't."

When Maggie and John Henry learned that Carollyn was not having a baby, Joe wrote from Vietnam assuring them that "it was us and our troubles that lost it. She did not have anything [an abortion] done. She loves me & our family so." [21]

In returning to Vietnam Joe overcame the Army's aversion to allowing heroes to go in harm's way again. As one recipient wrote, "Medal winners were few and far between, and those who survived their ordeals were to be protected and displayed." [22] Exactly how he did this is uncertain, though he had a good story, saying he appealed directly to Westmoreland and hinted that if he did not go back to the war, "I'd start marching with peacenik groups." General Westmoreland had no such communication from Joe. [23]

A more reasonable explanation was that by 1970 experienced non-commissioned officers willing to return to Vietnam were so scarce that Sergeant Hooper was a welcome commodity. Also, while President Johnson adamantly opposed allowing recipients to return to Vietnam, especially after World War II recipient Keith L. Ware was killed there, Nixon loosened the policy after strenuous lobbying by David C. Dolby. Once Dolby returned, others followed, including David H. McNerney, Delbert O. Jennings, and Franklin Miller. Some, such as Miller, were initially in staff positions but, as he said, "That lasted all of two months. I couldn't handle it. I craved action and excitement, and I sure wasn't getting either behind a desk. I made my demand—play me or trade me." [24]

No uncertainty surrounds *why* Joe wanted to go back. "Discipline was breaking down and guys were dying needlessly because of inexperienced leadership," he told a reporter. "I felt I could save lives." Flashing a Hooperesque grin, he added, "I was restless, too. I missed combat. That's where I was the best." He told another newspaperman that "I insisted on going back to Nam because the thing was in my blood and I knew that with my experience I could save the lives of some of our people." He looked forward to returning to his "jungle family," that is, to enjoying the comradeship of men in his unit.[25]

Seattle columnist Rick Anderson interviewed Joe extensively after the war about his second tour and discerned that "there was something about war. He was drawn to it. I got the impression he might have been drawn to the war itself, not the cause." Joe thought he was "a little smarter than some others out in the jungles" and could "at least save some of those young Americans in a worthless cause."[26]

In addition, Joe was thinking of applying for a direct commission as an officer, primarily because of pressure from Martin Barsky and, especially, Carollyn. While Joe was in Panama, Barsky wrote him an obsequious letter describing his amazing impact on "the entire business, political and social spectrum." Joe had an unusual gift "to communicate not only leadership and ability" but also "a humaneness and concern and honesty" that should not be wasted in the enlisted ranks. If his "impact as a non-com was so beneficial to our country, imagine how beneficial that could be as a commissioned officer." It behooved Joe to apply for a commission. As for Carollyn, she very much wanted him to become an officer even though "he didn't want to. He did that for me. I just thought he should be an officer and he really didn't want to."[27]

So Joe departed for Vietnam. Behind he left the Hollywood Bunker secure, nailing the windows partially shut to foil potential burglars and leaving one of his pistols with Carollyn. Ahead lay possible death. "He would never admit any weakness, *never!*" Carollyn exclaimed. "But when he got on the plane in Oakland to go back the second time he said, 'Do you think I'm going to make it back?' He was really scared."[28]

Whether Joe was scared or not, Carollyn was relieved to see him go. After the second abusive episode and miscarriage she looked in a mirror and thought, "I feel like I'm one hundred years old being around him. He just would drain all your energy, just drain the being out of you."[29]

She still loved him—too much—but now she could breathe, think, heal.

"We are veterans of the Vietnam War."

Thus began a statement of principles issued by the Vietnam Veterans

Against the War (vvaw). Founded by a handful of disaffected vets in 1967, it became the foremost antiwar veterans organization, though not the only one. The veterans believed in the freedom to think and speak, change their minds, and protest. "We join the dissent of millions of Americans against the war," the statement continued. "We support our buddies still in Vietnam. We want them home now. We want an end to the war now. We believe that this is the highest patriotism."[30]

Vets Larry Rottmann, John Kerry, and Bobby Muller personified the organization's membership. "It was clear to anybody who was looking that it was the wrong war at the wrong place at the wrong time against the wrong people for the wrong reasons," said Rottmann. "It was just a debacle of catastrophic proportions." Kerry asserted that "it is not patriotism to ask Americans to die for a mistake, and . . . it is not patriotic to allow a president to talk about not being the first president to lose a war, and using us as pawns in that game." A paraplegic, Muller believed the wound that left him paralyzed was no great tragedy. No, what he regretted was being "so totally naive and trusting. . . . I was an idiot because I never asked the question 'Why?' And that is my greatest tragedy—one which was shared by all too many Americans."[31]

The vvaw became prominent in the larger antiwar movement, which suffered a decline after Nixon's election as people waited for his "secret plan" to work. Troop withdrawals, Vietnamization, and pacification temporarily appeased the public. But periodically the antiwar movement regrouped. Huge demonstrations in October and November 1969, April 1970, and April–May 1971 revealed the frustrations with Vietnam, especially since the crowds were only the visible edge of a vast silent majority that opposed the war. Following the October 1969 Moratorium a high-level White House aide noted that the protest was a huge success. "The young white middle class crowds were sweet tempered and considerate: at times even radiant. . . . The movement lost no friends. It gained, I should think, a fair number of recruits and a great deal of prestige." The Nixon administration tried to smear the protest by portraying it as small, violent, and treacherous, but that was demonstrably untrue. During the fall 1969 protests, for the first time since the war began the national press portrayed demonstrators sympathetically.[32]

The vvaw spearheaded the April 1971 demonstrations in Washington, conducting Operation Dewey Canyon III (the Army conducted Dewey Canyon I and Dewey Canyon II in Vietnam in 1969 and 1970). The veterans' message of a complete and rapid withdrawal from Southeast Asia reached soldiers in Vietnam. "I heard about the Veterans in D.C.," wrote a grunt from I Corps in early May. "I agree with them in most ways." The VVAW's activities also commanded the attention of President Nixon who considered the organization a special threat because it proved that antiwar sentiments were neither un-American nor unpatriotic. As presidential speechwriter Patrick Buchanan understood, antiwar veterans were "being received in a far more sympathetic fashion than other demonstrators."[33]

Reflecting their constituency's changing mood, in 1970–71 even country and western singers, heretofore almost unanimously hawks, followed the path that rock 'n' roll and folk music traveled several years earlier and began questioning the war. In "What Is Truth" Johnny Cash suggested that opposing the war was not unpatriotic, and in "When You Gonna Bring Our Soldiers Home" Skeeter Davis criticized Nixon's war.[34]

By June 1971, 61 percent of Americans believed the war was a mistake, and the next month polls revealed that 65 percent favored withdrawal from Vietnam even if South Vietnam collapsed.[35] In essence, although antiwar activists remained unpopular, the public embraced their view that the war was wrong. Yet it continued.

Frustrated by the failure of the political process to end the conflict, a small number of activists went beyond peaceful protest to harassment, frequently targeting draft records. A Baltimore priest defaced draft records with pig's blood, and two Jesuit brothers along with seven others became the "Catonsville 9" when they destroyed draft records in that city with homemade napalm, burning, they said, paper instead of children. At least a dozen other well-publicized incidents occurred, culminating with the "Camden 28" in the late summer of 1971. Worse than harassment was a brief, violent spasm in 1969–71 that seemed to portend uncontrolled social disorder. Bombs exploded in America like artillery shells in Vietnam and arsonists struck at campus buildings, federal installations, banks, and corporate headquarters as militant fringe elements such as the Weathermen attacked the "establishment" with rage. The Nixon administration tried to discredit the antiwar movement by linking all of it to violence and terrorism, but most people understood that antiwar protests were overwhelming peaceful.[36]

Nixon was incapable of perceiving the truth about antiwar advocates. "We simply have to face the fact that we have large numbers of extremely well informed young people who are well educated and who think for themselves; that they tend to be overly idealistic and unrealistic does not alter the fact," wrote White House aide Tom Whitehead. Nixon accepted no such fact. Convinced that demonstrators were *his* enemies, he *knew* they must be Communist subversives. As did Johnson before him, he ordered the CIA and the FBI to investigate. When neither agency found any evidence of Communist influence, Nixon concluded the intelligence reports were faulty.[37]

As public support eroded, the administration had fewer military and diplomatic options and both the press and congressional opponents became increasingly bold in speaking against the war. "The reaction of the noisy radical groups was considered all the time," wrote Admiral Thomas Moorer, Chairman of the JCS. "And it served to inhibit and restrain the decision makers" in both the executive and legislative branches. Kissinger recalled that "the fear of another round of demonstrations permeated all the thinking about Vietnam in the Executive Branch that summer [1970]—even that of Nixon, who pretended to be impervious." [38]

Angered by its limited options and equating criticism with treason, the Nixon administration went to war against the peace movement. A special target was the VVAW. One way to defame the organization was to show that many of its participants were frauds. Despite vigorous efforts to discover false military credentials, only a handful of men were not legitimate veterans. Even though the administration knew that VVAW members were not impostors, it called them *alleged* veterans, thus implying that something was amiss. Government agents, sometimes acting as provocateurs, infiltrated the organization in ludicrous numbers; half the VVAW membership in Louisiana consisted of government infiltrators. FBI memos urged that at least one VVAW leader be "neutralized." [39]

Nixon did not attack just the VVAW. The administration infiltrated Quaker groups picketing the White House and tried to frame some Quakers with drug charges. It encouraged "hard hat" workers to beat up protesters and contemplated interning demonstrators in camps like those that housed Japanese Americans in World War II. The CIA's illegal Operation Chaos and the Army's domestic spying operation expanded. When the May Day Tribe tried to shut down the government between May 3 and 5, 1971, the administration responded with a military attack that "seemed more appropriate to Saigon in wartime than Washington." Wholesale violations of the Constitution occurred as city police, flak-jacketed troops, Marines, and helicopters swept through and over the streets. Among the victims were a couple on their way to their wedding and six psychiatric patients with their attendants. A subsequent class action lawsuit yielded $12 million for all those wrongfully arrested. Even Americans with no sympathy for the May Day rowdies felt uneasy over using military force and unconstitutional methods to keep the government functioning.[40]

Finally, the Justice Department abused the grand jury system to persecute the antiwar movement. "To silence the critics, the government accuses them of crimes they have not committed," editorialized the *St. Petersburg Times*. The Department of Justice, it continued, "has developed a sorry record of politically motivated prosecutions based on the amateurish pursuit of nebulous plots at which any first-year law student would scoff. . . . The suppression of legitimate dissent creates disrespect for laws which are abused and for the government which immorally exercises power." Trials bordering on the absurd occurred for, among others, the Boston 5, Chicago 7, Harrisburg 7, Camden 28, and Gainesville 8. Not a single sustained conviction emerged from any of these trials.[41]

When Joe kissed Carollyn goodbye at the Oakland airport, the country's attitude was dramatically less favorable toward the war from when the Delta Raiders deployed in December 1967.

The Army and the war awaiting him on the earth's far side were quite different, too.

By 1970 many soldiers no longer considered "The Star Spangled Banner" their national anthem.

They preferred "We Gotta Get Out of This Place," a 1965 song by the British rock group the Animals, who briefly rivaled the Beatles and the Rolling Stones in popularity. Originally written as an antipoverty song, with its insistent refrain that "We gotta get out of this place if it's the last thing we ever do," the song resonated not only in the ghettos and Appalachia, but also with all those GIs in Vietnam who, desperately, did not want to die for their country's mistake.

Arriving in Vietnam in late April 1970, Hooper encountered a different Army from what he experienced in 1967–68. Gone was the magnificent fighting machine of 1965–68 with its enthusiastic volunteers, soldiers who were shot to pieces pursuing Westy's flawed strategy or went home under the one-year rotation policy. In its stead stood an Army dominated by reluctant draftees, most of whom served honorably if unhappily. "We were the property of the government; they owned us, we were their pawns," wrote one dismayed soldier who nonetheless served loyally. "Those of us in the field knew that Vietnamization was a sham and a lie," wrote another man. "We were ordered to put our lives on the line for it. We did, but we also knew our leaders were lying to us and that we could no longer trust them (though we did obey them)." [42]

The Army deteriorated with exceptional speed after Nixon announced the first troop withdrawal, signaling American retreat. One general observed that the "hairline crack in the army's facade of morale and discipline which appeared in 1969 would become a visible fissure in 1970 and a yawning crevice in 1971." Succinctly summarizing the situation in November 1971, Brigadier General DeWitt C. Armstrong maintained that "the state of discipline among U.S. troops is generally appalling [and] has a great distance to rise before it can be termed acceptable." [43]

Difficulties arose in part because the draftee Army reflected the unruliness afflicting society in the late 1960s and early 1970s, prompted by what protesters viewed as the nation's warmongering, racial injustice, gender inequities, and environmental rapine.

Compounding the problem were grave leadership deficiencies. The "Study on Military Professionalism" ordered by Chief of Staff Westmoreland in 1970 revealed the Army's prevailing climate was far removed from the time-honored traditions of Duty, Honor, and Country. Moral and ethical transgressions were pervasive in the officer corps. A typical commander— ambitious, transitory, and marginally skilled in his duties—was "engulfed in producing statistical results, fearful of personal failure, too busy to talk with or listen to his subordinates, and determined to submit acceptably optimistic reports which reflect faultless completion of a variety of tasks at the expense of the sweat and frustration of his subordinates." Engaged in selfish career competition, senior officers routinely "sacrificed integrity on the altar of personal success"; were preoccupied with attaining "trivial short-term objectives even through dishonest practices"; stifled initiative and innovation among subordinates by stressing "trivial, measurable, quota-filling accomplishments"; and nourished self-deception by insisting on perfection, thus discouraging subordinates from relaying bad news and compelling them "to lie, cheat, and steal to meet the impossible demands of higher officers." [44]

Westmoreland had the study classified but concealing the truth did not hide the leadership problems in Vietnam. Wherever disciplinary difficulties existed, insisted one general, the primary cause was "ineffective leadership, in large part because many leaders made a career of their own careers rather than a career out of leading their own units."[45] Rather than exercising constructive leadership the high command cynically tried to placate the troops by handing out medals like Christmas toys, distributing more than half a million in 1970, or about two for every GI remaining in Vietnam. Soldiers took the measure of their so-called leaders and reciprocated this cynicism, derisively calling the medals "gongs."[46]

With little confidence in the nation's civil and military leadership, victory ceased to matter; survival, staying alive, trumped everything. Resenting the government and the high command, men no longer risked their lives to "kill a Commie for Mommie." Dying lost whatever nobility of purpose that prevailed before 1968. The typical grunt attitude was, "We just want to do our time"—that is, serve the one-year prison sentence and then be freed. After Tet the troops were, as future Chief of Staff Colin Powell commented, "no less brave or skilled, but by this time in the war, they lacked inspiration and sense of purpose."[47]

Soldiers, as one lieutenant put it, were not serving "for any reason or any cause that anybody could understand, other than brotherhood and camaraderie. There's no reason whatsoever in 1970 and 1971 for me to get anybody killed or to try to kill anybody." A sergeant concurred, saying that if replacements believed in search and destroy operations when they arrived, "they were soon believing in search and avoid." The 101st Airborne's commander, Major General John H. Hennessey, knew that with troop withdrawals underway "each soldier senses that he may be the last American casualty on the battlefield." No one wanted that privilege.[48]

Some soldier protests were comparatively innocuous. Men flashed the V sign, which now symbolized peace not victory, and wore peace medallions. They scribbled UUUU, IHTFP, or FTA on helmets and latrine walls: the Unwilling, led by the Unqualified, doing the Unnecessary, for the Ungrateful; I Hate This Fucking Place; Fuck The Army. Many GIs sympathized with antiwar demonstrators because they knew the protesters were right— or at least that peace would end their imprisonment.[49]

Officers told themselves that antiwar sentiments were the handiwork of a few malcontents, but this was self-deception. As early as the summer of 1968 even an enthusiastic soldier such as Delta Raider Jodey Gravett wrote

"END THE WAR IN VIET NAM!!" on the back of an envelope when mailing a letter. A *Life* magazine reporter interviewed 100 GIs from I Corps through III Corps, discovering that "many soldiers regard the organized antiwar campaign in the U.S. with open and outspoken sympathy" and did not consider home front protests demoralizing. Visiting I Corps in 1971, another reporter "found literally no young GIs in favor of the war, none who didn't think we should get out, few who didn't hate lifers [professional soldiers] almost as much as the 'dinks.'"[50]

But not all disciplinary problems were passive. A pandemic of desertions, fraggings, mutinies, race riots, and drug abuse ravaged the Army, mostly in rear areas but seeping into the field and prompting Colonel Robert D. Heinl Jr., a Marine with twenty-seven years of service, to publish an article on "The Collapse of the Armed Forces." "By every conceivable indicator" the armed forces were "approaching collapse, with individual units avoiding or having refused combat, murdering their officers and noncommissioned officers, drug-ridden, and dispirited where not near-mutinous." Military responses to this crisis were "confused, resentful, occasionally pollyana-ish, and in some cases even calculated to worsen the malaise that is wracking them."[51]

Desertion rates shot up from 14.9 per thousand in 1966 to 73.5 per thousand in 1971, and AWOL rates soared from 57.2 incidents per thousand in 1966 to 176.9 per thousand in 1971.[52]

Slang for the murder or attempted murder of aggressive (and hence unpopular) officers and noncommissioned officers, fragging was not unknown in previous wars, but became commonplace in Vietnam. The Pentagon confirmed ninety-six incidents in 1969, 209 in 1970, and 333 in 1971. These figures do not include what one Lieutenant General referred to as the "excessive number of 'accidental' shootings—too many of which appeared other than 'accidental'—and the promiscuous throwing of grenades that lent new meaning to the expression 'fragging' and that should leave all of us with an ill-at-ease feeling." Out in the field, said a lieutenant in the 23rd Division, "I was very frightened, not just of what was in front of me, but what was behind me." In rear areas officers moved their cots nightly to thwart assassination attempts.[53]

With their penchant for euphemisms that concealed ugly reality, officials called mutinies "combat refusals." The first large-scale mutiny occurred in mid-1969 when a company in the 196th Light Infantry Brigade sat down on the battlefield, and then the number escalated dramatically. The vaunted 1st Air Cav Division, for example, had three dozen refusal incidents in 1970. By 1971 the Army was using military police (MPs) to assault mutinous troops entrenched in bunkers and camps. "Nothing against you, Lieutenant, but this is just stupid," said one grunt who spoke for his platoon. "We move out and the point's getting ambushed before the rear squad's even cleared the laager. We've been hit day after day, and we're just not going." To avoid outright combat refusals, officers avoided ordering their men to undertake life-threatening actions, implicitly conspiring with them to go on "search and evade" missions. Noting the lack of aggressiveness, the Viet Cong delegation at the Paris Peace Conference announced that the VC had been ordered not to attack passive American forces.[54]

Racial friction flared primarily in rear areas. In the field, as a black rifleman with the 1st Air Cav understood, "everybody was the same. You can't find no racism in the bush. We slept together, ate together, fought together." Sergeant Mark Hawk, who served with Hooper in 1971, asserted that "there were no racial problems" in the jungle. But in base camps unofficial segregation and corrosive racial tension were omnipresent. At Camp Evans during his second tour in 1971, Dave Loftin discovered that black soldiers lived together in their huts and whites lived in theirs. "White guys didn't go in the black ones and blacks didn't go in the white ones." Racial conflicts, often full-fledged riots, erupted "murderously in all services," commented Colonel Heinl. Not all firefights were against the VC/NVA; some pitted white troops against African American soldiers.[55]

As with racial animosities, drug abuse occurred predominantly in the rear since drugs imperiled everyone, not just the users, on combat operations. But abuse reached such dangerous levels in base camps that it "would seriously have impaired combat efficiency had those locales been subjected to strong enemy attacks." Initially the major drug concern was marijuana but by 1969–70 cheap, high-grade heroin was the foremost culprit (actually alcoholism was the most serious problem, but the armed forces *encouraged* its use by providing subsidized alcohol through officers' club, enlisted men's clubs, and military retail liquor stores). The Army attacked drugs through confiscation, drug education, and amnesty programs. Nothing worked very well. Two servicemen a month died from drug overdoses in the spring of 1970, a rate that climbed to two *per day* by the fall when as many as 15 percent of all privates and corporals may have been heroin addicts.[56]

A "juicer" (alcohol user) rather than a "head" (drug user), Joe Hooper saw drugs in big base areas like Saigon and Da Nang, but believed reports of widespread abuse were exaggerated. Overwhelming evidence belied this. By August 1968, Fred Aronow considered the division rear area akin to Old Dodge City because so many men got "hopped up on dope and start shooting up the area. . . . I'd rather go back to charging NVA bunkers." Three years later another soldier still felt the same way, preferring duty in the bush to service in the rear where drug-crazed individuals "took their M-16[s] and leveled a whole basketball court full of guys." In their debriefings, many officers argued drugs were a more serious problem than the enemy.[57]

Even the 101st Airborne, once considered the Army's toughest division, was "as wary of combat, as reluctant to fight, as lax in discipline" as the worst American divisions. Nothing captured the 101st's malaise more than the 1971 cover of its magazine *Rendezvous with Destiny*. With defoliated trees in the background, three GIs stand on a truck reaching for a helicopter hovering overhead. Peace symbols are readily visible and the trees' twisted limbs form the letters FTA.[58]

"What the hell is going on," exclaimed General Abrams. "I've got white shirts all over the place—psychologists, drug counselors, detox specialists, rehab people, social workers, and psychiatrists. Is this a goddamned army or a mental hospital? Officers are afraid to lead their men into battle, and the men won't follow. Jesus Christ! What happened?"[59]

As Abrams understood, he needed "to get this Army home to save it."[60]

The period after the Tet Offensive, said VC village chief Trinh Duc, was "the worst time of the war."

Casualties were high, morale was low, allied forces reoccupied many areas, and the Americans sent "out guerrilla forces to ambush us in the jungle," lamented Trinh. During 1968–70, he was ambushed eleven times and wounded twice, indicating that the enemy had learned a lot about jungle fighting. Fortunately the Americans' habit was to strike, fall back, and call for external fire support, so the VC sometimes survived by staying so close to them "they couldn't hit us with artillery and air strikes." Still, so many of Trinh's men died that he had to reorganize his unit three times, the number of men progressively shrinking because getting new recruits was almost impossible. At one point his third reconstituted unit contained only twelve soldiers. From Trinh's perspective during 1969, "There was no food, no future

—nothing bright." Paradoxically 1969 "was also the time I was happiest." Trinh destroyed several tanks with mines made from unexploded American bombs. The peasants' "true heroism" shone during this dark period as they risked their lives bringing food to his isolated VC unit, their continued support being "one of the things that gave me courage to go on." Also encouraging "was the conviction that the Americans couldn't last. In 1969 they began to withdraw some of their troops. We believed that eventually they would have to withdraw altogether. We knew that even though we faced tremendous difficulties, so did they." By late 1970 the situation improved. "We started gaining more control," asserted Trinh. "I could feel the optimism starting to return." One reason was that "peasants felt more comfortable about contacting us and giving us support," including so much food and money that Trinh not only supplied his unit but also the NVA in his area.[61]

Plummeting into dire straits, tenaciously struggling on, then recovering —Trinh's experience personified the trajectory that Communist forces followed after the Tet Offensive and the follow-on offensives of May and August 1968 and February 1969. The VC/NVA had taken a beating, but had not been beaten. From the Communist high command's perspective, that year of sustained combat ultimately resulted in an unequivocal victory, though the immediate results often seemed ambiguous at best.

General Tran Van Tra encapsulated the ambiguity in his discussion of Tet and its aftermath. As the head of the Military Affairs Committee of the Central Office for South Vietnam (COSVN), which was the headquarters for all the VC forces operating in South Vietnam, Tra had keen insights into the post-Tet situation. "Despite our big victory," he wrote, "the general situation in the entire southern theater, especially in the cities, was no longer in our favor." Severe losses in troops and material caused "untold difficulties in coping with the enemy's frenzied counterattacks and rapid pacification activities in the 1969–1970 period when the Vietnamization policy was put into place." The Americans pushed the VC away from the cities, drove the NVA into border sanctuaries, and reclaimed many rural areas. In this difficult situation the VC/NVA "seemed to be on the decline." "Not a few people who judged things by their appearances, jumped to the conclusion that Tet was a failure." Confronted with intense enemy counterattacks and the wide-ranging pacification operations, even dedicated soldiers "were not aware of the extent of our victory and doubted the explanation from higher command." The short-term, superficial appearances of defeat shrouded Tet's strategic importance.[62]

PAVN's high command agreed with Tra's assessment. Tet and the follow-up offensives were too weak to achieve all the projected results, near-crippling losses drained the Communists' combat power, replacements were scarce, supplies were so difficult to obtain that soldiers grew their own food to avoid starvation, and the enemy's pacification program made rapid inroads, forcing some regiments to disperse down to the company, platoon, or even squad level. Despite the crippling losses and horrendous difficulties of 1968–70, PAVN leaders realized that Tet was a strategic victory that "struck a decisive blow that bankrupted the 'limited war' strategy of the American imperialists." And by early 1970 Communist forces were recovering, allowing strategists to contemplate once again taking the offensive.[63]

Communist leadership, which always had a much longer-range perspective than the Americans', considered Tet a crucial strategic turning point because it knocked the war off stalemate, tilting the conflict to the Communists' advantage and paving the way for their complete victory in 1975. In strategic terms, Tet shattered America's aggressive will by reducing public support for the war; showed the Americans that no matter how vast their resources were, they were not limitless; compelled the United States to de-escalate, gradually withdraw its troops, and embrace the questionable twin pillars of Vietnamization and pacification; induced the Americans to stop bombing North Vietnam; and forced the Johnson administration to pull up a chair at the peace negotiations. These achievements, as one enemy document phrased it, "indicated that the U.S. would [ultimately] lose and we would win." [64] Because of these strategic results even though the United States and ARVN significantly weakened the VC/NVA in 1968 and held the initiative in 1969–70, they could never generate sufficient power to drive their severely weakened adversaries completely from the battlefield.

Strategic results were visible only in the long run.

In the near term most VC/NVA, peering out of their hiding places, saw only their horrific casualties and the resurgent allied forces hunting them down.

In parallel with their American counterparts, VC/NVA morale deteriorated. Numerous captured documents attested to their defeatism, defections, desertions, unauthorized absences, suicides, self-inflicted wounds, inadequate recruiting efforts, supply shortages, mistreatment of villagers, and especially their fear of death resulting in a less than aggressive battlefield performance.[65] Even the postwar official history of PAVN, never eager to criticize the war effort, admitted that "Some of our cadre and soldiers became pessimistic and exhibited fear of close combat and of remaining in the battle zone. Some deserted their units to flee to rear areas, and some even defected to the enemy."[66]

In response to their immense losses and the consequent morale problems, Communist leaders undertook a public relations campaign to bolster their soldiers' fighting spirit, and changed strategy to conserve manpower while they replenished their strength. This dual track approach was incapable of generating decisive, war-winning action, but bought time while American strength and resolve diminished and the Communists rebuilt their manpower and fighting spirit.

Resurrecting morale involved undoing past promises of swift victory, explaining the difficult struggle that lay ahead, and reemphasizing traditional themes that would eventually result in victory.

In pre-Tet proselytizing the Communists emphasized *thoi co*, the idea that a rare opportune moment had arrived and striking hard in a General Offensive–General Uprising guaranteed immediate success. Now they backtracked, saying that many soldiers erroneously misinterpreted the General Offensive–General Uprising as a "one-blow affair," when in fact the attack represented just one of the war's many "transitional phases." A General Offensive–General Uprising was "a series of continuing offensive phases." "We did not fully realize," confessed the Hue City Party Committee, "that a General Offensive and General Uprising was a hard and fierce process consisting of many campaigns of continual and violent attacks and uprisings." Enemy leaders emphasized that "We secure victory not through a one-blow offensive . . . not even through a series of attacks culminating in a final kill. Victory will come to us, not suddenly, but in a complicated and tortuous way."[67]

Phrases such as "a complicated and tortuous way" dampened quick victory expectations. Because Americans were rich, powerful, perfidious, cunning, obstinate, and "the most bellicose and most cruel imperialist ringleaders in the world," they would never succumb easily or gracefully. Nonetheless the fighting *must* continue. The stakes were high, and "no agreement can be reached as long as we fail to win on the battlefield." A favorable negotiated settlement was unlikely since diplomatic activities merely supported military activities, which "will play the decisive role." Victory or defeat hinged on the battlefield's agonies, not the smooth, soft green felt of a conference table. Ho Chi Minh appealed to his people to maintain the struggle: "The sacred duty of our entire nation is now to increase our determination to fight on and to win, and we are resolved to liberate South Vietnam, defend North Vietnam, and advance toward peace and the unification of the Fatherland."[68]

To sustain the fighting spirit, enemy propagandists appealed to anti-imperialist sentiments and evoked the David versus Goliath element in Vietnam's martial past, in which high quality men blessed with superior élan and superb leadership overcame larger armies with better weapons. "Our people," wrote General Giap, "may be proud of being one of the nations possessing the most valiant anti-aggression and the staunchest anti-imperialism traditions." Moreover, the Vietnamese successively defeated "three great imperial powers on three continents" (the Japanese, the French, and now the Americans) by waging people's war, which was always protracted, filled with hardships, and complicated, but victorious. The present conflict, Giap continued, was "a just war, a national liberation war, or a Fatherland-protection war," a *"war of a brave, intelligent, stalwart, and resourceful people who use a small, weak, army to fight and defeat the great, strong aggressive army of an imperialist power whose country is vast and populous and which possesses great economic and military potential and modern technical equipment."* Weapons and equipment were important, but men were "the factors deciding victories in war." And with its superior men Vietnam knew how to use weakness to defeat strength, the few to defeat the numerous, and "our definite superiority in political and spiritual strength for winning over the enemy's iron and steel." With their creative resourcefulness, daring spirit, and perseverance, the Vietnamese always prevailed over mere weaponry and superior numbers.[69]

Just as both sides suffered morale problems, both sides also partially withdrew from the battlefield beginning in 1969. The United States did so to preserve morale on the homefront and the fighting front by reducing casualties, the Communists to conserve manpower while rebuilding their forces. Always considering time a powerful weapon, the VC/NVA reemphasized political *dau tranh* and reverted to the guerrilla warfare style of military *dau tranh* to protract the war while waiting for the Americans to withdraw.

In Tet's aftermath the infrastructure established "liberation committees" throughout South Vietnam to solidify its political support. The number of such committees leaped from 397 in September 1968 to 3,367 in mid-January 1969, many of them in areas the South Vietnamese government supposedly controlled. Although weakened militarily, politically the enemy maintained a firm grip on much of the countryside. Sabotage and terror against civilians, such as assassinations and abductions, rose from 7,566 in 1967 to 10,638 in 1969, and 12,056 in 1970 before dipping to 9,973 in 1971. "Political coercion," including distributing propaganda and holding meetings, also climbed substantially during these years. Terror intimidated or eliminated individuals the infrastructure considered a threat, and propaganda emphasized the terrorist incidents to demonstrate the vc's continued presence and resiliency. All this occurred despite pacification's alleged success in bringing security to the countryside.[70]

Battles, even firefights, became uncommon, especially after COSVN Resolution 9 was issued in July 1969 ordering the vc to preserve their strength and the NVA to disperse into small guerrilla-style units. By avoiding battles the vc/NVA negated American firepower and mobility, depriving U.S. troops of the rich targets they had enjoyed during Tet and the May offensive. Communist strategists believed that after the Americans left they could return to big-unit warfare and crush South Vietnam.[71]

In a sense, however, Resolution 9 merely ratified a transformation on the battlefield that occurred a year earlier. According to a 101st Airborne Division "lessons learned" report, after mid-June 1968 "contacts with and sightings of the enemy in groups larger than squad size were infrequent." Despite extensive search and destroy operations and numerous ambushes, the report continued, "contact with the enemy was infrequent and of short duration when he was engaged."[72]

In the second half of 1968 the Delta Raiders, for example, did a lot of patrolling and little fighting. Lieutenant T'Odon C. Leshikar endured months of "sheer boredom" interrupted by brief contacts in August and October. Three contacts punctuated Lieutenant John E. Frick's "tedious boredom"; in all three he saw only two enemy soldiers, "both of them quite dead."[73] "Nothing going on anywhere in the Brigade Area of Operations," Cleo Hogan regularly informed his wife after he was reassigned to brigade headquarters in early July 1968. Writing to Hooper in July 1969, the 101st Division's Sergeant Major explained that Joe's old regiment "hasn't been locked in any big fights since your battle—all small stuff." [74]

But enemy strategists believed "small stuff" was enough to counter the Vietnamization and pacification campaigns, to inflict enough casualties to hasten the Americans' departure, and to sustain the Communist position at the peace negotiations. In their small-scale economy-of-force operations the VC/NVA employed time-tested tactics such as snipers, mines, BBTS, standoff harassment (firing perhaps half a dozen projectiles), and standoff attacks (firing twenty to thirty rockets, mortar rounds, or artillery shells). In fulfilling COSVN Resolution 9 the enemy also conducted sapper assaults. Sappers were highly trained, proficient with modern weapons and high explosives, and suicidally determined. The press dubbed them "super-guerrillas" because they seemed to possess superhuman abilities. [75]

After Tet the number of enemy maneuver battalions remained constant but sapper battalions increased until they constituted a separate army. As emergency reinforcements, in Tet's wake North Vietnam dispatched ten sapper battalions and one hundred sapper companies and platoons to strengthen COSVN's battered sapper units, which had spearheaded many Tet attacks. By late 1969 sapper forces in South Vietnam consisted of one brigade, three regiments, thirty-eight battalions, seventy-one companies, more than one hundred platoons, and hundreds of "guerrilla sapper" teams. [76]

Sapper recruiting requirements were unusually stringent, their units enjoyed high priority for supplies and munitions, and sapper operations received considerably more attention than in the past. Representing an effective method of achieving significant results with a minimal expenditure, by late 1969 sappers were the enemy's most lucrative military undertaking. Their assaults "sustained the image of an effective VC/NVA fighting force despite heavy personnel losses" and gave the impression that allied forces were impotent. [77]

A classic sapper attack occurred at Fire Support Base Mary Ann on the night of March 27–28, 1971, when sappers, many of them dressed only in black shorts or naked, slipped through the defensive perimeter without alerting a single guard, killed thirty and wounded eighty-two Americans, and lost only fifteen of their own. Although most sapper assaults were not quite that successful, the "super-guerrillas" achieved a remarkable record of inflicting casualties while suffering few losses. [78]

"Thus COSVN Resolution 9 heralded the return of protracted guerrilla war," observed a perceptive MACV analysis, "with its emphasis on small-unit tactics, reliance on sappers, terrorism, and increased reliance on attacks by fire, as the most efficient means of wearing down the fighting capability of ARVN, heightening the demands by the U.S. public for withdrawal of U.S. forces, and eroding the Vietnamese people's faith in their government's ability to maintain their security." [79]

Combat during 1969–71 could be ferocious when the VC/NVA decided to fight. On April 1, 1970, for example, the VC/NVA launched a countrywide mini-offensive that included more than a dozen ground assaults, killing 279 Americans in two weeks.[80] When the NVA wanted to drive the Americans off Fire Base Ripcord, located about twenty-five miles west of Hue, they did. For more than three weeks in July 1970 they pounded the position, forcing the Americans to withdraw after heavy casualties and under heavy pressure in what Sergeant Mark Hawk sarcastically called "a strategic military withdrawal." As he well knew, American forces were "getting the shit kicked out of us," though official sources of course insisted that "Ripcord operations were highly successful." [81] During the Ripcord siege, the NVA also attacked the Delta Raiders atop Hill 805 about a mile and a half to the southeast. The Raiders held the hill for six days, lost nine killed and thirty wounded, and then—akin to Hamburger Hill—abandoned it.[82]

Still, nothing compared with the sustained combat during the first five months of 1968. Between 1969 and 1971 most contacts were meeting engagements, with the enemy quickly breaking contact to avoid decisive combat. U.S. operations repeatedly "drove an enemy trying to avoid contact [and] determined to avoid an engagement" from any particular area, though "drove" was hardly the appropriate verb.[83]

Joe Hooper was going to have fewer opportunities for heroic display during his second tour because the American public no longer countenanced high casualties, U.S. soldiers were reluctant to find and confront the enemy, and the VC/NVA were unwilling to fight pitched battles except in exceptional circumstances.

But Joe Hooper had a knack for finding trouble.

Joe claimed he was *under fire* for more than three hundred days during his second tour.

He never left the division, never went on R and R, killed about 115 enemy soldiers, and was wounded in the head, back, and legs by an exploding rocket only thirteen days after rejoining the 101st Airborne.[84]

So he said.

Arriving in "Eagle Country" in late April, Joe noticed that "It's not the same war." When the Raiders were in I Corps in 1968 "it was a free fire zone from Hue to the DMZ," but the enemy had been driven out of the lowlands, daily minesweeps along Highway 1 were no longer necessary, and Hue was thriving. Then the 101st was too busy fighting to devote attention to pacification; now the division was rebuilding the war-ravaged nation, the roads were safe, and "the people are able to plant their rice and raise their children in a little safety and freedom." The Screaming Eagle Replacement Training School at Camp Evans gave "replacements a better idea of what to expect and [helped] prepare them for anything they might face." Each replacement received a week of refresher training, which some thought was useless except to provide time to acclimatize to the heat and humidity.[85]

Not all the changes were positive. Joe lamented that "this modern Army is hell, and not like the old days at all." He was "seeing things that I cannot beli[e]ve. Don't really know if I can accept things as they are now. I think of all the good men who have given there lives, and these creeps reaping the beenies [benefits]." The creeps, who "got us in a world of hurt," included inexperienced captains and lieutenants and "instant NCOs" (or "shake 'n' bakes"), privates who went through basic and advanced infantry training and then received additional schooling at a Noncommissioned Officer Candidate School. The top 5 percent immediately became staff sergeant; the rest sergeants. In peacetime it normally took at least five years to become a sergeant, longer to become a staff sergeant.[86]

The shortage of experienced NCOs compromised platoons and squads in a combat environment. One lieutenant commanded a platoon with only four NCOs, none of whom had been in the Army for more than a year or was over twenty. Another said shake n' bakes were fine young men but "they just didn't have that expertise that you get when you're making a career out of it." In essence, novice captains and lieutenants led inexperienced shake 'n' bakes (many of whom knew they were inadequately prepared), who led unwilling draftees. The wonder is not that some shake 'n' bakes failed, but that so many served so well.[87]

Joe's return to Vietnam coincided with the Cambodian invasion in the III Corps region. Like the Communists who established "sanctuaries" there, the United States had long violated Cambodian neutrality with small cross-border infiltrations. But Nixon went much further. When the JCS assured him they could destroy COSVN and thus degrade Communist capabilities throughout III and IV Corps, he ordered B-52 raids that began on March 18, 1969. Code-named Operation Menu and kept secret from the public, the Congress, the Secretary of the Air Force, and the Air Force Chief of Staff, until the *New York Times* exposed it a few months later, the bombing ultimately involved 3,630 sorties.[88] The campaign, said General Palmer, "was a bad mistake" because "it placed the military in an impossible situation, having literally to lie publicly about a perfectly legitimate wartime operation." What made the deception especially reprehensible was that it had nothing to do with keeping the operation secret from the enemy or with enhancing aircrew safety. But Nixon preferred prevarication to the truth, insisting on May 11 that American policy "has been to scrupulously respect the neutrality of the Cambodian people."[89]

When the secret bombing was exposed and ended in late May 1970 (though bombing continued overtly), it had eliminated neither the sanctuaries nor COSVN. Irritable and overwrought, with alcohol slurring his speech and fortifying his truculence, Nixon ordered an invasion of Cambodia to destroy COSVN, disrupt enemy offensive plans by devastating the sanctuaries, and send a threatening madman message that "we will not be humiliated. We will not be defeated." He hoped the combined U.S.–ARVN operation, which began on April 29–30, might reverse the war's course so that the United States could "win" in some meaningful sense. The decision to invade Cambodia, he believed, was *tougher* than Kennedy's decision-making during the Cuban missile crisis. As the operation unfolded and then faltered, Nixon told aides to "keep an absolutely strong posture, show no sign of weakness" and to emphasize the president's courage.[90]

Next to the Tet Offensive, the Cambodia invasion was the war's second major turning point. As with Tet the United States suffered a strategic disaster. According to General Palmer, "Tet ended any hope of a U.S.-imposed solution, while Cambodia fatally wounded South Vietnam's chances to survive and remain free."[91]

Why was it so disastrous? For one thing, by engulfing Cambodia in the ground war it converted the Vietnam War into the Indochina War, with all of its intolerably sad consequences for Cambodia. As the NVA abandoned their border positions and retreated westward, the war went with them, spreading into the interior. The incursion also reignited domestic protest against the war. After the fall of 1969 the peace movement was quiescent since Nixon seemed to be ending the war through troop withdrawals, Vietnamization, and pacification. Although the president expected the invasion to generate protests he underestimated their extent and ferocity. Astounded and angered that Nixon was *widening* the war, not ending it, antiwar protesters were reenergized. Campus demonstrations and other protests drove the president to the edge of a nervous breakdown, and compelled him not only to end the incursion on June 30 but also to hasten the troop withdrawals.

Cambodia also revealed Vietnamization's limited progress and, conversely, inflicted only a temporary setback on the VC/NVA. ARVN did not fight well, repeatedly displaying its incompetent leadership and lack of battlefield aggressiveness. The invaders did not find, much less destroy, COSVN; the body count was low because Communists forces fled rather than fight; most of the captured weapons were obsolete (the Communists simply never bothered to transport them back up the Ho Chi Minh Trail); and the CIA estimated that the VC/NVA could replace their lost food and material within three months. As for disrupting an imminent Communist offensive, no conclusive evidence indicated they were planning one. Finally, North Vietnam did not quaver and quail when confronted with Nixon's madman gambit. For the Communists the raid was a temporary inconvenience, not a disaster.[92]

When one of his subordinates exalted that the invasion created "a hell of a problem" for VC/NVA, Abrams appraised the situation realistically, observing that the enemy was "*used* to a hell of a problem. He lives in an environment where he's got a hell of a problem. I get a certain amount of enjoyment, I must say, out of seeing the problem get *complicated*. But it isn't *worth* much."[93] The enemy agreed. "Nixon paid dearly for our temporary discomfiture by sustaining major political losses," wrote a high-ranking enemy political leader. Looking at it from a political and diplomatic as well as military perspective, the Cambodian excursion "resulted in a resounding victory for the National Liberation Front," giving the revolutionary movement "an enduring gift."[94]

With the Cambodian border ablaze, Joe began his second tour with the 101st Airborne in Thua Thien Province in I Corps, where things were comparatively quiet. On April 1, the division launched Operation Texas Star, which blended almost imperceptibly into the last major U.S. operation in the ground war, Operation Jefferson Glen, beginning on September 5. These operations were to maintain a protective shield between the canopied jungles and the lowlands by eliminating enemy forces, base areas, and cache sites, thus ensuring a secure pacification environment. To destroy the NVA and their logistical bases, U.S. forces conducted operations into the mountains whenever weather conditions permitted.

Although the NVA had filtered back into many positions it abandoned in 1969, presenting a growing threat during 1970–71, military intelligence correctly anticipated extensive probing of allied forces and installations, standoff mortar and rocket attacks, and occasional sapper assaults rather than a general offensive.[95]

Military intelligence also correctly predicted that the Viet Cong Infrastructure (VCI), which was the political arm of South Vietnam's Communist Party and was responsible for all noncombatant functions against South Vietnam (such as tax collecting and recruitment), would continue sabotage and terrorism in the lowlands while conducting hit-and-run tactics, all designed to discredit pacification. Despite intense pacification efforts the VCI carried out enough sabotage, kidnappings, assassinations, and other terror-inspiring activities to let the population know their security was precarious. For example, between May and August 1970, in Thua Thien Province it committed thirty-two acts of sabotage, a dozen kidnappings, seventeen assassinations, and thirty-eight other terrorist activities. Meanwhile, in June, July, and August the allies "eliminated" just sixty-five members of the VCI, only nineteen of them considered "significant." Approximately 2,000 VCI members remained in Thua Thien.[96]

The eighteen months of Operations Texas Star and Jefferson Glen cost the 101st Airborne 607 KIA and 3,145 WIA, a steady seepage of American blood into Vietnamese soil, much of it caused by mines and BBTs. In June, July, and August 1970, enemy forces initiated contact 859 times against the 101st Airborne, 211 of them via mines and BBTs; in the first three months of 1971 the analogous figures were 462 contacts, 350 of them mines and BBTs.[97] When a contact involved enemy soldiers they were usually in squad size or less, fired a few rounds, then retreated. Despite the paucity of battles, medals proliferated: four MOHS, five DSCS, 235 SSS, and 771 BS/VS either awarded or still pending when Texas Star ended and another fifteen DSCS, 292 SSS, and 1,002 BS/VS during Jefferson Glen.[98]

Joe's initial assignment was in the Headquarters and Headquarters Company of the 101st Aviation Group stationed at Camp Eagle, where conditions were so luxurious it "was almost like being stateside." The Aviation Group provided helicopter support for the 101st Airborne Division. For example, when a unit conducted a combat assault the Group supplied the helicopters that transported soldiers from the pickup zone to the LZ; it also controlled medevacs and provided Pathfinders.

Joe served in the Pathfinders.[99] Working in small teams, they helicoptered into an area ahead of a combat assault to set up and mark the LZ; if the area was "hot" Pathfinders had the responsibility to call in supporting firepower. They also served as weathermen, providing hourly reports from every fire base, an urgent task considering how quickly a sudden fog or clouds could sock in a fire base that was clear only minutes earlier. And they were air traffic controllers, directing helicopters on the LZs and fire bases, a difficult task since choppers sometimes swarmed around these areas like mosquitoes in a Louisiana bayou. Incredibly, as late as mid-summer 1970 Pathfinders used nonsecure FM frequencies; as one official "lessons learned" report observed, the enemy "can get sufficient warning of all approaching aircraft by monitoring [the] Pathfinder net and engage the aircraft from the most advantageous position."[100]

If or when Joe went into the field during his brief tenure with the Pathfinders is not known, but he probably remained in the rear. For one thing he complained about "too much free time."[101] Also, being a Pathfinder was dangerous and the high command was not eager to have an MOH recipient killed or injured. On April 1, 1970, for instance, one Pathfinder was KIA and another WIA when the division established Fire Base Ripcord.[102] A photograph shows Joe as a Pathfinder providing rifle training to a replacement at the Screaming Eagle Replacement Training School.[103] Moreover, Pathfinders normally completed a specialized Pathfinder Course at Fort Benning; without it Joe may not have been of much help. Finally, Joe had ample opportunities for drinking, visiting, and trying to salvage his relationship with Carollyn.

Being in the rear made drinking easy. Wherever Joe went people handed him a drink. Or if he was in a friend's hooch and they ran out of booze they walked over to the commanding general's quarters where an aide gave them access to the general's liquor supply. As one acquaintance said, Joe's MOH "got him a lot of special privileges that the ordinary NCO would not have gotten." He "was put on a pedestal," commented another soldier.[104] As a pedestal dweller his name was on a "watch list" of personnel who "may be of special interest to the news media" if they became casualties. Most of those on the list were related by blood or marriage to generals or politicians.[105]

Joe's celebrity status gave him the opportunity to visit the Delta Raiders on May 13 when they were at Camp Eagle for stand-down and battalion refresher training. Each battalion rotated through Camp Eagle on a more-or-less regular basis to re-zero weapons, replenish its ammo supply, receive routine medial care, attend to personal matters, and visit the PX and nearby Eagle Beach, a glistening strip of white sand on the South China Sea where men swam in the cool water and guzzled cold beer.

The Raiders were at Eagle Beach when Joe gave "a little speech for us," recalled Raider Ray Blackman who at the time had no idea who Joe Hooper was. "But not too many people were paying a lot of attention because they were getting relaxed and getting drunk." Of course Joe told whopping lies. "I'm sure you men will be glad to learn that President Nixon knows about you," he said. "One of the first things I did when I met him was give him a patch from the Delta Raiders of the 101st. He now keeps it under the glass top of his desk."[106]

One soldier who paid attention to Joe's talk was company commander Captain Christopher C. Straub, who saw the Raiders arrive at Cu Chi in December 1967. Straub sensed that the meeting between Joe, who looked very professional, and the Raiders, dressed in swimsuits and draining beer cans, was "a meeting of two cultures, two worlds." Joe was "an emissary from the past" who never left 1967–68 behind, which "was the distant past as far as our troops were concerned in 1970." "There was just a huge gulf between him and his gung-ho attitude and their view of the war," Straub concluded. Joe still sought medals, glory, heroism. But Straub's Raiders "were draftees and they were not interested in getting awards for valor," although "they were quite brave when circumstances required." All they wanted "was to get out of there, a trip home, to have done their duty but then go back and forget about Vietnam."[107]

As for Carollyn, although she was trying to break up with Joe, paradoxically she was still writing him and baking cookies for him, sending them packed in popcorn so they would not break. And they talked often over the MARS communications system, a joint venture between the military and civilian HAM radio operators who relayed calls through the Bell Telephone

System. Carollyn also received Joe's monthly paycheck and paid his bills. Thankful he was gone because he was "so uncontrollable socially," she also missed him. "It was," she said, "like a cord that couldn't be broken."[108]

Knowing their relationship was tenuous, Joe flooded her and Rolly with mementos, photographs, and letters, trying to rekindle her unadulterated love.[109] He sent a Vietnamese chieu hoi card with a notation reading "Come over to my side Blonde Mama-san—Please I love you. Will offer anything." A photo of a smiling Joe in his favorite white dress uniform bore a hand-written caption saying "this is one of the Last few that we were together. May they [there] be many more in the near future. Love you sweet have faith & trust. We will be one in the end. Love you Baby #10 GI Joe." Another photo, this one of Joe in Vietnam: "Love you forever Carollyn. Please don't give up. We will always be together. Take care of your wonderful son. Love Joe."

"Dear Carollyn," Joe wrote on June 2 in a poignant letter, "I know gifts won't win back your love, but I know you wanted this so bad," because she loved listening to music. "This" was a stereo turntable he bought for $91.50, which he hoped would bring her "some wonderful relaxing evenings." After sending his love to her and Rolly he added, "Last night I cried [in] my sleep for the forth straight night. I pray God gives me the strength to recover from this losing of your most precious love—All my love, Your #1 GI Joe." On ap-proximately the same day he wrote Rolly, wondering if he got some gifts Joe recently sent, asking how school was going, urging him to "keep the shoes spit-shined and the airborne haircut." and telling him not to "give the girls two hard of a time." "I look at you as my son," he told the lad, "and hope & pray that it comes true. Be good to the Mommy-san and mind her. She is the most wonderful mother in the world. Love her forever. Love, Daddy Joe."

On June 11 he wrote Carollyn again in a letter worth quoting at length:

> Rec[e]ived a letter from you today. As ever, I was happy to hear from you, good or bad news. Tonite you said it is I who should look in the mirror. You know what, I havent written you too much the past week, because that is what I have been doing. Looking in that glass, and I think for the first time, I seen the real Joe Hooper and I must admit what I looked at was not much of a person. You have thru love and hate showed me that, plus I my-self have seen somethings thats bad about me in my own eyes.

Now all I have to do, is face the hard clear facts, and be man enough to face them. You know there are a lot of men on skid row today, that have not had the guts to face life and try and make it better. You Carollyn gave me the most wonderful 1 1/2 years in my life. I will hope to ben[e]fit from it and try to be the man that I am capabile of.

I have always said if the woman leaves the man and he losses her love & respect, it is his fault. In someway he lost what he had gained. And if the woman loses the mans love it is her fault. I have lost your love—It [is] that simple. I screwed up. I nay [may] never regain your love. But to feel the self-respect & pride that I should it is up to me.

Even if we are never one, I hope to keep and share your friendship thru life. I hope that you will be able to look at me sometime in the future and see where the year and a half was not wasted with me. You have showed me so much good & love in life. Its up to me to grab it by the ass and do something with it.

Today I asked division to send me back to the line. This is my life and i know it is whats best and I desire.

The pathfinders are a great outfit and in away I regr[e]t leaving. But too much free time and the problems I have to work out, it was just not me.

So as the danger increases and if Mr Charles does get me, I pray that you will in no way feel responsibile. It is my decision and I know for the first time the right one. Where I will go I dont know until in the morning. . . .

I do still look forward to meeting you and Rolly in Hawaii for R & R. As friends & nothing more. Would you beli[e]ve two rooms. But we will wait for that decision and see what early Oct brings.

What ever you do with life sweet, I hope for the best of ever[y]thing.

If you don't care to handle my bills let me know, I will make other plans. But since I am going on line it would save me a lot of headaches.

Please take care, I will allway love the two of you and be concerned with your welfare. Good nite God Bless—

Love to the Mama-san & the Cpl [Corporal] Your GI Joe.
Remember <u>Yummy</u> <u>Yummy</u>."

That same day he sent Rolly an Army booklet entitled "Our Moral Heritage: Character Guidance Discussion Topics," which included topics such as "How to become a 'Real Person' in the choices and actions of everyday life" and "Responsibility is a process of decision making which helps a person meet his obligations." On the cover Joe scribbled, "To Cpl Rolly DeVore, As you get older you may want to read this. Their are a lot of wonderful ideas within—your mother has showed me some. If I had this book years ago—things may have been <u>better</u>."

Five days later Joe wrote Carollyn again, beginning with a note of sweet remembrance by recalling a time when both she and Rolly were sick and he "felt so much in love and happy to run from one room to the other doing first aid." Then he catapulted to the present: "Still no word on my tranfser. I take that back. A whole bunch of people are shook up. . . . I have begged them to let me be a normal GI and to forget about the medal. But everone wants to get their hand in." If he did not get transferred to a line company soon he was going straight to MACV to complain.

The next day, June 17, Joe penned a note sending his love and enclosing a will naming Martin Barsky as his executor, or Carollyn if he was unable or unwilling to serve. All pay and allowances due Joe at the time of his death went to Maggie and John Henry, but all the money held in joint savings and checking accounts at the Bank of America in Hollywood went to Carollyn, "the most dedicated person to my life and love." To Barsky went the book and movie rights to his life story, with the proceeds to be equally divided among his parents, Carollyn, Barsky, and a child welfare organization selected by Carollyn and Barsky. Nothing was to go to his estranged wife, Balbine, or to his son Robert Jay, who Joe believed had been adopted by a family with the surname of Domzee.[110]

These communications showed that Joe feared his relationship with Carollyn was shattered, primarily because of his drinking. But he held out hope for reconciliation by suggesting he could reform (unfortunately, despite the "skid row" reference his heavy drinking at Camp Eagle indicated he had not yet confronted his alcohol abuse). Even though Carollyn was blameless, Joe tried to make her feel guilty. Although his words seemingly absolved her of responsibility, Joe's implication was clear: he was going into the field and if he died it was her fault. She knew how dangerous I Corps was and could save him if she just said she loved him and took him back.

Joe became a squad leader in Company A, 2nd Battalion, 327th Regiment (A-2-327) on June 20. The battalion was patrolling and setting ambushes in the steep, dense jungles near Fire Bases Los Banos and Tomahawk along the border between Thua Thien and Quang Nam Provinces, and providing security for those fire bases.[111] Contact that summer was light and sporadic; between April 1–September 5 the entire battalion had eight killed and fifty-six wounded.[112]

In any event Joe was not in the field much. He returned to Camp Eagle with the battalion on June 29 for week-long refresher training, and was back in mid-July for a few days to take a physical examination for a direct commission as an officer (he was medically qualified).[113] In early August he was in the rear again, filling out an application for an appointment as a commissioned officer in the Army Reserve.[114] Then on August 7 he departed Vietnam on temporary duty to represent the 101st Airborne at its 25th Annual Reunion in Nashville from August 13 to 15. Joe also worked on legal matters in the United States, twice consulting with his lawyer about the divorce proceedings with Balbine.[115]

But his most important unofficial mission was wooing Carollyn. The mission was successful because she joined him in Nashville.[116] They had a wonderful time. Before departing California Joe bought her three new gowns so she looked smashing. He gave a brief speech at one of the official events and renewed acquaintance with his good buddy from the Delta Raiders, First Sergeant Scott.[117] Since Joe and Carollyn loved country music they visited "The Alley," where bands played nonstop. On Saturday night they were at the Grand Ole Opry where host Roy Acuff introduced Joe, his uniform sagging "a little on the left due to the medals hanging from it," to a prolonged standing ovation. After saying hello to his parents and praising country music as a morale booster for the troops, he called Carollyn on stage and "the crowd went crazy" again.

The newly reunited couple also drove to Fort Campbell to look at officers' military housing, which was much nicer than the quarters for enlisted men. They talked about living in that lush, green region after the war, where Carollyn could have more children and they could raise a Kentucky Derby horse that would be named "Hero."[118]

Sometime during the reunion Carollyn gave Joe a copy of Audie Murphy's *To Hell and Back* as a belated thirty-second birthday present. Joe had mentioned the book to her many times and was elated to have it because he so deeply admired Murphy. "Joe, my Boy Hero," she inscribed it, "I've been to hell and back with you. Love Carollyn, Blonde mama-san." [119]

Alas, Joe returned her to the netherworld the night before they left Nashville. At a pool party he got drunk, called Carollyn names, and was belligerent. Annoyed, she went to their room, though she was afraid "he would come back and hit me or accuse me of flirting with men. But he came into the room and fell asleep drunk."

Joe rejoined A-2-327, which was at Camp Eagle for another round of refresher training, on August 24. After the battalion returned to the Tomahawk–Los Banos region a week later, Joe wrote his parents saying he received "5 or 6 letters from Carollyn. All nice ones but dont really expect them to last long." Lying, he told Maggie and John Henry that he had "lost a lot of love for Carollyn and dont feel the same way about her as I did in the past. God knows I have tried to show her the way—But she is a very troubled girl." Then he contradicted himself, revealing exactly how much he still loved her. He would learn about his commission in a month and a half but did *not* want to become an officer. He was doing so only because he "hope[d] to hang on to Carollyn." [120]

The battalion saw little action during September, October, and November—for instance, on September 6 a reconnaissance team engaged a lone enemy soldier but for the next twenty-four days the battalion had no contact, and in October the battalion killed only three NVA. In early December 2-327 cycled through Camp Eagle again and then deployed to a new area of operations around Fire Base Birmingham, where action remained minimal throughout January 1971. [121]

All this was immaterial to Joe who was out of the field from mid-September through late November and for much of December. For September 19 to 27 the personnel daily summary for A Company cryptically stated "SSG Hooper Medical." Exactly what that meant was unclear since no evidence indicated Joe had medical problems. On September 28–29 the summary stated "SSG Hooper OJT XO PP"—he was undergoing on the job training as an executive officer, with his promotion pending. From September 30 to October 3 he was "Acting XO PP," and from October 4 to 11 the daily summary said "SSG Hooper PNDG [pending] COMMISSION." [122]

Then on October 13 Joe received thirty days emergency leave because of "pending court actions," undoubtedly referring to his divorce but also perhaps to a previous auto accident in Oakland. His leave address was 3321 Rowena Avenue—the Hollywood Bunker.[123] Three notable things happened during the emergency leave. The judge granted Joe and Balbine an annulment. On November 9 Carollyn and Joe taped a skit for a Bob Hope Special that aired a week later, for which each received $78. Most significantly, Carollyn told Joe that if she came to Vietnam for Christmas as she had done the past three years, she would *marry* him in the Camp Eagle chapel.[124]

Although Joe's leave expired November 11 he did not rejoin 2-327 until November 23. Even then he did not do much field duty, being at Camp Eagle for Thanksgiving, the battalion stand-down in December, and the Bob Hope show on December 22. Some of Hope's one-liners about drugs received boisterous responses. He heard, said the comedian, that many soldiers grew their own grass. "I was wondering how you guys were able to bomb Hanoi without planes." No wonder Johnny Bench, the Cincinnati Reds' Hall of Fame catcher who accompanied Hope, loved baseball. "Where else can you play eight months a year on grass and not get busted?" But Miss World, who was from Grenada, got the biggest ovation when Hope asked her what the island was like. It had "no pollution, no crime, and we've never had a war."[125]

Shortly after Joe departed the United States, Carollyn and Rolly recorded an audiocassette for him spanning several days. The tape revealed the travails of a single mother, struggling to make a living, worried about the bills and whether her son was eating the right food and getting proper discipline, helping Rolly with homework, and consumed with the details of daily life, made more stressful by holidays and unexpected events. "I get running in thirty directions at once," Carollyn said, "and I get pretty tired."[126]

Rolly spoke a lot, often prompted by his mother. They had attended the Super Nationals, which they enjoyed, Carollyn because "those cars really remind me of you" with all their delicious horsepower, Rolly because he bought lots of mementos and loved the noise and action, especially when a car flipped upside down and caught fire. Rolly named dozens of "Hot Wheel" toys he had or was going to get—Mongoose, Red Baron, Snake, Jackrabbit Special, and so on. He also told Joe about a Roadrunner patch they bought for him showing a coyote with his arms around the Roadrunner and a caption saying "Beep, beep, your ass!"

During the taping the phone rang and Rolly explained that he always answered the phone saying "DeVore residence." After his mother whispered something he said "Hooper residence." At one point Rolly used the phrase "what a fuckin' ass," vile language for a six-year-old. Since Carollyn laughed when he said it, her mild chiding of Rolly for being "naughty" probably did not do much good. Finally, the boy read Joe two of his favorite Dr. Seuss bed-time stories, then without prompting said "Good night, Joe. I love you."

What Carollyn said was probably of greater interest. She talked about Joe becoming a lieutenant, and, astoundingly, made light of his drinking. She promised to send him booze "so you can get blown away at Christmas" and wished he was there to help with Rolly's math homework about liquid measures since Joe was an expert on pints. She also wished that Sandra, his first wife, "wasn't so narrow-minded and would let Robert correspond with you and send you a card for your birthday or at Christmas, and seeing him even once a year would be nice." Perhaps Robert could spend a summer with them so she could "tell him about his Daddy. It's just one of the things that I'd like to see happen because I know it does mean a lot to you."

Two auto wrecks, one hers and the other his, were important topics. Carollyn accidentally rammed a "hippie wagon," resulting in extensive dam-age to her car, a bloody nose and lip, a sore jaw, and difficulty breathing. The good news was that Rolly was unhurt and that "I didn't bust up my face," a serious concern for an actress. Although it is unclear when it occurred, Joe's accident concerned a Hertz rental car he was driving in "an icky part of Oakland." A lawsuit was involved and Carollyn feared it could be a criminal case. She was sending the court papers to him via registered mail, urging him to check them carefully. Joe never talked much about the case but her "ESP tells me something is very wrong." Had Joe lied to the police? Who was the woman who was with him? Although he insisted she was "a nice girl," Car-ollyn knew nice girls were not out alone at 3:00 a.m. "Well, I'm not surprised that you were only back from Vietnam a couple of days when you pick up some girl. . . . I guess if I was a guy I'd do that, too. . . . Anyway, I don't care. I just don't want you to get in trouble." [127]

Most importantly, although Carollyn said she was not coming to Viet-nam for Christmas the marriage plans were still in effect because she would visit "Eagle Country" in February or March. When Joe left after his recent visit she definitely planned on going to Vietnam in December, but as soon as he was gone doubts arose. "Every day I kept thinking, 'Well, I will go, I won't go.'" She was afraid that if she went she would not resist getting married, and she remained deeply conflicted about marrying Joe. "If he was on the other side of the ocean, I could have willpower, but the minute I saw him I knew it would go out the window." [128]

"I really, really, really, really miss you," she purred seductively. "I'm just sitting here thinking about you. Yummy." As the tape ended the recorder resonated with feedback. "This thing is so sensitive this morning," Carollyn murmured. "It's sensitive like you are in the morning. Uhmmmm, nice. Take care, Boy Hero." Then she added, "This should get to you in December. One more Christmas without me."

Joe shared Carollyn's belief that they would soon be together permanently. When his return flight stopped in Japan he sent a postcard saying that "This is the last time we will be apart."

But by mid-December jealous doubts afflicted him. On the 9th, while at Camp Eagle for the battalion stand-down, he sent Carollyn four ceremonial swords as a Christmas present, a sentimental Christmas card, and a letter. He had just called the Hollywood Bunker where it was well after midnight, but she was not there. "I pray to God that you haven't left me again. Just when we are so close to being so happy. Please think about our love and plans before you do anything." Four days later he mailed a picture of the 101st Airborne Division Memorial Chapel where they planned on getting married and that emanated "such a feeling of comfort & closeness to God. To think I may marry the most wonderful girl in this great memorial brings tears of happiness to my eyes."

At some point Carollyn suddenly changed her mind about not going to Vietnam for Christmas and signed up with a USO tour, telling Joe they could meet in Saigon before going north to Camp Eagle. Joe flew to the capitol, rented a room, and adorned it with flowers and a portrait of Carollyn, Rolly, and himself that he had commissioned. Although Carollyn went to the airport in California with a wedding dress in her luggage, she stood him up again, just as she had done in Panama, and did not get on the plane. "I just didn't really want to get married, a legal type marriage. It just scared me, and just something told me not to go." [129]

Joe was distraught when Carollyn did not show up. "This may be the last time I write you," he wrote in a January 6, 1971, letter attached to the portrait of the three of them. "My mind won't let me think too clearly at this point." All he knew for sure was that he had "lived two years from the sunshine and warmth of these three beautiful smiles." Everything else was uncertain and unsure.

That same day he wrote Maggie and John Henry, sending them a duplicate of the portrait, though he told them that he, Carollyn, and Rolly "may never be one." In the letter he apologized for crying over the phone when he called them from Saigon shortly after Carollyn's nonarrival. But, he explained, he was terribly "upset the Blond Mama-san could not come over and I really felt alone."

"Don't worry about me over here," he assured them. "I [am] fine and will stay that way." [130]

Everything in the phone call to his parents and the letters to them and Carollyn belied that assurance.

February 1971 was a month of misfortune for the American and South Vietnamese cause, and for Joe Hooper.

Operation Lam Son 719, ARVN's invasion of Laos to capture Tchepone and disrupt enemy logistics in the area, began on February 8. Even though intelligence agencies indicated that NVA forces were concentrated near Tchepone, that the region contained dense air defenses, that the jungles were ill-suited for helicopter warfare, that no American troops or advisers would accompany ARVN, and that Hanoi *knew* about the invasion two weeks in advance, Nixon approved it, thus expanding the war for a second time. [131] The NVA defeated ARVN, with terrified South Vietnamese soldiers clinging to helicopter skids in a desperate effort to get out alive. Only American air power saved the invading force from annihilation.

Continuing the long history of self-delusion that characterized the military during the Vietnam War, Army officials involved with the operation considered it a rousing success. And with his penchant for prevarication, on April 7 Nixon publicly proclaimed that "Vietnamization has succeeded." General Davidson considered this assertion "an Orwellian untruth of boggling proportions. Lam Son 719 had demonstrated exactly the opposite, that Vietnamization had not succeeded." An ARVN general who participated in the invasion said none of his troops felt victorious, and General Alexander Haig, the deputy assistant to the president for national security affairs, realized that the raid "destroyed the cream of the South Vietnamese army." [132]

Joe's first misfortune was that he became an officer, receiving a direct commission as a 2nd Lieutenant in the Army Reserve on February 6. "I was the person who wanted him to be an officer, which he didn't want at all," Carollyn recalled. "That was my fault."[133]

And Audie Murphy's.

Because Murphy received a field commission and Joe was so obsessed with him, at times he thought he should emulate his hero by becoming an officer, too.

Joe was out of place as an officer. "Joe was so *basic*, he was such a basic, pretty simple person," Carollyn later realized, that he did not enjoy "all the formal protocol" associated with officership. "He was just used to being a soldier," she continued, "a sergeant, and he was getting to the top of his ranks being a sergeant. I think he was socially uncomfortable as an officer. He didn't want people to call him lieutenant, he just wanted to be a sergeant. I probably should have said just stay where you are. I don't care if there's an extra bedroom [in the quarters]."[134]

Joe also knew he was ill equipped to be an officer. "He always said he was a *combat soldier*," said Steve Hawk who served as Joe's platoon sergeant. "He told me one time, he said, 'The thing that's going to kill me the most was when there's not a war to fight.' He said, 'I am not a spit and polish soldier.'"[135]

An equally disastrous misfortune was that on February 14, 1971, Carollyn got married—not to Joe but to lawyer Dennis Haas who was about a dozen years older than she was. She met him at the Riverside Raceway when she went there to see her old boyfriend, driver Peter Revson, race. The romance was quick because Carollyn, "was really trying to get away from Joe and I thought if I married some attorney I might be protected."[136]

Joe's first assignment as a 2nd Lieutenant was with his old battalion, 2-501. He wanted to rejoin the Delta Raiders, which would "always be my favorit outfit," but "they were full and 'A' Co[mpany] was in a bind," so headquarters assigned him to it.[137] With its nickname of "Hard Luck Alpha," this was another misfortune.

The men in the company had a different name for themselves—the Alpha Avengers. But "Hard Luck Alpha" was more apt. The company's tough luck began at Cu Chi when an errant mortar round killed four of its members and wounded ten more. By 1970–71 its reputation was known at the Replacement School where the buzz among replacements was that a man wanted to avoid getting assigned to it. "Boy, this is your unlucky day," the school's assignment clerk told a replacement who was going to Alpha.[138]

"On the seventh day God opened the gates of Hell and out walked Hard Luck Alpha," a fellow GI wrote on Steve Hawk's helmet cover.[139] Considering its recent history, that was not much of an exaggeration. On May 13, 1969, Company A was securing the perimeter of Fire Base Airborne when sappers, some dressed in loin clothes or shorts and other naked, overran it, inflicting heavy losses.[140] Beginning on April 18, 1970, and continuing for more than a week, Hard Luck Alpha had numerous contacts, including the night of April 23 when an enemy attack on Alpha's NDP killed one and wounded eleven.[141]

By the time the company deployed to Fire Base Granite on April 29, it was only two-thirds of authorized strength. That night and all the next day the NVA subjected Granite to "a terrific firefight," in the words of 2-501's commander, Lieutenant Colonel Otis Livingston. "We got hit and hit hard." In particular "Alpha Company took a bad lick and was pretty badly mauled." For the next five days the fire base was under mortar attack. Reduced to seventy-five officers and men, on May 5 the company deployed to Fire Base Henderson to recuperate. But in another well-planned attack, in the wee hours of May 6 the NVA struck that fire base with rocket propelled grenades, small arms fire, satchel charges, and mortars, followed by a ground assault. NVA armed with flame-throwers ignited the ammo dump, detonating 1,000 rounds of 155 mm artillery shells. Company A again took brutal losses.[142] Between April 18 and May 7 Hard Luck Alpha had nineteen KIA, seventy-five WIA, and two MIA. For enduring such slaughter the Army recommended it for a Presidential Unit Citation.[143]

Of course Joe might not have looked at this mayhem unfavorably. According to a soldier in his new platoon, "Joe always said, when we were out in the field, his goal was to die in combat. That was his goal. He told us that his goal was to die in combat."[144]

Maybe he considered death a painless way to deal with the painful loss of Carollyn's love.

Twelve

Everybody thought he was so gung ho
that he wanted to get another medal,
and he'd get us all killed.

*James Jennette, expressing a common fear among soldiers
who served under Joe's command after his promotion to Second Lieutenant*

Joe may have lost Carollyn, but in joining A-2-501 he gained a soldier soul mate.

The battalion was at Camp Eagle for a stand-down when Sergeant Mark S. Hawk received word the captain wanted to see him. Friends called him Steve, or usually just Hawk. Since the company was short of lieutenants, Hawk had been serving as the 2nd Platoon leader for several months. After tucking the most recent *Playboy* under his stack of Sgt. Rock comic books, Hawk trudged over to Captain Loren Zimmerman's bunker. The sergeant was wearing shorts, unlaced jungle boots, no shirt, and a .45 in a shoulder holster, and wore his helmet backwards. Adorning the helmet cover were a peace symbol and three inscriptions: "What if they gave a war and nobody came?" "Kill by profession, love by choice, live by chance, 11B4P," which was a light infantryman's MOS (Military Occupational Specialty). "There will be peace in the Valley for me, oh Lord, I pray," with the valley referring to the A Shau, the long-time NVA stronghold that had been the deathbed for too many Americans.

"Captain Z, what to do you need?"

The captain had a new lieutenant for him.

"I don't need no goddamn butterbar lieutenant," Hawk exploded in an exasperated monologue, the "butterbar" referring to a 2nd lieutenant's single gold bar insignia. Every grunt knew that a 2nd lieutenant with a map and a .45 was more dangerous than the enemy. "He'll get out there and get shot up and you'll want to know how he got shot, why he got shot, who shot him. If they get shot at, the butter melts on their uniform and makes a mess. Then they start crying." And so on.

"Hawk, shut up! You don't have a choice. I want you to meet your new lieutenant, Lieutenant Joe Hooper."

Hawk had not noticed the second man in the bunker, but when he heard the name his brain clicked. Joe Hooper? Bob Hope introduced an MOH recipient with a name something like that during his Christmas show when Hawk had a front row seat and got a good look at the man.

Peering over, Hawk snapped to attention. "Good afternoon, sir! Please disregard all those remarks about lieutenants."

Laughing, Hooper assured the embarrassed sergeant he had made plenty of similar remarks—and still felt the same way.

A brief, intense comradeship was born.

As with many brave soldiers, Hawk was not adverse to spending time in the rear—he did not seem too upset when he fell off a cliff and hurt his ankle, when a falling tree injured his back, or when he ran a high fever since these injuries and illnesses put him in a hospital. He hoped for a "medical profile" confining him to the rear and angled for a REMF position. Halfway through his tour he was "jumpy" and scared to stay in the bush.[1] And he was indifferent to heroism. When Hoop told him, "Hawk, you stick with me, I'll get you a chestful of medals," he replied "Joe all I want to do is go home. You know what CMH stands for?" "Yeah, Congressional Medal of Honor." No, Hawk replied, "Casket with Medal Handles. I don't want one of those."[2]

Still, members of the platoon regarded Hawk as "a wild young guy" who excelled in the field. Bob Saal, known as "Rock," thought of Hawk "as this big Audie Murphy guy who knew a lot and was a damn good soldier." One grunt considered him "crazy. He'd just do about anything, anything dangerous he'd be the first one. He wouldn't ask any of us to do anything he wouldn't do." Another GI praised him as "one hell of a guy. If there was a poster boy for the U.S. Army, that guy was it."[3]

Linked by their "wild" personas and expert military skills, after their first meeting Hooper and Hawk, seemingly born of the same DNA, were nearly inseparable. Although Hawk was a shake 'n' bake, he was not some despicable "leg" serving in an airborne unit. Two days after graduating from the Noncommissioned Officer School at Fort Benning he moved across the fort and went to jump school. He enjoyed leaping from the 250-foot-high tower and, as he wrote his mother, was really "looking forward to Monday when we jump out of the plane." Equally exhilarating was the demolitions course, which he *loved*.[4]

Both men loved what they did and were good at it, recalled Saal, and the rest of the platoon "just kind of followed them and did what we had to do." They were in their "element out there. They were made for each other," said Wayne Anderson, nicknamed "Bear" because he could cut a trail like a bear when walking point.[5]

The Hawk-Hoop friendship began with a tour of the bunker, with Hawk introducing him to the platoon. At first men grumbled about being saddled with "a fucking cherry," a cherry being a soldier without combat experience. Then word spread that this butterbar had an MOH! "Oh, shit! Gung ho!" cried one soldier. "Fucking John Wayne," groused another disparaging voice.[6]

Joe was matter-of-fact with the men as he reviewed basic procedures, such as telling them to remember to cup their cigarettes in the field so the enemy could not see the glowing tips. But he became animated when discussing drugs. If he caught anyone smoking marijuana, that person was "only going to remember two sounds, and that's me yelling 'Frag out!' and then the explosion." After hearing Joe talk about fragging his men, Ned Kintzer thought that "maybe this guy isn't too sane."[7]

Not too sane. That was a common impression among the men of 2nd Platoon, who viewed Joe's hyperaggressiveness nervously. Most were draftees, reluctant soldiers, dismayed at being in a division with an aggressive reputation such as the 101st Airborne.[8] They preferred to search and evade, to serve their year, and make it back to the World. Joe wanted to search and destroy, fight and kill, so he could receive more medals. "He liked to kill people, so we're at opposite ends of the spectrum there," noted Patrick L. "Roonie" Runevitch, a "shake 'n' bake" who had no idea why the United States was in Vietnam but believed he should do what his country asked of him.[9] Another member of 2nd Platoon admitted, "We weren't searching real hard—until Hooper got there." "Everybody thought he was so gung ho that he wanted to get another medal, and he'd get us all killed," remembered James Jennette. According to Kintzer, Joe had an ego problem and "wanted to try and transfer some of that egotism to us, not necessarily to make us Medal of Honor winners, but to try and make us heroes, and I don't think that's what we were about." "Hooper was a wild man if there ever was one," said Bear Anderson. "I think he was certifiable. The man was fearless. He had to have a screw loose."[10]

Would a sane person *volunteer* for Vietnam and then want to be *first* into a firefight? Joe told his men that "I figure every GI is worth ten 'dinks.' So if we've got ten and they've got ninety, we've got them outnumbered!" Never wanting to miss the action—especially when the Americans had the enemy so badly outnumbered—Hooper always volunteered 2nd Platoon to go first. "He loved to be in the action," Rock Saal anxiously recalled. "He personally was first. He wanted to be first. He's always on the first bird." Another trooper agreed: "Anything that was kind of risky, he wanted to be right there, the first one to do it. That's the reason he was in the first helicopter." [11]

Learning what he did to receive the MOH reinforced the sentiment that Joe was crazy. And he made sure they knew because he was not shy about the medal. Not only did he carry a copy of his MOH file with him but he also had his men watch the Defense Department film of the White House ceremony during a stand-down on Fire Base Bastogne. Runevitch and Wayne Anderson summarized the general sentiment: "Holy shit! Here's a killing machine," said Roonie, "This is one *evil* person. We talked amongst ourselves —what the hell's wrong with this guy?" "Oh my God!" exclaimed Anderson in dismay, "What are we in for now?" [12]

The grunts of 2nd Platoon also learned that Joe drank too much and did not relish being an officer. He drank only in the rear, never out in the field. "Joe was a big lush," John Fair recalled, "and from the minute we hit the rear area till somebody went and drug him out of the NCO Club, he was drunk." Sometimes he was so hung over his men had to roust him from his cot and virtually drag him to a helicopter for a combat assault. [13]

Although he was an officer, Joe often drank at the NCO Club, not the Officers Club, because he felt more comfortable there. Even if he went to the Officers Club he usually dragged Sergeant Hawk along, forcing him to impersonate an officer. Most of the time, though, he was just "a regular guy. He partied with everybody in the rear not just with the 'uppers.'" First Lieutenant Frank Campagne, a graduate of OCS and jump school, considered Joe "a real soldier's soldier. He didn't like being an officer much." Or as a grunt phrased it, despite Joe's rank "he still felt like he was one of us." Insisting on being addressed as "Sarge" or "Hooper," if a man called him "Lieutenant" Joe would "dress your ass down in a heartbeat." [14]

The men had another view of Joe, too. Despite his craziness and drinking, many of them considered him a hero, looked at him with awe, and learned that in the field he was all business, thoroughly professional, and a superb leader when the lead was flying. "When it came to being in a combat situation, there was nobody I'd rather be with. He was maybe a little too aggressive, but I'd rather have somebody like that who showed no fear than have somebody who showed a lot of fear and indecisiveness," was how Anderson summed it up.[15]

Two days after Joe joined A Company, the entire battalion deployed to Fire Base Boise, staying there less than a week before moving to Fire Base Bastogne where it remained for the next several months.[16] The high command believed aggressive search and destroy operations around Bastogne would stop the NVA from moving out of the A Shau Valley along Highway 547 toward Hue and the populated lowlands. Recent intelligence summaries reported no traffic, either by foot or vehicle, on Highway 547, and contact in the area had been negligible during February, but the 6th NVA Regiment inhabited the area and the dry season was rapidly approaching, and no one knew what that would bring.[17] Little more than a dirt road that made wide loops and hairpin turns through the mountainous jungle, Highway 547 traversed such "steep-ass" terrain that Joe complained of aching knees and ankles as his unit mimicked mountain goats.[18]

Reinforced after its multiple disasters in 1970, on March 1 Hard Luck Alpha numbered 136 officers and men including four medics, three artillery personnel, two mortar forward observers, and five Kit Carson scouts. Joe commanded thirty men in 2nd Platoon. The company (and the battalion as a whole) had limited airmobility because of the heavy commitment of helicopters to support Operation Lam Son 719, where 108 were destroyed and another 618 damaged, many beyond repair.[19]

Fire Base Bastogne was so rat infested that Lieutenant Colonel Michael A. Boos, commander of 2-501, gave extra beer to those who killed the biggest and the most rats, and a "Rat Report" became a standard feature in the nightly briefings. "The goddamn rat traps went off all night," said Runevitch about his first night on Bastogne. "Bam! Bam! Bam! You'd catch two or three of them at a time." Rat hunting became intense competition, and like most competitive events it was not immune from cheating. Killing a large rat with a shovel, Runevitch stood on its head while pulling its tail with a pair of pliers, stretching it to win the biggest rat prize.[20]

While the rat hunting generated a huge body count, search and destroy operations in early March did not. "Things have been pretty quiet here," wrote Paul Gochnour, a platoon leader who went through ROTC while attending Gettysburg College, and who could not "understand how people can get so excited about killing." He realized he was "definitely in the wrong job." A week later he assured his parents that "The area we were working in showed no signs of the enemy which is really good." On March 11, Bob Saal told his folks the same thing: "Before I got here our company was called 'Hard Luck Alpha' because everywhere they went for awhile they were always getting hit." But "Everyplace we go now is pretty quiet."[21]

Paul and Bob spoke too soon. On March 9 a reconnaissance team spotted five NVA to the northeast of Bastogne, and was soon fighting in an enemy base camp area. The battalion initially committed Company A to relieve the reconnaissance team, but quickly withdrew all friendly forces from the area, designated it as a free fire zone, and pulverized it with artillery and air power for four days. When Company A moved back into the area the enemy had fled, leaving behind numerous hidden caches. The company went on a "treasure hunt," uncovering weapons, ammunition, medical supplies, and rice, all of it hidden in caves and hooches or buried under rocks and bunkers. "It seemed like every place you stopped, or whatever you did or looked in, you would find something," recalled Hawk. Gathering much of the captured booty into a huge pile, the treasure hunters destroyed it with 400 pounds of explosives, which shook the ground like a small earthquake. Hawk received the honor and pleasure of setting off the detonation, which he considered the highlight of his military career.[22]

Destroying the NVA's logistics "nose" was crucial in preempting its plans. Unlike the U.S. Army, which supplied its troops from the rear via a logistics tail, during the rainy season the NVA laboriously stockpiled weapons and equipment out in front of its troops. Discovering a large cache, General Abrams believed, was "just as important as defeating a communist battalion. In fact it is more important, because it never winds up in a big battle with a lot of destruction."[23]

A Company's treasure hunt was neither odor free nor cost free.[24] Along with supplies the Alpha Avengers also dug up graves, adding to the body count one rotting corpse at a time. Although the NVA fled, they left the base camp heavily booby-trapped. The first mishap occurred on March 18 when someone hit a tripwire and two ARVN and two men from Joe's platoon were injured. Headquarters flew in special mine dog teams trained to hunt BBTs like an English setter points quail, and the men became especially alert, but despite all precautions BBT detonations continued.

On the afternoon of March 20, for example, a bobby-trapped 60 mm mortar shell went off, wounding RTO Charles Shannon and First Lieutenant Campagne, known as "Skip." A platoon leader who in many ways personified small unit leadership in 1970–71, Campagne hated Vietnam, this "hellhole," he called it.[25] From his first day in the hellhole he looked forward to becoming a REMF after six months on line. Being in the field was awful, in part because he was unusually susceptible to jungle rot. "No sweat," he told his wife after experiencing a bout of the crud, "it just makes a miserable situation a little more miserable." He missed "everything civilized. I'm one step above an animal here." "Especially at night when I'm freezing cold and drenched to the skin," he explained to his wife, "I think about our warm bed, your beautiful body, Nikki [their infant daughter] in her cradle, *breakfast* the next morning, a toilet ahh (do you know what it's like crapping in the jungle in the rain—ugh!), dry clothes, lunch, no weight on your back, TV, supper, a day off, friendly people etc etc etc etc on and on!" After several weeks in the field he was haggard, gaunt, and bone tired, with a long scraggly beard and hollowed bloodshot eyes, and covered with cuts, sores, and rot.

As with so many other lieutenants and captains, he was happy to avoid contact. "Nobody wants to be the last man in Viet Nam killed," he explained. "My main job from now on is to get *me* first and my people home alive. Any mission he gives me comes second to that." "He" was Lieutenant Colonel Boos, a "lifer" who Skip detested because he "was playing with my peoples' lives for his own selfish reasons. He's trying to get promoted and wants to have a large 'body count' behind him. The only thing is he doesn't care if he kills Americans in the process." Twenty-five years later Campagne still seethed about the professional officer corps. "These sorry asses would go out of their way to get their ticket punched and show an increased body count. They didn't care who or how many guys got 'wasted' doing it, because these sorry asses stayed on the fire base or the rear area way in the back." The Army's own "Study on Military Professionalism" reached essentially the same conclusion.

Campagne considered Hooper "one lucky guy." They were walking along a trail in the base camp area when Hooper approached a fallen log and made a potentially fatal error. Instead of stepping on the log and taking a giant stride off of it to avoid snakes or, worse, a tripwire, Joe stepped right over it. Somebody yelled "Freeze!" "And he looked down and he was straddling an 82 mm mortar round with a tripwire that would've blow us all to Kingdom come had he set it off." Joe acknowledged his luck, saying "Boy, they can't get me. Boy, am I lucky." Incredibly, Hawk was even luckier. He tripped a BBT, but only the blasting cap of a B-40 rocket, not the rocket itself, went off.[26]

But Campagne believed that he, not Joe or Hawk, was the luckiest of them all because his BBT *did* detonate, giving him a million dollar wound. Hooper led a small knot of reinforcements, including a medic, to set up a perimeter around the injured men. Displaying his field skills and calmness under pressure, Joe remembered to grab a handcrafted bamboo-and-reeds stretcher from the NVA medical supplies. While the medic attended to Shannon, who was wounded in the gut, Joe treated Campagne. "Joe, you've seen a million wounds. Am I going home?" Frank never forgot his answer: "Skip, you're going home." They loaded Shannon on the stretcher and Campagne got a piggyback ride back to an LZ where they put them on a medevac. "As hurting as I was," recalled Campagne, "I was as happy as a pig in shit."

"Honey you can't imagine the relief I felt when that big C-141 took off from Da Nang headed for Japan," he informed his wife three days later. "It wasn't the freedom bird that I would have liked to get home in but the main fact is that I'm coming home, coming home and because God must have been watching over me, in one piece too." His legs were like a sieve from shrapnel wounds and he had a few broken bones, "But look at me—nothing!" With soaring spirits because his war was over, he happily let his wife know he would soon be home where "I can see you and kiss you and hug you and love you."[27]

While Campagne enjoyed liberation, Hard Luck Alpha remained in the field, searching for treasure during the day and setting ambushes at night, some manned and some mechanical. Hooper and Hawk were both avid ambushers, sometimes each leading one on the same night. However, they never sprang an ambush during Joe's time with Alpha.[28] Usually consisting of four claymore mines attached to a tripwire, a mechanical ambush was the American equivalent of a BBT, resulting in death and maiming from impersonal explosives. When a mechanical ambush detonated, preplanned fire from grenade launchers, mortars, and artillery saturated the area and then a small force swept it to collect weapons and documents and count the dead —which were sometimes water buffalo or, worse, other U.S. troops who blundered into the ambush.[29]

One night when they were in the NVA base camp a trip flare went off, which alerted everybody. Nobody saw anything but Joe ordered an on-line assault toward the dying flare. "You're fucking nuts!" Hawk told Hoop. "Come on, Hawk," Joe implored, "you gotta live dangerously." Disbelieving, the men in 2nd Platoon echoed Hawk's sentiments as they prepared to plunge into the pitch-black in an area laced with BBTs and, possibly, NVA. "Don't worry." Joe told them. "If you see 'em, just step on their fucking heads." No one knows how far they stumbled into the unknown before, thankfully, they encountered a small stream, bringing the movement to a halt.[30]

The troopers of Company A were not sorry when Company C replaced them in the base area on the morning of March 27. Depleted by death, injuries, and illness, the Alpha Avengers totaled only eighty-nine officers and men when they arrived back at Fire Base Bastogne.

After only three days of rats and rest, another calamity beckoned.

The battle that began on March 31–April 1 and extended into mid-April, said Steve Hawk, was just "a little disagreement over some land rights with the NVA."[31]

And the disagreement confirmed Hard Luck Alpha's hard-earned reputation.

In very late March, American reconnaissance elements discerned an enemy buildup along Route 547 west of an abandoned fire base named Veghel. After having been ghostlike for months, the NVA were suddenly "willing to engage in extended combat operations," which was "a definite change in enemy tactics." Ironically, 2-501 was planning raids into that area with hand-picked, specially trained twelve- to fifteen-man volunteer units. The idea was to operate on the edge of the dreaded A Shau Valley, hiding by day and harassing the NVA at night to stop infiltration along Route 547. Hawk was going to lead one of the raids, with almost all his volunteers coming from 2nd Platoon. Considering these operations extremely important, Captain Zimmerman canceled his R and R to Hawaii where he was to meet his wife. "These crazy lifers," wrote Lieutenant Gochnour in disbelief, "will do anything for browny points." The enemy's sudden aggressiveness compelled 2-501 to respond directly, canceling the raids.[32]

Trying to reconstruct what occurred on March 31–April 1 was subject to the same problems that prevailed at the Battle of La Chu, such as the frantic action and a man's narrow focus on the task at hand, inaccurate perceptions of time and distance, and distorted memories. "That day is kind of foggy in my mind," said Wayne Anderson, who did not see much "because I was laying so *low*." "A lot of that day is a blur to me," echoed Bob Saal. "I don't remember that much." Trying to visualize the size of one particular LZ all he could say was that "it *seemed* like a long way from one side to another. When you're getting shot at and mortared it's a long way to go across."[33]

But the general sequence of events was clear.[34]

Having operated in no more than platoon strength for months, the men were astonished that the whole company was going on the March 31 mission. "That's what was so odd about that day," remembered John Fair, a 6 foot 8 inch giant who carried an M-60 machine gun as easily as most men carried M-16s. "We were in company strength. And we never did that."[35] When Alpha's 1st Platoon led the combat assault into a small LZ near Fire Base Veghel, things went badly. As the choppers approached the LZ the crews spotted at least four enemy soldiers and took ground fire, so they aborted the mission and returned to Bastogne. Two troopers "went a little nuts" there, saying they were all going to die and refusing to return to the field, though Captain Zimmerman ultimately talked them out of their mini-mutiny.[36] While the area surrounding the intended LZ was "fired up" with air and artillery the company, joined by B Company, was airlifted from Bastogne to Veghel, only a mile from the LZ.

Veghel was a bare hill, the top having been leveled off by bulldozer-driving engineers who simply pushed the dirt over the precipitous sides. Perhaps as many as ten helicopters were shut down on the flat hilltop while the men watched the firepower saturating the intended LZ and awaited word to "saddle up" again for the combat assault. Hidden in the surrounding mountains, enemy soldiers sporadically sprayed Veghel with machine gun fire, which kept most men low to the ground, though not Joe Hooper who ambled over to Arvie LeBlanc's position. Arvie carried an M-203 (an M-16 with a grenade launcher mounted under the barrel) and Joe wanted him on the other side of the hill to fire grenades at a suspected enemy position. As they started across the hilltop Joe "was walking straight up like he was walking in a park. I was five to ten feet behind him and a burst of machine gun rounds went right between us. Me, I low-crawled the rest of the way and he just kept walking like it was nothing."[37]

Assuming the Americans might reuse Veghel because the region contained so few flat, open spaces, the NVA had it zeroed in with mortars. As Hooper's 2nd Platoon congregated near the helicopters to resume the combat assault—he undoubtedly volunteered them to go first ahead of 1st Platoon—the Communists unleashed an unexpected barrage and then lobbed intermittent rounds for the next several hours. More than a dozen men from Hard Luck Alpha (most of them from 2nd Platoon) and a few from Company B received shrapnel wounds while others sustained injuries jumping over the side of the hill—Bear Anderson, for example, broke an ankle. One of the wounded was Ron Rohs who opposed the war but "was too cowardly to go to Canada. So I served my country." "Everybody's grabbing their helmets and their nuts trying to stay low," said Ron, who had shrapnel in his thigh. Well, not quite everybody. He could see Hawk moving from man to man, helping the wounded. When a medevac arrived during a lull in the mortar fire, Rohs struggled onto the bird with four or five other wounded, several of them mangled, blood literally flowing out the open doors.[38]

To escape, both companies walked off the hill. At the bottom helicopters picked up Company B and took it to Bastogne. When they returned for Alpha they received ground fire and aborted, so the company marched to the Veghel pass where it set up a deeply dug NDP; everyone anticipated being mortared again. However nerve-racking, the night was quiet except for the artillery barrage going overhead to soften up the area for the morning's combat assault.

At 10:13 a.m. the air movement to the LZ began. Meanwhile the LZ, which was atop a hill near Veghel and big enough for only one chopper at a time, was doused with artillery, tactical air, and ARA (Aerial Rocket Artillery, which was rockets fired from helicopter gunships).

As often happened, neither the nighttime barrage nor the morning's firepower display did much good.

Joe wrote a brief account of that day to Cleo Hogan on April 10, the third anniversary of the Phuoc Dien cordon:

> On 1 April we CAd [combat assaulted] into the A-shaw [A Shau Valley]. I was [in] the lead ship and the only one to get in. Four

men & myself. We had six NVA at the hill top with us, so things were really jumping. We were there for six hrs alone and they final[ly] got 3 more birds in. We were under mortar fire and auto[matic] weapons all day. I lost one man and had three WIA's. We knocked out 2 [mortar] tubes 1 MG [machine gun] and killed 9 NVA but had to make a night withdraw[a]l, marr[y]ing up with the rest of the Co[mpany] at 2300 hrs. Quite a day.[39]

Although containing some exaggerations, this description was reasonably accurate.

To no one's surprise, 2nd Platoon led the combat assault and Joe was riding in the lead helicopter along with four other soldiers, including machine gunner John D. Tillitson who enlisted to beat the draft, believed he was just doing his job, and was proud to do his duty, and Rock Saal.[40] April 1 was "the worst day I can remember," recalled Saal, "we just got our asses *kicked* that day." Since enemy bunkers surrounded the LZ, since another unit tried the LZ several days before and could not get in, and since firing artillery at the area all night and into the morning did not impress Saal because the NVA were such expert diggers, he expected trouble. As helicopter skids brushed the ground, small arms and mortar fire began. Exactly how many NVA were within small arms range of the LZ was uncertain; Joe told Cleo six but in another account he mentioned four.[41] Exactly how many mortar rounds buffeted the LZ throughout the day was also uncertain. An official estimate was approximately fifty. But Saal's estimate was probably more accurate: "I don't know. I couldn't even guess. But a lot of them."

In any event the five men jumped out just as the chopper began whirling upward, and the other birds veered away.

Hooper and his men were stranded.

Saal and Tillitson took one side of the LZ, while Hooper, his RTO, and another soldier went to the other side. With his pack weighing at least 150 pounds because of all the extra ammo, Tillitson landed on his back leaping from the ascending helicopter and hurt himself. But he began firing his machine gun, "making noise more or less because if the enemy hears guns firing and the trees are snapping around them, they're not going to be standing up shooting back." During momentary lulls the men shouted back and forth to keep communications open. Saal heard Hooper on the radio discussing with headquarters whether they should be withdrawn. Joe was against it. "We got the hill, we can hold it," he barked. "We can hold it all night if you need us to." Bob and John looked at each other as if to say, "What is he talking about?!"

Joe's advice prevailed. Beginning a little more than an hour after his team landed—not the six hours he claimed—the rest of 2nd Platoon and all of 1st Platoon arrived. But the decision to hold the hill was unwise because, said Saal, "every time a bird came in they'd mortar us." All that flying lead created casualties. "And so they had to bring in medevac helicopters, and then they mortared more." Making the situation worse were heat casualties: the day was scorching, by late afternoon everybody was out of water, and men faltered.

Steve Hawk (who arrived on the second chopper into the LZ) and Joe Hooper relished the contact. Each took command of one side of the hill. Hawk incessantly moved along his expanding perimeter to make sure everyone was all right and ordering tactical adjustments. He directed Pete Winter, who came in on the same bird as Hawk, into a fighting hole when he emerged from the helicopter. As he settled into the position it took a direct hit from a mortar round, turning Winter "into a red mess." The only KIA that day, he may have had a premonition of impending death. Just before their helicopter headed to the LZ Pete handed Hawk a letter to his wife, asking him to mail it. For some reason Hawk never mailed the letter and still has it, unopened.

Even more noticeable than Hawk was Hooper, who was on the radio calling in air strikes and gunship support. Putting his former communications training to good use, Joe operated the radio without his RTO, allowing that lucky trooper to keep his head down. Tillitson saw Joe "crisscross the LZ several times because he wanted to make sure where the [enemy] fire was coming from. He wanted to get out and see it himself." Joe was "walking around on top of that damn hill, he had short red hair, didn't have a helmet on," remembered James L. Ayres, who was with 1st Platoon and was evacuated later that day with heat exhaustion. "I don't know who he was talking to, but he said 'Goddamn you motherfuckers, you sorry-ass son of a bitches, you better get me some goddamn shit and get it in here *now!*'" By "goddamn shit" he meant fire support. Ayres was astounded, not at the profanity but at Hooper's nonchalance. "I'm down behind a damn log and this son of a bitch is up walking around on top of that hill! I don't think it bothered him. Fear just didn't seem to be in him, or it didn't seem to be that day." Ayres cannot remember how long Joe was in the open except that "it was a pretty good while. Hell, who knows about that crazy son of a bitch!"

At one point an enemy machine gun was bedeviling the two platoons. Joe radioed Hawk asking if he saw the gun's location. Hawk thought he did but needed the machine gun to fire one more time to be sure.

"Well," replied Hooper, "on the count of three I'm going to run across the hill."

"Joe, don't do that!"

"You ready? You got anything that can take out a machine gun?"

"All I've got is a LAW."

"Get that son of a bitch ready! On the count of three I'm coming over the top."

"Joe, don't do it!"

"One, two, three!"

As Hooper raced across the hill the machine gun opened up. Hawk stood up and fired the LAW, destroying it.

"Boy, I'm getting too old for this shit," said Joe as he dove to the ground beside Hawk, panting.

Hawk may have felt he was getting too old, too, especially after a mortar round landed only a few feet from his position. Fortunately for him the shell was a dud. Staring at near death, Hawk noticed the words "United States Army Arsenal Harpers Ferry Virginia." He believed the round came from Fire Base Mary Ann, which NVA sappers recently overran.

While 1st and 2nd Platoons fought for their lives the battalion tried to relieve some of the pressure by inserting 3rd Platoon into a tiny nearby LZ that, like most scarce LZs, had been used before. The NVA were waiting. Along with seven other men, Platoon Leader Gochnour was aboard the first helicopter, which landed safely. But when the second bird was hit and crashed a couple hundred yards away, no others arrived.

James Jennette was one of the soldiers in that second chopper. "Tracer rounds were coming right through the helicopter," he said. "It was like a ball of fire coming right at you. It got within an inch of me and all I could do was watch." One of his buddies was not so fortunate, taking a round in his mouth, spewing bits of enamel, jawbone, and blood all over Jennette. With only a broken finger, Jennette helped get the injured men out after the crash.

As a Tennessean who did a lot of squirrel hunting, he believed the men on the nearby LZ were the squirrels, or sitting ducks. So when a medevac arrived he hopped on it even though his injury was not serious. Asked how he felt at the time, he answered "Scared." Those who were unhurt linked up with Gochnour's rump command.

Convinced that the NVA were trying to keep them on the hill so they could launch a nighttime assault, Hooper told Hawk "I don't know about you, but I don't want to stay on this hill tonight." "Hell," Hawk replied, "I don't want to be on here *now*." Joe relayed their concern to the battalion commander. Deciding the two separated LZs were not tenable, late in the afternoon he ordered the platoons to link up on Highway 547 near Veghel. Walking off the hill was an ordeal for 1st and 2nd Platoons even though they had a protective umbrella of jets and Cobra gunships. A few stray enemy shots bothered them, traversing enemy territory in near darkness was terrifying, and maneuvering through the dense vegetation was an ordeal. But the more serious problems were dehydration and the debilitating overdrive of the parasympathetic nervous system.

In such situations energetic leadership was crucial, and Hawk and Hoop provided it. Hawk cut point, hacking a path through the jungle because, said Rock Saal (whose was less than rocklike that evening), he was "the only one that seemed strong enough that day. Everybody was just wasted by the end of that day and Hawk took the machete and led us out." Meanwhile Hooper moved back and forth, uphill and downhill, along the line of stumbling men. "Keep on, keep on, keep on!" he encouraged them. "We can't stop, we can't rest here. We won't make it if we do." If someone tried to sit down, he had no sympathy, telling others to "just leave 'em, leave 'em there for the dinks." No one sat down long.

That night they dug in near the Veghel pass, close to where they spent the previous evening. Officials put the enemy body count for March 31–April 1 at twelve definite KIAS and forty to sixty KIA from air strikes and ARA; the latter was surely a WAG.[42] Hard Luck Alpha had only one KIA during those two days, but determining how many men were WIA, injured, or ill was difficult because the records were incomplete. For example, Department of the Army General Orders Number 3069, dated April 14, 1971, listed nine men as receiving Purple Hearts for April 1, but the list is surely incomplete.[43] Another source simply described the losses as "heavy," heavy enough that the battalion commander granted the company a one-day stand-down on Bastogne to recuperate.[44]

Awaiting Hard Luck Alpha on the fire base were the results of Major William G. Pagonis's personal efforts.[45] A superb logistician who later played a leading role in the buildup for Operation Desert Storm during the Gulf War, Pagonis readied hot showers, steaks, and plenty of beer. Also awaiting were medals for March 31–April 1: a bs/v, Army Commendation Medal, and Purple Heart for Pete Winter, posthumously of course, and plenty of impact awards for the living. The ceremony occurred on April 3 with Brigadier General Olin E. Smith presiding. Eight soldiers received bs/v, including Gochnour, Hawk, Saal, and Tillitson, and an equal number pinned on Army Commendation Medals with V device.

And Joe Ronnie Hooper received a second Silver Star.[46]

Beginning on April 2 the mission of 2-501 was to conduct search and destroy operations north of Route 547 and on the high ground south of the Veghel pass to determine if the enemy encountered on April 1 was moving eastward to Bastogne. Despite massive artillery and tactical air strikes (including b-52s) in the area during the next week, fighting flared wherever the Americans ventured as the enemy seemed determined to block any incursion along Route 547 into the A Shau Valley. Numbering only seventy-five officers and men, Alpha went back into the area, but according to Joe "dint reach 1st base." By April 10, however, contact slackened, which headquarters viewed as an indication the NVA had withdrawn from the area.[47]

During the morning of April 12 firepower saturated an LZ east of Veghel just before Company A's headquarters element and 3rd Platoon combat assaulted into the LZ.[48] The NVA had not withdrawn and they withstood the bombs, rockets, and shells. Alpha took casualties immediately and the battalion commander quickly ordered the unit extracted and more firepower applied. Before completing the extraction under heavy pressure, the Avengers had fifteen WIA and one KIA, Staff Sergeant Wentworth whose body they left behind.

The next day the Delta Raiders assumed the Alpha Avengers' mission, with the additional goal of recovering Wentworth's body. A harrowing ordeal ensued as the enemy hammered Joe's old unit on April 15–16, killing eight Raiders and badly wounding another fourteen. Hard Luck Alpha appreciated "what Delta did to go in and get Wentworth because he was sort of an icon in Alpha Company," but such thanks were small consolation for such devastating losses.[49]

After April 16 the NVA seemed to disappear. For the rest of the month little contact occurred anywhere in the Veghel-Bastogne area.

Looking at the platoon-size unit that remained of Company A, Bob Saal summed up the situation that had prevailed for a little more than two weeks. He and his comrades did not "hear too much out in the boonies except bullets and mortars and good stuff like that hitting all over." Continuing, "we have really been getting our butts kicked. Wow, our whole company's been just about wiped out. . . . I used to think I was a pretty unlucky guy but when I look at the company and see hardly anybody I know anymore because all the old guys have been replaced—wow I feel like the luckiest guy in the world."[50]

"What an example of blind xenophilia," wrote COSVN's General Tran Van Tra.

He was referring to the American hawks' "smug arguments" that the VC/NVA won the war in Washington and not on the battlefield, that only "internal conflicts and psychological panic," not the enemy's combat prowess, compelled the United States to withdraw.

"How could one accept the argument that we were crushed on the battlefield, beaten to rags and tatters, and then all of a sudden were handed a psychological and political victory by an enemy—the chieftain of all imperialist forces—who was paralyzed by its own frustrations and internal splits and who graciously bestowed this glorious victory on us? In fact, there is never an easy 'political' victory won by the grace of Heaven or through an enemy's mercy without first having to shed blood and scatter bones on the battlefield, especially in a big war such as ours."[51]

General Tra was doubly right.

No nation ever suffered a "military" defeat yet won a "political" victory through divine intervention or the enemy's goodwill. In every war the battlefield shaped political and diplomatic developments. A nation never obtained anything in a peace settlement that it did not earn in combat; the negotiating table always reflected battlefield realities.

To achieve victory, the Communists watered the battlefields with blood from the early 1960s through the mid-1970s.

Commencing with a coordinated three-pronged attack on March 30, 1972, the Easter Offensive was one of the foremost examples of the vc/nva's willingness to endure horrific losses to achieve a unified Vietnam.[52] The war's largest offensive, it represented Hanoi's decision to reverse the economy-of-force strategy that prevailed for the previous three years and escalate directly to the conventional warfare phase of military *dau tranh*. Supported by Soviet-made tanks and a huge artillery array, almost all of pavn's divisions participated. The Politburo hoped to deliver a knockout punch, to "defeat the American 'Vietnamization' policy, gain a decisive victory in 1972, and force the U.S. imperialists to negotiate an end to the war from a position of defeat." Since only about 70,000 U.S. troops remained, the vc/nva naturally concentrated their attacks against ARVN, which performed so dismally during Operation Lam Son 719 that Hanoi had a reasonable expectation of decisive success. But enemy strategists realized they might have to settle for less, such as improving their position inside South Vietnam by regaining territory and weakening pacification.[53]

U.S. military intelligence predicted an invasion but misjudged its timing, size, and location. Consequently pavn's offensive took ARVN and the Nixon administration by surprise. ARVN bordered on collapse, especially after May 1 when the Communists captured Quang Tri City, their first (and only) conquered provincial capital up to that point in the war. Calculating that he could not survive the 1972 presidential election if South Vietnam fell, the president responded vigorously, not by reintroducing troops but by mobilizing air power. Almost all the American troops who remained in Vietnam were serving in advisory roles, and scheduled withdrawals continued during the Easter Offensive so the number decreased during the spring and summer.

But air power was another matter. In June 1971, Nixon, at times angrily pounding his desk and shouting, insisted that he did not intend to "go out whimpering," that he was going to "bomb the livin' bejesus out of 'em," and that he wanted to "level the goddamn country!" Now in response to the enemy's offensive he began a massive air-power buildup in Southeast Asia, giving life to his previously failed "madman" strategy.[54] Under Operation Bullet Shot the b-52s in-theater climbed from forty-seven to 210, representing more than half of sac's strategic bombers. Operation Constant Guard increased the number of f-4 fighters from 185 to 374. Aircraft carriers in the Gulf of

Tonkin tripled from two to six, giving the Navy its greatest concentration of firepower during the war. By unleashing this formidable force Nixon hoped to smash the invasion, save his Vietnamization and pacification policies, and severely punish the North's homeland, compelling the Communists to sign a favorable treaty.[55]

Almost immediately Nixon authorized B-52 attacks north of the DMZ. The big bombers had never before struck Hanoi or Haiphong, but on April 16 twenty of them bombed oil storage facilities in Haiphong, trying, said Kissinger, to send "a warning that things might get out of hand if the offensive did not stop." Enraged and frustrated that the Communists were not letting him "win" the war, Nixon instructed Kissinger to be brutally frank in secret negotiations with the North Vietnamese on May 2. "In a nutshell you should tell them that they have violated all understandings, they [have] stepped up the war, they have refused to negotiate seriously. As a result, the President has had enough and now you have only one message to give them—Settle or else!"[56]

As usual the Communists did not respond to Nixon's threats. This time, however, the threats were not idle. He was determined "that for once we've got to use the maximum power of this country against a shit-asshole country to win the war." Even as the growing air power arsenal hammered PAVN divisions in the South, on May 8 the president announced the mining of Haiphong, a naval blockade, and Linebacker I, the sustained bombing of North Vietnam. Urging his military advisers to "recommend action which is very *strong, threatening,* and *effective,*" Nixon intended "to stop at nothing to bring the enemy to his knees." He even suggested to Kissinger that he'd "rather use a nuclear bomb" than bomb the Red River dikes (an act that would drown hundreds of thousands of people), and urged his national security adviser "to think big."[57]

The president settled for conventional bombs and sent few B-52s over North Vietnam, instead using the big bombers to support ARVN directly. But other aircraft flew north in large numbers. The renewed assault on North Vietnam was not entirely new to anyone except the American public; despite the bombing halt on November 1, 1968, some bombs still fell on the North. Throughout 1970–71 the United States flew a series of "protective reaction strikes," supposedly responding only in self-defense. And in Operation Proud Deep Alpha in late December 1971, U.S. aircraft flew more than 1,000 sorties attacking targets south of the 20th parallel.[58]

But Linebacker I was different—different from Rolling Thunder, the protective reaction strikes, and Proud Deep Alpha. As an official history of PAVN acknowledged, "This time the enemy employed larger forces and launched massive attacks that began on the first day of the operation, using many modernized, upgraded technical weapons and equipment." Consequently, "many of our units and local areas suffered heavy losses. Almost all of the important bridges on the railroad lines and on the road network were knocked out." Ground, coastal, and river transportation became difficult. The North's inability to defend important targets or shoot down very many enemy aircraft caused grave concern.[59]

For the first time, bombing was reasonably successful.

One reason was that détente with the Soviet Union and China reduced the chances of World War III, allowing Nixon to employ air power in ways Johnson never dared try. For the Communists superpowers, Vietnam was increasingly irrelevant, an irritant that might endanger their rapidly evolving relationships with the United States. Each was willing to tolerate more aggressive American action than ever before rather than undermine the détente policy.[60] Also, the Communists' conventional assault required substantial, sustained logistical support. Supplemented by the blockade and mining, bombing damaged the resupply effort, as did China's actions. In what the Vietnamese considered a betrayal, China delayed shipping goods to the North for three weeks and prevented Soviet goods destined for the North from crossing Chinese territory for three months. New weapons, especially laser-guided and electro-optically guided bombs and new jamming devices, made key contributions to the aerial assault's impact.

Most importantly, the bombing was successful because it supported a very limited policy objective. As often happened in warfare, the losing country reduced its war aims. While Johnson's goal was an independent, non-Communist South Vietnam that survived indefinitely, Nixon constricted the objective to an independent South Vietnam that did not immediately collapse following American withdrawal. By June 1970, the administration had decided to ultimately abandon South Vietnam to its fate. As Kissinger said in his secret talks in Paris with the North Vietnamese, "if we withdraw our troops unconditionally and quickly what happens in Saigon is *your* problem and you will have to decide whether you can win a war with the Saigon government or not." The national security advisor informed the Soviet ambassador that if renewed war broke out in Vietnam after America's withdrawal, "that conflict will no longer be an American affair; it will be an affair of the Vietnamese themselves, because the Americans will have left Vietnam. It will be beyond the scope of the Nixon administration." And he assured Chinese leaders that if the Saigon government was overthrown after the United States departed, "we will not intervene." All the administration wanted was for South Vietnam to survive for a "decent interval," which Kissinger defined as five years. Nixon hoped to use air power to insure its existence at least until early 1977 when his second administration ended, thus removing the slightest taint that he lost the war.[61]

Viewed from the administration perspective, the Easter Offensive was a failure, far from the decisive knockout blow the Communists envisioned in their most optimistic forecasts. Linebacker operations inflicted severe damage on the North, ARVN not only survived but in a few places fought well, and PAVN suffered at least 100,000 casualties. With their emphasis on the body count, Americans thought this was particularly significant. Officials told the American public (and often themselves) that Nixon's policy was working. In an astoundingly erroneous debriefing report, General Thomas M. Tarpley, who commanded the 101st Airborne Division in 1971–72, bragged that "Vietnamization is no longer a hopeful phrase but is, in fact, reality."[62]

Reports emphasizing Communist gains were withheld as unduly pessimistic, while "balanced" reports—those hued with rosy hopes—were leaked whenever anything negative appeared in the press.[63]

But leading Communists understood that their bloody effusion was a down payment on impressive strategic gains.[64] As the Easter Offensive sputtered to an end during the summer several indicators pointed to the Communists' ultimate success. Devastation in South Vietnam was immense and demoralizing, counterbalancing the destruction in North Vietnam. The combatants fired so much lead in Quang Tri Province that they destroyed nearly every building; one American feared "that if somebody flew over with a big magnet the whole goddamn province would just rise up in the air." Although recaptured, Quang Tri City was nothing but rubble. All told more than a million new refugees, some of them permanently displaced, roamed South Vietnam.[65]

Another strategic benefit was that the NVA established control over new territory. Referred to as the "Third Vietnam," the broad swath of terrain PAVN occupied inside South Vietnam along the Laotian and Cambodian borders was essential for subsequent offensives. "In South Vietnam our liberated areas expanded and linked up with the great rear area in the North," concluded PAVN's official history. "Our main force troops now held secure footholds in the important strategic areas. The interspersion of areas under our control within areas controlled by the enemy was gradually changing the balance of forces in favor of our side."[66]

In addition, as the South Vietnamese people realized, ARVN barely escaped defeat. The government's inability to protect the population was hardly conducive to pacification. "Until the current offensive the people became more and more committed to the Government of Vietnam," wrote an American adviser. "Now, many are measuring sides and their commitments waiting for the winner."[67]

Although praising those few South Vietnamese units that fought well, General Abrams admitted that Vietnamization was fragile, that only American air power saved ARVN. The government, he said on May 5, "would now have fallen, and this country would now be gone . . . if it hadn't been for the B-52s and the tac air." Two months into the offensive ARVN's leadership faltered badly and many ARVN units lost their will to continue fighting. Only a torrent of bombs compensated for this feeble fighting spirit. Abrams realized the problem was élan, not material. "*Equipment* is not what you need," he told General Cao Van Vien, chief of the Joint General Staff. "You need men that will *fight*. And you need *officers* that will fight and lead the men. No amount of *equipment* will change the situation." That was true in the spring of 1972 and would be true in the spring of 1975.[68]

In sum, the Easter Offensive revealed that pacification and Vietnamization could never compensate for South Vietnam's stillborn nationalism.[69]

As the fighting continued the negotiators maneuvered toward a settlement. After the battering from American warplanes during the Easter Offensive, the Communists' foremost goal was to get the United States out of the war as soon as possible. Nixon, too, felt a sense of urgency. All indications were that the upcoming Congress would be so dovish it might legislate an end to the war upon assuming office in January 1973.

Reflecting their urgent immediate concerns and the ambiguous battlefield situation in which each side suffered victory and defeat, both the Communists and the Americans made concessions. Since Nixon steadfastly maintained that Thieu must remain in power, the enemy's key concession was to drop its demand for his ouster and the creation of a coalition South Vietnamese government before reaching a settlement. Two lesser concessions were to sanction the release of all prisoners except for VC and to allow the Americans to resupply South Vietnam on a one-for-one replacement basis after they withdrew. The North Vietnamese not only partially betrayed their Southern allies, but also gave Thieu's government a better chance of surviving by allowing an ongoing materiel transfusion.

Nixon and Kissinger capitulated on several paramount issues. The single most significant concession by either side was the decision to permit NVA troops to remain *inside South Vietnam*. Although previously insisting on mutual American and NVA withdrawals, the United States brought its negotiating position in line with what was actually happening and accepted a unilateral withdrawal, thereby acknowledging that it had neither the will nor the ability to drive PAVN out of South Vietnam. As Kissinger stated, "no negotiations would be able to remove them if we had not been able to expel them with forces of arms." The Communists dropped their demand for Thieu's removal primarily because they recognized PAVN's presence in the South virtually guaranteed their ultimate success.[70]

Although Thieu remained in office, the Americans agreed to a Council of National Reconciliation and Concord, which sanctioned a Communist political presence in the South. Consisting of representatives from South Vietnam, the PRG, and a neutral "third force," the National Council was to exist side-by-side with Thieu's regime and organize elections for a new government, thus opening the way for a coalition government. Nor did the United States insist on denoting the DMZ as an international boundary, or demand that a settlement explicitly endorse two Vietnams. The agreement accepted the DMZ and Vietnam as recognized under the Geneva Convention—that is, it referred to a provisional demarcation line that was not a political or territorial boundary, and to a single Vietnam.

Finally, in a secret protocol the United States agreed to pay, without any political preconditions, at least $3.25 billion dollars in reparations to North Vietnam, a fate victors often imposed on the losing side. Naturally the Nixon administration kept this secret from the American people and Congress; in a bald-faced lie Secretary of State Rogers told a House Committee that "We have not made any commitment for any reconstruction or rehabilitation effort."[71]

The United States and North Vietnam finalized an agreement on October 8, agreeing to sign it on October 31. But one problem remained. Demonstrating the adage that "One country may support another's cause, but it will never take it so seriously as it takes its own," the United States conducted its retreat without fully consulting its ally—and with good reason since the United States conceded almost every key issue. "The real basic problem," wrote Nixon aide H. R. Haldeman, "boils down to the question of whether Thieu can be sold on it."[72]

When the United States handed Thieu a fiat accompli he reacted angrily, saying he "wanted to punch Kissinger in the mouth." Going to the heart of the matter, he understood that if NVA troops remained in the South "our struggle and the sacrifices we made during so many years would have been purposeless." He also feared that the National Council with its Communist representation was a coalition government in disguise, or was at the least an entering wedge for one. And Thieu was livid that the treaty did not denote the 17th parallel as an international boundary dividing two independent Vietnams.[73]

Having been the beneficiary of Thieu's sabotage in 1968, Nixon now discovered what being the victim was like.

The South Vietnamese president set out to kill the deal, just as he killed Johnson's deal-in-the-budding. But he had a problem, as Haldeman explained: "The settlement he's got is the best Thieu is ever going to get and unlike '68 when Thieu screwed Johnson, he had Nixon as an alternative." Now, however, the alternative was Democratic presidential candidate and avowed dove George McGovern, who would be a disaster for Thieu, "even worse than the worst possible thing that Nixon could do to him." Nonetheless, South Vietnam's president insisted the treaty required major changes embodying his "Four No's" policy: no recognition of the Communists, no neutralization of South Vietnam, no coalition government, and no surrender of territory. "It is hard to exaggerate the toughness of Thieu's position," Kissinger complained. "His demands verge on insanity." Nixon felt the same way. The October 8 agreement was better than the United States had any right to expect. If the American people knew its details, he told a late November JCS meeting, "they would never continue to support a prolongation of the war."[74]

To convince his recalcitrant ally to accept the treaty, the American ambassador to Saigon delivered a letter to Thieu in which Nixon repeated his "assurances to you that the United States will react very strongly and rapidly to any violation of the agreement. But in order to do this effectively it is essential that I have public support and that your Government does not emerge as the obstacle to peace which American public opinion now universally desires."[75]

Because the United States already had a deal with its enemy, its ally was *the* obstacle to peace. Thieu was skeptical of Nixon's assurances—"Who can know for sure?" he asked.[76] No one could, so he demanded substantial changes to the draft peace plan.

Nixon directed Kissinger to present Thieu's modifications to North Vietnam. Kissinger thought the changes were "preposterous." So did the North Vietnamese, especially since Kissinger had assured them that Thieu would sign the October 8 deal.[77] "We have been deceived by the French, the Japanese and the Americans, but the deception has never been so flagrant as now," responded the North's chief negotiator Le Duc Tho, who icily informed Kissinger that "If these are your last, unchangeable proposals, settlement is impossible." Deeply offended by Nixon's bad faith, the North Vietnamese refused to break the October 8 agreement, which it negotiated in good faith, or to yield on principles they had won on the battlefield as Thieu's modifications demanded. Eventually, negotiations broke off in mid-December. Demonstrating that he temporarily lost touch with reality, Kissinger lashed out at Tho and his entourage as "insolent," "ludicrous," and "tawdry, filthy shits," but he should have hurled those insults at a mirror.[78]

In a dark, malevolent mood, Nixon wanted to get tough.

He tried acting tough with Thieu, sending him a "Top Secret-Sensitive" message on November 23 threatening to move forward with the treaty "at whatever cost" and deploring Thieu's "dilatory tactics" in "an effort to scuttle the agreement." Several weeks later Kissinger reinforced the president's message, telling Thieu that if his "totally negative attitude continues it cannot but threaten the fundamental character of our future relationship."[79]

Thieu did not budge.

So Nixon got tough with North Vietnam, threatening another aerial attack.

North Vietnam did not budge.

At a loss as to what to do, Kissinger advised Nixon to "turn hard on Hanoi and increase pressure enormously through bombing and other means," but to also pressure Saigon "so that Thieu does not think he faced us down, and we can demonstrate that we will not put up with our ally's intransigence any more than we will do so with our enemy."[80]

Since bombing an ally to compel it to accept the peace treaty was unseemly, Nixon bombed the enemy that already agreed to a settlement. But the bombs were aimed as much at Saigon as they were at Hanoi.

Lasting from December 18 to 29, Operation Linebacker II relied primarily on B-52s, rearranged Linebacker I's rubble, devastated North Vietnam's air defenses, and inflicted some additional damage, especially on previously forbidden targets in Hanoi and Haiphong. Nixon provided no public explanation for the campaign. How could he explain that he was bombing North Vietnam because the United States and South Vietnam reneged on the October peace agreement?[81]

The results of the bombing campaign were these:

The United States endured terrible losses—fifteen B-52s and thirteen other warplanes, leaving ninety-three airmen missing (and presumed dead) and thirty-one more as new POWs.

It again demonstrated the American high command's flawed perception of war. Linebacker II, wrote General Phillip B. Davidson (who was in charge of MACV's military intelligence from 1967 to 1969), "had *no* military purpose. Nixon initiated it for purely psychological reasons—he wanted to send a message to North Vietnam to return to the negotiating table and reach an acceptable agreement."[82] As if psychological and military effects were ever separable! And without acknowledging the campaign's limited purposes and limited results, the Air Force accepted as gospel that it "proved" the validity of strategic bombing.[83]

Renewed bombing provoked outrage in the United States (particularly in Congress) and internationally, with even China and the Soviet Union reacting angrily in contrast to their acquiescence in Linebacker I.[84]

Responding to public sentiment, Congress vowed to cut off funding for the war, contingent upon the withdrawal of the remaining troops and the return of American POWs, thus putting pressure on Nixon to complete a deal quickly. Although the president warned North Vietnam he would unleash still another bombing campaign if a settlement did not occur swiftly, he admitted to Kissinger that "as far as our internal planning is concerned we cannot consider this to be a viable option."[85]

Rather than delay in the expectation of getting a better deal from

Congress, risking another strategic bombing campaign, or having its forces in the South further devastated, North Vietnam returned to the negotiating table, determined to get the United States out of the war by accepting a few cosmetic changes to the October 8 proposal.

Giving credence to Nixon's promise that the United States would punish North Vietnam if it violated an agreement, the bombing provided an incentive for South Vietnam to cooperate. Thieu still balked, forcing Nixon to apply the severe pressure Kissinger advised. He had "irrevocably decided" to sign an agreement, he wrote Thieu. "I will do so, if necessary, alone. In that case I shall have to explain publicly that your Government obstructs peace," in which case Congress would immediately terminate all military and economic assistance. Reluctantly, sullenly, rather than endure a public break with the United States, Thieu acquiesced.[86]

Although the president bombed the North primarily to impress the South, the so-called Christmas bombing created the myth that the Communists caved in to his toughness. The North Vietnamese merely continued agreeing to what they agreed to three months before. Thieu, not North Vietnam, caved in to Nixon, being bullied into accepting an armistice that was in America's best interest, not South Vietnam's.[87]

On January 23, 1973, all the parties signed the so-called Paris Accords, which were only slightly modified from the October 8 agreement, initiating a "peace" that was little different from what the United States could have achieved four years earlier. For the United States and South Vietnam the additional years of fighting and death bought one moderately important concession: Thieu survived, though the United States compelled him to share power with the PRG.

Four points.

Viewed in its best light, the truce was an unfavorable compromise that left South Vietnam only precariously alive. But that was the best light. Former Secretary of State Rusk, South Vietnam's General Vien, and South Vietnamese Vice President Ky assessed the accords more accurately. They were "in effect a surrender," said the American. General Vien believed "The Paris Agreement was served on South Vietnam like a death warrant." "Sellout" was how Ky described it.[88]

Although the president insisted the war ended with an honorable agreement, he knew otherwise, which is why he mobilized a public relations campaign to obscure reality.[89] Whether he treated the enemy or his ally more shabbily and with greater disdain in the negotiations was a coin toss. But according to Chief of Naval Operations Zumwalt, one thing was certain. Two words that could never be used to describe the outcome of Nixon's two-faced policy were "peace" and "honor." [90]

Only Nixon's intransigence, commitment to Thieu's dictatorship, and dedication to being tough delayed the agreement for so many years.[91]

The day before the cease-fire was signed Lyndon Johnson died in his bed from a heart attack.

Whether General Creighton Abrams perceived the war far differently from Westmoreland and introduced a new strategic approach after replacing him as MACV commander in July 1968 is unclear.

On the one hand, President Johnson urged Abrams to act just like Westy, to make the VC/NVA "feel the weight of everything you've got." In one of the general's first messages to his field commanders he emphasized that "the result I am looking for is a conscious, determined effort by all allied forces to seek battle with a will to win." During his command tenure some of the war's most vigorous operations—such as the Marines Corps' Operation Russell Beach, Major General Julian J. Ewell's frenzied pursuit of bodies (military and civilian), and the assault up Hamburger Hill—were indistinguishable from operations under Westmoreland.

When Abrams received new guidance in July 1969, changing his mission from defeating the enemy to pacification and Vietnamization, he issued no abrupt, new strategic guidance. What made it *seem* like he switched strategy was the war's changing nature as the enemy reverted to guerrilla warfare. Abrams wanted to fight big battles but the VC/NVA would not oblige, leaving him no choice but to resort to small unit patrols and raids. Little evidence indicated a heartfelt preference among his subordinates toward low-level violence instead of large-scale operations and high body counts.[92]

On the other hand, some historians argued that Abrams adopted a "one war" approach that ended Westmoreland's arbitrary dichotomy between the big unit war and pacification. Shortly after assuming command he ordered a Long Range Planning Task Group to study the situation. In a devastating critique of Westy's strategy, it observed that so far U.S. efforts had "made no significant, positive difference to the rural Vietnamese—for there is still no real security in the countryside." The problem was that destroying "NVA and VC units and individuals—that is, the 'kill VC' syndrome—has become an end in itself—an end that at times has become self-defeating." By ignoring pacification the United States allowed the VC to thrive because their goal was "to demonstrate that the Government of Vietnam is *not* capable of providing security to its citizens. And, *they have succeeded*." All the slaughter during Westmoreland's command was futile.[93]

"The enemy's operational pattern," asserted Abrams, who incorporated the Task Group's findings into his 1969 strategic objectives plan, "is his understanding that this is just one, repeat one, war. He knows there's no such thing as a war of big battalions, a war of pacification or a war of territorial security. Friendly forces have got to recognize and understand the one war concept and carry the battle to the enemy, simultaneously, in all areas of the conflict." At various times the MACV commander stressed that population security, not body count, was the true measure of success, firepower restraint must be used in populated areas, and neutralizing the VCI was more important than fighting battles. "It's a new and different war!" exclaimed Colonel Richard Prillaman in February 1969, after two previous tours in Vietnam. Small unit actions replaced battalion- and brigade-strength operations, Americans were working more closely with the Vietnamese, and the joint effort focused "on the enemy among the population rather than the forces hiding in the jungle."[94]

Although the strategic emphasis may have changed, some commanders failed to adapt to a "one-war" perspective. Several years after assuming command Abrams complained that the 4th Division still preferred multibattalion operations, and that U.S. forces relied too heavily on artillery, tactical air, and gunships in the populated lowlands.[95]

In any event Abrams's strategy made no difference. Signs of progress under his command were as illusory as they were under Westmoreland's.

When the United States signed the January 1973 accord, South Vietnam was still fragmented by regional, cultural, ethnic, religious, and political rivalries. Pacification programs had generated little political cohesion and loyalty. With the enemy preempting the issues of nationalism and anticolonialism, no ideology bound the South Vietnamese together. Anti-Communism was widespread, but was not an all-embracing ideology that could compensate for the perception that South Vietnam's leaders were "puppets," holding power only at the whim of a foreign power. "Perhaps the one message that came through repeatedly and insistently was the attitude of the people," observed Lieutenant General Collins. "It could almost be summed up in the words 'they don't care.'" The people did not care who won; they just wanted to be left alone. Their indifference and the flaccid dedication of the South's leadership was "no match for the determination and energy of the vc," whose dedication under the most trying circumstances was admirable. Compared to the vc/nva, the South Vietnamese government lacked "a will and a desire to win." [96]

Considerable evidence supported General Collins's perceptions. For example, when asked what they considered the most important problem facing the country, 52 percent of rural South Vietnamese and 45 percent of urbanites answered "Peace—end the war as soon as possible." Only 13 percent of the former and 11 percent of the latter thought the foremost problem was to "Fight the vc harder." [97]

Pacification generated little genuine enthusiasm for the South Vietnamese government, and what support existed was not principled but fragile and expedient, based primarily on the vc's temporary weakness. The enemy's current gloomy prospects, concluded a 1970 study, did not translate into permanent gains for Thieu's government. "Villagers are readily acknowledging that if the vc came back in force, a recalculation of behavior would be in order. In fact, the Government of Vietnam is surrounded by fair-weather friends." [98]

Most of the factors indicating "progress" in pacification were skewed if not false. "The result is a totally misleading and unbelievably optimistic view of the local elections," said an embassy official, disgusted with the documents being prepared for President Nixon on pacification's status. "This kind of dangerous diplomatic apologetics is what got us into Vietnam, and will one day make Vietnam an American tragedy." [99]

Scores from the Hamlet Evaluation System (hes) showed much of South Vietnam was secure, but deceit was blatant within the program. Many people living in "secure" villages were there only because they were the only places they were safe from American firepower. Moreover, those making the assessments responded to pressure from above to report success, and the military staged elaborate charades for visiting newsmen to convince them conditions in the countryside were improved. A crucial issue was that hes scores measured government military control, at least during daylight, not popular support. With good reason villagers felt less secure than HES ratings indicated.[100]

Although the Chieu Hoi, Phoenix, and Land to the Tiller programs caused the enemy problems, they were far from fatal. Few "ralliers" were important VC; many had been temporarily conscripted for unimportant tasks. Others were diehard VC who carried Chieu Hoi leaflets, pretending to rally if the situation became desperate. Still others considered the program akin to the Americans' R and R, an opportunity to take a brief break from the war, and some were participants in a VC effort to infiltrate the Chieu Hoi Centers.[101] The Phoenix program likewise eliminated few dedicated, high-ranking VC. Because of pressure to fill quotas, officials often apprehended or killed large numbers of those from the lowest ranks. Worse, when combined with poor military intelligence, the quota system often "neutralized" innocent victims.[102] Theoretically the land redistribution program should have generated widespread support for Thieu. But in many areas the program merely sanctioned what the Communists had done in the past, only to have the South Vietnamese government retract the redistribution to reward large landowners. Now the VCI asked why anyone should feel grateful to a thief (the government) who returned stolen property.[103]

The foremost example of South Vietnam's inability to fashion a political community was the 1971 presidential "election." Held in power by American guns and supported only by a wealthy elite, Thieu's government was undemocratic, authoritarian, and thoroughly militarized—as one U.S. officer said, South Vietnam was "not a country with an army but an army with a country." Despite ardent pacification efforts the populace did not embrace Thieu, who was unwilling to risk an honest election. Supported by the U.S. ambassador and the CIA, he rigged it. The Americans tried to make the fraudulent contest look legitimate by offering an opposition candidate a $3 million bribe to remain in the race, but the man had more scruples than that and withdrew. Running uncontested, Thieu garnered 94.3 percent of the votes, helped by the secret police who threatened to arrest citizens if they voted for anyone else and by the failure to provide voting cards in areas where Thieu was especially unpopular. To make doubly sure, province chiefs received orders to do whatever was necessary to ensure Thieu won. "It was a ridiculous election," said his vice president, "just like a communist one."[104]

If pacification's results were at best ambiguous, Vietnamization was also only marginally successful, as demonstrated by the Cambodian invasion, Lam Son 719, and the Easter Offensive. ARVN's problems were endemic: paralyzing immobility and passivity; lack of fighting spirit; disregard for the fundamentals of information security; a corrupt and incompetent officer corps that responded to political maneuvering rather than military professionalism; a promotion system that rewarded staff officers and discriminated against combat commanders; uninspiring leadership at all levels. Between 1968 and 1971 ARVN lost approximately one-third of its strength every year through desertion.[105]

"The fuckers are too corrupt, too lazy, too stratified (classwise), too indifferent, and too blasé to care," railed an American officer. "So we can continue to pour in the dollars and our nation's blood. But it will all go into a bottomless pit that will eat and eat and eat and then finally collapse." Without the profanity but with equal vehemence, Abrams made the same point: The South Vietnamese had "to correct their manpower situation, which is *bad*. And they've got to correct the leadership deficiencies. Those are the two main things. Those things cannot be solved by equipment. No way to solve them with equipment!"[106]

Despite their increased size, the Regional and Popular Forces were no more improved than ARVN. Although they varied tremendously from unit to unit, the overall quality was low. Soldiers in the Territorial Forces not only came from the rural masses, those who were most apathetic toward the war and only wanted peace, but also had relatives and friends among the VC. Political accommodations with the enemy and desertions were common, hard fighting was uncommon. As with ARVN, the Regional and Popular Forces were rarely guilty of excessive enthusiasm.[107] The same could be said of the People's Self Defense Force. "We all agreed," said one youthful member, "that if the V.C. ever come, we are going to throw down our weapons and run."[108]

Official military evaluations often downplayed the weaknesses in South Vietnam's armed forces. In what was a public relations campaign rather than an exercise in military professionalism, positive comments about ARVN and the Territorial Forces gushed forth, convincing the public that Nixon's plan was succeeding, that the United States was withdrawing from the war because Vietnamization would preserve an independent, non-Communist Vietnam.[109]

Since pacification and Vietnamization were, on balance, failures, the vc and vci not only survived the desperate years of 1969–70 when NVA "fillers" were necessary to sustain the revolutionary movement, but also began recovering by 1971–72. Americans misinterpreted the temporary disintegration of 1969–70 as defeat, forgetting that the revolutionary movement had once before all but collapsed but recovered. During Diem's purges in the late 1950s the Communist Party apparatus in the South virtually disappeared, yet, phoenixlike, it arose from the ashes.[110]

Out of the calamity of 1968–69 another phoenix was arising.

Among Vietnam veterans, including many from the 101st Airborne, a common axiom was that "We were winning the war when I left!"

Of course this was a delusion.

At no time between Kennedy's inauguration and the Paris Accords were the United States and South Vietnam winning. At best they maintained a precarious stalemate. Considering the vc/NVA's inexhaustible patience and far greater stake in the conflict, a stalemated war meant they were winning.

Thus, the 101st Airborne had no more substantive impact than a billowy cloud's passing shadow, only momentarily darkening the landscape.

Joe Hooper served in two places, briefly at Cu Chi in Hau Nghia Province, where the 25th Infantry served for much of the war, and in Thua Thien Province, where the 101st Airborne built Camp Eagle near the village of My Thuy Phuong.

In Hau Nghia the NLF was weakened by 1969–70, but the government remained weaker. Whatever "progress" Thieu's regime achieved resulted from force, not freely given loyalty, and the province remained contested, even in areas claimed as progovernment. Not a single government official ever dared sleep outside a barbed wire compound. Civic action programs in which the Americans took such pride were of little appeal to most people since they were incremental rather than distributive. That is, the rich got richer and the poor became less poor, but no revolutionary economic or political change occurred. High-ranking enemy officials rarely rallied and were rarely apprehended, meaning the Chieu Hoi and Phoenix programs had very limited value. The vc's faith in ultimate victory awed American province advisors. "The South Vietnamese were afraid of that tough enemy," concluded one adviser. "They were more afraid of the dedication, persistence, and uncompromising attitude of these people than they were of their numbers. It was just something we couldn't eradicate."[111]

The situation was no different in My Thuy Phuong where, despite the presence of thousands of American soldiers, the population remained disdainful of ARVN and sympathetic toward the NLF. For much of the war only a handful of elite landowners, tradesmen, and civil servants, collectively no more than 5 to 10 percent of the population and representing the same families who had favored the French and then Diem, supported Thieu. These villagers often praised strong leaders, such as Hitler. At least 80 percent of the villagers favored the NLF and the remaining 10 to 15 percent remained neutral. After the VC's losses during Tet, NLF support dropped to roughly 50 percent, but those favoring the government increased to only 10 to 15 percent. Those who temporarily turned from avowed support for the Communists moved into the noncommittal group (35 to 40 percent of the population). As in Hau Nghia, the majority of villagers resented civic action programs, which primarily benefited the wealthy. "How can I remember anything good about the Americans," asked one peasant, "when they did so much bad?" Indicating government weakness and a continuing insurgent presence, the Easter Offensive reinvigorated the revolutionary cause. By 1973–74, 70 percent of the population supported the NLF, 10 percent stood with Thieu's government, and 20 percent remained politically uncommitted.[112]

The long and devastating war, including more than three years of intense pacification, left the political orientation of Hau Nghia Province and My Thuy Phuong village little changed from ten years earlier.[113]

Joe Hooper was not involved in events after April 10, 1971, which was his last day in the field, his last day on a combat front.

Writing Cleo Hogan that day, he explained that "the action has really been [hot?] the last couple weeks and I've really had my hands full keeping my butt down." He soon headed to Australia for a week's R and R. After returning to Saigon, Joe, bedecked in all his medals and flashing an endearing Hooperesque grin, posed for photographer Richard Avedon, who captioned the picture as "Lt. Joe Hooper, the most decorated American soldier in Vietnam, Saigon."[114]

His second tour completed, Joe left Vietnam for the last time.

Now he would have to find a way to live in peace.

Thirteen

Lieutenant Hooper's service and contribution
to the Army and the nation
are deeply appreciated.

*The form letter that Medal of Honor recipient
Joe Hooper received dismissing him from the Army*

The first thing Joe did when he got back from Vietnam was head to the home of Red and Anna Combs. Looking gaunt, stressed, and exhausted, he showed up with a duffel bag and Neeltje Vanderploeg.

The duffel bag contained a copy of the annulment papers with Balbine, Joe's recent Silver Star, a couple of pictures of him and Bob Hope in Vietnam, clothes, and X-rated magazines. According to Red and Anna, Neeltje was his "Dutch girlfriend," who seemed like a surrogate Carollyn. She was not only blonde, busty, and "very nice" but also "had one or two children." Red and Anna did not know where Joe met Neeltje, but "anytime Joe would pop up there'd usually be a girl near, or around. Joe had no trouble having a girl with him." Still, his being with a new woman so quickly after returning to the United States amazed Anna.[1]

For Memorial Day weekend Red, Joe, and Neeltje headed to Las Vegas in Red's 1964 Fleetwood Cadillac. Their partying ended abruptly when they learned that a small plane carrying Audie Murphy had crashed in rugged West Virginia terrain on Friday, May 28.

Forty-six years old, in declining health, his once-boyish face turning tired and puffy, Murphy had fallen on hard times. Hoping to regain financial solvency, he went to Atlanta to meet with investors, and then the group was flying to Martinsburg to visit a company that constructed prefabricated buildings. But the plane never made it. Not until the afternoon of May 31 was the wreckage found; everyone in it was dead.[2]

Joe was crushed by the news, even crying for a few minutes in Red's presence.

"Today we lost a great American and Patriot—May our troops continue to serve God & Country," Joe wrote on the day the search party found Murphy's body.

There was another reason that Joe took the news so hard—he had hoped to enlist Murphy's help in emulating his Hollywood career. Joe was always dismayed that Audie got so much attention and he received so little. Perhaps with Audie's help his time would soon arrive.[3]

Although Joe claimed he and Audie were good friends, they had met only once and that was briefly. However, they were scheduled to participate together in "The Selling of America" on George Putnam's TV show the week after Murphy died. A long-time Los Angeles radio and television personality and superpatriot, Putnam became one of Murphy's close friends and anticipated using Audie and Joe to spread his hyper-Americanism.[4]

Joe undoubtedly expected to capitalize on "The Selling of America" to "Sell Hooper" but now Murphy was dead and that chance, perhaps his last, was gone.

"They thought I could make it in Hollywood," Joe said, lying about his failure to become a movie star, "but I chose not to, at least not at this time."

The truth was, of course, that Joe had no choice in the matter. By the early 1970s the American public had turned against the war. There would be no movie starring Joe or Steve McQueen or anyone else. Joe Hooper would never become the next Audie Murphy, not on the giant screen, anyway.

While Murphy's body was being returned to Los Angeles for a memorial service on June 4 at Forest Lawn Memorial Park in Hollywood Hills, Joe and Red visited Audie's second wife, former stewardess Pamela Archer, and their two sons to pay their respects. More than 600 people attended the service, including six MOH recipients. Red and Anna and Joe and Neeltje were there.

So was Carollyn.

Joe had called her to see if she was going, saying he wanted to talk to her. After the ceremony he ditched Neeltje, found Carollyn, and they arranged to meet nearby. The reunion did not go well because Joe "had been drinking and he was just being real strange. He just seemed really nervous and really uptight." Yet she still loved him and realized the marriage to Denny Haas was a mistake.[5]

Three days later Audie Murphy was buried with full military honors at

Arlington National Cemetery. Six black horses pulling a caisson brought the flag-draped walnut casket to the burial site, already adorned with a presidential wreath of red, white, and blue carnations and another wreath from the 3rd Infantry Division Association shaped like the division's shoulder patch. Those in attendance ranged from General Westmoreland in full dress uniform to Marty Benson, a race horse handler dressed in an orange knit shirt. Benson was a pallbearer, as was 6 foot 7 inch, 270 pound former prize fighter John Toole; horse trainer Harry Benson; Thomas Audie Peaveyhouse, the twenty-one-year-old son of Murphy's frequent movie stand-in; Terry Hunt, the white haired manager of Audie's favorite health club; and Joe Hooper. In the Vietnam War's backlash, even Audie's luster had faded. Of the three major news channels, only ABC covered the funeral.[6]

Eventually Joe created a small shrine in his apartment for Audie replete with a color picture, memorabilia, and candles.[7]

Shortly after the funeral Joe reported as a student to the Infantry Officer Basic Course at Fort Benning, Georgia. According to an officer who attended the course in the early 1970s, the training was tailored more to techniques, tactics, procedures, and equipment instead of teaching men to think and act like officers. The assignment bored Joe since he was being taught things he already knew by instructors who lacked even half his experience. What Joe needed was mentoring on how officers behaved. His academic report did not recommend him as an instructor at the school, rated him average in his ability to express himself, and under "special aptitudes" said "None Noted."[8]

After graduation from Officer Basic Course on August 22, Joe was assigned to Fort Polk. He took a little detour on the trip from Georgia to Louisiana.

He went to California.

Carollyn was working part-time at an advertising agency when she was not acting. While on her way to lunch one day, Joe was waiting outside the building, saying he loved her, that she should not be married to Haas because she still loved him, that he would quit drinking if she came back.

They went to Trancas Beach, one of their favorite seashore haunts, to walk and talk.

Carollyn was emotionally torn. "I wanted to be with him but I didn't want to be with him because I was still afraid of him." She was also married.

But the "wanted to be with him" side prevailed. They had dinner at a rustic bar along the beach, then went to Malibu and spent the night in a bungalow near Paradise Cove. It was just "that connection between the two of us that could never be broken." She was happy that night, guilty about it the next morning—but not all that guilty since Haas was also having an affair during their marriage. She learned about the affair from Joe, who hated Haas and was having one of his detective friends follow him. In any event, her husband was out of town on business so she did not have to explain her absence.[9]

Around Christmas 1971, Carollyn was starring in the popular TV show *The Rookies*. Arriving back at their apartment from the set, she discovered Haas and the furniture were gone. A divorce soon followed. Carollyn did not blame Haas in the least since she "*oozed* with Joe Hooper every day even if I didn't talk about him."

Approximately five months after she and Haas separated, on May 12, 1972, Carollyn gave birth to a daughter, Heather, who later became an actress and expert horsewoman. A publicity photo taken in the mid-1990s revealed a beautiful young woman with red hair and an irresistible smile.

Carollyn saw Joe again in 1975.

She had moved to Irvine, which was then semirural, close to the beach, "and a really nice place to raise kids," and was working a nighttime shift for the MPS at El Toro, the Marine Corps base in southern California. Since she loved the military and always "wanted to be a cop besides being an actress," the job was perfect. She served as a dispatcher and, with the ability to type 120 words a minute, did general office work. This particular evening someone said she had a phone call from the flight tower.

"Hello?"

"Hi Blonde Mama-san. Do you want to see me?"

They went to the officers club for a drink, he asked if she wanted to make love, she said no, and Joe was gone. That was the last time she saw him, though he called occasionally, always at odd hours and usually drunk, asking how she was doing, inquiring about Rolly, and pestering her about whether Heather was his child.

She always said no.

The breakup between Joe and Carollyn was prolonged and painful, much like the way the United States ended its relationship with Vietnam.

Still, Carollyn never regretted meeting Joe because he was "the person I loved most in my life."[10]

The Army had assigned Joe to the U.S. Army Infantry Training Center at Fort Polk, Louisiana, which in many ways was an unhappy experience.

He lived in a trailer park a few miles off post owned by retired Major Kurt Watkins. Joe roomed with Captain Frederick G. "Jerry" Hill, who he had met during his second tour. Jerry was already living in the trailer park when he overheard Watkins mention that Hooper was coming to Fort Polk and needed a place to stay. Having an extra bedroom, Jerry contacted Joe who soon arrived in his maroon Jaguar.

"Joe was a wild one, a work-hard, play-hard type," said Hill who was also a play-hard type. Both drank heavily, hosting drunken parties almost every Friday and Saturday night. Joe always invited enlisted men to join the festivities, and occasionally everyone, male and female, disrobed and painted each other with glow-in-the-dark paint. Watkins did not mind the loud partying, but when everyone washed the paint off by diving into the trailer park swimming pool he became a little aggravated.

Occasionally Joe's alcohol-fueled temper got the better of him at these parties. One time Jerry noticed Joe was missing and found him outside, holding an enlisted man bent over a car hood, the aerial wrapped around the man's neck, choking him. "So I had to knock Joe over the head," said Jerry, "almost knock him out just to get him off the guy." Another time when something—who knew what—provoked his ire he swung the vacuum cleaner wildly until the bag broke, flinging dust and dirt everywhere.

During quiet moments they discussed becoming mercenaries. Jerry declined because he "no longer had a death wish," but instinctively realized that Joe "belonged in a war." To stay tough for a future war Joe suggested they sleep on the floor rather than in their beds. Jerry declined. Then one day his bed disappeared. Rather than get mad at Joe or get tough, he bought a waterbed, which would be harder for his roomie to throw away. Although Joe sometimes slept in a bed, he often took to the floor—and slept soundly in either place, never suffering from nightmares or flashbacks.[11]

Joe was troubled and miserable at Fort Polk but not because of Vietnam memories. Indeed, he looked back on the war with nostalgia. "Jesus! Peace is a fuckin bore," exclaimed Eagan, a character in *The 13th Valley,* John Del

Vecchio's masterful novel about the war in I Corps. In real life Audie Murphy felt the same way, complaining that after World War II his life was a constant struggle "to keep from being bored to death."[12] Those were Joe's sentiments exactly. "The thing that's going to kill me the most," he told Steve Hawk, "is when there's not a war to fight."[13]

Hooper was so enthralled with war that nothing else ever again made him quite as contented. "An Infantryman spends countless weary days in the field," Joe wrote in one of his "Screaming Eagle" columns. "His hours ebb into many days of a continual cycle of torrid sun, driving rains, stinking mud, unrelenting mosquitoes and sleepless nights. His muscles are stretched, his mind made taut, his adolescence becomes manhood and his reflexes are conditioned to become instinctive. With this comes a new respect, the kind of respect men acquire for each other only while under the most critical situations."[14] Misery. Hardship. The indescribable joy of parading one's manhood. The vibrant bond among comrades. How he loved it!

"When you retire from guerrilla fighting it is not something you just walk away from without losing some part of you," Joe commented to Rick Anderson, a Seattle newspaper reporter. "In those days, you lived, almost thrived, on fear. Now there is no fear in my life, and I admit I'm a little flat." Trying to explain why he loved combat, he told another reporter that "In the heat of action, I was pushing all my capabilities to their peak," feeling strong, smart, unbeatable. Noncombat was a "downer" because he was not utilizing his capabilities fully. As a postwar friend discerned, Vietnam was "the place where he performed at his *absolute* highest level, and he knew he was good at it." Now he faced the dismaying prospect of doing things at which, at best, he was second best. Joe also longed for that special bonding combat soldiers shared, which he believed was "about the closest you can ever get to a person." Telling war stories, "recalling battles and tragedies as if they were pages out of a novel," garnered a lot of attention, but tall tales were a poor substitute for real war. So Joe mused about going back to Vietnam for a third tour—or becoming a mercenary.[15]

But he was stuck at Fort Polk. His duties were mundane, the relaxed discipline in the all-volunteer Army appalled him, and he did not like being an officer. After the exhilarating freedom of Vietnam, Joe now discovered that the foremost aspects of his life were forms in triplicate, delays and procrastination, rules and regulations, and more rules and regulations. Loving the hard-drinking, hell-raising, all-male Army of the 1960s, he disliked the all-volunteer force of the early and mid-1970s. He particularly despised having to "mollycoddle" new recruits and complained about the lack of discipline —an ironic complaint for someone so ill-disciplined in his own life. Potential soldiers needed tough training, he believed, testing their limits, preparing them for war's ordeal. But when it became too hot, training was canceled, as if some benign divine force would temper the sun when Americans again went to war.[16]

Being an officer added to Joe's unhappiness, which promotion to First Lieutenant on February 6, 1972, did not alleviate in the least. "Congress gave me this rank, and only Congress can take it away from me," he had told Hawk while he was still a butterbar, "but I'm still a staff sergeant at heart." Always preferring enlisted men to officers, he never stopped being a staff sergeant, which to his way of thinking was better than being a general. "I think it's fair to say," commented Joe's friend and fellow MOH recipient Roger Donlon, "that Joe might not have adjusted to the commissioned ranks as some people would have liked to see. His heart really was being an NCO. Had he had the right mentor and the right commander they could have taken that hard NCO and molded him into a really outstanding commissioned officer." Donlon was correct that Joe was an NCO at heart. Whether he could have been groomed—whether he had any interest in being groomed—as an officer is doubtful.[17]

Joe's disenchantment and heavy drinking manifested themselves in his job performance. Compare his last evaluation from Vietnam with his first from Fort Polk. In Vietnam, Captain Zimmerman praised Hooper's exemplary manner and superb leadership while "under extreme hostile fire," and Lieutenant Colonel Boos wrote that Joe was "a calm, cool officer who accomplished every task assigned in an outstanding manner," and that he "would fight to have LT Hooper in my command." Zimmerman and Boos rated him in the 99th percentile, graded him a "1" in virtually every category on a 1 to 5 scale, and believed he performed his duty better than any other officer they knew.

Those who rated Joe's first year at Fort Polk, where he was as an executive officer in a headquarters command, perceived him differently. One officer put him in the 80th percentile, the other in the 78th; both men gave him "2s" and "3s" on many important categories; and they believed he performed his duty only as well as most officers, which was the fourth best ranking. Joe lacked "the self-discipline and dependability expected of an officer," often being late for duty and needing continuous supervision. Superiors counseled him frequently, not only about his military duties but also his off-post behavior. He was running up debts and his driving was atrocious—the local police cited him twice for speeding and once for careless and reckless driving. A glimmer of hope was that Joe was being transferred "to better exploit his leadership traits." Although still serving as an executive officer, he would be in a training company.[18]

Joe's performance did not improve in his new assignment. One company commander he served under was Captain Bill Parsons, who was six years younger than Joe and served in Vietnam as a helicopter pilot during 1968–69. "If he made it to an appointed place three days out of five," said Parsons, "I considered that punctual for Joe." The problem was alcohol; a lot of people drank a lot, Parsons explained, but "Joe had a tendency to go to extremes." When he was drunk and unable to perform his duties the drill sergeants covered for him because they understood he was really one of them. The "drills" never lied directly to the captain, but they never told the whole truth while keeping Joe out of sight until he sobered up. When Joe was sober Parsons noticed "a certain degree of sadness about the guy," especially when reminiscing about comradeship in Vietnam.[19]

In mid-1973 Joe received a new assignment, this time providing rifle marksmanship instruction to 200 to 250 trainees each week; in late 1973 he became an officer-in-charge of a firing range. Getting out of an office and into the field improved Joe's performance because he had "a unique interest in the instruction of the younger soldier and his genuineness instantly gains and holds the attention of the trainees," inspiring them to do well. Still, with one exception his superiors rated him as "excellent," below the higher rankings of "superior" and "outstanding." In an era when ratings were highly inflated, being excellent was akin to failure.[20]

Not everything at Fort Polk was negative.

Undoubtedly one of his favorite activities was belonging to the Fort Polk Parachute Club, which allowed him to jump frequently, still providing the adrenaline rush that jolted him the first time he leaped from an airplane a decade earlier.[21]

As a hero-celebrity he was in demand for public relations and ceremonial events, which he enjoyed in moderation. As one superior observed, Joe "volunteered much of his spare time to speak to many organizations outside the military," and his professional military bearing was a credit to the Army. Among other public functions he spoke to the Lake Charles Rotary Club, participated in the 1972 Mardi Gras festivities, and attended the Congressional Medal of Honor Society's ceremony at the Waldorf-Astoria Hotel when the Honorable David J. Mahoney, the chairman of the American Revolution Bicentennial Commission, received the Society's Patriots Award.[22] Hooper also traveled to Reardan for Joe Mann Day in October 1972, an event occasioned when Kees Wittebrood presented a miniature pewter replica of the Joe Mann Monument to the town. A member of the Dutch underground in World War II and a postwar journalist, in 1954 Wittebrood wrote a story headlined "We Never Forgot Joe Mann," which inspired the city of Best to honor the American soldier. "Joe Mann Day," wrote Mann's sister Irene, "was a big day in this small town."[23]

When sober, Joe was a good public speaker as demonstrated by a fine speech he delivered to a Boy Scout convention on December 5, 1972. He undoubtedly had help preparing the talk, which revolved around three former Boy Scouts (Eugene Cernan, Ronald Evans, and Harrison Schmitt) who in approximately twenty-four hours would blast off in Apollo 17 on the last lunar landing mission. "In scouting," said Joe, "you often hear the words America and challenge." Thus it seemed appropriate that the crew named its landing craft the Challenger. In closing he praised the leaders and parents who taught and guided Scouts, showed them the moon and stars, and even related "this story of the Boy Scouts who went to the moon."[24]

Another excellent speech followed on May 28, 1973, when Joe spoke in Kinder, Louisiana, at the Memorial Day Dedication for First Lieutenant Douglas Fournet, who received a posthumous MOH in May 1968. "Our country never has in its history been involved in a war as frustrating as the bitter struggle in which we were engaged in Vietnam. No war has ever been fought under more trying circumstances," Joe intoned. "And yet our young men in the field of battle fought with courage and a high morale never before surpassed in the history of this Republic. The chance to serve one's country is a high privilege, not a worrisome sacrifice. I feel quite certain that the gallant man being honored here today never regretted the days he spent in the uniform of the United States." Joe plagiarized these (and other) sentiments in the Memorial Day speech from a speech Audie Murphy gave three years earlier. In another example of "borrowing" from Murphy, Joe uttered these words a week before he died: "All men are born to die, and if one man must go a few turns of the earth sooner than the next, what has he really lost? In life, it seems to me that quality is what counts—not quantity. Who among us, for example, would hang on for a few brief moments longer to leave a worse world behind—or refuse to depart a bit earlier, if he could leave a better world to his children and to posterity?" Originally Murphy's, the comments were no doubt heartfelt by both men.[25]

A highlight of his stay at Fort Polk was when the California legislature passed a resolution honoring him on September 22, 1971. The legislators packed an astounding number of factual errors into their resolution, repeating the myth that Hooper was critically wounded at La Chu and suffered from severe blood loss; saying he served seventeen months in Vietnam during 1968 and 1969 and was "under fire for as long as 129 straight days"; asserting that the March 20, 1968, ambush killed fifteen and wounded 132 Viet Cong; crediting Joe with killing sixteen more Viet Cong during his second tour, "some of them in hand-to-hand combat"; and giving official sanction to the canard that during 1970–71 Joe "never left his division, spending more than 300 of the 365 days under fire."[26]

As with many commentators, the California legislature acclaimed Joe as Vietnam's Audie Murphy, stating that he had "been awarded more decorations for courage, valor, and extraordinary service to his country and the cause of freedom than any other soldier in the Vietnam War."[27]

But what exactly did it mean to be the "most highly decorated" soldier? Exactly which medals counted? Did unit decorations count equally with individual awards? What about medals such as the Distinguished Flying Cross and the Air Medal, when not all combatants (especially infantrymen) were eligible for them? How were multiples of the same medal to be assessed—for instance, did two Silver Stars equal one DSC?

The most intractable problem was that the phrase was contradictory. "Most" referred to quantity (how many medals a soldier received), while "highly" referred to their quality (their relative importance, with the MOH being the most important). Some people tried to devise a formula to blend "most" with "highly" to reveal the soldier who was *the* most highly decorated. One medal aficionado, for example, suggested giving a point value to each medal—ten points for an MOH, nine for a DSC, eight for an SS, two for a PH, and so on. Even the author admitted his system was "not scientific, not definitive, and certainly subject to debate." Sure enough. Another medal buff immediately pointed out that equating five PHs to one MOH was absurd, suggesting that an MOH should be worth 1,000 points. To date, no universally accepted formula has been developed.[28]

MOH recipients Patrick Brady and Roger Donlon and the Department of the Army gave excellent advice when dealing with the "most highly decorated" issue. Be very wary of it, said Brady, because "there's just no way you can measure it." The claim of being the most highly decorated Vietnam soldier, Donlon warned, "is made every day for somebody different." The best that can be said of Hooper (or anyone else) was that he was "*amongst* the most highly decorated." The Army's long-standing policy was not to identify a soldier as the most highly decorated individual from a war because it had "no central source, index, or data base which contains information as to the highest decorated soldier, or information which would permit the comparison of awards of soldiers."[29]

Determining exactly what medals and awards Joe earned was difficult. In an official portrait taken on June 8, 1971, he wore thirty-five awards and decorations, thirty of them individual awards and five unit awards. However, in an official photograph taken on March 7, 1969, he had a United Nations Medal that was absent in the June 1971 photo; either he was not entitled to that medal and wore it erroneously, or he actually had thirty-six awards.

No paper record existed for some of Hooper's medals. For example, a 1989 Department of the Army inquiry that studied his personnel file attributed only one PH (for February 21, 1968) to Joe and no Army Commendation Medals. But in the June 1971 photo he wore a PH with three Oak Leaf Clusters (each OLC was akin to another award of that medal) and an Army Commendation Medal with V device and an OLC. The Army credited him with an Air Medal with two OLCs, but the photograph showed an Air Medal with four OLCs. Joe undoubtedly warranted more than one PH because he was wounded at least twice during late March 1968, though both "wounds were small." When he received the fourth wound is unknown, but medical records after his first tour detailed a gunshot wound on his right flank and shrapnel wounds to his right ankle, right thigh, right forearm, left knee, penis, and nose, so he shed plenty of blood to justify four PHs.[30] As for the Army Commendation Medals and possibly the Air Medals, the difficulty undoubtedly stemmed from impact awards, which officers freely distributed but then often failed to do the appropriate paperwork. (For a list of Joe's medals in June 1971 and the Army's 1989 compilation, see Appendix A.) [31]

Joe talked about his medals with seeming humility. "That's the only thing the medals mean to me," he alleged, "not that I killed but that I saved some of my men." [32]

This was false humility. Hooper liked his medals very much, particularly the MOH, and sought to exploit them to duplicate Audie Murphy's fame.

A stunningly beautiful redhead, her name was Winnie Faye Saint, though no one called her Winnie.

She came from a poor family in rural northern Alabama. During World War II her father deserted the family, leaving his wife with three small children, pregnant, and near destitute. To make ends meet Faye's mother worked in a brickyard six days a week, which left much of the child-rearing to her parents. The Saint kids worked, too, picking cotton, helping in the brickyard, clerking in a drugstore, and doing other odd jobs. "That was the way we were brought up," said Faye. "You worked. And if one job didn't pay the bills you worked two jobs." Money was still tight, but no one felt deprived since almost everyone in the region was poor. [33]

In high school Faye was active in the Future Homemakers of America, Pep Squad, and Glee Club, struggled in class because of dyslexia, displayed artistic talent, developed a rich imagination, and dated the son of a local preacher, William Wayne Guyse whom everybody called Wayne. [34]

Faye married Wayne right out of high school in 1958, though he was a dozen years older than she was. Faye's grandmother pushed her into the marriage, fearing Faye was becoming too wild and insisting that Wayne was "a good catch." "It was a horrible, horrible, *horrible* marriage, and I'm sure it was all my fault," recalled Faye. "I was not a very good wife. I still can't cook. I don't like housework. I don't like any of those things that you're supposed to do to be a good little wife." Wayne was a typical good ol' country boy, said Jack Saint, who considered him more of a brother than a brother-in-law. For several years he did odd jobs before going to welder's school; after that he took a steady job in a shipyard. Wayne also started drinking and became abusive—or at least that is what Faye told her brother, though he cannot verify the abuse. "I saw him drunk. I saw him mad and angry. But I never saw him physically beat her."

Shortly after her marriage, Faye went to Florence State University (now North Alabama), but "of course, I did not do well at all, being dyslexic and free-spirited." Meanwhile, she was displaying her artistic flair locally —"Faye has a lot of talent," according to her brother Jack. So many people complimented her artistic skills that in midsemester she moved to New Orleans with three friends (two girls and a boy). She planned to live in a loft and support herself as a street-corner painter. Discovering that loft living was expensive, the competition was ruthless, and many artists had more talent, she soon returned to Alabama.

Back in her home state, Faye worked at a factory that made undergarments, earning a respectable salary and saving much of it to finance her future aspirations ("I lived very frugally," she said, "and didn't even have a car"). Meanwhile, since she "always liked to fiddle with people's hair," Faye began working in a beauty shop and went to cosmetology school. After getting her license she taught in the school before opening her own beauty shop in Decatur in 1964. By then her career was taking off: modeling, teaching hairstyling, working at hairstyling contests, studying with noted designers, coordinating fashion shows, and continuing her artistic education. Faye received a degree from the Academy of Fine Arts in New York City, taking the first year by correspondence and going to the Big Apple for the second year, and attended a six-week beauty academy in England. She also starred in *Beauty Scope*, a syndicated weekly, half-hour TV program that provided the latest trends in fashions and cosmetics.[35]

Having higher aspirations than Wayne, Faye left him in the late 1960s though they were not divorced until March 15, 1972.[36] She liked attention and being "associated with people who have some type of 'mark' other than being just who they are," said Jack. Wayne was not that way. Faye "always wanted to do something better or bigger," continued her brother, "she's what I would say 'puttin' on airs.'" Because of her "airs" Jack never knew when she was telling the truth. "If the only thing I had to go on was Faye's word, I'd wait and document it and verify it in some other way" because she did not "quite live in a world of reality. She's more of a creative person and dances to a different tune. That's not good and that's not bad. That's just the way it is." Others confirmed that Faye had a Hooper-like capacity for spinning fantasies.[37]

On Saturday, October 23, 1971, Joe was attending a Medal of Honor Society convention in Birmingham.

He didn't have a date for the banquet that night, an unusual and embarrassing state of affairs that might compromise his reputation as a ladykiller. So he told Roger and Norma Donlon he was going shopping for a date at a nearby department store where he would find the prettiest woman at the cosmetics counter and bring her to the banquet. "And we laughed at him," said Norma. "Old crazy Joe Hooper, there he goes, out the door."

Faye was coordinating a department store fashion show for Revlon that day.

Spotting his "prey," Joe resorted to a tactic he had employed in the past. Without even knowing her name he gave Faye yellow roses, and said he was going to marry her. She was so impressed by this outrageously romantic gesture that she agreed to go to the banquet. "Boy, she was a head-turner! What a knockout!" smiled Roger Donlon as he recalled the scene when Joe arrived at the banquet with the statuesque Faye on his arm.

The Donlons believed Faye and Joe made an odd couple. Faye was delightful, "a lovely, typical Southern lady" who, thought Norma, was far too refined for Joe. Although the Donlons did not know it, they were mismatched for another reason: Faye opposed the Vietnam War.[38]

Perhaps in part because he was rebounding from Carollyn, Faye's beauty and charm snared Joe. He remained in Birmingham two more days, then continued the courtship long distance. A few days after leaving Birmingham Joe sent a booklet entitled *Being In Love Is The Nicest Way To Be,* inscribing it "To Love You is heaven—Please lets make it work." Another little book— *I Only Miss You Three Times a Day*—soon followed. "Jumping out of aircraft is not two safe when I have you on my mind—love & miss you so much," Joe wrote on the inside cover. "Love you so, you are all I think of and I dream [of] at nite. You are my destiny and I pray that you will let it be forever."[39]

One Friday night Joe and his roommate Jerry were having drinks when Joe decided they should go see Faye. After a quick call to Decatur, they drove nonstop in Jerry's car to get there. "The unique part," Jerry reminisced, "was that my lights didn't work so we drove from Louisiana to Alabama with no headlights—and not in the best shape, I might add, because of our drinking." Hobnobbing with elite society, Faye took them to a country club party where, unfortunately, Joe became surly after several guests made antiwar comments. Joe and Jerry were in civilian clothes, so other partygoers did not know they were Army officers.[40]

"When I met Joe," Faye recalled, "he wanted to get married, he wanted to settle down, and he wanted a family." Joe was indeed in a hurry to get married. By Christmas they were engaged, and Joe took her to Zillah for the holidays to meet his family.[41] Audrey liked Faye and thought Joe loved her, "but in a different way than he loved Carollyn. I think Carollyn was one of those all-consuming loves that you get."[42]

All-consuming passion or not, out of the blue Red Combs received a call from Joe asking him to come to Las Vegas because he was getting married there.[43]

Joe loved that city for weddings, having married Sandra and Balbine there, and often talking to Carollyn about getting hitched in the desert oasis. "So that's the first time I heard of Faye," Red recalled. Faye and Joe drove from Fort Polk, letting Red know where they were each night and when they expected to reach their destination. As they neared the sinful city, Red caught a flight to Las Vegas, where Joe and Faye picked him up at the airport. According to Red, Faye told him she was pregnant, which, if true, could explain the hasty marriage. Without thinking, Red asked if the baby was Joe's. Eyes flaring, Faye replied, "I ought to slap you," indicating that of course it was. If she was pregnant (she later denied it emphatically, saying "that's the craziest thing I've ever heard of") Faye evidently miscarried because the baby was never born.

After checking into the Stardust Hotel, where Joe exploited his fame to get complimentary rooms, they commenced partying. Faye and Red got along famously, with Red sensing that Faye really did not want to get married in Las Vegas by a justice of the peace. He suggested they get married in his home among friends. Faye loved the idea and Joe acquiesced.

That first night the trio partied until early the next morning. When Red awoke after a few hours sleep and called Joe and Faye's room, Faye answered. Joe was still sleeping off a hangover, so Red and Faye met for breakfast. Although he considered Joe a close friend, Red recognized his character flaws and asked Faye if she was sure about marrying him. "She seemed to be a very nice, well brought up girl. And I was subconsciously, if not consciously, concerned that she was biting off more than she could chew in getting connected with Joe Hooper." Red told her Joe was a "renegade" who marched to such a different drummer that "he was going to be extremely difficult to live with." Faye assured him that she knew Joe well enough despite their brief courtship.

When they linked up with Joe later that morning he was belligerent, demanding to know where they had been. "Joe had apparently imagined that Faye and I had gotten together, maybe in my room," Red recalled sadly. By afternoon the tension subsided, and that evening all of them gathered in Joe and Faye's room before going out. Faye and Red were joking and teasing when Joe's volcanic anger erupted. He slapped Faye, giving her a black eye—just as he had previously hit Sandra, Balbine, and Carollyn. Red told Joe he should be ashamed of himself, that he should beg forgiveness, which he did. But minutes later Joe hit her again. Not physically strong enough to restrain Joe, Red felt the best way of interceding was for him to leave, thus eliminating the cause of Joe's jealousy. Red was soon winging his way back to California, assuming there would be no wedding.

The next morning Joe called. He and Faye were in southern California, staying in a hotel. Red asked to talk to Faye, who said she was fine and still planned on getting married. Later Anna visited Faye at the hotel, noticed the black eye, and like her husband tried to talk Faye out of the marriage. Why did she want to bother with Joe and physical abuse? "She would have to be careful," Anna warned her, "she would have to know not to push his button, so to speak." But Faye was determined.

Soon Joe and Faye moved into Red's and Anna's home, with no settled marriage plan or date. While taking a walk they peered over a hillside, watched a garden wedding down below, and decided on a similar wedding of their own, but still did not set a date. A day or two later Joe appeared on George Putnam's TV show. Anna and Faye were watching the interview when Joe announced he was getting married on Father's Day, Saturday June 18, just three days away. "That was the first time that Faye or any of us knew the date that he was getting married," Anna remembered.

Although in the midst of hectic final preparations for her daughter's wedding the next week, Anna organized the wedding. At least fifty-eight people attended, including George Putnam, Audie Murphy's buddy Perry Pitt, Mark Aubel, Martin and Myrna Barsky—and Neeltje Vanderploeg who helped Faye fix her hair for the ceremony. Faye wore a lovely yellowish Hawaiian floral print summer dress; Joe was in a medal-bedecked full dress blue uniform. Anna served as matron of honor, Putnam gave Faye away, and the Reverend George D. Walters of the Northridge United Methodist Church performed the ceremony in Red's and Anna's back yard, the radiant couple standing under a floral arch as they affirmed their vows.[44]

That night the newlyweds headed to Fort Polk, the drive sufficing for a honeymoon. Aside from car trouble in Texas, the trip was fine, though hardly as exciting as a getaway to some exotic locale. A gracious thank you letter to the Red and Anna soon followed, along with another note from Joe enclosing a check for Reverend Walters, which Joe forgot to give him at the ceremony.[45]

"Oh my Heavens, what have I gotten myself into!" was Faye's reaction to Fort Polk.

She and Joe moved into a trailer, which was "a *tiny* little thing" propped up on rocks and coffee cans. Faye took a job at the PX, which she enjoyed, but she "didn't get along with the other Army wives. I tried not to have any contact with the other wives." For the first time in her life she began cooking, though not well. When the Hoopers invited a few people over for Thanksgiving, Faye unfortunately did not know the giblets were still inside the turkey and the bird never got completely cooked. Joe redeemed the dinner with peanut butter and jelly sandwiches, which the guests ate while sipping wine.[46]

As with almost everyone else who met her then or later, Jerry Hill admired Faye. She was far out of her element at Fort Polk, he said, but "never voiced any unhappiness at being there, or wanting to be back in Alabama." Like a good army wife, she soldiered on. Joe's boyhood pal Tom Johnson considered her "a real basic, nice person." Another acquaintance described Faye as "a very classy lady." "She was a southern lady," recalled MOH recipient Delbert O. Jennings, "and she was extremely patient. She put up with a lot of things."[47]

One thing she did not put up with was going airborne. Faye was venturesome enough to leap from the training tower. "Mom, this is Faye['s] 1st tower Jump," wrote Joe on a photograph he sent Maggie. "Wow is She Beautiful." However Faye was not Carollyn. She went up in an airplane but lacked the nerve to jump. Although Faye did not know of Carollyn's airborne exploits, she knew about the actress and was admittedly jealous. "I didn't like Carollyn because she was so gorgeous. There's not a woman in the world who would like Carollyn. She had long blonde hair and a great big chest." Joe lied about the other significant women in his life, telling Faye that Sandra and her baby both died in childbirth, that he lived with but did not marry Balbine, and that the boy at the MOH ceremony was some anonymous Boy Scout.[48]

Although Faye did not like military life, she enjoyed off-post events that did not require her to interact with other Army wives. She began teaching art lessons, which not only brought in a nice income but also was a lot of fun. For Halloween in 1972 the Army rented a house in nearby Leesville; Faye was in charge of putting on a scary show. More than 2,000 children attended. Dressed like Dracula and popping out of a coffin, Joe scared more than a few of them.[49] In January 1973, the Hoopers attended Nixon's second inauguration, an exciting few days marred only when a lady, obviously unimpressed by the impressive display of medals on his chest, mistook Joe for a hotel bell-hop. "Well, boy, are you going to take my bags up or are you just going to stand there?" Joe took the bags to the woman's room, and gleefully displayed the small tip he received.[50] Joe and Faye had a wonderful week at a 4-h camp during the summer of 1973. Joe gave a speech that received a standing ovation, signed hundreds of autographs, umpired softball games, and along with Faye judged a costume contest and presented awards to the winners.[51]

But life at Fort Polk, pleasant or otherwise, ended in early 1974.

Joe claimed he retired from the active service because he disliked the Volunteer Army's lax discipline, but this was untrue.

The active Army fired First Lieutenant Joe Ronnie Hooper.

Hoping to serve for at least twenty years for retirement purposes, in December 1973, Joe requested that his duty tour be extended for two years until February 5, 1976, which would give him almost twenty years. Fort Polk recommended approval and forwarded the request to the Military Personnel Center (MILPERSON). In a standardized form letter MILPERSON denied the request. "The strength of the Army is being reduced to conform with budgetary restraints and national policy," read the letter. "This action is not to be considered as having any derogatory connotations but rather is a reflection of the required reduction in the Army force structure. Lieutenant Hooper's service and contribution to the Army and the nation are deeply appreciated."[52]

MILPERSON was correct about the budgetary constraints in the post-Vietnam era. However, even an impersonal bureaucracy such as the Army usually granted special consideration to its celebrities. Ordinarily a hero did not receive a form letter saying "Sorry, the Army is down-sizing. Thanks. Good-bye."

The problem, as his sister Audrey understood, was that Joe "was not an officer and he definitely wasn't a gentleman. He couldn't conform to the role they wanted him to play." Her brother "just wasn't a real good guy. He was just wild and crazy."[53] A splendid wartime NCO and small unit officer, no evidence indicated he could adapt to a peacetime regimen as an officer, or that he had much interest in doing so. His excessive drinking and lack of self-discipline both on and off post were an embarrassment. Even with one bad efficiency report an officer was "on shaky ground," noted Cleo Hogan. "Two such reports that are less than glowing, less than maximum, you're gone at this time because the Army was drawing down."[54]

Joe also lacked a college degree at a time when a junior officer's educational level was crucial in determining who the Army kept. While at Fort Polk Joe said he enrolled in three classes at Northwestern State University, but that was an exaggeration. Northwestern State's main campus was in Natchitoches about fifty miles from Fort Polk, but it had a satellite campus at Leesville/Fort Polk where many military personnel took courses. In the fall semester 1972 Joe passed a Speech Discussion course and in the spring semester 1973 he passed a Military History class. Both were potentially important in professional development. Many of his superiors noted Joe's deficiency in oral communication, and officers routinely studied military history looking for "lessons" to guide their future conduct. But two classes were far from adequate; even had he taken three, that was still woefully short of a college degree.[55]

"The Medal of Honor," said a former officer who carefully studied the history of American medals, "can only carry you so far." In Joe's case, not far enough to overcome his limitations.[56]

Effective February 5, 1974, after seventeen years, six months, and four days of military active service, Joe Hooper was a civilian.[57]

Already famous for his best-selling *The Selling of the President, 1968,* Joe McGinniss titled his new book *Heroes.*

One of his subjects was Joe Hooper.

A more appropriate title for the book was *Non-Heroes.*

When the Hoopers left Fort Polk their ultimate destination was the seventeen-acre Hooper family farmstead in Zillah, but they detoured by way of New York City for a month-long vacation. While there they watched heavyweight champion Joe Frazier's rematch with Muhammad Ali.[58] And McGinniss conducted an extended interview with Joe.

For a July 1973 article in *Today's Health,* Dave Wolf interviewed Frazier, Chicago Bears linebacker Dick Butkus, and Hooper, trying to understand the minds of men who annihilated other human beings. "We may shudder at the ease with which these men inflict pain," wrote Wolf, "but their professions—boxing, football, and the military—are among the few areas in our society where varying and considerable degrees of violence are not only sanctioned, but demanded and admired." His interviewees relished their work, felt fulfilled only when engaging in violence, were prepared to endure pain as well as inflict it, and yet were "not insensitive men." [59]

Berry Stainback, the managing editor of the *New Times,* sent McGinniss a copy of Wolf's essay, saying that Hooper might be somebody he wanted to interview for his new book. Although unable to put his finger on a precise Hooper theme, Stainback believed something profound could be said about his future, "something about the American character, the pursuit and achievement of romantic dreams that result in no real hoopla of financial payoff." After achieving "superherodom," Joe was neither Sergeant York nor Audie Murphy and reaped no rewards from his fame. After Hooper's military career ended Stainback wondered what the man did for an encore. "What does he do in real life? And what does whatever he does do to him?" Phrased another way, "What does the early-achieved dream do to the rest-of-the-life dreams?" [60]

McGinniss was searching "for the vanished American hero." The country, he believed, no longer had heroes. No matter how the word was defined, the societal and political upheavals of the 1960s had eliminated heroes as potent cultural symbols. The military, politics, sports, entertainment, the astronauts—he did not expect to find heroes anywhere. [61]

The search fulfilled his expectation.

Democratic politicians George McGovern, Eugene McCarthy, and Ted Kennedy; novelist William Styron and playwright Arthur Miller; General Westmoreland and prisoner-of-war Tim Sullivan who endured five and a half years in captivity; conservative columnist William Buckley and liberal antiwar activist Daniel Berrigan; astronaut and senator John Glenn—not a single hero among them.

MOH recipient Joe Hooper was no hero either.

McGinniss met Joe and Faye on a warm February evening, a light drizzle dampening the sidewalks. They were staying in the McAlpin Hotel, a slightly shabby older establishment near Penn Station. Faye was already walking with a stoop, the result of ankylosis spondylitis, an incurable, degenerative spinal disease that, said McGinniss erroneously, would kill her within three years.[62]

The author took them to the Press Box restaurant for steaks, but Joe and Joe did more drinking than eating, not only at dinner but also in the Hooper's hotel room afterward and for three days and nights after that. "The consumption of alcohol, in fact, had become the apparent purpose of our lives," McGinniss wrote. "We drank through the daytime and we drank through the night, and our illusions grew in wisdom and strength."

Indeed, drinking was central to McGinniss's essay—that and Joe's self-centered attitude. Unlike many other recipients, Hooper was not bashful about letting people know who he was and that he wore an MOH. Joe's old battalion commander, Lieutenant Colonel Livingston, thought many recipients considered the medal an embarrassment because they know "there are other people who are equally deserving."[63] But Joe never suffered embarrassment and loved being the center of attention. So he made sure McGinniss understood he was the Vietnam War's most highly decorated soldier; drank; frequently displayed a wrinkled and stained $12,000 check he carried hidden in his shoe, which was his Army readjustment pay; drank; bragged about the hero's welcome he received when talking to the Boy Scouts or attending a Dodgers game; drank; boasted about the high paying job offers he turned down, including one for $300,000; drank; claimed he declined a starring role in a Hollywood movie because the film was antiwar; drank; gave McGinniss one of his pens with the MOH symbol and a facsimile signature just in case he forgot he was interviewing an MOH recipient; drank.

Amidst this booze-inspired blur, Hooper had a poignant insight. "The thing is, everybody wants me. Everybody wants to say, look, this here is Joe Hooper and we've got him. It gets to be kind of a burden, you know."[64]

Norma Donlon, who as Roger's wife spent a lot of time with MOH recipients, grasped how burdensome the MOH could be. Many of the men she met insisted their wartime exploits were not "nearly as difficult as what they've had to endure since they received the medal. And it's very true. Because it's an every minute of every day responsibility. When you go out you're always on display. People are watching you. You lose your own identity."[65]

After the New York City sojourn the Hoopers traveled west to California before turning north to Zillah.

While in California Joe spent most of his readjustment check on a pickup truck, horse trailer, and two race horses, Karsaii and Really. They drove the horses to the family farm, where Joe's brother Douglas still lived and raised beautiful Appaloosas. Joe and Faye stayed there for a few months, helping the family through an ordeal. Joe's half-sister Frances had brain cancer, which soon killed her.[66]

Comparatively at ease on the farm and passionate about horses and horse racing, a job linking Joe to the outdoors and horses would have been perfect. He often thought along those lines; for example, he told Sergeant Hawk that in retirement he was going to live near Louisville and raise thoroughbreds.[67]

But in a dreadful career choice, Joe went to work as a Veterans Administration contact representative, which is why he and Faye moved to Renton, right outside Seattle. They brought the horses, keeping them in a nearby pasture. Karsaii raced a few times but never won, though he occasionally finished second or third. Really eventually had a colt, Really Wow.[68]

With his shrewd understanding of Joe, Red Combs wrote a letter of recommendation to the VA saying Joe would be a valuable asset, but warning that his "energetic and somewhat independent approach to accomplish a given objective, although successful, will not endear him to the type of Superior who is either insecure or is inflexible in implementing standard operation procedures." With this less-than-enthusiastic recommendation, Joe may have gotten the job only because President Harry S. Truman had ordered that an MOH recipient could be appointed as a contact representative "without regard to the requirements of the Civil Service Rules." Starting at $12,057 a year, Joe gradually ascended the pay scale to $15,037. He was one of eighty-four Vietnam-era vets the Seattle Regional Office employed, representing 26 percent of the work force.[69] At the time Joe was in excellent health; he was a little over six feet tall, weighed 192 pounds, had 20/20 vision, and his hearing was considered normal.[70]

Joe's duties included helping veterans with home loans, education and training, and compensation and pension claims. At one level he was very good at his job because he related to genuine veterans as if they were longtime friends. "Some you feel like a brother to, some you feel like a father to and most you feel like a comrade," he commented. As fellow counselor and Vietnam vet Mike Sallis observed, Joe had a genuine *feeling* for combat vets.

Another coworker and Vietnam vet, Alex Vira considered Joe "our 'faith healer.' He was our 'Rambo' if you will. His presence and his words made us proud, before the memorial in D.C., before the parades, the books and the media hype." On the other hand, as Red Combs learned, Joe despised veterans who had "served a very short time in the military or maybe made an appearance in Vietnam in some rear echelon outfit, and they were full of gripes and complaints. Joe told me he felt like throwing them out the window. Yet he had to be there, and nod, and take notes, and just passively take all the crap they were giving him."[71]

A more severe difficulty was that Joe was no more comfortable in a civilian bureaucracy than he was in the peacetime Army. As the VA's regional director put it, "Joe had problems adapting to the bureaucratic environment" and found office work confining. An example occurred when Gary Foster visited Joe. A vet needed money but his check was not due for several days. Joe could not understand why the VA could not give him an advance, but a female bureaucrat insisted it went against the rules. Angered and disgusted, Joe gave the vet $20 from his own pocket and railed against "the bitch," suggesting that they should "send her ass over to Vietnam to see what it was like."[72]

Since Joe's inability to work within a bureaucracy was self-evident, and his charm, charisma, and celebrity status were invaluable assets, colleagues such as Vira and Larry Frank believed closeting him in an office was a mistake. The VA should have used him for PR duties and not worried about whether he showed up at the office every day or worked forty hours a week. The problem, Vira noted, was the VA "didn't have any kind of position like that. We should have invented one, I suppose."[73]

Instead of inventing a position to exploit Joe's talents, the VA reassigned him to a satellite office at Green River Community College. Because of generous educational benefits, in the 1970s many veterans attended college or vocational training programs. "We're the world's biggest scholarship fund," claimed one VA official. In the mid-1970s, for example, Green River's student body contained about 20 percent veterans, as did nearby Highline Community College. With veterans flooding institutions of higher learning, the VA established a "Vet Rep" program, stationing veterans' representatives on campuses to assist those eligible for benefits.[74]

As the Green River vet rep, Joe spent much of his time at Long Acres

Race Track, which was next to the Renton apartment complex where he and Faye lived. According to Green River's veterans' coordinator, John Arnhold, Joe often worked in the morning, then left for the track. "Of course, we would give him money to bet for us, and he would lose it. He liked racing, but I guess he wasn't too good at picking the horses." Along with horses, Arnhold observed that Joe loved alcohol. The Green River VA staff occasionally had parties during holiday seasons. "There'd be about twenty-five people or so in our little building, and he was the center of attention. He got that rum bottle going. I always thought something was a little amiss in his life, with that alcohol, and in a way I kind of felt sorry for him." In addition Arnhold noticed that Joe "was tinged with a little bit of B.S., and then there was the part about Joe that was real." Differentiating between the two was sometimes difficult.[75]

"What a wonderful, but disturbed fellow," commented Penny Norman, who was in charge of student loans at Green River and saw Joe three or four times a week. Penny liked him, though as a staunch conservative she was offended by his increasingly long hair, which made him look "hippie-ish." She believed a combination of emotional and physical pain fueled his alcohol abuse, and confirmed that he spent many afternoons at Long Acres.[76]

Despite his frequent absences and heavy drinking, Joe did his job. An occasional veteran came in during the afternoon and was aggravated by Joe's absence, but most student activity was in the morning. "So when all the morning work was done, you could sit around and be bored, or go do something," said Arnhold. "And Joe would go to the track." If an afternoon straggler came wandering in, the staff took his name and phone number and gave it to Joe the next morning. Joe also ably performed many social and ceremonial functions, though he considered some of them drudgery. Although not a part of his official duties, he was also an effective Army Reserve recruiter, helping the local unit maintain its strength, which was an important function since the Reserve had a hard time attracting and retaining people in the post-Vietnam malaise.[77]

Like the "drills" at Fort Polk, Arnhold and his staff covered for Joe's shortcomings. "The bottom line was that this was a farm boy who, somehow through the winds of fate, had become famous in his own way," commented Arnhold, "and he was having a tough time dealing with the notoriety." Nonetheless the situation was awkward. "After a while it became, is he here for veterans? What's he doing here?" The VA was in a difficult bind. "How do you discipline one of your most famous employees? They were in a tight pickle with that one."[78]

While Joe's VA career sputtered, far removed from Audie Murphy–like national fame, he remained a local celebrity and was an erratic participant in the Army Reserves. As a celebrity he continued giving speeches and participating in ceremonial events. In 1975, for example, he and Faye attended the Ruidoso Downs Race Track in New Mexico where the tenth race was named in his honor, though the main event was the 18th Annual All-American Futurity, the world's richest horse race at the time.[79]

The Bicentennial was an especially busy year for war heroes such as Hooper. In one of the numerous tributes that honored Vietnam vets, Washington governor Dan Edwards proclaimed April 2 as "Vietnam Era Vets Day," with many local colleges sponsoring programs to honor the vets. A featured speaker at Highline Community College, Joe parroted the military's postwar mythology that blamed the media for everything that went wrong, including the Vietnam veterans' alleged plight. By portraying them as undependable drug abusers the media "destroyed" Vietnam vets, Joe asserted with a dose of bitterness and a hint of self-pity. Now, however, "things are getting better because of the efforts of organizations like the National Alliance for Businessmen and various veterans groups."[80] A month later Joe was at the Bicentennial Patriots Award Dinner at the Century Plaza Hotel in Los Angeles. Sponsored by the Medal of Honor Society and with movie star George Peppard serving as master of ceremonies, the event conferred the Patriots Award on Bob Hope.[81]

In the fall of that year Joe spoke at the dedication of a memorial tree honoring Washington's forty-nine MOH recipients. He worked hard on the speech, writing a long draft incorporating much of what he said at Highland Community College. But the final draft eliminated the carping, plaintive tone that characterized that speech. He began by praising the states' MOH recipients. "A million words cannot describe the bitter hardships, pain, and self-sacrifice that earned these men this award," he said with self-knowing assurance. At the decisive moment, each man performed his duty in freedom's cause. Imploring his audience to emulate the recipients by being responsible citizens, he urged them to reaffirm those American values that seemed forgotten in the previous decade and to embrace freedom and love of country so that the Republic survived another two centuries. "Through faith and courage freedom was won," he concluded. "With faith we can maintain our freedom."[82]

Two weeks later Joe attended another tribute to the state's MOH recipients. The ceremony began in the capitol rotunda where a Marine Color Guard presented the colors and then the audience recited the Pledge of Allegiance, said prayers, sang hymns, and watched a solemn candle-lighting ceremony followed by the haunting sounds of "Taps." Then the throng moved to the State House grounds for music by the 9th Infantry Division Band, a skydiving exhibition, an Air Force and National Guard flyover, a few short speeches, and the unveiling of a granite obelisk monument with the names of all forty-nine recipients chiseled on it. A twenty-one-gun salute and a benediction closed the ceremonies.[83]

Despite numerous Bicentennial celebrity events, Joe's fame was waning. "I've dined with Kings and Queens, met the President, appeared on Johnny Carson and game shows," he lamented to a friend, "but now everything has stopped, and it seems like nobody needs me." Sensing he would never receive the long-term adulation the nation bestowed on York, Murphy, Jimmy Doolittle, and other military heroes, Joe was surprised and disappointed. As columnist Rick Anderson, who spent a lot of time with Joe, summed it up, Vietnam's "most decorated vet was almost instantly our most forgotten." "It's sort of like the war itself, now," Joe told Anderson as he slipped below the public's radar. "So many people wanted to forget it when I was fighting it. Why would they want to remember us now?"[84]

It may be that Joe was always less honored and more used than he understood. His colleague Alex Vira believed "everybody kind of mooched off Joe. Everybody around Joe was always sucking off that charisma from Joe. And if anybody ever offered him a deal, *guaranteed* it's for the benefit of the person who couldn't make it without Joe's prominence or celebrity. It was for their benefit, not Joe's." People basked in his reflected glory, and not just lesser hangers-on; as Vira understood, even Nixon and Bob Hope used Joe for their purposes but never gave anything back to him. "He got used by everybody else," Vira insisted. "What he got out of it was slow suicide."[85] Even Joe eventually understood that Nixon exploited his heroics to maintain support for continuing the war.[86]

Vira himself was not immune from using Joe, admittedly enjoying the reflected warmth when Joe joined his Army Reserve unit. Reserve duty obligated a soldier to spend twenty-four days a year (usually on weekends) in training, as well as to participate in an annual two-week exercise. Upon leaving the active Army Joe joined a U.S. Army Reserve unit in Spokane, undoubtedly assuming he would stay in the Zillah–Yakima–Moses Lake region. But when he went to work for the VA, Joe transferred to a Seattle unit, becoming the Executive Officer for a 12th Special Forces Group company even though he was not Special Forces qualified. He was, however, airborne qualified, and airborne operations were important for Special Forces operations. Shortly after Joe joined the company, seven members (including Joe) were recertified as jumpmasters.[87]

"Joe was much better out in the field than he was in garrison," said his company commander, Captain Peter E. McIntyre, who served with the Special Forces in Vietnam in 1967. If he asked Joe to do a simple administrative task, such as write a letter, he struggled because of his inadequate interest and education. But with a field mission "he'd be great. You couldn't beat him." McIntyre also learned that "In public relations, and if it wasn't too formal, Joe could do fine. But if it was a formal situation, then he was out of his comfort zone." Understanding Joe's weaknesses and strengths, McIntyre "tried to cover for him in the areas where he wasn't as strong, such as the administrative area."[88]

Another member of the company was former Navy corpsman Chris Luther who was a third grade teacher, excelled at long distance running, and held the record for doing jumping jacks in the Guinness Book of Records for 1979 and 1980. "I just loved the guy," he said about Hooper. "He was always extremely patient with soldiers. He was never condescending. He was always helpful, particularly with junior soldiers like myself and people who didn't have combat experience. The guy was very gracious. He made me feel like I had a lot of personal worth and value." Luther also felt sorry for Joe, who "really was trying to be one of the guys" rather than an officer. "I think it's sad. He should have stayed a sergeant." The Army's failure to help Hooper combat his drinking problem was, Luther thought, especially regrettable. Joe had to take some personal responsibility, "but by the same token, people never stepped up to say 'How can I help you?'"

Joe participated in annual two-week exercises in 1974 and 1975. The 1974 exercise staged out of Fort Chaffee, Arkansas, where the unit went into isolation, as Special Forces typically do before a mission. There they received their mission, devised a plan, and then executed it, beginning with an air drop into the desert region around White Sands, New Mexico. The jump did not go smoothly. Carrying a radio, which was a lot of extra weight, a man was badly injured when he inexplicably failed to follow standard procedure by dropping his rucksack on its special dropline approximately fifteen feet above the ground. A medevac flew the man to Fort Bliss for hospitalization.

The mission was to work against an aggressor force—in this case, a National Guard helicopter unit. Easily spotted from the air when moving in the desert during daylight, the Special Forces unit hid during the day and operated at night. Of course, this was not real war. One night the Special Forces men cheated. They slipped into a populated area, ate some decent food, slept in soft beds, then moved back into the desert. Moreover, after the war game's first week the referee told McIntyre that the aggressor force was going home for the weekend. So the referee trucked the Special Forces men to a nearby town where they spent a couple of pleasant nights, especially since the motel rooms were free thanks to Joe's smooth talking. Joe also drank for free after letting people in the bar know he was an MOH recipient.

The 1975 summer exercise was again conducted at White Sands, this time the unit deploying out of nearby El Paso. McIntyre again praised Joe's field skills. "LT Hooper is an experienced field soldier," he wrote, "and his experiences are exceptionally valuable to the detachment members." Joe eagerly shared his knowledge with younger soldiers; remained calm in all situations, providing a sense of stability to those around him; and completed rigorous activities on a tight time schedule.[89]

From February 1975 through January 1976, Captain McIntyre rated Hooper's performance as "Superior," not "Outstanding," and did not recommend accelerated promotion because he was deficient in administrative skills, had a lot to learn about being an officer, remained undereducated, and was unpredictable and undependable. For example, the unit had fifty-six assemblies scheduled during that year but Joe attended only thirty-eight, a terrible record, and never called McIntyre to let him know which ones he was going to miss.

In early 1976 Joe unexpectedly transferred to Captain Alexander Vira's company in the 104th Division (Training) because it was going to Fort Polk to run a basic training company for two weeks.[90] Should the Reserve unit ever be activated its mission was to conduct training, so this was a valuable exercise. About a month before the unit departed Vira half-jokingly asked Joe if he wanted to go. To his surprise, he said yes. When they arrived at the post the high command treated Joe like a pariah. Joe "was not regarded with favor on arriving at Fort Polk," which disappointed Vira because he was pleased with himself for bringing along a hero. Although none of the brass wanted anything to do with Joe, the trainees did. How they learned Joe was there was a mystery, but as they left the PX "we sort of got ambushed by a gaggle of about twenty or thirty of them," each holding a pamphlet about famous people from the 101st Airborne, including Joe, who graciously signed autographs and talked informally with the men.

During the day Joe was at the firing range, doing his duty. At one point he gave the trainees a pep talk about never giving up no matter how tough the situation became. The message captured their respectful attention, and his speaking ability in an informal setting impressed Vira. "I'm a very skeptical, cynical individual," he said, "but when I heard Joe speak I got goose bumps." At night Joe went drinking, though he never became fall-down drunk. Everyone in all the bars knew Joe and wanted to be his buddy.

Upon returning to Seattle, Vira realized the sole reason Joe joined his unit was to get to Fort Polk, which was disappointing since he wanted to sponge off Joe's image. He hoped the MOH recipient's luster would reflect favorably on the unit, entice volunteers to join, and sustain morale. "A guy like Joe would have had us swimming in volunteers," he mused. But Joe participated in no other company activities. For the rating period from January to August 1976, he attended nineteen of the thirty-two scheduled assemblies, and all were from the Fort Polk exercise: one for the day he signed up, one for each of the ten weekdays, and eight for the two weekends (each weekend day counted as two). Vira rated him "Superior" based on his work at Fort Polk, which was not a good ranking. "If you were an officer and your score wasn't in the 'Outstanding' range," wrote Vira, "you were a screw up."[91]

In the way of large bureaucracies, the Army promoted Joe despite his lackluster performance. Effective March 30, 1977, he was Captain Hooper.

Eighteen months later the Army discharged Captain Hooper because of his nonparticipation in Reserve activities.[92]

South Vietnam's collapse came with stunning swiftness, like a tree with shallow roots victimized by a sudden gust.

Because the Paris Accords did not solve the fundamental issue of South Vietnam's right to exist, Vietnam had no peace and Nixon and Kissinger achieved no decent interval. What Nixinger considered peace with honor was a thinly disguised defeat for the United States, quickly followed by South Vietnam's extinction.

The lone beneficiary of the January agreement was the United States, which grabbed its prisoners and withdrew from the war, allowing the Vietnamese civil war to continue without a foreign presence. For the other participants the accord was a sham peace that both sides shamelessly violated before the ink on the signatures dried. President Thieu stood stolidly behind his "Four No's," which were incompatible with the peace accord. Reassured by Linebacker I and II and by Nixon's promises, but fearful that the Americans might not support him forever, Thieu ordered his troops to reclaim as much territory as quickly as possible. The campaign reclaimed many of the areas "liberated" during the Easter Offensive, but by late 1974 ARVN was stretched thinly, a dangerous situation because, as always, the enemy could still choose the time and place to respond. Moreover, the VC/NVA yielded no territory without requiring a substantial sanguinary payment. ARVN's losses were high—25,473 KIA in 1973 and another 19,375 in the first eight months of 1974.[93]

"When we chased the American troops out," observed PAVN General Van Tien Dung, who was Giap's successor as chief of staff, "it finally created conditions for us to topple the puppets."[94] Confident of ultimate victory, the VC/NVA gradually escalated the violence, moving cautiously to avoid provoking another Linebacker campaign and buying time to rebuild their forces. Thanks to Soviet generosity in supplying new materiel, PAVN quickly recovered from the Easter Offensive. Even as ARVN temporarily reclaimed territory in the South, the American Defense Attaché Office in Saigon realized that "Hanoi had developed its strongest military position in the history of the war." Unhampered by U.S. aerial assault, it built better roads, constructed longer pipelines, and stockpiled more tanks and artillery. In I Corps PAVN began hammering the 1st ARVN Division, almost universally considered by Americans as Vietnam's best; by late 1974 U.S. analysts feared it could no longer withstand a major enemy assault. During 1974 the Communists also ousted the South Vietnamese from much of the land acquired in their immediate post-peace land grab. By late 1974, with desertions running about 24,000 per *month*, ARVN was dispirited and disintegrating.[95]

Increasingly confident that the United States was never returning to the war despite Nixon's promises (especially after he resigned in August 1974 because of criminal misdeeds during the Watergate scandal), encouraged by cuts in American economic aid that devastated the South's economy, and watching the popular unrest in South Vietnam against Thieu's dictatorship become more seething and widespread, North Vietnam adopted a two-year plan to unify the nation. It would begin with a series of offensives in the 1974–75 dry season to create favorable conditions for a decisive General Offensive–General Uprising in 1976. A few North Vietnamese leaders optimistically predicted the end might come more quickly.[96]

For once the optimists were correct. In mid-December, General Dung ordered COSVN's General Tran Van Tra to test American resolve and South Vietnam's capabilities by attacking Phuoc Long Province to the northwest of Saigon. The United States and South Vietnam failed the test. It took Tra's forces only three weeks to capture the province. Despite this blatant violation of the Paris Accords, the United States did not respond, and ARVN's defense had been inept.

Convinced that President Gerald R. Ford, Nixon's successor, was determined to steer clear of Vietnam no matter how severe the provocation, the Communist high command ordered an offensive in the Central Highlands, which commenced on March 10, 1975, with a five division assault on Ban Me Thout, the capital of Darlac Province. Although some ARVN defenders fought valiantly, Ban Me Thout was in Communist hands within a week. Since no substantial ARVN force now stood between PAVN and the sea, the enemy was poised to bisect South Vietnam.

Thieu made the task easier. Without any advance planning or warning, he suddenly ordered the remaining forces in the Central Highlands to retreat and establish a defensive line stretching from Tuy Hoa on the coast to the Cambodian border, in essence conceding the northern half of South Vietnam to the VC/NVA. Having no plans for a withdrawal, ARVN's retreat turned into a rout.

Meanwhile, in I Corps, where General Dung unleashed another five-division assault, a similar debacle occurred. Despite a few pockets of resistance, ARVN disintegrated. On March 26 the VC/NVA captured Hue—for good this time. Four days later they walked into Da Nang unopposed. The last flight from its airport, a World Airways 727, was emblematic of the disaster in I Corps as frightened soldiers from the 1st Division trampled women and children, some of them members of their own families, to get aboard. The overloaded plane took off only after soldiers who were angry at not getting on board fired shots and hurled grenades at it, damaging the left wing flaps. Some panic-crazed soldiers clung to the wheel wells and undercarriage as the airliner lifted off.[97]

Surprised but immensely pleased by the unexpected ease of its successes, the Politburo ordered General Dung to discard the two-year plan and complete the destruction during the current dry season. As Dung's forces plunged southward, ARVN was "losing the war faster than the Communists could win it," retreating so rapidly that no matter how fast the NVA moved they could not keep contact with their fleeing adversary.[98]

Suitably, the Communists high command named their final offensive, the one that completed the thirty-year struggle for independence and unification, the Ho Chi Minh Campaign. By mid-April Communist forces were rapidly approaching Saigon. Only a ferocious week-long stand by the 18th ARVN Division against four NVA divisions at Xuan Loc, a strategic crossroads astride Route 1, appreciably delayed them. After pausing for several days to let Americans and those Vietnamese who worked for the United States evacuate the city, the assault on South Vietnam's capital began. The Vietnam War's last battle started at 4:00 a.m. on April 29 when enemy rockets blasted Tan Son Nhut air base, MACV's former headquarters. One rocket hit the American Defense Attaché Office, killing two Marine guards, Lance Corporal Darwin Judge and Captain Charles McMahon Jr., the war's last two American deaths.[99] The next day South Vietnam unconditionally surrendered.

In the final campaigns the VC, who American military leaders insisted were destroyed during Tet and its aftermath, played a vital role. In January 1973, I Corps, where the fighting was always predominately a conventional war, contained 87,000 North Vietnamese and 9,000 VC combat, service, and administrative troops, but in IV Corps there were only 17,000 NVA and 23,000 VC; II and III Corps fell between these extremes. All told, 157,000 NVA and 62,000 VC troops were inside South Vietnam at the time of the Paris Accords, and the VC revived considerably after that. With good reason General Dung praised the local forces for their contributions in the final campaigns.[100]

President Thieu resigned on April 21 and fled the country. Unable to comprehend that the United States could invest so much effort, money, and blood in preserving his regime and then just abandon it, until the bitter end Thieu and other South Vietnamese leaders hoped the Americans would fulfill Nixon's promise and rescue him. But the promise was hollow from the start. As General Davidson observed, "In light of the prevailing opinions in Congress, the news media, and the country at large, Nixon must have known this was a fragile commitment indeed." On the day the combatants signed the Paris Accords a Gallup poll asked, "If North Vietnam does try to take over South Vietnam again, do you think the United States should bomb North Vietnam or not?" Only 17 percent said yes, 71 percent said no, and 12 percent had no opinion. Reflecting that overwhelming sentiment, in June 1973, Congress passed, and Nixon signed, a law prohibiting any direct or indirect combat activities over, on, or near Cambodia, Laos, and Vietnam, thus rendering any promise of continued support moot.[101]

In succession the VC/NVA had defeated America's special war, limited war, and Vietnamization/pacification strategies, and then forced South Vietnam's puppet dictator to flee for his life.

The Ho Chi Minh Campaign came on the heels of an unconventional, protracted conflict in which the enemy eroded the will and ability of their anti-Communist opponents, both American and South Vietnamese, to continue resisting. Consequently the Communists' final offensive was less a conventional coup de main than the coup de grace of a successful people's war.[102]

The scene in Fraunces Tavern in New York City on December 4, 1783, was suffused with emotion.

General George Washington was saying goodbye to a small group of his Continental Army officers. Each of these hard-bitten revolutionaries, their eyes momentarily daubed with tears, embraced their commander in a final farewell fraught with the special affection that developed among soldiers who prevailed against seemingly impossible odds.

For nearly a decade they waged a war of national liberation against England, the earth's greatest military power. Usually outnumbered, always short of supplies and weapons, oft-defeated in battle, and sometimes on the verge of collapse and defeat—how did they do it?

Even General Washington was not sure.

What he did know was that when later generations of historians described their victory, "it is more than probable that Posterity will bestow on their labors the epithet and marks of fiction: for it will not be believed that such a force as Great Britain has employed for eight years in this Country could be baffled in their plan of Subjugating it by numbers infinitely less, composed of Men sometimes half starved; always in Rags, without pay, and experiencing every species of distress which human nature is capable of undergoing."[103]

Two hundred and two years later, General Dung felt the same sense of astonishment and awe.

When word reached his headquarters that Saigon had surrendered, he and his staff, all hardened revolutionaries, shouted with glee, embraced each other, and became choked with emotion during "an indescribably joyous scene." Considering "the gigantic forces the enemy had mobilized" and "the extreme difficulties and complexities which our revolutionary sampan had had to pass through," they looked on their victory with profound wonderment. "This historic and sacred, intoxicating and completely satisfying moment was one that comes once in a generation, once in many generations," Dung wrote. "Our generation had known many victorious mornings, but there had been no morning so fresh and beautiful, so radiant, so clear and cool, so sweet-scented as this morning of total victory, a morning which made babes older than their years and made old men young again."[104]

Not all of them, and certainly not Joe Hooper.

"Mike, son-of-a-bitch," Joe said to his VA buddy Mike Sallis. "What was it all for, man?"

They were in a bar in late April 1975, eating sandwiches, swilling beer, and watching South Vietnam's death throes.

The pictures of Communist tanks rolling into Saigon precipitated an emotional upheaval. Three years previously Joe was certain the United States had stopped the Communists and protected South Vietnam's freedom.[105] Now, no matter what fictions the president had spewed about peace with honor, he and Mike knew the United States lost the war. Joe's immediate response was to rant and rave, insisting he was going to put all of his and Mike's medals in a shoebox "and mail it to the President and tell him to kiss our ass, we don't want them." Leaving the bar, they went to the VFW post in Renton and got thoroughly plastered, which helped them through the initial shock of defeat.[106]

All those lives, those broken bodies, Joe moaned. Wasted. Not a damned thing to show for a decade of effort. Defeat, he told a reporter, "made a mockery of the sacrifices of the American men who died fighting in Southeast Asia." [107]

Reflecting the blind Cold War ideology of his youth, Joe considered the Vietnam War a righteous cause. "I felt the Communists were oppressors, that it was right for the U.S. to aid South Vietnam," he stressed in 1973. "I think of myself as a professional. But the money isn't important. If there had been no pay, I'd still have been there." The Vietnamese people, he professed, wanted and needed U.S. help. But by late spring 1974 every inch of ground the Delta Raiders and Hard Luck Alpha fought over was in enemy hands, and he correctly predicted a complete Communist victory "as long as they are allowed to bring in equipment and arms." [108]

Embracing the Army's scapegoating then in full-throated roar, Joe blamed the war's politically imposed restrictions for defeat, not the military's inept strategy. He did wonder why the Army insisted on fighting a big unit war and on taking and retaking the same hills, but never pondered the implications of those questions. [109]

Instead he vented his ire on politicians. Sharing the military's erroneous assumption that bombing Hanoi and Haiphong into rubble in the 1960s and crossing the borders equaled victory, he gave no thought to the prospect that such actions might have resulted in a wider, larger, and more difficult war that endangered, not enhanced, America's security. Leave the war to the military and "we could be out of there in a week," he thought, never contemplating that leaving the war to the military might mean fighting Chinese or Soviet "volunteers" the next week. Like the Army, Joe's mantra was "we weren't allowed to win," and he was bitter about what he perceived as the government's "non-win policy." Accepting illusory progress reports about Vietnamization and pacification as gospel, Joe insisted the United States "left a year and a half too soon. The South Vietnamese were just gettin' good. I'm convinced they could have held their ground if we'd stuck around long enough to show them how." Sucked in by the deceits perpetrated by Nixon and Kissinger, he blamed Congress for South Vietnam's final crisis because it "tied the President's hands" by not authorizing more money and equipment, as if a few more dollars and bullets would magically foment an ardent nationalism and fighting spirit that had been absent for twenty years. [110]

Joe had long favored a lenient amnesty program for those who fled to

Canada to avoid the draft, but in the aftermath of defeat he went much further. "I'm a firm believer that every man should serve his country," he told a New Orleans reporter in 1972. "But they should let them come back to the U.S. and they should be punished, however, the punishment should be the lightest possible." After the Communists' victory, when asked if he would do it all over again, Joe said yes. He thought his skills helped save American lives —and of course he loved war. "But I would tell my children, if I were to do this over, go to Canada, don't fight. Don't fight a war you can't win. I would go back to help keep men alive, but I would tell my kids, it wouldn't make any sense. Run away, stay alive, that makes sense." [111]

Stunned by South Vietnam's collapse, Joe regretted the war ever happened. [112]

Joe and Faye had a daughter, Joey, a beautiful red-haired baby, born on January 13, 1976.

Faye never intended to have children because "there were too many things I wanted to do." While in Seattle she continued giving private art lessons and also worked for a design company in nearby Aurora, decorating or redecorating private homes, offices, and hotels, all of which she greatly enjoyed. [113]

But the best of intentions often go awry.

Had the child been a boy, he would have been John Donlon Hooper, John for Joe's father and Donlon for MOH recipient Roger Donlon. [114]

Holding a widely shared opinion, Penny Norman at Green River Community College considered Joey "the cutest girl you ever saw," and everyone agreed Joe loved the girl, taking her to work on occasions, cradling her in his arms at social functions, changing diapers and feeding her bottles, always fawning over the baby. If he went on a trip he sent "Caressables" cards, often adding his own decorative sketches of turtles, horses, and their dog Crickett. "We love & miss you," he scribbled on one of them. "Daddy, Crickett & Horsey." When people complimented Faye on having such a well-behaved child she explained that she "was not such a good mother. Joe was such a good father." "He was such a proud father," raved Anna Combs. "Talk about a trophy! He was just so proud of that little one, and showing her off." [115]

If warmth suffused the relationship between Joe and Joey, the relationship between Joe and Faye was another matter. According to Faye, Joe tempered his drinking and they had a loving, often idyllic marriage. Those who saw them intermittently, at times when Joe may have been on his best be-havior, thought Faye had a calming effect on him. Roger and Norma Don-lon believed Faye had "tamed" him, but they saw the Hoopers only at oc-casional MOH Society events. Arlene Foster, Gary's wife, was convinced that Faye "kind of tied him down and straightened him up," but the Fosters saw the Hoopers even less frequently than the Donlons. "He is a pleasant, coop-erative, intelligent, well educated man who's well oriented. No problems," read a medical examination report about Joe in May 1975, written by an individual who saw him for perhaps an hour when Joe was obviously pro-jecting his positive, likable side.[116]

But neither war, chronological maturity, marriage, nor fatherhood fun-damentally changed Joe, who was neither well oriented nor problem free. "No. Not a lot," said his sister Audrey when asked if Joe underwent a post-marriage metamorphosis. "Other than they had Joey and he was really into Joey. But as far as changing his drinking and all that stuff, he didn't change that." After spending many evenings drinking with Joe, fellow VA employee Larry Frank insisted, "There's no way he was changing his lifestyle for his baby, his wife, his friends, his job, any of them. He did what he wanted to do. That was one thing about Joe. He lived *exactly* the way he wanted to live. He wanted to drink, he wanted to run around, he wanted to gamble, he wanted to party, and he did. You don't tell Joe how to run his life, or do anything." Trying to keep up with Joe's excessive lifestyle left Frank burned out.[117]

Joe remained a man of extremes, a chameleon—wonderful yet dis-turbed, as Penny Norman put it, or a man with "two distinct sides," as an-other acquaintance phrased it. When acting wonderfully, Joe had a charis-matic magnetism that attracted people, but often his behavior was troubled, boisterous, obnoxious. World War II MOH recipient Donald Ross, who in-terviewed Hooper for a book about Washington's MOH recipients, saw the troubled Joe, one who "was on the verge of having some real serious prob-lems. We worked to keep him from falling apart. . . . He was a wild man."[118]

It may be that in Joe's mind the belief that he would not live long excused his aberrant behavior. "He didn't seem concerned about anything in the future," observed Floyd N. Greenwald who met Joe through the Reserves. "He didn't have any feeling toward the future at all. He *knew* he wasn't going to be around to collect any retirement." Having seen so many people die, Joe wanted "to max out every damn day," commented Alex Vira.[119]

Showing signs of immaturity, Joe often acted like a "spoiled brat" and always wanted to dominate a scene. For example, before the 1976 Patriots Award ceremony Joe threw a temper tantrum when he discovered the bow tie for his tux was missing. Witnessing the tirade, Anna Combs felt like shaking Joe and telling him to behave. "He had to be the center of attention, no matter how childish," said fellow Washington MOH recipient Delbert O. Jennings, who considered Joe "an extremely arrogant son-of-a-bitch." Hooper went to "ridiculous extremes to get that attention," including spinning certifiably false stories. His childhood friend Rusty Cutlip listened, enraptured, as Joe explained how "he was actually the man who captured Che Guevara, who was Castro's right hand man." Perhaps Cutlip believed Joe, but Jennings took his measure: "He was his own best press spokesman, and most of it was bullshit as far as I was concerned." [120]

In Joe's juvenile efforts to steal the limelight, he usually made a fool of himself, or at least so Jennings believed. But Joe could only make a fool of himself in the eyes of others, not his own. "Absolutely you could not embarrass him at all," commented Faye. "He would do absolutely anything." [121]

Alcohol and women were important aspects of Joe's wild craving for attention. He frequently enjoyed doing "some serious, get-down, get-drunk, get-loaded drinking," said Mike Sallis. "No matter how much he drank," recalled Vira, "he was just *thirsty*." Because of his celebrity-hero status, people thought they were doing their patriotic duty buying him a drink, and then another, and another. Although not a viciously mean drunk, Joe became loud and boisterous, perhaps a touch ornery. "If you caught him at a sober moment," Norma Donlon said, "he was just a pussycat, he was just a dear, sweet person." Unfortunately those sober moments were rare, and the outlandish things he did under alcohol's influence amazed her. Sometimes drinking until he could not walk out of a bar without help, he then drove home, putting himself and innocents at risk. Audrey Hooper and Rick Anderson were certain Joe was an alcoholic. "The first time I saw him he had a drink in his hand," said Anderson, "and the last time I saw him he had a drink in his hand." The only time he saw Joe without a drink was the one time he brought Joey to Anderson's office. [122]

To put Joe's drinking in context, alcoholism was a military-wide problem. "In the military," wrote one officer, "drinking fell into the same category as pussy: the more you could put away, the more macho you were among your buddies. The only problem was that the line between being a stud and an alcoholic was a fine one, and once crossed was really hard to reverse." [123] Joe never shifted into reverse.

As with his drinking, Joe never stopped womanizing. With his million-dollar smile and "rather amorous" ways, he rarely chased women because they chased him first. "Women chased him all the time," said Faye. "Even after we got married women called him all the time." Red Combs, who recounted one of Joe's frequent one night stands, "never saw Joe ever make an approach toward someone. He just happened to be there, and if they were there, and Joe was interested, well, things just seemed to happen." Mike Sallis realized Joe "never thought for a minute that there was a woman out there that didn't like him, including my wife," whom he tried to seduce, an event Mike did not learn about until after Joe died. [124]

Sallis knew Joe had a few one night stands plus a long-standing affair with a woman who "was not one of your bar girls. She had a lot of sophistication." VA coworker Larry Frank knew of a different more-or-less regular girl friend. According to Alex Vira, Joe spent one night at Fort Polk in a woman's apartment. When Faye, Joey, and Joe traveled to Moses Lake for a class reunion in 1977, Joe hooked up with a married woman. [125] One final example. When the Hoopers moved to Seattle, Joe (but not Faye) began partying with Rusty Cutlip and his wife and some other Moses Lake chums. As the incident with Mike Sallis's wife demonstrated, Joe felt no compunction about hustling the wives of friends. One time when he and Cutlip's wife were momentarily alone, he tried to kiss and fondle her. She told her husband but, said Rusty, "it wasn't like I was going to go try to kick his ass." Instead, he "accidentally" banged Joe with a car door, an effective but hardly gallant way of getting even. [126]

Joe's wildness, drinking, and womanizing threatened his marriage to Faye, who worked as an interior designer not only for hotels in Seattle and San Francisco but also for individuals. According to Joe's sister Kathryn, who witnessed some of the marital discord, Faye was "her own boss," "kind of headstrong," and "didn't put up with any of my brother's crap." Audrey Hooper concurred that Joe and Faye "had a lot of conflict. They had some real battles. I don't know about physical battles, but I know they had some real arguments." Both sisters heard divorce talk. [127]

According to some sources, the conflict became physical at least twice, though Faye denied that either of the incidents ever occurred. Supposedly, one time Faye came to a bar to pick Joe up, he wanted to drive home, and she said no. Enraged, Joe grabbed her shoulders and banged her head against the car window, leaving flecks of blood. Although details about another incident differed according to who related the story, during a bitter argument Faye shot at Joe, the bullet grazing his skull before entering the ceiling. Faye had long been comfortable around guns—"I have always liked shooting guns," she said, adding that she was a pretty good shot. When Joe first met Faye she was traveling a lot and often worked late at night and then went home alone. She had a little pearl-handled derringer for protection, but when Joe saw it he said, "You don't have a gun. What you have is a toy. If you happen to shoot somebody with it, it would make them angry and they'd take it away from you and probably beat your brains out." So he went to a gun shop and upgraded her firepower, but she lost the new gun. Joe replaced it with a .45 Colt, which she still had thirty years later.[128] Perhaps that was the gun she used when she shot at her husband.

Joe told Audrey, Maggie, Anna, and Mike Sallis (who saw the bullet hole in the ceiling) about the shooting incident; if Joe's account was the only source the story could be dismissed as a fabrication. But Red Combs said that Faye, not Joe, told him about the shooting.[129]

What kept the Hoopers together? Love was one explanation. Despite their difficulties, Red Combs had "no doubt that they loved each other. Just that at times certain things would occur that his button would be pushed." Joe's genuine concern to find medical help for Faye's worsening spinal condition impressed both Red and Anna. Extramarital sex for Joe, Sallis claimed, "was not for intimacy but for release"; for intimacy he relied on Faye, whom he loved. Kathryn thought Joey was crucial in maintaining the marriage because "she was my brother's pride and joy." While not disagreeing, Alex Vira believed Faye reveled in Joe's fame to such an extent that she "would have put up with anything. And she did." Faye's brother Jack concurred, pointing out that Faye "was involved with Medal of Honor activities as much or more so than Joe," and that they "meant more to her than to him in terms of the hoopla around the thing." A final explanation was Faye's stoicism in enduring Joe's antics, a trait both Vira and Larry Frank admired.[130]

His marriage on tenuous ground, Joe was out of the active Army, out of the Reserves, out of the military, and as of February 1, 1977, when he resigned, out of the VA.[131]

But he had a plan.

Fourteen

He wanted to live on this little piece of land
and raise horses, and that was
perfectly all right with me.

Faye Hooper, summing up Joe's postwar ambitions

Seeking an escape from four walls, bureaucracy, and suffocating rules, and to find redemption, Joe Hooper moved his family to Claremore, Oklahoma.

Some of Joe's friends believed that VA administrators hounded him into resigning. "Joe was driven out of his job," said Larry Frank, who worked with him in Seattle. "He was harassed." He drank hard, too hard, but "that's exactly what the VA is there for, people with problems like Joe's. They handled it by getting rid of him." Nobody at the VA tried to understand or help Joe, complained Mike Sallis. The higher administration was only interested in harassing him "with Gestapo-like tactics" until he quit.[1]

The truth was that Joe, bored, miserable, and restless, left the VA without being harassed into resigning. When asked which job he least liked and why, his answer was, "VA-counselor—inside & regimentation." And when asked what job he most liked, he responded, "Army—outdoors adventure."[2]

In a quest to get outdoors and turn his life around, Joe entered the Horse Management Program at Claremore Junior College (now Rogers State University, named after Will Rogers who was born near Claremore) in June 1978. He had also investigated the University of Arizona's Race Track Management major, but decided on Claremore, which required only two years rather than four years to get a degree. He intended to become a horse breeder and trainer, with an expected graduation date of July 1980.[3]

By the time Joe and Faye arrived in Claremore, many of the *myths* that encrusted and shrouded the Vietnam conflict were well on their way to being solidified, despite all the evidence to the contrary.

In a sense, societal memory was creative, acting like individual memory, selecting and distorting what it remembered to serve current needs and interests.[4]

Myth: Vietnam Was a Noble Cause

The war's rehabilitation began less than a month after Joe died when on May 28, 1979, President Jimmy Carter announced the start of the first Vietnam Veterans Week, but dramatically intensified the next year when Republican candidate Ronald Reagan, notable for his rich imagination (as befitting a Hollywood actor) and easy dismissal of inconvenient facts, declared that Vietnam "was, in truth, a noble cause," thus igniting a full-fledged national flight from reality.[5]

Instead of being noble, American policy was a hostage to an unquestioning anti-Communist ideology, a flawed domino theory, and presidential machismo, which often confused political expediency with national security. Ironically, the nation expended tens of thousands of lives and $150 billion in the name of freedom to sustain an unpopular, repressive regime.

Long before the war ended many individuals, both inside and outside the government and the armed forces, understood that the United States could live peacefully with the Soviet Union and China and that a victory by the Vietnamese revolutionaries would not precipitate a long row of toppling dominos. "The whole thing was a lie," said Sergeant Donald Duncan of the 5th Special Forces Group, who in 1965 became the first soldier to oppose the war publicly. Once a diehard anti-Communist, his Vietnam experience convinced him the United States was fighting a bad war. "We weren't preserving freedom in South Vietnam," he continued. "There was no freedom to preserve. . . . It's all there to see once the Red film is removed from the eyes. We aren't the freedom fighters. We are the Russian tanks blasting the hopes of the Asian Hungary." In April 1967, Martin Luther King spoke for many citizens, Afro-American and white alike, when he warned that the war threatened to drag the nation "down the long, dark and shameful corridors of time reserved for those who possess power without compassion, might without morality, and strength without sight." "This war is all wrong," wrote Sergeant Phillip Woodall, who served in the 101st Airborne, to his father: "We're fighting, dying, for a people who resent our being here."[6]

For others the realization came long after the war. The Vietnamese "just wanted to be left alone to do their little daily things, and live, raise rice and cook it, nothing spectacular," said Bobby Rakestraw in the late 1990s. "They just wanted to be alone." But during the war, "I was blinded. I didn't want to admit that it was a waste. I kind of thought it, but just didn't want to admit it. I wanted to think that I had done the right things." [7]

A distinction can be drawn between the cause and the soldiers who fought for it. "There is, and will continue to be throughout our lives, no end of controversy and name-calling about our Vietnam disaster," wrote John W. Palm, the father of Delta Raider Terry Palm who was KIA. Mr. Palm was addressing his son's Delta Raiders comrades in 1990. "But all the political and military decisions of those responsible were way over your heads. You were in no way responsible for the debacle. Your job was to carry out your orders as best you knew how. And in this effort I'm so proud to maintain that you gave it 'everything you had.' I salute you." [8]

Myth: The VC/NVA Did Not Defeat America

So strong, powerful, and righteous, only the United States could defeat the United States. The armed forces were especially fond of this myth. They could have won the war, *easily*, if weak-willed political leaders had not compelled them to fight with one hand tied behind their back and if the government had muzzled a traitorous press and treasonous antiwar protesters. "The reason we failed," read one typical Army general's comment, "was too much civilian interference in military matters—too many constraints. We were in essence handcuffed and not allowed to win." Another general complained of the "irrational limitations on the use of our national power." The Army's vitriol toward the media for allegedly undermining popular support was astounding: 89 percent of its generals despised the press and 91 percent loathed television. [9]

Akin to the German Army's stab-in-the-back theory following World War I, which ascribed defeat to a collapse on the home front rather than the fighting front, such scapegoating absolved the armed forces from any responsibility for the debacle.

In their insistence that a wider war was the path to victory, military leaders ignored the possibility of Chinese and Russian intervention and the acute difficulties in fighting a larger war on unfavorable terrain on the earth's far side.

For most of the war much of the press and television were cheerleaders, lap dogs rather than watch dogs, paper soldiers in tune with national policy, reporting what the administration and the military said (including the calculated lies designed to mislead and manipulate public opinion), and presenting a World War II/John Wayne image of a great crusade. Most war reporting simply parroted the official viewpoint. A random sample of 2,850 front-page stories from the *New York Times* and the *Washington Post* between 1949 and 1969 revealed that 78.1 percent relied on an official pronouncement, news release, or interview. In TV coverage prior to Tet, spokespeople favoring the war appeared five times more often than antiwar critics. As Brigadier General Winant Sidle, the chief of MACV's Office of Information in the mid-1960s, later attested, the vast bulk of the reporting was either advantageous to the government's policies or reasonably neutral.[10]

Although not formally censored—the State Department and Westmoreland's headquarters both objected to censorship—the media in Vietnam worked under military-imposed "voluntary" guidelines that carried severe penalties if violated, and rarely were.[11] Early in the war some veteran reporters criticized the administration and the military, but that was because they feared the nation's strategy was failing; sharing the government's staunch anti-Communism, the reporters thought the war was well worth winning.

After Tet media criticism became more widespread, but that reflected changes among government officials, the public, and the troops as deep misgivings emerged in these collective groups. For instance, a random sample of 779 TV broadcasts between August 1965 and January 1973 showed that 49 percent of the criticism of the administration's war policy came from public officials who had developed doubts about the war.[12] To repeat, the media *reflected* but did not *cause* the pervasive national despondency. Declining morale resulted from the war's evident failure and endlessness, a less gullible public that refused to be mislead any longer by official optimism and deceptions, the perception that defeat would have no impact on America's security, and the metamorphosis then underway in the great power relationships. An anti-Communist crusade in a tiny third world country was increasingly irrelevant. Simply put, the escalating casualties for seemingly no good purpose were dismaying.

Conservatives claimed television projected blood into living rooms every evening and thus demoralized a squeamish population. But TV had a limited influence and expressly refrained from showing gore. In 1969, 57 million households had TV sets, but on any given night only 24.3 million were tuned to the evening news. Moreover, one survey showed that an hour after the news, 51 percent of the people who watched it could not recall a single story! Between August 1965 and August 1970, TV news carried 2,300 reports originating in Vietnam. The author of a study on the media and the war commissioned by the Army's Center of Military History discovered that only seventy-six "showed heavy fighting—soldiers in combat, incoming artillery, or American dead and wounded within sight on the ground."[13] Many broadcasts showed lots of commotion and distant smoke, but nothing gruesome. For carnage viewers turned to *Gunsmoke* and *Kojack*, two of the day's popular TV dramas. Although the military accused the media of an antiwar bias, a Louis Harris poll commissioned by *Newsweek* in 1967 revealed that by more than two to one, TV coverage made respondents support the troops more, not oppose the war.[14]

As for public support, the military emphasized the loss of will, the lack of tenacity. But as Henry Kissinger noted in a postwar memorandum, Vietnam "was the longest war in American history, the most distant, the least obviously relevant to our nation's immediate concerns, and yet the American people supported our involvement and its general objectives until the very end."[15] Antiwar protesters began as an insignificant minority reviled by the general public and the media as filthy, foul-mouthed, long-haired radicals, and would have remained that way had the armed forces been winning the war. Military stalemate and defeat spurred antiwar sentiment, not just among college students but more importantly among middle Americans and Vietnam vets who discerned that the armed forces' strategy was inept and the war was marginal to national security.

"Following their own third course, exercising their own independence of mind, and displaying a substantial measure of contempt for all those in the press and government who sought to manipulate them over the years," concluded the most careful study of the war's media coverage, "Americans had used their common sense. If more bombing and more killing had earlier proved to be of no avail, and if the South Vietnamese had shown few of the traits necessary for survival, why prolong the struggle? Enough was enough."[16]

Most military leaders remained unwilling to admit that their dismal performance had little to do with politicians, protesters, and the press. Their own conduct (as detailed, for example, in the Army's "Study on Military Professionalism") hindered the war effort, as did their inept strategy and penchant for using excessive firepower as a substitute for wise tactics. Equally significant in explaining America's defeat was the enemy's strategic brilliance and superior morale, which flowed from a cause perceived to be more righteous.

Only a few, too few and usually too late, acknowledged the wisdom of political restraints, the Army's failings, and the enemy's genius. Westmoreland eventually realized that Johnson's "strategy of avoiding a larger and possibly uncontrollable war and at the same time protecting our strategic interest" has been sustained by history. Perhaps the armed forces were, as the generals complained, "handcuffed." But the cuffs fettered unruly prisoners with the capacity to do grave harm to the national interest if left unrestrained. Westmoreland's deputy, General Palmer, decried the military's tendency to blame the political leadership because "our top-level military leaders must share the onus of failure." And General DuPuy admitted that he had lacked perspicacity, that he should have thought through the military problems more systematically. As for the media, at least one general acknowledged that the armed forces caused most of the problems: "We placed too much emphasis on the positive, and were over-sensitive to criticism, while engaging in false reporting to cover up setbacks. This, in time, led to our losing credibility." [17]

Of course the North Vietnamese followed America's domestic situation closely and took comfort from it. "Every day our leadership would listen to the world news over the radio at 9 a.m. to follow the growth of the American antiwar movement," said Colonel Bui Tin who was an influential wartime newspaperman. Still, the NVA and VC never expected the American people to win the war for them. They relied instead on the support of the Vietnamese people, both North and South, on assistance from China and the Soviet Union, and most of all on their own military prowess. [18]

The victors had it right. America did not defeat America. The VC/NVA defeated America. "The intelligence and will of our nation had won completely," crowed General Dung. "Because we were fighting for a just cause," noted the official history of PAVN, "our army enjoyed absolute superiority over the enemy in political and spiritual matters." "Ours was a just war against foreign aggression and a traitorous puppet regime, against brutality and injustice, for national independence and freedom, and for human dignity," observed General Tra. "Our aggregate forces were therefore stronger than those of the enemy, and the difference was hardly determinable by arithmetic calculation."[19] Whether the Communists brought less brutality, more justice, and greater freedom and human dignity to the Vietnamese was, of course, debatable. But that they had defeated the United States was not.

A Liberation Radio broadcast best summed up the victors' perspective: "Why has every U.S. strategy and tactic gone bankrupt? It is highly obvious that the White House and Pentagon, though possessing vast amounts of dollars, are so stupid that they have been unable to grasp the basic factors determining victory in the war. They have only taken into account the numerical strength of their army, while failing to realize its quality. They have only taken into account the quantity of weapons, while failing to grasp the human and combat morale factors. They have only taken into account military forces, while failing to realize the political forces."[20]

Years after the war General Davidson and many of lesser rank agreed with this assessment, paying well-deserved homage to the enemy. Throughout the war, Davidson wrote, "the Politburo held to a clear and concrete mission, developed flexible and innovative concepts employing all facets of power to accomplish this mission, and executed these concepts and plans with skill and resolution." Philip Caputo was dismayed whenever he heard "some general who spent his tour looking at maps and flitting around in helicopters claim that we could have won the war." Recalling a difficult platoon-sized patrol he commanded near a place called Charlie Ridge, Caputo believed that had the generals been there with him on the ground, fighting a highly motivated, skillful adversary at close quarters, they would have known better.[21]

Myth: South Vietnam Could Have Been Saved If Congress Authorized More Aid in 1974–75

Of all the disingenuous propositions Nixon propagated, this one was among the cleverest. The White House promised to support Thieu but kept the pledge secret because the president knew Congress would not approve it. Then when Congress refused to fulfill the secret promise, Nixon and Kissinger blamed the legislature for sabotaging South Vietnam!

Despite decreasing support South Vietnam was hardly defenseless. Immediately after the truce the United States flooded South Vietnam with such plentiful military supplies and equipment that it deprived its active duty and Reserve forces of many prime assets. And in the countryside ARVN fired sixteen rounds for every one the VC/NVA fired. As it had done for the previous decade, the enemy continued doing far better with much less.[22]

Once again the victors accurately perceived the situation. "No matter how much more the United States had supplied to the quislings in weapons and munitions in 1975," wrote General Dung, "they would certainly still have collapsed and our troops would have confiscated all the more war booty."[23]

"Even if the United States had continued its military assistance at the 1972–73 level," General Davidson admitted in his postwar history of the conflict, "the combination of the inherent debilities of the Thieu government and the power and determination of the North Vietnamese would have eventually destroyed the Republic of Vietnam."[24]

Myth: The United States Left Behind More Than Two Thousand Men Who Were Missing in Action (MIA)

Immediately after the return of the 591 American POWs, the Defense Intelligence Agency calculated the number of MIAS as approximately 1,200, but that was an inflated number. Intent on getting a high enemy body count and keeping the American body count low, commanders preferred to list a man as MIA rather than KIA even though the evidence was often clear that the soldier or airman was dead. A House of Representatives committee that investigated the MIAS one-by-one concluded that in forty of the first fifty-three cases it reviewed, the "missing" individual could have justifiably been declared KIA. The number of genuine MIAS, where nobody really knew what happened to the man, was in the low hundreds, a remarkably low number for such a big, long war.

Then something curious happened. Bowing to the pressure of families who would not give up hope that their loved ones were somehow still alive, in the late 1970s the Defense Department arbitrarily added to the MIAS another category, those approximately 1,100 individuals originally listed as KIA/BNR: Killed in Action/Body Not Recovered. Never before lumped with the MIAS, these men were "missing" only in the sense that their bodies had not been recovered, oftentimes because no body remained—for example, after an airplane disintegrated in a fireball and no one saw any parachutes.

Adding the 1,100 KIA/BNRs to the already inflated list of 1,200 MIAs yielded more than 2,000 MIAs. But the vast majority of those listed as MIA were never missing in the first place, and of the others the jungles and muck had long since overgrown or swallowed up the bodies, or rendered them into their natural constituent elements.[25]

The MIA myth kept the hopes of families painfully and artificially alive, provided self-righteous politicians a patriotic soapbox, unnecessarily delayed the normalization of relations with Vietnam, made wonderful escapist fodder for numerous Hollywood movies, and was an example of ethno-centric hypocrisy. After all, Vietnam had some hundreds of thousands of MIAs, in part because Americans treated enemy bodies so callously. Cleo Hogan had three regrets about the war: he did not put his men in for enough medals, a few POWs captured by the Raiders were ill treated, and enemy "bodies were treated as if they were garbage," often just flung over a hill-side with no effort to bury them or mark grave sites. Sometimes purpose-ful, mass, anonymous destruction of enemy remains occurred. U.S. soldiers gathered them up in a cargo net slung below a helicopter and dumped them far out at sea, or stacked bodies in alternate layers with logs, soaked the whole pile in gasoline, and set it aflame.[26]

Myth: Vietnam Veterans Were Neglected, Maladapted, and Permanently Scarred, Tormented Losers, a Frightening Number of Them Afflicted with a Novel Malady, Posttraumatic Stress Disorder

Instead of being bums, addicts, drunks, and derelicts, the overwhelming ma-jority of Vietnam veterans were well-adjusted men and women who looked back on their military service fondly and lived productive lives.[27] They took unprecedented advantage of the G.I. Bill's benefits (education and voca-tional training, low-interest home loans, preference in federal employment, VA health care, the right to loans from the Small Business Administration, and so on) to become well-educated and as successful, or even more suc-cessful, than individuals who did not serve. An insignificant percentage was in prison, a low percentage was unemployed, only a tiny fraction was home-less, they did not commit suicide in unprecedented numbers, they did not father a distressingly large number of children with birth defects, nor did they suffer catastrophic health problems—greater hearing loss and a lower sperm count were the only differences between Vietnam vets and veterans who served elsewhere, though the Vietnam vets still fathered a similar number of children.[28]

At the heart of the Vietnam vets' regnant image was Posttraumatic Stress Disorder (PTSD), which purported to explain their alleged postwar adjustment difficulties and mental health problems. In veterans suffering from PTSD, the past (an unpleasant memory or memories) constantly relived itself in the present—for example, through intrusive images and a compulsion to replay old events. Unlike normal memories that weakened, decayed, and became scrambled with other memories over time, these traumatic memories remained intact, perpetually renewing themselves in the present.

Historically, large numbers of soldiers from any conflict had temporary readjustment problems and at least some suffered severe, enduring mental wounds. In *The Aeneid* the Roman poet Virgil maintained that:

> *It is easy to go down into hell;*
> *Night and day, the gates of dark death stand wide;*
> *But to climb back up again,*
> *To retrace one's steps to the open air,*
> *There lies the problem, the difficult task.*[29]

Combat soldiers often found it difficult to ascend to the open air, to overcome a sense of aimlessness and alienation. One problem was near-terminal boredom. One of the Delta Raiders, Ava James, revealed that although he would not go back to Vietnam he enjoyed himself there. After the war he had a lot of different jobs and owned several businesses because "I've got a low threshold on boredom. I get bored pretty easy. Once you get into the action, everything else is pretty boring." "For all its disappointments and raw realities," noted another solider, enunciating a widespread sentiment, "I find it difficult not to look upon my months in Vietnam as the most meaningful of my life."[30]

Much of the alienation emerged from "the incommunicable experience of war."[31] Combat could not be communicated to civilians. "Such bloody scenes can never be realized without an actual sight," wrote the Japanese soldier Tadayoshi Sakurai in his memoir of the Russo-Japanese war. "My pen is powerless to describe it." "In part we couldn't describe our feelings because the language failed us," wrote Vietnam vet William Broyles Jr. "The civilian-issue adjectives and nouns, verbs and adverbs, seemed made for a different universe." Writing his mother, another veteran understood the failure of mere language: "I feel different now after seeing some horrible things, and I'll never forget them. It makes you glad you're just existing. I can't say what I mean, but some of the things you see here can really change a man or turn a boy into a man." One combatant urged his family not to ask questions when he arrived home. What he experienced was "something you don't feel like discussing and can't begin to write about." "Maybe when I go home," commented still another soldier, "I'll just crawl back inside myself, and not say a word. Things are so violent nobody would believe it. And I don't want to die of frustration trying to convince them."[32]

As soldiers realized, civilians would consider what was normal in war as crazy and repulsive because they had not traveled the combatant's journey from numbing to coarsening and toughening and finally to brutalization.[33] Sakurai was amazed at how insensitive soldiers became to war's horrors. "What is shocking and sickening," he wrote, "becomes a matter of indifference. Familiarity takes off the edge of sensibility. If we should continue to be shocked and disgusted we could not survive the strain." Drawing an analogy between hunting and killing in war, a soldier wrote his friend that "I know I'm after souls, but I get all excited when I see a VC, just like when I see a deer. I go ape firing at him. . . . Civilians think such thinking is crazy, but it's no big deal." A fellow combatant realized he "actually enjoyed some of the things I've done which would be repulsive to a healthy mind. This place does make you sick in the head. When one starts to enjoy the sickness of war, he is sick."[34]

While feelings of boredom and alienation invariably faded, war sometimes inflicted permanent damage on the psyche. From "nostalgia" during the Civil War to "shell shock" in World War I and "combat fatigue" in World War II, they endured crippling, invisible battle wounds, what the Russians called "diseases of the soul." The jargon changed, but the symptoms remained the same: loss of one or more of the senses, paralysis of one or more limbs, memory loss, exaggerated startle reactions ("jumpiness"), survivor guilt, panic attacks, nightmares and flashbacks, uncontrollable rage, irritability, spiritual lassitude.

What caused these psychological maladies was a puzzle, but they afflicted cowards and heroes alike. Everyone, not just the timid or weak, had a breaking point, and it usually came inside of sixty days of continuous combat—except for the approximately 2 percent in World War II who were aggressive psychopathic personalities. "Thus it is not too far from the mark," as one author put it, "to observe that there is something about continuous, inescapable combat which will drive 98 percent of all men insane; the other 2 percent were crazy before they got there." Sometimes mentally broken men never recovered. When World War II began, 65 percent of the patients in veterans' hospitals were World War I shell shock victims.[35]

During the Vietnam War soldiers had a lower neuropsychiatric casualty rate than previous wars—only 12 cases per 1,000 as opposed to as many as 101 per 1,000 in World War II and a rate of 37 per 1,000 in Korea. The reasons for the low rate were obvious. In Vietnam soldiers served for only a year rather than the duration thus relieving the foreboding sense of interminable helplessness; they did not endure unremitting artillery barrages that created a feeling of abject helplessness, which damaged the mental stability of so many men in the World Wars; they frequently rotated out of the field to rear areas, thus mitigating the utter exhaustion that undermined mental health; often had hot food and cold beer even while in the field; received prompt medical care; and enjoyed a one-week R and R vacation to an exotic locale. Many soldiers also became expert at "ghosting," hiding out in the rear for a few extra days or even weeks. The net effect was that in many crucial ways those serving in Vietnam had it easier than those who fought in previous wars.

Yet avowedly antiwar psychiatrists and psychologists such as Robert Jay Lifton, Chaim Shatan, and other proponents of PTSD, who acted as veterans' advocates rather than neutral scientists, asserted that Vietnam was uniquely stressful. Soldiers were younger and therefore less resilient than in previous wars, engaged in a surreal and unprecedented guerrilla war, suffered severe guilt because they routinely committed atrocities, and felt unappreciated because of low public support and a hostile reception when they returned. Most of this was untrue, which was not surprising since Lifton and his fellow advocates based their studies not on representative samples or scientific methods, but on anecdotal evidence from antiwar vets, many of them intent on horrifying America into ending the war.[36] Polls revealed how inaccurate the antiwar psychiatrists and psychologists were. Vietnam vets were overwhelmingly proud of their service, were warmly embraced by family and friends when they returned home, and while the public had rejected the war, it did not blame those who fought it.

The result of Vietnam's supposedly dire and unique circumstances was PTSD, a special trauma that manifested itself months or even years after the traumatic experiences. In 1980 the American Psychiatric Association gave this new "disease" its official blessing, incorporating it into the *Diagnostic and Statistical Manual of Mental Disorders* (*DSM–III*) despite numerous methodological problems.[37] What "disease process" within the body or brain caused PTSD? Were the underlying causes biological, cognitive, behaviorist, psychoanalytic, or developmental? Was PTSD chronic or transitory? Since no one knew the answers to these and other questions, no consensus developed on exactly what the disease was, how to define it, or how to treat it.

Moreover, PTSD was a self-reported debility. Health professionals relied on what veterans told them concerning their traumatic experiences, when their mental suffering began, and the intensity of the symptoms. Did a veteran's psychiatric problems originate in the war, or before or after it? Did the war cause the symptoms, or did something else? Who could tell for sure? Self-reporting was subject not only to forgetfulness but also to willful reconstruction and embellishment, especially since substantial monetary disability checks were at stake. Finally, prolonged feelings of guilt, dread, and melancholy intermingled with nightmares and flashbacks might be the normal human reaction to privation, chaotic violence, and unnatural death, not some abnormal disease.

PTSD advocates overstated the uniqueness (or "singularity") of the Vietnam veterans' postwar suffering and exaggerated the magnitude of the problem, especially since PTSD's symptoms were easily faked. A delayed reaction to wartime stress was not unique to Vietnam vets. Unable to shake their gruesome experiences and unpleasant memories, some Civil War soldiers exhibited symptoms identical to those associated with PTSD and ended up in mental institutions long after the war. In 1951 Dr. Samuel Futterman and others published a study chronicling the rising number of World War II veterans seeking help for the first time because of psychological trauma. And researchers who tracked World War II veterans for two decades detailed a "chronic stress syndrome" that the former soldiers endured. Yes, some Vietnam veterans suffered acutely after the war. But so did veterans of other wars even though, according to Lifton, Shatan, and others of their ilk, they fought a less onerous war, had more sustained home front support, and marched in warmly received welcome-home parades.[38]

Estimates as to how many vets had PTSD varied widely from 3.5 percent to 50 percent. One supposedly authoritative study, the National Vietnam Veteran Readjustment Survey (NVVRS), concluded that approximately 26 percent of all Vietnam vets suffered from full or "partial" PTSD, whatever "partial" meant since DSM–III listed acute, chronic, or delayed PTSD, but not "partial." However, one problem was that researchers did not check what an individual told them against his service record for accuracy. Another was that initially many of the interviewees did not meet the criteria established in DSM–III, so researchers created a much broader definition, one that made PTSD so amorphous and all-inclusive that if a combat soldier had an occasional squeamish twinge he qualified. A Centers for Disease Control study found that only 15 percent of Vietnam vets experienced "some" PTSD symptoms at some point *during or after* military service; hence, the 15 percent included men who might have had a single flashback shortly after a firefight but experienced no long-lasting posttraumatic stress. Consequently, even the 15 percent estimate, much less the 26 percent, was inflated.[39]

PTSD symptoms were easy to simulate, yet VA mental health professionals had little incentive to expose frauds. Landy Sparr and Loren D. Pankratz published the first study of "factitious" PTSD in 1983. They investigated five men treated at the Portland, Oregon, VA medical center, three of whom claimed to be former POWs. All were fakes. None was a POW, four had never been in Vietnam, and indeed two were never even in military service.[40] VA counselor Richard Burns, who served two tours in Vietnam in the Special Forces and the Pathfinders, believed many of his clients were fakes. "Most of them are just damn lazy," he observed. "They're doing drugs, drinking alcohol, they don't want to get jobs." "These guys," he continued, "can do anything—tell the psychologists to go fuck themselves, beat their wives, lay around the house—because they've been traumatized. They have no job except to show up for their [VA] appointment."[41]

Men lied to make their otherwise mundane lives more exciting, to provide excuses for a failed and miserable existence, to gain sympathy or respect, and to milk the VA cash cow for benefits that in the mid-1990s could be more than $35,000 per year tax free, not to mention Social Security bene-fits, spousal benefits, tuition for children, and other benefits conferred by in-dividual states. "Wouldn't you rather be diagnosed a hero suffering from war trauma," asked VA counselor Burns, "and [be] given three thousand dollars a month than diagnosed as somebody who's got an antisocial disorder?" "The most important thing to realize about your benefits," observed *The Viet Vet Survival Guide*, "is that the VA Regional Office is essentially a bank." Pretenders and malingerers making monthly withdrawals cost taxpayers tens of millions of dollars a year in disability benefits and salaries for VA health experts.[42]

Frauds were often obvious. They misused acronyms, mispronounced places in Vietnam, misunderstood unit organizations, claimed service in a unit at a time when that unit was not deployed to Vietnam, and described preposterous events that a cursory knowledge of the war revealed as un-true. But because the VA system thrived on PTSD few officials challenged the pretenders; as a careful investigation of the topic concluded, "The VA doesn't cure PTSD; it teaches PTSD." "We are judged by the number of people we see, not by the quality of our treatment," said Burns in criticizing his employer. "It's a number game. You keep your jobs, your funding, by the numbers." An ample supply of PTSD patients meant job security for VA employees.[43]

Also, veterans' organizations found the image of scorned, maligned vets useful in lobbying for more extensive benefits. Veterans became a privileged class with their own extensive welfare system, observed one scholar.[44] Saying "no" to the veterans' lobby was tantamount to committing political suicide, akin to a politician admitting he or she hated babies, kittens, puppies, and nursing home residents.

Men who served with Joe Hooper generally agreed that PTSD was exag-gerated. Cleo Hogan suffered no ill effects from the war but believed others did, though not as many as claimed: "I think there are some people who have played it, or over-played it, in order to gain sympathy or other benefits, claiming stress." Wayne Horne, who became chairman of his county's Vet-erans Assistance Commission, realized that PTSD was susceptible to fraud; he thought wartime memories might be discomforting on occasion, but not necessarily incapacitating. Most PTSD "sufferers" were fakes, said Ned Kint-zer bluntly. "I don't think you'd find more than 5 percent of the true grunts that suffer from PTSD." T'Odon C. Leshikar concurred, believing "that a lot of people use PTSD as an excuse, as a crutch, in order to get by." Dave Bischoff and Bobby Rakestraw also agreed, the former asserting that "a lot of people have used PTSD as an excuse to not necessarily participate in society, or to be just on the fringes of weird." Rakestraw had several buddies who *claimed* they had it, but they "were dragging everything they could out of the Veterans Administration. I think they use it as a big crutch to take a free ride." Although claiming he had PTSD, Roy Barber admitted he "was doing fine until my wife died." That is, his wife's death, not the war, caused his trauma. Delta Raider Jodey Gravett abused drugs, but only long after he left the Army when he "began running around with the wrong people, the wrong crowd. Vietnam didn't have anything to do with it." [45]

Looking back at Joe's life, some of his friends said he suffered from PTSD.[46] But this was unlikely. His heavy drinking long antedated the war, thus undercutting the argument that he used alcohol as a form of self-medication to numb traumatic memories. Those who had the best opportunity to know how he slept — Carollyn, Faye, Jerry Hill — insisted he had no nightmares or flashbacks. Joe told Buck Johnson he could close his eyes and see the faces of some of the men he killed, but that he did not have nightmares about it.[47] Yes, Joe was troubled, but he manifested disturbing personality traits as a teenager long before he joined the Army. Upon leaving the active Army his problem was not psychological trauma but that he was poorly educated with no useful peacetime skills. It took several years of floundering before Joe settled on a suitable career path, horse management.

The biggest struggle looming in Joe's future was not PTSD, but alcohol abuse.

With an insider's knowledge of VA benefits, when Joe went to Oklahoma to study horse breeding and training he applied to the VA's vocational rehabilitation program for disabled veterans for financial assistance.

Based on the results of several vocational tests, a personal interview, and the "School College Ability Test," his VA counselor in Oklahoma, Robert Spencer, believed Joe was well suited for the program and had the intellectual ability to perform at the junior college level. Indeed, Joe told him he had already completed seven credit hours, receiving an "A" in six and a "B" in the seventh. For once in his life Joe understated his achievements; he had passed three classes (Introduction to Work Experience, U.S. History to 1865, and American Federal Government) and received nine credit hours.[48]

Spencer described Joe as a "husky 39 year old Caucasian disabled vet." "Husky" was a polite way of saying that while still robust and healthy, Joe was no longer a hard, lean soldier, but had developed the flabby midriff common to men approaching middle age. "Disabled" referred to the 60 percent service disability compensation Joe received beginning as of February 6, 1974, when he left the active Army. His disability exam detailed Joe's multiple wounds, the remaining scars, the permanent damage done to underlying muscle groups, and his tinnitus, a constant ringing, whistling, or roaring in his ears.

Badly scarred, his left elbow was painful to extend and the left arm as a whole was weak. Shrapnel wounds to his right ankle, knee, thigh, hip, elbow, and shoulder went deep and in some cases hit bones, leaving permanent tenderness in those areas. The finger bitten by an angry Marine when Joe was in the Navy still caused problems, as did his right wrist, which he broke in a parachuting accident at Fort Polk. A right-handed man his size normally had a right-hand grip of one hundred pounds and a left-hand of eighty-five pounds, but Joe could only do sixty-five pounds right-handed and seventy-five pounds left-handed, a considerable loss of strength in both hands. About the only military-related injuries that did not hurt were the penis wound and a gunshot wound to his right forehead that left a small scar. Sometime during his first tour a bullet hit him there and ricocheted instead of penetrating—either an incredibly fortunate angle or a "spent" projectile near the end of its trajectory that had lost its penetrating power.[49] Despite the scars and aches, Joe realized he was lucky because at least "all my limbs are functional."[50]

Although the disabilities affected Joe's ability to lift, push, pull, climb, reach, stand, and hear, they would not prevent him from having a horse management career, especially considering "the vet's positive attitude and high motivation."[51]

Joe's academic career progressed well. In the fall semester he passed a General Biology class and three courses in the Horse Management Program (Care and Nutrition, Groom and Show, and Anatomy and Physiology). Joe enjoyed all of these classes, except for the anatomy class. Struggling in that course, he requested the VA to pay for a tutor, Jori Allen, who received $3 per hour. A fellow student, Allen was also a nurse who was married to a doctor and shared Joe's passion for horses. From September 14 through December 7, she tutored him for fifty-eight hours, helping him turn a failing grade into at least a "B."[52] Enthusiastic about his ability to handle the academic workload, Joe enrolled for nineteen credit hours in the Spring Semester, with four courses in the Horse Management Program (Disease and Prevention, Brood Mare, Breeding and Genetics, and Stallion Management) and two in the Cabinetry Program (Furniture Refinishing and General Wood).[53]

As Joe sped through the Horse Management Program the Hoopers settled into the Chalet Apartments complex, which consisted of eight two-story buildings on West Blue Star Road. They lived toward the back, in apartment number 2F, a ground level unit with two bedrooms, a bath and a half, kitchen, eating area, living room, and lots of closet space.[54] Right by the door was a small table where Joe left some change almost every day so Joey could visit the ice cream truck that cruised the neighborhood. One day while playing outside, perhaps awaiting the bell on the ice cream truck, Joey fell and cut her head on a concrete step. A neighbor man took Faye and Joey to the emergency ward while his wife went to find Joe at school. As the doctor began stitching Joey, Faye closed her eyes and said a little prayer. Fearing she was going to faint, the doctor tried to escort her out of the room but she refused to go, insisting she was fine. Just then Joe arrived, so the doctor turned back to his work. Suddenly he heard a tremendous "Thump!" At the sight of his little girl in pain, MOH recipient Joe Hooper fainted.[55]

The Hoopers brought their three horses to Oklahoma, keeping them in a pasture they rented. Since Faye did not like horses and wanted nothing to do with them, Joe and Joey took care of Karsaii (who developed a bad foot and no longer raced), Really, and Really Wow. Although Joey was too young to do any of the real work she accompanied her dad as he cared for them.

In the spring of 1979, Really was again pregnant, and Joe was going to be gone for a few days in early May to attend the Kentucky Derby. He left behind a note telling Faye and Joey that "Really is due to foal in two to four days. It will Happen in earley morn—so nothing you can do—But check each day." This was true. A mare normally foaled between 1:00 and 6:00 a.m., the process taking thirty to sixty minutes if everything went smoothly, The note gave specific directions for feeding the horses, saying "Joey will do it but watch her close." Faye was also to let Joey brush and pet the animals. If problems arose, she should call fellow horse lover Jori Allen or the local veterinarian, Jimmy Shipman. Standard procedure was to have a veterinarian on call when a mare was ready to foal in case of an emergency.[56]

Shipman was new to Claremore, having moved there in late 1978, but he and Joe became good enough friends that they occasionally went out to lunch or dinner with a few other fellows, who sat around transfixed listening to Joe's war stories. Speaking in a raspy voice, thick with alcohol and cigarettes, using animated gestures and facial expressions, when Joe told a story "you could almost see a picture of it as he was telling it," recalled Shipman. As Joe recounted them, his exploits were amazing, "almost too good to be true," since it seemed impossible "that a person could live through all those things and still be sitting there telling us about it." Although the men gave Joe the benefit of the doubt, they wondered if everything he said was true.[57]

Jori Allen, Jimmy Shipman, and other people associated with horses represented one of several "worlds" Joe inhabited at Claremore. An entirely different "world" coalesced around Dewey "Buck" Johnson, the Claremore police chief, who met Joe at the community college where Buck was a frequent guest speaker in a criminal justice class. One time when Johnson was walking across campus, Joe approached him and began a conversation, saying he was interested in law enforcement and knew a lot of men in the Los Angeles Police Department. "And the conversation just went from there," Buck recalled. Soon Joe was spending a lot of time with the police chief, riding shotgun in his patrol car, becoming active in his reelection campaign, and visiting his home.[58]

"Congressional Medal of Honor Recipient Joe Hooper Endorses Dewey Buck Johnson," blared the headline of an ad featuring Joe in full dress uniform.[59] But Joe did more than appear in local advertising. During the campaign he spoke at various civic groups on Buck's behalf and was at the Johnsons' home two or three times a week helping to organize people to go door-to-door, shaking hands, extolling Buck's virtues, and handing out campaign literature. Joe even did some of this "laying it on" himself.

Buck lost the election, but the defeat harmed neither his law enforcement career nor his friendship with Joe. Buck went to the sheriff's office as a criminal deputy until 1984 when the voters elected him sheriff. Meanwhile, at their home "the door was always open to Joe." The Johnsons believed "Joe was a super nice guy. He quickly became part of the family," fitting in wonderfully not only with Buck and Mrs. Johnson, but also their four children, Jannelle, Karla, Dewey Jr., and Andrea. Born in 1963 and sharing Joe's passionate interest in Audie Murphy, young Dewey considered Joe a hero. "I knew what a hero was," he said. "Even by age sixteen I'd watched every Audie Murphy movie there was, and so considered him in that category." The young man thought Joe was exceptionally modest. Joe participated in Dewey's Explorer Scout group and advised him to get at least two years of college education before joining the military, always speaking to him one-on-one, man-to-man.

No one in the Johnson family met Faye or Joey. Buck thought Joe and his wife might be separated, and a friend of Buck's believed Joe's wife lived elsewhere, maybe in California. For whatever reason, the Hoopers did not socialize. One possible explanation came from Joe's former supervisor at Green River Community College. "To be kind of brutal about it," commented John Arnhold, "I think, in a strange way, he might have been somewhat embarrassed about his wife's physical condition." On the other hand, if Joe was womanizing, the Johnsons never saw even a hint of it. Nor did any of his other friends, who believed he was being faithful to Faye.[60]

The Johnsons were twice beholden to their friend Joe Hooper. Buck liked to fish at Claremore Lake, built in 1929 when Dog Creek was dammed, and Joe frequently joined him. As with many older impoundments, the water clarity was more accurately water *un*clarity; only under ideal conditions could a person see even ten inches into the water. Not liking boats, Buck fished from a huge rock slab jutting into the water, which was deep there. On a typical outing he brought rods and reels, a beer-stuffed cooler, and much of his family. Joe was not much of a fisherman but enjoyed sitting on the rock talking with Buck and playing with the kids. On one such outing two-year-old Whitney, Karla's daughter, accidentally slid off the rock into the water. She did not yell and sank like a rock. No one saw her disappear into the murk—except Joe who leaped into the water, the sudden huge splash nearly scaring everyone to death. Surfacing, he cradled Whitney in his hands. More than twenty years later Buck's voice still quivered as he recounted this tragedy averted.

Then on a Sunday evening in late March 1979, tragedy did strike. A drunk driver killed Jannelle, the oldest child, leaving behind two young daughters who the Johnsons raised. "Joe hung with us *real* tough through the accident," recalled Buck. Yes, said Dewey Jr., "We were all down when my sister died, and boy, Joe wouldn't let us frown too long. He was very, very encouraging and always had the right words to pick somebody up. He'd come up here and get our minds off of our troubles, our grief. It was kind of like an angel coming by for us."

While Joe hobnobbed with the police chief and other law enforcement personnel, he also moved in Claremore's underworld, a world inhabited by professional gamblers such as Oliver "Ironman" Humble and Jerry "Black Bart" McCollum. More than twenty years older than Joe in 1978, Ironman, who got his nickname because he had been an iron worker, died in an auto wreck in 1987 while returning from a high stakes poker game in Muskogee. McCollum considered Humble "an old tough dude, but a real honorable guy." "Honorable" in Black Bart's lexicon was someone who paid his gambling debts. "I sure hated to see him get killed," said Black Bart, "because he owed me $16,000 when he died."

Two years younger than Joe, McCollum owned the Orbit Club, which was a bar in the front and a bookie joint in back. Jerry came from a dirt-poor Oklahoma family, had ten brothers and six sisters, and an eighth grade education. His nickname came from his close association with African Americans; as a child he picked cotton side-by-side with black children and during adulthood he preferred to play poker in black bars, especially down in Texas where, unlike white bars, they never closed. Convicted of operating an illegal sports booking operation in the mid-1980s after federal wiretaps recorded him taking a $40,000 bet on the 1984 Orange Bowl, McCollum spent six months in jail.

When Black Bart met Joe in 1978 he thought his last name was Cooper, so he always called him "Cooper," which aggravated Hooper no end. Joe frequently fermented in the Orbit Club where he studied the daily racing form and sometimes became so drunk that Jerry had to drive him home, which was no problem since he also lived in the Chalet Apartments.[61]

Unlike Ironman and Black Bart, who were hard-core gamblers, Joe was just a small-time gambler who rarely wagered more than a few bucks. He did not like poker and never bet on sports, but enjoyed betting a few dollars on the horses, doing it for fun, not to make money. Despite their different gambling habits, the three men decided to attend the 1979 Kentucky Derby together.[62]

As it turned out, Really gave birth to a colt named Really Joey without any problems, so no emergency call to Jori Allen or Jimmy Shipman was necessary.

As it also turned out, Faye soon sold Karsaii, Really, Really Wow, and Really Joey.[63] In part this was because, financially, the sky had fallen.

In mid-March 1979, Joe learned the VA made two errors "in prior award and rating actions which have now been corrected." Instead of 60 percent his disability should have been 70 percent, meaning he would get $2,600 for retroactive pay as well as a larger monthly check. Unfortunately, the VA had failed to withhold any money to recoup 75 percent of his $15,000 readjustment pay, which, by law, it should have been doing once he began receiving a disability check. Only after the 75 percent (that is, $11,250) was recouped could a veteran receive disability compensation. Consequently, the $2,600 check was going to the recoupment and, effective April 1, his disability compensation would be withheld until the government recouped the remaining $8,450.[64]

The VA's adjudication officer apologized to Joe for the VA's past errors and any inconvenience the new changes caused. But for the Hoopers this was not just an inconvenience. The VA's errors represented a severe financial hardship that put Joe's education and aspirations at risk.

Faye and Joe had no business income, stocks or bonds, bank deposits, annuities, rental income, or real estate. Although they had few debts, they were barely making it financially, with average monthly expenditures of approximately $1,000 and an income of $806 for Joe's disability, $200 for his MOH, and a modest subsistence allowance.[65]

While assessing his situation, Joe contacted the VA in Seattle to see if he could be reemployed there, certainly a disheartening prospect; investigated several other employment possibilities, including some in Claremore; submitted a statement of financial hardship to the VA, asking that only $300 a month be withheld for the recoupment; and, unable to concentrate on his studies, withdrew from school on April 13, his dream of completing the Horse Management Program on hold. Fortunately for Joe both the regional VA director and the Veterans Services Officer took a direct interest in his case. The VA authorized a special $806 payment covering April and a letter was soon on its way to Washington DC, requesting special permission to collect the readjustment pay at a rate of only $300 per month. By the end of the month arrangements were in place so that Joe could resume his studies in the summer if he was still unemployed. Joe was interested in returning to school, and suggested he might get some credit hours transferred from Northwestern State University.[66]

In this uncertain milieu only one thing was certain.

Joe and Ironman were driving to Louisville in Humble's brown Oldsmobile Royal.

The phone call to Carollyn seemed bizarre.

It was around 5:00 a.m., California time, several days before Joe was planning to leave for Louisville. Although Joe was incoherent, probably drunk, the gist of the conversation was clear. He was asking Carollyn to meet him at the Derby, offering to pay for the flight and suggesting that she bring her children along. "Just like nothing ever happened!" she marveled. As if they last saw each other four days instead of four years ago! Carollyn said no, but in retrospect she regretted not going.[67]

On Wednesday morning around 10:30, May 2, Ironman and Joe headed for Louisville, with Joe behind the wheel.[68] Black Bart was going to drive with them, but when they stopped by his apartment he was arguing with his "old lady" so he told them to go ahead, that he would catch a plane the next day and meet them at the race track paddock. With Joe driving the entire trip, he and Humble arrived at Ft. Knox early the afternoon of May 3 and checked into Room 204, Building 2604 of the Steindam Apartments at Ft. Knox. What they did that afternoon was unknown, except that they did not go to the paddock. That evening they were at the Ft. Knox Officers Club drinking.

Dressed in a black coat and black hat and with $10,000 stuffed into each of his boots and a few extra bucks in his pocket, Black Bart bought a one-way ticket from Tulsa to Louisville. Since he was not carrying a suitcase he took a taxi directly to the track and went to the paddock, where he waited all afternoon. Finally realizing his friends — "those sorry assholes" — were not going to show up, he was "pissed because I ain't got no room." After taking a taxi to the worst part of downtown Louisville, he acted as if he was virtually penniless to deceive potential thieves, hoping to find cheap lodging. He settled for a tiny room above a bar — seven floors above it, with no elevator up there. The room had no door and lots of peeling wallpaper, but Jerry felt safe since no robber would look for someone with $20,000 in such a hovel.

The next day Jerry took a taxi back to the track and found Joe and Iron-man at the paddock, right where they were supposed to meet the previous day. The three men spent the day at the track, went to the Officers Club that evening, then returned to the Steindam Apartments. Since the room had only two beds, Black Bart got the floor, fashioning a cushion out of the pillows from the room's two stuffed chairs.

Saturday May 5 was Derby Day. Alert with anticipation, the men were up early and by 10:00 a.m. Joe was drinking bourbon nonstop as they awaited the day's main event. According to Black Bart, Ironman was going to bet $10,000 on Spectacular Bid, but after some discussions with Joe placed the money on another horse. Spectacular Bid won in 2:02 2/5, a comparatively slow time, well off the record pace of 1:59 2/5 that Triple Crown winner Secretariat set six years previously. "But Ironman's a gambler," said McCollum. Losing $10,000 "didn't mean nothing to him."

After the races they took a shuttle to Ironman's car. The shuttle was packed and Joe was one of those standing in the aisle. When another man asked him to move down, he turned surly, refusing to move until Black Bart persuaded him to behave. After they left the parking lot they stopped at a cafe where Joe devoured a plate of biscuits and gravy and drank two pints of buttermilk, his favorite nonalcoholic beverage. Then they went to the Officers Club where they settled around a table with a Reserve major who Joe and Ironman first met there on Thursday night. Joe resumed drinking alcohol and Black Bart joined him; Ironman remained sober.

By midnight Joe was so drunk his head slumped—or was he feeling sick? When he asked someone to take him to the Steindam Apartments, Ironman volunteered. After drinking another hour with the major, Jerry arrived at the apartment around 1:30 a.m., none too sober himself. With Joe laying "dead naked" on one bed and Ironman snoring in the other, Black Bart settled onto the floor for the second straight night.

Ironman awoke first, around 8:00 a.m., and went to use the bathroom. The door normally opened inward, but moved only a few inches when he pushed it. Peering through the crack, he saw Joe lying on the floor, face down, his buttocks against the door. The older man awoke Black Bart, kicking him on the foot, complaining that "that damn Hooper, he's in there drunk, shit all over himself. I can't go to the bathroom. He's up against the door. I just ain't going to mess with some drunk. See if you can't get in there and get him cleaned up so we can get out of here."

Like Ironman, Jerry thought Joe had passed out drunk. After years of running a bar, he knew cold water often revived a drunk so he muscled the door open a bit more and threw water on Joe's back, yelling at him to wake up. No response. Sensing something was seriously wrong, Jerry reached in to lift Joe's head. He heard a "gurgling" sound, halfway between heavy breathing and choking. Joe's eyes were closed, he had a fresh knot above his right eye, his face was "blue, so blue, I mean just flat blue," and white-ish vomit trickled from his mouth. As Black Bart held his head, the MOH recipient took a deep, rasping breath, then exhaled.

"Ironman," Jerry yelled, "Cooper's dead!"

Stepping onto the balcony they saw a man walking below and called for help. Within minutes an ambulance and the MPS were on the scene.

Joe had a faint pulse when the medics arrived, but as they put him in the ambulance they could no longer detect it.

At 9:02 a.m., Sunday May 6, 1979, Joe Ronnie Hooper was pronounced Dead on Arrival at Ireland Army Hospital, the apparent victim of a heart attack.

Trained to be suspicious, the MPS were not so sure. They learned Joe had a wad of $100 bills in the Officers Club the previous night, he had two nasty bruises (one above the right eye, the other adjacent to the left eye), the money was missing, and they found Joe's empty wallet in Ironman's trunk. They quizzed Ironman and Black Bart not only about Joe's health, wondering whether he had heart problems, but also about the contusions and the money. If Joe had health problems, Ironman and Black Bart assured the MPS, they did not know about them; nor did they know how Joe got the bruises or where his money was.

Neither a murderous robbery nor a fatal heart attack occurred.

The MPS found $1,230 in Joe's jacket, which was hanging on the coat rack just inside the apartment door.

The Army's official investigative report, including the autopsy results, concluded Joe died from natural causes, a massive subarachnoid brain hemorrhage due to an aneurysm of a blood vessel in the brain. A blood vessel burst, causing the brain hemorrhage, which in turn caused Joe to fall and hit his head, perhaps on the bathroom sink or the stool and then the floor.

When Ironman and Black Bart left Ft. Knox that day they believed the Army was going to conclude Joe died of a heart attack since the MPS questioned both of them about that possibility. Understanding that the Army might want a sanitized death for a war hero, they agreed not to challenge that verdict even though they disagreed with it.

Twenty years later, with Ironman dead, Black Bart explained how he thought Joe died. "If I was on a witness stand, under oath," he said during a long interview with Buck Johnson sitting at the table, "and they asked me how Joe Hooper died, I would say Joe Hooper went into the bathroom, sick, started vomiting, slipped and fell, hit his head, and when he fell the vomit was still in his throat and he strangled to death in his own vomit." Alcohol followed by biscuits and gravy and buttermilk followed by more alcohol— it made sense that Joe got sick. The individual who performed the autopsy mentioned the "smell of vomitus in Mr. Hooper's mouth," and Buck declared that Jerry's description of Joe's death was consistent with someone drowning in his own fluids.[69]

Faye learned of Joe's death early Sunday morning when a Claremore policeman knocked on the door, told her the grim news, gave her a number to call at Ft. Knox, and then left. She dialed the number and a male voice told her Joe was barely alive when he was transported from the room and that an investigation was underway because his money was missing. Shortly thereafter an Army officer arrived, confirming her husband's death.[70]

The official finding of an aneurysm-induced brain hemorrhage was fortunate for Faye in terms of death benefits. Ordinarily the VA paid no more than $250 for a veteran's funeral expenses, plus another $150 for a burial plot. But if the death was from a service connected disability the VA allotted $800, plus an additional amount to pay for transporting the body to a national cemetery. After reviewing his records, three ratings specialists determined Joe's death was service connected. They discovered that on November 24, 1958, while Joe was in the Navy, he was "struck from behind by an unknown object and knocked unconscious." Ten years later a bullet hit him in the head and ricocheted. Since a hard blow to the head can weaken a blood vessel, making it more likely to burst, "The brain hemorrhage causing death cannot be satisfactorily disassociated from the head injuries in the service without resorting to speculation."[71]

Ironically, by mid-May the VA had angled around its regulations and stopped trying to recoup Joe's readjustment pay. Had Joe still been alive he could have continued at Claremore.[72]

Carollyn was sound asleep on May 6 when some mysterious force startled her bolt upright.

Suddenly she was standing in the middle of the bedroom sobbing, scared. May 6 was her father's birthday and she feared something was wrong with him. A quick call confirmed that he was fine.

Four or five days later Nancy Sprayberry, wife of MOH recipient Michael Sprayberry, called. She had learned of Joe's death through the MOH grapevine. His passing went so unnoticed in the national media that Nancy was certain Carollyn did not know.

Better sit down, she told Carollyn.

After Nancy's call Carollyn gathered up Heather, then seven years old, and went to Trancas Beach. While the energetic little girl splashed in the water and dug in the sand, the Blonde Mama-san sat frozen, tearfully remembering how often she and Joe walked in the surf there, especially those special times when they were alone and made love.[73]

Joe's funeral was held in a chapel at Arlington, Thursday afternoon, May 10. A small gathering was in attendance. Faye, genuinely bereaved, Joey, and Faye's brother Jack were there. Maggie and John Henry flew in, both frail, grief-stricken, and poor, living only on their social security checks. Joe's sister Audrey and her son Clifton D. White, who was then in Army boot camp, attended. Sister Kathy did not. Nor was Joe's brother Douglas at the service; he remained in Oklahoma where he had recently moved from New Mexico. Red Combs arrived from California. Representing the Congressional Medal of Honor Society were Lloyd "Scooter" Burke (who received his MOH for heroism in Korea) and John L. Levitow (a Vietnam War MOH recipient). Official military personnel, including a general, a chaplain, and the pallbearers, completed the mourners.[74]

The funeral ceremony was short, quiet, and uncomfortable since the afternoon was hot and humid and the chapel's air conditioning was not working. A horse drawn caisson—Arlington is the only national cemetery authorized to use horses and caissons—carried the flag-draped casket from the chapel to the grave.

A prayer.

A twenty-one-gun salute.

The precise folding of the flag, solemnly handed to the widow.

The lowering casket.

As with all headstones at Arlington, the simple upright white slab, rounded at the top, marking Joe's grave contained no epitaph. But Joe deserved one. Actually, as befitting such a complex man, more than one:[75]

> Joe himself: "The fortunes of war are always difficult to assess or justify and can never be fully explained to the satisfaction of everyone."
>
> Alex Vira: "If Joe hadn't had the Medal, what would he have? He'd be a loser."
>
> Don Ross, World War II MOH recipient: "His problem was that he couldn't survive peacetime. He had become a soldier forever. They should have had a war going on all the time for people like him."
>
> Chris Luther: "He was a good man who did a tough job. His life choices were not always the best, but he always placed the needs of soldiers ahead of his own safety and needs."
>
> Rusty Cutlip: "Thank God we had guys like him defending our country."
>
> Faye: "He wanted to live on his little piece of land and raise horses, and that was perfectly all right with me."
>
> Carollyn: "I will love him always."

Friends learned of Joe's death the way Carollyn did, by word of mouth in hushed phone calls, because about the only publicity it generated was a brief announcement in the June 1979 issue of The Medal of Honor Historical Society's *The Annals,* hardly as widely read as the *New York Times.*

But thanks to a proselytizing trio Joe did receive posthumous recognition beginning in the late 1980s. By then the weathering effects of passing time and myth making had eroded the sharp spikes of defeat down to nubs, making the Vietnam War increasingly palatable.

The lead sword-bearer for Joe's postwar memorialization was fellow Vietnam vet and VA employee, Mike Sallis, who had been in the Marines.

Another of Joe's Seattle friends, Larry Frank who served with both the 1st Air Cavalry and the 173rd Airborne Brigade in Vietnam, later teamed with Mike in the effort. Sallis wanted Joe honored not only because of his special virtues as a warrior, but as a symbol of all Vietnam veterans. "What can I do for Joe that will reflect on the warrior, versus necessarily the man, the warrior part of Joe, and the good part of Joe?" he asked himself. Sallis also believed that if the nation honored Joe, "in a round about way it will show the other Vietnam vets that, hey, this country respects what you did." Others shared Mike's sentiments. Honoring Joe, wrote Alex Vira, would establish links between the broader public and "those vets still burdened with feelings that society wants to forget them and doesn't care. We see this effort as part of a healing process to erode the barriers that still exist between Vietnam vets, vets of other wars and the community. At last, 'Nam vets would have their own hero, a public tribute that all of us can share." [76]

Knowing the VA was remodeling its Seattle medical facility, Sallis wanted the refurbished building named in Joe's honor, just like the Audie L. Murphy Memorial Veterans Hospital in San Antonio or the VA facility in Murfreesboro, Tennessee, named after Alvin York. In February 1982, Sallis wrote Washington Senator Henry M. Jackson, explaining why the Seattle VA Medical Center should carry Hooper's name. Jackson forwarded Sallis's suggestion to VA officials. [77]

Then things became complicated. So many requests arrived at the VA to name facilities after individuals, replied Donald L. Custis, the VA's chief medical director, that rather than make difficult decisions itself, the VA passed the buck to Congress. Yes, Hooper was a fine candidate, but the VA named facilities for individuals only after Congress passed a bill mandating it. Then the VA "will be pleased to assist in every possible way." Senator Jackson's office forwarded a copy of Custis's letter to Sallis, saying that "if legislation regarding Mr. Joe Hooper reaches the Senate floor for a vote, Senator Jackson will keep your views in mind," which was not very helpful. [78]

When Senator Jackson died in 1983, Sallis wrote his replacement, Daniel J. Evans, renewing his request. In the way that bureaucracies constantly reinvent the wheel, Evans forwarded the letter to the VA, which repeated the gist of the Custis's earlier response, and suggested the Senate Veterans Affairs Committee as the appropriate starting point. While forwarding copies of this correspondence to Sallis, Evans indicated he had expressed interest in the project to that committee. But Mike was not especially encouraged when the senator later referred to "Mr. Joe Harper."[79] Although Evans wanted to help, bureaucratic inertia compounded by lethargy delayed progress.

With great persistence, Sallis now tried Washington Representative Thomas S. Foley, who responded quickly. The House Veterans Affairs Committee, he discovered, had specific guidelines for renaming VA facilities, which included having the support of a state's congressional delegation, Veterans Affairs Department, and major veterans' organizations. In view of these stringent requirements, Foley alerted Sallis that although the VA no longer named entire facilities after an individual, it retained the authority to name separate wings or departments within a veterans' institution. If Sallis accepted a wing rather than an entire building, Foley would contact the VA.[80]

Believing Joe was the Vietnam's most highly decorated soldier, just as Audie Murphy was for World War II, Sallis insisted upon an entire medical center, not just a wing. Events, however, shunted aside his views.

In July 1988, Washington senator Brock Adams wrote Seattle newspaperman Rick Anderson, who admired Joe, found his ongoing story fascinating, and had written several columns centered on the question of "What's going to happen to his life?" Now Adams informed the columnist that he recently learned of previous efforts to name a *wing* of the Seattle VA Medical Center after Hooper, and discovered what Representative Foley already knew, that congressional legislation was unnecessary to name a facility wing. The senator believed honoring Joe was not only long overdue but also "important for all Vietnam veterans who have common bonds with Joe Hooper's experiences." The Seattle facility had a "Wing 100," which Adams wanted renamed the "Joe Hooper Wing."

Before making a formal request, however, he needed letters of support from veterans groups, the community as a whole, and Washington's congressional delegation. "If you can work with groups in the state," the Senator told Anderson, "I'll work with other members of the delegation to get support. I will also make the formal request for the designation and my staff will track the request to make sure it doesn't get lost in the bureaucratic maze."[81]

Using the power of the press, Anderson did his part, receiving more than 250 letters and petitions favoring the proposal. Ronald E. Stuby and Jim Cooper expressed typical sentiments. "I couldn't think of a person who deserves to have his name on that wing more than Mr. Hooper, a true American hero," said Stuby. "It's certainly better than putting some god-damn politician's name on it." "By all means name the VA wing, or anything, for our brother Joe Hooper," two-tour Special Forces veteran Jim Cooper wrote. "It's just too bad that we have to be dead to be recognized. Thank you for what you're doing." [82]

Given the widespread support, Adams and Representative Rod Chand-ler, a recent convert to the cause, plunged ahead, adopting a two-pronged approach because of the VA's "mixed signals on the best way to pursue the matter." Adams spearheaded the effort outside of Congress to have the VA name a wing for Joe, while Chandler introduced a bill to name the Medical Center's Alcohol and Substance Abuse Treatment wing after him. The dual effort yielded results. In April 1989, officials at the Seattle VA Medical Center requested formal approval to name the facility's alcohol and drug treatment unit in Joe's honor. [83]

These developments embittered Sallis and Frank, not only because they wanted something more grandiose but also because the choice of an alco-hol and substance abuse ward appalled them. "I said you're slapping Joe in the face," recalled Sallis, "and by doing that you're slapping the rest of us in the face. You're acknowledging only one side, one part of Joe, the part that he couldn't help, that he had no control over. That's not right." Mike and Larry wanted Joe remembered for battlefield exploits, not alcoholism. They pre-ferred that nothing be named for Joe rather than the current plan, which was "misguided and wrong and does not befit Joe's memory as Vietnam's most decorated soldier." [84]

In a strange twist, an unexpected first fruit of their efforts pleased Mike and Larry because it honored Joe as they wanted him remembered, as a sol-dier, not a drunk. On May 6, 1989, the Staff Sergeant Joe R. Hooper United States Army Reserve Center, a new $4.8 million facility in Bothell, Wash-ington, was dedicated. The Center housed six Reserve units, including the Headquarters of the 3rd Training Brigade of the 104th Division (Training). While the Center was being built, the brigade's Command Sergeant-Major, Richard Detjen, had the responsibility of finding a suitable name for it. He and others were reading Anderson's columns about Hooper and the VA Medical Center and someone remembered Joe's brief service with the Bri-gade when he joined Alex Vira's company for the Fort Polk exercise. Higher authorities swiftly approved Joe's name. "Now all of this started with your articles," Detjen praised Anderson, "and for this we will be forever grateful, so will a lot of Vietnam Vets who still serve as citizen soldiers as members of the US Army Reserve." [85]

Colonel Dennis M. Cunneen, the Brigade commander, gave the opening remarks, followed by a formal address by Washington MOH recipient, Brigadier General Patrick H. Brady who was the Chief of the Secretary of the Army's Public Affairs Office. Lieutenant Colonel William F. Aronow, the Delta Raiders' executive officer back in 1968 and now commanding a battalion in the 104th Division presented personal reflections about Joe. Finally members of the Hooper family—Faye and Joey, Douglas, Audrey, and Kathy, and John Henry (Maggie died in April 1982)—unveiled the plaque and cut the ribbon. No one noticed the plaque had Joe's birth date wrong, 1939 instead of 1938. Numerous dignitaries (including the governor, Washington's two senators, the Sixth Army commander, and the 104th Division commander) applauded. The chaplain's benediction completed Joe's first formal postwar recognition. Watching the ceremony were Sallis and Frank, who were "much gratified" because this initial public recognition emphasized Joe's heroism. [86]

The event, wrote Rick Anderson, meant that "Vietnam's most decorated soldier will not remain one of its least remembered." [87]

Other commemorations soon followed. In late September 1989, Fort Campbell's new bowling alley, the Kegelbahn, received a second name, the Hooper Bowling Center. "Hooper risked his life at a time when some people were demonstrating against the war and others fled to Canada to avoid the draft," said Major General J. H. Binford Peay III, the 101st Airborne's commander who spoke at the dedication. An information sheet erroneously gave Hooper's birthday as August 8, 1939, credited him with thirty-seven citations (the most Joe claimed was thirty-five), and said he had only one Silver Star. The sheet did not note that Joe loved bowling from boyhood when he set pins, through young adulthood when he gave his first wife Sandra a bowling ball, to his days in Seattle when he and Larry Frank were on the local VA bowling team. [88]

On August 17, 1990, Wing 100 of the Seattle Medical Center officially became the Joe Hooper Inpatient Addictions Treatment Center, which was a thirty-bed inpatient alcoholism and drug dependence rehabilitation program with an outpatient follow-up component. The official plaque again had his birth date a year late, but accurately described Joe as "one of the most highly decorated soldiers of the Vietnam era" and praised "his exemplary service to his country." Although Sallis and Frank did not approve, dedicating this wing to Joe was as appropriate as naming the Reserve Center and the Fort Campbell bowling alley for him. The VA might not have helped Joe, but linking his name to the treatment center might make it easier for other addicted vets to get assistance. As Senator Adams said in a news release, naming the wing after Joe was "a proper way to acknowledge both dimensions of his life; his valor in the field and his difficulties at home." [89]

Honors came to Joe not only in Seattle and Fort Campbell, but also in his home town. Late in 1991 the Moses Lake American Legion Post 209 became the Joe R. Hooper American Legion Post 209, thus recognizing the local origins of the man who the townsfolk believed was "the most decorated U.S. soldier in history"—in *history*, not just Vietnam. One reporter astutely recognized this was more than a name change. The act was also symbolic because it welcomed "the stigmatized veterans of the divisive Vietnam era to the ranks of those who served in less controversial conflicts," such as World War II vets. [90]

Mike Sallis lost his limited war against the VA, but in the Joe R. Hooper Peace Memorial he achieved a complete victory. Like Joe, Mike had lived in Moses Lake and he wanted their home town to honor Joe, and indirectly all its veterans. Along with Larry Frank, Mike testified before the Moses Lake Parks and Recreation Advisory Commission in November 1988, and then for more than four years wrapped himself around the project like an anaconda, squeezing, never letting go until finally, in May 1993, the city dedicated the memorial in a grassy city park. Mike spent the night before the ceremony guarding the site to make sure no vandals defaced it. [91]

Fred Aronow was there, describing Hooper as "a hell-raising son of a gun" who led a charmed life, repeatedly escaping near-death in Vietnam. Joe's childhood chum, now State Senator Harold Hochstatter, maintained that even as a boy Joe was "the kind of guy who would bite off more than he could chew and proceed to chew it." And Faye and Joey came from Alabama so that Faye could lay a wreath and give a brief speech. She quoted the words from one of Joe's speeches, the one he plagiarized from Audie about no one wanting to live a few moments longer to leave behind a worse world. Then the widow added some remarks of her own, recalling all the "bright, beautiful young men who died half a world away in the jungles of Asia. These bright, beautiful young men, willing to fight and die. They did not refuse their country's call. They marched into battle accepting death as their constant companion."[92]

"Joe R. Hooper Peace Memorial," read the inscription chiseled into the memorial's center marble slab. "Dedicated to all the men and women of Moses Lake who served in the armed forces of the United States during times of war and peace so that others might enjoy the rights and freedoms that we as a nation hold so dear." The left side slab honored James P. Fleming, a 1961 Moses Lake High School graduate and Air Force captain who received an MOH on November 26, 1968, and, like Joe, lived to receive it.

Joe was memorialized on the right-hand panel, where the text provided an inaccurate date for his MOH action (February 11, 1968, instead of February 21) and credited him with six Bronze Stars and eight Purple Hearts (instead of two and four respectively). But it gave both his birth year and the total number of his medals correctly.

That was about right for Joe.

Half legend, half truth.[93]

Another memorial service occurred after Joe's funeral. Some of his old buddies from the 101st Airborne came to a hotel to give their condolences to the family. Little Joey Hooper was taken back to the room by her grandparents early. When Faye came back to the room later, she picked up Joey's coat from the floor. Some packets fell out of the pockets: a one dollar bill paper-clipped over a one hundred dollar bill. These $101 packages were the 101st's way of taking care of a fallen comrade's family.

Was Joe Hooper a hero?

Was he a tragic hero in the sense of the Greek epics? Certainly he was an Achilles-like warrior with an Achilles heel—alcohol. Or was a medieval hero more apt? Joe displayed few traits that were chivalrous, except for his doubtless charm with the ladies, and yet was certainly a Roland at the bridge —when the time for combat came he was heroic and unyielding. Perhaps Shakespeare's complicated and flawed heroes were better models—something of Prince Hal lurked in Joe, and he did become a Henry V when war called.

Looking at a specifically American model might be more fruitful. James Fenimore Cooper's characters are available—loners, skilled in woodscraft, men of action. Or was Joe more of a Huckleberry Finn, endlessly drifting down a river of his own imagination, searching for freedom? In a mid-twentieth-century model, Joe most resembled the heroes of novelist James Jones's World War II trilogy—the troubled, hard-drinking career soldiers who fought so bravely and could not come to terms with peace.

But Joe, essentially uneducated in academic matters, knew nothing of the Greek epics or Roland or Henry V. Nor did he know who James Fenimore Cooper, Mark Twain, and James Jones were. No, for inspiration Joe looked not to the distant past, not to literature, but to film, especially to Audie Murphy and John Wayne—and James Dean. Joe's pursuit of Audie's heroic fame was palpable, but so were his Dean-like anti-heroic attributes. Joe was neither Murphy nor Dean, but both: a military hero and an individualistic anti-hero.

Like the Vietnam War, Joe Hooper evades easy answers, remaining elusive, ambiguous, mysterious. Looking for Joe is akin to looking at funhouse mirrors—what you see depends on who you are and where you're standing, and the images are distorted, only occasionally reflecting reality, and that only fleetingly. Joe was in this hall of mirrors, his image reflected back through the prism of too many other people's images: hero, drunk, soldier, lover, lout, husband, hero, father, son, comrade, public figure, officer, hero. In the end, these distorted pieces never quite fit together.

It may well be that Joe, too, was looking for Joe, and never found him whole.

Epilogue

... the most decorated soldier of the Vietnam War.

Tour guide at Arlington National Cemetery,
pointing out Joe's gravesite to visitors

America has few sacred sites.

Independence Hall, Gettysburg, Pearl Harbor, and now the World Trade Center site, but especially Joe's final destination, Arlington National Cemetery.

While the nation underwent its Vietnam ordeal, Arlington experienced its own crisis. The problem was space: too many bodies, too little land.

The cemetery was born in mid-1864. Three years earlier, in one of the first major movements of the Civil War, Union troops stationed in Washington slipped across the Potomac River and occupied Arlington, Virginia. The Union commander, General Irvin McDowell, converted Arlington House mansion, the prewar home of Confederate General Robert E. Lee, into the Army of the Potomac's headquarters. During the war the magnificent house hosted many gala social events. Then in early 1864 the mansion was officially confiscated, sold at auction, and bought by the U.S. government for $26,800. At the same time, stung by surging criticism about the treatment of dead Union soldiers, the War Department was assessing federal land for potential cemeteries. The Union Army's Quartermaster General asked Secretary of War Edwin M. Stanton to designate two hundred acres near the mansion as a national cemetery "and to encircle the residence with graves thereby making it unsuitable for private habitation"—that is, making sure that the traitor Bobby Lee never lived in the house again. By year's end more than seven thousand Union soldiers were buried there.[1]

When the original wooden grave markers deteriorated in the early 1870s the government introduced the standardized gleaming white marble headstones still used in all national cemeteries. Built in 1874, the original amphitheater held 1,500 people; the new Memorial Amphitheater completed in 1920 held more than three times that many. A year later the government added the Tomb of the Unknown Soldier, where sentinels of the 3rd U.S. Infantry maintain eternal vigil. Each soldier paces twenty-one steps down a mat, pauses for twenty-one seconds, then returns. A new guard takes over every hour, except from April through September when the shifts are only half an hour.[2]

As improvements occurred, Arlington expanded by 142 acres in 1889 and another 56 in 1897. But by the 1960s space was at a premium. To conserve it, Arlington abolished side-by-side burials for family members and adopted a tier system in which the bodies of a veteran, spouse, and all dependents could be stacked one atop the other in a single gravesite. Other space-saving measures followed, including strict eligibility requirements for burial there. The new requirements were immensely unpopular among veterans, and in 1980 the cemetery opened its first columbarium, with a second completed five years later. Perhaps most important in the battle for space, in 1966 the cemetery annexed another 190 acres.[3]

The "little piece of land" Joe wanted so he could raise horses would surely have been a reverent place for him, just as a national reverence hovers over Arlington National Cemetery even with thousands of tourists and a myriad tour buses roaming the grounds.

No private vehicles have been permitted on the grounds since 1970, and people speak in muted tones and walk gingerly as they peek and probe amidst the more than 230,000 headstones, each smartly standing at attention.

Joe's remains reside in Section 46, Grave 656-17, the third headstone in from the end of a row running perpendicular to Memorial Drive. With its gold lettering, made available only to honor MOH recipients, the marker stands out from the hundreds that surround it. Looking east from the headstone, in the spring a coppice of cherry trees, richly adorned in robust pink blossoms, shields the grave from the traffic on Memorial Drive and obscures the Memorial Amphitheater just across the blacktop. To the north and northwest, readily visible beyond several dozen rows of matching headstones, are memorials commemorating national heartaches: the Challenger space shuttle, the failed Iran hostage rescue mission, and the USS *Maine*, sunk in Havana's harbor with heavy loss of life from an accidental internal explosion back in 1898. To the west is a vast green expanse, the grass neatly stitched with white grave markers.

And to the south, about sixty feet away, lies Audie Murphy. Although Arlington's tourist pamphlet insists that flags can decorate a gravesite only on Memorial Day weekend, no one confiscates the tiny American flag nestled against Audie's headstone.

In 1995, as an open-sided tour bus headed from south to north along Memorial Drive the guide informed his passengers that if they looked to their left they could see the grave of Audie Murphy, "the most decorated soldier of World War II," and that a little farther on they could see the grave of Joe Hooper, "the most decorated soldier of the Vietnam War." When flagged down, a subsequent tour guide averred that mentioning both Audie and Joe was part of the routine presentation. But many tour guides became so long-winded in extolling Audie's fame that they had to skip Joe so they could talk about the Challenger, the hostage rescue mission, and the *Maine*.

Standing near Grave 656-17 for an hour or so further emphasized the comparative fame of Audie and Joe. Dozens of tourists wandered by, scanning the headstones, looking for Audie. When shown Joe's grave and informed that he was often acclaimed as the Vietnam War's equivalent of Audie Murphy, several took snapshots and a few more paused to read the gold lettering. Most, however, hastened southward to Audie's grave with its miniature flag.

Despite the near-anonymity, Joe undoubtedly feels reasonably secure here and likes the company he keeps. If he was on patrol, protecting his back are the men and women who died aboard the Challenger, the military personnel who ventured into Iran on an audacious rescue mission, and—harkening back to his first days in uniform—the *Maine*'s sailors.

For eternity Joe's left flank will be anchored by two fine men, Sergeant Major Elmer H. Kettler and First Sergeant Lambert W. Deshetler Jr., both career NCOs and veterans of World War II, Korea, and Vietnam. To his right, well, maybe that flank needs special attention because an officer—a colonel no less—rests there.

And to his front, walking point, is Audie Murphy.

Awards and decorations displayed on his uniform for an official Army portrait taken on June 8, 1971:[1]

Right Breast (thirty individual awards)

Combat Infantryman Badge
Medal of Honor
Silver Star with Oak Leaf Cluster (OLC)
Bronze Star Medal with V device and OLC
Air Medal with four OLCs
Army Commendation Medal with V device and OLC
Purple Heart with three OLCs
Army Good Conduct Medal with Bronze Clasp, two knots
Navy Good Conduct Medal
National Defense Service Medal
Armed Forces Expedition Medal
Republic of Vietnam Service Medal with Silver Star
    (equivalent to five campaigns)
Republic of Vietnam Gallantry Cross with Palm
    [according to the official citation, this should
    be a Silver Star, not a Palm]
Republic of Vietnam Campaign Medal
U.S. Master Parachutist Jump Wings

Left Breast (five unit awards)

South Vietnamese Special Forces Parachute Wings at the novice level
    [why he wore this was a mystery since he was undoubtedly authorized to wear the South Vietnamese Army Airborne Wings]
Presidential Unit Citation
South Vietnamese Presidential Unit Citation (presented to the 2nd
    Brigade, 101st Airborne for service in early 1968)

Republic of Vietnam Gallantry Cross with Palm Unit Citation
Republic of Vietnam Civil Actions Unit Citation with Palm

The Army's compilation of his awards in July 1989:[2]

Medal of Honor
Silver Star with OLC
Bronze Star Medal with V device and OLC
Air Medal with two OLCS
Purple Heart
Good Conduct Medal, Bronze with three loops
Vietnam Service Medal with six Bronze Service Stars
Combat Infantryman Badge
Republic of Vietnam Campaign Ribbon with Device (1960)
National Defense Service Medal
Republic of Vietnam Gallantry Cross with Palm Unit Citation
Republic of Vietnam Gallantry Cross with Silver Star
Republic of Vietnam Civil Actions Honor Medal, First Class Unit
    Citation Badge
Parachutist Badge
Expert Badge with Automatic Rifle Bar
Sharpshooter Badge with Rifle Bar

Acknowledgments

To all those listed in the Bibliographical Essay who shared their personal papers and consented to interviews we send a robust "Thank You!" In every case we approached these people as strangers and, at least from our perspective, left as friends. Although each of these individuals was vital in reconstructing Joe's life, we owe a special debt to seven people, named here in alphabetical order.

Carollyn DeVore graciously consented to multiple interviews, allowed us to rummage through the extensive material she had relating to Joe, openly discussed both Joe's good and bad sides, and had an astoundingly accurate memory. Steve Hawk's extensive collection of wartime material and detailed recollections were instrumental in understanding Joe's service with A-2-501 and how the war had changed by 1971. Along with an initial interview that lasted the better part of two days, Cleo C. Hogan Jr. was tireless in answering "just one more question." In addition, he permitted us to read his almost-daily letters to his wife Glynna (who had the good sense to keep them), shared his encyclopedic knowledge of the Delta Raiders' first six months in Vietnam, and wrote his memoirs, which are indispensable in understanding Joe's first tour. Everything in this book flowed from the first interview we did, which was on August 12–13, 1994, when we met with Faye Hooper in her Decatur, Alabama, home. Not only did Faye answer as many questions as we asked (both then and in subsequent phone calls), but she also gave us access to Joe's surviving papers, memorabilia, and photographs. Aside from what we discovered about Joe from these materials, we also first learned of Carollyn DeVore and the Delta Raiders of Vietnam Association, and through that Association we contacted Cleo Hogan, Captain McMenamy, and so many other Raiders. For insight into the last year of Joe's life, our interviews with Dewey "Buck" Johnson (and his family) were indispensable, especially since it was through "Buck" that we met Jerry McCollum, who was with Joe the day he died. Captain Mac literally went hoarse talking with us for eight straight hours about the Raiders' formation, deployment to Vietnam, and their first two months in-country, and—after considerable prodding—about his own remarkable military career. To say that he is a dynamic personality and truly inspirational leader does not do justice to the gentleman's character. Finally, through both personal and telephone interviews, and through written responses to our inquiries, Alex Vira allowed us to better understand Joe's years in the Seattle region when he worked for the VA, and introduced us to Mike Sallis and Larry Frank.

To Noah and Joyce Rockel, thanks for the lessons in devotion and courage.

The book benefited immensely from the critiques provided by three exceptionally talented historians who read an initial draft of the manuscript: Professor Mark Clodfelter, a former Air Force officer who now teaches at the National War College; Professor Jerry Cooper, who recently retired after a distinguished career at the University of Missouri–St. Louis; and David M. Toczek, an Army officer and author of a fine book on the Battle of Ap Bac. Although we accepted almost all of their suggestions, we did not incorporate them all. Consequently, any errors in the book are ours alone.

Thanks to John F. Sanders, who is Professor Maslowski's neighbor and frequent fishing companion, many of the photographs in this book are better quality than the originals. John is a professional photographer who is a genius at converting less-than-perfect photos—sometimes no more than aging, fading snapshots—into truly splendid black-and-white prints.

Without generous support from the University of Nebraska–Lincoln, this book could not have been written. The project benefited from several grants-in-aid from the Research Council that funded travel costs for trips to the National Archives and to conduct interviews. Also Professor Maslowski's faculty development leave in the fall semester, 2002, permitted the authors to complete the text.

Numerous hard-working, knowledgeable individuals at various institutions, repositories, and libraries provided invaluable assistance. Our debt runs especially deep to the following: Gretchen Holten Poppler at the University of Nebraska–Lincoln's Love Library, a historian at heart who is unfailingly and enthusiastically helpful; Jeffrey Clarke, Romana Danysh, and Erik Villard at the U.S. Army Center of Military History at Fort McNair, all of whom readily responded to inquires about often-obscure matters; John Slonaker (now retired) and Richard Sommers at the U.S. Army Military History Institute at Carlisle Barrack, Pennsylvania, both of whom know the records there like the proverbial backs of their hands; Eric V. Voelz, with an assist from Carl Paulson, at the Military Personnel Records, National Personnel Records Center at St. Louis, who guided us through the records there and "translated" into English the acronym-laden military-speak used in many official documents; Mrs. Skip Munson of the City of Moses Lake Library, who graciously loaned us the *Columbia Basin Herald* on microfilm; Dr. Chris Maggio, director of alumni affairs at Northwestern State University, for identifying the classes Joe took there; Dr. Dannette Boyle for identifying the classes Joe took at Claremore Junior College (now Rogers State University); and most especially, Clifford L. Snyder of the Textual Reference Branch, Archives II, National Archives at College Park, who understands the records from the Vietnam War better than anyone else and is tireless in sharing his knowledge.

Working with the following people at the University of Nebraska Press has been a joy: Elizabeth A. S. Demers, the history acquisitions editor; Margie Rine, the proposal writer; Renae Carlson, the project editor; and Sandra Johnson, the marketing manager. In addition, freelance copyeditor Dawn Hall did a masterful job in polishing the manuscript. All authors should be so lucky to benefit from the efforts of such talented people.

On the home front, morale and encouragement remained high throughout the many years we spent fighting to understand Joe Hooper and the Vietnam War. To Jean and Thomas Joel, and to Pern, Jed, and Laurel, our gratitude will always be inadequate, our love unremitting. Professor Maslowski also thanks his father, Karl H. Maslowski, who at age ninety-one still regularly hunts and fishes (and reads history!), for his love, support, and inspiration.

We would be seriously remiss if we did not thank Jim Rome and "The Jungle," and especially one memorable day when XR4TI appeared. When we needed humorous relief, "The Jungle" is often where we found it. The Clones may be unemployed and still living in their parents' basement, but some of them are amazingly clever and witty. By the way, we never forget Mark Mulder.

War Jake Porter.

War the Tillman brothers.

War Nebraska.

We're out.

A Few Words Concerning the Text

We have done a very modest amount of editorial work to make the text easier to read by avoiding the constant use of [*sic*], brackets, and ellipses. For example, we corrected most misspelled words and grammatical errors, except in what Joe Hooper wrote, where we left the original intact, correcting only his most egregious errors with bracketed material. As an example of the types of changes we made, Cleo Hogan wrote, "I could not even phantom what a DSC or Medal of Honor would be like to receive or recommend." Since he obviously meant "fathom" rather than "phantom," we made the change. Or Dale Urban said, "I never seen Joe again until after we got done," which we modified to "I never saw Joe again until after we got done." As a final example, Noah Rockel was no scholar but he got his point across when he wrote about "the most proudest fighting unit the U.S. has, the 101st Airborne Division, the Screaming Eagles there the most proudest paratroopers there are. And we were asked to do a job here. So were doing it." Without losing the flavor of what he said, we changed the first "there" to "they're" and the second "were" to "we're."

Interviewees sometimes made points in an awkward or "wordy" manner, so we occasionally modified quotes to make them read more smoothly. For instance, Ava James said, "And we were the only two guys that I saw up there. I didn't see anybody else. There was nobody else up there at all." Leaving out the middle sentence, which was redundant, we rendered this as "And we were the only two guys that I saw up there. There was nobody else up there at all." Or Chris Luther said, "I just felt comfortable knowing this guy, yeah, he had fear like everybody else but he knew how to control it." In the text this appears as "I just felt comfortable knowing this guy had fear like everybody else but knew how to control it." That is, we omitted three unnecessary words: "yeah," "he," and "he."

In a few cases when interviewees told us what Joe said, we put those words in quotation marks as if he actually spoke them. These quotes should not be taken literally but as an approximation of what Joe said.

To limit the number of acronyms, we often wrote out those that appeared infrequently. For example, General Westmoreland wrote that Tet "has dealt the GVN a severe blow," which we changed to "has dealt the Government of Vietnam a severe blow," and General Abrams wrote that he hoped to "ensure a free RVN," which we changed to "ensure a free Republic of Vietnam."

In July 1970, the United States changed the four Corps Tactical Zones to Military Regions, but we used Corps for the entire war. Thus, in the text it remained "I Corps," never Military Region I (or the acronym, MRI). Also, fire bases and fire support bases were technically different, but soldiers often used "fire base" for either a fire base or a fire support base, and so have we.

Abbreviations and Acronyms

AAR	After Action Report
Abn	Airborne
ACS	Assistant Chief of Staff
ARA	Aerial Rocket Artillery
ARVN	Army of the Republic of Vietnam
Bde	Brigade
BDJ	Battalion Daily Journal
Bn	Battalion
BS	Bronze Star
BBT	Booby trap
CBH	Columbia Basin (Moses Lake) Herald
CIA	Central Intelligence Agency
COSVN	Central Office for South Vietnam
Div	Division
DROVA	Delta Raiders of Vietnam Association
DRV	Democratic Republic of Vietnam
DSC	Distinguished Service Cross
Infy	Infantry
JCS	Joint Chiefs of Staff
JRHP	Joe Ronnie Hooper Papers
LL	Lessons Learned
LZ	Landing Zone
MACV	Military Assistance Command, Vietnam
MILPERSON	Military Personnel Center
MOH	Medal of Honor
MOS	Military Occupational Specialty
NARA	National Archives and Records Administration
NDP	Night Defensive Position
NLF	National Liberation Front
NVA	North Vietnamese Army (synonymous with PAVN)

PAVN	People's Army of Vietnam (synonymous with NVA)
PH	Purple Heart
PLAF	People's Liberation Armed Force
PRG	Provisional Revolutionary Government
RG	Record Group
SS	Silver Star
VARO	Veterans Administration Regional Office
VC	Viet Cong
VCI	Viet Cong Infrastructure

Notes

Prologue

1. A copy of the Medal of Honor file is in the Joe Ronnie Hooper Papers (henceforth JRHP). The file can also be viewed online at http://www.nara.gov/cgi-bin/starfinder/ 5725/complete.txt.

2. Mark S. Hawk interview, June 21, 1997.

Chapter 1

1. For the development of Moses Lake, see Rita G. Seedorf and Martin F. Seedorf, "Runways & Reclamation: The Influence of the Federal Government on Moses Lake," *Columbia: The Magazine of Northwest History* (Summer 1994), and the *Columbia Basin (Moses Lake) Herald* (henceforth CBH) for the relevant years.

2. This account of the Hooper household relies heavily on the interviews with Audrey Hooper, March 2, 1996, July 19, 1999, and May 16, 2000; Kathryn D. Hendricks (nee Hooper), June 16, 1999 and July 28, 1999; and Michael R. Grimm, September 19, 1999.

3. Mavis Withers (nee Opp) interview, April 16, 1996.

4. Copies of "Marriage Certificate" for Raymond Roy Sweatt and Maggie L. Garrison and "Certificate of Death" for Raymond Roy Sweatt, Michael R. Grimm Papers; copy of "Marriage Certificate" for John Henry Hooper and Maggie Sweatt, Audrey Hooper Papers.

5. Audrey Hooper interview, March 2, 1996.

6. James R. Gumm interview, July 2, 1995.

7. "How the Town Stands," CBH, June 22, 1950, 1; "Moses Lake Census Hits 9,053," CBH, April 1, 1955, 1; "Hospital Fund Drive Set for Next Friday," CBH, February 4, 1949, 1; "Council Approves Sidewalk and Curb Project," CBH, April 15, 1949, 1; "City Bus Line Begins Service," CBH, April 26, 1955, 1.

8. Harold A. Hochstatter interview, April 12, 1996.

9. Thomas M. Johnson interview, April 14, 1996.

10. Johnson interview.

11. "Certificate of Achievement," JRHP, and Joe's eighth grade report card, Audrey Hooper Papers.

12. Rusty Cutlip interview, June 17, 2000.

13. "We Can Do Something on Juvenile Delinquency," CBH, July 20, 1955, 4.

14. On James Dean, see David Hofstede, *James Dean: A Bio-Biography* (Westport CT: Greenwood Press, 1996); the reviewer's quote is on page 45.

15. Michael C. C. Adams, *The Best War Ever: America and World War II* (Baltimore: Johns Hopkins University Press, 1994), 78, and Arthur Schlesinger Jr., "The Crisis of American Masculinity," *Esquire*, November 1958, 63–65.

16. The discussion of manhood relies on E. Anthony Rotundo, *American Manhood: Transformation in Masculinity from the Revolution to the Modern Era* (New York: Basic Books, 1993); Michael Kimmel, *Manhood in America: A Cultural History* (New York: The Free Press, 1996); George L. Mosse, *The Image of Man: The Creation of Modern Masculinity* (New York: Oxford University Press, 1996); Michael A. Messner, *Power at Play: Sports and the Problem of Masculinity* (Boston: Beacon Press, 1992); and Ralph D. Donald, "Masculinity and Machismo in Hollywood's War Films," in Steve Craig, ed., *Men, Masculinity, and the Media* (Newbury Park CA: Sage, 1992).

17. Tobin Siebers, *Among Men* (Lincoln: University of Nebraska Press, 1998), 104–5.

18. Joe's tenth grade report card, Audrey Hooper Papers.

19. Ron Isakson interview, May 13, 1998.

20. Withers interview, April 16, 1996.

21. "Chief Grid Practice Set," CBH, August 14, 1955, 8; "18 Chiefs End High School Play Friday," CBH, November 9, 1955, 8; "Moses Lake Roster," CBH, November 10, 1955, 7.

22. "Chief Sophs Win by 38–21," CBH, September 19, 1955, 8; "Chief Jayvees Bow to Ephrata B Team, 18–7," CBH, October 25, 1955, 7; "Jayvees Lose to Wenatchee," CBH, November 1, 1955, 8; Cutlip interview, June 17, 2000.

23. For examples, see Mark Melson, "Vietnam's Most-Decorated U.S. Soldier: Joe Hooper, Number One G.I.," *Shreveport Times*, September 16, 1973, clipping in the JRHP, and Dave Wolf, "Probing the Minds of Men Paid to Annihilate Other Men," *Today's Health*, July 1973.

24. "Amateur Athletic Union" certificate, JRHP. The relevant school yearbooks do not show Joe on either the track or varsity football teams; see *The Nineteen Fifty-Four Tyee*, *Through the Years with the 1955 Tyee*, and *Tyee 1956*, all in the Thomas M. Johnson Papers.

25. Withers interview, April 16, 1996.

26. Roy Wayne Miller interview, April 11, 1999. Joe's other high school pals—Isakson, Perez, Cutlip, and Mason—confirm his penchant for gambling.

27. "Local Negro Church Only One over Widespread Area," CBH, October 7, 1955, 11.

28. Our thanks to Kevin Redding for sending a Xeroxed copy of Joe's Social Security Account Number application. Redding wrote a brief essay on Joe; see "A Guy Named Joe," *American Iron Magazine*, January 2002, 18.

29. Isakson interview, May 13, 1996.

30. Inscription in *Through the Years with the 1955 Tyee*, Mavis Withers Papers, and inscription in *Through the Years with the 1955 Tyee*, Thomas M. Johnson Papers.

31. Alfred D. Mason interview, April 14, 1998.

32. Pete Perez interview, May 11, 1998, and Isakson interview, May 13, 1998.

33. Cutlip interview, June 17, 2000.

34. Mason interview, April 14, 1998.

35. Miller interview, April 11, 1999.

36. For the militarization of American society and the Cold War, see Michael S. Sherry, *In the Shadow of War: The United States Since the 1930s* (New Haven: Yale University Press, 1995); Stephen J. Whitfield, *The Culture of the Cold War*, 2nd edition (Baltimore: Johns Hopkins University Press, 1996); Walter J. Hixon, *Parting the Curtain: Propaganda, Culture, and the Cold War, 1945–1961* (New York: St. Martin's Press, 1997); and J. Fred MacDonald, *Television and the Red Menace: The Video Road to Vietnam* (New York: Praeger, 1985).

37. Whitfield, *Culture of the Cold War*, 24–25.

38. "Base Renamed for Yakima Pilot Killed over Germany," CBH, June 15, 1950, 1.

39. "As Big as 3 High School Gyms," CBH, March 1, 1955, 1; "First B-52 Delivered from Larson," CBH, June 29, 1955, 1.

40. Whitfield, *Culture of the Cold War*, 96.

41. Carlos Arnaldo Schwantes, *The Pacific Northwest: An Interpretive History*, revised and enlarged edition (Lincoln: University of Nebraska Press, 1996), 473–75.

42. Whitfield, *Culture of the Cold War*, 55–57.

43. Whitfield, *Culture of the Cold War*, 81, 99.

44. Audrey Hooper interview, July 19, 1999; Hendricks interview, July 28, 1999; Melson, "Vietnam's Most-Decorated U.S. Soldier."

45. Audrey Hooper interview, July 19, 1999; Hendricks interview, July 28, 1999; Withers interview, June 17, 2000. The CBH printed regular TV schedules, which not only show the TV stations that could be seen in Moses Lake, but also the programming. For an excellent discussion of Cold War TV, see MacDonald, *Television and the Red Menace.*

46. Other military programs that appeared on Moses Lake TV were *Air Force Film Magazine* and *Navy Log.*

47. Carl von Clausewitz, *On War*, ed. Michael Howard and Peter Paret (Princeton: Princeton University Press, 1976).

48. The CBH regularly ran ads for all the movie theaters in Moses Lake.

49. Perez interview, June 17, 2000, and Cutlip interview, June 17, 2000.

50. For Audie Murphy, see Don Graham, *No Name on the Bullet: A Biography of Audie Murphy* (New York: Viking Penguin, 1989); Colonel Harold B. Simpson, *Audie Murphy: American Soldier* (Hillsboro TX: The Hill Junior College Press, 1975); Roger J. Spiller, "The Price of Valor," MHQ, *The Quarterly Journal of Military History* (Spring 1993); Thomas B. Morgan, "The War Hero," *Esquire*, December 1983; Audie Leon Murphy Personnel File, Military Personnel Records, National Personnel Records Center, St. Louis, Missouri.

51. Graham, *No Name on the Bullet*, 22.

52. The quotes are from a July 1945 interview by Murphy published in the "Audie Murphy Research Foundation Newsletter" (Spring 1998), and Hal Boyle, "Audie Lost His Zest for Hunting," *CBH*, August 30, 1955, 10.

53. Audie Murphy, *To Hell and Back* (New York: Grosset and Dunlap, 1949), 15, 179, 77, 158.

54. Murphy, *To Hell and Back*, 210, 273.

55. Boyle, "Audie Lost His Zest for Hunting," 10.

56. Michael Evans and Alan Ryan, eds., *The Human Face of War: Killing, Fear and Chaos in Battle* (St. Leonards NSW, Australia: Allen and Unwin, 2000), 48–49.

57. Ron Kovic, *Born on the Fourth of July* (New York: Pocket Books, 1977), 54.

58. Morgan, "War Hero," 602.

59. July 1945 interview published in the "Audie Murphy Research Foundation Newsletter" (Spring 1998).

60. On Wayne, see Randy Roberts and James S. Olson, *John Wayne: American* (New York: The Free Press, 1995), and Garry Wills, *John Wayne's America* (New York: A Touchstone Book, 1998).

61. Roberts and Olson, *John Wayne*, 240.

62. Philip Caputo, *A Rumor of War* (New York: Ballantine, 1978), 6.

63. James R. Ebert, *A Life in a Year: The American Infantryman, 1965–1972* (Novato CA: Presidio Press, 1993), 9.

64. Roberts and Olson, *John Wayne*, 211.

65. Graham, *No Name on the Bullet*, 326, 327.

66. Michael Bilton and Kevin Sim, *Four Hours in My Lai* (New York: Viking, 1992), 11.

Chapter 2

1. Carollyn DeVore to the authors, c. fall 1994. The "Report of Medical Examination," July 20, 1970, in the Joe Ronnie Hooper Medical Records, Claim Folder 24965568, VARO, Muskogee, Oklahoma, confirms the presence of the lips.

2. Except where otherwise noted, this account of Hooper's naval service relies on the Joe Ronnie Hooper Naval Personnel Records, National Personnel Records Center, St. Louis, Missouri; Gary Foster interviews, March 7, 1995 and February 28, 1996; Arlene Foster interview, February 28, 1996; and Miller interview, April 11, 1999. We are indebted to Captain Frank H. Tryon Jr. (Retired) for help in understanding some of the information relating to Joe's naval service in his Personnel File; Tryon interview, May 23, 1995.

3. "3 Moses Lake Youths Enlist for Navy Duty," *CBH*, December 30, 1955, 1.

4. "Report of Medical Examination," January 17, 1956, Hooper Medical Records, Claim Folder 24965568.

5. On the *Wasp* and its history, see James L. Mooney, ed., *Dictionary of American Naval*

Fighting Ships, 8 vols. (Washington DC: Navy Department, Office of the Chief of Naval Operations, Naval History Division, 1959–1981), and Gareth L. Pawlowski, *Flat-Tops and Fledglings: A History of American Aircraft Carriers* (New York: A. S. Barnes and Company, 1971).

6. Audrey Hooper interview, March 2, 1996, and Hendricks interview, July 28, 1999.

7. On the *Hancock* and its history, see Mooney, *Dictionary*, and Pawlowski, *Flat-Tops and Fledglings*.

8. Joe's Naval Personnel Records say that three civilian males attacked him, but Gary Foster said a Marine bit Joe's finger. The "Chronological Record of Medical Care" and a "Veterans Administration Regional Office, Portland, Oregon, Administrative Decision," December 10, 1975, both in the Hooper Medical Records, Claim Folder 24965568, confirm Foster's account.

9. On homosexuality during the Cold War, see Sherry, *Shadow of War*, 152–55, and Kimmel, *Manhood in America*, 100.

10. For example, see the *CBH*'s editorial cartoons of September 28, 1954, 16; February 1, 1955, 8; and April 27, 1955, 4.

11. Tryon interview, May 23, 1995.

12. "Report of Medical Treatment, Hospitalization, and Allied Services," November 26, 1958, Hooper Medical Records, Claim Folder 24965568.

13. Buis and Ovnand were the second and third Americans to die in Vietnam; the first was Captain Harry Cramer, who perished in a Viet Cong mortar barrage in October 1957.

14. "NSC-68. A Report to the National Security Council" by the Executive Secretary on United States Objectives and Programs for National Security, April 14, 1950, reprinted in the *Naval War College Review*, May–June 1975, 69, 60.

15. *CBH*, February 11, 1955, 12.

16. "NSC-68," 61, 54; *CBH*, February 18, 1955, 14.

17. "NSC-68," 56, 63.

18. "NSC-68," 80.

19. Michael D. Pearlman, *Warmaking and American Democracy: The Struggle over Military Strategy, 1700 to the Present* (Lawrence: University Press of Kansas, 1999), 337.

20. William Darryl Henderson, *Why the Vietcong Fought: A Study of Motivation and Control in a Modern Army in Combat* (Westport CT: Greenwood Press, 1979), 53.

21. This account of the war between France and the Viet Minh, followed by America's increasingly important role in South Vietnam, comes from the following: Gerard J. DeGroot, *A Noble Cause? America and the Vietnam War* (New York: Pearson Education, 2000); William J. Duiker, *Sacred War: Nationalism and Revolution in a Divided Vietnam* (New York: McGraw-Hill, 1995); George C. Herring, *America's Longest War: The United States and Vietnam, 1950–1975*, 3rd edition (New York: McGraw-Hill,

1996); James S. Olson and Randy Roberts, *Where the Domino Fell: America and Vietnam, 1945 to 1995*, 2nd edition (New York: St. Martin's Press, 1996); Robert D. Schulzinger, *A Time for War: The United States and Vietnam, 1941–1975* (New York: Oxford University Press, 1997); William S. Turley, *The Second Indochina War: A Short Political and Military History, 1954–1975* (New York: Mentor, 1987); Marilyn B. Young, *The Vietnam Wars, 1945–1990* (New York: HarperCollins, 1991); George Donelson Moss, *Vietnam: An American Ordeal*, 4th edition (Upper Saddle River NJ: Prentice Hall, 2002); and Robert J. McMahon, ed., *Major Problems in the History of the Vietnam War: Documents and Essays*, 2nd edition (Lexington MA: D. C. Heath, 1995).

22. Olson and Roberts, *Where the Domino Fell*, 29.

23. William J. Duiker, *Ho Chi Minh: A Life* (New York: Hyperion, 2000), 379.

24. Duiker, *Ho Chi Minh*, 28.

25. State Department "Statement of U.S. Policy toward Indochina, 1948," in McMahon, *Major Problems*, 76–77, and "NSC Paper No. 64, 1950: The Position of the United States with Respect to Indochina," in McMahon, *Major Problems*, 82. Also see Robert Buzzanco, *Masters of War: Military Dissent and Politics in the Vietnam Era* (New York: Cambridge University Press, 1996), 32, 47.

26. Olson and Roberts, *Where the Domino Fell*, 37.

27. Duiker, *Sacred War*, 67.

28. "Final Declaration of the Geneva Conference on Indochina, 1954," in McMahon, *Major Problems*, 125.

29. Jane S. Werner and Luu Doan Huynh, eds., *The Vietnam War: Vietnamese and American Perspectives* (Armonk NY: M. E. Sharpe, 1993), 235. The commander was General Tran Van Tra.

30. Duiker, *Ho Chi Minh*, 509.

31. Duiker, *Ho Chi Minh*, 511–16, 521.

32. Military History Institute of Vietnam (translated by Merle L. Pribbenow), *Victory in Vietnam: The Official History of the People's Army of Vietnam, 1954–1975* (Lawrence: University Press of Kansas, 2002), 48–50.

33. Military History Institute of Vietnam, *Victory in Vietnam*, 528.

34. Buzzanco, *Masters of War*, 29–30.

35. Buzzanco, *Masters of War*, 45–46.

36. Olson and Roberts, *Where the Domino Fell*, 47.

37. Graham Greene, *The Quiet American* (New York: Penguin, 1982); the following quotes are on 58, 12, 31, 33, 62, 163, 107, 94, 97, 176, 86, 124.

38. Kevin Hillstrom and Laurie Collier Hillstrom, eds., *The Vietnam Experience: A Concise Encyclopedia of American Literature, Songs, and Films* (Westport CT: Greenwood Press, 1998), 244–45.

39. Except where noted, this account of Joe's relationship with Sandra relies primarily on

the Sandra L. Horwege interview, February 27, 1997; Ruby G. Schultz interview, February 27, 1997; and Robert Jay Hooper interview, February 27, 1997.

40. Audrey Hooper interview, March 2, 1996. Gary Foster made the same point: Foster interview, March 7, 1995.

41. Gary Foster interview, March 7, 1995.

42. Arlene Foster interview, February 28, 1996.

43. "Marriage Certificate No. 494174, Reno, Nevada," in the Sandra L. Horwege (nee Schultz) Papers. The marriage is also detailed in the back pages of a Bible given to Joe when he entered the Navy; the Bible is in the JRHP.

44. "Interlocutory Judgment of Divorce No. 117600," Sandra L. Horwege Papers. The "Final Judgment of Divorce No. 117600" dissolving the marriage was dated August 2, 1961, Sandra L. Horwege Papers.

Chapter 3

1. Johnson interview, April 14, 1996. Joe told many people he joined the Army only because the Navy's recruiting station was closed.

2. Except where otherwise indicated, this account of Joe's Army career from May 1960 until September 1967 relies on the Hooper Military Personnel Records and the Morning Reports for Company E, 20th Infantry, for the Headquarters and Headquarters Company, 3rd Battalion (Airborne), 508th Infantry, and for Company B, 3rd Battalion (Airborne), 508th Infantry. All the Morning Reports are on microfilm in the Military Personnel Records at the National Personnel Records Center in St. Louis.

3. Christopher S. DeRosa, "A Million Thinking Bayonets: Political Indoctrination in the United States Army" (PhD diss., Temple University, 2000), 214–28.

4. Handwritten notations on a page torn from a "Calendar of Birthdays & Anniversaries" in a scrapbook that Joe gave to his parents. The scrapbook is in the Kathryn D. Hendricks Papers.

5. Tobias Wolff, *In Pharaoh's Army: Memories of the Lost War* (New York: Vintage, 1994), 52.

6. E-mail from Romana M. Danysh, U.S. Army Center for Military History, August 9, 1999, and *Directory and Station List of the United States Army (U) 15 August, 1963* (a copy of this is in the Military Personnel Records at the National Personnel Records Center), 106.

7. Much of the information about Company E and its duties relies on an interview with a veteran of that unit who served with Joe, Kenneth K. Sugawara, July 20, 2000.

8. Sugawara interview.

9. E-mail from Benjamin F. Dansby, October 6, 2001.

10. Captioned picture of Joe with the dog, Audrey Hooper Papers.

11. E-mails from Dansby, October 6 and October 17, 2001.

12. Dansby e-mails.

13. Dansby e-mails.

14. Audrey Hooper interview, March 2, 1996. The Audrey Hooper Papers contain the woman's address, where Maggie sent baby clothes. Sandra Horwege confirmed that Joe had at least one child by a Korean woman; Horwege interview, February 27, 1997.

15. This discussion of Korean prostitution relies on Katharine H. S. Moon, *Sex among Allies: Military Prostitution in U.S.-Korean Relations* (New York: Columbia University Press, 1997); for the gonorrhea rate, see p. 170.

16. "Report of Medical Examination," May 8, 1962, in the Hooper Medical Records, Claim Folder 24965568.

17. Department of the Army, *Army Regulations 611-201 (Personnel Selection and Classification: Manual of Enlisted Occupational Specialties)*, 23–24; a copy of this book is in the Military Personnel Records at the National Personnel Records Center.

18. Audrey Hooper interview, March 2, 1996.

19. Michael R. Beschloss, ed., *Taking Charge: The Johnson White House Tapes, 1963–1964* (New York: Simon and Schuster, 1997), 248–50.

20. McMahon, *Major Problems*, 198.

21. Olson and Roberts, *Where the Domino Fell*, 96, and Buzzanco, *Masters of War*, 136.

22. Truong Nhu Tang, with David Chanoff and Doan Van Toai, *A Vietcong Memoir* (New York: Vintage, 1986), 47.

23. Eric M. Bergerud, *The Dynamics of Defeat: The Vietnam War in Hau Nghia Province* (Boulder CO: Westview Press, 1991), 3–5; Turley, *Second Indochina War*, 198–201; Senator Mike Gravel, ed., *The Pentagon Papers: The Defense Department History of United States Decisionmaking in Vietnam*, 5 vols. (Boston: Beacon Press, 1971), II, 595.

24. Almost all historians agree on this point. For example, see John M. Carland, *United States Army in Vietnam: Combat Operations: Stemming the Tide, May 1965 to October 1966* (Washington DC: Center of Military History, 2000), 9–10, and H. R. McMaster, *Dereliction of Duty: Lyndon Johnson, Robert McNamara, the Joint Chiefs of Staff, and the Lies That Led to Vietnam* (New York: HarperCollins, 1997), 41.

25. Buzzanco, *Masters of War*, 156.

26. Neil Sheehan and others, eds., *The Pentagon Papers as Published by The New York Times* (New York: Bantam Books, 1971), 243–44; Fredrik Logevall, *Choosing War: The Lost Chance for Peace and the Escalation of War in Vietnam* (Berkeley: University of California Press, 1999), xx; Gravel, *Pentagon Papers*, III, 109

27. Sheehan, *Pentagon Papers*, 283–84.

28. For a detailed discussion of events between November 1963 and March 1965, see Logevall, *Choosing War*.

29. For the draft resolution, which went through several subsequent variations, see Sheehan, *Pentagon Papers*, 286–88.

30. David M. Barrett, ed., *Lyndon B. Johnson's Vietnam Papers: A Documentary Collection* (henceforth *LBJ's Vietnam Papers*) (College Station: Texas A&M University Press, 1997), 54.

31. Gareth Porter, ed., *Vietnam: A History in Documents* (New York: New American Library, 1981), 271–75.

32. A copy of the resolution is in Porter, *Vietnam*, 286–87. For a detailed discussion of the events surrounding the Tonkin Gulf, see Edwin E. Moise, *Tonkin Gulf and the Escalation of the Vietnam War* (Chapel Hill: University of North Carolina Press, 1996).

33. Beschloss, *Taking Charge*, 493–95, 499, 509, and Olson and Roberts, *Where the Domino Fell*, 116.

34. Timothy S. Lowry, *And Brave Men, Too* (New York: Crown Publishers, 1985), 25.

35. Sheehan, *Pentagon Papers*, 265–67, 289–91.

36. BDM Corporation, "A Study of Strategic Lessons Learned in Vietnam. Omnibus Executive Summary," IV-13, in *U.S. Armed Forces in Vietnam 1954–1975. Part Two. Vietnam: Lessons Learned* (microfilm, reel V).

37. For the arrival of Marines and the 173rd Airborne, see Shelby L. Stanton, *The Rise and Fall of an American Army: U.S. Ground Forces in Vietnam, 1965–1973* (Novato CA: Presidio Press, 1985), 31–35, 45–46. A copy of National Security Action Memorandum 328 is in Sheehan, *Pentagon Papers*, 442–43.

38. This language is in the memorandum.

39. Olson and Roberts, *Where the Domino Fell*, 149.

40. Gravel, *Pentagon Papers*, III, 461–62.

41. Gravel, *Pentagon Papers*, III, 468, and IV, 294.

42. General Wheeler quoted in Lewis Sorley, *Honorable Warrior: General Harold K. Johnson and the Ethics of Command* (Lawrence: University Press of Kansas, 1999), 211; for the "Wise Men," see Robert Dallek, *Flawed Giant: Lyndon Johnson and His Times, 1961–1973* (New York: Oxford University Press, 1998), 272–73; McNamara's memo is in Barrett, *LBJ's Vietnam Papers*, 215–22.

43. Sorley, *Honorable Warrior*, 211.

44. Dallek, *Flawed Giant*, 273.

45. McMahon, *Major Problems*, 217, and George C. Herring, *"Cold Blood": LBJ's Conduct of Limited War in Vietnam* (Colorado Springs: U.S. Air Force Academy, 1990), 13.

46. Military History Institute of Vietnam, *Victory in Vietnam*, 148.

47. Barrett, *LBJ's Vietnam Papers*, 226.

48. Leon Festinger, "Cognitive Dissonance," *Scientific American*, October 1962. See Richard Beringer and others, *Why the South Lost the Civil War* (Athens: University of Georgia Press, 1986), 280–85 for a discussion of how Southerners suffered from cognitive dissonance and the badly flawed reasoning they used to try to alleviate it.

49. Beschloss, *Taking Charge*, 365, 372.

50. Logevall, *Choosing War*, 377–83.

51. Thomas W. Miburn and Daniel J. Christie, "Effort Justification as a Motive for Continuing War: The Vietnam Case," in Thomas W. Milburn, Daniel J. Christie, and Betty Glad, eds., *Psychological Dimensions of War* (Newbury Park CA: Sage, 1990).

52. Olson and Roberts, *Where the Domino Fell*, 90.

53. Olson and Roberts, *Where the Domino Fell*, 97–98, and Andrew F. Krepinevich Jr., *The Army and Vietnam* (Baltimore: Johns Hopkins University Press, 1986), 81. For the Battle of Ap Bac, see David M. Toczek, *The Battle of Ap Bac: They Did Everything but Learn from It* (Westport CT: Greenwood Press, 2001).

54. General Bruce Palmer Jr., *The 25-Year War: America's Military Role in Vietnam* (New York: A Touchstone Book, 1985), 11.

55. Loren Baritz, *Backfire: A History of How American Culture Led Us Into Vietnam and Made Us Fight the Way We Did* (New York: William Morrow, 1985), 122.

56. Beschloss, *Taking Charge*, 300. For the views of high-ranking Johnson administration officials, see Barrett, *LBJ's Vietnam Papers*, 264–65, 447.

57. Neil Sheehan, *A Bright Shining Lie: John Paul Vann and America in Vietnam* (New York: Random House, 1988), 339–42.

58. Buzzanco, *Masters of War*, 262–63.

59. Cleo C. Hogan Jr. interview, August 4, 2000, explained each of the schools.

60. For the 3rd Battalion's duties, see Headquarters, 3rd Battalion (Airborne), 508th Infantry, Fort Kobbe, Canal Zone, Annual Historical Supplements for Calendar Year 1966 and for Calendar Year 1967, located at the U.S. Army Military History Institute; the quote is from the 1967 Historical Supplement. Also important in understanding what the 508th did were interviews with two soldiers who served there with Joe— Eugene E. Robertson, October 27, 1995 and January 9, 1997, and Edward J. Petitt Jr., July 24, 1998.

61. For an overview of the 1959 and 1964 riots and the School of the Americas, see Walter LaFeber, *The Panama Canal: The Crisis in Historical Perspective* (New York: Oxford University Press, 1978).

62. *Army Regulations 611-201*, 288.

63. First Lieutenant Knud B. Jorgensen to Mrs. J. H. Hooper, 23 August 1967, Audrey Hooper Papers.

64. McMahon, *Major Problems*, 301.

65. Truong, *Vietcong Memoir*, 50–51.

66. For this account of events in Vietnam, in addition to the sources cited in Chapter 2, note number 21, see Duiker, *Ho Chi Minh*, 535ff.

67. Military History Institute of Vietnam, *Victory in Vietnam*, 126. The regiments were the 18th, 95th, and 101st, all of them from the 325th Division.

68. Truong, *Vietcong Memoir*, 58.

69. Phillip B. Davidson, *Vietnam at War: The History, 1946–1975* (New York: Oxford University Press, 1988), 327–28, and Jeffrey Record, *The Wrong War: Why We Lost in Vietnam* (Annapolis: Naval Institute Press, 1998), 7.

70. John Morton Blum, *Years of Discord: American Politics and Society, 1961–1974* (New York: W. W. Norton, 1991), 233.

71. Military History Institute of Vietnam, *Victory in Vietnam*, 83, 137.

72. John M. Gates, *The U.S. Army and Irregular Warfare* (www.wooster.edu/history/jgates/book-contents.html, March 29, 2000), chapter 7, unpaginated.

73. Gates, *U.S. Army*, chapter 7, and Bergerud, *Dynamics of Defeat*, 112.

74. Tom Engelhardt, *The End of Victory Culture: Cold War America and the Disillusioning of a Generation* (New York: Basic Books, 1995), 223.

75. Young, *Vietnam Wars*, 189, also see 6–8, 30. Bergerud, *Dynamics of Defeat*, and Duiker, *Sacred War* also have much to say about the social and economic revolution.

76. Truong, *Vietcong Memoir*, 319–28, reprints the "Manifesto."

77. Ted Gittinger, ed., *The Johnson Years: A Vietnam Roundtable* (Austin: Lyndon Baines Johnson Library, 1993), 156–58.

78. Barrett, *LBJ's Vietnam Papers*, 250, 253. Also see Gravel, *Pentagon Papers*, III, 472.

79. Michael R. Beschloss, ed., *Reaching for Glory: Lyndon Johnson's Secret White House Tapes, 1964–1965* (New York: Simon and Schuster, 2001), 181–82, also see 238.

80. Sheehan, *Pentagon Papers*, 253–54, and Barrett, *LBJ's Vietnam Papers*, 469–75.

81. Buzzanco, *Masters of War*, 125.

82. Beschloss, *Reaching for Glory*, 212–13, 316; also see 194, 216.

83. Robert S. McNamara, *In Retrospect: The Tragedy and Lessons of Vietnam* (New York: Vintage, 1996), 107, also see 100. The one option the United States never seriously considered was pulling out of Southeast Asia; see Secretary of State Dean Rusk's comments in Beschloss, *Taking Charge*, 382.

84. Barrett, *LBJ's Vietnam Papers*, 259.

85. McNamara, *In Retrospect*, 114.

86. Gordon H. Chang, *Friends and Enemies: The United States, China, and the Soviet Union, 1948–1972* (Stanford: Stanford University Press, 1990), 235, 255.

87. Barrett, *LBJ's Vietnam Papers*, 108, and Sheehan, *Pentagon Papers*, 432.

88. Melvin Small, *Democracy and Diplomacy: The Impact of Domestic Politics on U.S. Foreign Policy, 1789–1994* (Baltimore: Johns Hopkins University Press, 1996).

89. Beschloss, *Taking Charge*, 73, 213–14.

90. Beschloss, *Taking Charge*, 370. The administration was often quite cynical about the situation. In early 1964 Bundy sent a memo to Johnson asking, "Question: in terms of domestic U.S. politics, which is better: to lose now or to lose after committing 100,000 troops? Tentative answer: the latter." See Record, *Wrong War*, 10.

91. Beschloss, *Taking Charge*, 395, 364–65, 370, and Beschloss, *Reaching for Glory*, 204.

92. Buzzanco, *Masters of War*, 68–69.

93. Olson and Roberts, *Where the Domino Fell*, 82, also see 92–93.

94. Beschloss, *Reaching for Glory*, 133, 408; Beschloss, *Taking Charge*, 266; Dallek, *Flawed Giant*, 254–55.

95. Barrett, *LBJ's Vietnam Papers*, 87–88, and Carland, *United States Army in Vietnam*, 16–17.

96. McMaster, *Dereliction of Duty*, 275, and Doris Kearns, *Lyndon Johnson and the American Dream* (New York: Signet, 1977), 278.

97. In any event, by the mid-1960s Le Duan replaced Ho as the leading policy voice in North Vietnam. With his health declining seriously, Ho's role was increasingly limited to that of a policy *adviser*, various ceremonial duties, and "fulfilling his growing image as the spiritual father of all the Vietnamese people and the soul of the Vietnamese revolution." See Bui Tin, *Following Ho Chi Minh: Memoirs of a North Vietnamese Colonel* (London: Hurst and Company, 1995), 65, and Duiker, *Ho Chi Minh*, 508, 533, 553.

98. Alexander DeConde, *Presidential Machismo: Executive Authority, Military Intervention, and Foreign Relations* (Boston: Northeastern University Press, 2000), and Kristin L. Hoganson, *Fighting for American Manhood: How Gender Politics Provoked the Spanish-American and Philippine-American Wars* (New Haven: Yale University Press, 1998).

99. Sherry, *Shadow of War*, 242; also see 302–3.

100. Just as Kennedy concealed the country's growing involvement in Vietnam, he also lied about his health, pronouncing it "excellent" at a time when he was under the care of an allergist, an endocrinologist, a gastroenterologist, an orthopedist, and a urologist, as well as an internist and pharmacologist who treated his back pain, a physician on the White House staff, and a German émigré doctor who treated numerous celebrities with amphetamines. See Robert Dallek, "The Medical Ordeals of JFK," *Atlantic Monthly*, December 2002.

101. Michael H. Hunt, *Lyndon Johnson's War: America's Cold War Crusade in Vietnam, 1945–1968* (New York: Hill and Wang, 1996), 50–51, 70, and Thomas C. Reeves, *A Question of Character: A Life of John F. Kennedy* (New York: The Free Press, 1991), 62–68, 311.

102. Baritz, *Backfire*, 118.

103. Baritz, *Backfire*, 131.

104. Dallek, *Flawed Giant*, detailed Johnson's erratic behavior. Also see Beschloss, *Reaching for Glory*, 378.

105. On Johnson's military "career" see Barrett Tillman and Henry Sakaida, "LBJ's Silver Star: The Mission That Never Was" (http://www.b-26marauderarchive.org/MS/MS1709/MS1709.htm, May 2001), and Arnold R. Isaacs, *Vietnam Shadows: The War, Its Ghosts, and Its Legacy* (Baltimore: Johns Hopkins University Press, 1977), 36.

106. Dallek, *Flawed Giant*, 500, and Beschloss, *Reaching for Glory*, 390.

107. Beschloss, *Taking Charge*, 403; Kearns, *Lyndon Johnson*, 264; Dallek, *Flawed Giant*, 491; Sherry, *Shadow of War*, 301. McNamara shared the president's desire to appear tough. "Ho Chi Minh is a tough old sob," he said. "I'm as tough as he is." See Tom Wells, *The War Within: America's Battle over Vietnam* (New York: Henry Holt, 1996), 101.

108. Beschloss, *Reaching for Glory*, 444; Logevall, *Choosing War*, 393; Young, *Vietnam Wars*, 141; James W. Gibson, *The Perfect War: The War We Couldn't Lose and How We Did* (New York: Vintage, 1988), 435. Johnson used to tell his subordinates that if they engaged in any wrongdoing, "I'll cut your balls off." See Dallek, *Flawed Giant*, 611.

109. McMahon, *Major Problems*, 225, and Young, *Vietnam Wars*, 179. Logevall argues that Johnson's concern for his reputation was *the* decisive factor in his decision for war.

110. Turley, *Second Indochina War*, 138, and Gibson, *Perfect War*, 407.

111. Beschloss, *Taking Charge*, 369.

Chapter 4

1. Michael Watson interview, July 12, 1996.

2. Except where otherwise noted, this account of McMenamy's career relies on the following sources: McMenamy's 201 (personnel) file; "Sylvester Stallone Has Nothing on Wayne McMenamy," undated clipping; "Dr. Wayne's Violent Years," undated clipping; "McMenamy Proves You Can't Keep a Good American (Flyer) Down," undated clipping. All in the McMenamy Papers. Charles Wayne McMenamy interviews, February 10, 1995 and August 23, 2000. McMenamy, "Background Notes on the 'Birth' of the Delta Raiders," in Delta Raiders of Vietnam Association (henceforth DROVA), *Delta Raiders: D Company, 2nd Battalion, 501st Infantry, 101st ABN Division* (St. Petersburg FL: Southern Heritage Press, 1998).

3. Major General O. M. Barsanti, Senior Officer Debriefing Report, August 14, 1968, U.S. Army Military History Institute; "Birth of the Army's Second Airmobile Division—The 101st Airborne Division (Airmobile)," 101st Airborne Division (henceforth Abn Div), Organizational History, Box 1, Record Group (henceforth RG) 472.

4. George L. MacGarrigle, *United States Army in Vietnam. Combat Operations. Taking the Offensive, October 1966 to October 1967* (Washington DC: Center of Military History, 1998), 348.

5. Lieutenant General John H. Cushman, "'Ready to Go!' A Personal Memoir: An Account of the 2nd Brigade and 2nd Brigade Task Force, 101st Airborne Division, September 1967 through June 1968," (unpublished draft of July 8, 1996); Chief of Staff Harold K. Johnson to Barsanti, October 14, 1967, Olinto M. Barsanti Papers, U.S. Army Military History Institute; *101st Airborne Division Screaming Eagles* (Paducah KY: Turner Publishing, 1995), 55; "Annual Historical Supplement, Calendar Year

1967," Headquarters 3rd Battalion (Airborne), 508th Infantry, Fort Kobbe, Canal Zone, in the U.S. Army Military History Institute; Eugene E. Robertson interview, January 9, 1997.

6. "Delta Raiders Newsletter," 20 (December 1989). We are indebted to Ray "Blackie" Blackman, longtime editor of the "Newsletter," for providing us with a copy of every issue.

7. No one knows exactly how many Raiders had an 11-B MOS. Cleo Hogan believes at least 50 percent did, but McMenamy believes the percentage was far less than that.

8. Roy L. Barber II interview, February 28, 1997, and Al Mount interview, July 12, 1996.

9. Robert L. Rainwater interview, July 22, 2000, and Salvator Bongiorno interview, July 12, 1996.

10. Richard Ryan interview, July 8, 1995; also, George R. Parker Jr. interview, March 23, 1995, and William D. Loftin interview, August 13, 1995.

11. William Fred Aronow interview, April 9, 1995.

12. "Lieutenant Colonel Richard J. Tallman, Commanding Officer 2-501st (Airborne) Infantry," Infantry (henceforth Infy) Units, 2nd Battalion (henceforth Bn), 501st Infy, Organizational History, Box 1, RG 472.

13. "Our training seemed a lot more difficult than everybody else's," said Wayne A. Horne. "We were always the last one off the [training] field. We were always doing one more march." Horne interview, July 22, 2000.

14. "After Action Report, Operation Detroit," 101st Abn Div, 2nd Brigade (henceforth Bde), Assistant Chief of Staff (henceforth ACS), S-3, After Action Reports (henceforth AARs), Box 1, RG 472.

15. Carollyn DeVore interview, February 11–12, 1995.

16. George R. Parker Jr. 201 (personnel) file, Parker Papers; Parker interview, March 23, 1995; Dale A. Urban interview, April 7, 1995; Aronow interview, April 9, 1995; Bobby L. Rakestraw interview, June 24, 1997.

17. Samuel Ayala interview, May 9, 2000.

18. Both McMenamy and Parker confirm this story.

19. Lonnie Nale Jr. interview, July 13, 1995.

20. Tex W. Gray interview, October 30, 1995.

21. Although many variations exist, the story involved either one of his soldiers who was on drugs and for whom Joe could not get adequate treatment, or, surprise, a woman. In his fabricated tale, Joe always ended up punching an officer in defense of the unfortunate drug user or the woman, and getting court-martialed. The real story of his court-martial as related in chapter 3 was more mundane.

22. Ava G. James interview, January 14, 1996.

23. Rakestraw interview, June 24, 1997. The variations come from James, from Rakestraw, and from James R. Kearns interview December 15, 1997.

24. Cushman, "A Biographical Note," unpaginated, in "'Ready to Go!'"

25. Cushman, "'Ready to Go!'" 3; Barsanti, Senior Officer Debriefing Report; "Campbell Unit Plans Exercise," undated clipping, Cleo C. Hogan Jr. Papers.

26. Kearns interview, December 15, 1997.

27. Gray interview, October 30, 1995; William Erbach interview, March 20, 1996; Cushman, "'Ready to Go!'" 6.

28. Tallman to To Whom It May Concern, June 5, 1969, in McMenamy's 201 file.

29. Quoted in "Dr. Wayne's Violent Years."

30. Westmoreland's career can be followed in Samuel Zaffiri, *Westmoreland: A Biography of General William C. Westmoreland* (New York: William Morrow, 1994), which portrays the general in an excessively favorable light. McNamara, *In Retrospect*, 121, called Westy a "casting director's dream for the role of a general." On his penchant for self-promotion, see Palmer, *25-Year War*, 134, and Davidson, *Vietnam at War*, 371, 380. Also see Robert Pisor, *The End of the Line: The Siege of Khe Sanh* (New York: Ballantine, 1993), 19–21.

31. Davidson, *Vietnam at War*, 379.

32. Zaffiri, *Westmoreland*, 107.

33. Zaffiri, *Westmoreland*, 93–94.

34. BDM Corporation, "Study of Strategic Lessons," Appendix C: Characteristics of the American Way of War, C-2.

35. General William C. Westmoreland, *A Soldier Reports* (Garden City NY: Doubleday, 1976), 277–78.

36. Edward F. Murphy, *Dak To: America's Sky Soldiers in South Vietnam's Central Highlands* (New York: Pocket Books, 1995), 85.

37. Davidson, *Vietnam at War*, 382, and Palmer, *25-Year War*, 40, 135.

38. Clausewitz, *On War*, 110, 119.

39. For an excellent account of all this, see Douglas Pike, *PAVN: People's Army of Vietnam* (New York: Da Capo Press, 1986), and Michael Lee Lanning and Dan Cragg, *Inside the VC and the NVA: The Real Story of North Vietnam's Armed Forces* (New York: Ivy Books, 1992). Dong's quote is in Pisor, *End of the Line*, 127.

40. Thomas C. Thayer, *War without Fronts: The American Experience in Vietnam* (Boulder CO: Westview Press, 1985), 17; John C. Schlight, ed., *The Second Indochina War: Proceedings of a Symposium . . .* (Washington DC: Center of Military History, 1986), 18–24.

41. Robert A. Doughty, Ira D. Gruber, et al., *Warfare in the Western World*, 2 vols. (Lexington MA: D. C. Heath, 1996), II, 903.

42. Sheehan, *Bright Shining Lie*, 204.

43. Pike, *PAVN*, 3, 191, 248–49; also see Schlight, *Second Indochina War*, 153.

44. BDM Corporation, "Study of Strategic Lessons," I-13; also see VI-24.

45. Colonel David H. Hackworth and Julie Sherman, *About Face* (New York: A Touchstone Book, 1990), 569–70; Murphy, *Dak To*, 328–29; Ronald H. Spector, "The Evacuation of Kham Duc," in Calvin L. Christman, ed., *America at War: An Anthology of Articles from* MHQ . . . (Annapolis: Naval Institute Press, 1995), 544; Robert Saal interview, June 26, 1997.

46. BDM Corporation, "Study of Strategic Lessons," EX-6.

47. Thomas C. Thayer, *How to Analyze a War without Fronts: Vietnam, 1965–1972* (Washington DC: Office of the Assistant Secretary of Defense (PA & E), declassified on December 31, 1978), 259.

48. This whole matter can be followed in Thomas C. Thayer, ed., *A Systems Analysis View of the Vietnam War: 1965–1972*, 12 vols. (Washington DC: OASD (SA) RP Southeast Asia Intelligence Division, Pentagon, 1975), VIII, 225–35.

49. Otis W. Livingston interview, July 10, 1995.

50. Lieutenant Colonel Leo R. Kennedy, "An Examination of Vietnam War Senior Officer Debriefing Reports: An Individual Essay," (U.S. Army War College Military Studies Program Papers, Carlisle Barracks PA: May 12, 1986), U.S. Army Military History Institute, 7, and Gates, *U.S. Army*, Chapter 6, unpaginated.

51. Douglas Kinnard, *The War Managers* (Hanover NH: University Press of New England, 1977), 110–12.

52. Stuart H. Loory, *Defeated: Inside America's Military Machine* (New York: Random House, 1973), 46; Eric M. Bergerud, *Red Thunder, Tropic Lightning: The World of a Combat Division in Vietnam* (Boulder CO: Westview Press, 1993), 302. The U.S. Army War College, "Study on Military Professionalism" (Carlisle Barracks PA: June 30, 1970) contains a scathing indictment of the high command's rampant careerism.

53. Good accounts of this affair are in William M. Hammond, *United States Army in Vietnam. Public Affairs: The Military and the Media, 1962–1968* (Washington DC: Center of Military History, 1988), 280–82, and Buzzanco, *Masters of War*, 283–87.

54. Barrett, *LBJ's Vietnam Papers*, 394, 399–400.

55. Colin L. Powell, with Joseph E. Persico, *My American Journey* (New York: Ballantine, 1996), 144.

56. Baritz, *Backfire*, 301.

57. Westmoreland's comments are in the documentary *Hearts and Minds*.

58. For revolutionary warfare, see John Shy and Thomas W. Collier, "Revolutionary War," in Peter Paret, ed., *Makers of Modern Strategy from Machiavelli to the Nuclear Age* (Princeton: Princeton University Press, 1986), 815–62; John M. Gates, "Two American Wars in Asia: Successful Colonial Warfare in the Philippines and Cold War Failure in Vietnam," *War in History* (January 2001); Gates, "People's War In Vietnam," *Journal of Military History* (July 1990); Gates, *U.S. Army*; Pike, *PAVN*, chapter 5, "Strategy," which contains the best explanation of *dau tranh*; Werner and Huynh, *Vietnam War*, 116–20.

59. Duiker, *Ho Chi Minh*, 261.

60. An excellent discussion of the cadres' role and their propaganda themes is in Bergerud, *Dynamics of Defeat*, 60–68.

61. For an excellent discussion of the role of women, see William J. Duiker, "Vietnam: War of Insurgency," in Nancy Loring Goldman, ed., *Female Soldiers—Combatants or Noncombatants? Historical and Contemporary Perspectives* (Westport CT: Greenwood Press, 1982).

62. Gary D. Solis, *Son Thang: An American War Crime* (Annapolis: Naval Institute Press, 1997), 144–45. On the militarization of women and children, see Sandra C. Taylor, *Vietnamese Women at War: Fighting for Ho Chi Minh and the Revolution* (Lawrence: University Press of Kansas, 1999); despite the title chapter 5 is on "Youth at War."

63. Olson and Roberts, *Where the Domino Fell*, 145.

64. Gates, *U.S. Army*, Chapter 8, unpaginated; Wray R. Johnson, "War, Culture, and the Interpretation of History: The Vietnam War Reconsidered," *Small Wars and Insurgencies* (Autumn 1998): 83–113.

65. Military History Institute of Vietnam, *Victory in Vietnam*, 8.

66. Donald J. Mrozek, *Air Power and the Ground War in Vietnam: Ideas and Actions* (Maxwell Air Force Base: Air University Press, January 1988), 23.

67. Pike, *PAVN*, 218–19.

68. Werner and Huynh, *Vietnam War*, 70–74.

69. Thomas M. Huber, "Napoleon in Spain and Naples: Fortified Compound Warfare," in *The History of Warfighting: Theory and Practice. Term 1 Syllabus/Book of Readings* (Fort Leavenworth KS: Combat Studies Institute, July 1999).

70. Palmer, *25-Year War*, 25, 201.

71. George C. Herring, one of the war's foremost scholars, makes this point repeatedly; see, for example, *LBJ and Vietnam: A Different Kind of War* (Austin: University of Texas Press, 1994), 40–41, 49, 182–83.

72. Barrett, *LBJ's Vietnam Papers*, 414–15.

73. Dallek, *Flawed Giant*, 341–42; Kearns, *Lyndon Johnson*, 264; McNamara, *In Retrospect*, 160, 275.

74. Gravel, *Pentagon Papers*, IV, 414, 485–86, and John Prados, *The Blood Road: The Ho Chi Minh Trail and the Vietnam War* (New York: John Wiley and Sons, 1999), 360–61; also see 209–11.

75. Barrett, *LBJ's Vietnam Papers*, 548.

76. Turley, *Second Indochina War*, 197; Pisor, *End of the Line*, 124; Davidson, *Vietnam at War*, 364.

77. Barrett, *LBJ's Vietnam Papers*, 460.

78. On the relationship between China and the Soviet Union, see Chang, *Friends and Enemies*.

79. For China's role in the Vietnam War, see Qiang Zhai, *China and the Vietnam Wars*,

1950–1975 (Chapel Hill: University of North Carolina Press, 2000); Chen Jian, "China's Involvement with the Vietnam War, 1964–1969," *China Quarterly* (June 1995); Xiaoming Zhang, "The Vietnam War, 1964–1969: A Chinese Perspective," *Journal of Military History* (October 1996); Gittinger, *Johnson Years*, 10.

80. Ilya V. Gaiduk, *The Soviet Union and the Vietnam War* (Chicago: Ivan R. Dee, 1996).

81. Gravel, *Pentagon Papers*, IV, 442, and Barrett, *LBJ's Vietnam Papers*, 617.

82. Gittinger, *Johnson Years*, 76. At the same time Admiral Thomas Moorer, who became JCS Chairman, was still moaning that "Westy's hands were tied"; see page 85.

83. Herring, *America's Longest War*, 168.

84. Carland, *United States Army in Vietnam*, 363.

85. Davidson, *Vietnam at War*, 799.

86. Westmoreland, *Soldier Reports*, 83, and Davidson, *Vietnam at War*, 348.

87. Olson and Roberts, *Where the Domino Fell*, 113.

88. Gravel, *Pentagon Papers*, IV, 387–88. The armed forces also used body counts as the measure of success in the Korean War; see Scott Sigmund Gartner and Melissa Edson Myers, "Body Counts and 'Success' in the Vietnam and Korean Wars," *Journal of Interdisciplinary History* (1995).

89. Krepinevich emphasizes this theme; Westmoreland's firepower quote is on 197. Also see Thayer, *How to Analyze a War without Fronts*, 780.

90. Baritz, *Backfire*, 242.

91. Gravel, *Pentagon Papers*, III, 393–95, 469, 479–81, and Krepinevich, *Army and Vietnam*, 141.

92. Krepinevich, *Army and Vietnam*, 222; Carland, *United States Army in Vietnam*, 363; Lieutenant General W. B. Rosson, Senior Officer Debriefing Report, October 11, 1968, U.S. Army Military History Institute.

93. Schlight, *Second Indochina War*, 123. Also see Thayer, *How to Analyze a War without Fronts*, 784.

94. Sorley, *Honorable Warrior*, 242.

95. Gravel, *Pentagon Papers*, II, 596, and IV, 398–99.

96. Krepinevich, *Army and Vietnam*, 198; Carland, *United States Army in Vietnam*, 360–61; Gibson, *Perfect War*, 103.

97. Arnold R. Isaacs, *Without Honor: Defeat in Vietnam and Cambodia* (Baltimore: Johns Hopkins University Press, 1983), 126.

98. Carland, *United States Army in Vietnam*, 359; Charles A. Krohn, *The Lost Battalion: Controversy and Casualties in the Battle of Hue* (Westport CT: Praeger, 1993), 89; Michael Clodfelter, *Vietnam in Military Statistics: A History of the Indochina Wars, 1772–1991* (Jefferson NC: McFarland and Company, 1995), 232. When one general eliminated harassment and interdiction fire in his region "no noticeable increase in enemy activity or vitality could be detected." See Kennedy, "An Examination of Vietnam War Senior Officer Debriefing Reports."

99. Krepinevich, *Army and Vietnam*, 201.

100. Palmer, *25-Year War*, 168, and Lieutenant General A. S. Collins Jr., Senior Officer Debriefing Report, January 6, 1971, in *U.S. Armed Forces in Vietnam 1954–1975. Part Four. Vietnam U.S. Army Senior Officer Debriefing Reports* (microfilm, Reel IV).

101. Krepinevich, *Army and Vietnam*, 188–92, and Guenter Lewy, *America in Vietnam* (New York: Oxford University Press, 1978), 68.

102. Tin, *Following Ho Chi Minh*, 60.

103. Olson and Roberts, *Where the Domino Fell*, 164.

104. On refugees, see Lewy, *America in Vietnam*, 65, 107–14.

105. Record, *Wrong War*, 86–87.

106. Hackworth and Sherman, *About Face*, 735.

107. Lewy, *America in Vietnam*, 100; Olson and Roberts, *Where the Domino Fell*, 170; Jonathan Schell, *The Real War: The Classic Reporting on the Vietnam War with a New Essay* (New York: Pantheon, 1987), 65. Some generals retrospectively recognized firepower's counterproductive nature; see Palmer, *25-Year War*, 167.

108. Olson and Roberts, *Where the Domino Fell*, 164.

109. Truong, *Vietcong Memoir*, 134.

110. Major General John H. Cushman, Senior Officer Debriefing Report, December 4, 1972, U.S. Army Military History Institute.

111. Olson and Roberts, *Where the Domino Fell*, 143.

112. Noah R. Rockel interview, June 28, 1997.

113. Christian G. Appy, *Working Class War: American Combat Soldiers and Vietnam* (Chapel Hill: University of North Carolina Press, 1993), 27.

114. Appy, *Working Class War*, 26.

115. Ayala interview, May 9, 2000; Petitt interview, July 24, 1998; Jodey Gravett interview, July 21, 2000.

116. Arnold Barnett, Timothy Stanley, and Michael Shore, "America's Vietnam Casualties: Victims of a Class War?" *Operations Research* (September–October 1992).

117. M. Giovanna Merli, "Socioeconomic Background and War Mortality during Vietnam's War," *Demography* (February 2000).

118. Ronald E. Phillips to To Whom It May Concern, August 1, 1995, in Grady L. Towns Jr. Papers.

119. Noah Rockel to Joyce, September 28, 1967, Rockel Papers.

Chapter 5

1. For Eagle Thrust and its aftermath, see "Birth of the Army's Second Airmobile Division—The 101st Airborne Division (Airmobile)," 101st Abn Div, Organizational History, Box 1, RG 472; "Base Camp Development After Action Report," March 23, 1968, 101st Abn Div, 2nd Bde, ACS, AARS, Box 1, RG 472; "Memorandum for the Record—Subject: Republic of Vietnam Call 290700 November 1967," November 29, 1967, and "101st Airborne Division Circular Number 600-251" December 7, 1967,

both in the Olinto M. Barsanti Papers, U.S. Army Military History Institute; *Rendezvous with Destiny*, June 1968, 5 and July 1968, frontispiece; Ava G. James Diary, November 19–December 23, 1967, James Papers.

2. Aronow to his wife, December 17, 1967; Hogan to his wife, December 18, 1967; Aronow to Everyone, December 18, 1967; Aronow to his wife, December 18, 1967; Hogan to his wife, December 20, 1967.

3. Aronow to his wife, December 18, 1967.

4. "Organization of Airborne Division and Comparison to Infantry Division," December 5, 1967, 101st Abn Div, 2nd Bde, Organizational History, Box 1, RG 472; Delta Company Roster "The Delta Raiders," Roster Number 1, c. December 10, 1967, Cleo C. Hogan Jr. Papers; Christopher C. Straub interview, July 22, 2000.

5. Parker interview, March 23, 1995, and Rockel to Joyce, December 14, 1967.

6. Rakestraw interview, June 24, 1997.

7. Rockel to his wife, December 18, 1967; Aronow to his wife, December 18, 1967 and December 19, 1967; Hogan to his wife, December 20, 1967.

8. Cushman, "'Ready to Go!'" 7.

9. Barsanti, Senior Officer Debriefing Report; "Birth of the Army's Second Airmobile Division"; Hogan to his wife, December 21, 1967; Aronow interview, April 9, 1995; Aronow to his wife, December 20 and December 24, 1967.

10. McMenamy interview February 10, 1995.

11. For accounts of the war in the Cu Chi vicinity see Tom Mangold and John Penycate, *The Tunnels of Cu Chi* (New York: Berkley Books, 1986), and Bergerud, *Red Thunder, Tropic Lightning* and *Dynamics of Defeat*.

12. Mangold and Penycate, *Tunnels of Cu Chi*, 12, 17, and Bergerud, *Dynamics of Defeat*, 45.

13. Mangold and Penycate, *Tunnels of Cu Chi*, 66, 141–42.

14. Cushman, "'Ready to Go!'" 9–11.

15. Cushman, "'Ready to Go!'" 12, and Hogan to his wife, December 29, 1967.

16. Hogan interview, March 21–22, 1995.

17. DROVA, *Delta Raiders*, 30, and McMenamy interview, February 10, 1995.

18. James interview, January 14, 1996; Roy L. Barber II interview, February 29, 1997; Straub interview, July 22, 2000.

19. Barber interview, February 29, 1997.

20. Rockel to Joyce, December 26, 1967.

21. Loved ones at home could never understand this. As Dale Urban's girlfriend wrote, "What do you mean you don't hardly ever wear your bullet proof vest??! Now listen here, you had better, because when you're home I'm going to 'wring your neck.' . . . So wear it! That's an order!" Janet to Urban, January 9, 1968, Dale Urban Papers.

22. Rockel to Joyce, January 1, 1968.

23. DROVA, *Delta Raiders*, 40.

24. DROVA, *Delta Raiders*, 40.

25. Hooper to Mom & Dad, January 6, 1968, Kathryn D. Hendricks Papers. When he returned home Joe spoke to his sister Audrey about how amazing the tunnels were and about how much he admired the VC who built and used them; Audrey Hooper interview, March 2, 1996.

   As explained in "A Few Words Concerning the Text," whenever quoting Joe's writings we have corrected only his most egregious spelling and grammatical errors with bracketed material so that readers can get a "feel" for his writing style.

26. Hogan to his wife, January 1, 1968, and Rockel to Joyce, December 31, 1967.

27. Hooper to Mom & Dad, January 6, 1968, JRHP; Hogan to his wife, January 4, 1968; DROVA, *Delta Raiders*, 40–41.

28. Hogan to his wife, January 15, 1968; Aronow to his wife, January 15, 1968; DROVA, *Delta Raiders*, 41.

29. Barsanti, Senior Officer Debriefing Report, and "Combat Notes No. 1. Defense Discipline," January 15, 1968, Barsanti Papers.

30. Cushman, "'Ready to Go!'" 13.

31. Hogan to his wife, January 19, 1968, and Aronow to his wife, January 19 and January 21, 1968.

32. McMenamy interview, February 10, 1995, and Hogan to his wife, January 15, 1968.

33. Hogan interview, March 21–22, 1995, and James interview, January 14, 1996.

34. Aronow to his wife, December 25 and 27, 1967 and January 7, 1968; Hogan to his wife, December 22, 1967 and January 1, 1968.

35. Except where otherwise noted, this account relies on DeVore to the authors, c. fall 1994, July 1, 1995, c. mid-April 2002, and several brief, undated notes; DeVore's "Brief Memoir" and her "Memories," copies in the authors' possession and both dated February 1995; DeVore interviews, February 11–12, 1995, February 15, 1995, March 6, 2002, and June 21, 2002. For her modeling, beauty contests, and career, see several different publicity sheets about her, copies in the Carollyn DeVore Papers. For the quote about Marilyn Monroe see Alec Blasco-Ibanez, "Viet Nam's Blonde Bombshell," *Los Angeles Herald-Examiner*, "California Living," May 9, 1969, Carollyn DeVore Papers.

36. Hogan interview, March 21–22, 1995, and Rockel to Joyce, December 20, 1967.

37. Cushman, "'Ready to Go!'" 5, and McMenamy interview, February 10, 1995.

38. Hogan interviews, October 27, 1995 and July 25, 1999; Cushman, "'Ready to Go!'" 1, 45, 66, 174; speech delivered by Brigadier General John Cushman to the 33rd Annual Convention Banquet, Italian-American Veterans of the United States, Inc., August 17, 1968, copy in the Barsanti Papers; "Major General Olinto Barsanti," 101st Abn Div, 2nd Bde, Organizational History, Box 1, RG 472.

39. "Fundamentals of Infantry Tactics," Barsanti Papers; also see Barsanti, Senior Officer Debriefing Report.

40. Erbach interview, July 29, 1996; also see Cushman, "'Ready to Go!'" 66.

41. DROVA, *Delta Raiders*, 30, and McMenamy interview, February 10, 1995.

42. Gravel, *Pentagon Papers*, III, 482–83.

43. Herring, *LBJ and Vietnam*, 20.

44. For a virtual case study of much of the following, see James F. Humphries, *Through the Valley: Vietnam, 1967–1968* (Boulder CO: Lynne Rienner, 1999).

45. Barrett, *LBJ's Vietnam Papers*, 197, and McNamara, *In Retrospect*, 208–9.

46. Davidson, *Vietnam at War*, 404–5, and Kim Willenson, *The Bad War: An Oral History of the Vietnam War* (New York: New American Library, 1987), 81.

47. John Frick to his wife, July 25, 1968, Frick Papers.

48. Davidson, *Vietnam at War*, 427–28, and Lanning and Cragg, *Inside*, 95.

49. Gibson, *Perfect War*, 104; "Combat After Action (Feeder) Report Covering the Period 1 Oct–31 Oct 1970 of Operation Jefferson Glen," December 1, 1970, 101st Abn Div, 1st Bde, AARS, Box 3, RG 472; James R. McDonough, *Platoon Leader* (New York: Bantam, 1986), 162.

50. Lanning and Cragg, *Inside*, 158, 203; Bergerud, *Red Thunder, Tropic Lightning*, 109; Parker interview, March 23, 1995; "Know Your Enemy: The Viet Cong (DOD Gen-20)," March 8, 1966, copy in the Carollyn DeVore Papers.

51. Ray Blackman interview, August 17, 1994; Murphy, *Dak To*, 241; Lanning and Cragg, *Inside*, 207.

52. Davidson, *Vietnam at War*, 405–6, and Richard A. Hunt, *Pacification: The American Struggle for Vietnam's Hearts and Minds* (Boulder CO: Westview Press, 1995), 56.

53. Sorley, *Honorable Warrior*, 282.

54. "Birth of the Army's Second Airmobile Division," and Lieutenant General John J. Tolson, *Vietnam Studies: Airmobility, 1961–1971* (Washington DC: Department of the Army, 1973), 88.

55. Tolson, *Vietnam Studies*, 27.

56. Carland, *United States Army in Vietnam*, 361, and "Birth of the Army's Second Airmobile Division."

57. For example, see "Feeder After Action Report Covering the Period 1 Oct–31 Oct 70 of Operation Jefferson Glen/Monsoon Plan 70," November 30, 1970, 101st Abn Div, 2nd Bde, ACS, S-3, AARS, Box 2, and "Feeder After Action Report Covering the Period 5 Sept–30 Sept 1970 of Operation Jefferson Glen," Oct 31, 1970, 101st Abn Div, 1st Bde, AARS, Box 3, both in RG 472. Also see MG Melvin Zais, Senior Officer Debriefing Report, May 25, 1969, in *U.S. Armed Forces in Vietnam 1954–1975* (microfilm, Reel I).

58. "Birth of the Army's Second Airmobile Division"; "Operational Report—Lessons Learned (henceforth LL), Period Ending 30 April 1971," May 24, 1971, and "Operational Report of the 101st Air Cavalry Division for the Period Ending 31 July 1968,"

August 15, 1968, both in 101st Abn Div, ACS, G-3, Operations Reports—LL, Box 2, RG 472; "Feeder After Action Report Covering the Period 1–31 Jan 1971 of Operation Jefferson Glen/Monsoon Plan 70," March 2, 1971, 101st Abn Div, ACS, G-3, AARS, Box 2, RG 472; "Operational Report—Lessons Learned for the Period 1 Nov 70–30 Apr 71," April 30, 1971, 101st Abn Div, 3rd Bde, ACS, S-3, Operations Reports—LL, Box 1, RG 472.

59. "Diary of an Infiltrator, December 1966," in *Vietnam Documents and Research Notes Series: Translations and Analysis of Significant Viet Cong/North Vietnamese Documents* (6 reels, A Microfilm Project of University Publications of America) Reel I; Robert Mason, *Chickenhawk* (New York: Penguin, 1984), 122; Frederick Downs, *The Killing Zone: My Life in the Vietnam War* (New York: W. W. Norton, 1993), 25; Clodfelter, *Vietnam in Military Statistics*, 227–28.

60. Mason, *Chickenhawk*, 275; Lewy, *America in Vietnam*, 60; Pisor, *End of the Line*, 13; Paddy Griffith, *Forward into Battle: Fighting Tactics from Waterloo to Vietnam* (Strettington House, England: Antony Bird Publications, 1981), 116.

61. Gibson, *Perfect War*, 107.

62. John D. Bergen, *United States Army in Vietnam. Military Communications: A Test for Technology* (Washington DC: Center of Military History, 1986), 402.

63. Bergen, *United States Army in Vietnam. Military Communications*, 403.

64. Ronald H. Spector, *After Tet: The Bloodiest Year in Vietnam* (New York: The Free Press, 1993), 79–81, and John Prados, *The Hidden History of the Vietnam War* (Chicago: Ivan R. Dee, 1998), 198–99.

65. Rosson, Senior Officer Debriefing Report, and Palmer, *25-Year War*, 37, 167. Also see "Operations Security Report," June 6, 1970, 101st Abn Div, 2nd Bde, ACS, S-3, Command Reports, Box 1; "Operational Report—Lessons Learned for Period Ending 31 July 1970," 101st Abn Div, 101st Aviation Group, Command Reports, Box 17; "Feeder After Action Report Covering the Period 1–31 1970 of Operation Texas Star," August 30, 1970, 101st Abn Div, 3rd Bde, ACS, S-3, AARS, Box 2; "Feeder After Action Report Covering the Period 1 Aug 051800H Sept 70 of Operation Texas Star," September 10, 1970, 101st Abn Div, 2nd Bde, ACS, S-3, AARS, Box 2; S-3 Daily Journal, April 3, April 8, June 22, 1970, 101st Abn Div, 101st Aviation Group; all in RG 472.

66. Pisor, *End of the Line*, 47.

67. Krepinevich, *Army and Vietnam*, 192; Thayer, *How to Analyze a War without Fronts*, 767–68, 801; Schlight, *Second Indochina War*, 124–25.

68. MacGarrigle, *Combat Operations*, 175–77, 288, 309; Mike Watson interview, July 12, 1996; Murphy, *Dak To*, 69; "Operations Report—Lessons Learned for the Period Ending 30 Apr 70," May 5, 1970, 101st Abn Div, 3rd Bde, ACS, S-3, Operations Reports—LL, Box 1, RG 472; Parker interview, March 23, 1995.

69. Pisor, *End of the Line*, 51–52.

70. "Fundamentals of Infantry Tactics."

71. Keith W. Nolan, *Sappers in the Wire: The Life and Death of Firebase Mary Ann* (College Station: Texas A&M University Press, 1995), 81, 91; Ebert, *Life in a Year*, 135–37; John E. Frick to his wife, August 28, 1968, Frick Papers.

72. MacGarrigle, *Combat Operations*, 306, and Pisor, *End of the Line*, 141–42.

73. Thayer, *How to Analyze a War without Fronts*, 853; BDM Corporation, "Study of Strategic Lessons," VI-35; Kennedy, "An Examination of Vietnam War Senior Officer Debriefing Reports," 6–7; Livingston interview, July 10, 1995; Record, *Wrong War*, 99.

74. Michael Lee Lanning, *The Only War We Had: A Platoon Leader's Journal of Vietnam* (New York: Ivy Books, 1987), 200; Downs, *Killing Zone*, 189; "Operational Feeder Report—Lessons Learned for Period Ending 31 October 1970," November 3, 1970, "Operations Report—Lessons Learned for Period Ending 30 April 1971," May 3, 1971, both in 101st Abn Div, 2nd Bde, ACS, S-3, Operations Reports—LL, Box 1, RG 472; Palmer, *25-Year War*, 53, 73–74; Mason, *Chickenhawk*, 145–46.

75. Carland, *United States Army in Vietnam*, 358; Davidson, *Vietnam at War*, 454; Ebert, *Life in a Year*, 210.

76. Gravel, *Pentagon Papers*, IV, 321.

77. Saal interview, June 26, 1997, and Charles Gadd, *Line Doggie: Foot Soldier in Vietnam* (Novato CA: Presidio Press, 1987), 150.

78. Bergerud, *Red Thunder, Tropic Lightning*, 73, and Griffith, *Forward into Battle*, 117.

79. John Schlight, *The United States Air Force in Southeast Asia. The War in South Vietnam: The Years of the Offensive, 1965–1968* (Washington DC: Office of Air Force History, 1988), 293.

80. Griffith, *Forward into Battle*, 130–31; Lanning and Cragg, *Inside*, 208–9, 235; Alfred S. Bradford, *Some Even Volunteered: The First Wolfhounds Pacify Vietnam* (Westport CT: Praeger, 1994), 75.

81. "Operational Report—Lessons Learned for the Period 1 Nov 70–30 Apr 71," April 30, 1970, 101st Abn Div, 3rd Bde, ACS, Operations Reports—LL, Box 1, RG 472; Bergerud, *Red Thunder, Tropic Lightning*, 84; Mike Watson interview, July 12, 1996.

82. "Diary of an Infiltrator, December 1966"; Tolson, *Vietnam Studies*, 145–46; Watson interview, July 12, 1996; Murphy, *Dak To*, 67–69, 200; Lanning and Cragg, *Inside*, 255; Barsanti, "Combat Notes No. 5 [Incident (From Friendly Supporting Fires)]," Barsanti Papers; David Chanoff and Doan Van Toai, *Portrait of the Enemy* (New York: Random House, 1986), 155; "Operational Report—Lessons Learned, Headquarters, 101st Abn Div, Period Ending 31 July 1970 (U)," April 8, 1971, Ray Blackman Papers.

83. Frick to his wife, August 22, 1968.

84. For an example, see Bergerud, *Red Thunder, Tropic Lightning*, 142.

85. "Feeder After Action Report Covering the Period 1–31 March [1971] of Operation

Jefferson Glen/Monsoon Plan 70," April 21, 1971, 101st Abn Div, 2nd Bde, ACS, S-3, AARS, Box 2, RG 472.

86. Lanning and Cragg, *Inside*, 254; Tim O'Brien, *If I Die in a Combat Zone, Box Me Up and Ship Me Home* (New York: A Laurel Edition, 1979), 125; Thayer, *A Systems Analysis View of the Vietnam War*, VIII, 141.

87. Lanning and Cragg, *Inside*, 254, and Bernard Edelman, ed., *Dear America: Letters Home from Vietnam* (New York: Pocket Books, 1988), 184-85.

88. Thayer, *How to Analyze a War without Fronts*, 803-4, and Thayer, *War without Fronts*, 47.

89. DROVA, *Delta Raiders*, 176.

90. Gravel, *Pentagon Papers*, IV, 370-71. Also see Thayer, *How to Analyze a War without Fronts*, 834-36; Thayer, *War without Fronts*, 90-91; Carland, *United States Army in Vietnam*, 356-57.

91. BDM Corporation, "Study of Strategic Lessons," EX-8; Davidson, *Vietnam at War*, 422; MacGarrigle, *Combat Operations*, 215.

92. "Troop Training and Combat Competition Campaign—An Emulation Plan," Document No. 15, in *Vietnam Documents and Research Notes Series*, Reel I.

93. Henderson contains an excellent discussion of the three-cell's importance; the quote is on page 41.

94. Pike, *PAVN*, 173-75, 196; Lanning and Cragg, *Inside*, 73, 109, 200-201, 233-34; Gravett interview, July 22, 2000.

95. "Out of Rice, Ammo & Bandages: Notes of a VC Veteran," Document No. 13, and "The Problems of a Dispensary," Document No. 16, both in *Vietnam Documents and Research Notes Series*, Reel I; Mangold and Penycate, *Tunnels of Cu Chi*, 176-79.

96. For example, see "Diary of an Infiltrator," Document No. 1, and "Problems of a North Vietnamese Regiment," Documents Nos. 2-3, both in *Vietnam Documents and Research Notes Series*, Reel I.

97. Chanoff and Toai, *Portrait of the Enemy*, 209.

98. Carland, *United States Army in Vietnam*, 365-66, and Lanning and Cragg, *Inside*, 236.

99. Hogan interview, March 21-22, 1995.

100. James R. Kearns interview, December 15, 1997; Rick Anderson, "GI Hero Unwinds from Vietnam," *Seattle Post-Intelligencer*, May 7, 1974, A5, in Richard ("Rick") G. Anderson Papers; "Medal Winner," undated clipping, Audrey Hooper Papers.

101. Joe to his parents, April 12, 1968, JRHP.

102. Downs, *Killing Zone*, 149; McDonough, *Platoon Leader*, 160; Edelman, *Dear America*, 53; Nolan, *Sappers in the Wire*, 51; John Keegan and Richard Holmes, *Soldiers: A History of Men in Battle* (New York: Elisabeth Sifton Books, 1986), 267; Lanning and Cragg, *Inside*, 226-27; "Pass It On" by Lieutenant Colonel David H. Hackworth,

enclosed with "17 Sep 70-Subject: Lessons Learned" in 101st Abn Div, 3rd Bde, ACS, S-3, Command Reports, Box 1, RG 472.

103. Craig Sturges interview, March 5, 1996.

104. "Delta Raiders Newsletter," 13 (July 1988); Schell, *Real War*, 154; Bergerud, *Red Thunder, Tropic Lightning*, 267.

105. Cushman, "'Ready to Go!'" 13–15, and Hogan to his wife, January 24, 1968.

106. Gravel, *Pentagon Papers*, IV, 426; Spector, *After Tet*, 118; Zaffiri, *Westmoreland*, 268.

107. The buildup in I Corps can be followed in Lieutenant General Willard Pearson, *Vietnam Studies: The War in the Northern Provinces, 1966–1968* (Washington DC: Department of the Army, 1975).

108. Pisor, *End of the Line*, 72.

109. Pisor, *End of the Line*, 121, 153.

110. Cushman, "'Ready to Go!'" 16–17; "After Action Report (Offensive Operations 22 Jan 10–Mar 1968)" and "Jeb Stuart I," both in Headquarters, U.S. Army Vietnam, Command Histories, AARS, Box 15, RG 472.

111. DROVA, *Delta Raiders*, 30; McMenamy interview, February 10, 1995; Aronow to Mom and Dad, January 22, 1968; Aronow to his wife, January 23, 1968.

112. DROVA, *Delta Raiders*, 30; McMenamy interview, February 10, 1995; Rockel to Joyce, February 1, 1968.

113. Cushman, "'Ready to Go!'" 22–24.

114. DROVA, *Delta Raiders*, 30, 43.

115. DROVA, *Delta Raiders*, 43, and Hogan to his wife, January 31, 1968.

116. Hogan to his wife, January 19, 1968.

117. Prados, *Hidden History*, 135, and James J. Wirtz, *The Tet Offensive: Intelligence Failure in War* (Ithaca: Cornell University Press, 1991), 173–75.

118. Barrett, *LBJ's Vietnam Papers*, 436.

119. Barrett, *LBJ's Vietnam Papers*, 389–90.

120. Gravel, *Pentagon Papers*, IV, 424–25, 442, and Wirtz, *Tet Offensive*, 119.

121. Zaffiri, *Westmoreland*, 245, and Porter, *Vietnam*, 352–54.

122. Sorely, *Honorable Warrior*, 288–89.

123. McNamara, *In Retrospect*, 283; Gravel, *Pentagon Papers*, IV, 518; MacGarrigle, *Combat Operations*, 442–43.

124. MacGarrigle, *Combat Operations*, 431–32.

125. MacGarrigle, *Combat Operations*, 57; Krohn, *Lost Battalion*, 140; Erbach interview, March 20, 1996.

126. Gibson, *Perfect War*, 120, and Kinnard, *War Managers*, 75.

127. Murphy, *Dak To*, 86, 210; MacGarrigle, *Combat Operations*, 419; Powell, *Journey*, 142.

128. Gibson, *Perfect War*, 141, and Barrett, *LBJ's Vietnam Papers*, 434.

129. Thayer, *How To Analyze a War without Fronts*, 846, and Thayer, *A Systems Analysis View of the Vietnam War*, VIII, 31–34.

130. Kinnard, *War Managers*, 75, and U.S. Army War College, "Study on Military Professionalism."

131. A good account of the controversy over the enemy's OB is Sam Adams, *War of Numbers: An Intelligence Memoir* (South Royalton VT: Steerforth Press, 1994). Also see Thayer, *How to Analyze a War without Fronts*, 785; Thayer, *War without Fronts*, 28–32; Spector, *After Tet*, 75–76; MacGarrigle, *Combat Operations*, 22; Prados, *Hidden History*, 123–26; Christopher Andrew, *For the President's Eyes Only: Secret Intelligence and the American Presidency from Washington to Bush* (New York: HarperPerennial, 1996), 329–38.

132. Andrew, *President's Eyes Only*, 330.

133. Andrew, *President's Eyes Only*, 337.

134. Record, *Wrong War*, 82, and Young, *Vietnam Wars*, 214–15.

135. Wirtz, *Tet Offensive*, 139, 157, 163, 170–79, 223, 259, 268–69, and Zaffiri, *Westmoreland*, 261.

Chapter 6

1. Edelman, *Dear America*, 48, 131–32.

2. "USO Information Vietnam," Carollyn DeVore Papers.

3. Patrick L. Runevich interview, April 11, 1996.

4. McMenamy interview, February 10, 1995.

5. Downs, *Killing Zone*, 63, and Caputo, *Rumor of War*, 80.

6. Saal to Hi Folks, April 15, 1971, Robert Saal Papers. Another soldier put it this way: "The weather here has been bad as it always seems to be." Paul Gochnour to his parents, January 11, 1971.

7. Bernard E. Grady, *On the Tiger's Back* (Brunswick ME: Biddle Publishing Company, 1994), 119, and Caputo, *Rumor of War*, 62.

8. Jimmy L. Emory, "Borrowed Time," *The American Legion* (November 1995): 28; Downs, *Killing Zone*, 109; Grady, *Tiger's Back*, 158; John Frick to his wife, October 8, 1968; Lanning, *Only War We Had*, 254–55.

9. DROVA, *Delta Raiders*, 222.

10. Urban interview, April 7, 1995, and Edelman, *Dear America*, 23.

11. Olinto M. Barsanti, "Methods of Combat on the Coastal Plains," Barsanti Papers, and McDonough, *Platoon Leader*, 172.

12. *101st Airborne: Vietnam [19]69*, 19, copy in the Ray Blackman Papers, and Gary Foster interview, February 28, 1996.

13. Ryan interview, July 8, 1995.

14. Thayer, *War without Fronts*, 14; Thayer, *How to Analyze a War without Fronts*, 776–77, 855; Thayer, *A Systems Analysis View of the Vietnam War*, VIII, 124–26, 129–30.

15. Clodfelter, *Vietnam in Military Statistics*, 238; Thayer, *A Systems Analysis View of the Vietnam War*, VIII, 113.

16. Thayer, *War without Fronts*, 11–13.

17. Hogan interview, March 21–22, 1995.

18. Sturges interview, March 5, 1996; Hogan interview, March 21–22, 1995; Aronow interview, April 9, 1995; Aronow to his wife, January 25–26, 1968.

19. "Congressional Medal Winner . . ." undated clipping, Kathryn D. Hendricks Papers.

20. MacGarrigle, *Combat Operations*, 255, and Hogan to his wife, February 9, 1968.

21. Gibson, *Perfect War*, 233; Schell, *Real War*, 198–202, 246–49; Hogan interview, March 21–22, 1995; Aronow interview, April 9, 1995.

22. "War Hero Never Fought Viet Cong," undated clipping, Kathryn D. Hendricks Papers; also, Gary Foster interviews, March 7, 1995 and February 9, 1996.

23. Hogan interview, March 21–22, 1995; Blackman interview, August 17, 1994; Parker interview, March 23, 1995.

24. Nale interview, July 13, 1995; James interview, January 14, 1996; Al Mount interview, July 12, 1996; Eugene E. Robertson interview, October 27, 1995; Sturges interview, March 5, 1996.

25. Bongiorno interview, July 12, 1996.

26. Parker interview, March 23, 1995, and Gary Foster interview, March 7, 1995.

27. Hogan interviews, March 21–22, 1995, and June 9, 1996, and Loftin interview, August 13, 1995. To protect the guilty we have omitted the name of the individual who experimented with "grass."

28. Herring, *LBJ and Vietnam*, 140.

29. Sorley, *Honorable Warrior*, 292; Kearns, *Lyndon Johnson*, 319; Charles DeBenedetti and Charles Chatfield, *An American Ordeal: The Antiwar Movement of the Vietnam Era* (Syracuse: Syracuse University Press, 1990), 187.

30. Schulzinger, *Time for War*, 243; Wells, *War Within*, 137; Young, *Vietnam Wars*, 210.

31. Lewy, *America in Vietnam*, 73; MacGarrigle, *Combat Operations*, 440; Pearlman, *Warmaking*, 358; Thayer, *How to Analyze a War without Fronts*, 770, 807.

32. Hammond, *Military and the Media, 1962–1968*, 105.

33. Powell, *Journey*, 128–29.

34. Barrett, *LBJ's Vietnam Papers*, 289, 418, 534; Gravel, *Pentagon Papers*, IV, 506; Herring, *"Cold Blood,"* 19; MacGarrigle, *Combat Operations*, 443.

35. McNamara, *In Retrospect*, 252–53, and BDM Corporation, "Study of Strategic Lessons," IV-1.

36. Unless otherwise noted, this account of the antiwar movement relies on DeBenedetti and Chatfield, *American Ordeal;* Wells, *War Within;* Melvin Small, *Covering Dissent: The Media and the Anti-Vietnam War Movement* (New Brunswick NJ: Rutgers University Press, 1994); Melvin Small, *Antiwarriors: The Vietnam War and the Battle for America's Hearts and Minds* (Wilmington DE: Scholarly Resources, 2002); and David W. Levy, *The Debate over Vietnam* (Baltimore: Johns Hopkins University Press, 1995). Olson and Roberts, *Where the Domino Fell*, contains a fine, brief discussion of the dissent, as does Herring, *America's Longest War*.

37. McNamara, *In Retrospect*, 269.

38. Davidson, *Vietnam at War*, 440.

39. Wells, *War Within*, 257.

40. They were just two of the eight Americans who burned themselves to death in protest against the war; see Small, *Antiwarriors*, 21.

41. Small, *Antiwarriors*, 172.

42. DeBenedetti and Chatfield, *American Ordeal*, 152.

43. Levy, *Debate*, 77–79, 93, 102–11 is particularly strong on these matters. King's quote is in McMahon, *Major Problems*, 471, and Ali's is in Isaacs, *Vietnam Shadows*, 18.

44. Pearlman, *Warmaking*, 353.

45. Sorely, *Honorable Warrior*, 274.

46. Howard Jablon, "General David M. Shoup, U.S.M.C.: Warrior and War Protester," *Journal of Military History* (July 1996): 532.

47. David M. Barrett, *Uncertain Warriors: Lyndon Johnson and His Vietnam Advisers* (Lawrence: University Press of Kansas, 1993), 71.

48. Kearns, *Lyndon Johnson*, 327.

49. Wells, *War Within*, 183–84, 276; Dallek, *Flawed Giant*, 486–87; Engelhardt, *End of Victory Culture*, 247.

50. Mitchell Hall, *The Vietnam War* (New York: Longman, 2000), 96–97; Barrett, *LBJ's Vietnam Papers*, 537–39, 774–76, 779–80; Dallek, *Flawed Giant*, 489; DeBenedetti and Chatfield, *American Ordeal*, 204.

51. Herring, *"Cold Blood,"* 21; Herring, *LBJ and Vietnam*, 141–45; Dallek, *Flawed Giant*, 497.

52. Gittinger, *Johnson Years*, 113–14; Adams, *War of Numbers*, 218; Barrett, *LBJ's Vietnam Papers*, 524–29.

53. Barrett, *LBJ's Vietnam Papers*, 469–75.

54. McNamara, *In Retrospect*, 305–9.

55. Palmer, *25-Year War*, 75, and Sorley, *Honorable Warrior*, 289.

56. The July 1967 data is in George H. Gallup, *The Gallup Poll: Public Opinion, 1935–1971*, 3 vols. (New York: Random House, 1972), III, 2074. The November data was inadvertently omitted from this volume, but was confirmed in a conversation with Ms. Maura Strausberg, Data Librarian for the Gallup Poll, on July 9, 2001.

57. Hunt, *Pacification*, 35; Barrett, *LBJ's Vietnam Papers*, 363–66; Gravel, *Pentagon Papers*, IV, 385.

58. Barrett, *LBJ's Vietnam Papers*, 412, and Sorley, *Honorable Warrior*, 267.

59. Barrett, *LBJ's Vietnam Papers*, 534.

60. *LBJ's Vietnam Papers*, 568–69.

61. Herring, *LBJ and Vietnam*, 25, 32, 36–37, 44, 47–48, 51, 62.

62. Except where otherwise noted, the following discussion relies on McMaster, *Dereliction of Duty*, and Buzzanco, *Masters of War*.

63. Barrett, *LBJ's Vietnam Papers*, 89.

64. Palmer, *25-Year War*, 34–35, 201; also see McNamara, *In Retrospect*, 175, and Willenson, *Bad War*, 89.

65. Buzzanco, *Masters of War*, 349.

66. Gravel, *Pentagon Papers*, IV, 347.

67. Gravel, *Pentagon Papers*, IV, 364.

68. Lieutenant General Carroll H. Dunn, *Vietnam Studies: Base Development in South Vietnam, 1965–1970* (Washington DC: Department of the Army, 1972), 1–12; Prados, *Hidden History*, 104–8; Barrett, *LBJ's Vietnam Papers*, 447.

69. Sorley, *Honorable Warrior*, 263–64.

70. For discussions of the Reserve issue see Kinnard, *War Managers*, 117–24, and Record, *Wrong War*, 146–49.

71. Gittinger, *Johnson Years*, 69, 100; Wells, *War Within*, 41; Gravel, *Pentagon Papers*, IV, 385. The best account of the National Guard's mobilization during Korea is William M. Donnelly, *Under Army Orders: The Army National Guard during the Korean War* (College Station: Texas A&M University Press, 2001), which asserts that most communities considered the mobilization undesirable but necessary, but that many Guardsmen considered it unfair and feared the Regular Army would mistreat Guard units. In addition, the Guard suffered from equipment, personnel, training, and leadership problems and had difficulty adjusting to combat. "Guardsmen and their supporters," wrote Donnelly, "were not shy about voicing their displeasure over real or imagined injuries and insults to mobilized units and individuals"; see 183.

72. Beschloss, *Reaching for Glory*, 410–11; also see 382–83.

73. Buzzanco, *Masters of War*, 264, 269; Gittinger, *Johnson Years*, 100–101; Barrett, *LBJ's Vietnam Papers*, 510.

74. Sorley, *Honorable Warrior*, 291.

75. Gravel, *Pentagon Papers*, II, 576–78; Sorley, *Honorable Warrior*, 227–36; Davidson, *Vietnam at War*, 409–10.

76. Gravel, *Pentagon Papers*, IV, 463–68, 477–89, 498–501.

77. For a discussion of many of the issues involving the Marines, see Allan R. Millett, *Semper Fidelis: The History of the United States Marine Corps*, revised and expanded edition (New York: The Free Press, 1991). Also see Millett, "Why the Army and the Marine Corps Should Be Friends," *Parameters* (Winter 1994-95).

78. Lewy, *America in Vietnam*, 86–87.

79. Sorley, *Honorable Warrior*, 240; Sheehan, *Bright Shining Lie*, 630–36; Zaffiri, *Westmoreland*, 169; Buzzanco, *Masters of War*, 250–51; Gravel, *Pentagon Papers*, II, 517, 533–35.

80. Francis J. West Jr., "Stingray '70," *United States Naval Institute Proceedings* (November 1969).

81. Krepinevich, *Army and Vietnam*, 175.

82. Hooper to his parents, April 7, 1968, JRHP.

83. Prados, *Blood Road*, 241–46; Wirtz, *Tet Offensive*, 204–5, 239; Andrew, *President's Eyes Only*, 341; Zaffiri, *Westmoreland*, 283.

84. Werner and Huynh, *Vietnam War*, 45.

85. Sheehan, *Bright Shining Lie*, 709–10.

86. Wirtz, *Tet Offensive*, 224, 238; Palmer, *25-Year War*, 78; Westmoreland, *Soldier Reports*, 320.

87. Pike, PAVN, 17–20, 224–25; Wirtz, *Tet Offensive*, 23; Shy and Collier, in Paret, *Makers of Modern Strategy*, 820, 825–27.

88. "'Time Opportunity': The Uprising Appeal of VC Leaflets," Document No. 22, and "'The Decisive Hour': Two Directives for Tet," Documents No. 28-29, both in *Vietnam Documents and Research Notes Series*, Reel I.

89. George C. Herring, "'Peoples Quite Apart': Americans, South Vietnamese, and the War in Vietnam," *Diplomatic History* (Winter 1990), and Werner and Huynh, *Vietnam War*, 86.

90. Werner and Huynh, *Vietnam War*, 41, 83–87, and Duiker, *Sacred War*, 210–13. Also see Ang Cheng Guan, "Khe Sanh—From the Perspective of the North Vietnamese Communists," *War in History* (January 2001).

91. For the Battle of Hue, see George W. Smith, *The Siege at Hue* (Boulder CO: Lynne Rienner, 1999), and Pearson, *Vietnam Studies*. Also, "Achievements of the Hue City Party Committee, Tri-Thien-Hue Region," an enemy document dated December 1968, the U.S. Army Center of Military History. We are indebted to Dr. Erik Villard for calling our attention to this document.

92. Krohn, *Lost Battalion*, 60–61. Overall, Krohn is the best account of the relief effort.

93. Krohn, *Lost Battalion*, 61; Barsanti, "Methods of Combat on the Coastal Plains"; "Jeb Stuart I," Headquarters, U.S. Army Vietnam, Command Historians, AARS, Box 15, RG 472. The latter two sources differ on exactly which NVA regiments stood in the way of a relief force.

94. Krohn, *Lost Battalion*, 75.

95. McMenamy interview, February 10, 1995.

96. Aronow interview, April 9, 1995. Also Parker interview, March 23, 1995, McMenamy interview, February 10, 1995, and Ryan interview, July 8, 1995.

97. Hogan interview, March 21–22, 1995; Hogan to his wife, February 9, 11, 14, 1968; Cushman, "'Ready to Go!'" 27; Krohn, *Lost Battalion*, 52, 55, 60.

98. Battalion Daily Journal (henceforth BDJ), February 8–12, 1968, Infy Units, 2nd Bn, 501st Infy, ACS for Operations (S-3), RG 472, and DROVA, *Delta Raiders*, 44–45.

99. DROVA, *Delta Raiders*, 31–32, 44, and "Gunship Gagne—Gutty Grenadier," undated clipping in the Ray Blackman Papers.

100. Krohn, *Lost Battalion*, 6, 59; DROVA, *Delta Raiders*, 45; Robertson interview, October 27, 1995; Aronow to his wife, February 12, 1968.

101. DROVA, *Delta Raiders*, 45–46; BDJ, 2-501, February 14, 1968; Mount interview, July 12, 1996; Parker interview, July 13, 1996; Richard L. Buzzini interview, August 14, 2001.

102. McMenamy interview, February 10, 1995.

103. Aronow to his wife, February 14, 1968.

104. Mount interview; Rakestraw interview, June 24, 1997; Rainwater interview, July 22, 2000.

Chapter 7

1. Except where otherwise noted, this account of the February 15 battle relies on the following: Robertson interview, October 27, 1995; McMenamy interview, February 10, 1995; Ryan interview, July 8, 1995; Loftin interview, August 13, 1995; Sturges interview, March 5, 1996; Rainwater interview, July 22, 2000; Watson interview July 12, 1996; Bongiorno interview, July 12, 1996; Rockel interview, June 28, 1997; Aronow interview, April 9, 1995; Kearns interview, December 15, 1997; "Report of Engagement by D/2/501 Inf, 15 February 1968," in the BDJ, 2-501, February 15, 1968; DROVA, *Delta Raiders*, 32–35, 46.

2. Melson, "Vietnam's Most-Decorated U.S. Soldier," JRHP. The NVA also emphasized recovering their dead and wounded; see "Problems of a North Vietnamese Regiment," Documents Nos. 2-3, *Vietnam Documents and Research Notes Series*, Reel I.

3. Collins, Senior Officer Debriefing Report.

4. Clifford C. Sims Military Personnel Records, Military Personnel Records, National Personnel Records Center, St. Louis, Missouri.

5. Buzzini interview, March 1, 1997.

6. Krohn discusses the logistical system collapse in *Lost Battalion;* especially see 131, 153, 165–66.

7. Along with the Aronow interview, he wrote detailed letters to his wife and his parents about February 15; see the letters to his wife on February 17, February 18, and April 6, 1968, and to his dad on February 21 and March 31, 1968.

8. James interview, January 14, 1996.

9. Aronow to his parents, May 12, 1968, and Aronow interview, May 19, 1995.

10. Aronow to his wife, February 17, 1968; also see Aronow to his mom and dad, February 25, 1968.

11. Rockel to Joyce, February 16, 1968.

12. "After Action Report (Offensive Operations 22 Jan 10–Mar 1968)," Headquarters, U.S. Army Vietnam, Command Historian, AARS, Box 15, RG 472. Aronow wrote his wife on February 18, 1968, that "the NVA soldiers up here are elite hard-core professionals. Many of the them are 6'2" 200 pounds, some even 6'4"."

13. Hogan to his wife, February 15, 1968, and BDJ, 2-501, February 16, 1968; also see Hogan to Blackman, January 17, 1990, Ray Blackman Papers.

14. Aronow to his wife, February 18, 1968.

15. The lists of the wounded and those deserving medals are in the McMenamy Papers. The elegy is in DROVA, *Delta Raiders*, 21.

16. Ebert, *Life in a Year*, 138.

17. Clausewitz, *On War*, 227, 258; Spiller, "Price of Valor," 104; Sturges interview. March 5, 1996.

18. Edelman, *Dear America*, 24.

19. Gerald F. Linderman, *The World within War: America's Combat Experience in World War II* (New York: The Free Press, 1997), 48–55; Aronow to his wife, February 17, 1968; Nale interview, July 13, 1996; "2 More Citations Received by Medal of Honor Winner: Vietnamese, U.S. Government's [*sic*] Decorate Sgt. Joe Hooper for Heroism in Combat," undated clipping, Hendricks Scrapbook. Another reason veterans said so little about combat was that they did not remember much of what occurred; see Chapter 8 for a discussion of this point.

20. Rakestraw interview, June 24, 1997; McDonough, *Platoon Leader*, 14–15; Hawk interview, June 21, 1997; Edelman, *Dear America*, 62.

21. Grady, *Tiger's Back*, 203, and Hogan interview, March 21–22, 1995.

22. McMenamy interview, February 10, 1995.

23. DROVA, *Delta Raiders*, 46, and McMenamy interview, February 10, 1995.

24. BDJ, 2-501, February 17, 1968, and Cushman, "'Ready to Go!'" 47.

25. DROVA, *Delta Raiders*, 47, and Cushman, "'Ready to Go!'" 48.

26. This account of February 19 relies on the following sources: BDJ, 2-501, February 19, 1968; DROVA, *Delta Raiders*, 35–36; McMenamy interview, February 10, 1995; Rockel interview, June 28, 1997; Kearns interview, December 15, 1997; Loftin interview, August 13, 1995; Sturges interview, March 5, 1996; combined interview with Hogan and Loftin, July 13, 1996.

27. For Hogan's assumption of command, see Cleo C. Hogan Jr., "The Delta Raiders: February July 1968, A Personal History," 1–2; Hogan to his wife, February 27, 1968; Hogan to McMenamy, May 16, 1990, all in Cleo C. Hogan Jr. Papers; Hogan interviews, March 21–22, 1995 and July 21, 2000; Hogan/Loftin interview, July 13, 1996.

28. Erbach interview, July 29, 1996; Rockel interview, June 28, 1997; Nale interview, July 13, 1995; Aronow interview, April 9, 1995.

29. Watson interview, July 12, 1996.

30. Samuel Hynes, *The Soldier's Tale: Bearing Witness to Modern War* (New York: Penguin, 1997), 27–28; John Keegan, "Natural Warriors," *Wall Street Journal*, March 27, 1997, A20; Lieut. Col. Dave Grossman, *On Killing: The Psychological Cost of Learning to Kill in War and Society* (Boston: Little, Brown, 1996), 43–44, 180–81.

31. John Del Vecchio, *The 13th Valley* (New York: Bantam, 1983), 160–61.

32. Aronow interview, April 9, 1995.

33. Hogan interview, March 21–22, 1995.

34. Ryan interview, July 8, 1995.

35. Buzzini interview, March 1, 1997.

36. Rockel interview, June 28, 1997.

37. Aronow to Father Leary, May 8, 1968, Aronow Papers.

38. Saal interview, June 26, 1997, and Buzzini interview, March 1, 1997.

39. Brady is quoted in "Reserve Center Dedicated in Memory of Joe Hooper," undated clipping, Frank M. Campagne Papers.

40. "The Story of Joe Hooper, War Hero," *Cumberland (MD) Times/News*, February 20, 1986, Red and Anna Combs Papers; Parker interview, March 23, 1995; Audrey Hooper interview, March 2, 1996.

41. Sturges interview, March 5, 1996, and James interview, January 14, 1996.

42. Hooper interview, March 2, 1996; Aronow interview, April 9, 1995; Ryan interview, July 8, 1995. Hogan believed Joe had a guardian angel (Hogan to the author, January 23, 1996) as did Patrick L. Runevitch (Runevitch interview, April 11, 1996). Chaplain Erbach thought Hooper "was one dag-gummed lucky guy," Erbach interview, March 20, 1996.

43. Clausewitz, *On War*, 85, and Nicholas Rescher, *Luck: The Brilliant Randomness of Everyday Life* (New York: Farrar Straus and Giroux, 1995), 7.

44. Hawk interview, June 21, 1997.

45. Kearns interview, December 15, 1997; Sturges interview, March 5, 1996; Aronow interview, April 9, 1995.

46. William Ian Miller, *The Mystery of Courage* (Cambridge: Harvard University Press, 2000), 159.

47. Rakestraw interview, June 24, 1997, and Wayne Anderson interview, July 29, 1999.

48. Fax from Brian Oak to the authors, January 31, 1997, and Ryan interview, July 8, 1995.

49. Except where otherwise indicated, this account of courage relies on Miller's brilliant book *Mystery of Courage*.

50. Murphy, *Dak To*, 80, and Tim O'Brien, *The Things They Carried* (New York: Penguin, 1991), 62.

51. Stanley C. Marcieski, "Eagle Dustoff" ("Delta Raiders Newsletter," 59 [1996]) wrote of "having a dumb attack or a surge of John Wayne fever." Looking back on the brave/dumb things he did, his main thought was "Curse you John Wayne."

52. Aronow to his wife, April 6, 1968.

53. Eisenhower is quoted in Miller, *Mystery of Courage*, 197; Towns interview, July 13, 1996.

54. Robert L. O'Connell, "Courage," *MHQ* (Autumn 1990): 62–66.

55. George Putnam, "Reminiscences of Audie Murphy," June 1, 1971, copy in JRHP.

56. O'Brien, *If I Die in a Combat Zone*, 45, and Kovic, 218–19; also see Michael Clodfelter, *Mad Minutes and Vietnam Months: A Soldier's Memoir* (n.p.: Pinnacle Books, n.d.), 126–27.

57. Richard Holmes, *Acts of War: The Behavior of Men in Battle* (New York: The Free Press, 1986), 141.

58. For a superb discussion of comradeship, see Linderman, *World within War*, 263–99. Also see Herbert Spiegel, "Psychiatry with an Infantry Battalion in North Africa," in William S. Mullins, ed., *Neuropsychiatry in World War II. Vol. II. Overseas Theaters* (Washington DC: n.p., 1973).

59. McDonough, *Platoon Leader*, 140–41.

60. "Delta Raiders Newsletter," 13 (1988); "Delta Raiders Newsletter," 51 (1995); videotape of the Delta Raiders' Memorial Service, July 13, 1996, copy in the authors' possession.

61. Hooper to his parents, March 11, 1968, JRHP, and Blackman, "Thoughts of War," Ray Blackman Papers. The enemy also understood the family-like feelings that accompanied comradeship; see Chanoff and Toai, *Portrait of the Enemy*, 172.

62. Erbach interview, March 20, 1996, and McMenamy interview February 10, 1995.

63. Linderman, *World within War*, 298, and Hooper to his parents, May 3, 1968, JRHP. Also see Rakestraw interview, June 24, 1997.

64. Miller, *Mystery of Courage*, 12.

65. Murphy, *Dak To*, 96, and Luther interview, May 30, 2000. Hooper always readily admitted to friends and colleagues that in battle he was scared. For example, see the interview with Jerry McCollum, September 24, 1999.

66. Hawk interview, June 21, 1997.

67. Except where otherwise noted, the following discussion relies on William DeMyer, *Neuroanatomy*, 2nd edition (Baltimore: Williams and Wilkins, 1998); Jack Fincher, *The Brain: Mystery of Matter and Mind* (New York: Torstar Books, 1984); S. David Gertz, *Liebman's Neuroanatomy Made Easy and Understandable*, 5th edition (Gaithersburg MD: Aspen Publishers, 1996); Gerard J. Tortora, *Principles of Human Anatomy*, 8th edition (New York: Addison Wesley Longman, 1998); Joseph LeDoux, *The Emotional Brain: The Mysterious Underpinnings of Emotional Life* (New York: A Touchstone Book, 1998); Antonio R. Damasio, *Descartes' Error: Emotion, Reason, and the Human Brain* (New York: Avon Books, 1994); John J. Ratey, *A User's Guide to the Brain: Perception, Attention, and the Four Theaters of the Brain* (New York: Pantheon, 2001).

68. Some pioneering work on the amygdala's role was conducted by Fred J. Helmstetter, "The Amygdala Is Essential for the Expression of Conditional Hypoalgesia," *Behavioral Neuroscience* (June 1992).

69. Grossman, *On Killing*, 70–71.

70. The concept of an emotional hijacking is from Daniel Goleman, *Emotional Intelligence* (New York: Bantam, 1995).

71. *Time* magazine, January 26, 1987, 61.

72. Goleman, *Emotional Intelligence*, 215–21.

73. Karl Taro Greenfield, "Life on the Edge," *Time* magazine, September 6, 1999, 29–36; especially see the insert titled "For Our Ancestors, Taking Risks Was a Good Bet," 32–33.

74. George R. Uhl, Ichiro Sora, and Zaijie Wang, "The μ Opiate Receptor as a Candidate Gene for Pain: Polymorphisms, Variations in Expression, Nociception, and Opiate Responses," *Proceedings of the National Academy of Sciences of the United States of America*, July 16, 1999, and "Study: Gene May Be Used to Treat Pain," *Lincoln Journal Star*, July 20, 1999, 1A, 4A.

75. James M. Dabbs Jr., and Robin Morris, "Testosterone and Antisocial Behavior in a Sample of 4,462 Men," *Psychological Science*, May 1990; Dan Olweus, Ake Mattsson, Daisy Schalling, and Hans Low, "Testosterone, Aggression, Physical, and Personality Dimensions in Normal Adolescent Males," *Psychosomatic Medicine*, March 1980; Joel Ehrenkranz, Eugene Bliss, and Michael H. Sheard, "Plasma Testosterone: Correlation with Aggressive Behavior and Social Dominance in Man," *Psychosomatic Medicine*, November December 1974.

76. On 17-OHCS, see Cynthia Gimble and Alan Booth, "Who Fought in Vietnam?" *Social Forces*, June 1966; Capt. Peter G. Bourne, Capt. Robert M. Rose, and John W. Mason, "Urinary 17-OHCS Levels: Data on Seven Helicopter Ambulance Medics in Combat," *Archives of General Psychiatry*, July 1967, and "17-OHCS Levels in Combat: Special Forces 'A' Teams under Threat of Attack," *Archives of General Psychiatry*, August 1968; Peter G. Bourne, *Men, Stress, and Vietnam* (Boston: Little, Brown, 1970), especially chapter 7, "The Green Berets."

77. Audrey Hooper interview, March 2, 1996, and Mike Sallis interview, March 1, 1996.

78. Earl J. Hess, *The Union Soldier in Battle: Enduring the Ordeal of Combat* (Lawrence: University Press of Kansas, 1997), 73–74.

79. Hooper to his parents, March 15, 1968, JRHP.

Chapter 8

1. John C. Fitzpatrick, ed., *The Writings of George Washington . . .* , 39 vols. (Washington DC: United States Government Printing Office, 1931–1944), 24: 487–88.

2. Except where otherwise noted, this brief history of medals relies on Philip K. Robles, *United States Military Medals and Ribbons* (Rutland VT: Charles E. Tuttle Company, 1971); Lawrence H. Borts, and Col. (Ret.) Frank C. Foster, *United States Military Medals 1939 to Present*, 3rd edition (Fountain Inn SC: Medals of America Press, 1995); Boston Publishing Company, *Above and Beyond: A History of the Medal of Honor*

from the Civil War to Vietnam (Boston: Boston Publishing Company, 1985); *America's Medal of Honor Recipients: Complete Official Citations* (Golden Valley MN: Highland Publications, 1980); Timothy S. Lowry, *And Brave Men, Too* (New York: Crown Publishers, 1985); Edward F. Murphy, *Heroes of World War II* (Novato CA: Presidio Press, 1990).

3. Regulation Number 672-1, February 20, 1967 Change No. 3 to November 12, 1965 version, dated May 2, 1966.

4. Two organizations chartered by Congress in the 1950s protect and promote the MOH's elite status and the ideals it represents. Being Cold War creations, they aggressively extolled patriotism and Americanism. An explicit objective of the Legion of Valor of the United States of America was to "stimulate patriotism in the minds of our youth," and one of the purposes of The Congressional Medal of Honor Society of the United States was to "foster and perpetuate Americanism."

5. Geoffrey Perret, *There's a War to Be Won: The United States Army in World War II* (New York: Random House, 1991), 475.

6. Cushman, " 'Ready to Go!' " 52.

7. Dale A. Urban File, Headquarters, U.S. Army Vietnam, Adjutant General, Military Personnel Division, Awards Branch, Military Awards Case Files, Box 404, RG 472.

8. The concept of the "institutionalization of valor" comes from Spiller, "Price of Valor," 101; also see Jeffrey W. Anderson, "Military Heroism: An Occupational Definition," *Armed Forces and Society* (Summer 1986); S. L. A. Marshall with Bill Davidson, "Do the Real Heroes Get the Medal of Honor?" *Collier's*, February 21, 1953; Holmes, *Acts of War*, 359.

9. Regulation Number 672-1, as cited above.

10. Major General John M. Wright Jr., May 11, 1970, *U.S. Armed Forces in Vietnam, 1954–1975*, Reel III. Another commander, Major General Zais, considered medals "a real morale builder," May 25, 1969, *U.S. Armed Forces in Vietnam, 1954–1975*, Reel I. And like Napoleon, Westmoreland cynically believed that "A bolt of ribbon will win many battles"; Westmoreland, *Soldier Reports*, 305.

11. Barber interview, February 29, 1997.

12. Doyle Urban to Urban, c. late September 1968, and his parents to Urban, April 9 [1968], Dale Urban Papers, and Caputo, *Rumor of War*, 73.

13. James W. Johnston, *The Long Road of War: A Marine's Story of Pacific Combat* (Lincoln: University of Nebraska Press, 1998), 114–15, and Marshall with Davidson, "Real Heroes."

14. Regulation Number 672-1, as cited above; McMenamy interview, February 10, 1995; Erbach interview, April 12, 1997; Jack Saint interview, April 12, 1997 (Mr. Saint was Joe Hooper's brother-in-law).

15. Gary Foster interview, February 28, 1996.

16. Harold Leinbaugh and John D. Campbell, *The Men of Company K: The Autobiography of a World War II Rifle Company* (New York: William Morrow, 1985), 236.

17. Bradford, *Some Even Volunteered*, 115, and Grady, *Tiger's Back*, 201.

18. Powell, *Journey*, 141, and Livingston interview, July 10, 1995; also see Erbach interview, July 29, 1996.

19. Frick interview, September 21, 1995, and Frick to his wife, January 24, 1969, Frick Papers. Colin Powell, *Journey*, 141, believed that "writing the justifying citations became a minor art form."

20. Cushman, "'Ready to Go!'" 153.

21. Hogan interview, March 21–22, 1995, and Hackworth and Sherman, *About Face*, 675.

22. William M. Hammond, *Reporting Vietnam: Media and Military at War* (Lawrence: University Press of Kansas, 1998), 194, and Erbach interview, July 29, 1996.

23. Frick to his wife, January 24, 1969, and Loftin interview, August 13, 1995. Frick had previously turned down a Bronze Star with V device that his commanding officer wanted to give him because he did not "consider laying on the ground and crawling around a very valorous act, especially when all my crawling was to the rear"; Frick to his wife, September 26, 1968.

24. DeGroot, *Noble Cause*, 294.

25. Gravett interview, July 21, 2000.

26. These figures are compiled from *The Congressional Medal of Honor: The Names, The Deeds* (Forest Ranch CA: Sharp and Dunnigan Publications, 1984), which is a readily available source. However, the number of MOH recipients is fluid, even in peacetime. Since that book's publication, Congress has awarded after-the-fact MOHs to a former slave for action during the Civil War, to Theodore Roosevelt for the Spanish-American War, to twenty-one Asian Americans and seven African Americans for heroism during World War II, and to two men who served in Vietnam.

27. "Delta Raiders Newsletter," 32 (May 1992).

28. "Jeb Stuart I," Headquarters, U.S. Army Vietnam, Command Histories, Box 15, RG 472; DROVA, *Delta Raiders*, 47; Hogan interview, March 21–22, 1995.

29. Hogan interview, March 21–22, 1995, and Hogan, "The Delta Raiders, February–July 1968: A Personal History," 3–4.

30. Erbach interview, March 20, 1996.

31. Mount interview, July 12, 1996.

32. Hogan interview, March 21–22, 1995; Hogan, "The Delta Raiders," 5–6; Hogan to the authors, undated [c. 1996].

33. Erbach interview, March 20, 1996.

34. Petitt interview, July 24, 1998.

35. Hogan interview, August 1, 1996; Sturges interview, March 5, 1996; David Bischoff interview, January 13, 1997; Parker interview, March 23, 1995; Rakestraw interview, June 24, 1997; Bongiorno interview, July 12, 1996.

36. Parker interviews, March 23, 1995 and April 17, 1995.

37. Barber interview, February 29, 1997; Hogan to the authors, January 23, 1996; Ryan interview, July 8, 1995.

38. Gravett interview, July 21, 2000; Bongiorno interview, July 12, 1996; Sturges interview, March 5, 1996; Buzzini interview, March 1, 1997.

39. Comments by Dr. Jeffrey Clarke, Chief Historian, U.S. Army Center of Military History, during the 1998 annual meeting of the Department of the Army's Historical Advisory Committee, October 30, 1998.

40. Aronow to his wife, February 21, 1968.

41. Hogan to the authors, January 23, 1996.

42. Donlon interview, February 9, 1996.

43. Hogan to his wife, February 27, 1968, and Hogan's diary, entry for February 21, 1968, Cleo C. Hogan Jr. Papers.

44. Hogan interviews, March 21–22, 1995 and July 25, 1999. Hogan also commented on what he saw in two videotaped interviews. One was for Cushman and appeared in his video autobiography of his Vietnam tour (copy in authors' possession). The other was for Marty Callaghan who was then working for MPI Teleproductions (copy in authors' possession).

45. Parker interviews, March 23, 1995, April 17, 1995, and July 13, 1996.

46. Erbach interviews, March 20, 1996 and July 29, 1996; Erbach to the authors, c. April 3, 1996. The inscribed Bible is in the JRHP. Bobby Rakestraw (interview, June 24, 1997) and Richard Buzzini (interview, March 1, 1997) confirm that Erbach was wounded in the rice paddy, not in the village.

47. Gray interview, October 30, 1995, and James interviews, January 14, 1996 and April 10, 1996.

48. Petitt interview, July 24, 1998.

49. Urban interview, June 8, 1995; Sturges interview, March 5, 1996; Grady Towns interview, July 13, 1996; T'Odon C. Leshikar interview, October 28, 1995; Aronow interview, April 9, 1995.

50. Urban interview, April 7, 1995. He also made this point in a second interview on June 8, 1995.

51. The following discussion of memory depends heavily on Fincher, *The Brain*; LeDoux, *Emotional Brain*; Ratey, *User's Guide*, especially chapter 5 on "Memory"; Robert E. McGlone, "Deciphering Memory: John Adams and the Authorship of the Declaration of Independence," *Journal of American History* (September 1998), 411–38; and especially Daniel L. Schacter, ed., *Memory Distortion: How Minds, Brains, and Societies Reconstruct the Past* (Cambridge: Harvard University Press, 1995) and Schacter, *Searching for Memory: The Brain, the Mind, and the Past* (New York: Basic Books, 1996).

52. Fincher, *The Brain*, 82.

53. Ratey, *User's Guide*, 192, says that "brain wave activity in the hippocampus during dreaming actually rehearses memory patterns, either to harden newer experiences into long-term memories or to keep fading connections alive."

54. LeDoux, *Emotional Brain*, 239, 243.

55. Tadayoshi Sakurai, *Human Bullets: A Soldier's Story of Port Arthur*, trans. Masujiro Honda ([1907] Lincoln: University of Nebraska Press, 1999), 232, 236.

56. Urban interviews, April 7, 1995 and June 8, 1995; Rakestraw interview, June 24, 1997; Barber interview, February 29, 1997; Buzzini interview, March 1, 1997; Bischoff interview, January 13, 1997.

57. Barber interview, February 29, 1997; Urban interview, April 7, 1995; James interview, January 14, 1996; Rakestraw interview, June 24, 1997.

58. LeDoux, *Emotional Brain*, 203.

59. Schacter, *Searching for Memory*, 129.

60. Schacter, *Searching for Memory*, 52.

61. Ratey, *User's Guide*, 31, 191–92, and Richard Restak, *Mozart's Brain and the Fighter Pilot: Unleashing Your Brain's Potential* (New York: Three Rivers Press, 2001), 15–20.

62. McGlone, "Deciphering Memory," 418.

63. Schacter, *Searching for Memory*, 114.

64. John McCrone, "Reasons to Forget: Scientists Count the Ways We Get It Wrong," *Times Literary Supplement*, January 30, 2004, 3–4, emphasizes this point.

65. Schacter, *Searching for Memory*, 21.

66. Restak, *Mozart's Brain*, 35.

67. Schacter, *Searching for Memory*, 76.

68. Stan H. Smith, "Medal of Honor Recipients—A Profile," Stan H. Smith Papers, and Erbach interview, March 20, 1996.

69. Hogan to the authors, January 3, 1996, and Hogan interview, March 31, 1996.

70. The following account of how Hooper's MOH file was compiled relies on Hogan to the authors, January 3, 1996 and January 23, 1996; Hogan interview, March 21–22, 1995; Aronow interview, April 9, 1995; and Aronow to Blackman, February 16, 1990, copy in the Cleo C. Hogan Jr. Papers.

71. Professor Allan R. Millett of the Ohio State University to the authors, November 11, 1998; Miller, *Mystery of Courage*, 120–26; Anderson, "Military Heroism."

72. Both citations are in Hooper's MOH file.

73. Hooper to his parents, May 6, 1968, JRHP. On Joe leaving the service, see his letters to his parents on March 11 and April 7, 1968, JRHP.

74. The quote about "another day at the office" was from the Aronow interview, April 9, 1995. Sal Bongiorno (interview, July 12, 1996) summed this up, saying that after February 14 firefights were common "and I can't put it altogether chronologically as to what happened on down the line."

75. Kearns interview, December 15, 1997.

76. Rakestraw interview, June 24, 1997.

77. Erbach (interview, July 29, 1996) believed "Joe was a central character in the general play prior to that [February 21, 1968] just because of his personality," which made a difference between being recognized or being ignored.

78. Keirn C. Brown interview, January 11, 1997.

79. Except where noted the following account relies on Hogan to his wife, February 27, 1968; Hogan interviews, March 21–22, 1995, May 13, 1995, July 14, 1996, August 1, 1996, and July 25, 1999; Hogan to the authors, undated [c. 1996] and January 3, 1996; Hogan's videotaped interviews with Cushman and Callaghan; Hogan, "The Delta Raiders," 3–11. Hogan's accounts contain some inconsistencies, but they do not relate to significant events.

80. Loftin interview, August 13, 1995, and Hooper to his parents, March 15, 1968, JRHP.

81. Watson interview, July 12, 1996.

82. Barber interview, February 29, 1997.

83. James interview, April 10, 1996.

84. Erbach interview, March 20, 1996.

85. Bischoff interview, January 13, 1997, and Bischoff to the authors, January 20, 1997.

86. Bongiorno interview, July 12, 1996, and Sims's MOH file, which can be viewed online at http://www.nara.gov/cgi-bin/starfinder/5725/complete.txt.

87. After the war Hogan suspected that Urban was in the gap, though he was never sure; Hogan to the authors, January 23, 1996, and Hogan interview, July 14, 1996. The following account relies on the Urban interviews, April 7, 1995 and June 8, 1995. Unlike many veterans who expressed doubts about their memory and despite some vagueness about time and distance, Dale was confident his recollections were accurate. In all cases where corroboration was possible, what he said fit with the other evidence.

88. For the location of Urban's DSC file, see note 7. Scott has not been located, so it cannot be stated with certainty that his signature was a forgery.

89. James interviews, January 14, 1996, and April 10, 1996.

90. Ayala interview, May 9, 2000.

91. Rockel interview, June 28, 1997.

92. Ryan interview, July 8, 1995, and Mount interview, July 12, 1996.

93. Rakestraw interview, June 24, 1997; Barber interview, February 29, 1997; Buzzini interview, March 1, 1997.

94. The document is in the Audrey Hooper Papers; a copy is in the authors' possession.

95. Hogan interview, July 13, 1996.

96. Nancy Gould, "A Vietnam Hero—His Story," *Kent News Journal*, April 1, 1976, in JRHP; Bob Burnett, "I always had the will to live," *Wenatchee World*, February 28, 1975, in the Maxine L. Bohn Papers; Jay Berman, "Two Weapons Fail in Hero's Exchange," undated clipping, Hendricks Scrapbook; Gary Foster interview, March 7, 1995; Johnson interview, April 14, 1996; Arden D. Hardison interview, July 7, 2000.

97. Gould, "A Vietnam Hero."

98. Aronow interview, April 9, 1995.

99. Wolf, "Probing the Minds," 64; "Medal Winner," undated clipping, Audrey Hooper Papers; Gary Foster interview, March 7, 1995; Floyd N. Greenwald interview, August 5, 1996.

100. Hawk interview, June 21, 1997.

Chapter 9

1. Hogan to his wife, February 27, 1968; Aronow to his wife, February 22, 1968; BDJ, 2-501, February 21, 1968.

2. Ayala interview, May 9, 2000, and Hogan interview, March 21–22, 1995.

3. Hogan, "The Delta Raiders," 11, and Hogan interview, March 21–22, 1995.

4. Bongiorno interview, July 12, 1996; Ayala interview, May 9, 2000; Rakestraw interview, June 24, 1997.

5. Urban interview, April 7, 1995.

6. Hogan interview, March 21–22, 1995; also Hogan interview, July 13, 1996.

7. "Most decorated soldier takes XO post here," undated clipping, JRHP; Records for Joe R. Hooper in Casualty Information System (TAGCEN), 1961–1981, the Center for Electronic Records, NARA; "U.S. Army Casualty Report Format," Audrey Hooper Papers.

8. Hogan, "The Delta Raiders," 12.

9. Hogan, "The Delta Raiders," 12–13; Hogan interview, March 21–22, 1995; Hogan to his wife, February 27, 1968; BDJ, 2-501, February 22, 1968.

10. Aronow to his wife, February 23 and February 25, 1968.

11. Hogan to his wife, February 27, 1968; Hogan, "The Delta Raiders," 13–14; DROVA, *Delta Raiders*, 50.

12. Keith William Nolan, *Battle for Hue, Tet, 1968* (Novato CA: Presidio Press, 1983), 171; Smith, *Siege at Hue*, 161, 165; Krohn, *Lost Battalion*, 126; "Jeb Stuart I," Headquarters, U.S. Army Vietnam, Command Historian, AARS, Box 15, RG 472.

13. Aronow interview, April 9, 1995, and Aronow to his wife, February 26, 1968.

14. Hogan interview, March 21–22, 1995.

15. Aronow to his parents, March 14, 1968.

16. Aronow to his wife, February 26, 1968.

17. Aronow to his wife, February 26, 1968.

18. Hogan, "The Delta Raiders," 16, and Hogan to his wife, February 28, 1968.

19. "After Action Report (Offensive Operations 10 Mar 68–17 May 68)," 101st Abn Div, ACS G-3, AARS, Box 1, RG 472.

20. Cushman, "'Ready to Go!'" 57–58.

21. Hogan, "The Delta Raiders," 16–18; DROVA, *Delta Raiders*, 64–65; Hogan to his wife, February 28, March 1, March 4, and March 8, 1968; "After Action Report (Of-

fensive Operations 22 Jan–10 Mar 1968)," Headquarters, U.S. Army Vietnam, Command Histories, AARS, Box 15, RG 472.

22. "After Action Report (Offensive Operations 10 Mar 68–17 May 68)," and "Combat Operations After Action Report Operation Carentan," both in 101st Abn Div., ACS G-3, AARS, Box 1, RG 472.

23. Joe to his parents, March 11, 1968, JRHP; Nale interview, July 13, 1995; Gumm interview, July 2, 1995; Erbach interview, March 20, 1996; James interview, April 10, 1996.

24. Robertson to Jackie and Jim, February 18, 1968, Eugene Robertson Papers.

25. Frank M. Campagne interview, January 8, 1996; Gumm interview, July 2, 1995; Erbach interview, March 20, 1996; Aronow interview, April 9, 1995; Buzzini interview, March 1, 1997.

26. Mr. Eric Voelz, Archivist, Military Operations Branch, Military Personnel Records, searched the relevant hospital records but found no charge out information for Hooper; Voelz to the authors, September 15, 1995. Richard Buzzini took two pictures of Joe in his hospital gown and generously gave the pictures to the authors.

27. Joe to his parents, March 11, 1968, JRHP.

28. Joe to his parents, March 15, 1968, JRHP.

29. Joe to his parents, March 11 and 15, 1968, JRHP; DROVA, *Delta Raiders*, 65; Hogan to his wife, March 8, 1968.

30. Palmer, *25-Year War*, 59, and "Proverbs and Reflections from Viet Nam Foxholes," copy in the Mark S. Hawk Papers.

31. Barsanti, "Combat Notes No. 2, Night Combat," January 20, 1968, Barsanti Papers, and Cushman, "'Ready to Go!'" 41, 68.

32. Parker interview, March 23, 1995; Urban interview, April 7, 1995; Petitt interview, July 24, 1998; Hogan interview, March 21–22, 1995; Robertson interview, October 27, 1995.

33. Soldiers might not have known about cones and rods, but they knew, as Urban put it, that "you never look directly at anything, you kind of look away from it, and you can actually see it out of your peripheral vision"; interview, April 7, 1995.

34. Aronow interview, April 9, 1995. When asked about keeping one eye closed, Robertson said, "That sounds familiar, but I'll guarantee you I didn't do that"; interview, October 27, 1995.

35. Sturges interview, March 5, 1996; Ebert, *Life in a Year*, 250; Gadd, *Line Doggie*, 81.

36. Urban interview, April 7, 1995.

37. DROVA, *Delta Raiders*, 222.

38. Parker interview, March 23, 1995. Eugene Robertson was either on the same ambush or on one that was similar when approximately 100 NVA passed through the kill zone unmolested; interview, October 27, 1995.

39. The account of this "ambush" and its aftermath relies on Hogan, "The Delta Raid-

ers," 18–20; Hogan interview, March 21–22, 1995; BDJ, 2-501, March 18, 1968; Hogan to his wife, March 19, 1968.

40. Aronow to his wife, March 19, 1968, and Parker interview, March 23, 1995.

41. Aronow to his wife, March 19, 1968.

42. Aronow to Blackman, February 16, 1990, Ray Blackman Papers, and Sturges interview, March 5, 1996.

43. The account of this ambush relies on Urban interview, April 7, 1995; Buzzini interview, March 1, 1997; Rakestraw interview, June 24, 1997; Hogan interview, March 21–22, 1995; Aronow interview, April 9, 1995; BDJ, 2-501, March 20, 1968. The quote about not "getting anybody killed" was from Urban.

44. The citation is in Joe's Military Personnel Records. For his fabrications, see SSG Joe R. Hooper, "The Screaming Eagle," undated clipping, JRHP, and Bob Burnett, "I Always Had the Will to Live," *Wenatchee World*, February 28, 1975, clipping in the Maxine L. Bohn Papers.

45. Hogan interview, March 21–22, 1995.

46. Except where otherwise noted, this account of the battle for Hill 309 relies on Hogan, "The Delta Raiders," 21–26; Hogan interviews, March 21–22, 1995 and August 1, 1996; Hogan to his wife, March 23, 1968; Loftin interview, August 13, 1995; Aronow interview, April 9, 1995; "After Action Report (Offensive Operations 10 Mar 68–17 May 68)"; DROVA, *Delta Raiders*, 67–68; and BDJ, 2-501, March 21–25, 1968.

47. Dale Stengel interview, August 2, 1996. The Raiders received their first replacements in early March, but those men were airborne qualified. "They're green," Aronow wrote, "but at least they're not legs. In a month's time they'll be veterans like everyone else"; Aronow to his wife, March 8, 1968.

48. Stengel interview, August 2, 1996; Aronow interview, April 9, 1995; Ebert, *Life in a Year*, 17.

49. Sturges interview, March 5, 1996. Stengel interview, August 2, 1996, and Aronow to his wife, March 24, 1968, both attest to the terror they endured that night.

50. Before typing up his "Delta Raiders," Hogan wrote much of his history in longhand and sent it to us. This exact language is in the undated handwritten draft; the typed version has slightly different wording. Along with the sources cited below, the battle for Hill 100 can be followed in DROVA, *Delta Raiders*, 69–70; BDJ, 2-501, March 26–29, 1968; and "After Action Report (Offensive Operations 10 Mar 68–17 May 68)."

51. Hogan interview, March 21–22, 1995.

52. Hooper to his parents, March 25, 1968 and March 11, 1968, JRHP.

53. Stengel interview, August 2, 1996, and Towns interview, July 13, 1996 both attest to the shock of the ambush.

54. Hogan, "The Delta Raiders," 26–27.

55. Hogan, "The Delta Raiders," 27, and Loftin interview, August 13, 1995.

56. Stengel interview, August 2, 1996.

57. In August 1968 Hogan explained this event in a six-page typewritten account, which is in the Cleo C. Hogan Jr. Papers. For the Raiders shooting VC as they slept, see Hogan to his wife, June 13 and 19, 1968; Red Combs interview February 8, 1995.

58. Hogan, "The Delta Raiders," 27, and Aronow to his wife, March 27, 1968.

59. Hogan interview, August 1, 1996, and Hogan to his wife, March 28, 1968.

60. Hogan, "The Delta Raiders," 28.

61. Hooper to his parents, March 31, 1968, JRHP.

62. Barrett, LBJ's Vietnam Papers, 636.

63. Clarence R. Wyatt, Paper Soldiers: The American Press and the Vietnam War (Chicago: University of Chicago Press, 1995), 187.

64. Buzzanco, Masters of War, 312.

65. Buzzanco, Masters of War, 311, and Marc Jason Gilbert and William Head, eds., The Tet Offensive (Westport CT: Praeger, 1996), 234–35.

66. Garth Porter, "The 1968 'Hue Massacre,'" http://www.shss.motclair.edu/english/furr/porterhue1.html (and porterhue2.html for the second part of the essay), and Gilbert and Head, Tet Offensive, 243.

67. Gilbert and Head, Tet Offensive, 234–35; BDM Corporation, "Study of Strategic Lessons," EX-5; Thayer, How to Analyze a War without Fronts, 835.

68. Gilbert and Head, Tet Offensive, 236, and Barrett, LBJ's Vietnam Papers, 601–5.

69. Gilbert and Head, Tet Offensive, 237–38; Barrett, LBJ's Vietnam Papers, 605–11; Gravel, Pentagon Papers, IV, 539–42; Westmoreland, Soldier Reports, 352.

70. Gravel, Pentagon Papers, IV, 546–49, and Barrett, LBJ's Vietnam Papers, 629–34.

71. Davidson, Vietnam at War, 505–6.

72. Barrett, LBJ's Vietnam Papers, 624–25, 638, and Gravel, Pentagon Papers, IV, 550–52.

73. Barrett, Uncertain Warriors, 129; Krepinevich, Army and Vietnam, 245; Herring, LBJ and Vietnam, 159.

74. For Clifford's study group, see Gravel, Pentagon Papers, IV, 549–84.

75. Spector, After Tet, xvi.

76. Barrett, LBJ's Vietnam Papers, 643–51.

77. Barrett, LBJ's Vietnam Papers, 634, 708, and Schell, Real War, 34.

78. Jim Mann, "Declassified Files Reveal U.S. Feared War in Korea in 1968," Lincoln Journal Star, January 28, 2001, 9A.

79. Gravel, Pentagon Papers, IV, 541, and Barrett, LBJ's Vietnam Papers, 599.

80. Gravel, Pentagon Papers, IV, 585–88.

81. Barrett, LBJ's Vietnam Papers, 688, 709; Young, Vietnam Wars, 225; Gilbert and Head, Tet Offensive, 225; Powell, Journey, 119–20.

82. D. Michael Shafer, ed., The Legacy: The Vietnam War in the American Imagination (Boston: Beacon, 1990), 142, and Kearns, Lyndon Johnson, 352.

83. Pisor, *End of the Line*, 238, and Young, *Vietnam Wars*, 228.

84. Barrett, *LBJ's Vietnam Papers*, 713–15, and Gilbert and Head, *Tet Offensive*, 245.

85. Gravel, *Pentagon Papers*, IV, 596–602.

86. Barrett, *LBJ's Vietnam Papers*, 604.

87. Barrett, *LBJ's Vietnam Papers*, 720.

88. Herring, *LBJ and Vietnam*, 163–64.

89. Baritz, *Backfire*, 265.

90. Gibson, *Perfect War*, 165–66.

91. Buzzanco, *Masters of War*, 339. Although Buzzanco is the strongest advocate of this interpretation, others agree with it; for example, see Record, *Wrong War*, 4–5.

92. Barrett, *LBJ's Vietnam Papers*, 600.

93. Gilbert and Head, *Tet Offensive*, 24, and Barrett, *Uncertain Warriors*, 112.

94. Gallup, *Gallup Poll*, III, 2135.

95. Hogan to his wife, March 29, 1968.

96. Hooper to his parents, April 7 and 12, 1968, JRHP. "Reconnaissance-in-force" was a euphemism for "search and destroy"; the operations remained the same, only the name was changed so it at least seemed as if the Americans were doing less destroying.

97. Hooper to his parents, April 7 and 12, 1968, JRHP.

98. Hooper to his parents, April 12, 1968, JRHP, and three photos of the service in the Cleo C. Hogan Jr. Papers.

99. Hooper to his parents, April 7, 1968, JRHP.

100. Except where otherwise noted this account of the Battle of Phuoc Dien relies on Hogan, "The Delta Raiders," 30–33; Hogan to the authors, January 23, 1996; Hogan interview, March 21–22, 1995; Hogan's unpublished typewritten account in the Cleo C. Hogan Jr. Papers; Hogan's videotaped interviews with Cushman and Callaghan; Hogan to his wife, April 12, 68; DROVA, *Delta Raiders*, 73–74; BDJ, 2-501, April 9–11, 1968; Cushman, "'Ready to Go!'" 105–8, though this account varies from the 1995 version when he wrote of "a coordinated battalion attack" on Phuoc Dien (in the 1996 version he ignores whether the attack was preplanned or ad hoc). As often happened, the official accounts of this battle were written after the fact, making the battle seem preplanned and orderly. "As I recall," Hogan wrote, "the after action report was written in June 1968. These reports were cleaned up, embellished to make the unit look good, errors that were made were not often included since they reflect poorly on the command. Eagles and stars could be made or lost based on how successful a mission was, and the after action report was written in the best light possible, for obvious reasons." But, cautioned Hogan, "keep in mind that these documents are written by people at Brigade Headquarters from reports received by Battalion Headquarters and Company Headquarters. By the time in-

formation has gone through three Headquarters things get changed, garbled, mis-stated, mis-understood." These comments are in Hogan to the authors, January 23, 1996; also see Appy, *Working Class War*, 161, for another example of how official reports made the military's performance seem better than it was.

101. DROVA, *Delta Raiders*, 171–72; Caputo, *Rumor of War*, 105–6, 277–78; Aronow interview, April 9, 1995; Parker interview, March 23, 1995.

102. Hogan to his wife, March 29 and April 8, 1968.

103. "Combat Notes No. 8 [Chemical Operations]," February 18, 1968; "Combat Notes No. 9, Increasing the Effectiveness of Preparatory Fires," February 18, 1968; "Combat Notes No. 12, E8 Tactical CS Launcher," March 28, 1968; all in Barsanti Papers. Subsequent 101st commanders agreed; see Wright, Senior Officer Debriefing Report, 17.

104. Hooper to his parents, April 12, 1968, JRHP.

105. Spec 4 Dennis Thorton, "Encore for Medal of Honor Winner Hooper," *Pacific Stars and Stripes*, June 11, 1970, clipping in the JRHP. Joe repeated the same story, with slightly different embellishments, in Wolf, "Probing the Minds," 27.

106. The citation is in the Hooper Military Personnel Records.

107. Hooper to his parents, April 12, 1968, JRHP. Hogan was just beginning the process of upgrading Joe's Silver Star. Where or when Joe received the Army Commendation Medal is unknown; his Military Personnel Records contain no record of it.

108. For cordons, see Cushman, "'Ready to Go!'" 79–87; Barsanti, "Methods of Combat on the Coastal Plains," Barsanti Papers; "Operational Report of the 101st Air Cavalry Division for the Period Ending 31 July 1968," 101st Abn Div, ACS, G-3, Operations Reports—LL, Box 2, RG 472; "Combat Operations After Action Report Operation Carentan," 101st Abn Div, ACS, G-3, AARS, Box 1, RG 472.

109. Robertson interview, October 27, 1995.

110. "2nd Brigade 101st Airborne Division . . . Inscription Ceremony at the 101st Airborne Division Memorial," Arlington Cemetery, May 29, 1994, Cushman Papers.

111. Cushman, "'Ready to Go!'" 130–34.

112. *The 101st Airborne 1968 Vietnam Yearbook*, 27, 97, and Zais, Senior Officer Debriefing Report, 19.

113. Unit Order No. 11, April 14, 1968, Aronow Papers; Aronow to Blackman, February 16, 1990, Aronow to Hogan, June 7, 1990, and Hogan to Aronow, June 20, 1990, all in the Cleo C. Hogan Jr. Papers; Hogan to the authors, July 5, 1996; Hogan interviews, March 21–22, 1995 and July 14, 1996; Aronow interview, April 9, 1995; Aronow to his wife, June 5, 1968. According to Aronow's Officer Efficiency Report for January 19–June 21, 1968, he preferred "combat operations in the field over more mundane administrative tasks required in the rear area. This attitude was generally reflected in his work"; this document is in the Aronow Papers.

114. Aronow to his wife, June 3, 8, and 10 and July 3, 1968; Aronow to his parents, April 17, 1968; Aronow to his wife, April 17, 1968; Aronow to his Dad, March 31, 1968; Aronow to his parents, March 29, 1968; Aronow to his parents, May 12, 1968.

115. Cushman, "'Ready to Go!'" 113–17; DROVA, *Delta Raiders*, 75–76; "Combat Operations After Action Report Operation Carentan," June 15, 1968, and "After Action Report (Offensive Operations 10 March 68–17 May 68)," 101st Abn Div, ACS, G-3, AARS, Box 1, RG 472.

116. Thayer, *How to Analyze a War without Fronts*, 813–14, and BDJ, 2-501, February 8 and March 18, 1968.

117. Cushman, "'Ready to Go!'" 80, and "Operational Report of the 101st Air Cavalry Division for the Period Ending 31 July 1968," August 15, 1968, 101st Abn Div, ACS, G-3, Operations Reports—LL, Box 2, RG 472.

118. Hogan interview, March 21–22, 1995.

119. Aronow to his wife, March 2, 1968. On Aronow's doubts, see his letter to his wife, March 27, 1968 where he wrote that "nearly everyone I know is *against* the general idea of the war and knows we can't win here. I was really surprised, no kidding. But they're right. . . . Too many men have died already for *seemingly no reason.*"

120. Parker interview, March 23, 1995; Rakestraw interview, June 24, 1997; Ryan interview, July 8, 1995.

121. "The Battle of Phuoc Yen," Barsanti Papers; DROVA, *Delta Raiders*, 77–78; Cushman, "'Ready to Go!'" 83–84, 122–28; BDJ, 2-501, April 28–May 3, 1968; "Combat Operations After Action Report Operation Carentan," June 15, 1968, 101st Abn Div, ACS, G-3, AARS, Box 1, RG 472; Aronow to Hogan, June 7, 1990; Aronow interview, April 9, 1995.

122. Stengel interview, August 2, 1996, and Rakestraw interview, June 24, 1997.

123. Spector, *After Tet*, 319, and Barrett, *LBJ's Vietnam Papers*, 744–45.

124. The following paragraphs are based on Hooper to his mother, April 27, 1968, and Hooper to his parents, May 3 and May 6, 1968, all in JRHP.

125. Audrey Hooper interview, March 2, 1996, said Joe "liked to go to Saigon and party, and talked about his mama sans, his girl friends, and just go in and party and getting drunk and being crazy on leave." Another source, who wishes to remain anonymous, confirmed Hooper's partying in Saigon. For the promotion see the Morning Report, Company D, 2nd Bn, 501st Regiment, May 19, 1968, National Personnel Records Center, St. Louis, Missouri.

126. Comparison of the Raiders' Roster No. 1, c. December 10, 1967, Cleo C. Hogan Jr. Papers and the Raiders' Roster No. 6, June 6, 1968, Dale Urban Papers. Also, Hogan to the authors, c. early June 1995.

127. Robertson to Jackie and Jim, May 15 and July 17, 1968, Robertson Papers. For others who wanted out of the bush, see Barber to his parents, May 24, 1968, Barber Papers, and Rakestraw interview, June 24, 1997.

128. Buzzini interview, March 1, 1997.

129. DROVA, *Delta Raiders*, 12–13 contains a list of the Raiders who died in Vietnam and the date of their death.

130. Robertson interview, October 27, 1995.

131. DROVA, *Delta Raiders*, 81.

132. John Keegan, *The Face of Battle* (New York: Viking, 1976), 16.

133. Except where noted, this account relies on the interview with Noah and Joyce Rockel, June 28, 1997, and on a telephone interview with Noah Rockel on August 1, 1997.

134. Joyce to Noah, January 27, 1968 and, as an example, Noah to Joyce, October 8, 1967, both in the Rockel Papers.

Chapter 10

1. For DeVore, see the sources cited in chapter 5, note 35.

2. Arduous research but someone had to do it: "Honey in the Bank: Christa Speck," Playmate of the Month, *Playboy*, September 1961, and "Playmate of the Year" Pictorial, *Playboy*, April 1962.

3. Except where otherwise noted, this account of Balbine and Joe depends on an interview with Peter Boenigk and his wife Susan, March 5, 1996, and on a second interview with Peter, June 1, 2002.

4. Gary Foster interview, March 7, 1995.

5. The date of the marriage is in dispute. Balbine said they married on July 28, Joe on July 17.

6. Hooper's "Statement of Personal History," January 3, 1969, in his Military Personnel Records.

7. "Burbank Honors GI," undated clipping, Audrey Hooper Papers; Audrey Hooper interview, March 2, 1996; Hendricks interview, June 16, 1999.

8. Gumm interviews, July 2, 1995 and August 6, 1995.

9. Isakson interview, May 13, 1998.

10. Relevant records in Hooper's Military Personnel Records.

11. Gary Foster interview, March 7, 1995, and Cheryl Riley, "How the Saugus Hero Won Medal of Honor," undated clipping, Audrey Hooper Papers.

12. James McNamara to Lt. Colonel Richard Laurer, April 16, 1969; Howard F. Bergherm to Laurer, May 23, 1969; Bill Compton to Laurer, June 9, 1969; John Wagner to General William C. Westmoreland, June 11, 1969, all in Hooper's Military Personnel Records.

13. Arlene Foster interview, February 28, 1996.

14. Del Vecchio, *13th Valley*, 408.

15. *Newsweek*, March 11, 2002, 6.

16. Lewis Sorley, *A Better War: The Unexamined Victories and Final Tragedy of America's Last Years in Vietnam* (New York: A Harvest Book, 2000), 129; Blum, *Years of*

Discord, 462; Stanley I. Kutler, ed., *Abuse of Power: The New Nixon Tapes* (New York: The Free Press, 1997), which transcribes White House conversations. Another historian wrote that Nixon "lacked the character for public office," "believed that power and those who used it were not accountable—not accountable to the people, not accountable to the law," and therefore he "encouraged and committed wholesale violations of federal law and of the Constitution." Still another proclaimed the president "was paranoid, moody, devious, and insecure" and lacked moral compunction about ethical matters. See Blum, *Years of Discord*, 436, 474, 477, and Jeffrey Kimball, *Nixon's Vietnam War* (Lawrence: University Press of Kansas, 1998), 65.

17. Engelhardt, *End of Victory Culture*, 252; James Rosen, "Nixon and the Chiefs," *Atlantic Monthly*, April 2002, 59; Kimball, *Nixon's Vietnam War*, 3–14; Schulzinger, *Time for War*, 276; Sherry, *Shadow of War*, 309, 313, 319–20; Kutler, *Abuse of Power*, 173.

18. McMahon, *Major Problems*, 461; Rosen, "Nixon and the Chiefs," 53–59; Blum, *Years of Discord*, 31.

19. Davidson, *Vietnam at War*, 591; Kimball, *Nixon's Vietnam War*, 12, 14, 177–79, 204; Sherry, *Shadow of War*, 308, 318; Engelhardt, *End of Victory Culture*, 204; Larry Berman, *No Peace, No Honor: Nixon, Kissinger and Betrayal in Vietnam* (New York: The Free Press, 2001), 76.

20. Kimball, *Nixon's Vietnam War*, 12–13, 204; Schulzinger, *Time for War*, 291; Kutler, *Abuse of Power*, 8, 11, 21, 97, 491.

21. Blum, *Years of Discord*, 450; Rosen, "Nixon and the Chiefs," 57; Christopher Hitchens, "The Case against Henry Kissinger. Part One: The Making of a War Criminal," *Harper's Magazine*, February 2001, 33–58, and "The Case against Henry Kissinger. Part Two: Crimes against Humanity," *Harper's Magazine*, March 2001, 49–74; Schulzinger, *Time for War*, 301; Kimball, *Nixon's Vietnam War*, 135, 287–89, 335; Berman, *No Peace, No Honor*, 46.

22. Excellent accounts of this tawdry affair are Kimball, *Nixon's Vietnam War*, 55–61, 89–90; Hitchens, "The Case against Henry Kissinger, Part One"; Dallek, *Flawed Giant*, 575, 584–88; and Berman, *No Peace, No Honor*, 27–36, 47 (see page 30 for the conversation with Abrams).

23. Barrett, *LBJ's Vietnam Papers*, 827, 829.

24. Berman, *No Peace, No Honor*, 34, and Dallek, *Flawed Giant*, 588.

25. Gaiduk, *Soviet Union and the Vietnam War*, 199.

26. Berman, *No Peace, No Honor*, 45; Kimball, *Nixon's Vietnam War*, 52, 100–101; DeGroot, *Noble Cause*, 204; Blum, *Years of Discord*, 349.

27. Kimball, *Nixon's Vietnam War*, 75, 86; Schulzinger, *Time for War*, 282; Blum, *Years of Discord*, 349.

28. Sherry, *Shadow of War*, 313, and Truong, *Vietcong Memoir*, 209.

29. Kimball, *Nixon's Vietnam War*, 163.

30. Kimball, *Nixon's Vietnam War*, 94.

31. Porter, *Vietnam*, 373–80.

32. For the linkage efforts, see Chang, *Friends and Enemies*, and especially, Gaiduk, *Soviet Union and the Vietnam War*.

33. Kimball, *Nixon's Vietnam War*, 23, 76–77, 80; Jeffrey Kimball, *The Vietnam War Files: Uncovering the Secret History of Nixon-Era Strategy* (Lawrence: University Press of Kansas, 2004), 103; Doughty and Gruber, *Warfare*, II, 929.

34. Davidson, *Vietnam at War*, 598; Berman, *No Peace, No Honor*, 56–57; Kimball, *Nixon's Vietnam War*, 164–65.

35. William Burr and Jeffrey Kimball, "Nixon's Secret Nuclear Alert: Vietnam War Diplomacy and the Joint Chiefs of Staff Readiness Test, October 1969," *Cold War History*, January 2003, 113–56.

36. Hunt, *Pacification*, 151; Clodfelter, *Vietnam in Military Statistics*, 144, 155; Kimball, *Nixon's Vietnam War*, 128; Sorley, *A Better War*, 105, 125; Bergerud, *Dynamics of Defeat*, 246.

37. Blum, *Years of Discord*, 320–21; Kimball, *Vietnam War Files*, 79–80.

38. Zais, Senior Officer Debriefing Report; Lewy, *America in Vietnam*, 145; Erbach interview, March 20, 1996; Rakestraw interview, June 24, 1997; Gibson, *Perfect War*, 211. An earlier example of this absurdity was abandoning Khe Sanh, a position Westmoreland had insisted was vital, in July 1968. To avoid a public outcry, razing the base was done secretly.

39. Kimball, *Nixon's Vietnam War*, 220; John B. Wilson, *Maneuver and Firepower: The Evolution of Divisions and Separate Brigades* (Washington DC: Center of Military History, 1998), 341–46; Jeffrey J. Clarke, *Advice and Support: The Final Years, 1965–1973* (Washington DC: Center of Military History, 1992), 524; Thayer, *War without Fronts*, 36–37; Hunt, *Pacification*, 209–10.

40. Sorley, *A Better War*, 113.

41. "Vietnamization . . . The Path Leading to Collapse," Document No. 74, *Vietnam Documents and Research Notes Series*, Reel II.

42. Campagne interview, January 8, 1996; Kimball, *Nixon's Vietnam War*, 161; Prados, *Blood Road*, 292; Herring, *America's Longest War*, 253; Sorley, *A Better War*, 137, 161, 187.

43. Turley, *Second Indochina War*, 134; Thayer, *War without Fronts*, 155–67; Clodfelter, *Vietnam in Military Statistics*, 152.

44. Scott Sigmund Gartner, "Differing Evaluations of Vietnamization," *Journal of Interdisciplinary History* (Autumn 1998): 243–62.

45. Wright, Senior Officer Debriefing Report; Brigadier General Henry M. Mueller, June 9, 1970, *U.S. Armed Forces in Vietnam 1954–1975. Part Four. Vietnam U.S. Army-Senior Officer Debriefing Reports;* "Operational Report—Lessons Learned, Headquarters, 101st Airborne Division, Period Ending 31 July 1970 (U)," April 8, 1971, copy in the Ray Blackman Papers.

46. "The Decline of VC Capabilities in Sub-Region 5, COSVN, in 1969–1970," Document No. 92, *Vietnam Documents and Research Notes Series*, Reel III.

47. Hunt, *Pacification*, 109–10, and Thayer, *War without Fronts*, 205.

48. Dale Andrade, *Ashes to Ashes: The Phoenix Program and the Vietnam War* (Lexington MA: Lexington Books, 1990) is an excellent account; the figures for those killed and apprehended are on 287.

49. "Command Information Pamphlet 9-70, March 1970," copy in the Carollyn DeVore Papers, and Thayer, *War without Fronts*, 195–98.

50. Wright, Senior Officer Debriefing Report; for an example of the tallies, see "Combat Operations AAR, Operation Texas Star, 1 Apr 70–5 Sept 70" enclosure 5, 101st Abn Div, AARS, Box 34, RG 472.

51. Thayer, *War without Fronts*, 152.

52. Zais, Senior Officer Debriefing Report; Wright, Senior Officer Debriefing Report; Thayer, *War without Fronts*, 144–45.

53. Tin, *Following Ho Chi Minh*, 63; also see Chanoff and Toai, *Portrait of the Enemy*, 168–69.

54. Except where otherwise noted, this account of the MOH ceremony relies on an MOH file in the Presidential Libraries Materials (Nixon), RG 950, National Archives, which contains a guest list, sequence of events, the president's scenario, and the president's prepared remarks, and on a 16 mm color motion picture of the event produced by the U.S. Army Photographic Agency (a copy is in the JRHP). Why Joe invited McMenamy and not Hogan is a mystery since Cleo commanded the company that day.

55. McMenamy interview, February 10, 1995, and "Congressional Medal Winner . . . ," undated clipping, Hendricks Scrapbook.

56. Boenigk interview, March 5, 1996, and Al Stump, "Peace Is Worth Fighting For," *Los Angeles Herald-Examiner*, May 23, 1971, copy in Weldon and Anna Combs Papers.

57. Erbach interview, March 20, 1996.

58. Sandi Dolbee, "He's a Hero to Everyone but Himself," undated clipping, and Peter Baumann, "New Vet's Representative a Vietnam Hero," *Green River Current*, May 6, 1976, both in Rick Anderson Papers.

59. "Application for Enrollment on the Medal of Honor Roll and for the Pension Authorized by the Act of Congress Approved August 14, 1961," dated March 7, 1969, in Hooper's Medical Records, Claim Folder 24965568; "Congressional Medal Winner . . . ," undated clipping, Hendricks Scrapbook; Hooper business card, JRHP; Gary Foster interview, March 7, 1995; Command Sergeant Major Robert A. Young to Hooper, July 3, 1969, Don F. Pratt Museum, Fort Campbell, Kentucky.

60. Except where otherwise noted, this account relies on Gina Townsend interviews, February 21, 2002 and June 10, 2002; Mary Grace Sims to the authors, c. June 10, 2002; and relevant papers in Sims's Military Personnel Records.

61. Gina was the biological daughter of Mary's sister.

62. Hogan interview, July 21, 2000.

63. Tim Croft, "Veterans' Home to be Named for Port St. Joe's Clifford Sims," *The Star*, April 4, 2002, clipping in Gina Townsend Papers.

64. This account relies on the Boenigk interviews.

65. Audiocassette from Carollyn and Rolly to Joe, recorded November 23–25, 1970, JRHP.

66. Audrey Hooper interview, March 2, 1996.

67. The five postcards are in the Carollyn DeVore Papers.

68. Program for the "Third Annual Salute to The Armed Forces," Carollyn DeVore Papers, and Hooper, "The Screaming Eagle," *Downtowner*, c. mid-June 1969, Audrey Hooper Papers.

69. Except where noted, the following account depends on the Red and Anna Combs interviews, February 8, 1995.

70. Hooper, "The Screaming Eagle," *Downtowner*, c. mid-June 1969, Audrey Hooper Papers.

71. Red and Anna Combs interviews, February 8, 1995.

72. DeVore to the authors, May 4, 2002.

73. Martin Barsky, "About a 'Concerned' American," undated clipping, and "War Hero Never Fought Viet Cong," undated clipping, both in Hendricks Scrapbook.

74. Roger and Norma Donlon interviews, February 9, 1996. A photograph in the JRHP shows Joe with his arms around two of the miniskirted lovelies.

75. "Hero to Be Parade Leader," undated clipping; "Less Than 3 Months Ago . . . ," undated clipping; "Welcome Home, Son," undated clipping; "Hooper Returns to California," undated clipping; "Hero to be Feted," undated clipping; "Zillah Hero Leads Fete," undated clipping; "Zillah Day Has Everything," undated clipping. All in the Hendricks Scrapbook.

76. Withers interview, April 16, 1996; Johnson interview, April 14, 1996; Perez interview, May 11, 1998.

77. "Standard Form 85," April 23, 1974, Official Personnel Folder, United States Office of Personnel Management, OPF/EFM Access Unit, St. Louis, Missouri; "Congressional Medal Winner . . . ," undated clipping, Hendricks Scrapbook; Baumann, "New Vet's Representative a Vietnam Hero"; Sturges interview, March 5, 1996.

78. For Joe's comment see Putnam, "Reminiscences of Audie Murphy," copy in the JRHP. For Perry Pitt see Simpson, *Audie Murphy*, 137.

79. Gary Foster interview, March 7, 1995; DeVore, "Brief Memoir"; DeVore interview, February 11–12, 1995; John Whiteside, "It's Not Something You Just Walk Away From . . ." undated clipping, Combs Papers; James D. Snyder, "Our Most Decorated Servicemen, *Parade*, November 16, 1969; Rick Anderson, "Joe Hooper—Forgotten Hero in a Forgotten War," *Seattle Times*, September 25, 1977, clipping in the JRHP.

80. This account relies on Case No. 759160 in the Superior Court of the State of California for the County of Los Angeles and on the David Darr interview, March 6, 1996.

81. "Delta Raiders Newsletter," 22 (April 1990).

82. Combs interview, February 8, 1995.

83. Red Combs confirmed that Joe was a very jealous person; interview, February 8, 1995.

84. Bischoff interview, January 13, 1997.

85. This account relies primarily on Irene Bennett to the authors, July 22, 1997. But also see Rick Anderson, "Joe Hooper's Supporters Write from across Nation," *Seattle Times*, September 14, 1988, copy in the Larry Frank Papers, and an information sheet on the PFC Joe E. Mann Army Reserve Center in Spokane, Washington, dedicated on January 25, 1975, copy in the Rick Anderson Papers.

86. Martin Barsky to Awards Branch, The Adjutant General's Office, Washington DC, March 15, 1971, JRHP.

87. "Editorial," *Downtowner*, c. late April 1969, Audrey Hooper Papers.

88. Copies of six of the columns are in both the JRHP and the Combs Papers; the Audrey Hooper Papers contains a copy of a seventh column.

89. Boenigk interviews, March 5, 1996 and June 1, 2002, and Melson, "Vietnam's Most-Decorated U.S. Soldier," JRHP.

Chapter 11

1. Department of the Army, Office of the Adjutant General, International Travel Orders, November 19, 1969, and "USO Information Vietnam," both in the Carollyn DeVore Papers.

2. "Johnny Delivers the Goodies: Grant's Great for Grunts," *Pacific Stars and Stripes Sunday Magazine*, July 27, 69, and Alec Blasco-Ibanez, "Viet Nam's Blonde Bombshell," *Los Angeles Herald-Examiner*, "California Living," March 9, 1969, both in the Carollyn DeVore Papers.

3. "Zillah Legion Greets Hero and His Fiancee," undated clipping, Hendricks Scrapbook, and Blasco-Ibanez, "Viet Nam's Blonde Bombshell."

4. USO Information Sheet about Johnny Grant's 1969 tour and the Polaroids are in the Carollyn DeVore Papers.

5. Christmas (1969) Menu, Carollyn DeVore Papers.

6. The card and the photo are in the Carollyn DeVore Papers.

7. For the Saigon wedding, see DeVore's "Brief Memoir" and DeVore interview, February 11–12, 1995.

8. DeVore interviews, February 11–12, 1995 and June 21, 2002, and "Farewell Party Held For Medal of Honor Winner," undated clipping, Hendricks Scrapbook.

9. DeVore interview, February 11–12, 1995; Morning Reports, Company A, 3rd Bn, 5th Infy, October 20, 21, 1969 at the National Personnel Records Center, St. Louis,

Missouri; postcard from Joe to Carollyn, October 25, 1969, Carollyn DeVore Papers; "Headquarters 3rd Bn 5th Infy Fort Kobbe, Canal Zone Annual Historical Supplement Calendar Year 1969" and "3rd Bn, 5th Infy CY [19]70," both in the U.S. Army Military History Institute.

10. All these are in the Carollyn DeVore Papers. Sometimes they spelled Sarah without an "h."

11. DeVore interview, February 11–12, 1995, and DeVore's "Brief Memoir."

12. Morning Reports, Company A, 3rd Bn, 5th Infy, November 12, 1969, and postcard from Joe to Carollyn, Carollyn DeVore Papers.

13. Morning Reports, Company A, 3rd Bn, 5th Infy, November 24, 1969 and January 22, 30, 1970.

14. A note from the flower shop, which read, "Welcome Home & Happy New Year Love Joe," and the telegram are in the Carollyn DeVore Papers.

15. "Application for and Approval of Advance Authorization to Enter the Canal Zone—Visitors," Carollyn DeVore Papers; DeVore's "Brief Memoir"; DeVore interview, February 11–12, 1995.

16. Morning Reports, Company A, 3rd Bn, 5th Infy, March 19, 1970.

17. *Key Magazine* (Los Angeles), May 17–21, 1970; *Southern California Guide*, June 1970; ticket stubs for the Academy Awards; all in the Carollyn DeVore Papers; DeVore's "Brief Memoir"; DeVore interview, February 11–12, 1995.

18. Except where otherwise noted, this account of the Zillah visit depends on the written communications from and interviews with DeVore listed in chapter 5, note 35.

19. Audrey Hooper interview, March 2, 1996, and Hendricks interview, June 16, 1999.

20. "War Hero, Pin-Up Girl Guests of Zillah Legion" and "Zillah Legion Greets Hero and His Fiancee," undated clippings in Hendricks Scrapbook.

21. Joe to his parents, September 1, 1970, Audrey Hooper Papers.

22. Franklin Miller with Elwood J. C. Kureth, *Reflections of a Warrior* (Novato CA: Presidio Press, 1991), 193.

23. Stump, "Peace Is Worth Fighting For"; Weldon Combs interview, February 8, 1995; Westmoreland to the authors, April 16, 1995.

24. Delbert O. Jennings interview, October 19, 1996, and Miller, *Reflections*, 193. Ware was a lieutenant colonel in December 1944, when he performed the actions for which he received the MOH; he was commanding the 1st Infantry Division on September 13, 1968, when ground fire hit his helicopter, which crashed, killing him.

25. Wolf, "Probing the Minds," 27; Stump, "Peace Is Worth Fighting For"; Thomas J. Dolan, "This Christmas, He's Going Home," *Chicago Sun Times*, December 25, 1971, clipping in the JRHP.

26. Rick Anderson interview, July 9, 1996.

27. Barsky to Hooper, December 10, 1970, JRHP, and DeVore interview, March 6, 2002; also see "Congressional Medal Winner . . . ," undated clipping, Hendricks Scrapbook.

28. DeVore interview, February 11–12, 1995, and DeVore's "Brief Memoir."

29. DeVore interview, March 6, 2002.

30. Richard R. Moser, *The New Winter Soldiers: GI and Veteran Dissent during the Vietnam Era* (New Brunswick NJ: Rutgers University Press, 1996), 102. Two other antiwar veterans groups were the American Servicemen's Union and the Movement for a Democratic Military.

31. Gerald Nicosia, *Home to the War: A History of the Vietnam Veterans Movement* (New York: Crown Publishers, 2001), 39, 72, 146.

32. Wells, *War Within*, 375–76, 395–96, and Small, *Antiwarriors*, 98–99.

33. Gochnour to his parents, May 5, 1971, Gochnour Papers, and Wells, *War Within*, 493.

34. Peter Dennis Hoffman and Kent Anderson, "Songs of War: Popular Music and Vietnam," *Vietnam Magazine* (August 1996): 26–32.

35. DeBenedetti and Chatfield, *American Ordeal*, 310.

36. Young, *Vietnam Wars*, 202; Andrew, *President's Eyes Only*, 364; Levy, *Debate*, 152, 157; DeBenedetti and Chatfield, *American Ordeal*, 392.

37. Wells, *War Within*, 312, 351.

38. Kimball, *Nixon's Vietnam War*, 221; Wells, *War Within*, 579; DeBenedetti and Chatfield, *American Ordeal*, 285.

39. Nicosia, *Home to the War*, 101, 109, 222, 276.

40. Wells, *War Within*, 311, 345, 503–5; Sherry, *Shadow of War*, 298; DeBenedetti and Chatfield, *American Ordeal*, 247, 305; Nicosia, *Home to the War*, 230; Small, *Antiwarriors*, 157–59.

41. Nicosia, *Home to the War*, 247, 252–53, 265, 281.

42. DROVA, *Delta Raiders*, 221, and Bradford, *Some Even Volunteered*, 189.

43. Davidson, *Vietnam at War*, 619, and Brigadier General DeWitt C. Armstrong, Senior Officer Debriefing Report, November 2, 1971, *U.S. Armed Forces in Vietnam 1954–1975*, Reel IV.

44. U.S. Army War College, "Study on Military Professionalism."

45. Kinnard, *War Managers*, 112.

46. Rick Atkinson, *The Long Gray Line* (Boston: Houghton Mifflin, 1989), 301.

47. Nolan, *Sappers in the Wire*, 106–7, and Powell, *Journey*, 128.

48. Campagne interview, January 8, 1996; Ebert, *Life in a Year*, 219; Major General John H. Hennessey, Senior Officer Debriefing Report, March 24, 1971, U.S. Military History Institute, U.S. Army War College.

49. Baritz, *Backfire*, 314; Ebert, *Life in a Year*, 187; DeBenedetti and Chatfield, *American Ordeal*, 232.

50. Jodey Gravett to Dale Urban, c. mid-June 1968, Dale Urban Papers; Jerry Lembcke, *The Spitting Image: Myth, Memory, and the Legacy of Vietnam* (New York: New York University Press, 1998), 47; Donald Kirk, *Tell It to the Dead: Stories of a War*, revised edition (Armonk NY: M. E. Sharpe, 1996), 111–12.

51. Originally published in *Armed Forces Journal* (June 7, 1971): 30–37, and reprinted many times since.

52. Olson and Roberts, *Where the Domino Fell*, 228.

53. Olson and Roberts, *Where the Domino Fell*, 228; "Trauma Grips War Widow," *Cincinnati Enquirer*, October 23, 1996, 1; Lieutenant General A. S. Collins Jr., Senior Officer Debriefing Report; Nolan, *Sappers in the Wire*, 96; Powell, *Journey*, 129.

54. Clodfelter, *Vietnam in Military Statistics*, 193; Nolan, *Sappers in the Wire*, 103; Appy, *Working Class War*, 245–46.

55. Al Santoli, *Everything We Had: An Oral History of the Vietnam War by Thirty-Three American Soldiers Who Fought It* (New York: Ballantine, 1982), 157; Hawk interview, June 21, 1997; Loftin interview, August 13, 1995.

56. BDM Corporation, "Study of Strategic Lessons," VII-3, VII-14; Loory, *Defeated*, 204; Hennessey, Senior Officer Debriefing Report, U.S. Army Military History Institute; Armstrong, Senior Officer Debriefing Report and Major General Thomas M. Tarpley, Senior Officer Debriefing Report, July 13, 1972, both in *U.S. Armed Forces in Vietnam*, Reel IV; Spector, *After Tet*, 276–78; Otis W. Livingston interview, July 10, 1995.

57. "Hooper against Total Amnesty," *Times-Picayune*, undated clipping in the JRHP; Aronow to his wife and parents, August 6, 1968; Songer interview, July 28, 1999; Kennedy, "An Examination of Vietnam War Senior Officer Debriefing Reports," 8–9.

58. Kirk, *Tell It to the Dead*, 117.

59. Olson and Roberts, *Where the Domino Fell*, 229. The disintegration also afflicted the American Seventh Army in Europe, which had been "destroyed as a fighting force," as one general put it, supplying the forces in Vietnam with men, officers, material, and money. By 1970–71 it was less an Army than an armed mob. "They are supposed to protect us," editorialized a German magazine. "But they rob, murder, and rape. American soldiers in Germany arouse naked fear." See Palmer, *25-Year War*, 94, and Atkinson, *Long Gray Line*, 363–68.

60. Sorley, *A Better War*, 289. Also see Record, *Wrong War*, 58–59.

61. Chanoff and Toai, *Portrait of the Enemy*, 107–10. Huong Van Ba, a southern artillery officer, gave essentially the same account; see Chanoff and Toai, *Portrait of the Enemy*, 157.

62. Werner and Huynh, *Vietnam War*, 48–62.

63. Military History Institute of Vietnam, *Victory in Vietnam*, 221–57; the quote is on page 223.

64. Many enemy documents stressed these themes. The quote is from "The Study of

COSVN Resolution 10," Document No. 99, *Vietnam Documents and Research Notes Series*, Reel IV, but for other examples, see the following documents in the same source: "Indoctrination Notes on Peace Talks: A Call for 'Violent Revolution' to the End," Document No. 39, Reel I; "Summer 1969: A VC Study of the Situation and Prospects," Document No. 64, Reel I; Giap's "The Party's Military Line Is the Ever-Victorious Banner of People's War in Our Country," Document No. 70, Reel II; "An Elaboration of the 8th Resolution Central Office of South Vietnam," Document No. 67, Reel II; "Vietnamization . . . The Path Leading to Collapse," Document No. 74, Reel II.

65. See the following documents in *Vietnam Documents and Research Notes Series:* "Fighting at Tet: A VC 'After Action Report,'" Document No. 27, Reel I; "After Tet: 3 VC Assessments," Documents Nos. 30–32, Reel I; "On Political and Ideological Indoctrination Vs Desertion and Surrender," Document No. 46, Reel I; "A COSVN Directive for Eliminating Contacts with Puppet Personnel and Other 'Complex Problems,'" Document No. 55, Reel I; "It Is Better to Return Home and Cultivate the Land Than to Join the Revolutionary Army," Documents Nos. 56–57, Reel I; "Self-Sufficiency: A Duty of Cadre and Combatant," Documents Nos. 58–59, Reel I; "Ideological Deficiencies and Lowered Combat Effectiveness," Document No. 73, Reel II; "COSVN's Preliminary Report on the 1969 Autumn Campaign," Document No. 82, Reel III; "The Decline of VC Capabilities in Sub-Region 5, COSVN, in 1969–1970," Document No. 92, Reel III; "The Study of COSVN Resolution 10." Also see "Achievements of the Hue City Party Committee."

66. Military History Institute of Vietnam, *Victory in Vietnam*, 247.

67. "An Elaboration of the 8th Resolution"; "Summer 1969"; "Achievements of the Hue City Party Committee."

68. "An Elaboration of the 8th Resolution"; Colonel General Van Tien Dung, "Under the Party's Banner, Viet-Nam's Military Art Has Constantly Developed and Triumphed," *Vietnam Documents and Research Notes Series*, Document No. 71, Reel II; Giap, "The Party's Military Line"; "The Study of COSVN Resolution 10"; "The 'Local Task' In North Viet-nam," Document No. 89, Reel III; "Indoctrination Notes on Peace Talks." Ho's quote is in Military History Institute of Vietnam, *Victory in Vietnam*, 232.

69. Giap, "The Party's Line." General Dung made the same points in "Under the Party's Banner."

70. Hunt, *Pacification*, 200–201, and Thayer, *War without Fronts*, 48–49.

71. Sorley, *A Better War*, 154–55, and Hunt, *Pacification*, 218–20.

72. "Operational Report of the 101st Air Cavalry Division for the Period Ending 31 July, 1968," August 15, 1968, 101st Abn Div, ACS, G-3, Operations Reports—LL, Box 2, RG 472.

73. DROVA, *Delta Raiders*, 85–137; Leshikar interview, October 28, 1995; Frick interview, September 21, 1995; Frick to his Dad, November 20, 1968, Frick Papers.

74. Numerous letters from early July through November 1968, Cleo C. Hogan Jr. Papers, and CSM Robert A. Young to Hooper, July 3, 1969, Don F. Pratt Museum, Fort Campbell, Kentucky.

75. Thayer, *War without Fronts*, 45–47, and Pike, *PAVN*, 228.

76. Military History Institute of Vietnam, *Victory in Vietnam*, 243.

77. "The Impact of the Sapper on the Vietnam War: A Background Paper," unnumbered document, *Vietnam Documents and Research Notes Series*, Reel II. Also see Gerald Ellis, "Fighting Forces," *Vietnam Magazine* (June 1997), and Chanoff and Toai, *Portrait of the Enemy*, 161–62 for discussions of sapper training, organization, and audacity.

78. Nolan, *Sappers in the Wire*, recounts this debacle.

79. Sorley, *A Better War*, 156–57.

80. Clodfelter, *Vietnam in Military Statistics*, 175.

81. Hawk interview, June 21, 1997; Hawk to his mother, July 6, 1970, Mark S. Hawk Papers; "Operational Report—LL, Headquarters, 101st Abn Div, Period ending 31 July 1970 (U)," Ray Blackman Papers.

82. DROVA, *Delta Raiders*, 199–201, 207–9.

83. "Feeder AAR for 5 Sept–30 Sept 1970 of Operation Jefferson Glen," October 31, 1970 and "Feeder AAR for 1 Oct–31 Oct 1970 of Operation Jefferson Glen," December 1, 1970, both in 101st Abn Div, 1st Bde, AARS, Box 3, RG 472.

84. Wolf, "Probing the Minds," 24, and Stump, "Peace Is Worth Fighting For."

85. Spec 4 Dennis Thorton, "Encore for Medal of Honor Winner Hooper," *Pacific Stars and Stripes*, June 11, 1970, clipping in JRHP; "Medal of Honor Recipient Rejoins 101st," *Army Reporter*, June 22, 1970, clipping in Combs Papers; "SSG Joe Hooper Writes Home," undated clipping, Hendricks Scrapbook; *The 101st Airborne 1968 Vietnam Yearbook* (Oklahoma City: The Paseo Press, 1985), 77; Leshikar interview, October 28, 1995.

86. Hooper to DeVore, June 16, 1970, Carollyn DeVore Papers, and Schlight, *Second Indochina War*, 177–78.

87. Hennessey, Senior Officer Debriefing Report; McMenamy interview, February 10, 1995; Lanning, *Only War We Had*, 133–34; Straub interview, July 22, 2000; Keirn C. Brown interview, January 11, 1997; John C. Walton interview, April 9, 1996; Blackman interview, August 17, 1994.

88. Isaacs, *Without Honor*, 194–97; Sorley, *A Better War*, 118–20; Berman, *No Peace, No Honor*, 50–51.

89. Palmer, *25-Year War*, 97, and DeGroot, *Noble Cause*, 221.

90. Kimball, *Nixon's Vietnam War*, 204–6, 211–12.

91. Palmer, *25-Year War*, 103–4.

92. Kimball, *Nixon's Vietnam War*, 215–25; Sorley, *A Better War*, 211–13; DeBenedetti and Chatfield, *American Ordeal*, 279; Duiker, *Sacred War*, 229; Schulzinger, *Time for War*, 285–86; Hammond, *Reporting Vietnam*, 213–14.

93. Sorley, *A Better War*, 203.

94. Truong, *Vietcong Memoir*, 183, 212.

95. See 101st Abn Div, ACS, G-2, Monthly Intelligence Summaries, Box 1, RG 472.

96. See the relevant summaries in 101st Abn Div, ACS, G-2, Monthly Intelligence Summaries.

97. See the relevant summaries in 101st Abn Div, ACS, G-2, Monthly Intelligence Summaries.

98. For Texas Star, see: Hennessey, Senior Officer Debriefing Report; "Combat Operations AAR, Operation Texas Star, 1 April 1970–5 September 1970," 101st Abn Div, AARS, Box 34, RG 472; "Combat Operations After Action Feeder Report, Operation Texas Star," June 30, 1970, and similar titles dated July 30, 1970 and August 30, 1970, all in 101st Abn Div, 2nd Bde, ACS, S-3, AARS, Box 2, RG 472; "Operational Feeder Report—LL for Period Ending 31 October 1970," November 3, 1970, 101st Abn Div, 2nd Bde, ACS, S-3, Operations Reports—LL, Box 1, RG 472; "Combat Operations AAR, Operation Texas Star," May 27, 1970 and June 27, 1970, "Feeder AAR Covering the Period 1–30 June of Operation Texas Star," July 30, 1970, and "Feeder AAR Covering the Period 1–31 July 1970 of Operation Texas Star," August 30, 1970, all in 101st Abn Div, 3rd Bde, ACS, S-3, AARS, Box 2, RG 472; *101st Airborne Division Screaming Eagles*, 73–74. For Jefferson Glen, see: Hennessey, Senior Officer Debriefing Report; "Feeder AAR Covering the Period 051800H–30 Sep of Operation Jefferson Glen/Monsoon Plan 70," and similar titles for other months of the operation in 101st Abn Div, ACS, G-3, AARS, Box 2, RG 472; "2nd Bn (Airmobile) 327th Infy . . . ," 101st Abn Div, 1st Bde, Organizational History, Box 3, RG 472; "Combat Operations AAR, Operation OPORD 13-70 (Jefferson Glen/Monsoon Plan 70), 5 September 1970–8 October 1971," November 3, 1971, 101st Abn Div, 2nd Bde, ACS, S-3, AARS, Box 2, RG 472.

99. For Pathfinders, see: "Operational Report—LL for Period Ending 31 July 1970," 101st Abn Div, 101st Aviation Group, Command Reports, Box 17, RG 472; the BDJ, 101st Abn Div, 101st Aviation Group, S-3 Daily Journal; "SSG Joe Hooper Writes Home," undated clipping, Hendricks Scrapbook; "Pathfinders Guide Move," *Screaming Eagle*, March 1, 1971, clipping in the Steve Hawk Papers; Brown interview, January 11, 1997; Patrick L. Runevitch interview, April 11, 1996; Hennessey, Senior Officer Debriefing Report; *101st Airborne: Vietnam [19]69*, copy in the Ray Blackman Papers.

100. Enclosure 1 "LL—FSB Ripcord (U) to Feeder AAR Covering the Period 1–31 July 1970 of Operation Texas Star (U)," 101st Abn Div, 3rd Bde, ACS, S-3, AARS, Box 2, RG 472.

101. Joe to Carollyn, June 11, 1970, Carollyn DeVore Papers.

102. BDJ, 101st Aviation Group, April 1, 1970.

103. The photograph is in the JRHP.

104. Brown interview, January 11, 1997, and Arden D. Hardison interview, July 7, 2000.

105. Division Circular Number 600-7, "Personnel—General: Watch List," March 16, 1971, JRHP, and November 16, 1970, Carollyn DeVore Papers.

106. Blackman interview, August 17, 1994, and "Medal of Honor Recipient Rejoins 101st."

107. Straub interview, July 22, 2000.

108. DeVore interviews, February 11–12, 1995 and March 6, 2002, and DeVore to the authors, August 15, 2002.

109. Except where noted all the items mentioned in the text are in the Carollyn DeVore Papers.

110. A copy of the will is in the Carollyn DeVore Papers. Sandra married a man named Donze, but divorced him in September 1969.

111. John C. Walton interview, April 9, 1996, and the "Combat Operations After Action Feeder Reports, Operation Texas Star," dated June 30, July 30, August 30, and September 10, 1970, 101st Abn Div, 2nd Bde, ACS, S-3, AARS, Box 2, RG 472.

112. Enclosure 3 of "Combat Operations AAR, Operation Texas Star, 1 April 1970–5 September 1970," 101st Abn Div, AARS, Box 34, RG 472.

113. "Report of Medical Examination," Hooper Medical Records, Claim Folder 24965568, and the "A Company Personnel Daily Summary," BDJ, 2-327, July 22–23.

114. "Application for Appointment," Hooper's Military Personnel Records.

115. "A Company Personnel Daily Summary," BDJ, 2-327, August 7–23. Joe signed documents in Darr's office on August 13 and 18.

116. Except where noted this account relies on the DeVore interview, February 11–12, 1995; DeVore's "Brief Memoir"; "Opry Stage for Hero's Welcome," *Nashville Tennessean*, August 17, 1970, clipping in the Carollyn DeVore Papers.

117. Michael Collins interview, June 15, 1997, and Hooper to Hogan, April 10, 1971, Cleo C. Hogan Jr. Papers.

118. DeVore to the authors, May 4, 2002.

119. DeVore interview, June 21, 2002.

120. Joe to his parents, September 1, 1970, Audrey Hooper Papers.

121. "2nd Battalion (Airmobile) 327th Infy, 101st Abn Div: 'No Slack.' Unit History 5, September 1970–30 June 1971, Republic of Vietnam," 101st Abn Div, 1st Bde, Organizational History, Box 3, RG 472.

122. BDJ, 2-327, September 19–Oct 11, 1970.

123. "Emergency Leave Orders," JRHP.

124. "Local Actress Has Cameo Role in Hope Special," *Record-Ledger*, November 15, 1970, clipping in the Carollyn DeVore Papers; copies of the checks in the Carollyn DeVore Papers; DeVore interview, February 11–12, 1995.

125. BDJ, 2-327, November 17–23, 1970. Joe tape-recorded the Hope show; the tape is in

the JRHP. Also see Sgt. John Mueller, "Bob Hope Shows 'em He's Still with It," un-dated clipping, Audrey Hooper Papers.

126. The audiocassette is in the JRHP.

127. DeVore also discussed this accident in an interview on August 19, 2002.

128. DeVore interview, August 19, 2002.

129. DeVore interview, February 11–12, 1995.

130. Joe to his parents, January 6, 1971, Audrey Hooper Papers.

131. Sorley, *A Better War*, 236, 243, and Prados, *Blood Road*, 323.

132. Tarpley, Senior Officer Debriefing Report; "Operational Report—LL, Period Ending 30 April 1971," May 24, 1971, 101st Abn Div, ACS, G-3, Operations Reports—LL, Box 2, RG 472; Davidson, *Vietnam at War*, 659–69; Kimball, *Nixon's Vietnam War*, 246–48.

133. DeVore interview, February 11–12, 1995.

134. DeVore interview, February 11–12, 1995.

135. Hawk interview, June 21, 1997.

136. DeVore interview, June 21, 2002.

137. Hooper to Hogan, April 10, 1971, Cleo C. Hogan Jr. Papers.

138. Patrick L. Runevitch interview, April 11, 1996, and Hawk interview, June 21, 1997.

139. Hawk interview, June 21, 1997.

140. Leshikar interview, October 28, 1995, and "AAR, Sapper Attack on Firebase Airborne," July 2, 1969, Infy Units, 2nd Bn, 501st Infy, ACS for Operations (S-3), Command Reports, Box 17, RG 472.

141. "Combat Operations AAR, Operation Texas Star, 1 April 1970–5 September 1970."

142. For Granite and Henderson, see: Otis W. Livingston interview, July 10, 1995; "Combat Operations AAR, Operation Texas Star," May 27, 1970 and June 27, 1970, 101st Abn Div, 3rd Bde, ACS, S-3, AARS, Box 2, RG 472; "Combat Operations AAR, Operation Texas Star, 1 April 1970–5 September 1970."

143. "Recommendation for Award of the Presidential Unit Citation," August 12, 1970, 101st Abn Div, Adjutant General, Unit Commendations, 2nd Bn, 501st–801 Maint. Bn., Box 3, RG 472.

144. Songer interview, July 28, 1999. Also see Wayne Anderson interview, July 29, 1999.

Chapter 12

1. Hawk to his mother, August 22, November 21, December 8, December 10, 1970 and January 12, 1970 [1971], Mark S. Hawk Papers.

2. Hawk interview, June 21, 1997.

3. Gochnour interview, July 6, 2000; Saal interview, June 26, 1997; John D. Tillitson interview, July 19, 1999; Ronald F. Rohs interview, July 27, 1999.

4. Hawk to his mother, February 25, 1970, Mark S. Hawk Papers, and Hawk interview, June 21, 1997.

5. Saal interview June 26, 1997, and Wayne Anderson interview, July 29, 1999.

6. Saal interview, and Wayne Anderson interview.

7. Ned T. Kintzer interview, January 29, 1996.

8. Ray Blackman said getting assigned to an airborne unit was like having a nightmare come true; Blackman interview, September 17, 1994. When Paul Gochnour, who adorned his letters with peace symbols and the phrase "Love & Peace," learned he was going to the 101st he wrote that "I can't say I am terribly happy"; Gochnour to his parents, October 24, 1970, Gochnour Papers. Wayne Anderson "was pretty intimidated" when he received orders to the 101st; Wayne Anderson interview, July 29, 1999. "I wouldn't say I was overjoyed" at the prospect of joining the 101st, said Ned Kintzer; Kintzer interview, January 29, 1996.

9. Patrick L. Runevitch interview, April 11, 1996.

10. Saal interview, June 26, 1997; James Jennette interview, February 8, 1998; Kintzer interview, January 29, 1996; Wayne Anderson interview, July 29, 1999. Also see Songer interview, July 28, 1999; James L. "Ted" Ayres interview, June 22, 1999; and Runevitch interview, April 11, 1996.

11. Saal interview, June 26, 1997, and Jennette interview, February 8, 1998.

12. Saal interview, June 26, 1997; Runevitch interview, April 11, 1996; Wayne Anderson interview, July 29, 1999. Also see Hardison interview, July 7, 2000; Jennette interview, February 8, 1998; Campagne interview, January 8, 1996.

13. John Fair interview, August 6, 1999; Campagne interview, January 8, 1996; Kintzer interview, January 29, 1996; Saal interview, June 26, 1997; Gochnour interview, July 6, 2000; Wayne Anderson interview, July 29, 1999.

14. Hawk interview, June 21, 1997; Saal interview, June 26, 1997; Campagne interview, January 8, 1996; Tillitson interview, July 19, 1999; Fair interview, August 6, 1999.

15. Fair interview, August 6, 1999; Kintzer interview, January 29, 1996; Gochnour interview, July 6, 2000; Wayne Anderson interview, July 29, 1999; Tillitson interview, July 19, 1999.

16. "Feeder AAR Covering the Period 1–28 February 1971 of Operation Jefferson Glen/ Monsoon Plan 70," March 30, 1971, 101st Abn Div, ACS, G-3, AARS, Box 2, RG 472, and "Bastogne Area of Operations (25 Feb–7 May 1971)," Infy Units, 2nd Bn, 501st Infy, Organizational History, Box 1, RG 472.

17. Monthly Intelligence Summaries, January and February, 1971.

18. Campagne interview, January 8, 1996.

19. Roster No. 2, March 1, 1971, A-2-501, Frank M. Campagne Papers; Campagne interview, January 8, 1996; Spencer C. Tucker, ed., *The Encyclopedia of the Vietnam War: A Political, Social, and Military History* (New York: Oxford University Press, 1998), 218.

20. Gochnour interview, July 6, 2000, and Runevitch interview, April 11, 1996. Also see Hawk interview, June 21, 1997, and Saal to his parents, March 11, 1971.

21. "Bastogne Area of Operations"; Gochnour to his parents, January 31, March 2, 9, 1971, Gochnour Papers; Gochnour interview, July 6, 2000; Saal to his parents, March 11, 1971, Robert Saal Papers.

22. "Bastogne Area of Operations," and Hawk interview, June 21, 1997. Also see Wayne Anderson to his parents, March 24, 1971, Wayne Anderson Papers; Saal to his parents, March 22, 1971, Robert Saal Papers; "Cache a Day," *Drive On Weekly*, March 28, 1971, Mark S. Hawk Papers.

23. Sorley, *A Better War*, 21, 42, 138–39.

24. Much of the following account relies on the BDJ, 2-501, March 18–25, 1971, and "Feeder AAR Covering the Period 1–31 March 1971 of Operation Jefferson Glen," May 1, 1971, 101st Abn Div, 1st Bde, AARS, Box 3, RG 472.

25. The following account relies on the letters Campagne wrote his wife between December 3, 1970 and March 25, 1971, Frank M. Campagne Papers, and on the Campagne interview, January 8, 1996.

26. Hawk interview, June 21, 1997, and Saal interview, June 26, 1997.

27. Not all BBT incidents ended as happily. For instance, on March 23 a detonation resulted in one KIA and another WIA.

28. Hawk interview, June 21, 1997.

29. "AAR—Mechanical Ambush (U)," February 22, 1971, 101st Abn Div, 2nd Bde, ACS, S-3, AARS, Box 2, RG 472; Hawk interview, June 21, 1997; Nolan, *Sappers in the Wire*, 124.

30. Hawk interview, June 21, 1997; Saal interview, June 26, 1997; Wayne Anderson interview, July 29, 1999.

31. Hawk interview, June 21, 1997.

32. "Bastogne Area of Operations"; "Operations Report—LL for Period Ending 30 April 1971," May 3, 1971, 101st Abn Div, 2nd Bde, ACS, S-3, Operations Reports—LL, Box 1, RG 472; summary of Hawk to his mother, March 29, 1971 (since his fiancée could read his handwriting better than his mother could, she often summarized the letters for her), and Hawk to his mother, April 5, 1971, both in the Mark S. Hawk Papers; Hawk interview, June 21, 1997; Gochnour to his parents, March 30, 1971.

33. Wayne Anderson interview, July 29, 1999, and Saal interview, June 26, 1997. Everyone else interviewed about these two days made similar comments.

34. For these two days as a whole, see "Bastogne Area of Operations"; BDJ, 2-501, March 31–April 1, 1971; Gochnour to his parents, April 3, 1971, Gochnour Papers.

35. John Fair interview, August 6, 1999.

36. Rohs interview, July 27, 1999.

37. Arvie LeBlanc interview, August 4, 1999.

38. Saal interview, June 26, 1997; Wayne Anderson interview, July 29, 1999; LeBlanc interview, August 4, 1999; Rohs interview, July 27, 1999. Also see Gochnour interview, July 6, 2000; Fair interview, August 6, 1999; Ayres interview, June 22, 1999.

39. Hooper to Hogan, April 10, 1971, Cleo C. Hogan Jr. Papers.

40. In addition to the sources noted in note number 33, this account is reconstructed primarily from the following interviews: Tillitson, July 19, 1999; Ayres, June 22, 1999; Hawk, June 21, 1997; Gochnour, July 6, 2000; Jennette, February 8, 1998.

41. "Lt. Foils Red Attack on Helos," *Pacific Stars and Stripes*, April 26, 1971, clipping in JRHP.

42. BDJ, 2-501, April 2, 1971.

43. A copy is in the Mark S. Hawk Papers.

44. The "heavy" estimate is in "Bastogne Area of Operations."

45. In general for the events of April 2–3, see the BDJ, 2-501. Also see Saal to his parents, April 4, 1971, Robert Saal Papers.

46. "Awards Ceremony," *Drive On Weekly*, April 4, 1971, Mark S. Hawk Papers. A second soldier also received an SS, but his name is illegible. On April 23, General Smith sent a letter describing the ceremony and enclosing a photograph of Joe receiving the award; the letter is in the Audrey Hooper Papers.

47. DBJ, 2-501, April 2, 1971; "Bastogne Area of Operations"; Hooper to Hogan, April 10, 1971, Cleo C. Hogan Jr. Papers.

48. For April 12 and the subsequent few days, see BDJ, 2-501, April 12–16, 1971; "Bastogne Area of Operations"; "Operations Report—LL for Period Ending 30 April 1971," May 3, 1971, 101st Abn Div, 2nd Bde, ACS, S-3, Operations Reports—LL, Box 1, RG 472.

49. DROVA, *Delta Raiders*, 238–39; Michael Kelley, "Delta Raiders' Costly Recovery Mission," *Vietnam Magazine* (June 1999); Gochnour interview, July 6, 2000.

50. Saal to Civilians, April 20, 1971; on the same day he wrote much the same to his brother. Both letters are in the Robert Saal Papers.

51. Werner and Huynh, *Vietnam War*, 57–58.

52. The best account of the campaign is Dale Andrade, *America's Last Vietnam Battle: Halting Hanoi's 1972 Easter Offensive* (Lawrence: University Press of Kansas, 2001).

53. Military History Institute of Vietnam, *Victory in Vietnam*, 283–84.

54. Kimball, *Vietnam War Files*, 163–65, 206.

55. Mark Clodfelter, *The Limits of Air Power: The American Bombing of North Vietnam* (New York: The Free Press, 1989), 152–54.

56. Clodfelter, *Limits of Air Power*, 154–56.

57. Clodfelter, *Limits of Air Power*, 156–57, and Kimball, *Vietnam War Files*, 214–17, 221.

58. Kimball, *Nixon's Vietnam War*, 196, 293; Hammond, *Reporting Vietnam*, 275; Palmer, *25-Year War*, 126; Gibson, *Perfect War*, 384; Clodfelter, *Limits of Air Power*, 151.

59. Military History Institute of Vietnam, *Victory in Vietnam*, 298–300.

60. Isaacs, *Without Honor*, 27–28.

61. Excellent discussions of these matters are in Clodfelter, *Limits of Air Power*, 167–74, and Earl H. Tilford Jr., *Crosswinds: The Air Force's Setup in Vietnam* (College Station:

Texas A&M University Press, 1993). The Kissinger quotes are in Kimball, *Vietnam War Files*, 135, 139, 187, 190–91. Kissinger also referred to a "healthy interval," "reasonable interval," and "sufficient interval"; see Kimball, *Vietnam War Files*, 197, 322. Berman, *No Peace, No Honor*, repeatedly asserts that Nixon planned to support South Vietnam with air power through 1976; see, for example, 8–9, 154, 174, 179.

62. Tarpley, Senior Officer Debriefing Report.

63. Kimball, *Nixon's Vietnam War*, 323–24.

64. Truong, *Vietcong Memoir*, 211–12.

65. Isaacs, *Without Honor*, 25–26, and Hunt, *Pacification*, 257–58.

66. Sorley, *A Better War*, 342; Davidson, *Vietnam at War*, 706; Lewy, *America in Vietnam*, 198, 201; Berman, *No Peace, No Honor*, 133; Military History Institute of Vietnam, *Victory in Vietnam*, 298, 311.

67. Andrade, *America's Last Battle*, 486.

68. Sorley, *A Better War*, 324–30, 335.

69. Andrade, *America's Last Battle*, 489.

70. Berman, *No Peace, No Honor*, 80, and Sorley, *A Better War*, 351.

71. Isaacs, *Without Honor*, 133, and Engelhardt, *End of Victory Culture*, 257–58.

72. Clausewitz, *On War*, 603, and Berman, *No Peace, No Honor*, 159.

73. Berman, *No Peace, No Honor*, 145, 161, 164–65, 185; Kimball, *Nixon's Vietnam War*, 342; Davidson, *Vietnam at War*, 715, 722.

74. Berman, *No Peace, No Honor*, 146, 160–61, 169, 196, 203, and Hunt, *Pacification*, 215–16.

75. Berman, *No Peace, No Honor*, 187.

76. Berman, *No Peace, No Honor*, 213.

77. Berman, *No Peace, No Honor*, 67.

78. Berman, *No Peace, No Honor*, 189, 191, and Kimball, *Nixon's Vietnam War*, 360.

79. Berman, *No Peace, No Honor*, 192–93, 214–15.

80. Clodfelter, *Limits of Air Power*, 182.

81. Along with the account of Linebacker II in Clodfelter, *Limits of Air Power*, see Marshall L. Michel, *The Eleven Days of Christmas: America's Last Vietnam Battle* (San Francisco: Encounter Books, 2002), who demonstrates that "the United States came close to suffering a major defeat in Linebacker II," 236.

82. Davidson, *Vietnam at War*, 726–27.

83. Clodfelter, *Limits of Air Power*, 201.

84. Herring, *America's Longest War*, 280.

85. Clodfelter, *Limits of Air Power*, 192.

86. Clodfelter, *Limits of Air Power*, 200–201.

87. Berman, *No Peace, No Honor*, 218, and Kimball, *Nixon's Vietnam War*, 264.

88. Record, *Wrong War*, xv, and Sorely, *A Better War*, 360.

89. Clodfelter, *Limits of Air Power*, 195, and Kimball, *Nixon's Vietnam War*, 368.

90. Berman, *No Peace, No Honor*, 204.

91. Berman, *No Peace, No Honor*, 244–46 emphasized how closely the January agreement resembled the vc's 1969 peace proposal on all major issues.

92. Sorley, *A Better War*, 31, 87; Kimball, *Nixon's Vietnam War*, 151; Davidson, *Vietnam at War*, 571; Krepinevich, *Army and Vietnam*, 253–57; Hunt, *Pacification*, 221–33.

93. Krepinevich, *Army and Vietnam*, 254, and Hunt, *Pacification*, 212–13.

94. Sorley, *A Better War*, 18, 22, 28–29, 42, 59, 77, 103, 124, 134–35, 145.

95. Sorley, *A Better War*, 191–92, 219.

96. BDM Corporation, "Study of Strategic Lessons," II-1, II-6, and Collins, Senior Officer Debriefing Report.

97. Thayer, *War without Fronts*, 178. The other options were "Security" (16 percent and 14 percent) and "Economic" (13 percent and 20 percent).

98. Isaacs, *Without Honor*, 119.

99. Kinnard, *War Managers*, 145.

100. Hunt, *Pacification*, 186, 206, 261; Lewy, *America in Vietnam*, 192–93; Kinnard, *War Managers*, 108; Thayer, *How to Analyze a War without Fronts*, 881.

101. Bergerud, *Dynamics of Defeat*, 158, and Thayer, *War without Fronts*, 201.

102. Hunt, *Pacification*, 199, 249–51; Thayer, *How to Analyze a War without Fronts*, 915; Prados, *Hidden History*, 215–18.

103. Bergerud, *Dynamics of Defeat*, 299, and Hunt, *Pacification*, 265.

104. Isaacs, *Without Honor*, 102; Kimball, *Nixon's Vietnam War*, 276; Berman, *No Peace, No Honor*, 99–100.

105. Collins, Senior Officer Debriefing Report; Armstrong, Senior Officer Debriefing Report; Sorley, *A Better War*, 180–86; Lewy, *America in Vietnam*, 172; Kennedy, "An Examination of Vietnam War Senior Officer Debriefing Reports," 18–20; Clarke, *Advice and Support*, 502–3; Thayer, *War without Fronts*, 61–75.

106. Hackworth and Sherman, *About Face*, 717, and Sorley, *A Better War*, 276.

107. Collins, Senior Officer Debriefing Report; Hunt, *Pacification*, 258–60; Bergerud, *Dynamics of Defeat*, 263.

108. James W. Trullinger, *Village at War: An Account of Conflict in Vietnam* (Stanford: Stanford University Press, 1994), 170–71.

109. Clarke, *Advice and Support*, 506; DeGroot, *Noble Cause*, 211–12; Lewy, *America in Vietnam*, 221.

110. Military History Institute of Vietnam, *Victory in Vietnam*, 44–45, 246, 249–50; Spector, *After Tet*, 290; Gilbert and Head, *Tet Offensive*, 8, 105; Hunt, *Pacification*, 262; Thayer, *How to Analyze a War without Fronts*, 918, 938.

111. Bergerud, *Dynamics of Defeat*; the quote is on 304.

112. Trullinger, *Village at War*.

113. A recent study demonstrated virtually the same outcome in My Tho Province (which is in the Mekong Delta), where "though the revolutionaries were often knocked down, they were never knocked out. They seemed to find ways of recovering from every setback by devising new approaches when old tactics faltered, from the French period right through to the end." The revolutionary movement in the province "did not progress in an upward linear manner and did not recede in a terminal reverse direction. Large groups of people remained latent supporters even when they could not or would not act on their sympathies. This group was clearly smaller at the end of the war than in its earlier stages, but still remained significant throughout the entire period." See David W. P. Elliott, *The Vietnamese War: Revolution and Social Change in the Mekong Delta, 1930–1975,* 2 vols. (Armonk NY: M. E. Sharpe, 2003); the quotes are in vol. I, page 9, and vol. II, page 1395.

114. Hooper to Hogan, April 10, 1971, Cleo C. Hogan Jr. Papers; Permissive Orders for Out-of-Country Travel, JRHP; Richard Avedon and Doon Arbus, *The Sixties* (New York: Random House, 1999), 183.

Chapter 13

1. Combs interview, February 8, 1995; DeVore interview, February 11–12, 1995; picture of Joe and Neeltje in the Combs Papers.

2. Graham, *No Name on the Bullet,* 334–35, and Simpson, *Audie Murphy,* 287–88.

3. Melson, "Vietnam's Most-Decorated U.S. Soldier"; Rick Anderson interview, July 9, 1996; Larry Frank interview, March 2, 1996.

4. Greenwald interview, August 5, 1996; Putnam, "Reminiscences of Audie Murphy," JRHP; Graham, *No Name on the Bullet,* 311–12, 335.

5. Red and Anna Combs interviews, February 8, 1995, and DeVore interviews, February 11–12, 1995, August 19, 2002.

6. "Disparate Worlds of Audie Murphy Join to Bury War Hero in Arlington," undated clipping, Carollyn DeVore Papers, and Graham, *No Name on the Bullet,* 338–39.

7. Combs interview, February 8, 1995; Hooper to Combs, May 31, 1971, Combs Papers; Floyd N. Greenwald interview, August 5, 1996.

8. Bill Parson interview, July 30, 1996, and "Academic Report," August 23, 1971, in Hooper's Military Personnel Records.

9. DeVore to the authors, August 18, 20, 2002.

10. DeVore interviews, February 11–12, 1995, June 21, 2002, and August 19, 2002, and DeVore, "Brief Memoir."

11. Frederick G. "Jerry" Hill interview, February 1, 1996.

12. Del Vecchio, *13th Valley,* 97, and Graham, *No Name on the Bullet,* 305.

13. Hawk interview, June 21, 1997. For an example of another MOH recipient fearing peace, see Miller, *Reflections,* 194.

14. "The Screaming Eagle," undated clipping, JRHP.

15. Rick Anderson, "Joe Is Honored at Last," undated clipping, Combs Papers; Wolf,

"Probing the Minds," 27; Larry Frank interview, March 2, 1996; Dolbee, "He's a Hero to Everyone but Himself"; Anderson, "GI Hero Unwinds from Vietnam," clipping in the Rick Anderson Papers. Aside from Jerry Hill, Joe talked about being a mercenary with many other people, including Carollyn and fellow veteran Mike Sallis.

16. Powell, *Journey*, 197; Bob Burnett, "I Always Had the Will to Live," *Wenatchee World*, February 28, 1975, clipping in Maxine L. Bohn Papers; "The Story of Joe Hooper, War Hero," *The Cumberland (MD) Times/News*, February 20, 1986, clipping in Combs Papers; Johnson interview, April 14, 1996; Gary Foster interview, March 7, 1995; Combs interview, February 8, 1995.

17. Hawk interview, June 21, 1997; Rick Anderson interview, July 9, 1996; Hill interview, February 1, 1996; Bill Parsons interview, July 30, 1996; Stump, "Peace Is Worth Fighting For"; Donlon interview February 9, 1996.

18. These documents are in Hooper's Military Personnel Records.

19. Bill Parsons interview, July 30, 1996. Also see the February 1973 evaluation in Hooper's Military Personnel Records, which noted that, "LT Hooper has been tardy on several occasions."

20. See the evaluations for November 1973, and March 1974, in Hooper's Military Personnel Records.

21. "Sport Parachuting: The Sport of Space for the Age of Space," undated clipping, and Letter of Appreciation from Lieutenant Colonel James L. Allen to Hooper, October 13, 1971, both in JRHP.

22. November 1973, evaluation, Hooper's Military Personnel Records; Fred W. Nodler to Colonel Jim Allen, December 7, 1971, JRHP; Lieutenant Colonel Paul L. Munier to 1st Lieutenant Joseph [sic] Hooper, February 23, 1972, JRHP; audiotape, evidently recorded by Joe, of the Society's awards ceremony in the JRHP.

23. "Posthumous Recognition of PFC Joe E. Mann," in the Irene Bennett Papers, and Bennett to the authors, July 22, 1997.

24. A copy of the speech is in the JRHP.

25. A copy of Hooper's speech is in the JRHP. For Murphy's speech see Putnam, "Tribute to Audie Murphy," May 31, 1971, copy in the JRHP. Joe's widow Faye wrote that Joe spoke about all men being born to die a week before his death; she did not know they were really Murphy's words. See Faye's undated, handwritten speech in the JRHP.

26. A copy of the resolution is in the Don F. Pratt Museum, Fort Campbell, Kentucky.

27. For just a few other examples, see Putnam, "Reminiscences of Audie Murphy," JRHP; Melson, "Vietnam's Most-Decorated U.S. Soldier"; "War Hero: 'He couldn't survive peacetime,'" undated clipping in the Hendricks Scrapbook; Clint Claybrook, "High Medal Changed Life for War Hero," *Decatur (AL) Daily*, June 6, 1983, clipping in the JRHP.

28. Suggested by Stan Smith but written by Edward F. Murphy, "The Most Decorated?"

The Annals (June 1990): 92–94; Charles F. Sughrue, "More on the Most Decorated," *The Annals* (March 1991): 60–62; Brett A. Gookin, "More on the Most Decorated," *The Annals* (June 1991): 92–93. The authors thank Mr. Stan H. Smith for providing copies of these articles. Also see "Letter to the Editor" from Lieutenant Colonel David T. Zabecki, MHQ (Summer 1993): 7. A debate rages over whether Audie Murphy or Lieutenant Colonel Matt Urban was the most highly decorated World War II soldier; see Stan H. Smith to George J. Zoscsak, copy provided by the Audie Murphy Research Foundation of Santa Clarita, California.

29. Major General Patrick Brady interview, May 28, 1996; Donlon interview, February 9, 1996; Chief Warrant Officer James T. Garrett to Mr. W. Michael Sallis, January 27, 1989, W. Michael Sallis Papers.

30. Earl Yowell, Chief, Special Actions Branch, to Stan H. Smith, July 5, 1989, Stan H. Smith Papers; Joe to his parents, March 31, 1968, JRHP; Report of Medical Examination, May 30, 1968, Hooper's Medical Records, Claim Folder 24965568.

31. The authors are indebted to Colonel Frank C. Foster for his detailed discussion of Joe's medals; Frank Foster interview, October 9, 1996. Colonel Foster is the coauthor (with Lawrence H. Borts) of *United States Military Medals 1939 to the Present*, 3rd edition (Fountain Inn SC: MOA (Medals of America) Press, 1995).

32. Rick Anderson, "Ten Years Later, It's Time to Un-Bury Staff Sgt. Joe Hooper," *Seattle Times*, May 5, 1989, clipping in Audrey Hooper Papers.

33. Except where noted, this account relies on the Faye Hooper interviews, August 12, 1994, and September 19, 2002, and the Jack and Paula Saint interviews, April 12, 1997 (Jack is Faye's brother and Paula is his wife).

34. For Faye's high school activities, see *The Hazelnut 1958*, which was a high school yearbook; a copy is in the Jack and Paula Saint Papers.

35. "Former Fashion Coordinator Works on BPW Style Show," undated clipping in the JRHP.

36. The divorce decree is in the Alabama Center for Health Statistics.

37. Audrey Hooper interview, March 2, 1996, and Red and Anna Combs interviews, February 8, 1995.

38. Roger C. and Norma Donlon interviews, February 9, 1996. In her August 12, 1994, interview Faye said she was against the war and Gary Foster confirmed it in his interview on March 7, 1995. Red Combs verified the story about the yellow roses and the instant marriage proposal; interview, November 13, 1995.

39. The booklets are in the JRHP.

40. Hill interview, February 1, 1996.

41. Faye Hooper interview, June 1, 2002, and Thomas J. Dolan, "This Christmas, He's Going Home," *Chicago Sun Times*, December 25, 1971, clipping in JRHP.

42. Audrey Hooper interview, March 2, 1996.

43. Except where noted, this account relies on the Red and Anna Combs interviews, February 8, 1995. Faye denied much of what Anna and Red said, but much of their account makes sense.

44. The wedding guest book and wedding pictures are in the JRHP.

45. Both letters are in the Combs Papers.

46. Faye Hooper interview, August 12, 1994.

47. Hill interview, February 1, 1996; Johnson interview, April 14, 1996; Chris Luther interview, May 30, 2000; Jennings interview, October 19, 1996.

48. The picture is in the JRHP. Faye Hooper interview, August 12, 1994.

49. Faye Hooper interview, August 12, 1994; "The Other Life . . ." *Leesville Leader*, November 2, 1972 (which has three photos illustrating the story), clipping in the JRHP; a photo of Joe as Dracula is in the JRHP.

50. Clint Claybrook, "High Medal Changed Life for War Hero," *Decatur Daily*, June 26, 1983, clipping in the JRHP.

51. Dalton M. Waldrop Jr. to Lieutenant Colonel Ralph Schmitz, August 14, 1973, in Hooper's Military Personnel Records; "Hooper Cited for 4-H Work," *Leesville Leader*, February 21, 1974, clipping in the JRHP; thirteen pictures of camp events in the Hendricks Scrapbook.

52. A copy of all this correspondence is in the JRHP.

53. Audrey Hooper interview, March 2, 1996.

54. Hogan interview, July 13, 1995; Loftin interview, July 13, 1995; Michael Collins interview, June 15, 1997; Keirn C. Brown interview, January 11, 1997.

55. "Personal Qualifications Statement" in Hooper's Military Personnel Records; e-mail to the authors from the Northwestern State University's registrar's office, August 8, 2002; e-mails from Dr. Chris Maggio, Director, Alumni Affairs, Northwestern State University to the authors, August 8, 12, 2002. Later Joe also claimed that he had three credit hours from Stanford and thirty-two semester hours through the CLEP program; see "Standard Form 85," April 23, 1974, Official Personnel Folder, United States Office of Personnel Management, OPF/EMF Access Unit, St. Louis, Missouri. The authors have been unable to verify these claims.

56. Frank Foster interview, October 9, 1996. As MOH recipient Delbert O. Jennings put it, an MOH recipient who became an officer was "normally kept unless they really screw up"; Jennings interview, October 19, 1996.

57. Special Orders Number 015, Extract, Headquarters US Army Training Center, Infantry and Fort Polk, January 15, 1974, in Hooper's Military Personnel Records.

58. Frazier won their first fight in 1971.

59. Wolf, "Probing the Minds."

60. Stainback to McGinniss, July 13, 1973, copy in JRHP.

61. Joe McGinniss, *Heroes* (New York: Viking, 1976), 12, 16–19.

62. Years later an auto accident that did a lot of nerve damage compounded the disease problem. "I just don't get around very well, sometimes a lot better than others," she said. But she was still getting around. Interview, August 12, 1994.

63. Livingston interview, July 10, 1995.

64. McGinniss, *Heroes*, 128–39 for the essay on Joe; the drinking quote is on 138 and the "everybody wants me" quote in on 135–36. A "Readjustment Pay" form, January 15, 1974, Hooper's Medical Records, Claim Folder 24965568, indicated his readjustment pay was $15,000, but the government withheld $3,000 for taxes.

65. Norma Donlon interview, February 9, 1996. For confirmation of this point, see Miller, *Reflections*, 192–93, 198; Stan H. Smith, "Medal of Honor Recipients—A Profile," Stan H. Smith Papers; Boston Publishing Company, *Above and Beyond*, 3.

66. Faye Hooper interview, September 19, 2002.

67. Faye Hooper interview, July 12, 2000, and Hawk interview, June 21, 1997.

68. Faye Hooper interview, July 12, 2000.

69. Copy of the letter of recommendation in the Combs Papers; "Notification of Personnel Action" forms in Hooper's Military Personnel Records; "Veterans Administration News," May 5, 1974, Combs Papers; "Authorizing the Appointment to Positions of Contact Representative, Veteran Administration, without Regard to the Requirements of the Civil Service Rules," copy in Hooper's Official Personnel Folder, United States Office of Personnel Management, OPF/EMF Access Unit, St. Louis, Missouri.

70. "Certificate of Medical Examination," May 6, 1974, Hooper's Employee Medical Folder, United States Office of Personnel Management, OPF/EMF Access Unit, St. Louis, Missouri.

71. Dolbee, "He's a Hero to Everyone but Himself"; Sallis interview, March 1, 1996; Alex Vira to Red Combs, July 30, 1985, Combs Papers; Combs interview, February 8, 1995.

72. John Whiteside, "It's Not Something You Just Walk Away From . . ." undated clipping in the Combs Papers; Rick Anderson, "Joe Is Honored at Last," undated clipping in the Combs Papers; Gary Foster interview, March 7, 1995.

73. Larry Frank and Alex Vira interviews, March 2, 1996, and Sallis interview, March 1, 1996.

74. Harry Brooks, "Viet Vets: The Same Plight 200 Years Ago," *News-Journal*, April 4, 1976, clipping in JRHP, and John Arnhold interview, April 16, 1996.

75. Arnhold interview. Mike Sallis agreed that Joe was not good at picking winners at the track; Sallis interview, March 1, 1996.

76. Rick Anderson, "Hooper Hospital Gains Support as Readers Exercise Their Writes," *Seattle Times*, undated clipping, Larry Frank Papers, and Penny Norman interview, April 3, 1996.

77. Arnhold interview, and Floyd N. Greenwald interview, August 5, 1996.

78. Arnhold interview.

79. "Most Decorated VN Soldiers," undated clipping in Hendricks Scrapbook, and audiotape of some of the races in the JRHP. In 1974 Joe claimed that, "In the past five years I have made over 600 speaking engagements and over 100 television appearances. Audiences ranged from heads of state, civic groups, schools of all levels, and many youth groups"; see "Standard Form 85," April 23, 1974, Official Personnel Folder, United States Office of Personnel Management, OPF/EMF Access Unit, St. Louis, Missouri.

80. Nancy Gould, "A Vietnam Hero—His Story," *Kent (WA) News Journal,* April 1, 1976, and Brooks, "Viet Vets: The Same Plight as 200 Years Ago," both clippings in the JRHP.

81. "Notice to All Medal of Honor Society Members Announcing the Annual Patriots Award Dinner," and Joe's memo requesting administrative leave to attend the event (marked "approved"), both in JRHP.

82. Copies of the long draft and final speech are in the JRHP.

83. *Veterans News,* January–February, 1977, in JRHP.

84. Typewritten page of quotes about Joe assembled by W. Michael Sallis, in the Sallis Papers; "Joe's Legacy: He Gave Everything," in "Delta Raiders Newsletter," 22 (April 1990); Rick Anderson, "Our Most Decorated Vet Is Our Most Forgotten," *Seattle Times,* Memorial Day 1988, clipping in Larry Frank Papers; Rick Anderson interview, July 9, 1996; "Forgotten Hero Would Fight Again," *Daily News,* undated clipping in the Hendricks Scrapbook.

85. Vira interview, March 2, 1996. Others also believed Joe was badly used; Michael Collins interview, June 15, 1997, and Arnhold interview, April 16, 1996.

86. Rick Anderson interview, July 9, 1996.

87. "Jumpmaster Re-Certification," July 21, 1974, Hooper's Military Personnel Records.

88. The following account relies on the Peter E. McIntyre interview, June 11, 2000, and Chris Luther interview, May 30, 2000.

89. The evaluation is in Hooper's Military Personnel Records.

90. The following account relies on interviews with Alex Vira on March 2, 1996, May 9, 1996, July 9, 1996, and August 1, 1996, and the Floyd N. Greenwald interview, August 5, 1996.

91. The evaluation is in Hooper's Military Personnel Records; Vira to the authors, July 31, 1996.

92. The promotion and discharge papers are in his Military Personnel Records.

93. Schulzinger, *Time for War,* 311; Military History Institute of Vietnam, *Victory in Vietnam,* 335; Isaacs, *Without Honor,* 310–11. Because of a bookkeeping error, the United States was led to believe the losses were only half those numbers, which seemed to be proof that South Vietnam was holding its own.

94. Van Tien Dung, *Our Great Spring Victory: An Account of the Liberation of South Vietnam* (New York: Monthly Review Press, 1977), 257; for a similar assessment, see Military History Institute of Vietnam, *Victory in Vietnam*, 330.

95. Isaacs, *Without Honor*, 145, 327–29, and Clodfelter, *Vietnam in Military Statistics*, 207.

96. Herring, *America's Longest War*, 294, and Duiker, *Sacred War*, 244.

97. Isaacs, *Without Honor*, 366–71, described this bizarre episode.

98. Pearlman, *Warmaking*, 392, and Isaacs, *Without Honor*, 401.

99. Isaacs, *Without Honor*, 447–48.

100. William E. Le Gro, *Vietnam from Cease-Fire to Capitulation* (Washington DC: U.S. Army Center of Military History, 1985), 28; Dung, *Great Spring Victory*, 244, 248–49; Gates, "Two American Wars in Asia" and "People's War in Vietnam."

101. Herring, "Peoples Quite Apart," 20; Davidson, *Vietnam at War*, 723, 741; Berman, *No Peace, No Honor*, 262.

102. Gates, "Two American Wars in Asia," 14, and "People's War in Vietnam," 342.

103. Allan R. Millett and Peter Maslowski, *For the Common Defense: A Military History of the United States of America*, revised and expanded edition (New York: The Free Press, 1994), 81–82.

104. Dung, *Great Spring Victory*, 236, 245–46.

105. "Hooper against Total Amnesty," *Times-Picayune*, undated clipping in the JRHP.

106. Sallis two-page memoir, undated, copy in the Rick Anderson Papers, and Sallis interview, March 1, 1996.

107. Paul Henderson, "We Left a Year and a Half Too Soon," undated clipping in the JRHP. For similar sentiments, see "You Should Know Joe Hooper," reprinted from the *Joliet Herald-News*, in the "Delta Raiders Newsletter," 22 (April 1990).

108. Wolf, "Probing the Minds," 27; Spec 4 Dennis Thornton, "Encore for Medal of Honor Winner Hooper," *Pacific Stars and Stripes*, June 11, 1970, clipping in the JRHP; Anderson, "GI Hero Unwinds from Vietnam," clipping in the Rick Anderson Papers.

109. Rick Anderson interview, July 9, 1996.

110. Anderson, "GI Hero Unwinds from Vietnam"; Audrey Hooper interview, March 2, 1996; Paul Hopkins, "Medal of Honor Winner Visits New Orleans East," undated clipping in the JRHP; Faye Hooper interview, August 12, 1994; DeVore interview, February 11–12, 1995; Clint Claybrook, "High Medal Changed Life for War Hero," *Decatur Daily*, June 26, 1983, clipping in the JRHP; Henderson, "We Left a Year and a Half Too Soon."

111. "Hooper against Total Amnesty," and Anderson, "Joe Hooper—Forgotten Hero in a Forgotten War." Many other veterans expressed the same ambiguity about the war. For example, Tex Gray, whom Hooper may have rescued at La Chu, said he

would do it all over again because he believed in fighting "for your country, right or wrong." But "I would advise my own son to get the hell out of Dodge [City]." Gray interview, October 30, 1995.

112. Diane Tod, "'It's a Day to Remember': Memorial Day Is Special for Most-Decorated State GI," undated clipping in the JRHP.

113. Faye Hooper interview, September 19, 2002.

114. Faye Hooper interviews, August 12–13, 1994 and November 29, 1995.

115. Norman interview, April 14, 1996; Major General Patrick Brady interview, May 28, 1996; Sallis interview, March 1, 1996; Faye Hooper interview, August 12–13, 1994; Anna Combs interview, February 8, 1995. Several of the "Caressables" cards are in the JRHP.

116. Roger and Norma Donlon interviews, February 9, 1996; Arlene and Gary Foster interviews, February 28, 1996; "Report of Medical Examination for Disability Evaluation, May 7, 1975," in Hooper's Medical Records, Claim Folder 24965568.

117. Audrey Hooper interview, March 2, 1996, and Larry Frank interview, March 2, 1996.

118. Parson interview, July 30, 1996, and Rick Anderson, untitled draft column, Rick Anderson Papers.

119. Greenwald interview, August 5, 1996, and Vira interview, March 2, 1996.

120. Anna Combs interview, February 8, 1995; Delbert O. Jennings interview, October 19, 1996; Cutlip interview, June 17, 2000.

121. Faye Hooper interview, August 12–13, 1994.

122. Michael Collins interview, June 15, 1997; Sallis interview, March 1, 1996; Norma Donlon interview, February 9, 1996; Larry Frank interview, March 2, 1996; Audrey Hooper interview, March 2, 1996; Rick Anderson interview, July 9, 1996.

123. Hackworth and Sherman, *About Face,* 320.

124. Roger Donlon interview, February 9, 1996; Faye Hooper interview, August 12–13, 1994; Combs interview, February 8, 1995; Sallis interview, March 1, 1996.

125. Sallis interview, March 1, 1996; Larry Frank interview, March 2, 1996; Vira interview, March 2, 1996; Johnson interview, April 14, 1996.

126. Cutlip interview, June 17, 2000.

127. Hendricks interview, June 16, 1999, and Audrey Hooper interview, March 2, 1996.

128. Faye Hooper interview, September 19, 2002.

129. Audrey Hooper interview, March 2, 1996; Red and Anna Combs interviews, February 8, 1995; Sallis interview, March 1, 1996.

130. Red and Anna Combs interviews, February 8, 1995; Sallis interview, March 1, 1996; Hendricks interview, June 16, 1999; Vira interview, March 2, 1996; Jack Saint interview, April 12, 1997; Larry Frank interview, March 2, 1996.

131. At that point Joe had twenty years, three months, and eight days of government service, seventeen years, six months, and five days in the military and two years, nine

months, and three days for the VA. See "Employee Service Statement," February 1, 1977, Official Personnel Folder, United States Office of Personnel Management, OPF/ EMF Access Unit, St. Louis, Missouri. Under government regulations, he would not be eligible for deferred retirement payments until age sixty-two.

Chapter 14

1. Rick Anderson, "Joe Is Honored at Last," undated clipping in the Combs Papers; Mike Sallis's two-page memoir in the Rick Anderson Papers; Sallis to "Dear Gentlemen," October 9, 1987, also in the Rick Anderson Papers.

2. "Counseling Record—Personal Information," July 20, 1978, Hooper's Medical Records, Claim Folder 24965568. Also see "Veterans Administration Counseling Record —Appraisal—Selection of Objective," August 2, 1978, in Hooper's Medical Records, Claim Folder 24965568.

3. "Counseling Record—Personal Information," July 20, 1978, and "Training Program and Progress Record," undated, both in Hooper's Medical Records, Claim Folder 24965568.

4. Schacter, *Memory Distortion*, 330–51. The following five myths are representative, not an all-inclusive list.

5. Isaacs, *Vietnam Shadows*, 48–49.

6. Moser, *Winter Soldiers*, 43; Young, *Vietnam Wars*, 192; Edelman, *Dear America*, 225.

7. Rakestraw interview, June 24, 1997.

8. "Delta Raiders Newsletter," 24 (September 1990). Schell, *Real War*, 192, also makes this point.

9. Kinnard, *War Managers*, 31, 132, and Marc Leepson, "Perspectives," *Vietnam Magazine* (December 1996): 62.

10. Hammond, *Military and the Media, 1968–1973*, 9–11, and Hammond, *Reporting Vietnam*, 291. In additon, for the complex subject of the military and the media, see the essay by Hammond cited in note 14; Small, *Covering Dissent;* Wyatt, *Paper Soldiers;* Daniel C. Hallin, *The "Uncensored War": The Media and Vietnam* (Berkeley: University of California Press, 1989).

11. Hammond, *Reporting Vietnam*, 61, and Hammond, *Military and the Media, 1968– 1973*, 4–5.

12. Hammond, *Military and the Media, 1968–1973*, 11.

13. Hammond, *Reporting Vietnam*, 75, 159.

14. William M. Hammond, "The Press in Vietnam as Agent of Defeat: A Critical Examination," *Reviews in American History* (June 1989): 315–16, and Wyatt, *Paper Soldiers*, 147–48, 218.

15. Berman, *No Peace, No Honor*, 279.

16. Hammond, *Reporting Vietnam*, 295–96.

17. Gittinger, *Johnson Years*, 189–92; Palmer, *25-Year War*, 200–201; Kinnard, *War Managers*, 41, 133.

18. Sorley, *A Better War*, 93, and Kimball, *Nixon's Vietnam War*, 221.

19. Dung, *Great Spring Victory*, 252; Military History Institute of Vietnam, *Victory in Vietnam*, 438; Werner and Huynh, *Vietnam War*, 63.

20. "Vietnamization . . . The Path Leading to Collapse," Document No. 74, *Vietnam Documents and Research Notes Series*, Reel II.

21. Davidson, *Vietnam at War*, 791, and Caputo, *Rumor of War*, 138.

22. Werner and Huynh, *Vietnam War*, 207.

23. Dung, *Great Spring Victory*, 260.

24. Davidson, *Vietnam at War*, 792.

25. For a splendid brief account of the MIA issue, see Isaacs, *Vietnam Shadows*, 101–16.

26. Olson and Roberts, *Where the Domino Fell*, 279; Hogan interview, October 18, 1999; William C. Meacham, *Lest We Forget: The Kingsmen, 101st Aviation Battalion* ([1968] New York: Ivy Books, 1999), 85–88.

27. Except where noted this discussion relies closely on the splendid books by Eric T. Dean Jr., *Shook over Hell: Post-Traumatic Stress, Vietnam, and the Civil War* (Cambridge: Harvard University Press, 1997), and Allan Young, *The Harmony of Illusions: Inventing Post-Traumatic Stress Disorder* (Princeton: Princeton University Press, 1995). B. G. Burkett and Glenna Whitley, *Stolen Valor: How the Vietnam Generation Was Robbed of Its Heroes and Its History* (Dallas: Verity Press, 1998) is also extremely valuable on this subject.

28. Burkett and Whitley, *Stolen Valor*, is the best book on the Vietnam veterans' postwar adjustment; for the specific points, see 66, 72, 305–8; 317; 529–33; 543–44.

29. "101st Airborne Division Vietnam Veterans Newsletter" (March 1995).

30. James interview, April 10, 1996, and Clodfelter, *Mad Minutes and Vietnam Months*, 21.

31. The phrase was from Supreme Court Justice Oliver Wendell Holmes Jr., who served in the Civil War; quoted in Hess, *Union Soldier in Battle*, 21. Linderman, *World within War*, 318ff, brilliantly details the nuances of a soldier's inability to explain his experience.

32. Sakurai, *Human Bullets*, 133; William Broyles Jr., "Why Men Love War," *Esquire*, November 1984, 56; Edelman, *Dear America*, 122–23; Schell, *Real War*, 231.

33. For a discussion of this transition, see Linderman, *World within War*, 75–83.

34. Sakurai, *Human Bullets*, 61, and Edelman, *Dear America*, 78–79.

35. For excellent discussions of these points, see the following essays by Roger J. Spiller: "Isen's Run: Human Dimensions of Warfare in the 20th Century," *Military Review* (May 1988); "Shell Shock," *American Heritage* (May/June 1990); "In Review: Breakdown on the Battlefield," *MHQ* (Winter 1992); "Violent Collisions: The Advent of the

Psychological Battlefield" (unpublished, copy in the authors' possession). Also see Paul Wanke, "American Military Psychiatry and Its Role among Ground Forces in World War II," *Journal of Military History* (January 1999). The 98 percent/2 percent comment is in Evans and Ryan, *Human Face of War*, 7.

36. Burkett and Whitley, *Stolen Valor*, 145.

37. *Diagnostic and Statistical Manual of Mental Disorders (Third Edition)* (Washington DC: American Psychiatric Association, 1980), 236–38.

38. Along with Dean, *Shook over Hell*, see Wanke, "American Military Psychiatry," 143–44.

39. Burkett and Whitley, *Stolen Valor*, 223–33.

40. Landy Sparr and Loren D. Pankratz, "Factitious Posttraumatic Stress Disorder," *American Journal of Psychiatry* (August 1983). Also see Loren D. Pankratz, "Continued Appearance of Factitious Posttraumatic Stress Disorder," *American Journal of Psychiatry* (June 1990).

41. Burkett and Whitley, *Stolen Valor*, 255–61, 281.

42. The best discussion of the fakers and the VA's reluctance to expose them is Burkett and Whitley, *Stolen Valor;* the Burns quote is on 261. For the VA being a bank see Dean, *Shook over Hell*, 186.

43. Burkett and Whitley, *Stolen Valor*, 265, 280.

44. Dean, *Shook over Hell*, 186–87.

45. Hogan interview videotaped by Marty Callaghan, 1999; Horne interview, July 22, 2000; Kintzer interview, January 29, 1996; Leshikar interview, October 28, 1995; Bischoff interview, January 13, 1997; Rakestraw interview, June 24, 1997; Barber interview, February 29, 1997; Gravett interview, July 21, 2000. Many other soldiers interviewed for this book expressed skepticism that PTSD was widespread.

46. "VA Wing Dedicated to War Hero Hooper," undated clipping in the Sallis Papers, and Sallis interview, March 1, 1996.

47. Dewey "Buck" Johnson interview, September 24, 1999.

48. For information about Joe's academic record, we are indebted to Dr. Danette Boyle, who in September 1999 was the vice president for development at Rogers State University; with appropriate regard for privacy concerns, she allowed a secretary in her office to release the titles of the classes Joe took and whether he passed them, but not the specific grades.

49. "Report of Medical Examination for Disability Evaluation," May 7, 1975; "Orthopedic Examination," May 7, 1975; "Rating Decision," December 9, 1975; all in Hooper's Medical Records, Claim Folder 24965568.

50. Nancy Gould, "A Vietnam Hero—His Story," *Kent (WA) News Journal*, April 1, 1976, clipping in the JRHP.

51. "Disabled Veterans Application for Vocational Rehabilitation," June 5, 1978; "Veter-

ans Administration Counseling Record—Appraisal—Selection of Objective," August 2, 1978; Memo from Robert Spencer, Counseling Psychologist, to Chief, Counseling and Rehabilitation Section, August 14, 1978; "Counseling Record—Medical Information—Related Findings," August 2, 1978; all in Hooper's Medical Records, Claim Folder 24965568.

52. Along with the source cited in note number 48, also see Richard Hix, "Special Report of Training," September 13, 1978 (this contains Joe's statement that he was getting at least a "B" in the anatomy class); "Authorization and Certification of Entrance or Reentrance into Training and Certification of Trainee Status," September 13, 1978; "Application and Enrollment Certification for Individualized Tutorial Assistance," December 12, 1978; all in Hooper's Medical Records, Claim Folder 24965568. Also see Jimmy Shipman interview, September 1, 1999; Shipman was a Claremore veterinarian who knew Jori Allen.

53. Along with the source cited in note number 48, see "Enrollment Certification," January 23, 1979, in Hooper's Medical Records, Claim Folder 24965568.

54. On September 24, 1999, the occupants of number 2F graciously allowed us to tour the apartment.

55. Joey Hooper interview, August 12–13, 1994, and Faye Hooper interview, August 12–13, 1994.

56. Faye Hooper interview, July 12, 2000; the note is in the JRHP; Shipman interview, September 1, 1999.

57. Shipman interview.

58. Except where otherwise noted, the following discussion depends on Dewey "Buck" Johnson interview, August 1, 1999; Mrs. Dewey Johnson interview, August 2, 1999; Dewey Johnson Jr. interview, August 2, 1999. In addition they were all present for another interview on September 24, 1999.

59. The ad appeared in the *Claremore Progress*, Sunday, March 18, 1979, clipping in the JRHP.

60. Arnhold interview, April 16, 1996, and Jerry McCollum interview, August 2, 1999.

61. McCollum interviews, August 2, 1999, September 24, 1999, and October 1, 1999.

62. McCollum interview, August 2, 1999.

63. Faye Hooper interview, July 12, 2000.

64. "Rating Decision," January 1, 1979; E. B. Webb, Adjudication Officer, to Joe Hooper, March 15, 1979; "Special Report of Training," March 19, 1979; all in Hooper's Medical Records, Claim Folder 24965568.

65. "Income-Net Worth and Employment Statement," June 21, 1978, and "Statement in Support of Claim," April 20, 1979, both in Hooper's Medical Records, Claim Folder 24965568.

66. "Special Report of Training," April 9, 1979; Ray E. Smith, Director, to Field Director,

Central Region, VARO, April 23, 1979; "Special Report of Training," April 27, 1979; Lorin M. Drain, Finance Officer, to Joe Hooper, April 27, 1979; "Special Report of Training," April 30, 1979; all in Hooper's Medical Records, Claim Folder 24965568.

67. DeVore to the authors, May 4, 2002, and DeVore interview June 21, 2002.

68. The following account relies on interviews with Jerry McCollum on August 2, 1999, August 3, 1999, September 24, 1999, September 25, 1999, October 1, 1999, and the U.S. Army Criminal Investigation Command (USACIDC) Report of Investigation (ROI) No. 79-CID032-11227-5H8, U.S. Army Crime Records Center, Fort Belvoir, Virginia; obtained through a Freedom of Information Act request, the document was sanitized to protect the names of the agents involved and the privacy of individuals mentioned in the report.

69. Dewey "Buck" Johnson interview, September 24, 1999.

70. Faye Hooper interview, August 12–13, 1994.

71. "Rating Decision," May 24, 1979, and E. E. Webb, Adjudication Officer, VARO, Muskogee, to Faye Hooper, June 27, 1979, both in Hooper's Medical Records, Claim Folder 24965568.

72. J. C. Peckarsky, Director, VA Compensation and Pension Service, to Director (21) VARO, Muskogee, May 15, 1979, Hooper's Medical Records, Claim Folder 24965568.

73. DeVore's "Brief Memoir"; DeVore to the authors, c. fall 1994; DeVore interview, February 11–12, 1995.

74. Faye Hooper interview, August 12–13, 1994; Audrey Hooper interview, March 2, 1996; Congressional Medal of Honor Society *Newsletter* (Fall 1979), copy in the Audrey Hooper Papers.

75. The following quotes come from a fragment in Joe's handwriting in the JRHP; Vira interview, March 2, 1996; Anderson, "Ten Years Later, It's Time to Un-bury Staff Sgt. Joe Hooper"; Luther to the authors, June 5, 2000; Cutlip interview, June 17, 2000; Faye Hooper interview, August 12–13, 1994; DeVore's "Brief Memoir."

76. Sallis interview, March 1, 1996, and Vira to Red Combs, July 30, 1985, Combs Papers.

77. Sallis to Jackson, February 4, 1982, and Jackson to Sallis, February 12, 1982, both in the Rick Anderson Papers.

78. Donald L. Custis, Chief Medical Director, VA, Department of Medicine, to Senator Jackson, March 12, 1982, and Vicki J. Boyle, Seattle Office of Senator Henry M. Jackson, to Sallis, March 18, 1982, both in the Rick Anderson Papers.

79. Senator Daniel J. Evans to Sallis, April 5, 1984; Jerome R. Dolezal, Director, VA Medical Center, Seattle, to Evans, April 18, 1984; Evans to Sallis, May 11, 1984; Evans to Sallis, December 21, 1984; all in the Rick Anderson Papers.

80. Sallis to Representative Thomas S. Foley, February 25, 1987, Rick Anderson Papers.

81. Senator Brock Adams to Rick Anderson, July 11, 1988, Rick Anderson Papers.

82. Anderson, "Hooper Hospital Gains Support as Readers Exercise Their Writes." Also

see Anderson, "Joe Hooper's Supporters Write from across Nation." Many of the original letters are in the Rick Anderson Papers. An interesting fraud occurred during this campaign. "I knew Joe Hooper and handled some of his legal problems," a Seattle lawyer allegedly wrote in a letter that Anderson published. "I feel it is an obscene travesty to even consider naming this wing after a psychotic sociopath such as Joe Hooper. Like Lt. Calley and other violence-prone individuals, he had the best moments of his life in Vietnam. Nothing made him happier or gave him greater satisfaction than exercising his instinctive talent for killing. What you refer to as bravery in this 'American hero' was really a combination of psychosis and stupidity." In fact, an unknown person sent the letter using the lawyer's name; after the lawyer provided a writing sample proving he was not the author the paper published a retraction. Interview with the lawyer who wished to remain anonymous since the original letter created a "nightmare" for him, August 26, 2002.

83. Congressman Rod Chandler press releases, January 31, April 4, 1989, Rick Anderson Papers.

84. Frank to Anderson, May 11, 16, 1989; Frank and Sallis to James T. Krajeck, Director, VA Medical Center, Seattle, June 8, 1990; Frank and Sallis to Senator Adams, June 12, 1990; Frank and Sallis to Anderson, June 12, 1990; all in the Rick Anderson Papers. Also, Sallis interview, March 1, 1996.

85. Detjen to Anderson, February 3, 1989, Rick Anderson Papers, and an e-mail from Dennis M. Cunneen to the authors, May 3, 2000.

86. "Staff Sergeant Joe. R. Hooper United States Army Reserve Center Memorialization Ceremony," May 6, 1989; "Information Pamphlet," May 6, 1989; numerous snapshots of the ceremony; all in the James R. Gumm Papers; Press Release about the memorialization ceremony, May 1, 1989, Rick Anderson Papers; "Reserve Center dedicated in memory of Joe Hooper, CBH, May 8, 1989, clipping in the Audrey Hooper Papers; Frank to Anderson, May 11, 1989, Rick Anderson Papers.

87. Anderson, "Ten Years Later, It's Time to Un-Bury Staff Sgt. Joe Hooper."

88. "Memorialization Ceremony In Honor of Staff Sergeant Joe R. Hooper," September 28, 1989, Combs Papers, and Steve Zolvinski, "Bowling Alley Named to Honor Vietnam Hero," *Screaming Eagle* (November/December 1989), clipping in the Irene Bennett Papers.

89. "Joe R. Hooper (1939 [sic]–1979) Dedication: Joe R. Hooper Inpatient Addictions Treatment Center," August 17, 1990, and "VA Wing Dedicated to War Hero Joe Hooper," undated clipping, both in the Mike Sallis Papers; "Moses Lake War Hero Hooper Finally Gets Some Recognition," undated clipping in the Audrey Hooper Papers.

90. "Dedication of Post 209 in Memory of Medal of Honor Winner Joe R. Hooper," December 10, 1991, and David U. Andrews, "Joe R. Hooper Remembered in Moses

Lake," CBH, December 11, 1991, both in the Audrey Hooper Papers. Also see "Legion Post Named for Hero Joe Hooper," *Wenatchee World*, December 6, 1991, clipping in the Hendricks Scrapbook.

91. Jean Parietti, "New Efforts Are Made for Hooper Memorial," *Moses Lake Herald*, November 10, 1988, clipping in the Rick Anderson Papers; Sallis interview, March 1, 1996; Alex Vira interview, March 13, 1996.

92. Michael Wagar, "Peace Memorial Unveiled," CBH, June 1, 1993, and Charles Siderius, "Memorial to a Hero," *Wenatchee World*, May 31, 1993, both clippings in the Aronow Papers; fragments of Faye Hooper's speech in the JRHP.

93. For two brief accounts of Joe that are heavily laced with legends, see Kregg J. Jorgenson, *Very Crazy G.I.: Strange but True Stories of the Vietnam War* (New York: Ballantine, 2001), 122–44, and Donald K. Ross and Helen Lou Ross, *Washington State Men of Valor*, revised edition (Port Orchard WA: Rokalu Press, 1994), 220–24.

Epilogue

1. Philip Bigler, *In Reporting Honored Glory: Arlington National Cemetery, The Final Post*, 2nd edition (Arlington VA: Vandamere Press, 1994), 23–28.

2. Bigler, *In Reporting Honored Glory*, 37, 50.

3. Bigler, *In Reporting Honored Glory*, 42, 105, 127.

Appendix A

1. Compiled with the assistance of retired Colonel Frank C. Foster, an expert on U.S. military medals.

2. Earl Yowell, Chief, Special Actions Branch, Personnel Services Division, U.S. Army Reserve Personnel Center, to Mr. Stan H. Smith, July 5, 1989, copy in the Stan H. Smith Papers.

Bibliographic Essay

This bibliographic essay discusses only the unpublished primary sources used in the book. Published sources, both primary and secondary, are cited only in the notes.

The Joe Ronnie Hooper files in various official repositories contain a great deal of information unavailable elsewhere. These files include: Employee Medical Folder, United States Office of Personnel Management, OPF/EMF Access Unit, St. Louis, Missouri; Official Personnel Folder, United States Office of Personnel Management, OPF/EMF Access Unit, St. Louis, Missouri; Military Personnel Records, National Personnel Records Center, St. Louis, Missouri; Naval Personnel Records, National Personnel Records Center, St. Louis, Missouri; Medical Records, Claim Folder 24965568, VARO, Muskogee, Oklahoma; Casualty Information System (TAGCEN), 1961–81, the Center for Electronic Records, NARA. In addition the Don F. Pratt Museum, Fort Campbell, Kentucky, has a small collection of records and the U.S. Army Crimes Records Center at Fort Belvoir, Virginia, contains the U.S. Army Criminal Investigation Command (USACIDC) Report of Investigation (ROI) 79-CID032-11227-5H8, which deals with Joe's death.

Looking for a Hero would have been impossible without the many individuals who allowed us to interview them, either in person or by phone (and some by both methods). The following are the people we interviewed in person, listed alphabetically: E. James Alford, March 2, 1996; William Fred Aronow, April 9, 1995; Roy L. Barber II, February 28, 1997; Raymond H. Blackman, August 17, 1994; Peter Boenigk, March 5, 1996; Salvator Bongiorno, July 12, 1996; Richard L. Buzzini, March 1, 1997; Anna Combs, February 8, 1995; Weldon E. ("Red") Combs, February 8, 1995; David Darr, March 6, 1996; Carollyn DeVore, February 11–12, 1995; Roger C. Donlon, February 9, 1996; Norma Donlon, February 9, 1996; Gary W. Foster, March 7, 1995, February 28, 1996; Arlene Foster, February 28, 1996; Larry Frank, March 2, 1996; John E. Frick, September 21, 1995; Jodey Gravett, July 21, 2000, July 22, 2000; Mark S. Hawk, June 21, 1997; Cleo C. Hogan Jr., March 21–22,

1995, October 27, 1995, July 13, 1996, July 14, 1996, July 21, 2000; Cleo C. Hogan Jr., videotaped by Marty Callaghan of MPI Teleproductions, 1999 (copy in authors' possession); Cleo C. Hogan Jr., videotaped by General John H. Cushman for a video autobiography of his Vietnam tour entitled "2nd Brigade, 101st Airborne Division, September 1967–June 1968" (copy in authors' possession); Audrey Hooper, March 2, 1996; Faye Hooper, August 12–13, 1994; Joey Hooper, August 12–13, 1994; Robert Jay Hooper, February 27, 1997; Sandra Lorenzen Horwege, February 27, 1997; Wayne A. Horne, July 22, 2000; Dewey ("Buck") Johnson, September 24, 1995; Dewey Johnson Jr., September 24, 1995; Gwen Johnson, September 24, 1995; T'Odon C. Leshikar, October 28, 1995; William David Loftin, July 13, 1996; Jerry McCollum, September 24, 1999; Charles Wayne ("Captain Mac") McMenamy, February 10, 1995; Alfred M. Mount, July 12, 1996; Lonnie Nale Jr., July 13, 1996; George R. Parker Jr., March 23, 1995, July 13, 1996; Robert L. Rainwater, July 22, 2000; Bobby L. Rakestraw, June 24, 1997; Eugene E. Robertson, October 27, 1995; Joyce Rockel, June 28, 1997; Noah R. Rockel, June 28, 1997; Richard Ryan, July 8, 1995; Robert Saal, June 26, 1997; Jack Saint, April 12, 1997; Paula Saint, April 12, 1997; Warren Michael Sallis, March 1, 1996; Ruby G. Schultz, February 27, 1997; Roger J. Spiller, February 9, 1996; Dale L. Stengel, August 2, 1996; Christopher Straub, July 22, 2000; Craig Sturges, March 5, 1996; Grady L. Towns Jr., July 13, 1996; Frank H. Tryon Jr., May 23, 1995; Dale A. Urban, April 17, 1995, June 8, 1995; Alex Vira, March 2, 1996; Michael Watson, July 12, 1996.

We conducted the following telephone interviews, listed in alphabetical order: Richard ("Rick") Anderson, July 9, 1996; Wayne C. Anderson, July 29, 1999; John Arnhold, April 16, 1996; William Fred Aronow, May 19, 1995; Samuel Ayala, May 9, 2000; James L. ("Ted") Ayers, June 22, 1999; David G. Bischoff, January 13, 1997; Peter Boenigk, June 1, 2002; Maxine L. Bohn, April 14, 1996; Dr. Dannette Boyle, September 14, 1999; Major General Patrick Henry Brady, May 28, 1996; Keirn C. Brown, January 11, 1997; Richard L. Buzzini, August 14, 2001; Frank Campagne, January 8, 1996; Michael Collins, June 15, 1997; Weldon E. ("Red") Combs, November 13, 1995; Rusty Cutlip, June 17, 2000; Carollyn DeVore, March 6, 2002, June 21, 2002, August 19, 2002; William W. Erbach, March 20, 1996, July 29, 1996; John Fair, August 6, 1999; Frank C. Foster, October 9, 1996; Paul Gochnour, July 6, 2000, August 1, 2000; Floyd N. Greenwald, August 5, 1996; Tex. W. Gray, Oc-

tober 30, 1995, April 10, 1996; Michael R. Grimm, September 19, 1999; James
R. Gumm, July 2, 1995, August 6, 1995; Arden D. Hardison, July 7, 2000;
Mark S. Hawk, August 9, 1997; Kathryn D. Hendricks, June 16, 1999, July 28,
1999; Frederick G. ("Jerry") Hill, February 1, 1996; Harold A. Hochstatter,
April 12, 1996; Cleo C. Hogan Jr., April 17, 1995, May 13, 1995, November 29,
1995; August 1, 1996, August 17, 1997, July 25, 1999, October 18, 1999, August 4,
2000; Audrey Hooper, July 19, 1999, May 16, 2000; Faye Hooper, August 16,
1994, November 12, 1995, August 30, 1999, July 12, 2000, June 1, 2002, September 19, 2002; Ron Isakson, May 13, 1998; Ava G. James, January 14, 1996,
April 10, 1996; James Jennette, February 8, 1998; Delbert O. Jennings, October 19, 1996; Dewey ("Buck") Johnson, August 1, 1999; Dewey Johnson Jr.,
August 2, 1999; Gwen Johnson, August 2, 1999; Thomas M. Johnson, April 14,
1996, June 28, 2000; James R. Kearns, December 15, 1997; Ned Kintzer, January 29, 1996; Arvie LeBlanc, August 4, 1999; Otis W. Livingston, July 10, 1995;
William David Loftin, August 13, 1995; Christopher Luther, May 30, 2000;
Jerry McCollum, August 2, 1999, August 3, 1999, September 25, 1999, Octo-
ber 1, 1999; Peter E. McIntyre, June 11, 2000; Charles Wayne ("Captain Mac")
McMenamy, August 23, 1994, August 23, 2000; Alfred D. Mason, April 14,
1998; Roy Wayne Miller, April 11, 1999; Penny Norman, April 3, 1996, April 14,
1996; George R. Parker Jr., April 17, 1995; William Parson, July 30, 1996; Pete
Perez, May 11, 1998, June 17, 2000; Edward J. Petitt Jr., July 24, 1998; Eugene
E. Robertson, January 9, 1997; Noah R. Rockel, September 19, 1997; Ronald
F. Rohs, July 27, 1999; Patrick L. Runevitch, April 11, 1996; Jimmy Shipman,
September 1, 1999; Rod Songer, July 28, 1999; Roger J. Spiller, April 11, 1995;
Kenneth K. Sugawara, July 20, 2000; John D. Tillitson, July 19, 1999; Gina
Townsend, February 21, 2002, June 10, 2002; Alex Vira, March 13, 1996,
May 9, 1996, July 9, 1996, August 1, 1996; John C. Walton, April 9, 1996; Mavis
Withers, April 16, 1996, June 17, 2000.

In addition to the interviews, many individuals let us examine their personal papers (although these remain in private hands, in almost all cases
the owners allowed us to Xerox them): Richard ("Rick") G. Anderson, correspondence and clippings relating to efforts to have Joe Hooper memorialized after his death; Wayne C. Anderson, letter collection; William Fred
Aronow, very large letter collection; Roy L. Barber II, small collection of
official documents, a few letters; Irene Bennett, small letter collection, newspaper clippings, photographs, and other documents relating to her brother,

Joe E. Mann; Raymond H. Blackman, extensive collection relating to the Delta Raiders' history, including a complete file of the Raiders' "Newsletter" and a copy of "Operational Report—LL, Headquarters, 101st Abn Div, Period Ending 31 July 1970 (U)"; Maxine L. Bohn, newspaper clippings; Frank M. Campagne, letter collection; Weldon E. ("Red") and Anna Combs, small collection including photographs, official documents, and newspaper clippings; Lieutenant General John H. Cushman, includes a copy of his unpublished memoirs ("'Ready to Go!' A Personal Memoir . . . ") and a videotape of "2nd Brigade, 101st Airborne Division, September 1967–June 1968," which includes footage of the La Chu Battlefield; Carollyn DeVore, very extensive collection of letters, newspaper clippings, event programs, and photographs; Larry Frank, newspaper clippings relating to efforts to memorialize Joe Hooper; John E. Frick, extensive letter collection; Paul Gochnour, extensive letter collection; Tex W. Gray, small collection of letters and official documents; Michael R. Grimm, genealogical material relating to the Hooper family; James R. Gumm, small collection of clippings, photographs, and documents relating to Hooper's postwar memorializations; Mark S. Hawk, extensive collection of letters, newspaper clippings, official documents, and artifacts; Kathryn D. Hendricks, scrapbook filled with newspaper clippings, photographs, letters, and miscellaneous documents; Harold A. Hochstatter, small collection relating to Moses Lake's early history; Cleo C. Hogan Jr., extensive letter collection, many photographs, numerous official documents and newspaper clippings, and a copy of his memoirs ("The Delta Raiders: February–July 1968, A Personal History"); Audrey Hooper, extensive collection of letters, photographs, newspaper clippings, and official documents; Joe Ronnie Hooper (in Faye Hooper's possession), very extensive collection of letters, official documents, newspaper clippings, photographs, and memorabilia; Sandra L. Horwege, small collection of official documents and photographs; Ava G. James, consists of a brief diary he kept; Thomas M. Johnson, copies of the Moses Lake High School yearbooks for 1954, 1955, and 1956; Charles Wayne ("Captain Mac") McMenamy, collection of wartime documents, newspaper clippings, and photographs, plus a copy of his Military Personnel Records; George R. Parker Jr., small collection of official documents and photographs; Eugene E. Robertson, letter collection; Noah R. and Joyce Rockel, letter collection; Robert Saal, extensive letter collection; Jack and Paula Saint, small collection of clippings and photographs relating the Saint family history; Warren Michael Sallis, small collection of news-paper clippings, documents, and photographs, especially relating to efforts to memorialize Joe Hooper; Stan H. Smith, small collection relating to the MOH and Joe Hooper, including three essays in *The Annals* in 1990 – 91 trying to assess the "weight" of various medals; Grady L. Towns, consists of a single letter, Ronald E. Phillips to To Whom It May Concern; Gina Townsend, small collection of newspaper clippings and photographs relating to Clifford C. Sims; Dale A. Urban, letter collection and a few photographs.

Numerous people also sent us invaluable personal communications in response to various questions that we sent them: Irene Bennett, July 22, 1997; David Bischoff, January 20, 1997; Dennis Burgess, June 14, 2000 (e-mail); Dennis M. Cunneen, May 3, 2000 (e-mail); Benjamin Franklin Dansby, October 6, 17, 2001 (e-mails); Romana M. Danysh, August 9, 1999 (e-mail); Carollyn DeVore, c. fall 1994, "Brief Memoir," February 1995, "Memories," February 1995, July 1, 1995, c. mid-April 2002, May 4, 2002, August 15, 18, 20, 2002, numerous undated notes; William W. Erbach, c. April 3, 1996; Cleo C. Hogan Jr., c. early June 1995; undated [c. 1996]; January 3, 1996; January 23, 1996; July 5, 1996; Chris Luther, June 5, 2000; Dr. Chris Maggio, August 8, 12, 2002 (e-mails); Allan R. Millett, November 11, 1998; Northwestern State University's Registrar Office, August 8, 2002 (e-mail); Brian Oak, January 31, 1997 (fax); Mary Grace Sims, c. June 10, 2002; Alex Vira, July 31, 1996; Eric Voelz, September 15, 1995; William C. Westmoreland, April 16, 1995.

In addition to the interviews, documents in RG 472, NARA: United States Army, Vietnam, were instrumental in reconstructing events during Joe's two tours. The records consulted included: Headquarters, U.S. Army Vietnam, Adjutant General, Military Personnel Division, Awards Branch, Military Awards Case Files, Box 404; Headquarters, U.S. Army Vietnam, Command Histories, AARS, Box 15; Infy Units, 2nd Bn, 327th Infy, ACS Intelligence/Operations (S2/3), Daily Journal, Boxes 30-40; Infy Units, 2nd Bn, 501st Infy, ACS for Operations (S-3), Command Reports, Box 17; Infy Units, 2nd Bn, 501st Infy, ACS for Operations (S-3), Daily Journal, Boxes 4-5 and 10-11; Infy Units, 2nd Bn, 501st Infy, Organizational History, Box 1; 101st Abn Div, Adjutant General, Unit Commendations, 2nd Bn, 501st-801 Maint. Bn., Box 3; 101st Abn Div, AARS, Box 34; 101st Abn Div, ACS, G-2, Monthly Intelligence Summaries, Box 1; 101st Abn Div, ACS, G-3, AARS, Boxes 1-2; 101st Abn Div, ACS, G-3, Operations Reports—LL, Box 2; 101st Abn Div, Organizational

History, Box 1; 101st Abn Div, 1st Bde, AARS, Box 3; 101st Abn Div, 1st Bde, Organizational History, Box 3; 101st Abn Div, 2nd Bde, ACS, S-3, AARS, Boxes 1-2; 101st Abn Div, 2nd Bde, ACS, S-3, Command Reports, Box 1; 101st Abn Div, 2nd Bde, ACS, S-3, Operations Reports—LL, Box 1; 101st Abn Div, 2nd Bde, Organizational History, Box 1; 101st Abn Div, 3rd Bde, ACS, S-3, AARS, Box 2; 101st Abn Div, 3rd Bde, ACS, S-3, Command Reports, Box 1; 101st Abn Div, 3rd Bde, ACS, S-3, Operations Reports—LL, Box 1; 101st Abn Div, 101st Aviation Group, Command Reports, Box 17; 101st Abn Div, 101st Aviation Group (S-3), Daily Journal, Box 11.

Also at the NARA, RG 950, Presidential Library Materials (Nixon) contains a file on the Presentation of the Medal of Honor Ceremony, The White House, Friday, March 7, 1969.

The U.S. Army Military History Institute at Carlisle Barracks, Pennsylvania, has a number of diverse records relating to Joe's life: the Annual Historical Supplements for the 3rd Bn (Airborne), 508th Infy, Calendar Years 1966, 1967, and the 3rd Bn, 5th Infy, Calendar Years 1969, 1970; the Olinto M. Barsanti Papers; the Senior Officer Debriefing Reports for Major General Olinto M. Barsanti, August 14, 1968, Lieutenant General W. B. Rosson, October 11, 1968, Major General John J. Hennessey, March 24, 1971, and Major General John H. Cushman, December 4, 1972. The Institute also has a copy of U.S. Army War College, "Study on Military Professionalism," (Carlisle Barracks PA: June 30, 1970).

The National Records Personnel Records Center in St. Louis, Missouri, contains Audie Leon Murphy's Military Personnel Records; the Clifford C. Sims Military Personnel Records; the Morning Reports for the units in which Joe served—those we consulted were for Company A (Abn), 3rd Bn, 5th Infy; Company E (Rifle), 20th Infy; Company A, 2nd Bn, 501st Infy; Company D, 2nd Bn, 501st Regiment; Company B, 3rd Bn (Abn) 508th Infy; and Headquarters and Headquarters Company, 3rd Bn (Abn), 508th Infy.

Two large microfilm collections contain significant material. *U.S. Armed Forces in Vietnam 1954–1975. Part Two. Vietnam: Lessons Learned* (Reel V) contains BDM Corporation, "A Study of Strategic Lessons Learned in Vietnam. Omnibus Executive Summary," while *U.S. Armed Forces in Vietnam 1954–1975. Part Four. Vietnam U.S. Army Senior Officer Debriefing Reports* (4 reels) includes the debriefing reports of Major General Melvin Zais,

May 25, 1969 (Reel I), Major General John M. Wright, May 11, 1970 (Reel III), Brigadier General Henry J. Muller, June 9, 1970 (Reel III), Lieutenant General A. S. Collins Jr., January 7, 1971 (Reel IV), Brigadier General DeWitt C. Armstrong, November 2, 1971 (Reel IV), and Major General Thomas M. Tarpley, July 13, 1972 (Reel IV). For understanding the enemy's perspective, *Vietnam Documents and Research Notes Series: Translation and Analysis of Significant Viet Cong/North Vietnamese Documents* (A Microfilm Project of University Publications of America, 6 reels) is indispensable. Another captured document that provided insight into the enemy was "Achievements of Hue City Party Committee, Tri-Thien-Hue Region," (dated December 1968, and captured on January 22, 1969), which is archived at the U.S. Army Center of Military History, Fort McNair.

Two legal documents were useful. Case No. 759160, Superior Court of the State of California for the County of Los Angeles, deals with Joe's divorce from Balbine, while the "Report of Divorce" between William Wayne Guyse and Faye Guyse, Alabama Center for Health Statistics, provides the raw data for the divorce between Wayne and Faye.

As for specialized newspapers and newsletters, the "Audie Murphy Research Foundation Newsletter" presents a lot of information about Audie; the *Columbia Basin Herald* (Moses Lake, Washington) helps to provide the context for Joe's childhood; and the "Delta Raiders Newsletter" (published as the "Delta Company Newsletter" from no. 1 through no. 50) provides a great deal of information about that remarkable group of soldiers (we are indebted to Ray "Blackie" Blackman, longtime editor of the "Newsletter" for a complete file of all the issues). Broader in focus and thus less directly relevant, was the "101st Airborne Division Vietnam Veterans Newsletter."